*David Bellamy's*

# Complete Guide to Landscapes

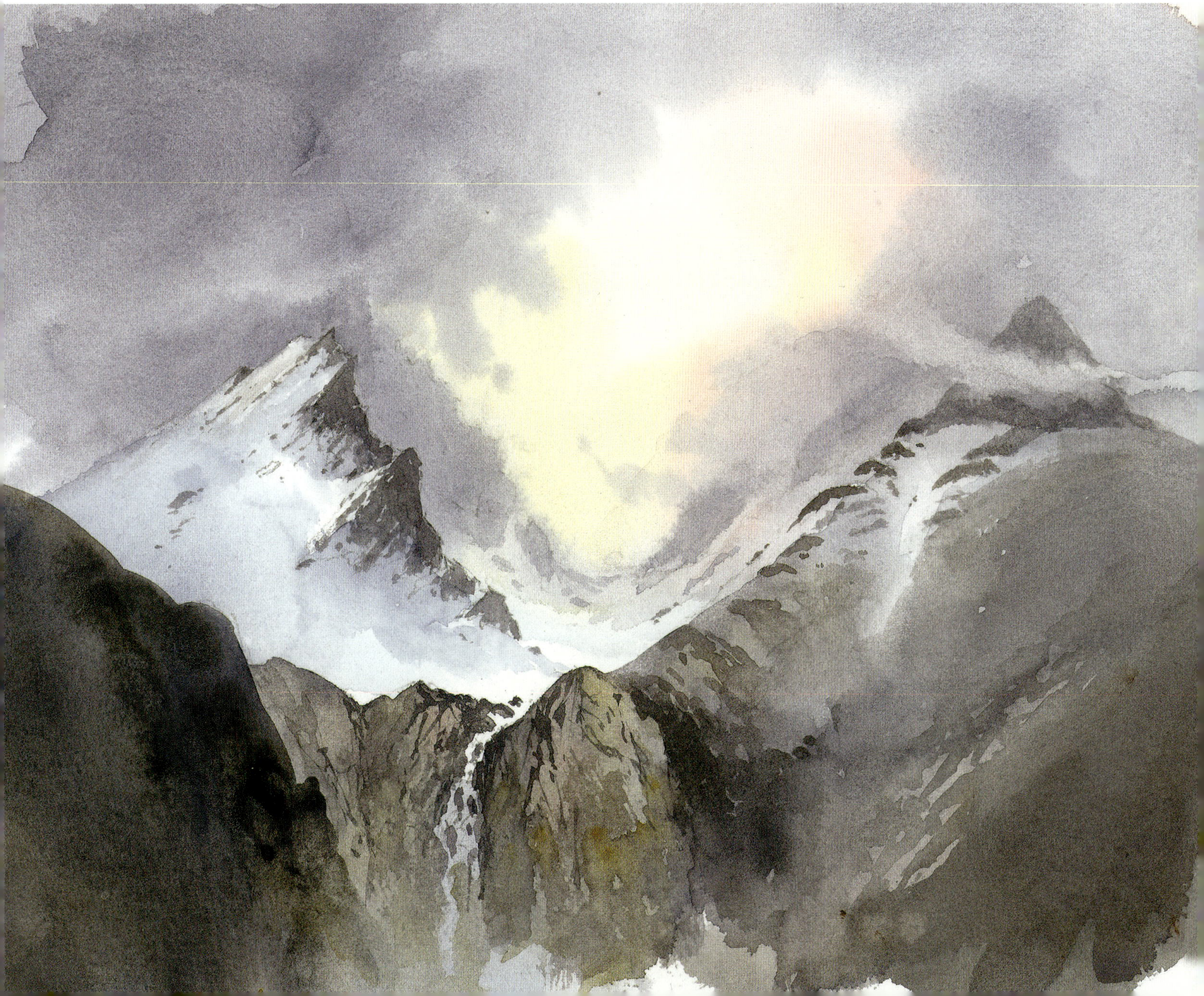

# Dedication

Every summer over the past 30 years or so, at the fabulous Patchings Art Festival in Nottinghamshire, I have had the great pleasure to meet hundreds of readers of my books, and you all give me such a heart-warming response. This book is therefore dedicated to all my readers, with grateful thanks for all your support over so many years.

*Front cover*

GALWAY COAST
*28 x 40.5cm (11 x 16in)*

*Page 1*

MOODY MOUNTAIN, SNOWDONIA
*17 x 23cm (6¾ x 9in)*

*The inter-relationship between skies, light and atmosphere is shown in this watercolour, where the moody peaks and crags run into the sky area and the light is concentrated in certain parts of the composition. In places it is almost impossible to judge whether a shape is a mountain peak or a cloud.*

*These pages*

FARM, STAFFORDSHIRE MOORS
*23 x 30cm (9 x 11¾in)*

*Overleaf*

HAROLDSTON CHINS
*44.5 x 30.5cm (17½ x 12in)*

*The cliffs are at their most interesting when they are crumbling away, thus providing a focal point in this watercolour.*

*David Bellamy's*

# Complete Guide to Landscapes

## PAINTING THE NATURAL WORLD IN WATERCOLOUR

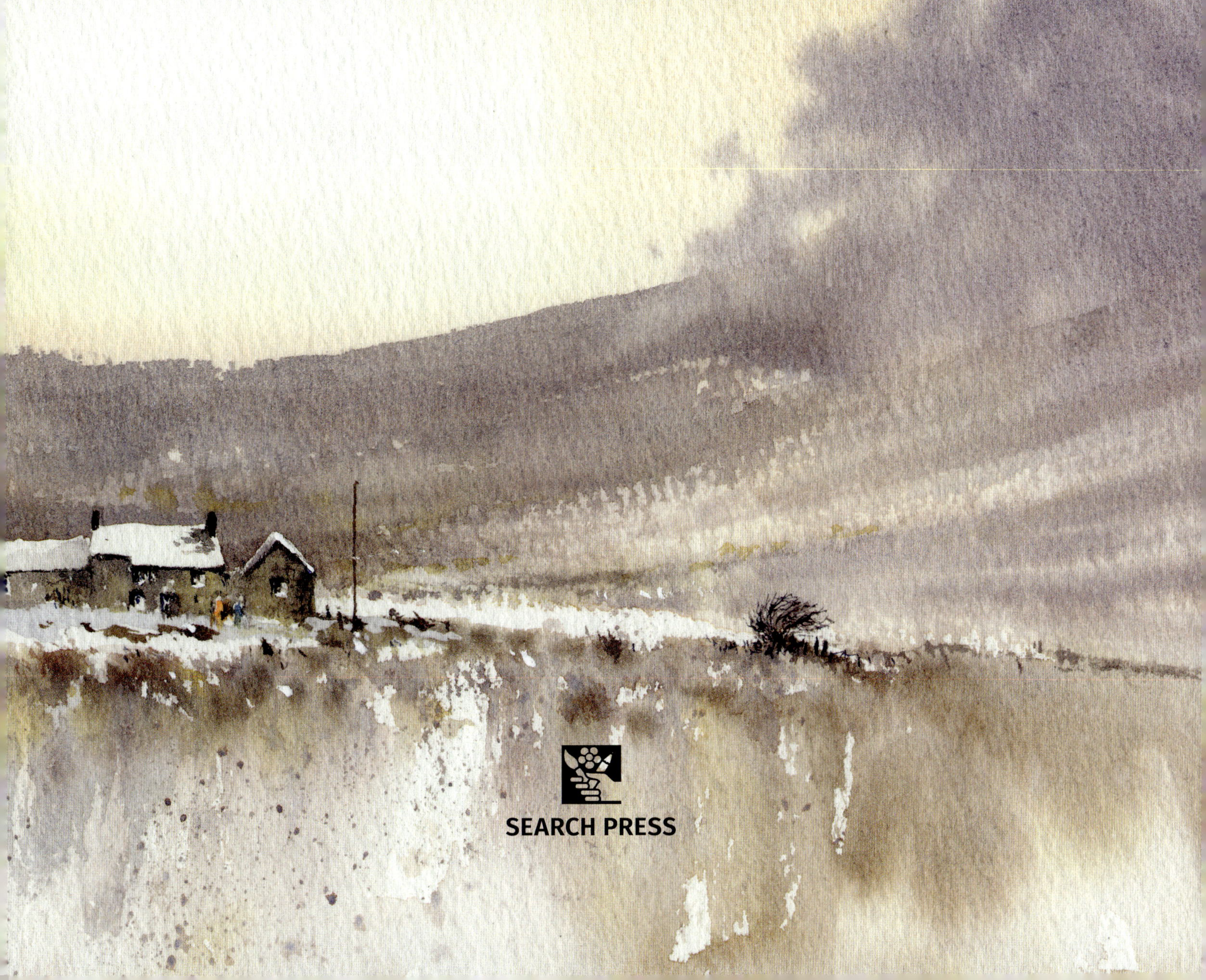

SEARCH PRESS

# Contents



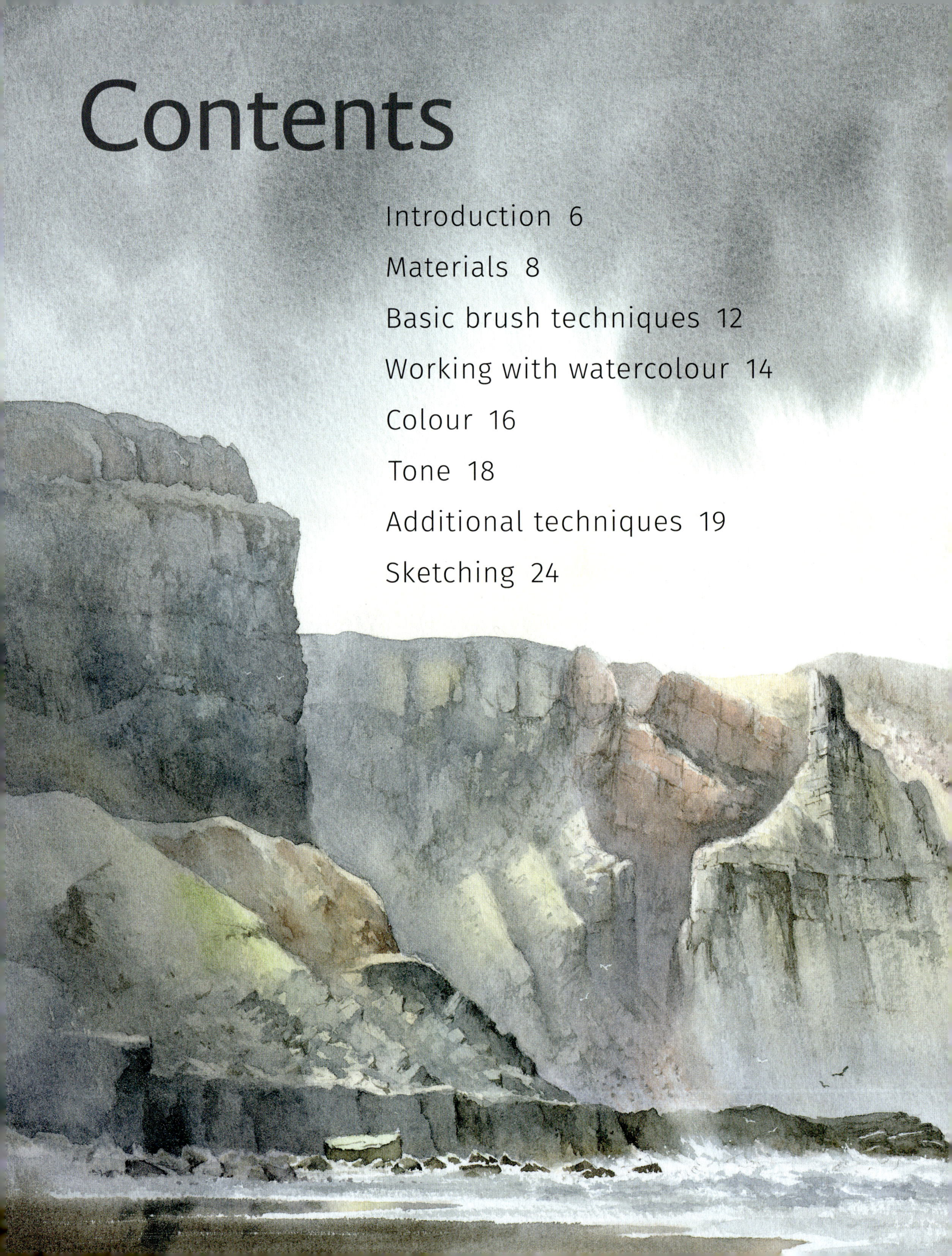

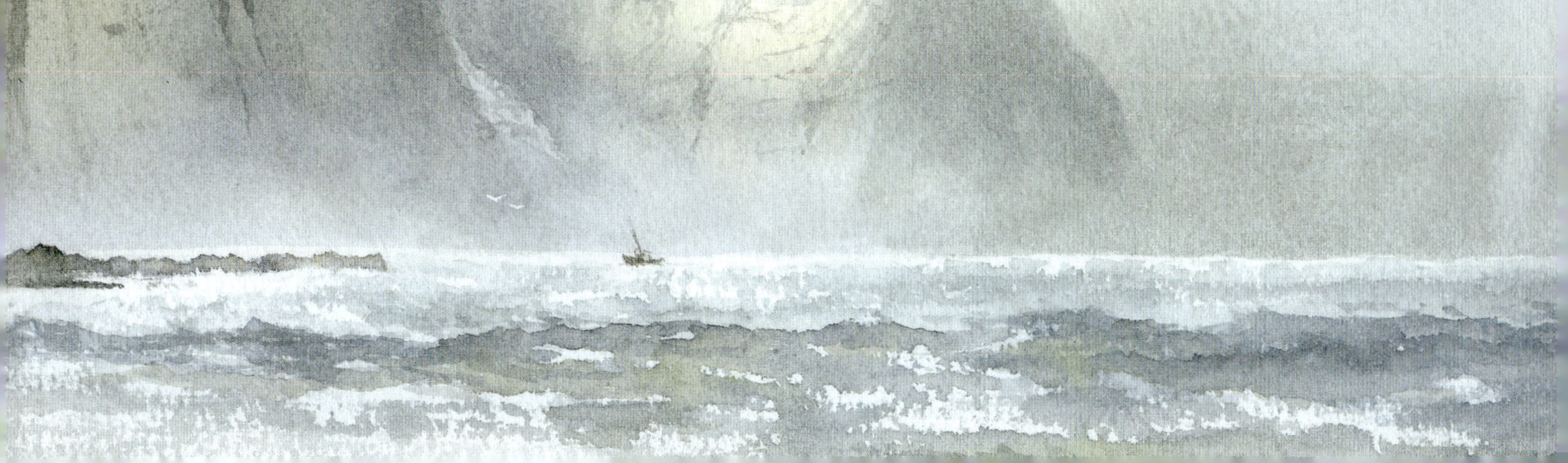

# Introduction

This book brings together in one volume the four books in my previous series in an updated format, and begins with the three vital ingredients to breathing life and energy into your landscapes: skies, light and atmosphere. For the landscape painter, these elements are all inextricably bound together, and by fusing them into a sense of empathy with the scene being painted you will enhance your painting considerably. However good your composition may be, it will fall short if it lacks the passion and inspiration with which these three ingredients can enrich your work. Even the most mundane of subjects can be transformed by the right lighting and mood, so whatever you may wish to paint, the techniques and devices you find here will greatly enhance your paintings. You will find a wide variety of scenery and seasons, and a whole range of different skies to try out. One of the advantages of being able to render a large selection of skies, moods or various forms of lighting is that you can paint the same subject time and time again in a completely different way, so this will provide you with many excellent ideas for tackling your favourite subjects.

We then move on to the more uncultivated landscapes of mountain and moor, which have always held great fascination as subject matter for landscape painters. However, there is much more to these stunning locations than just the raw peaks and crags, and if you relish painting the less developed scenery there is much to interest you even. Many moorland scenes will provide you with quite simple compositions, which can be extremely helpful for those with little experience. Trees, streams, lakes and waterfalls all hold tremendous appeal, and the examples shown in this section should help you improve your work even if you prefer to remain in the lowlands.

Seas and shorelines form the next section, covering a wide variety of coastal scenery, including boats, harbours and seabirds, with further examples of interesting skies. Exciting new approaches, sometimes with non-standard additives and textural effects that will push your work in slightly new directions are included here, and these should provide you with new ideas. The final section covers a variety of landscapes through the various seasons, and is again well-stocked with techniques to enhance your watercolours.

Enjoy your painting.

**PENBERRY HILL**
*16.5 x 24cm (6½ x 9½in)*

*I sketched this in early summer when the greens were much in evidence on the hill, but here I have brought the warmer colours further down the hillside and reduced the foreground greens with flowers and patches of red. The middle section was pretty much colour-faithful with a sort of faded green. I left out a caravan and electricity poles and added in chickens.*

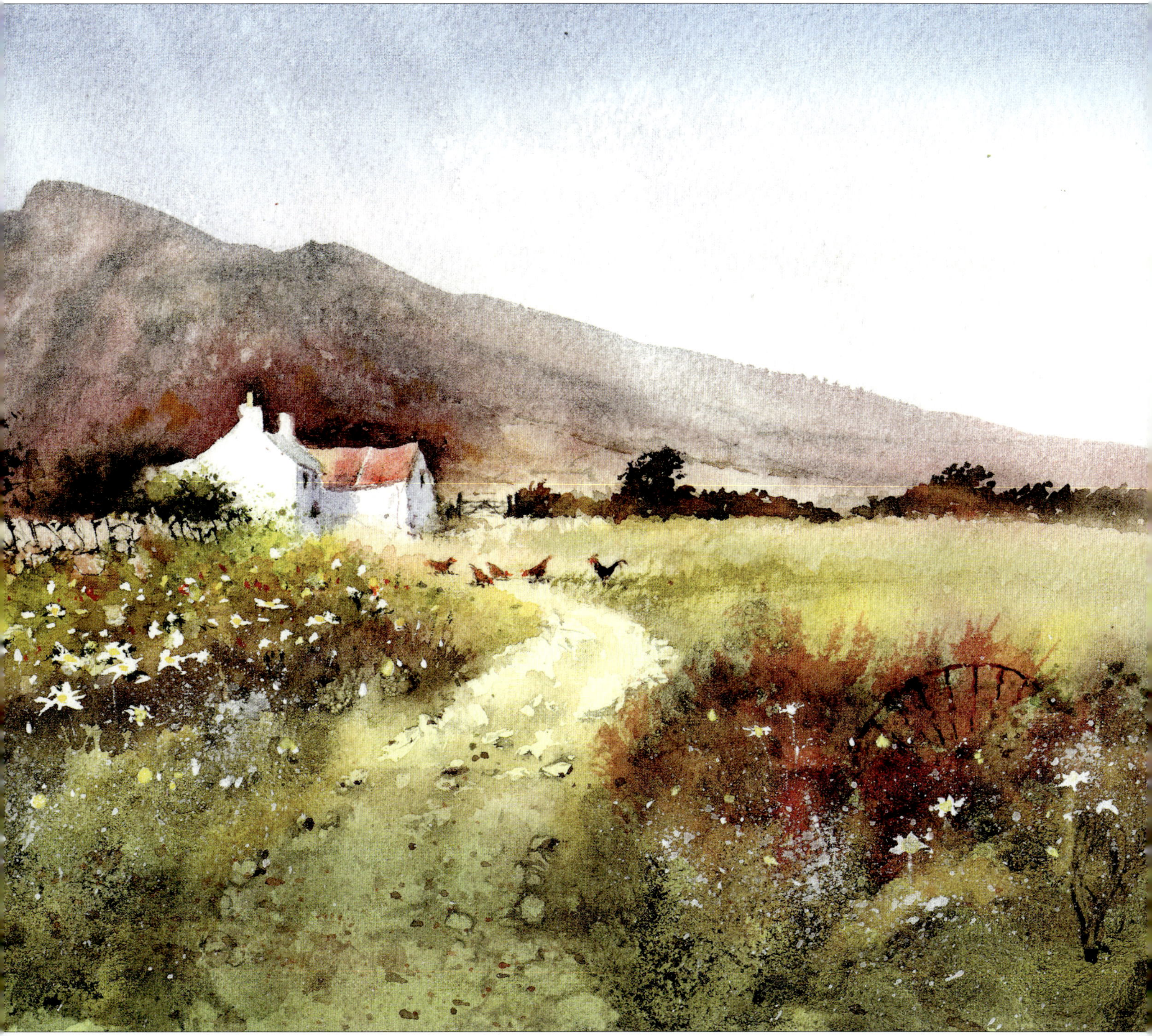

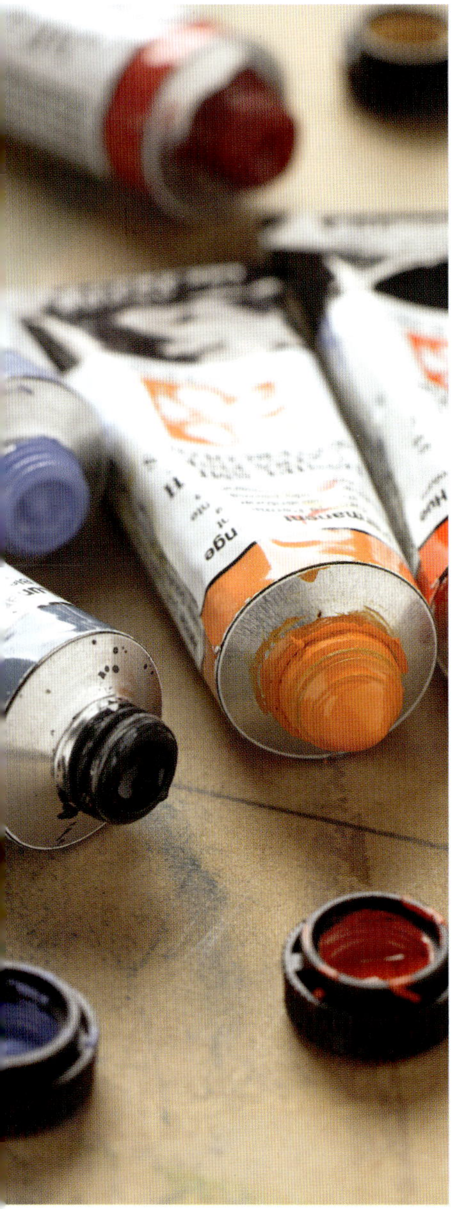

# Materials

## PAINTS

Watercolour paints are available in tubes, pans and half-pans. I normally use half-pans for outdoor sketching, supplemented with tube colours on expedition or travel abroad. For the larger studio paintings, tube colours are essential, as one can quickly mix large washes. Choice of colours is up to the individual. I always work with artists' quality paints as they are more powerful and finely ground, but the students' variety are cheaper and there is not a great difference in quality with many colours.

If you are new to painting, start with a few colours and get to know them before adding more. My basic colours are: French ultramarine, burnt umber, cadmium yellow pale, cadmium red, cobalt blue, Winsor blue or phthalo blue, alizarin crimson or quinacridone red, new gamboge, light red and yellow ochre, plus white gouache for minor highlights. Add the following colours when you feel confident, but preferably not all at once: burnt sienna, raw umber, aureolin, viridian, indigo, cerulean blue, Naples yellow, cadmium orange, raw sienna and vermilion.

I use the Daniel Smith Extra Fine range of watercolours for their wide range of granulating colours, as well as some of the spectacular new pigments. Colours that I particularly like and have used in some of the demonstrations in this book are: transparent red oxide, sodalite genuine, zoisite genuine, Aussie red gold, green apatite genuine and lunar blue. Always study the manufacturers' labels and leaflets and avoid any fugitive colours. These will also tell you if the colour is transparent, opaque or falls between the two, whether it granulates, and the degree of staining.

I sometimes use Daniel Smith watercolour ground to create textured effects in foregrounds (see page 223).

If you are not using Daniel Smith colours, you can approximate the colours as follows:

- Nickel titanate yellow: Naples yellow.
- Sodalite genuine: a mixture of burnt umber and French ultramarine (note that sodalite genuine induces much stronger granulation).
- Green apatite genuine: French ultramarine mixed with cadmium yellow pale for light greens; and raw sienna or yellow ochre for duller greens.
- Transparent red oxide: light red.
- Aussie red gold: cadmium orange, but this is more opaque and not quite so vibrant.
- Lunar blue: this is really quite unique, with strong granulations that can vary unpredictably, and often in a delightful way. There is no simple replacement.

# PAPER AND SKETCHBOOKS

Watercolour paper is best bought in imperial-sized sheets: full imperial (76 x 56cm/38 x 22in), half imperial (38 x 56cm/15 x 22in) and quarter imperial (38 x 28cm/15 x 11in), which are cheaper and can be cut to whatever size and configuration you wish. Pads, and blocks that are glued all round the four edges so that you don't have to stretch the paper, are good for working away from home. Usually the paper comes in weights of 190gsm (90lb), 300gsm (140lb), 425gsm (200lb) or 640gsm (300lb), with some manufacturers having a more extended range. The 640gsm (300lb) paper is as thick as cardboard; the 190gsm (90lb) version rather flimsy and prone to cockling. The 300gsm (140lb) paper will most likely need stretching before painting unless you work on really small sizes, so many people find the 425gsm (200lb) paper the ideal weight, as it does not need stretching unless you are painting larger works, and it is less expensive than the 640gsm (300lb) type.

Most papers come in three types of surface: Rough, Hot Pressed (smooth) and Not (or Cold Pressed). Hot Pressed paper is excellent for fine detail, but you may find it best to leave this surface until you are more experienced, as it dries rather more quickly. A Rough surface is extremely effective for creating textures or ragged edges, or for laying a broken wash with the dry-brush technique, although it is not best for fine detail. The most popular paper is the Not surface, which falls between the other two types in degree of smoothness.

Buy a few sheets from different manufacturers to test which suits you best. Most of the paintings in this book were done on Saunders Waterford paper.

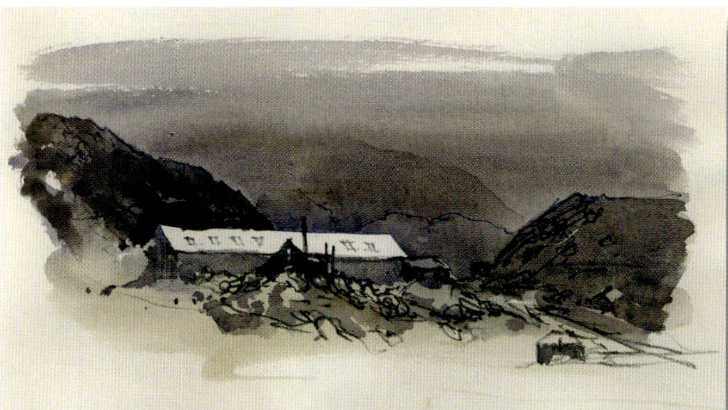

*This watercolour sketch of quarry buildings shows the crisp, sharp edges that can be achieved using Hot Pressed (smooth) watercolour paper.*

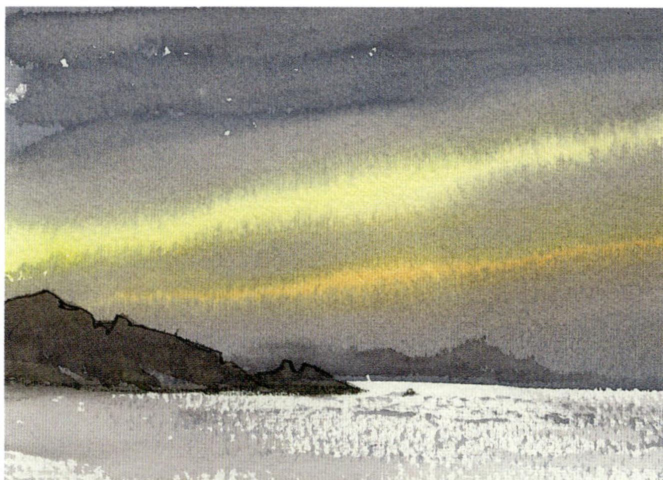

EVENING LIGHT, NAXOS

*15 x 10cm (6 x 4in) 640gsm (300lb) Rough paper*

*This watercolour sketch done on Rough paper shows how you can achieve sparkling light on the water with a brush loaded with pigment but very little water, and dragged across the surface.*

## BRUSHES

The finest brushes for watercolour are undoubtedly sable, though there are excellent synthetic brushes on the market. Kolinsky sable brushes have a fine tip, a large belly to hold copious amounts of paint, and the ability to spring back into shape and not lie limp after one brush stroke. A good compromise, if you find sables too expensive, is to buy a brush of mixed sable and synthetic hairs. Large squirrel-hair mops make lovely wash brushes, although they are prone to losing the odd hair now and then.

The minimum brushes would be a large squirrel mop for washes, a no. 7 or 8 round, a no. 4 round, a no. 1 rigger and a 13mm (½in) flat brush. Add a no. 10 or 12 round and a no. 6 round when you feel the need and you are well set up. More specialized brushes for certain applications, such as a fan brush, can also help on occasion, but are not essential. Take care of your brushes and they will last well. Wash them out with clean water after use. I use the superb brushes from Rosemary & Co. which are of excellent value and unrivalled quality.

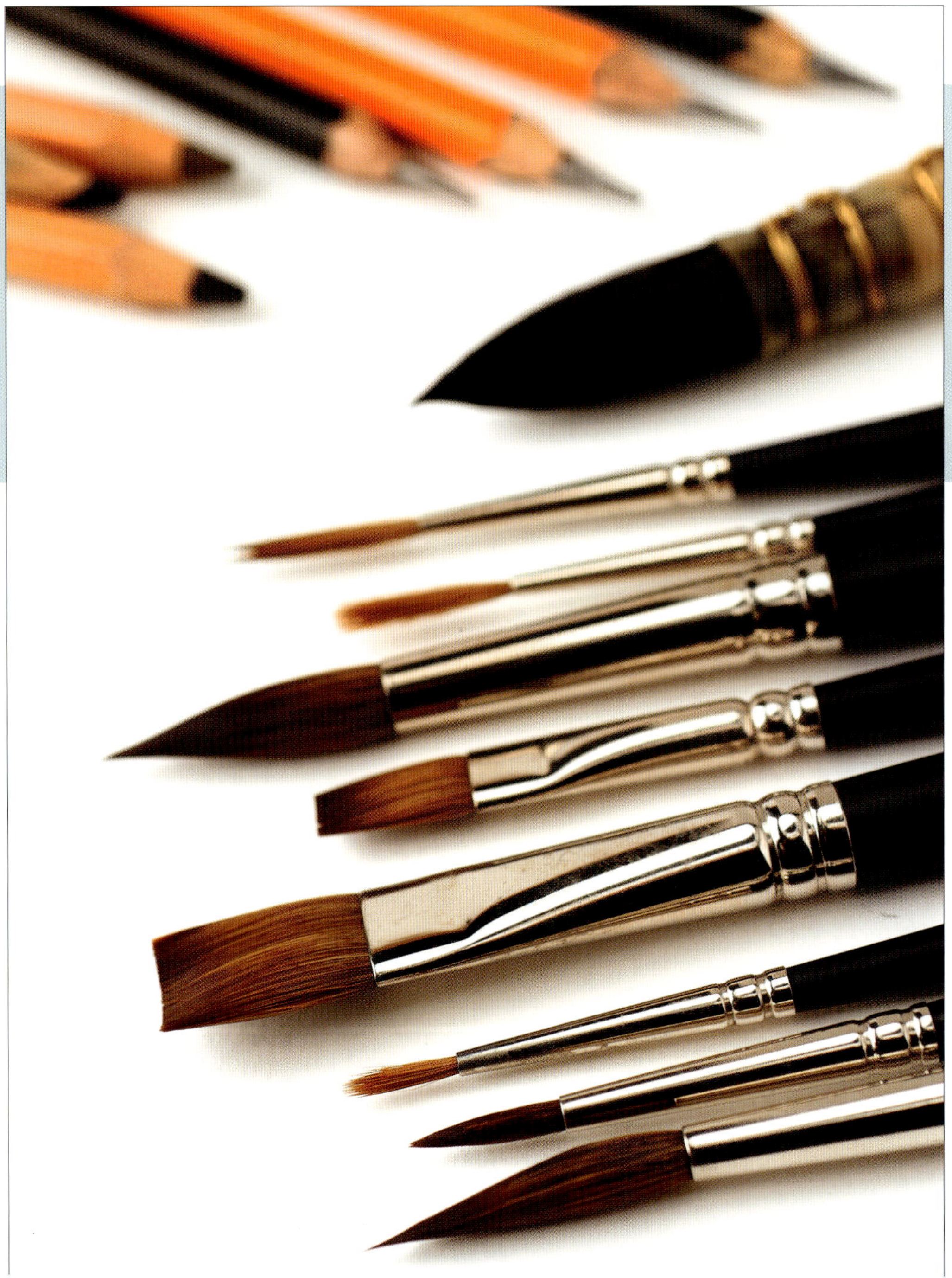

*Some of the brushes used in the step-by-step demonstrations in this book, from front to back: a no. 7, no. 4 and no. 1 round (nos 8 and 6 were also used), a 13mm (½in) flat, a 6mm (¼in) flat, a no. 10 round and a no. 2 and no. 1 rigger, with a squirrel mop.*

## OTHER MATERIALS

At least one drawing board, a selection of pencils from 2B to 4B, a putty eraser, a soft sponge, at least one large water pot, masking fluid and a scalpel are all essential items. Also useful are bulldog clips, an old toothbrush for spattering, tissues and rags. I find a plant spray is useful to speed up the mixing of colours accurately, and occasionally for spraying over a damp wash to create a speckled effect. If you intend stretching paper, then a roll of gummed tape will be required.

You will need a large palette on which you can lay out the colours you are using, many of which will be for small areas of detail, and some for slightly larger areas. A palette with deep wells is needed for mixing up pools of colour for the main washes. Many artists prefer to use a saucer, butchers' tray or large plate, and so long as it is white and does not affect the way you see the colours, this is perfectly fine. For a large wash, the whole saucer would be needed, but for small detail, many mixes can take place on one dinner plate.

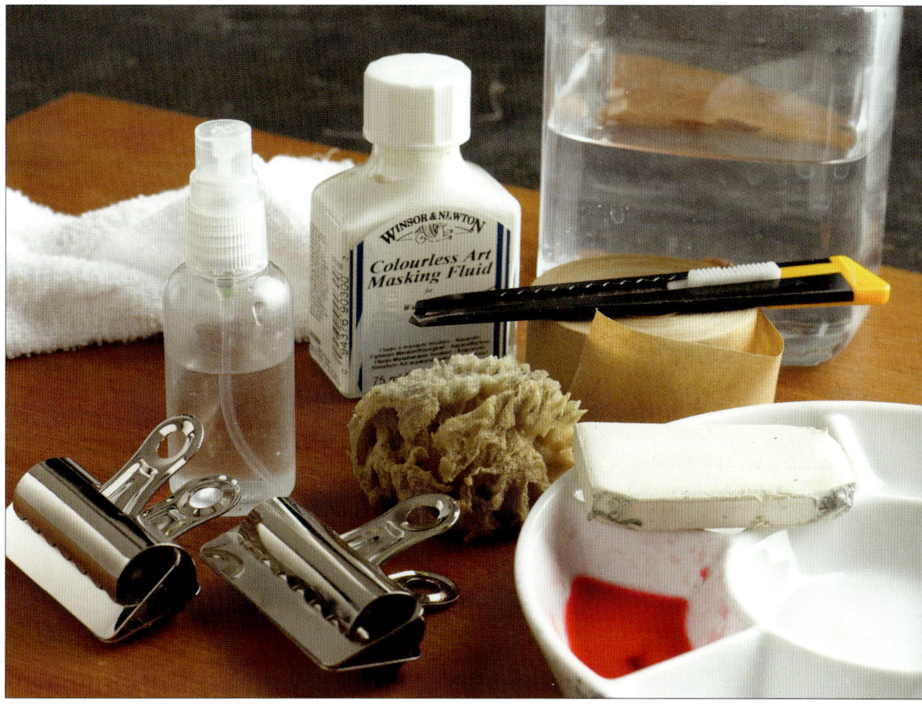


## SKETCHING OUTDOORS

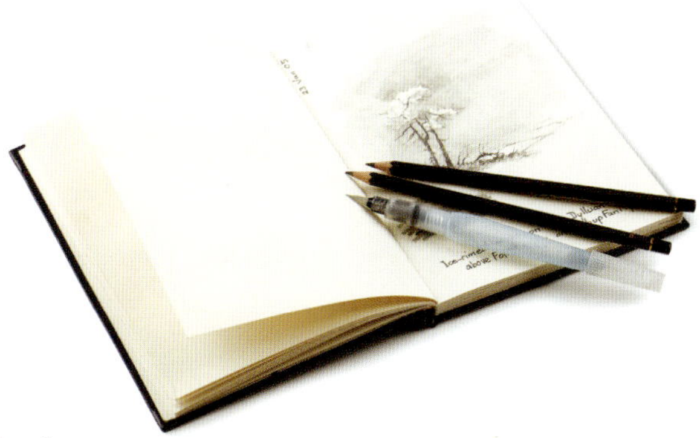

If you are tentative about sketching outdoors, then start with a minimal kit (shown right) of an A5 (21 x 15cm/8¼ x 5¾in) cartridge pad, a couple of graphite water-soluble pencils and a water brush, which contains its own water supply in the handle. This enables you to work quickly, wet or dry, without fuss. Try working with this, and when you gain confidence, add a small box of watercolours in half-pans, a few brushes and a water pot. Most watercolour boxes include an integral palette in the lid. I sometimes use Derwent Inktense blocks, water-soluble ink blocks, for sketching. Cartridge paper can be difficult to work on with watercolours until you are used to it, so you might prefer a small book of watercolour paper. All this is stored in a belt bag, with gloves to keep out the cold. Later you can expand this kit to suit your needs. I also carry larger sketchbooks and additional materials in a rucksack.

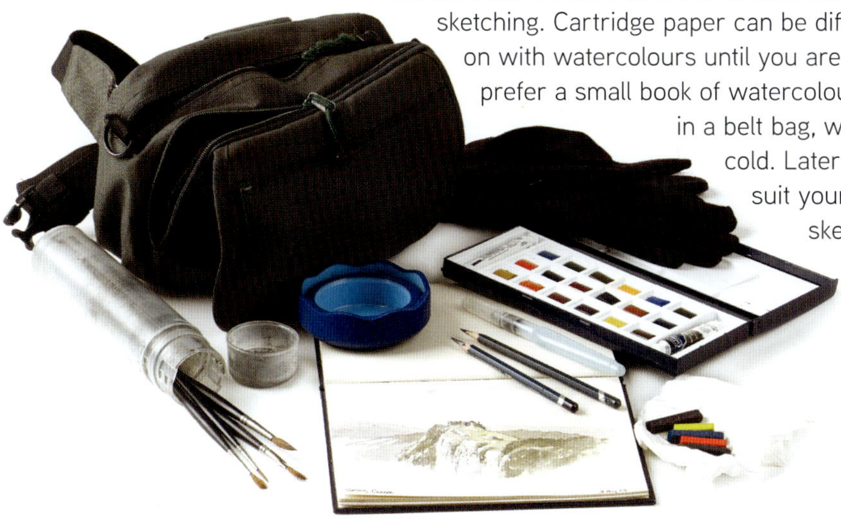

# Basic brush techniques

How you handle your brush is critical to the success of your painting, and time spent practising various brush techniques will be well rewarded. For some techniques, such as creating texture with the side of the brush, or the stabbing technique, for example, you can happily use an old, worn brush – in fact it makes sense to do so, as you don't want to wear out those marvellous new, well-pointed sables too quickly – while for delicate, detailed work, you need to reserve your best brushes and keep them in good order. I also use an old, large brush for mixing colours. In this section we look at a few basic techniques on how to achieve certain effects with your brushes.

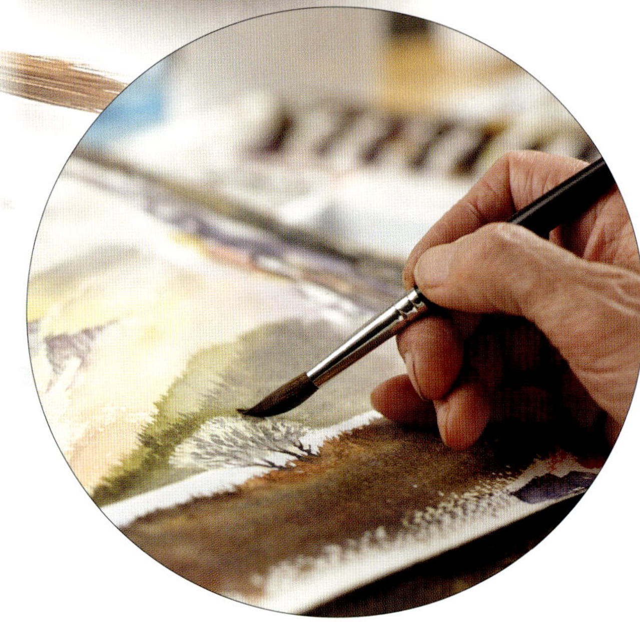

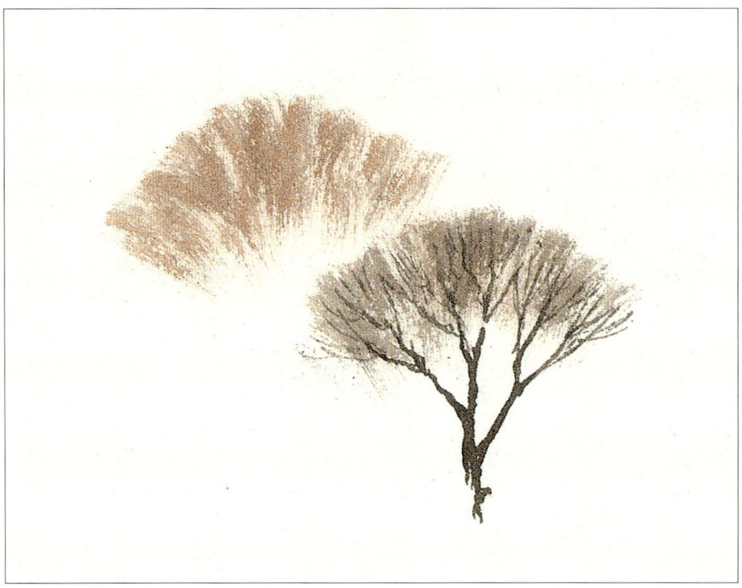

## STABBING METHOD

This is extremely useful for suggesting masses of twigs with a few strokes. Simply stab the brush down onto the paper at the point where you want the extremity of the twigs to start, and then drag it towards the centre of the bush or tree. Doing it this way gives an energetic effect. Practise it on scrap paper first to ensure the brush contains the right consistency of paint. The left-hand example was done with a no. 4 round brush, the right-hand pair with a 6mm (¼in) flat brush.

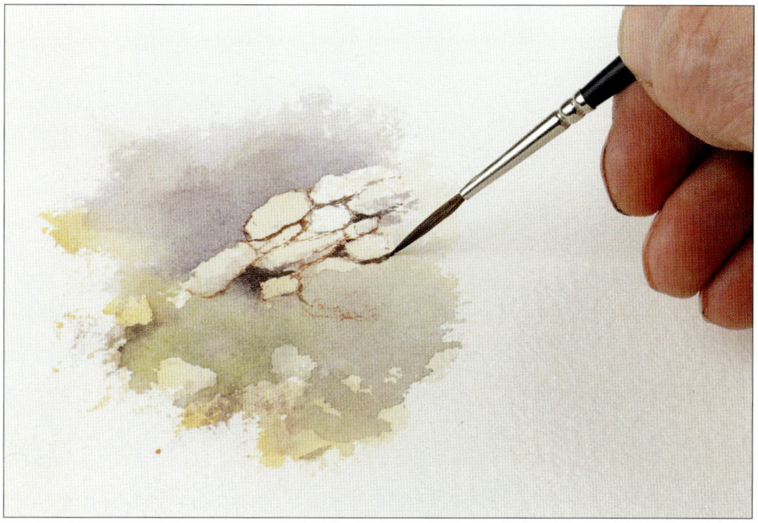

## VARYING MARKS AND LINES WITH A RIGGER

By putting varying pressure on a brush, you can create more interesting marks and lines, as in this section of a dry-stone wall painted with a fine rigger brush.

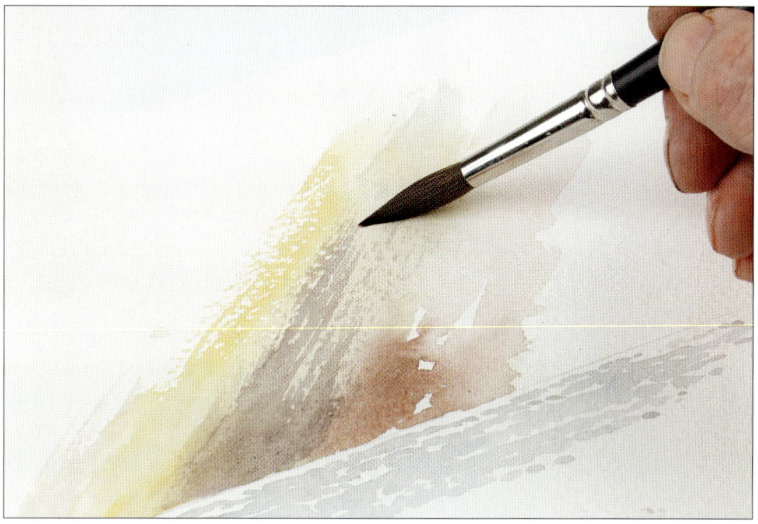

## CREATING TEXTURES WITH THE SIDE OF A BRUSH

With this technique, sometimes called dry-brush technique, the brush is dragged across the paper on its side, as shown here where a rough mountain slope descends to a lake. By testing the effect on spare paper, you can assess how liquid to make the mixture. On Rough paper, this method is extremely effective in creating broken washes, but it still works well on a Not surface. It is hard to beat when you need rough or broken texture, sparkle on water or boulder scree tumbling down below a crag.

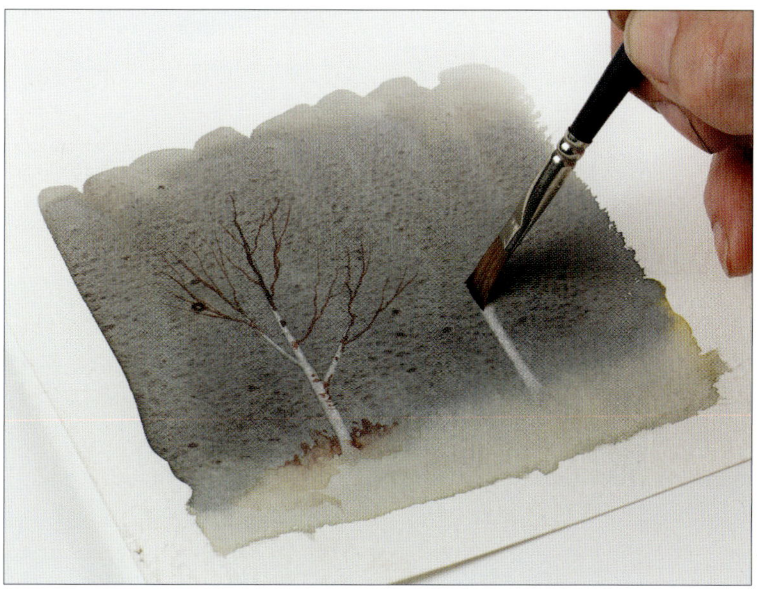

## FLAT BRUSHES FOR LIFTING OUT PAINT

Flat brushes are extremely effective for lifting out paint when brushed sideways as shown. It is fairly easy to create light tree trunks in this way without having the chore of working round the tree shapes with a dark wash in a negative fashion. They are also useful for removing unwanted paint. For this type of technique, you need to ensure the brush is one of the thinner flats, as this will ensure more delicate results.

# Working with watercolour

## HANDLING FLUID WASHES

Mixing and applying watercolours are two of the greatest problems facing the inexperienced artist, and there is no alternative to practising laying washes as often as you can. I would emphasize that testing your mixtures out on scrap paper first, before laying on the wash, is vital.

The amount of water you use in a mix is critical, and for larger washes you need to mix a pool of fluid watercolour that will more than cover the area you wish to paint: there is nothing worse than running out of colour halfway through the application and having to stop to mix more colour while the already-laid colour is rapidly drying. The most likely result then is ugly runbacks forming as a new wet wash is introduced to a drying one.

As you apply the paint, it is better to get it right first time than to apply multiple coats of washes, or you risk creating a muddy result. The mixture also needs to be strong enough in tone to give the result you desire, bearing in mind that watercolour tends to play the nasty trick of drying lighter than it appears when wet. Only experience will give you the expertise to overcome this.

The answer is to waste a lot of paper conducting test washes before you tackle the real thing on your composition. Make your mistakes on scrap paper, or on the back of failed watercolours. Use as large a brush as you feel confident with, for the fewer the strokes you apply, the cleaner your wash will appear.

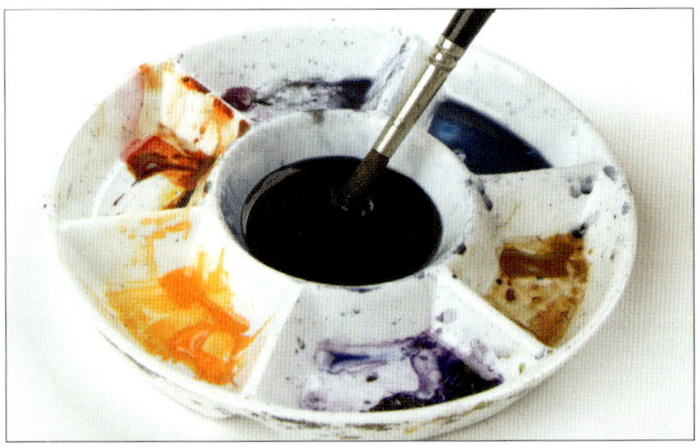

CREATING A WATERCOLOUR WASH

*In order to lay down an area of colour you need to mix a fluid pool of paint to apply with a reasonably large brush. Use an old brush that you save only for mixing.*

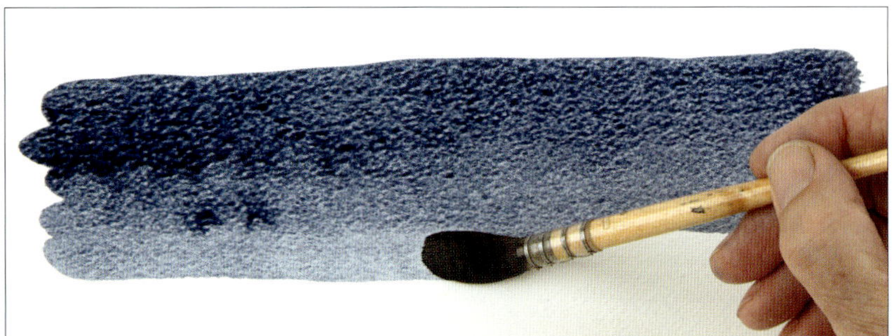

LAYING A WATERCOLOUR WASH

*Apply the wash quickly, preferably working down the paper with the board at a shallow angle, so that the fluid paint runs down gently towards you – a pile of books works well for this – each stroke of the brush slightly overlapping the previous one.*

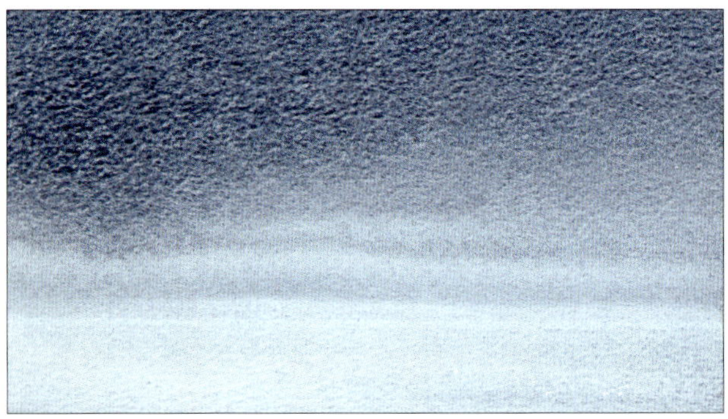

ALTERING THE TONE

*If you want to lighten the wash as you progress, then simply add a little more water to the mixture. If you wish to darken it, then add more of the appropriate colour.*

## WET-INTO-WET TECHNIQUE

This popular and exciting technique takes some experience to achieve good results, but is an excellent way of creating moody scenes and soft effects in a painting. First of all you need to lay out and mix all the colours you will need, as timing is critical – searching for tubes of paint while a wash is drying is a recipe for disaster. If that does happen, it is best to leave the first wash to dry completely (use a hairdryer to speed up the drying process if you wish, but be aware that this will spoil any granulations you may want to leave present).

Once the wash has dried, re-wet it with clean water then apply the second application, watching for the right moment. Getting the timing right to introduce the second application of paint can be tricky: too soon and it will spread out weakly and lose its shape; too late and it may well induce ugly cabbage-like runbacks into the wash. After applying the wash, look for reflected light showing up the sheen on the drying surface. When you see the sheen starting to dry, that is usually the optimum moment to introduce the second application of colour.

Testing it on the side of the painting, or a point where any error can be overlaid, is a sensible way of assessing the result. With the introduction of the second wash of colour, make sure that the consistency is strong enough and that you don't have much water on the brush, as this will also encourage runbacks. With time and experience in laying wet-into-wet washes, you will find your expertise will improve.

### Misty cliffs wet into wet

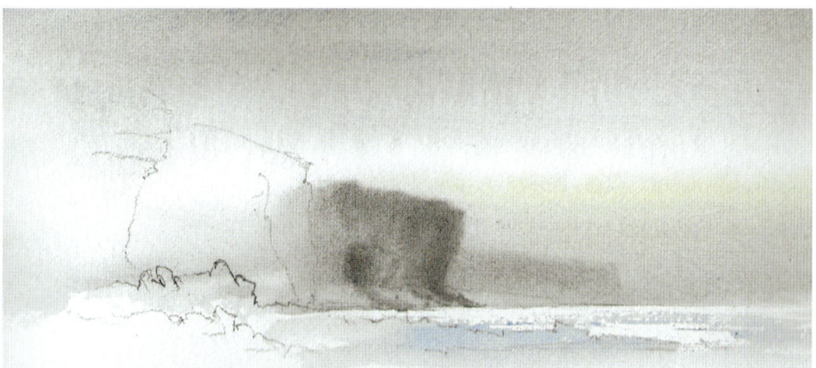

1 Firstly, paint the sky with a really fluid wash, bringing it right down to the horizon, then allow it to start drying before applying paint to the distant faint headland – too soon and the headland wash would spread out too weakly and too far; while if left till too late, the edge would become hard, thus bringing the headland too close to the viewer. There is also the danger of runbacks forming, especially if you introduce too much water in the second wash.

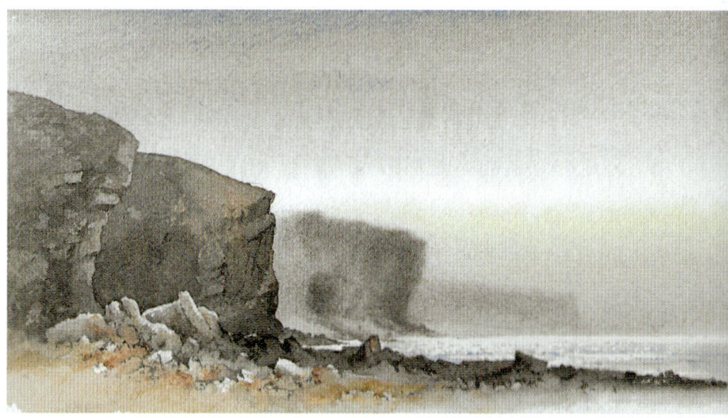

2 Add the darker tones of the closer cliffs and rocks once the paper has dried. Some light red was dropped into the foreground to complete the painting.

# Colour

## COLOUR MIXING

With watercolour we need to mix various colours to create the exact one that we require. Mixing more than two colours can be fraught with a tendency to produce a muddy effect, but sometimes a third colour is required, in which case only a touch of colour is generally needed.

As with so many aspects of working in watercolours, testing the results of your mixtures on scrap paper is vital before diving into the fray. Try out a variety of colours for mixing for the passage you are working on. It's possible to obtain similar results with combinations of different colours. Create charts of your favourite mixtures – it is frustrating to find a brilliant combination of colours and then forget which ones you used when next you wish to achieve that end colour.

## COLOUR TEMPERATURE

Choice of colours can depend on whether you desire a warm or cool effect. While it is easy to see that a red is warmer than a blue, blues – indeed, all other colours – can vary in temperature. The examples below show the warmer colour in each case on the right.

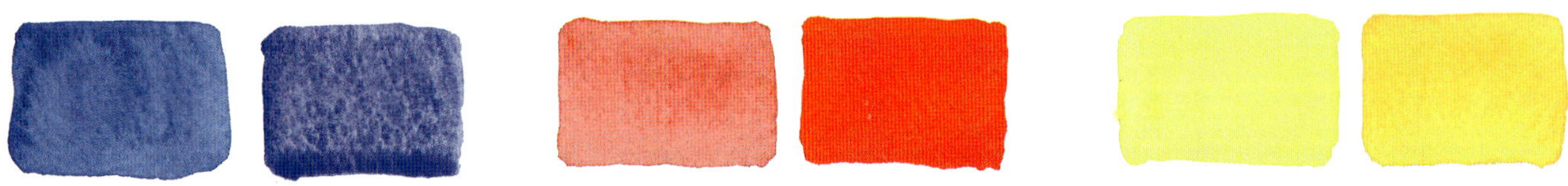

Phthalo blue (cool blue) | French ultramarine (warm blue) | Alizarin crimson (cool red) | Cadmium red (warm red) | Cadmium yellow pale (cool yellow) | New gamboge (warm yellow)

## EFFECTS OF ADJACENT COLOURS

When you place a colour next to one already laid down, the colours are affected by each other. For example, a cool colour such as phthalocyanine blue placed beside warm Aussie red gold will make that colour appear even warmer.

Other effects can also be achieved. Placing an intense indigo alongside Aussie red gold will create a strong contrast – extremely useful in highlighting a centre of interest, for example; while if warm sepia is adjacent to the Aussie red gold, it has the opposite effect, creating a sense of harmony as the two colours lie close together on the colour wheel.

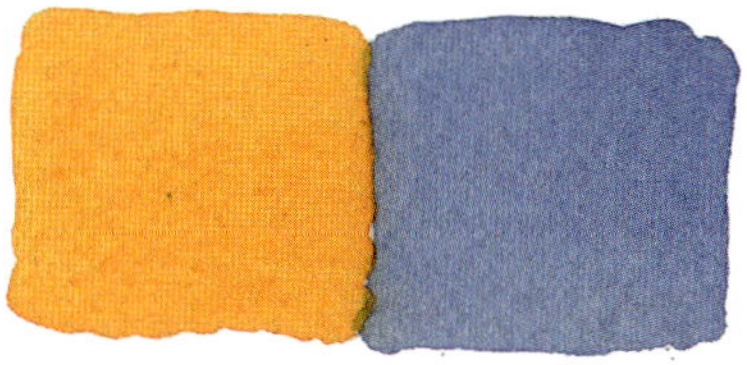

Aussie red gold Phthalo blue

*The cool blue makes the Aussie red gold appear to be even warmer.*

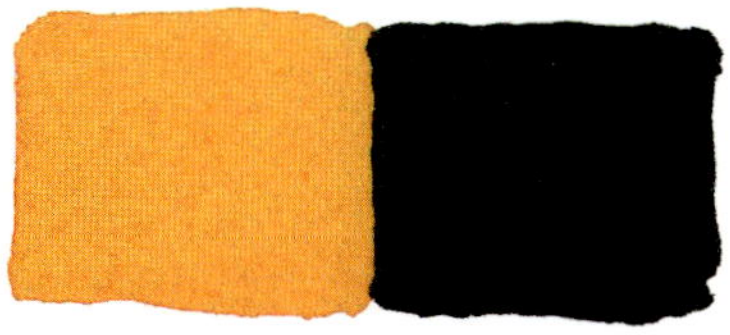

Aussie red gold Indigo

*The intensely dark indigo creates a striking contrast when set against Aussie red gold.*

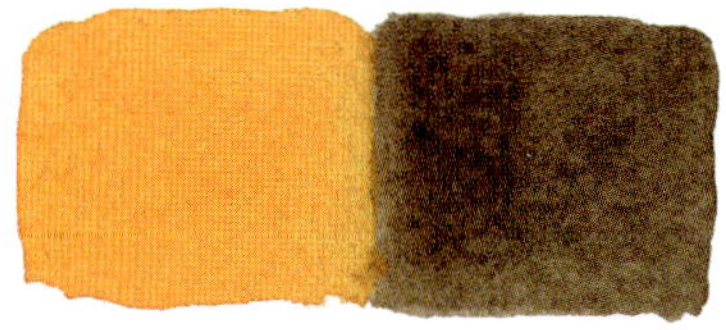

Aussie red gold Warm sepia

*A sense of harmony is created by having another warm colour next to the Aussie red gold.*

## DROPPING IN COLOURS

In addition to mixing paints on the palette an effective way of introducing colour is to drop it into a wash already laid on the paper; in other words, mixing it on the paper. This technique needs to be done immediately after laying the main wash, otherwise runbacks may well rear up out of the drying colours. As with the wet-into-wet applications (of which this method is a variant), you need to restrict the amount of water on the brush as you drop in the additional colour.

This technique can really liven up an area and add considerable interest without the need to introduce strong detail. While you can try any colours in this role, I find excellent ones to drop in are yellow ochre, cadmium orange, phthalo blue, cadmium red, Aussie red gold, transparent red oxide and quinacridone gold. Yellow ochre is especially effective as it is something of a bully, pushing other colours aside and thus often inducing spontaneous happy accidents.

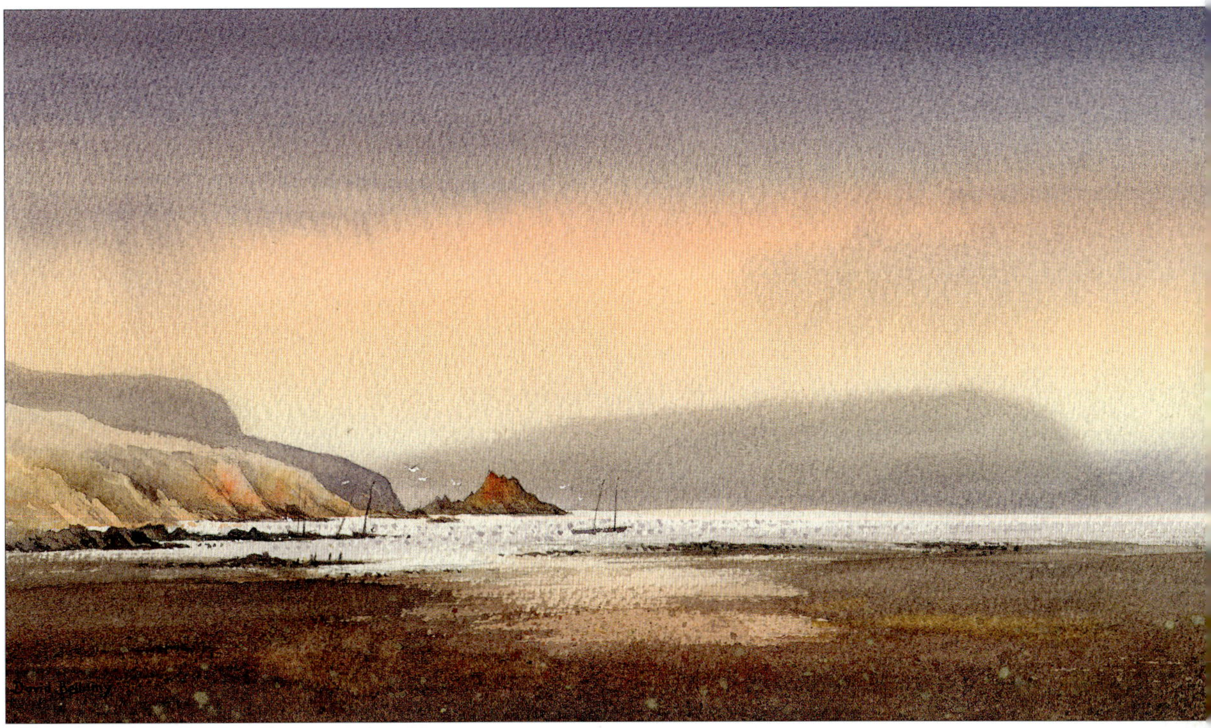

CAT ROCK

*23 x 30.5cm (9 x 12in)*

*By dropping a strong red into the wet colour on the rock this feature has been enlivened and strengthened as a focal point.*

# Tone

Tone is the degree of lightness or darkness in a colour and is controlled by how much water you include in the mixture. Adding more water will lighten the tone.

The range of tones you can achieve in different colours varies considerably: indigo, for example, being a dark colour, has a wide range of tones, whereas cadmium yellow light, being inherently such a light colour, allows much less scope for tonal variation.

Strong tones will make a feature appear to come forward towards the viewer, while weak ones recede. In a landscape we use this to suggest an illusion of space and distance, often exaggerating the degree of tonal variation to highlight a feature, or bring it more forward than it actually appears in real life.

When considering how we are going to paint a passage we need to consider what we have already laid on the paper – if there is to be a strong contrast in tones, then this is going to draw the eye towards that feature, which is an excellent method of highlighting your centre of interest. If, however, you wish to play down a feature, then painting with a fairly similar tone to the adjacent passage will achieve this.

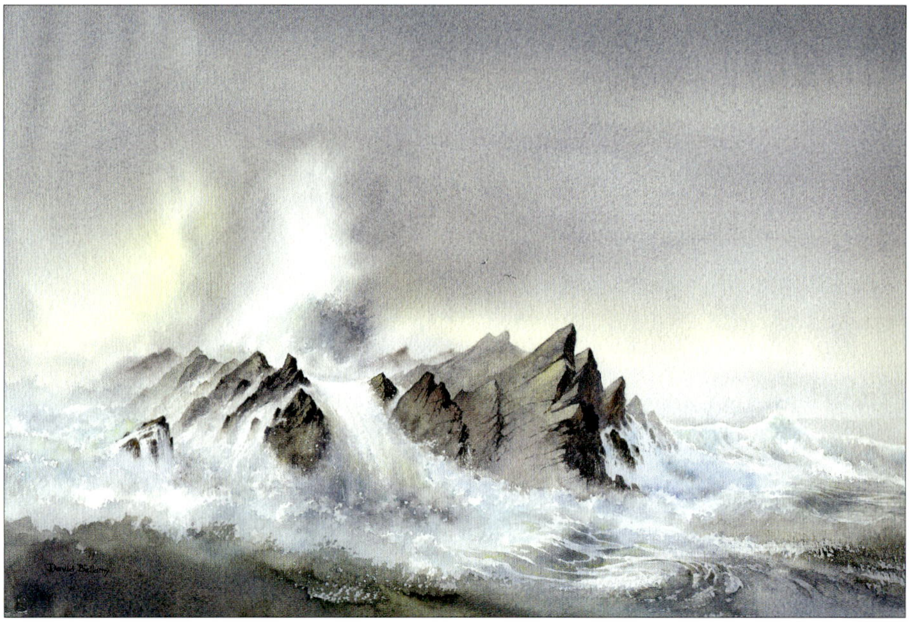

DETAIL FROM ATLANTIC FURY

*Here I have exaggerated the tonal range on the right-hand rocks by making those slightly further away much lighter than they actually appeared, to emphasize that they are receding and thus giving more depth to the scene.*

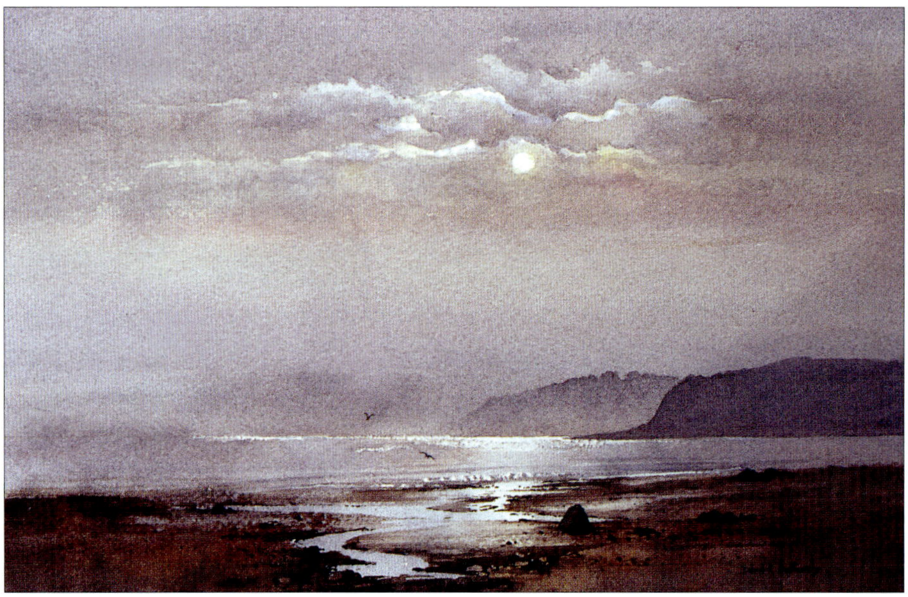

NOVEMBER AFTERNOON LIGHT

*21.5 x 30.5cm (8½ x 12in)*

*The backlit effect increases the mood, with hardly any colour. The composition relies on tonal variation to suggest distance. Note that the dark rock in the foreground stands close to the light rivulet, the contrast in tones accentuating the focal point.*

# Experimental techniques

A number of watercolour additives are available now and these seem to be on the increase. While some are effective, others have only limited value. If you like the effect of granulation in a wash, bottles of granulation medium are available which you can introduce into your mixtures, although you do need quite a considerable amount to produce really strong granulations.

It's great fun to experiment with materials to hand, such as credit cards, cut-up pieces of mount-board or watercolour paper, plastic food wrap, odd pieces of material mono-printed onto your composition with a roller, and whatever your imagination suggests. Having an occasional day experimenting can be liberating!

## PULLING OUT COLOUR

This rock shows me pulling out the colour while still damp, using a credit card.

In this particular example I have enhanced the effect by mixing the colour with Winsor & Newton Aquapasto medium, which adds body to the mixture and makes lifting out easier.

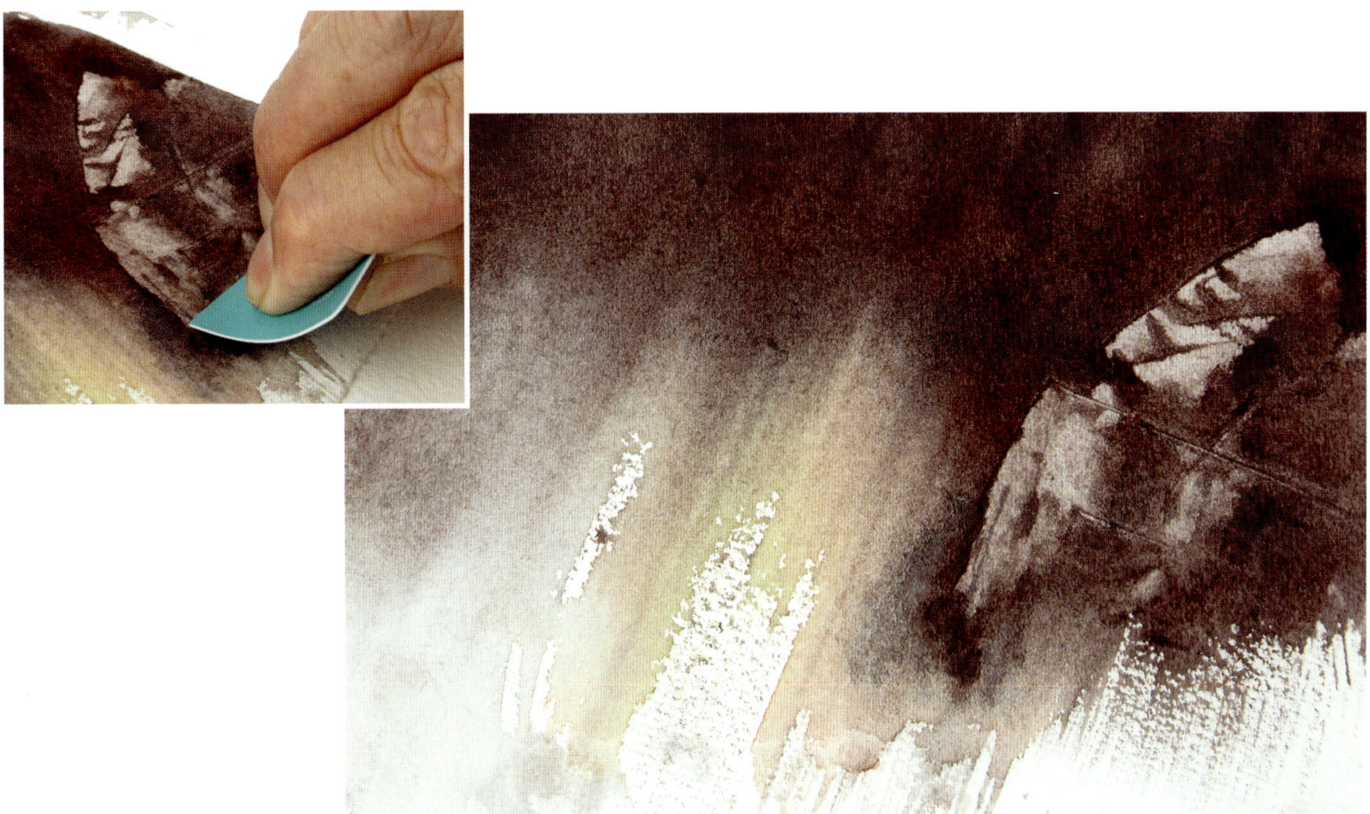

## MONOPRINTING

The pattern of netting on a lobster pot can be achieved by painting the pot dark, and then either scratching the netting out with a scalpel, or painting it on with white gouache. Small areas can also be suggested by negative painting, but here I use monoprinting with a small section of netting that comes with washing products.

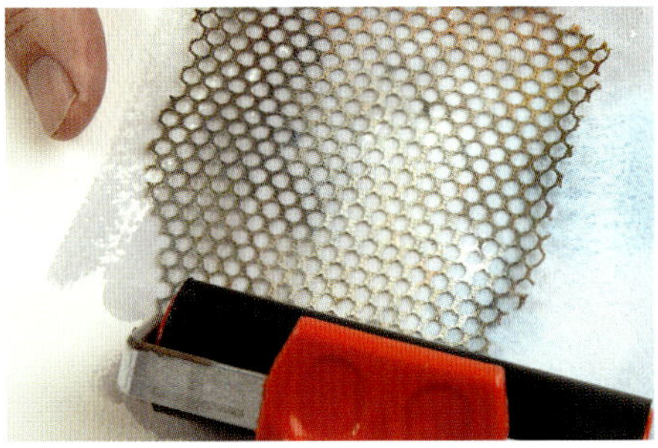

1 Liberally coat the net with a mixture of white gouache and a touch of Naples yellow to take off the stark whiteness. Place it on a piece of scrap watercolour paper covered in a fairly dark colour, and press it down with the roller. This gives an idea of how the result will appear and gets rid of the excess paint. You may need to do this more than once.

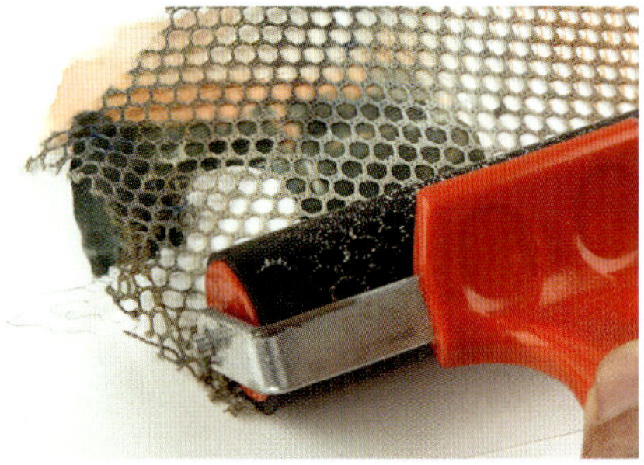

2 As soon as you are happy with the result, lay the netting over the image of the pot and roll over it; making sure that the outline of the pot, the buoy and the light foreground are masked off, and the dark background covered with paper to avoid any of the gouache spreading beyond the lobster pot.

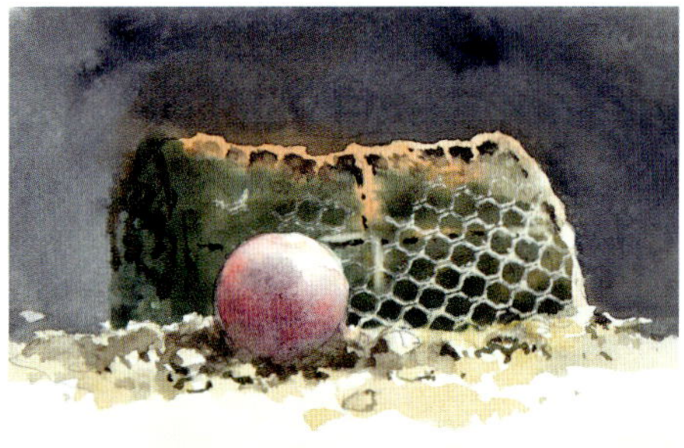

3 The result in this instance has been reasonably effective. You may find that you need to tidy up the edges of the monoprint a little with a damp brush and tissue.

## TEXTURAL EFFECTS

There are numerous ways of introducing texture into watercolour paintings, from the simple manner of brushing across a Not or Rough surface with the side of a brush, to introducing materials specifically aimed at creating textures.

After laying a wash of lightish colour (raw sienna or Naples yellow, for example) and allowing it to dry, you can apply broken colour of a darker tone with the side of the brush. As you draw it across, it will pick up the texture of the paper. You can change to the point of the brush in places to create variation as well.

I often spatter my work, to induce texture and spontaneity. This can be done by dragging your finger or thumb across the hairs of a loaded brush or a palette knife. Spattering using a toothbrush loaded with either paint or just water works well over a damp wash that is almost dry. Spattering over a dry wash using a toothbrush, round or flat brush loaded with paint also works well. You can also apply the spatter with a chopping motion, or strike the brush downwards onto a finger.

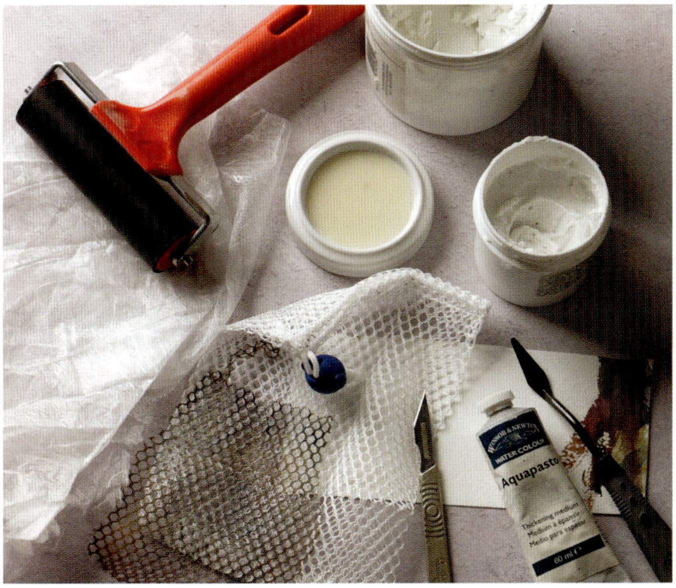


### MATERIALS FOR ADDING TEXTURE

*Heavy texture can be striking but beware of over-doing the effect. I often use white Daniel Smith Watercolour Ground applied with a painting knife. Once allowed to dry overnight, you can paint over it, and this can produce exciting textures. Gesso is similar, though watercolour does not take so well. Having said that, the more unpredictable results can have a charm of their own. Schminke texture paste produces a rougher finish that can be appealing on features like rocks, cliffs, rough ground and so forth. It is best applied with a knife or piece of card. A scalpel is most effective for scratching out highlights, while the roller, netting and aquapasto pictured above are used for the technique on page 20.*

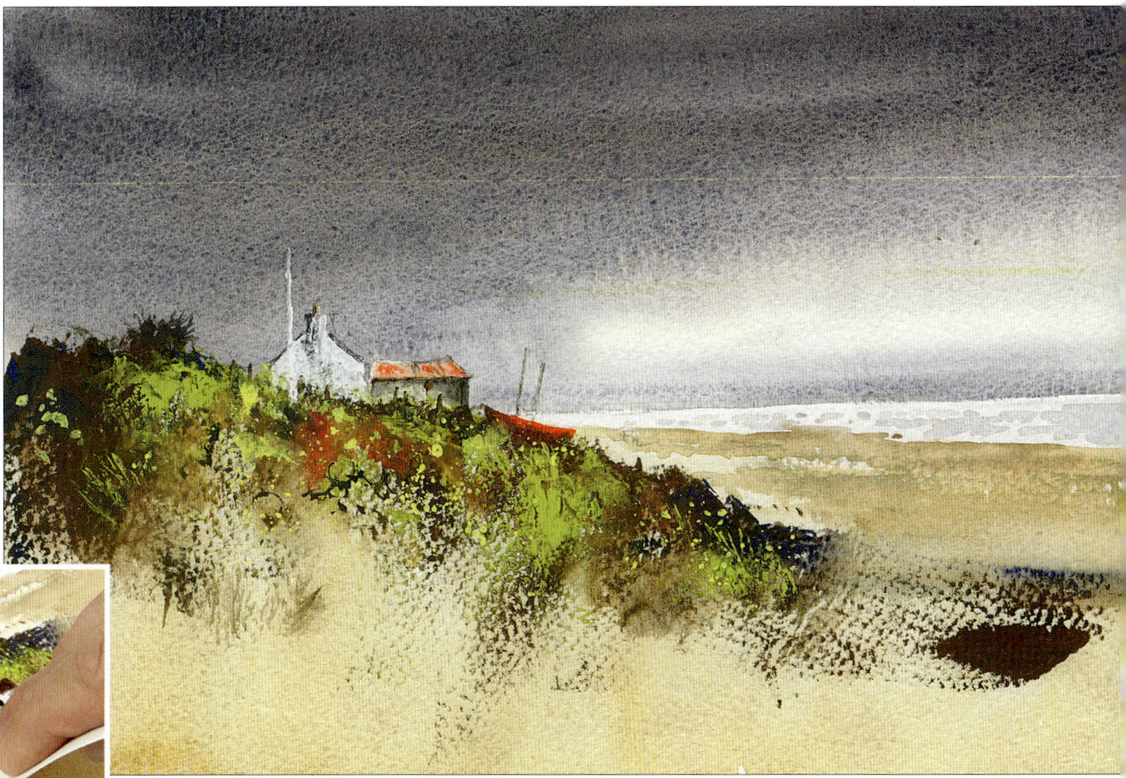

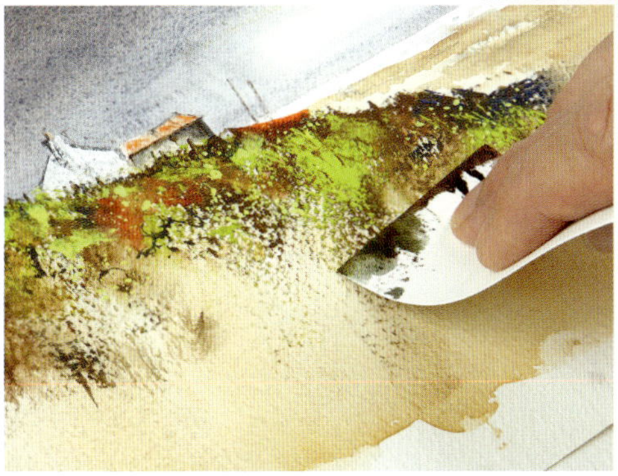

### THE RED BOAT

*12.5 x 23cm (5 x 9in) 425gsm (200lb) Not surface*

*After painting the sky and beach washes in the normal manner, I then used a small piece of card to apply paint, effectively working its straight edge to define the cottage with white gouache, then the dark masts and fenceposts, and finally on its side to suggest rough ground in the foreground in the style of a dry-brush (see inset). The Bockingford Not surface helped to achieve this effect. I then applied the darks with a no. 8 round brush. The final flourish was to plaster thick light green and yellow gouache in places with a few dabs here and there to indicate individual grasses with the edge of the card.*

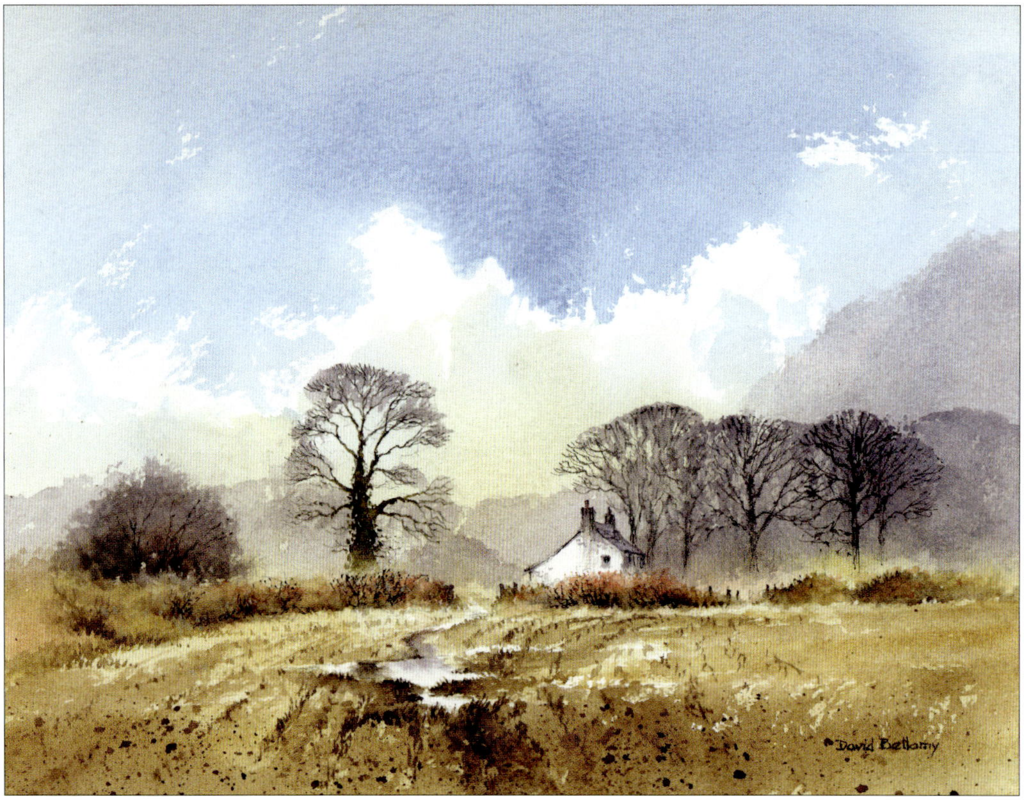


**PEMBROKESHIRE FARM**

*20.3 x 28cm (8 x 11in), 300gsm (140lb) Not paper*

*In this painting of a farm in Wales, I used a no. 8 round sable brush, charged with a fluid mix of French ultramarine and burnt umber, and I brought the brush down sharply onto the handle of another brush to induce a jolt which spattered the wet paint across the foreground. Sometimes I use more than one colour to spatter an area.*

**EDGE TOP FARM, LONGNOR – WATERCOLOUR SKETCH ON CARTRIDGE PAPER**

*I don't normally spatter over snow, but in this watercolour sketch done on the spot in the English Peak District, I felt it would liven things up a little. The character of spatter is greatly affected by the type of brush you employ, the angle of approach, and whether you strike the brush against another object, as in the painting above, or use your finger or a knife to drag through the bristles of the brush. Here I simply loaded a no. 6 round sable with fluid paint, and holding it a couple of inches above the paper, flicked the brush with my first finger, adjusting the angle of the brush and flick of the finger to create a slightly more horizontal trajectory for the left-hand spattering.*

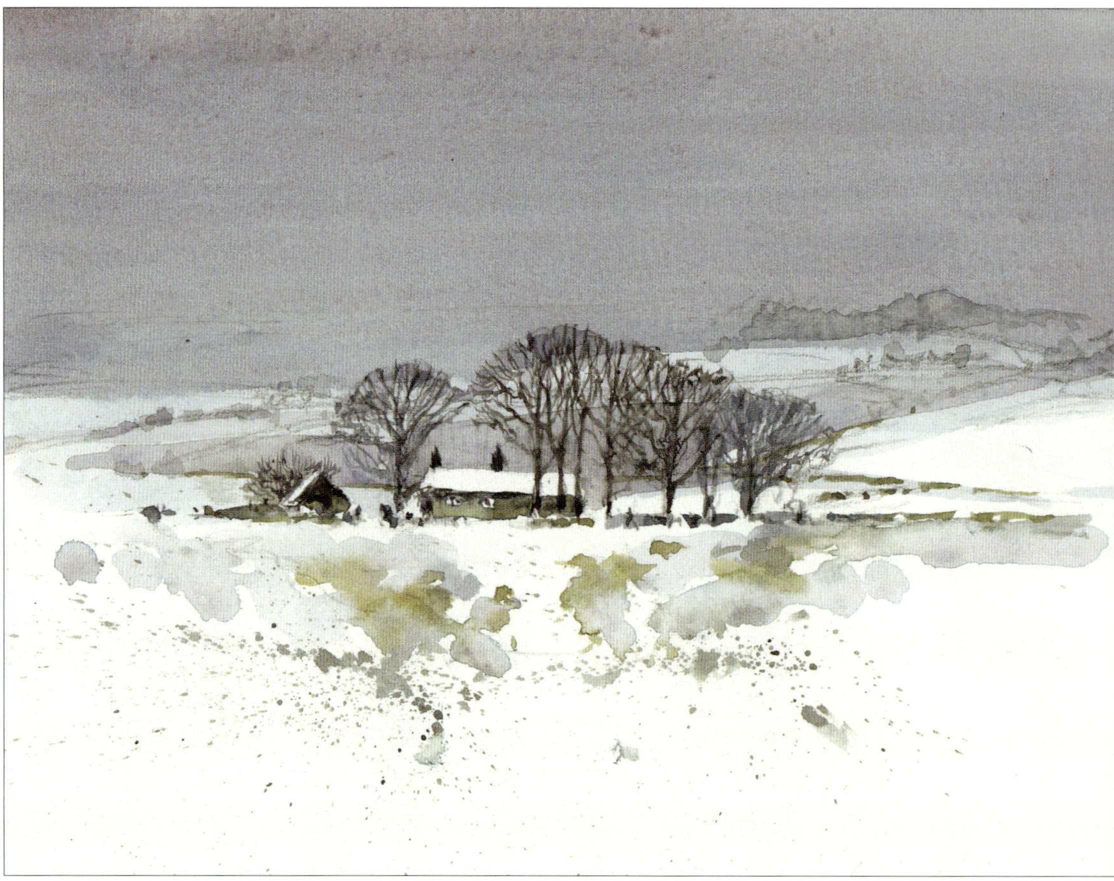

### BOATS AT BEER, DEVON

*25.5 x 38cm (10 x 15in)*

*One of the problems of painting the beach at Beer is the heavily contrasting cliff detail which is often overdone and spoils many a painting of this lovely scene. In this watercolour I wanted to portray the beautiful cliff scenery but place the emphasis on the boats as a centre of interest. I also wanted to portray the lovely sunlight falling on the cliffs, and after some deliberation decided to use Daniel Smith Watercolour Ground applied with a painting knife across the cliff area. In places I created a heavier impasto effect, varying the application throughout. The next day I began the watercolour washes, leaving white highlights in places to enhance the sense of sunlight, and playing down the strongly contrasting vegetation which would introduce a tatty leopard-spot appearance. The overall effect formed a fine background to the boats, without being intrusive and drawing too much attention.*

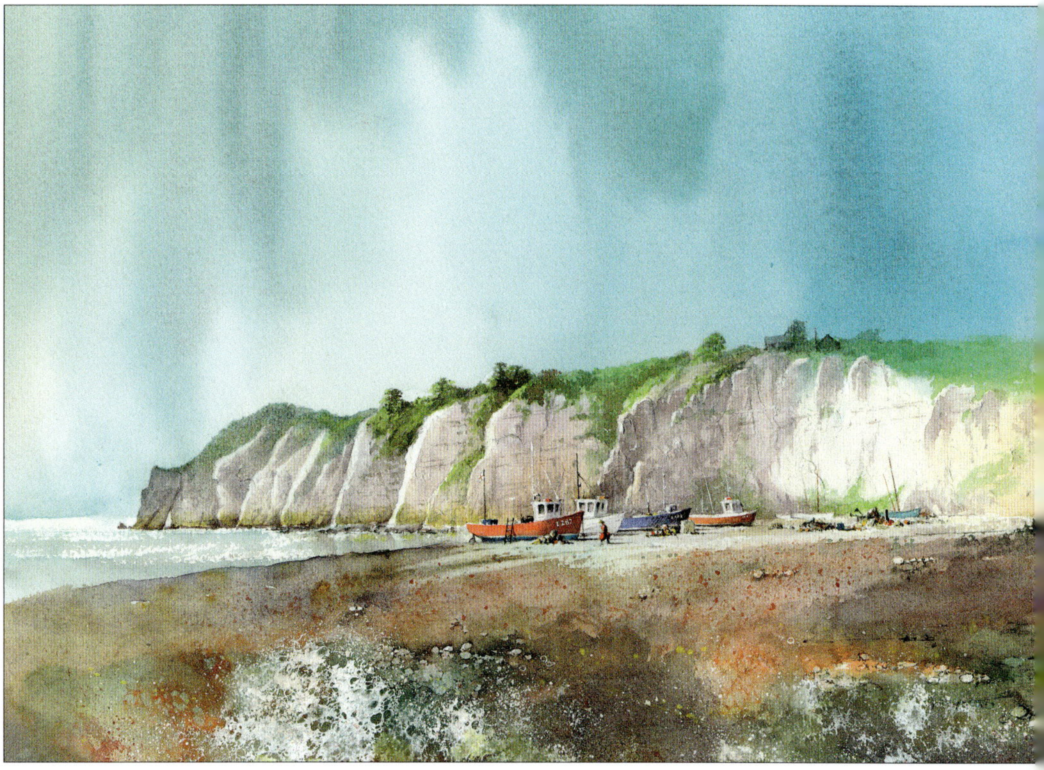

### TEXTURE PASTE FOR ROCKS

*Here Schminke heavy texture paste was spread across the rocks with a knife (see detail below) and, when dry, painted over. This can produce striking textures in rocks, walls or ground detail, and even foliage, although it needs care where you wish to depict fissures.*

*The sea was painted with a scrub-and-scratch method, where the brush was held almost parallel with the paper and in line with the horizon, then with a wriggling motion dragged across the sea area, leaving white strips here and there. When the sea was dry, further highlights were scratched out with a scalpel.*

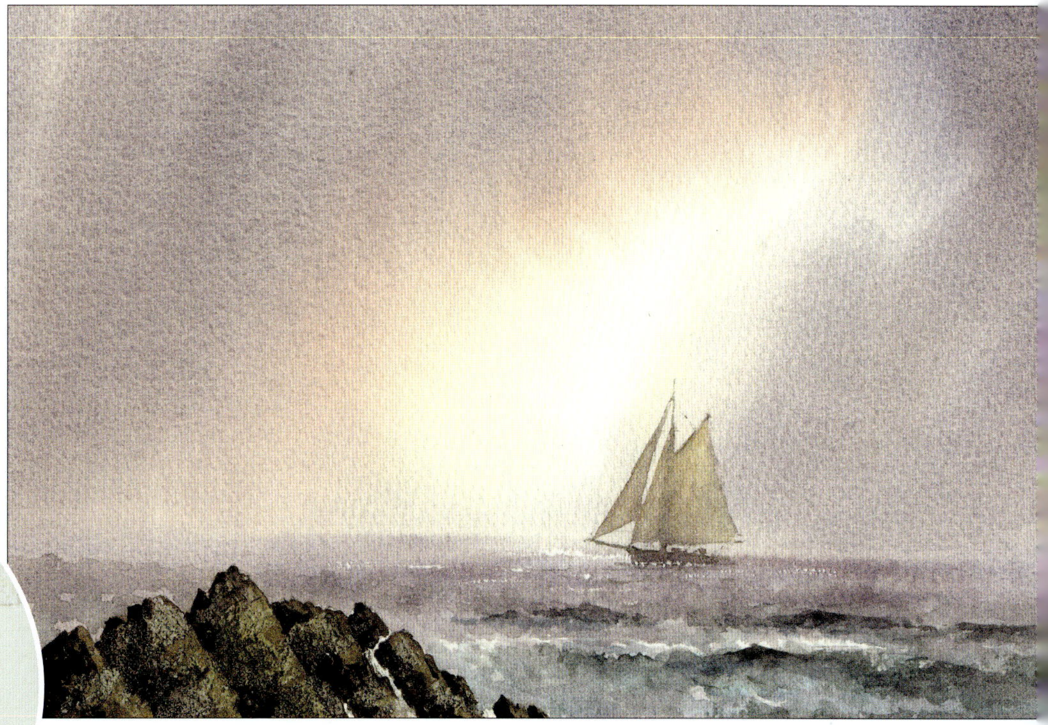

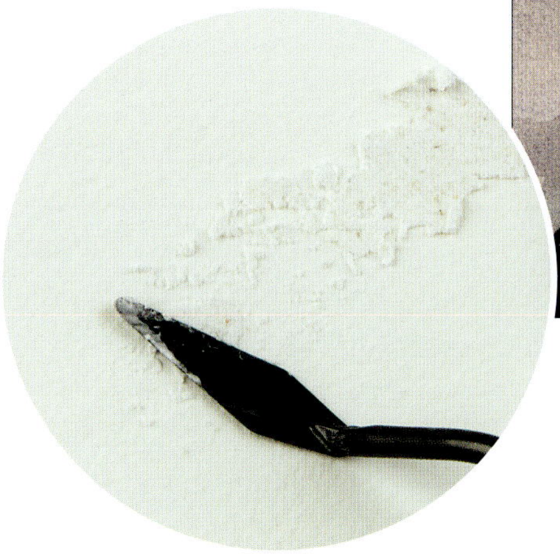

# Sketching

Finding subjects to paint can be one of the chief joys of being an artist. Many people are reluctant to go out and sketch and it warms the heart to see the enthusiastic reaction of many coming on a course for the first time and discovering this way of working. Going out and seeking what you especially want to paint is rewarding, whether it's your mum's cottage, friends climbing a mountain, or maybe some favourite old moorland boulder. Believe me, there are distinctive rocks and crags all over the country which I regard as old friends, and have painted many times, with some appearing in paintings from Killarney to Kathmandu.

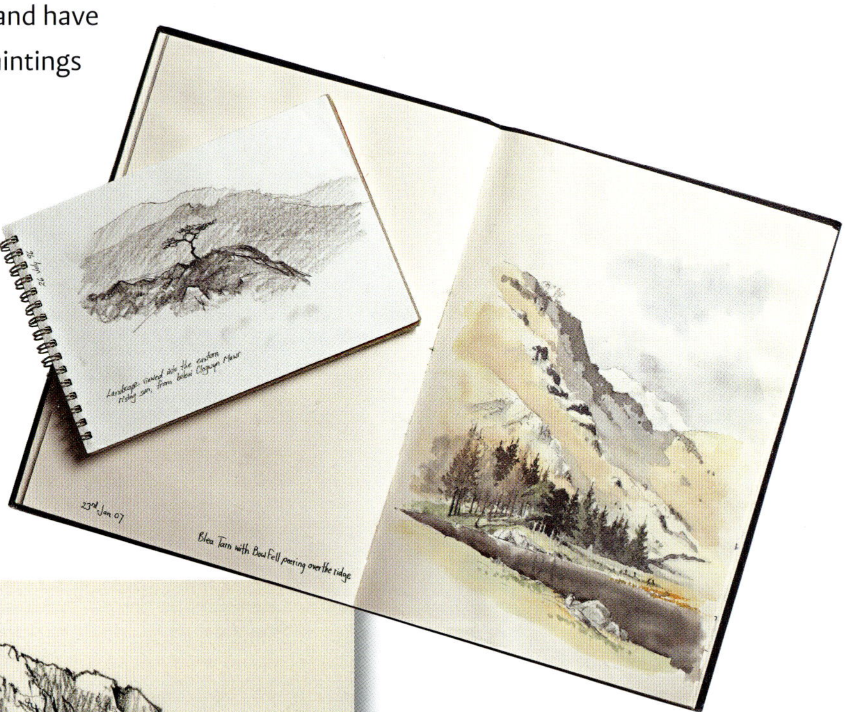


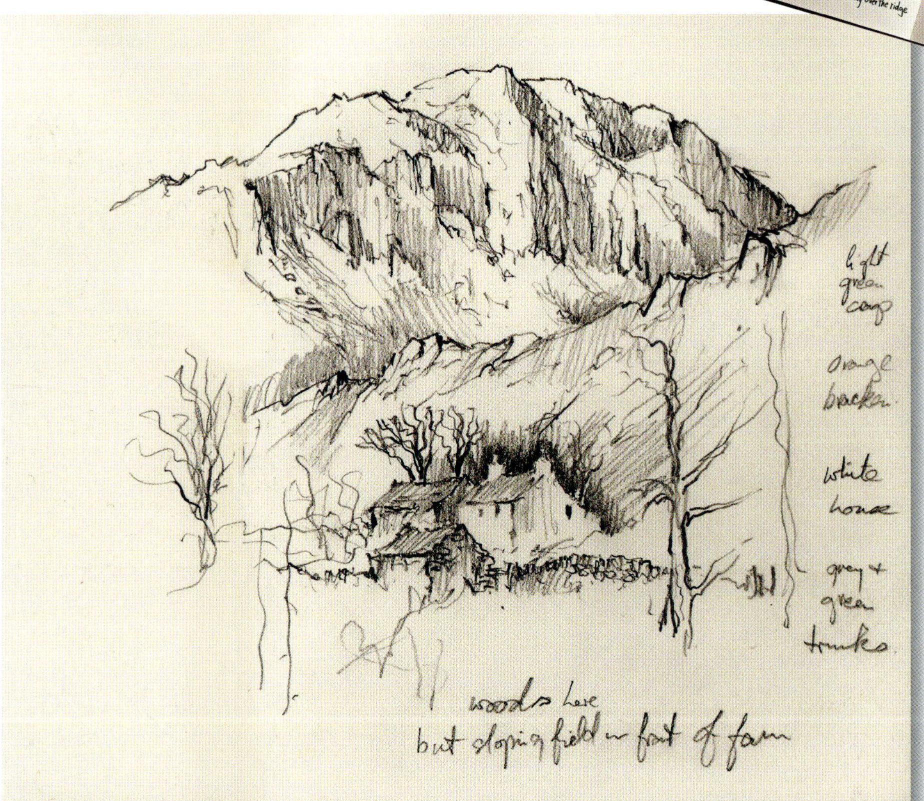


*This subject was impossible to photograph properly because it was hidden by trees. However, by moving around I could easily see between the trunks of the trees and created a pencil sketch of the farm without difficulty. It pays to have a sketchbook and a few pencils with you all the time.*

## SKETCHING FROM A CAR

Many subjects worth sketching can easily be seen from the car, although finding a parking space can at times be difficult. I sometimes stop in a field gateway for a short while to carry out a quick sketch, but make sure I stay with the car and am ready to move on if someone wants to get through. Often the road itself can act as an excellent lead-in to a composition, and many is the time I have turned a major road into a dirt track. Whatever you do, safety and consideration for other people are paramount and I have never had any problems in this respect. Some maps indicate unfenced roads with dotted lines on each side, and this will give you a fair idea of roadside parking possibilities.

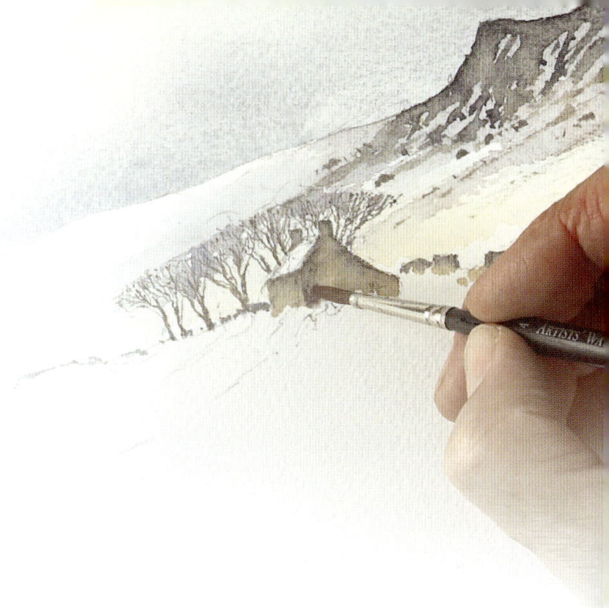

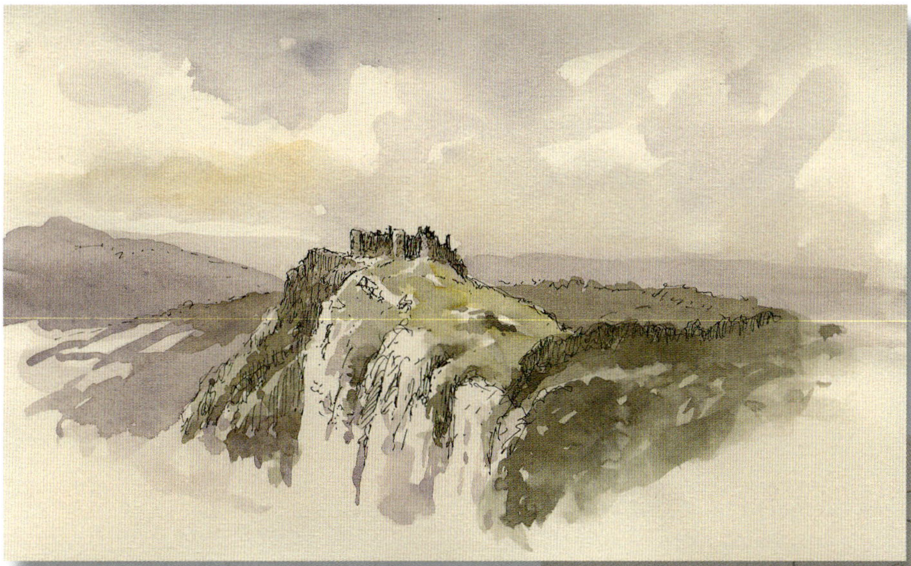

*Subjects like this castle, set in dramatic moorland that seems to attract the most glorious atmospheric conditions, can be seen for miles from many directions, and are easily sketchable from a car.*

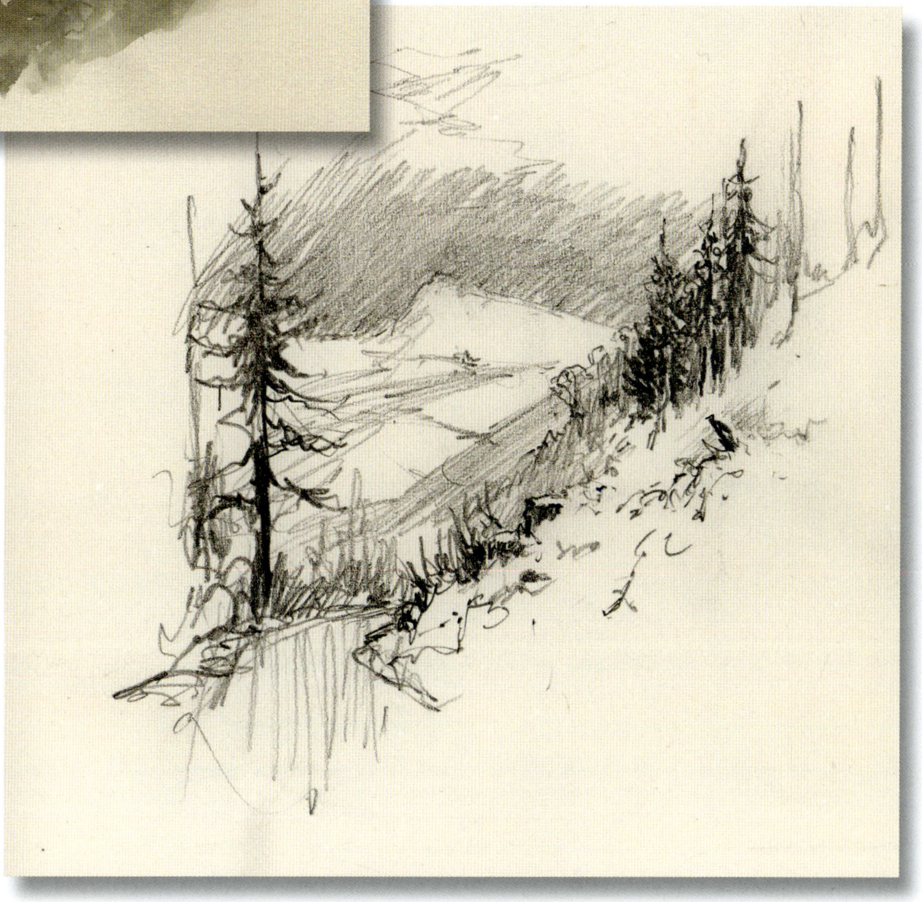

*How often we see scenes from a busy main highway while driving along. Many of these can be captured safely from a lay-by, using the road as a lead-in, as in this case. Often I downgrade a major highway to a rustic old lane.*

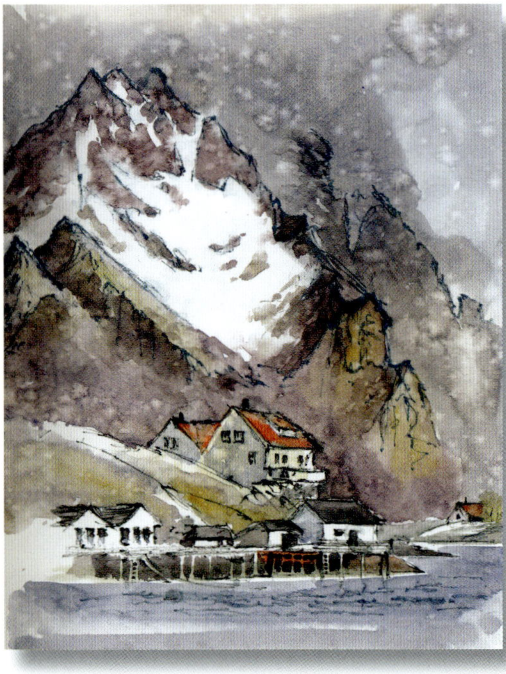

*This watercolour sketch of Festvagtinden in Norway's Lofoten Islands was carried out with light rain falling on the paper, so I used watercolour pencils to strongly define the detail. Don't let the weather deter you when you're in front of a good subject – rain can often add a sense of spontaneity to an alfresco watercolour that cannot be achieved any other way.*

## SKETCHING IN BAD WEATHER

While sketching inside a vehicle can make you feel safer and insulated from people who want to see what you are up to, there is nothing like getting out and wandering around for the optimum viewpoint. While it is good to go out in fine weather, don't always pick the sunny days: heavy rain gives waterfalls a much greater appeal and you may be able to sketch in between showers. Distant rain squalls can create a strong sense of mood and lose unwanted features. If a few rain spots spatter your sketch, it is no cause for alarm, and often it helps to suggest a spontaneous response to the scene. I sometimes draw into wet washes with a dark watercolour pencil (black, dark grey, indigo or sepia) to capture detail, and this works when the sketchbook is being spattered with rain.

Many waterfalls stand close to a road and make ready-made subjects needing little alteration in a great many cases. Study the maps to find them.

For the house-bound, acquiring subjects is not so easy. Friends and relatives might be cajoled into taking photographs of scenes for you, but this depends on how resourceful they are. Copying from books, calendars, magazines, etc, is an alternative, but lacks personal input. Maybe you have old photographs, or even memories that can be evoked. In each of these cases it pays to do some studio sketches to rough out the composition and make changes before deciding on the final design.

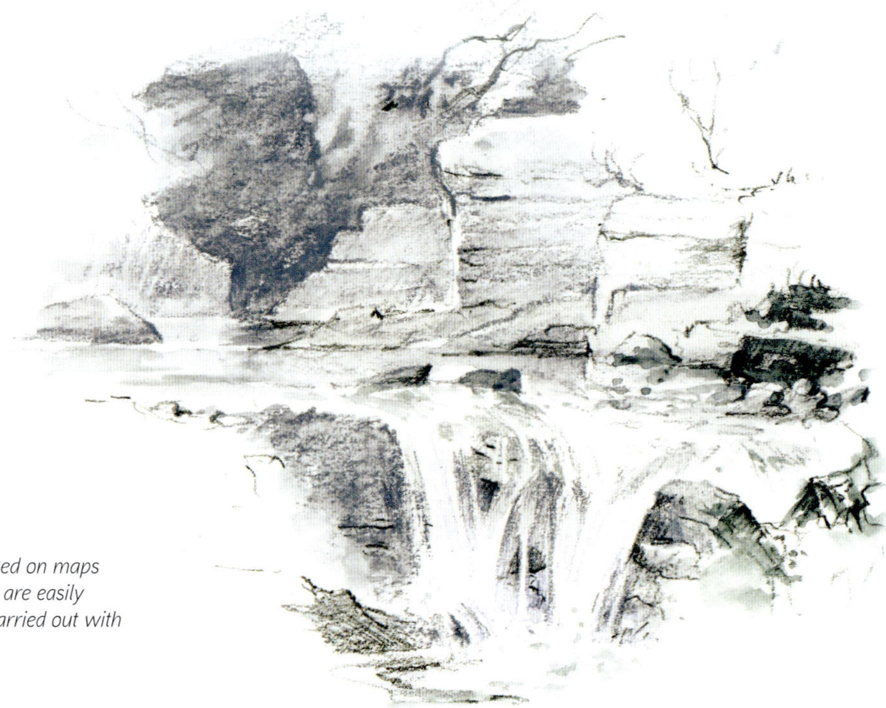

*Waterfalls are normally marked on maps of 1:50,000 scale, and many are easily accessible. This sketch was carried out with a water soluble pencil.*

## SKETCHING FIGURES

Some places, such as villages, call out for figures, while at other times you may wish to show the immense scale of a mountain by including tiny figures. Where you position them is critical: too close to the foreground and the figures may well dwarf the rest of the composition; too distant and they may become lost in the mass of scenery. A lone figure in a vast panorama is an excellent way of suggesting a sense of loneliness. If you are nervous about adding figures, keep a jar of clean water nearby so that if you make a mistake you can immediately wash it out with a large round brush. Dab the area with a tissue, wait for it to dry and have another go. It helps if you do not have any strong detail beside the figure. Be aware that if you include figures, they will instantly become the centre of interest.

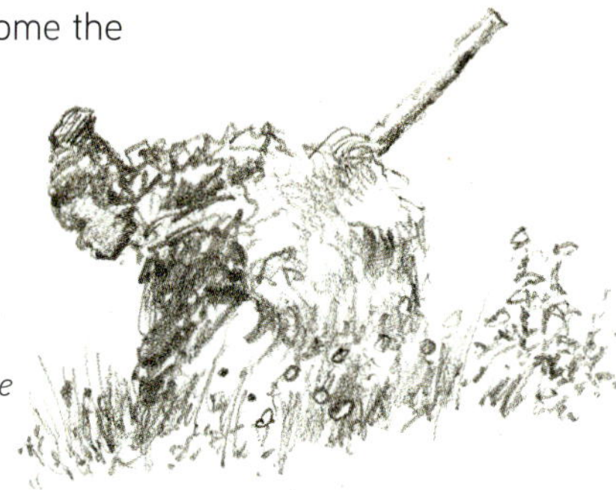

*It took me some time to work out what this Ladakhi woman, from the northernmost state of India, was doing, as she was wrapped up in furs while weeding crops. Capturing poses like this is a delight.*

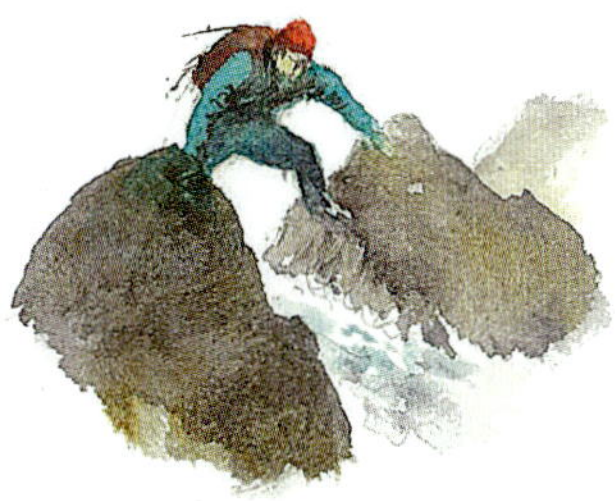

*Figures are at their most convincing when seen doing something rather than standing dummy-like. Try to include some action if you can.*

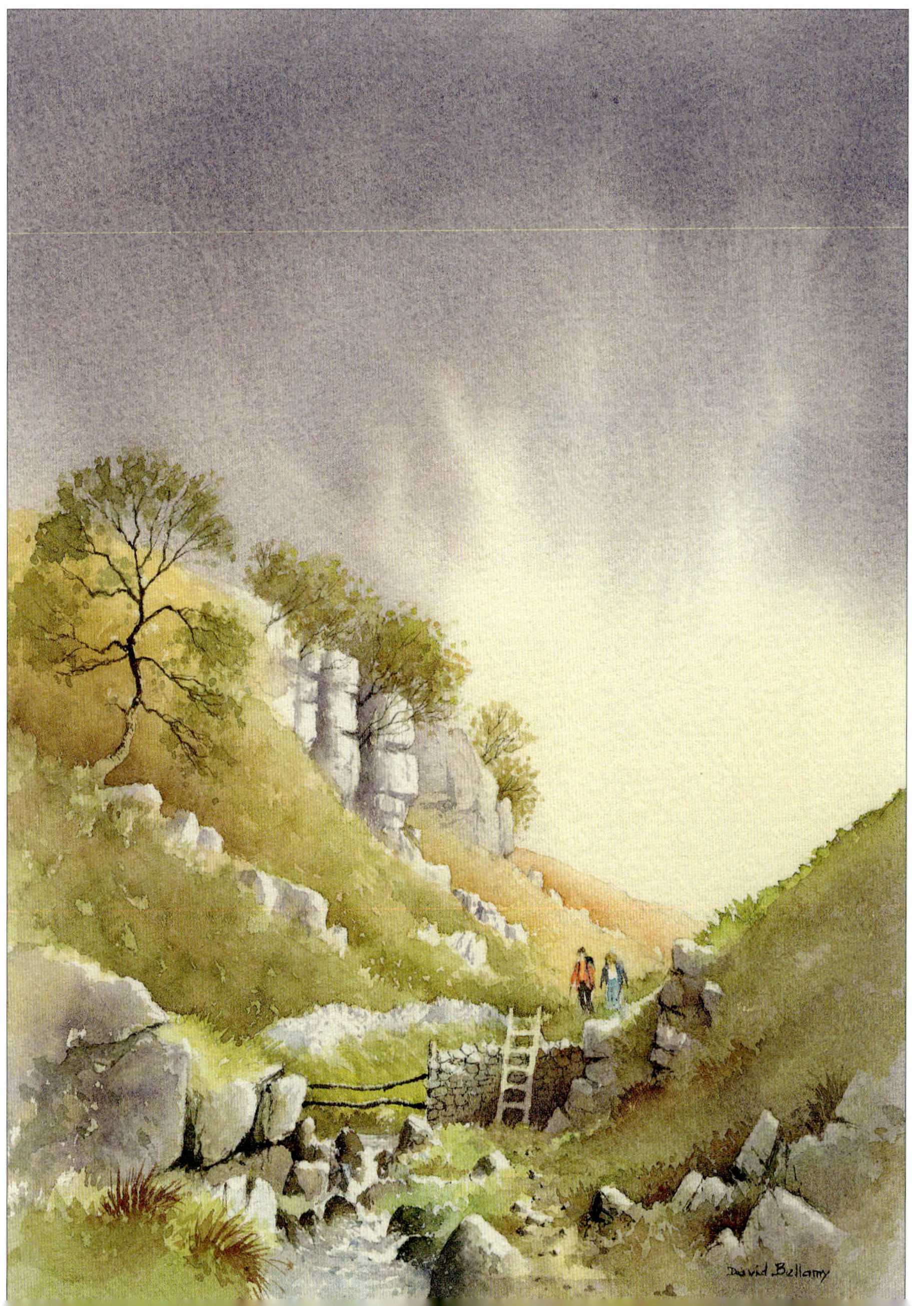


**TROLLER'S GILL, YORKSHIRE**
*23 x 18cm (9 x 7in)*

*Sometimes a landscape calls out for figures, and this was one such scene. As I had included a ladder stile, the picture seemed empty without someone climbing it, or about to do so as in this case.*

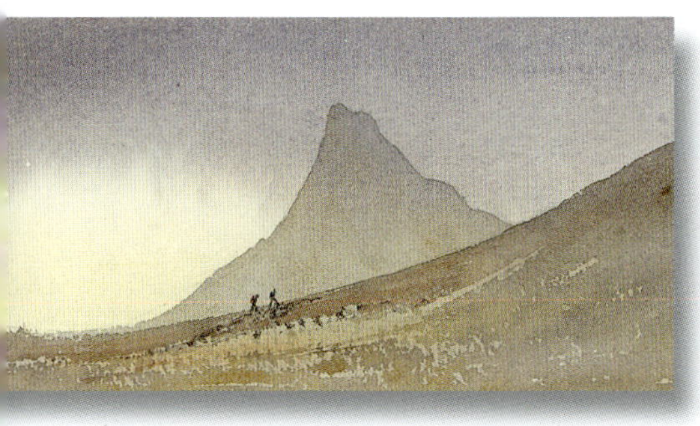

*Placing tiny figures in a mountain landscape dramatically emphasizes the massive scale of a peak, and at this range figures should present no difficulty.*

## SKETCHING ANIMALS

Like figures, animals will add life, scale and interest to your landscapes and it is worth building up a library of animal images in sketches and photographs to include in your scenes. If you position them against a fairly bland, uncluttered hillside, or perhaps mist, they will stand out. By altering the light and shadow you can turn them into a silhouette or light them up. When out capturing images of wild animals, I like to sketch as much as I can, but also take many photographs. Once, while stalking musk-oxen in Greenland, all my photographs turned out to be under-exposed rubbish, but my sketches, done through binoculars mounted on a tripod, saved the day. The biggest danger of painting animals from photographs is that of making the beasts appear like wooden carvings.

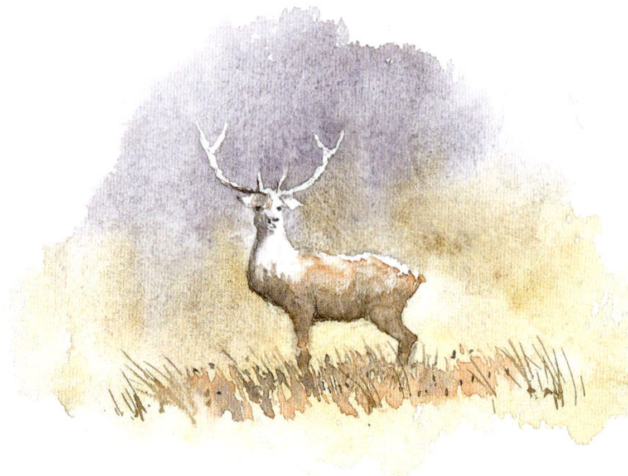

*Animals can enhance a scene, or act as the centre of interest, so I do studies of all manner of wildlife when the opportunity arises. This stag appeared from behind vegetation and boldly posed long enough for me to carry out a sketch and take photographs.*

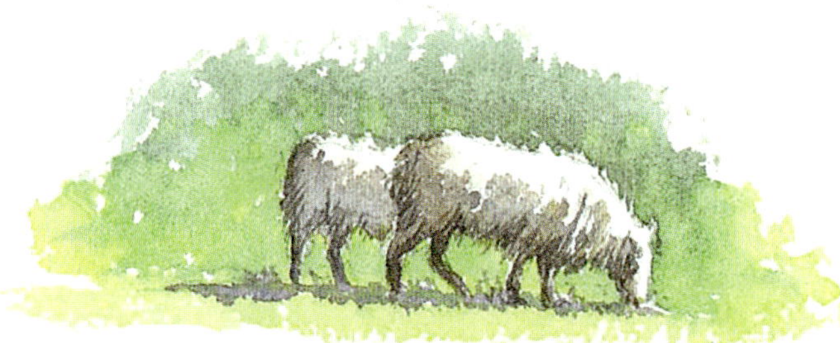

*Sheep add life and interest to scenes on the lower mountain slopes. Bunch some of them together, overlapping them as in this study, as they are extremely gregarious creatures.*

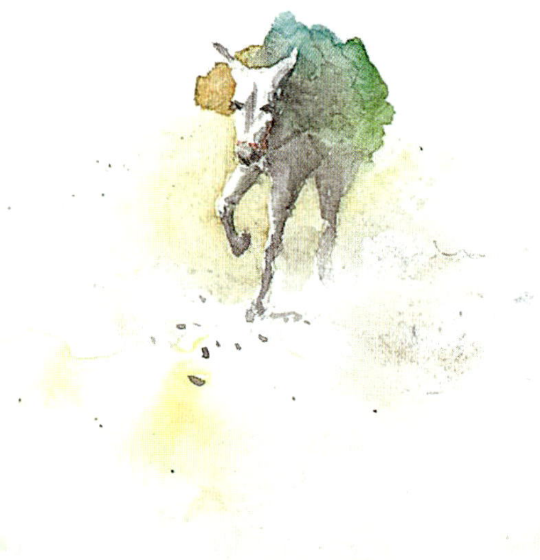

*I take many photographs of moving animals but I find there is nothing like sketching to capture the actual sense of movement. A slight blurring of the legs or wings will suggest a moving limb, as well as creating a pose that shows the beast with its legs in a moving position, as in this case.*

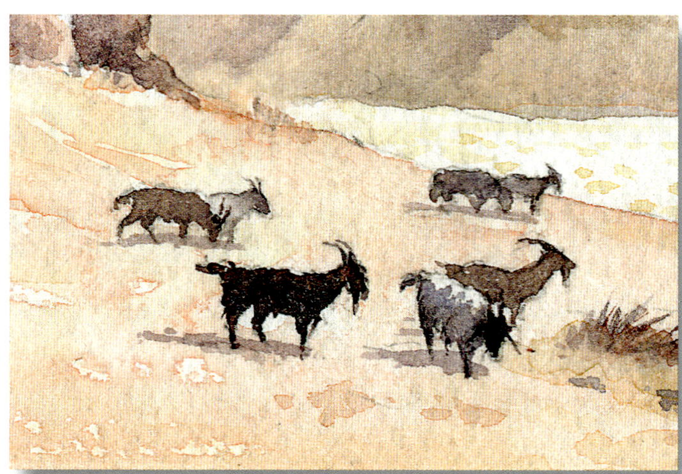

# Working from photographs

The ease with which we can photograph a scene now makes the camera a versatile tool for the landscape artist. Even my small compact camera has a powerful zoom lens which can bring distant images close-up. Make good use of this facility and take a number of photographs of the scene from different ranges and angles. If the lighting is tricky, then take several shots with different settings to over- and under-expose the image, as this technique will doubtless make one part of the image much better exposed.

When working from photographs back at home, it helps to do a studio sketch from the photograph first. This will help you work out the composition, as you will see in the example. In this way you can change emphasis or tones, rearrange the image and add and subtract features before you do the final drawing. Try to avoid slavishly following the detail when working directly from a photograph.

*The reference photographs for the painting. Right: the overall scene.*

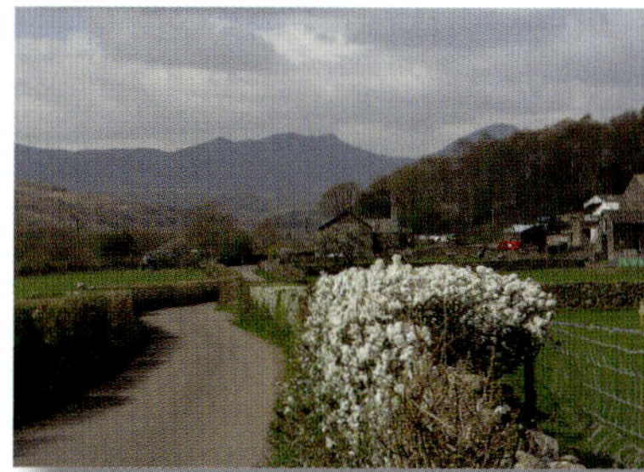

*Right: a close-up of the building. Close-up shots, like small detailed sketches of part of a scene, can provide useful information for the finished work. Take some from a slightly different angle to gain a better understanding of complicated features.*

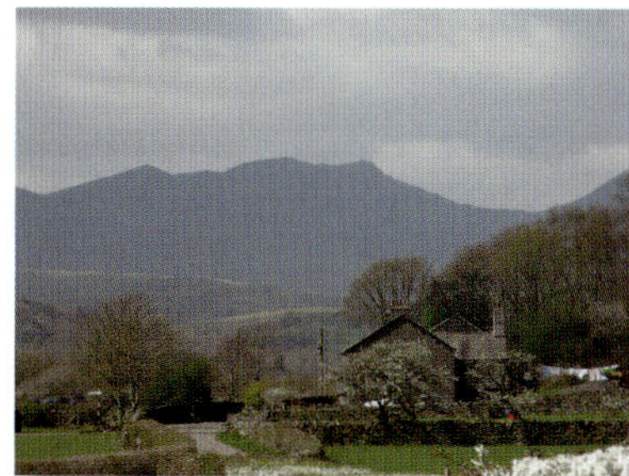

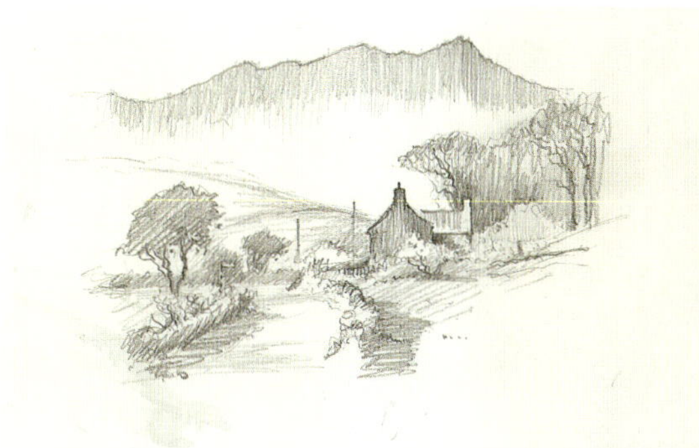

*A studio sketch is an excellent way to work out your composition from photographs. In the sketch I have simplified the building and omitted those at the extremities of the photographs, as well as one of the walls crossing the right-hand field. The lane has also been made simpler.*

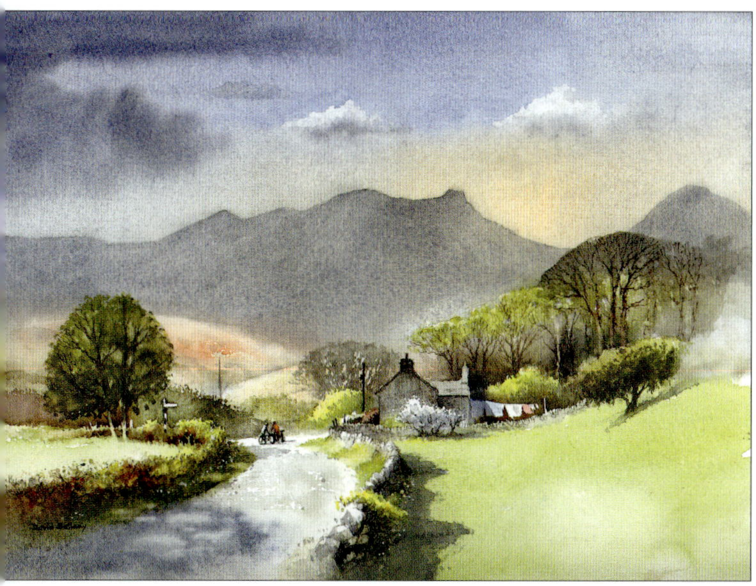

FARM NEAR CONISTON
*20.3 x 25.5cm (8 x 10in)*

*In the painting I have tried to put across the sense of a sunny spring day, with the foreground shadows emphasizing the feeling of sunlight. The main addition is the inclusion of two cyclists consulting near the farmhouse. Minor changes are always worth considering, and here you will see that I have swivelled the signpost round to point into the picture instead of in the opposite direction, moved some trees and avoided the manicured look of the left-hand hedgerow. I felt the foreground mass of blossom was just too overwhelming to include.*

# Composition

While there are a few landscape scenes that may work well without any changes, most need to be composed to a degree before they make a good image. This re-arrangement of the scene can be subtle or involve drastic alterations to the various elements and their relationships with each other. The best way to work out the composition is to do one or more thumbnail sketches in soft pencil, charcoal, watercolour or whatever suits you. Try to include the main tones as strong tonal areas have a considerable influence on how we view the composition.

I usually start with the focal point, or centre of interest, as this is the single most important feature in the scene. While you can have more than one focal point, the composition is stronger with just one, with perhaps minor ones to create a sense of balance. The focal point must stand out, and this can be done convincingly by creating your most striking tonal contrasts at that point. Bright colours and detail can also help, but by far the most powerful way is judicious use of tones.

My second concern is supporting the centre of interest with other features, such as trees around a building, a bush or prominent rock beside a waterfall, and so on. Figures and wildlife can be introduced, but they then become the focal point, so they need to be positioned near some feature of interest if possible, but not lost in detail. A further manner of support is by providing a lead-in in the form of a stream, track, dry-stone wall, or whatever suits you. This should lead from the foreground directly to or close to the focal point. Gullies and ridges descending a mountainside towards the focal point also help.

Before you begin painting, check your composition for balance. If everything is placed on one side it helps to find a feature to add to the other side. Often just a simple post will suffice, but shapely bushes, trees, rocks, farm implements, or whatever seems appropriate, should fit the bill, provided they are in character with that type of landscape.

When planning a painting, consider what sort of mood you wish to convey. If you wish to suggest a peaceful, tranquil mood then a more horizontal composition would work best, using strong horizontal emphasis in the scene and perhaps an elongated (panoramic) type format. To emphasize drama, a vertical format works well, perhaps with cliffs or an abyss. A strong diagonal bias within the composition will suggest a dynamic approach and this can easily be achieved with rising mountain ridges, fallen pine trees or a series of rising crags.

### Adding interest to foregrounds

Features that may be added:

- Puddles, preferably with a simple reflection
- Posts, perhaps festooned with vegetation
- Flowers and plants
- Rocks and boulders (in appropriate locations)
- A lead-in such as a path, road, stream, fence or wall
- Fallen tree trunk

Useful techniques to enhance foregrounds:

- Spatter with a round brush or toothbrush
- Broken colour allowing an initial wash to show through
- Dry-brush effect over a lighter colour
- Shadow glaze over all or part of the foreground
- Warm colours and strong tones to help suggest depth
- Abstraction or semi-abstraction of features

### GREAT STAPLE TOR, DARTMOOR, 1 (HOW NOT TO DO IT)

*This is a fairly faithful rendering of the scene, but shows a too literal response. Although the area beneath the tor is littered with rock debris, it is too overwhelming to include it all. People scattered in a variety of places as though tossed like seed will detract from any painting, and the foreground is too busy with boulders. Additionally the different parts of the tor have equal prominence.*

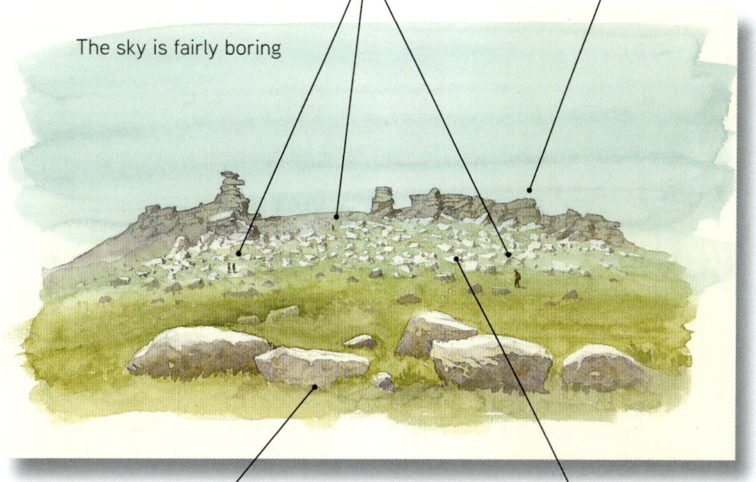


### GREAT STAPLE TOR, DARTMOOR, 2 (AN IMPROVED RESPONSE)

*This is a stronger composition, with much of the rock debris eliminated. The higher part of the tor has been pushed towards the centre of the composition and the other side subdued. I now have only two tiny figures and they are positioned clearly near the left-hand tor rocks to support this as the focal point. This is further emphasized by creating a lighter track leading up to them. The foreground boulders have mainly been eliminated and the cloud structure not only improves the sky, but helps to highlight the tor.*

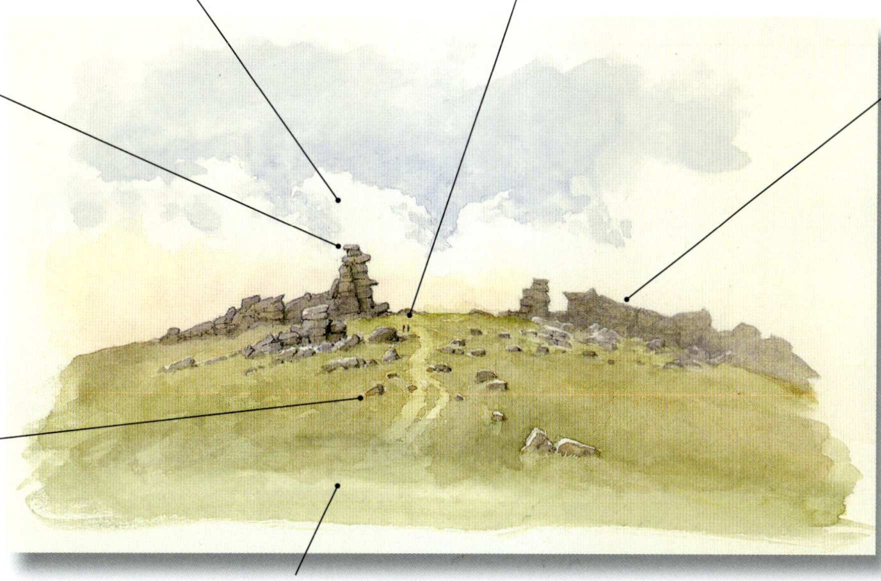

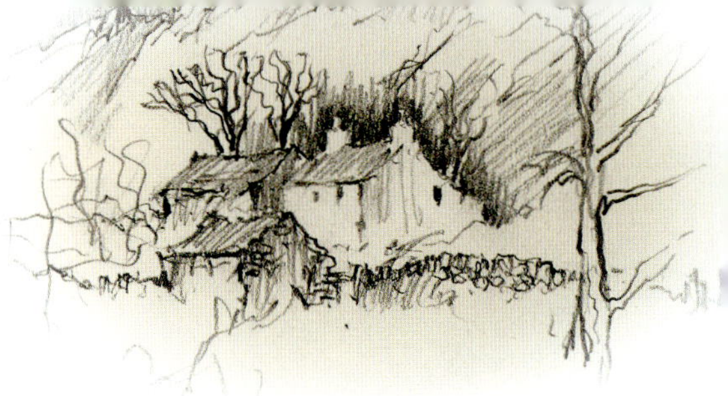

# Buildings

If you enjoy painting rustic old buildings then you are probably more likely to find good examples of these in the mountain regions than anywhere else. The added complication here, though, is that many of them are built on uneven ground, sometimes with almost every side appearing to be at a slightly different level. This is not necessarily a great problem, and rather than correct it so that the building looks as though it has been built on flat ground, use these sloping angles to advantage, even exaggerating them if you like.

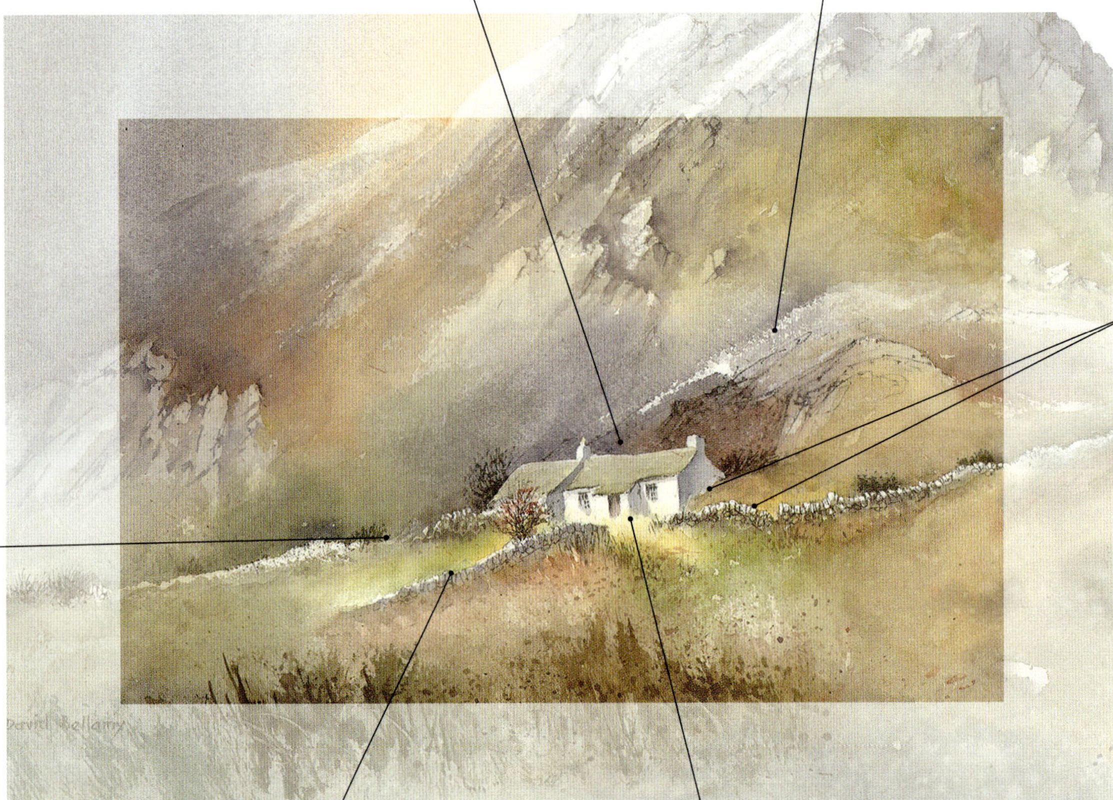


COTTAGE IN THE HILLS

*How often I see students painting a stone cottage scene on a mountain slope, but totally ruining the effect by placing the building itself on what looks like a billiard table! As with rocks and boulders, we need to make hillside buildings look as though they are growing out of rough, uneven ground.*

# PERSPECTIVE ON HILLSIDE BUILDINGS

In many situations where the ground is rough and sloping, keen observation of the structure lines is more important than following rigid perspective rules. I normally prefer to enhance the sense of character instead of correcting any wonkiness, but a simple studio sketch or two will usually guide you to the right answer.

The further away you are from a building, the more the perspective problems will diminish, but in the scene below, the viewer is well below the subject, so the closer barn needs particular care.

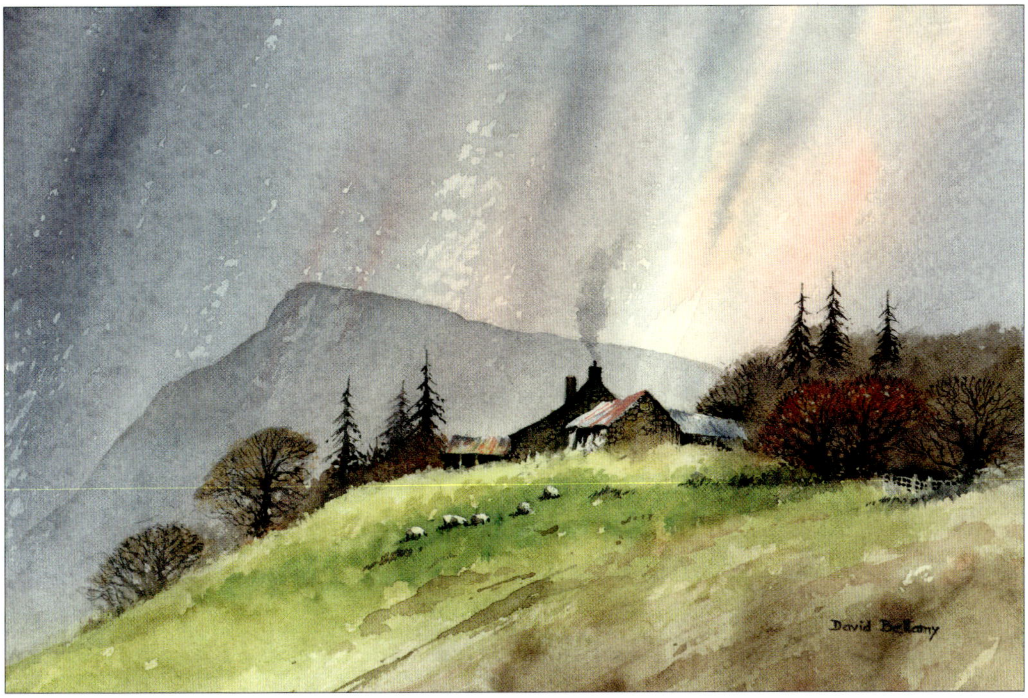


**HILL FARM**
*18 x 23cm (7 x 9in)*

*The barn in this painting is set at a different angle to the house, with two sides showing, so we need to portray the roof lines as sloping slightly downwards as they recede to the left. The accompanying diagrams illustrate how to tackle this, but many of these ancient rustic buildings do not conform exactly to the laws of perspective, which often adds to their charm. Make full use of the sloping ground to show up the uneven floor levels.*

**PERSPECTIVE DIAGRAMS**

*These diagrams give an idea of how the angles of the horizontal lines (mainly on the roof here) are seen by the viewer both below and above the subject.*

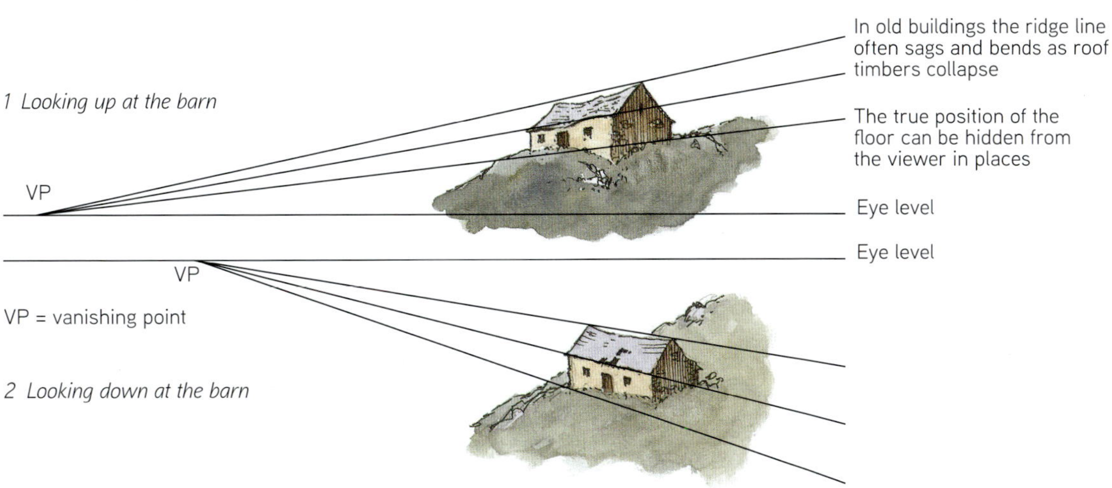

# SKIES

Skies set the mood of a landscape painting and greatly influence the light, yet many artists barely give them any consideration. In this book you will find skies of all sorts, and they are not limited to this section. Time spent carefully considering how you will tackle the sky in a painting is never wasted, and in this section my aim is to show you a range of skies with the techniques used to create them, and also how to consider the composition of the sky and how it should relate to the landscape.

Occasionally I will come across a sky that fits in well with the scene I am sketching or painting, but most of the time I need to introduce a completely different type of sky to get the most out of the composition in terms of mood, lighting, logic and compositional considerations. This is where experience plus a wide selection of sky reference material is vital to success. The problem can be

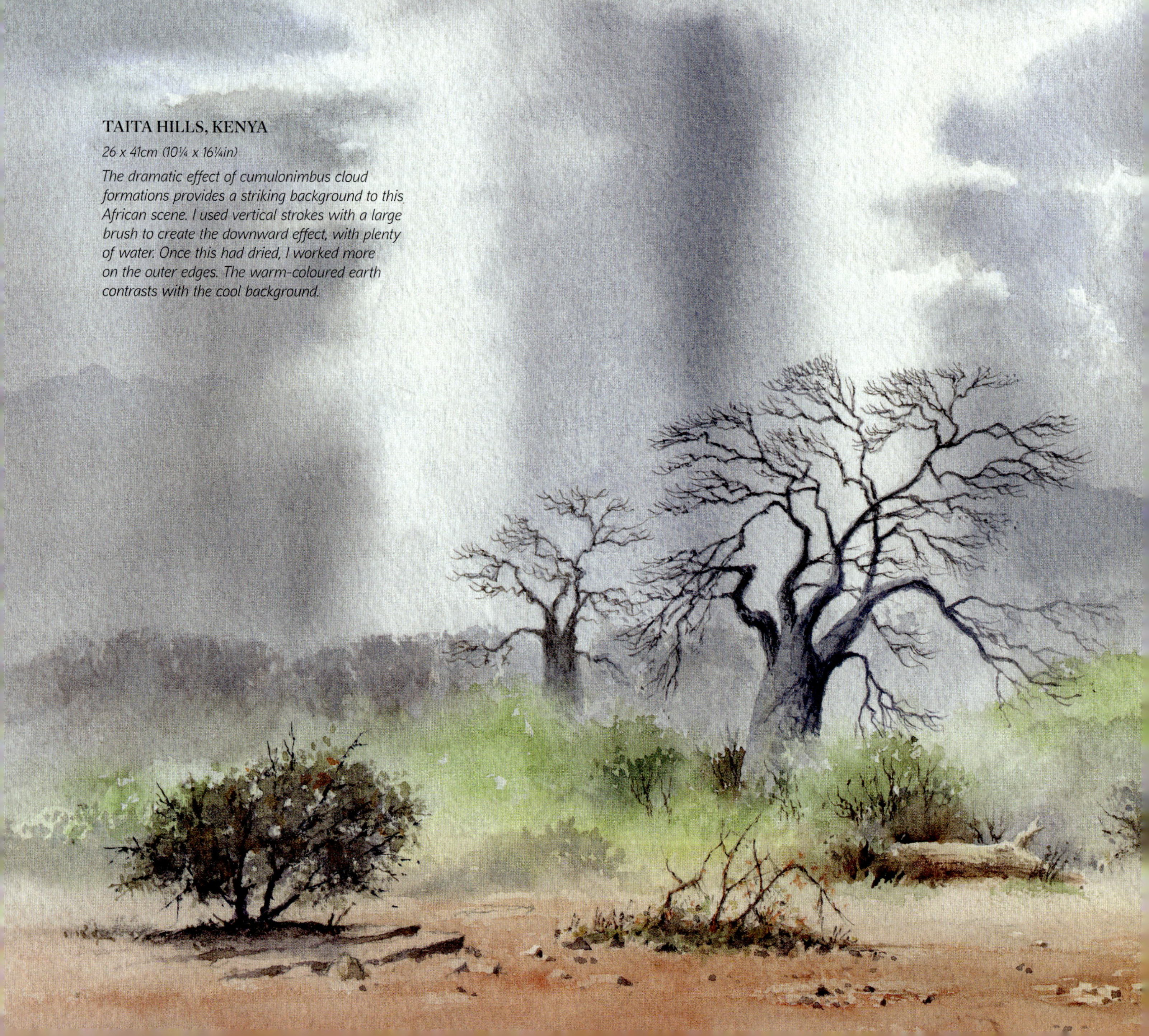

TAITA HILLS, KENYA

*26 x 41cm (10¼ x 16¼in)*

*The dramatic effect of cumulonimbus cloud formations provides a striking background to this African scene. I used vertical strokes with a large brush to create the downward effect, with plenty of water. Once this had dried, I worked more on the outer edges. The warm-coloured earth contrasts with the cool background.*

effectively solved in many ways, and there is rarely just one answer. So before starting a painting, I ask myself a number of questions: what sort of mood do I wish to create that would work with this composition? Do I want a cool, warm or neutral sky? What time of day do I want to suggest? Is there a need for the sky to be used to balance the composition? Can the clouds or light in the sky be arranged to highlight a prominent landscape feature? How should the sky relate to the landscape, especially where the two elements meet? Do I want intense light coming from some part of the sky and if so, where?

These questions may seem to introduce over-complication, but after a while they become second nature and most are instantly resolved. Once that has been done, you need to consider which colours to use, whether to work on wet or dry paper and the order of working. With just a little forethought and knowledge you can turn your skies into absolute gems, and as with so much to do with painting, it is often the simplest ones that have the most impact.

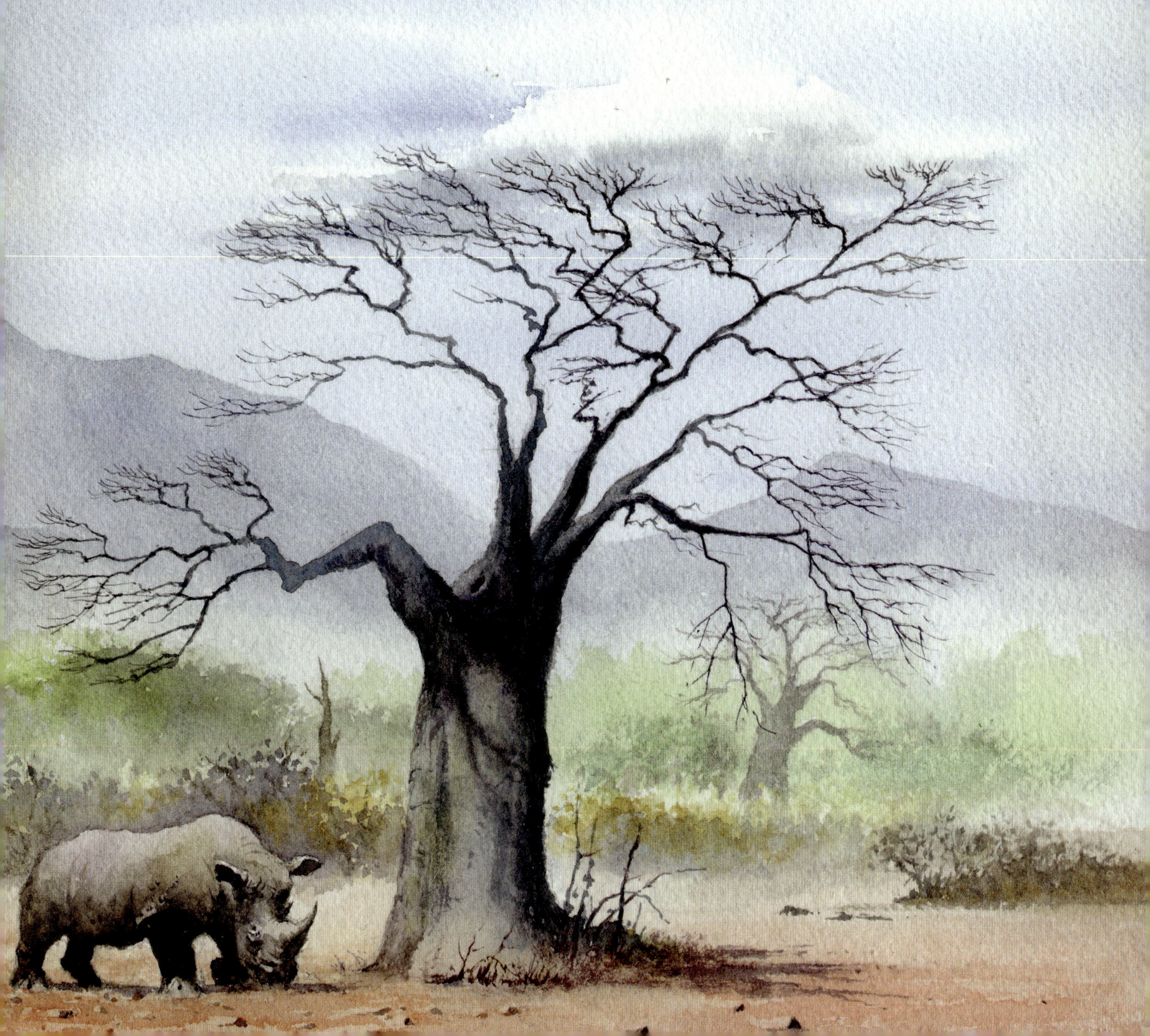

# BASIC TECHNIQUES FOR SIMPLE SKIES

Try out these methods on scrap paper before you start using them in a full painting. With watercolour, timing is often so critical, especially when you are working into wet paint as with the wet-in-wet technique shown opposite. The secret is to use as few brush strokes as you can get away with, and this will create a lovely freshness in your work. Naturally this means working with the largest brush you feel comfortable with for any particular passage. Limiting your brush strokes will also help you to avoid getting those embarrassingly green skies – often artists include yellow and blue in a sky and wonder why they get green. The answer is to apply them as separate colours and not blend them in with overbrushing, which will almost certainly guarantee a green sky.

In each of the following illustrations a generous pool of liquid colour was mixed in a deep well on the palette, and applied with broad strokes with a large brush, working horizontally across the paper and slightly overlapping each horizontal stroke to keep a uniform application of colour.

## Lifting out

*Immediately the dark wash was laid, a paper tissue was pressed into it for a few seconds. The paper was allowed to dry, then I washed over the lower part of the clouds with a light grey wash, softening it up into the white cloud with a damp brush. Finally, when it was dry, the darker clouds were introduced below.*

## Scrub-washed clouds

*Using a round brush on its side, scrub it across the paper as shown to create rough and ragged edges to a cloud. This works well on a Not surface, but even better on a Rough one.*

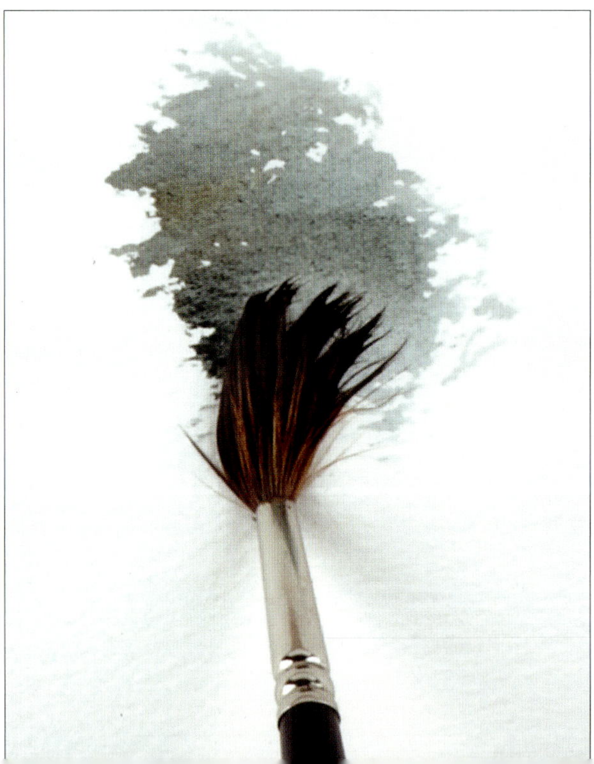

## Dark wet-in-wet clouds

*The dark line of clouds was added while the sky was still damp. For this it is vital that you have very little water on the brush, and a strong mix of colour, otherwise it will spread out and possibly create ugly cabbage-like runbacks. Timing is critical, so practise this on scrap paper first to gain experience.*

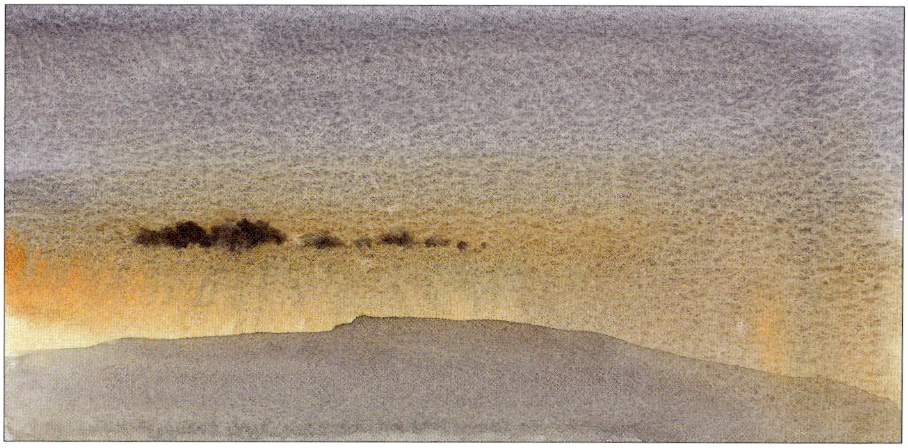

## Negative clouds

*The blue sky has simply been worked round the shapes of the white clouds on dry paper to create crisp edges. I added a slightly darker wash to the undersides of the clouds afterwards.*

### CASCADING SKY EFFECT

*This lovely effect is achieved by wetting the paper liberally and dropping a medium to dark coloured wash into the top part, to allow the effect to run down the paper. Try it while holding the paper at shallow and steep angles, and several points in between. Note that this effect can be laid on to a passage that you have already painted.*

# TWO-STAGE SKY

Many skies are painted with just one application of colour and allowed to dry, with nothing further being done to the sky area. However, with more complicated skies, and where you want dark, hard-edged clouds to appear in front of more distant ones, for example, you will need to lay washes in further stages. On this page you can see how a greater depth is suggested in the sky by painting it in two stages. The third illustration simply shows the land features completed.

1 I applied an initial wash of cerulean blue to the sky, working round the clouds, and then washed a weak application of permanent rose over most of the white areas. Lower down I dropped in a mix of cobalt blue and cadmium red while it was all wet.

2 When the paper was dry, I painted a mixture of French ultramarine and cadmium red to represent the darker left-hand cloud, softening the edge in places with a damp brush. Once this second stage of this type of sky is complete, the sky reveals considerably more depth.

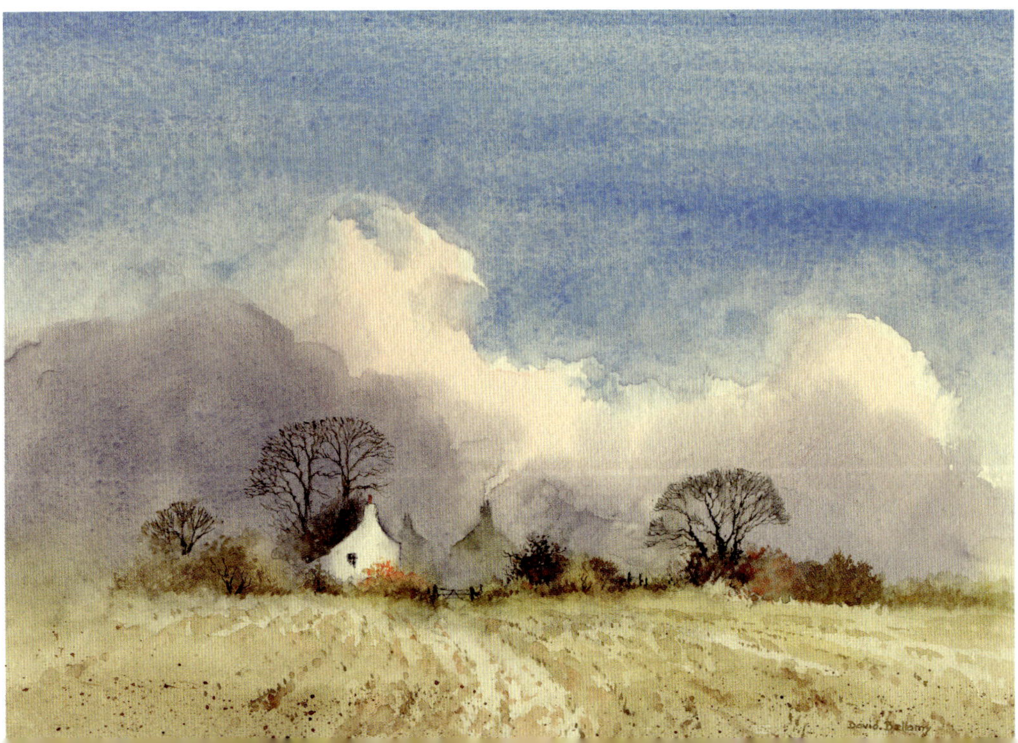

3 At this final stage the ground detail was painted in to complete the work.

## PLANNING A SKY

Your skies will always benefit from some planning beforehand. In most landscapes the sky should enhance the land features without trying to dominate, and help to highlight the centre of interest, especially in those features that extend up into the sky, such as mountains, crags, castles, trees and so on. The positioning of elements such as large cloud masses, the brightest part of the sky, or the most colourful, can greatly affect the overall composition of the painting. On the other hand, you may wish to play down an area, most commonly the extremities of the painting, and in this case a glaze of transparent colour may be applied over that part of the scene you wish to subdue, as will be shown later in the book.

In certain cases you may wish to make the sky the focal point, and where you want to paint an extremely striking sky composition, it pays to make the land element take a subsidiary role, as in the case of the second painting below. I enjoy studying skies and occasionally a really powerful one will suggest a painting which is primarily a skyscape with just a minor role for the landscape below. It pays to carry out sky sketches whenever you can, and for this I often use watercolour pencils or the water soluble graphite ones.

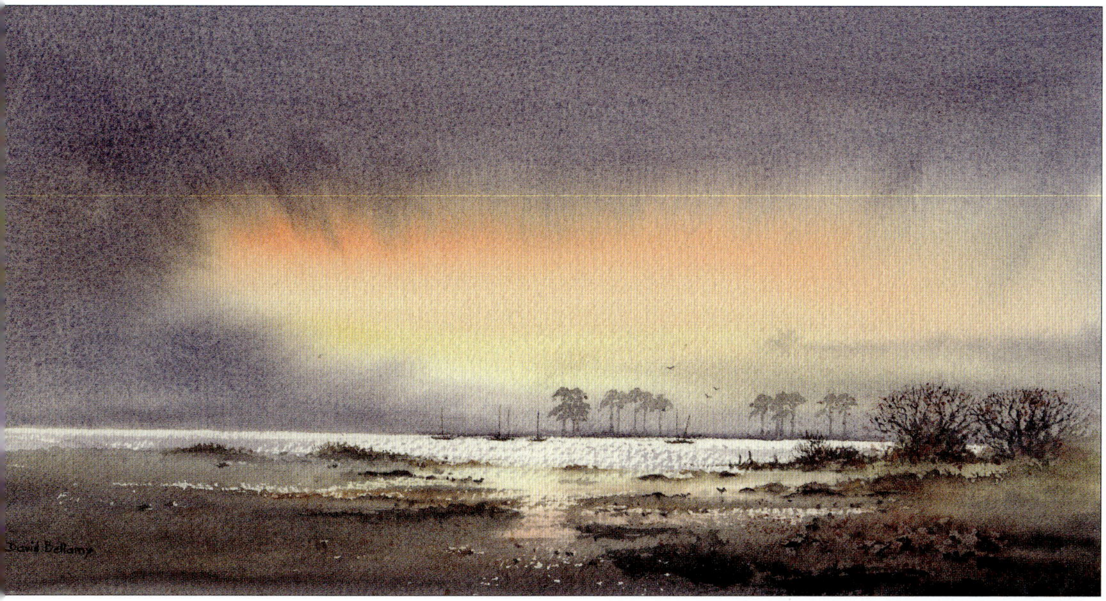



**BEAULIEU RIVER ESTUARY**
*18 x 29cm (7 x 12½in)*
*Here the sky is composed to highlight the focal point, which is the distant trees and boats. These are emphasized by the brightest part of the sky – a simple, yet effective ruse.*

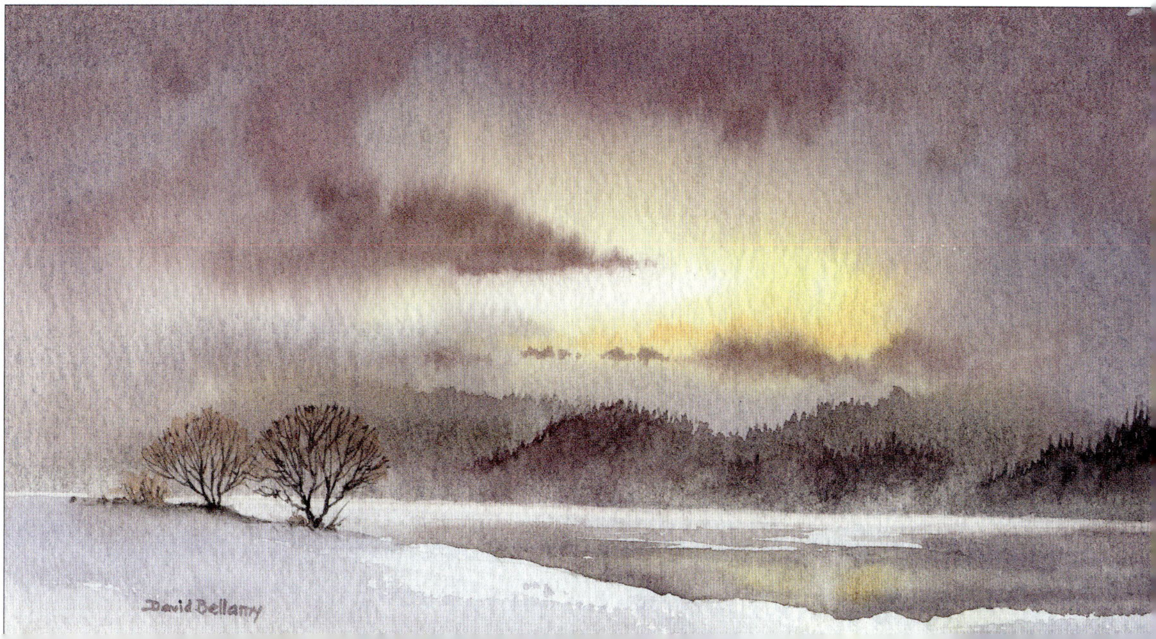



**FEBRUARY SUNLIGHT**
*12 x 21cm (4¾ x 8¼in)*
*In this watercolour the sky is so strongly rendered that it effectively becomes the centre of interest itself – and why not?*

# TYPES OF CLOUD

With just a little thought and application, you can improve and vary your skies considerably. So many artists are content to simply apply a standard wash across their sky areas, and this can appear rather repetitive in an exhibition. Small or thin, streaky clouds can be used to break up large expanses of sky, wispy cirrus clouds can be bent to direct the eye towards a focal point, and dense stratus is useful where you want to throw the attention elsewhere on to a land feature. Cumulus clouds come in such a variety of shapes and sizes that they can be made to range from dark, threatening masses to light, airy white puffs scudding across a blue sky.

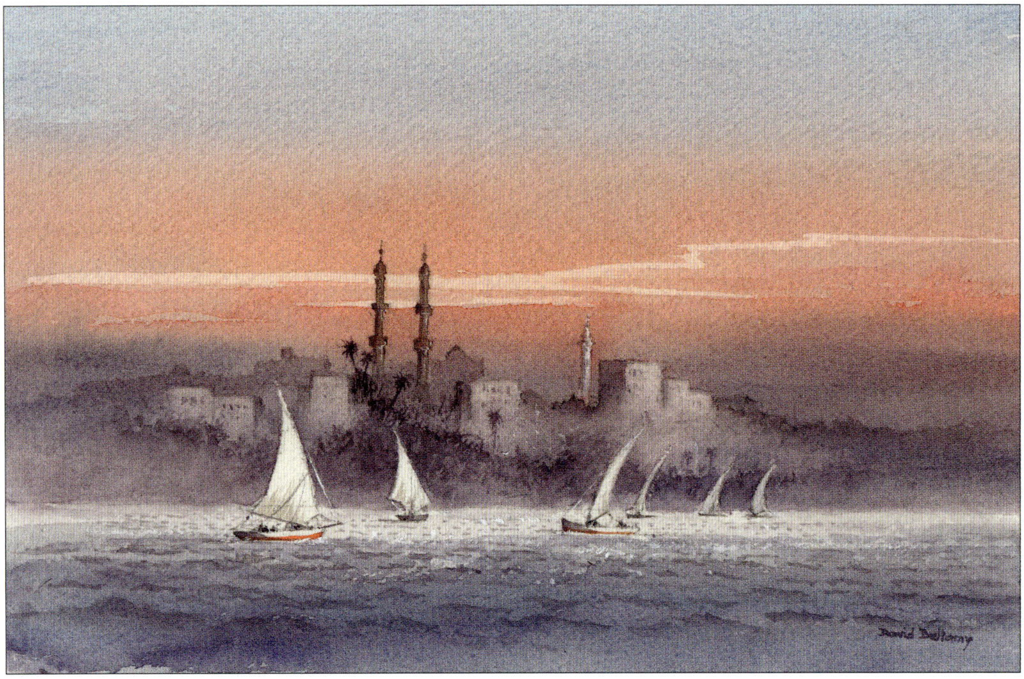

**APPROACHING DUSK, ASWAN** *15 x 22cm (6 x 8¾in)*

*Fibratus – streaky clouds – can add interest to a sky, while at the same time intimating a restful serenity, as in this painting, so long as they are not overworked. This type of cloud is especially striking when viewed through tall trees, pinnacles or minarets, as in this scene in Aswan, Egypt.*

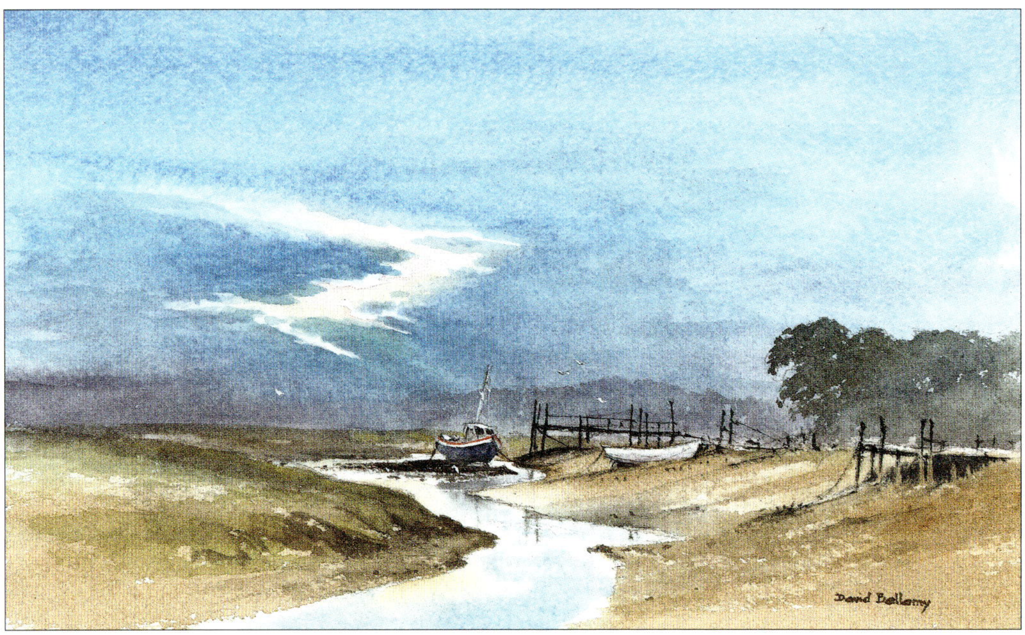

**NORFOLK CREEK**
*13 x 20cm (5 x 8in)*

*I like using cirrus, or wispy clouds, to highlight a focal point by pointing at it, rather in the manner of a stream or track leading into the composition. I often bend or zigzag these little gems to fit my scheme or mood.*

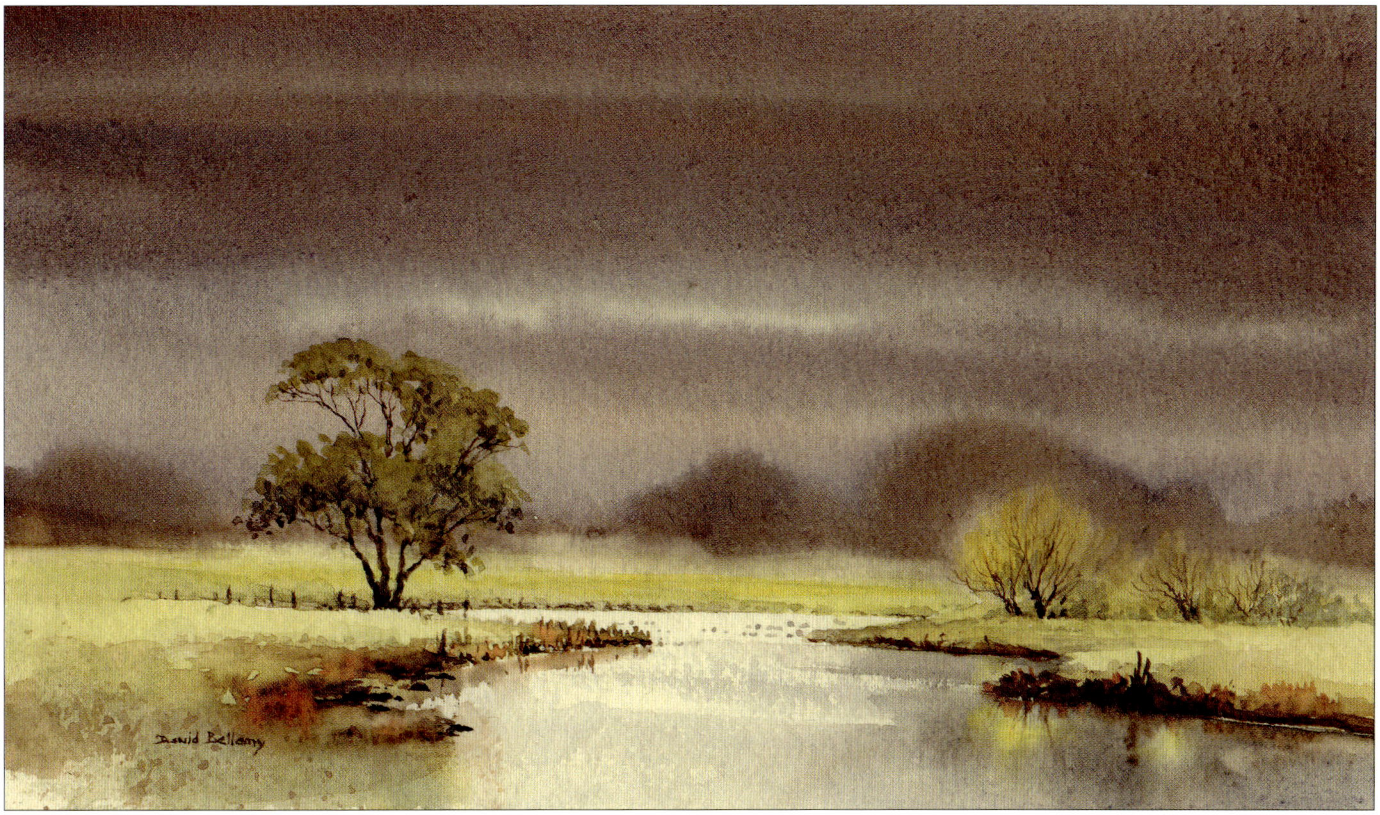

**RIVER TEST, HAMPSHIRE**
*11 x 19cm (4½ x 7½in)*

*Densely layered stratus can provide a supremely dull backdrop where you want to throw the emphasis elsewhere and increase the sense of light on certain ground features. It can also create the mood of an impending storm or something horrible about to happen.*

**OFF GATEHOLM ISLAND**
*12 x 24cm (4¾ x 9½in)*

*Cumulus can appear light and airy when set against a blue sky, or dark, angry and threatening in towering masses, and thus are excellent for setting the mood. Note the complete change of colour from the manganese blue hue above the clouds to the weak cadmium orange below.*

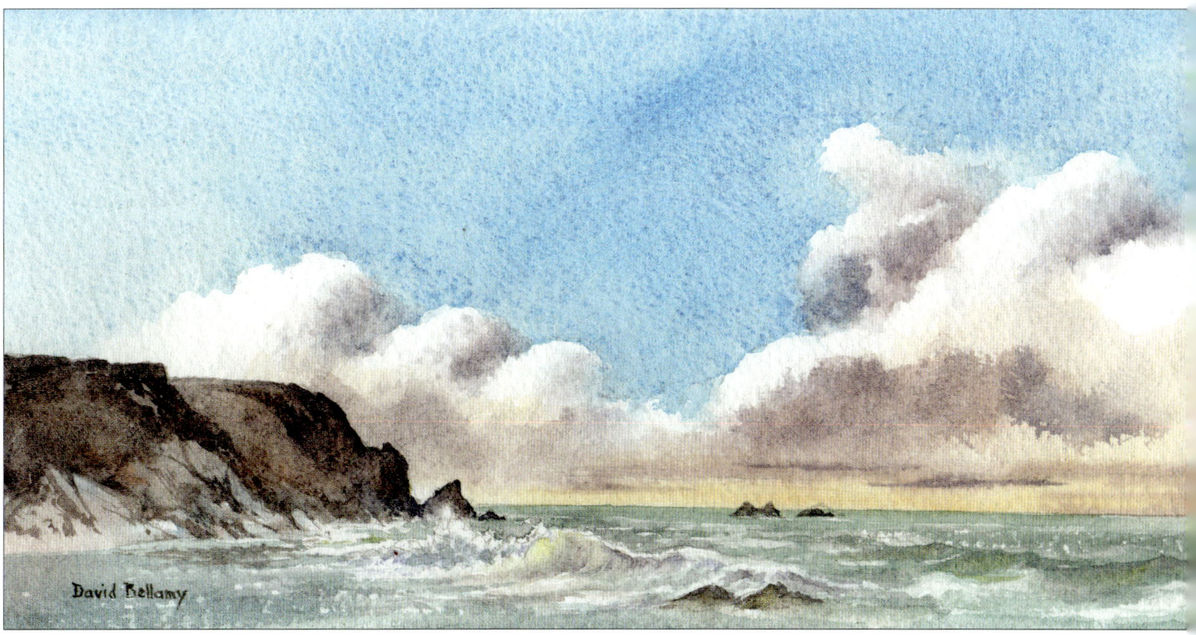

## SILVER LININGS

Creating silver linings can add sparkle to your skies, but it is best not to overdo the effect: a few simple ones tend to work better than a lining on every cloud. It also pays to break them up by making them intermittent rather than continuous for long stretches across the sky. Try not to make all your silver linings hard-edged, as including too many hard edges tends to spoil the overall effect.

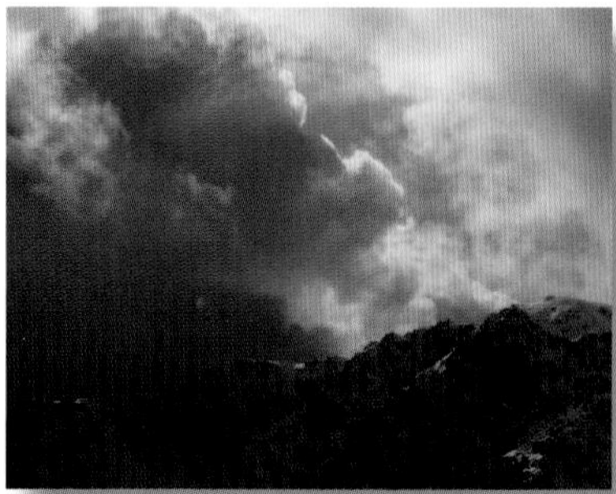

*Often the cloud structures are too complicated to include everything, as in this photograph where clouds were boiling up all around me. The energy and atmospheric power of the constantly shifting scene offered a challenge, but you have to identify the parts that excite you most – and render them quickly.*

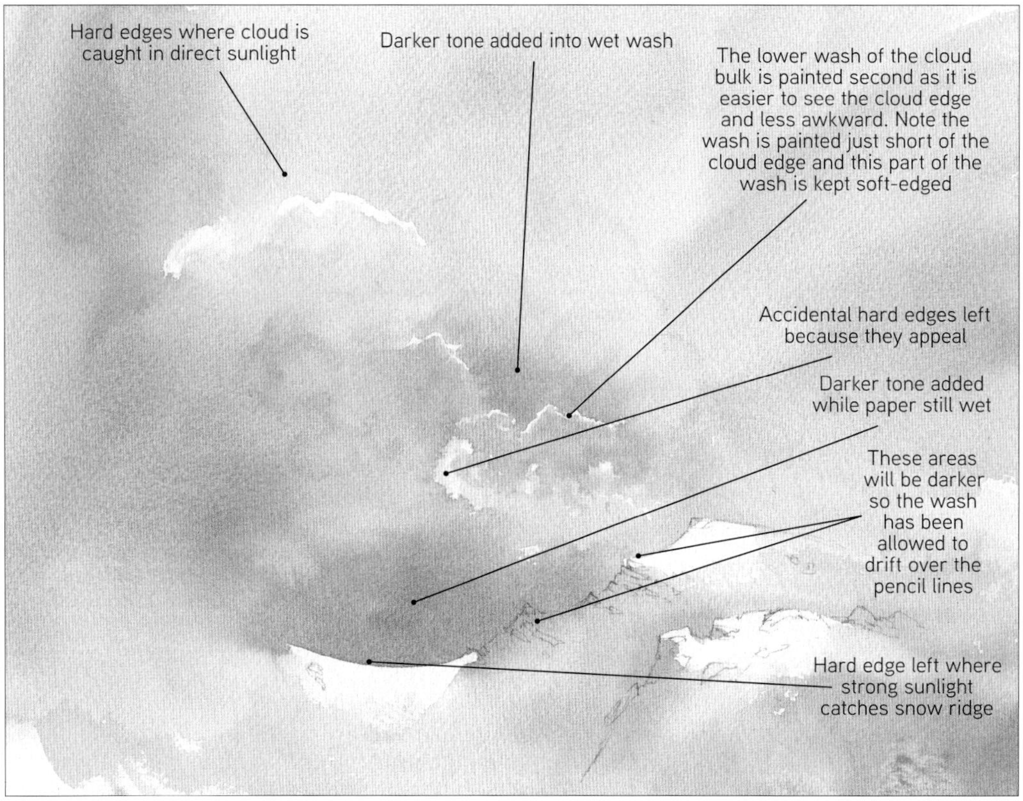


**1** To keep things simple, I have subdued the urge to put too much energy into this watercolour, as I want to illustrate how the silver linings are achieved. Firstly the upper part of the sky is painted with a wash of weak cobalt blue plus cadmium red on dry paper, working round the tops of the cloud edges, and running the wash under them for a short distance. The edge of the wash under the linings is softened off with a damp brush. While this is wet, Naples yellow is drifted into the area between the cloud masses, then cobalt blue and perylene red to give the clouds a sharp edge.

**2** When the paper is completely dry, clean water is brushed over the areas under the tops of the clouds, over the end of the previous wash, taking it out into the sky beyond the silver-edged clouds. Next, a darker grey, made up of French ultramarine and perylene red, is applied carefully – I prefer to use a no. 10 or 12 round sable for this, as the fine point helps to retain a thin rim of white at the tops of the clouds. This wash runs into the wetted areas and thus creates a soft transition below the silver linings, but the cloud limit is indicated by the soft-edged darker mass. Then the mountain ridge is added.

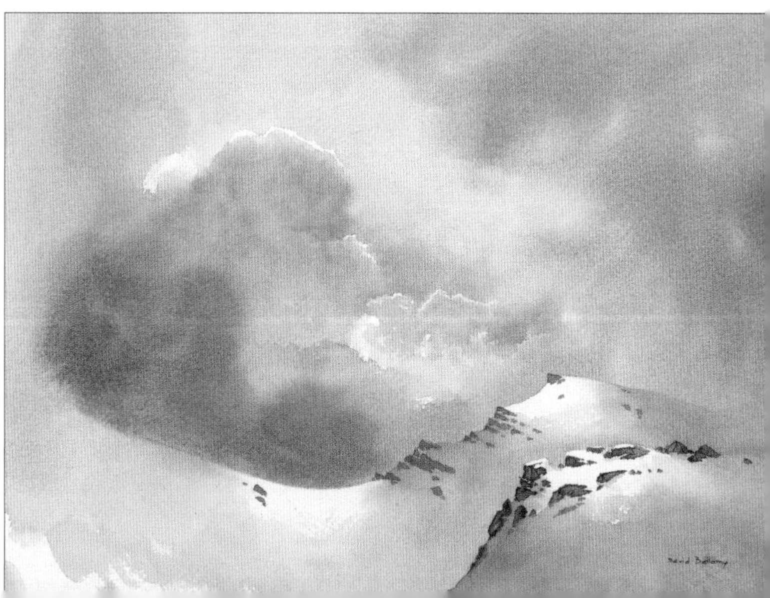

## SUNSETS AND FIERY SKIES

Sunsets can make exciting paintings but can appear garish if too many bright reds and yellows are included. Like most things in painting, they usually need to be simplified. Often they are best painted in two or three stages, normally allowing each stage to dry before going on to the next. You need to fix clearly in your mind the exact point where the sun will be, whether you are including it or not. This helps you to determine if any silver lining will appear at the top or the bottom of a cloud, for example, or when rays of sunshine are emanating from a particular point. Note that distant objects on or near the horizon are usually starting to get lost in strong atmosphere, while closer objects may stand out strongly as silhouettes. In very strong atmospheric conditions, the horizon may disappear completely and sky will gradually merge into land. With so much colour in the sky, you will need to play down any strong colours in the land element.

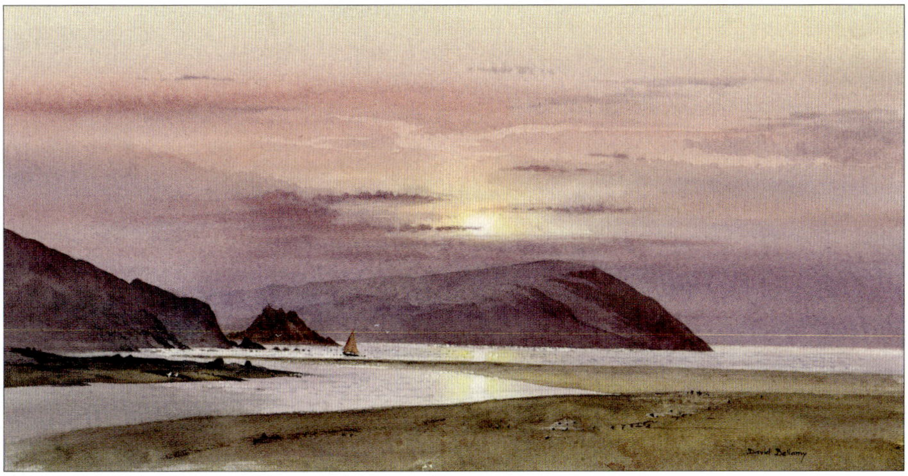

**SUNSET, NEWPORT BAY**
*18 x 32cm (7 x 12½in)*

*Sunsets are often so complicated that they need considerable simplification. This sky was done in two stages. Firstly I laid a weakish wash of permanent alizarin crimson in the upper sky, running it down into the centre where I laid in some Naples yellow. While this was still wet, I worked in some new gamboge, blending it into the Naples yellow and describing the shape of the sun. When the paper had dried, I applied a stronger wash of permanent alizarin crimson with a touch of French ultramarine into the upper part of the sky, leaving streaks of untouched paper to reveal the earlier lighter wash of alizarin. Lower down I introduced much more ultramarine into the mix, taking it down over the headland, and while the paper remained wet, I added strings of horizontal clouds with an even stronger mix of the same colours. For the headland, I included permanent alizarin crimson in the mix to retain a sense of unity.*

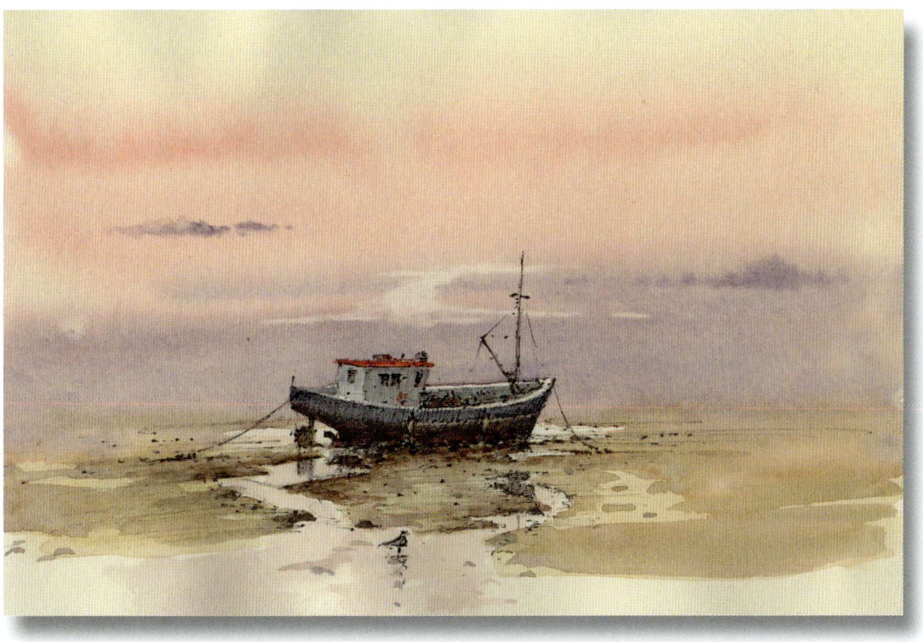

**BOAT AT TENBY – WASH AND LINE SKETCH ON CARTRIDGE PAPER**

*On moody evenings the horizon is often obscured in the misty atmosphere, and here I ran the colour of the sky into the sand. This throws great emphasis on to the focal point. The dark clouds were added wet in wet, while the streaky one was taken out with a thin flat 13mm (½in) brush.*

# SHAFTS OF SUNLIGHT

A powerful tool for highlighting a centre of interest is a shaft of sunlight, and it is also useful for breaking up less interesting passages and creating variety. These can be achieved in a number of ways, and occasionally I employ two different techniques on the same lighting effect.

Firstly the stopping-out method, as shown in the upper illustration, involves laying a dark or medium-dark wash across the area where the shafts of light will appear, and then immediately lifting out the shafts with a tissue or large damp brush. To create an authentic-looking light shaft, it is best to repeat the lifting out process down the centre of the shaft of light so that the beam seems to be more intense there. The second method employs a stencil technique and this is done after the dark or medium-dark wash has dried, as in the case of the lower illustration. Take two strips of thin card or watercolour paper and lay them along the lines where the shaft of light will appear, one on either side, revealing where the centre of the shaft will be created. Draw a soft sponge and clean water down between the two strips of card as many times as are needed to create the shaft, then dab with a tissue to remove excess water. Reposition the card strips at the same angle but slightly further out from the centre-line of the shaft, and sponge again gently. The idea is to create soft edges to the shafts, so one gentle stroke might be sufficient, otherwise continue until the required result is achieved.

Shafts can also be created by painting them with white gouache. This is best done on a rough surface, and is an excellent method when painting on tinted paper. A fourth method, of working negatively with a dark wash down each side of the sunlight shafts, can also produce the effect desired. When you wish to include several shafts of light, they should all start from the same point in the sky, whether you include the sun or not.

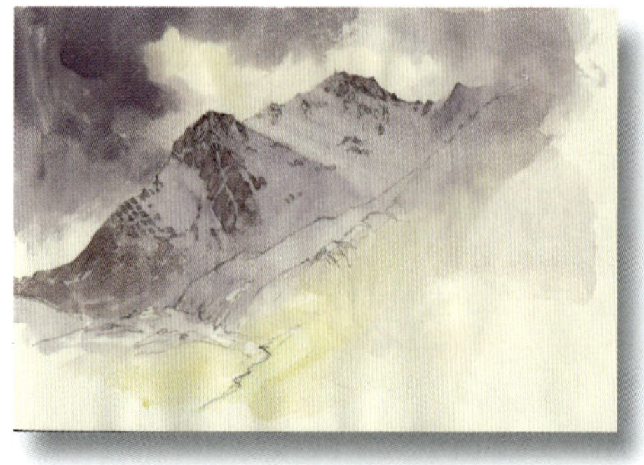

**SHAFTS OF SUNLIGHT ACROSS AONACH BEAG, SCOTLAND**

*In this watercolour sketch on cartridge paper my main objective was to record the effects of how the slanting shafts of sunshine created light and shadow areas across the face of the mountain, together with the cloud formation that was causing this phenomenon. Speed was essential, as this sort of effect does not last long, and also it was spitting with rain. I actually painted the whole face in the shadow colour, then immediately pulled out the lighter shafts with a damp no. 10 brush. As I wanted to preserve my efforts, I stopped sketching once the rain became heavier.*

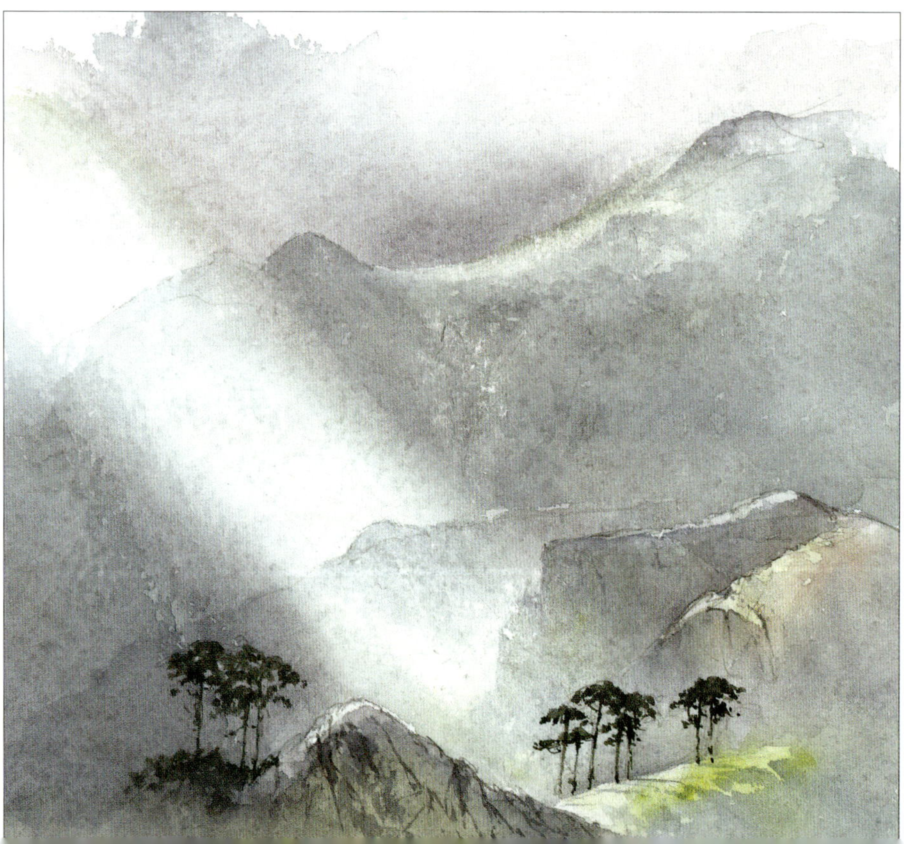

**SUNBEAMS IN THE OGWEN VALLEY**
*15 x 18cm (6 x 7in)*

*In this small watercolour of a valley in Snowdonia, Wales, the background mountains were painted first and allowed to dry. Then a soft, natural sponge was rubbed diagonally over the area where the shaft appears, shielding each side of the shaft initially with thin card, then softening the edges caused by the card. Doing these procedures in this order enabled me to achieve a soft transition at the edges of the shaft of sunlight. Once all this was dry, I added details of the trees and closer crags.*

## GRADUATED SKIES

Graduating your sky washes is a simple and effective way of adding interest and variety to both the main part of the sky and to small passages between clouds. This is such a common phenomenon in skies that the technique should be in every artist's repertoire. Note how in the illustration below the sky is really dark at the top and much lighter where it meets the distant hill. Had I left it as dark throughout, the hill would be lost in the dark mass. Also, the graduation method has been used on the crag to throw the emphasis on to the part nearest the centre of the composition.

Graduation is vital if you include the sun in your sky as it can suggest the intensity of light close to the sun, gradually revealing the sky to become darker, however slightly, as the distance increases. In the vertical plane, especially with almost clear, blue skies you will see the tone graduate from a darker blue at the top to a much lighter one at the horizon, although this can depend on the position of the sun. The trick is to observe these effects when you are out and about, as you can learn so much even without a sketchbook.

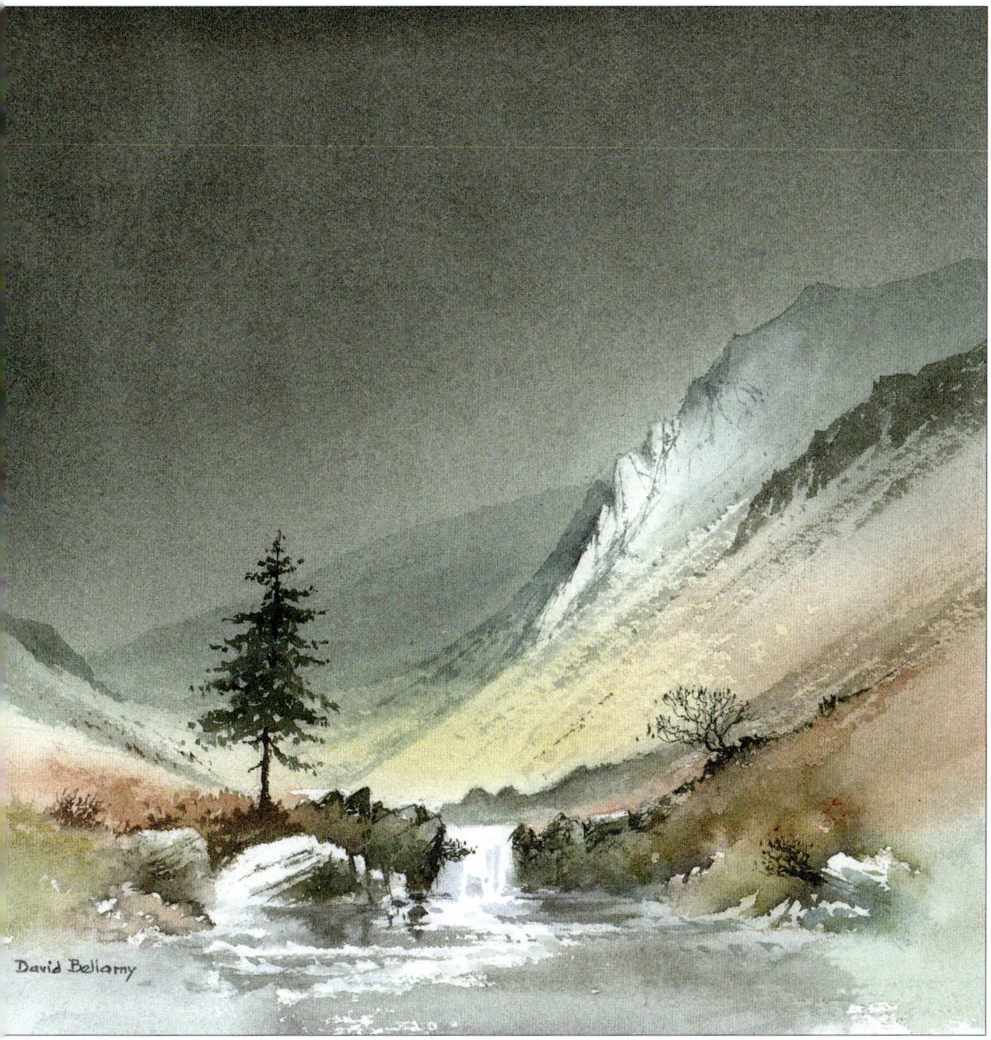


**IRFON VALLEY**
*19 x 19cm (7½ x 7½in)*

*In this Welsh scene, I wanted to create a simple, graduated sky to throw the attention on to the crag and cascade, while suggesting a brooding atmosphere. The distant hill was painted first using indigo with a touch of burnt umber. When this had dried, I completely wet the sky, the dark top of the crag on the right, and the hill I had just painted. A strong mixture of indigo with some burnt umber was then washed down the sky. I made it extremely dark at the top, adding a little more water to the wash lower down, and much more water near the bottom of the sky. I worked hard to keep the light part of the crag from being over-run, and it needed a lot of mopping up at the bottom where I ran in some cadmium yellow pale.*

## CREATING A SKY TO COMPLEMENT A LANDSCAPE

When you consider what type of sky you wish to include with a particular scene, think of the effect as a whole and not just the two main elements in isolation. The light and atmosphere will affect both sky and landscape equally, and where you position clouds and the light source may have a profound effect on a landscape feature. It pays to do little thumbnail sketches to ascertain the optimum position for the main clouds and light, and make sure you do this in conjunction with the ground features. If there is a strong mist, take care not to have any hard edges on distant objects, as this will jar with the overall impression. Puddles suggest a rainy or showery day, so include clouds that also suggest this. Strong directional clouds, as in the photograph opposite, can be used to point towards a landscape feature.

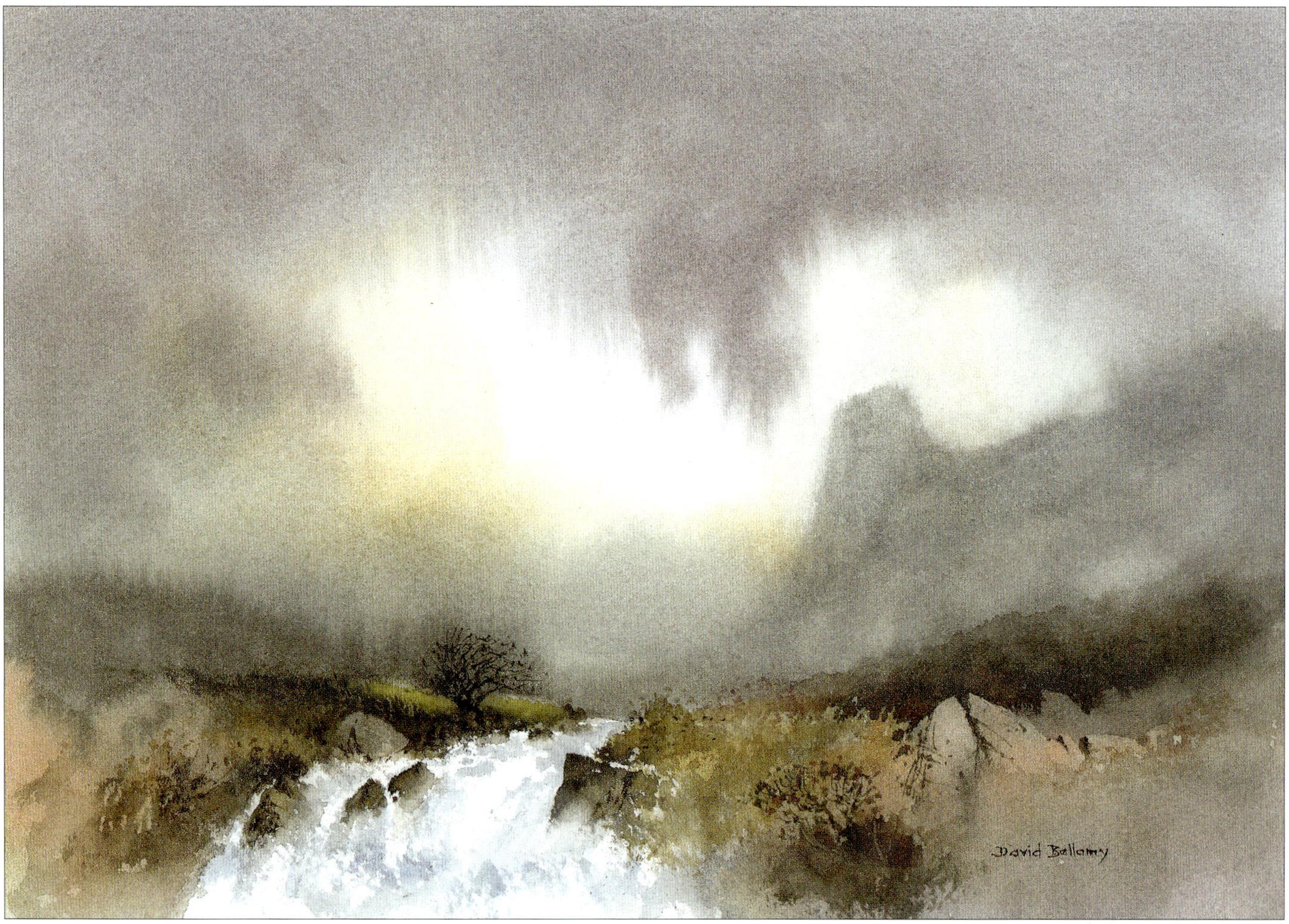


**LOWERING SKY**
*17 x 24cm (6¾ x 9½in)*

*A device I commonly use with skies is to create a swirl of cloud around a prominent ground feature, such as a castle on a hill, a shapely mountain summit or, as in this case, a crag thrusting out from a ridge. I have not included any detail on the crag because it is not the focal point. Giving the sky a more interesting composition that complements part of your landscape will add more power to your painting.*

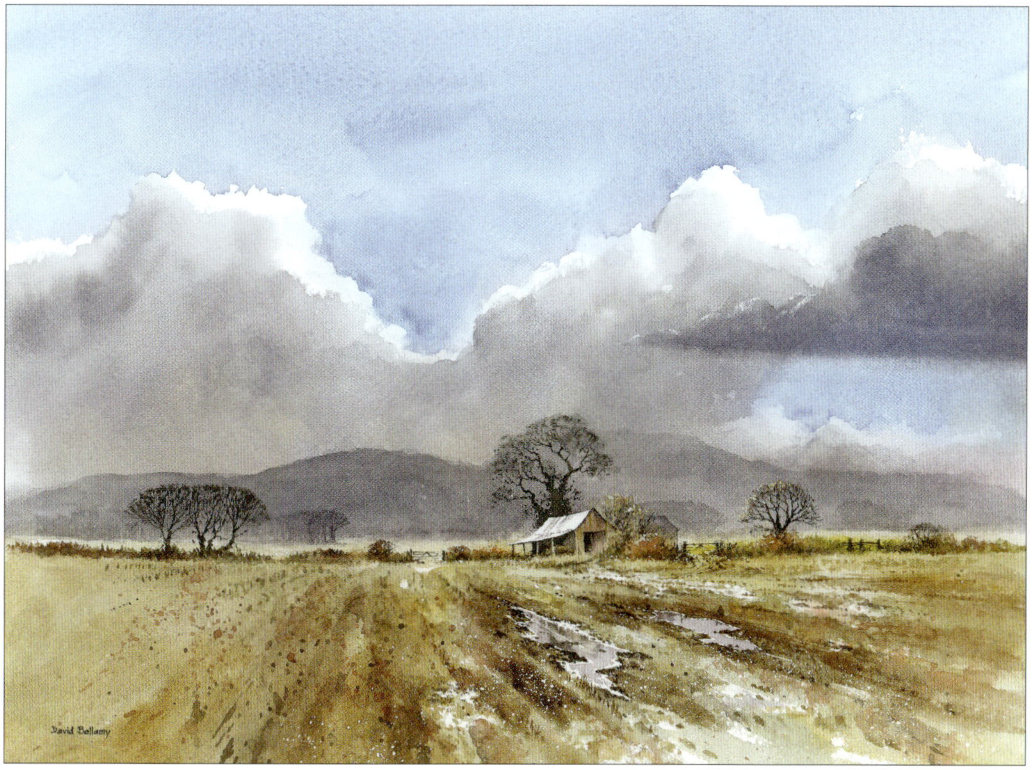


SHOWERY MORNING
*28 x 37cm (11 x 14½in)*

*Varied and fairly heavy clouds imply a showery day, and in this watercolour my aim was to give the impression that the rain had just stopped and the sun had come out. The effect I have tried to achieve is that of high backlighting from the late-morning sun which causes a sparkling effect on the rims of puddles and beads of moisture on the ground. Painting in a light to medium wash of French ultramarine and cadmium red over the puddles, I stopped just short of the edges to leave a white rim, and then dropped in a few touches of reflections while the wash remained wet. The dark, muddy outer edges emphasize the white rim further. For the sparkling beads I spattered white gouache over the ground area.*

## BEEFING UP A SKY THAT LACKS IMPACT

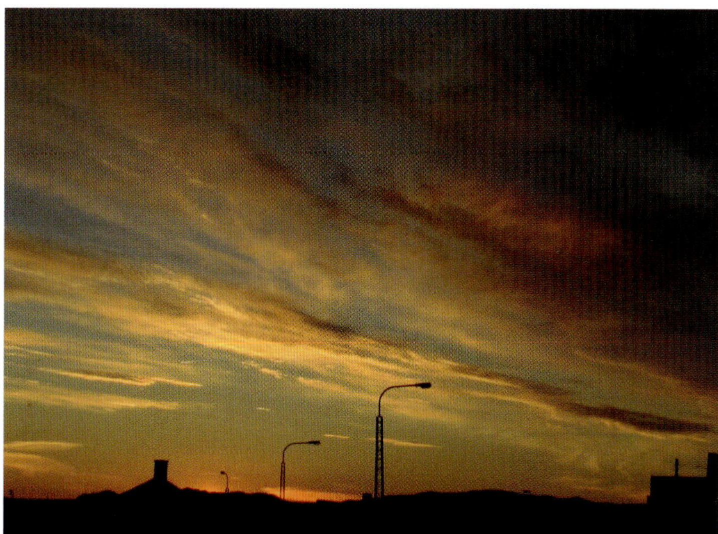

EVENING SKY

*This photograph shows a sky that has a strong directional pull, and this effect can be useful for highlighting a feature such as a castle or mountain peak, which could be positioned at the lower end of the cloud formation, in this case the bottom right.*

# DRAMATIC SKY

While many skies can be rendered with just a single wash, I shall now demonstrate a more complicated sky where more than one application is necessary. You will also see how important it is to re-adjust certain washes while they are still wet, by using a damp brush to pull out straggles of paint that have strayed too far.

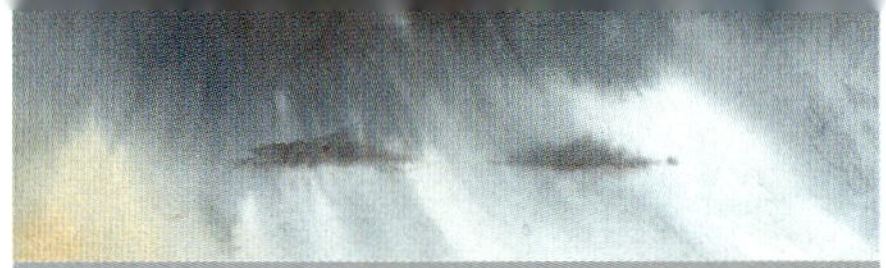

**MATERIALS USED**

Saunders Waterford 640gsm (300lb) Rough watercolour paper

Brushes: squirrel mop, no. 10 round, 6mm (¼in) flat, no. 7 round, no. 1 rigger

Colours: Naples yellow, cadmium orange, cerulean blue, indigo, cadmium red, yellow ochre, cadmium yellow pale

Masking fluid and old brush

Paper tissue

Craft knife

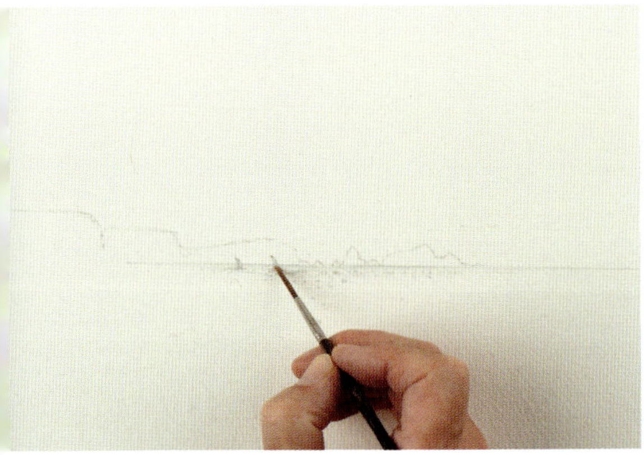

1 Draw the scene. Use an old, fine brush to apply masking fluid to the water's edge and the two yachts. Add a few tiny dots lower down to suggest sparkles in the water.

2 Wet the sky, and use the squirrel mop to drop in Naples yellow in the centre and at the bottom. Drift cadmium orange into the left-hand side, then cerulean blue at the top, working round untouched paper to suggest clouds. Wetting the paper first gives soft edges. Allow to dry.

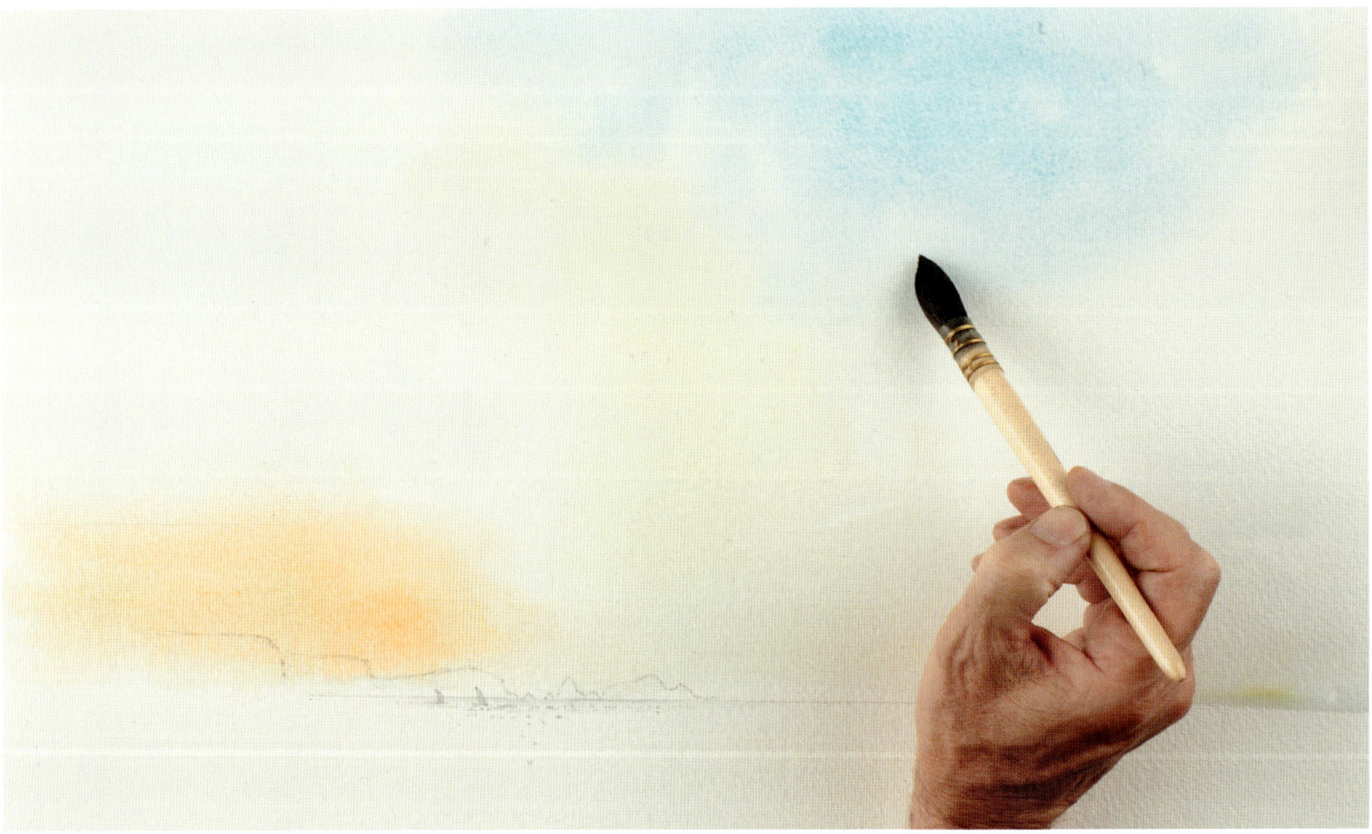

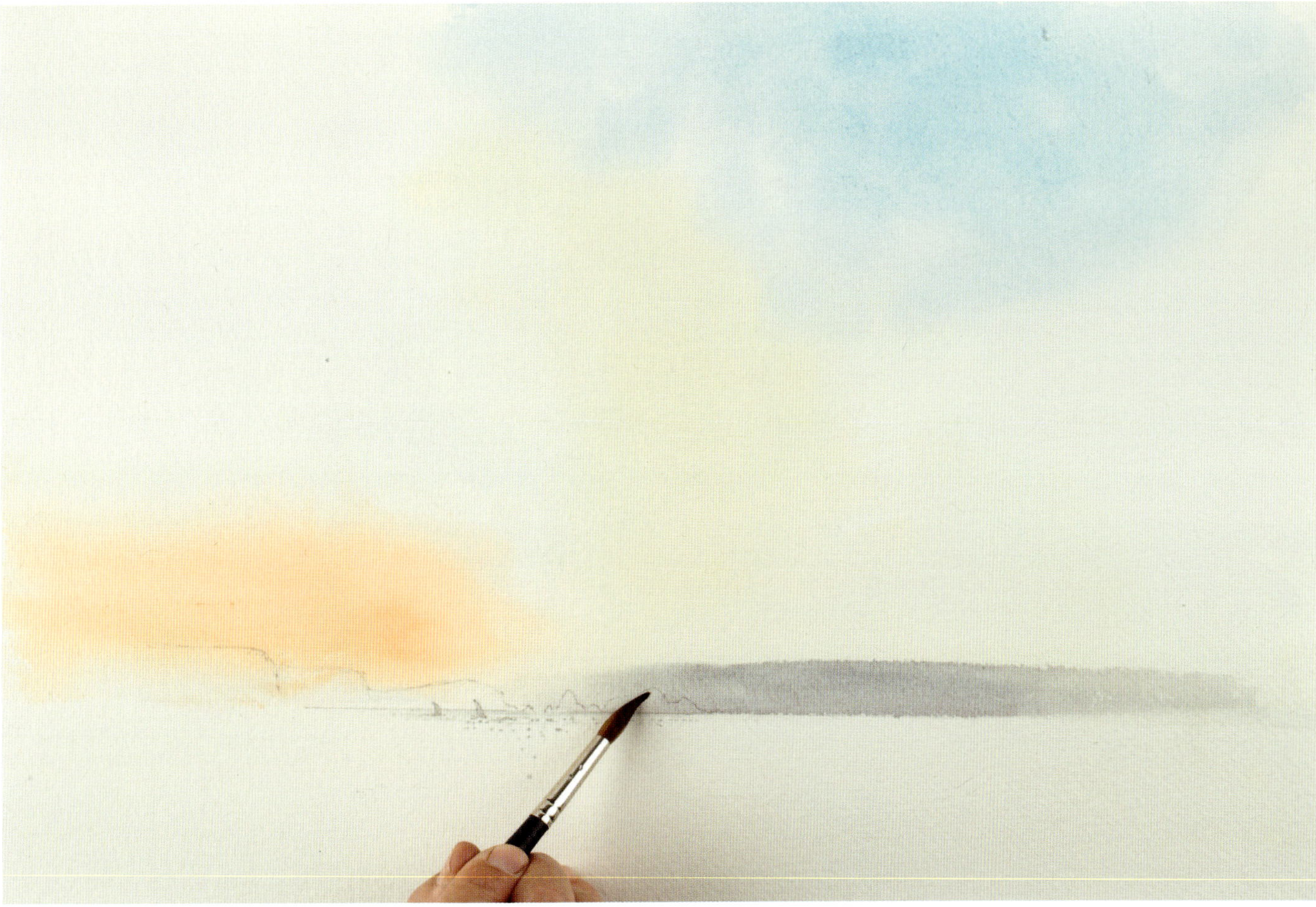

3 Use the no. 10 round brush to paint the distant mainland with a pale grey mix of indigo and cadmium red. Fade either edge and soften the top a little with a damp brush. Allow to dry.

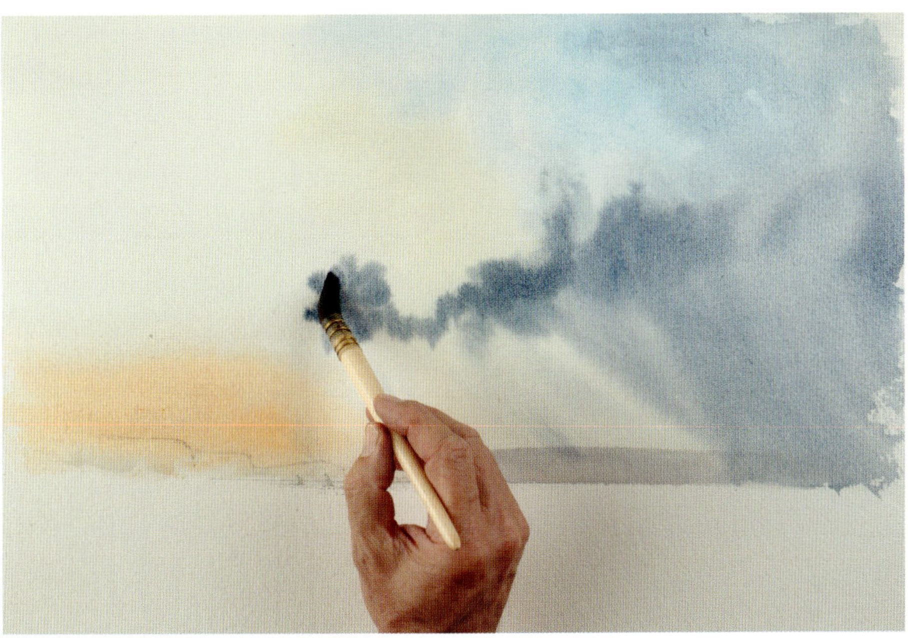

4 Wet the whole sky area again. Use the squirrel mop with indigo and a little cadmium red to paint dark clouds running into the cerulean blue area. Make the clouds stronger in places and paint shafts of light and dark down to the sea. The shafts of sunlight should all begin from the same (unseen) point, but as they spread out, they will be at slightly different angles.

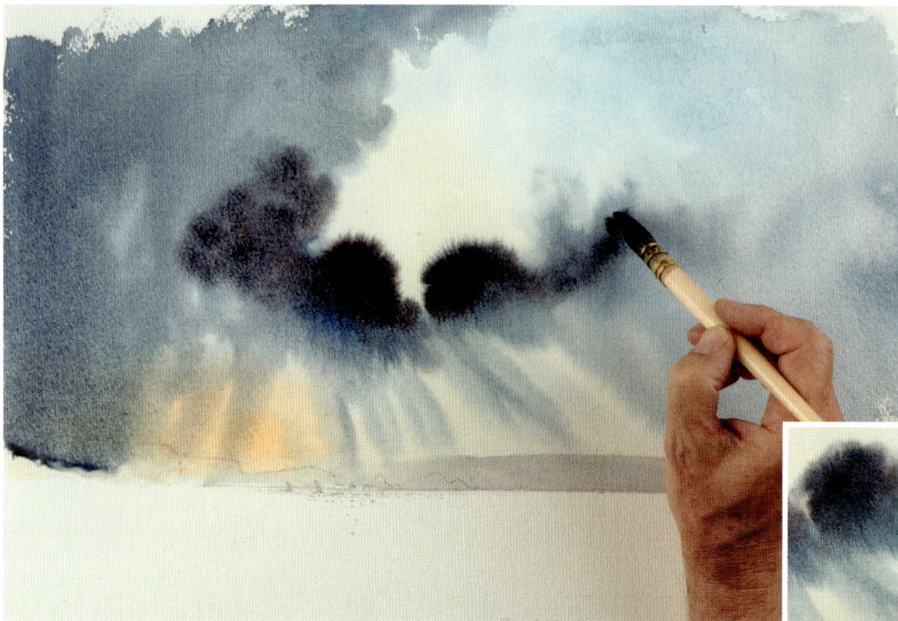

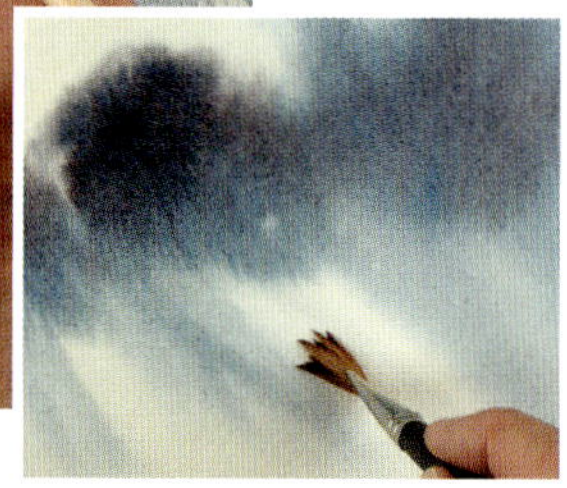

5 Continue painting cloud shapes and shafts of light and dark. Paint very dark clouds in the centre with indigo and neat cadmium red. Use the 6mm (¼inch) flat brush to pull out colour and correct any hard lines that appear as the sky develops. This is especially important with the shafts of sunlight (see inset).

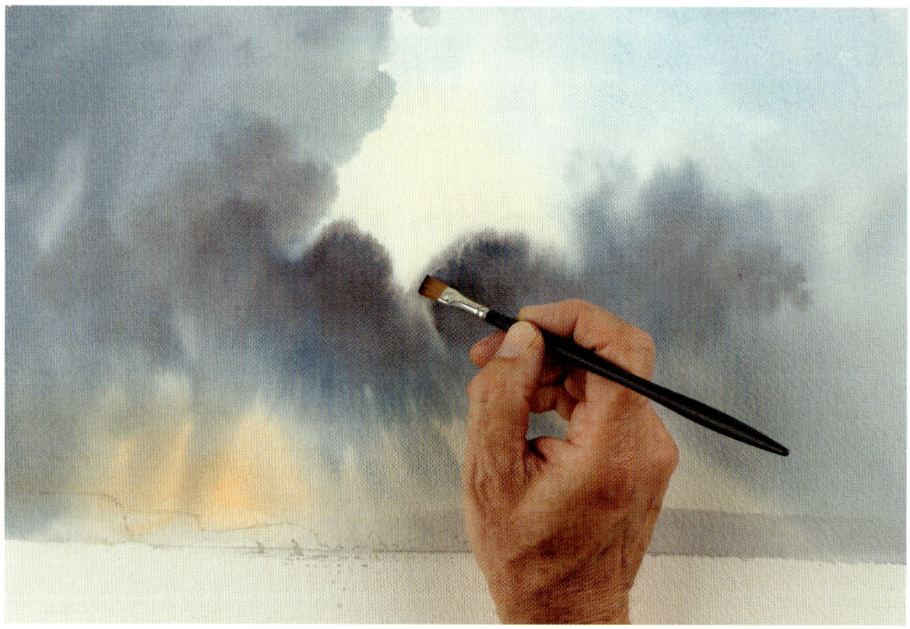

6 Lift out some colour at the edges of the central very dark clouds with the 6mm (¼in) flat brush, to show where light is catching the cloud edges. Allow the painting to dry.

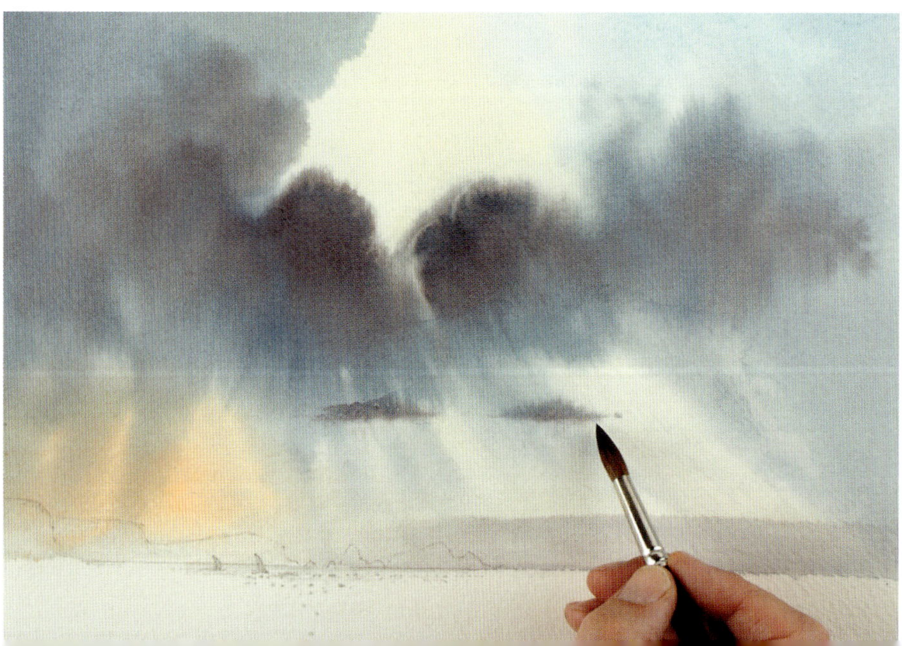

7 To introduce a couple of smaller clouds in front of the shafts of sunlight, re-wet the central area of sky carefully, brushing the water in the direction of the light shafts. Take the no. 10 brush and a mix of indigo and cadmium red, then drop in small lateral clouds below the darkest clouds. Blot out the bottoms of the clouds with paper tissue.

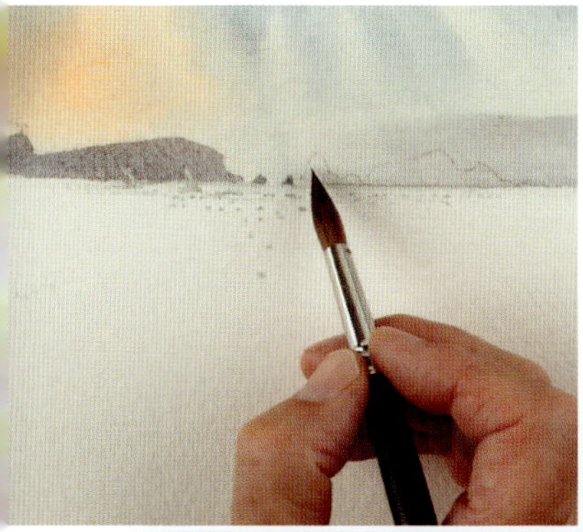

8 Put a little more cadmium red in the mix and paint in the headland and islands with the no. 10 brush. Tidy the waterline with a damp 6mm (¼in) brush.

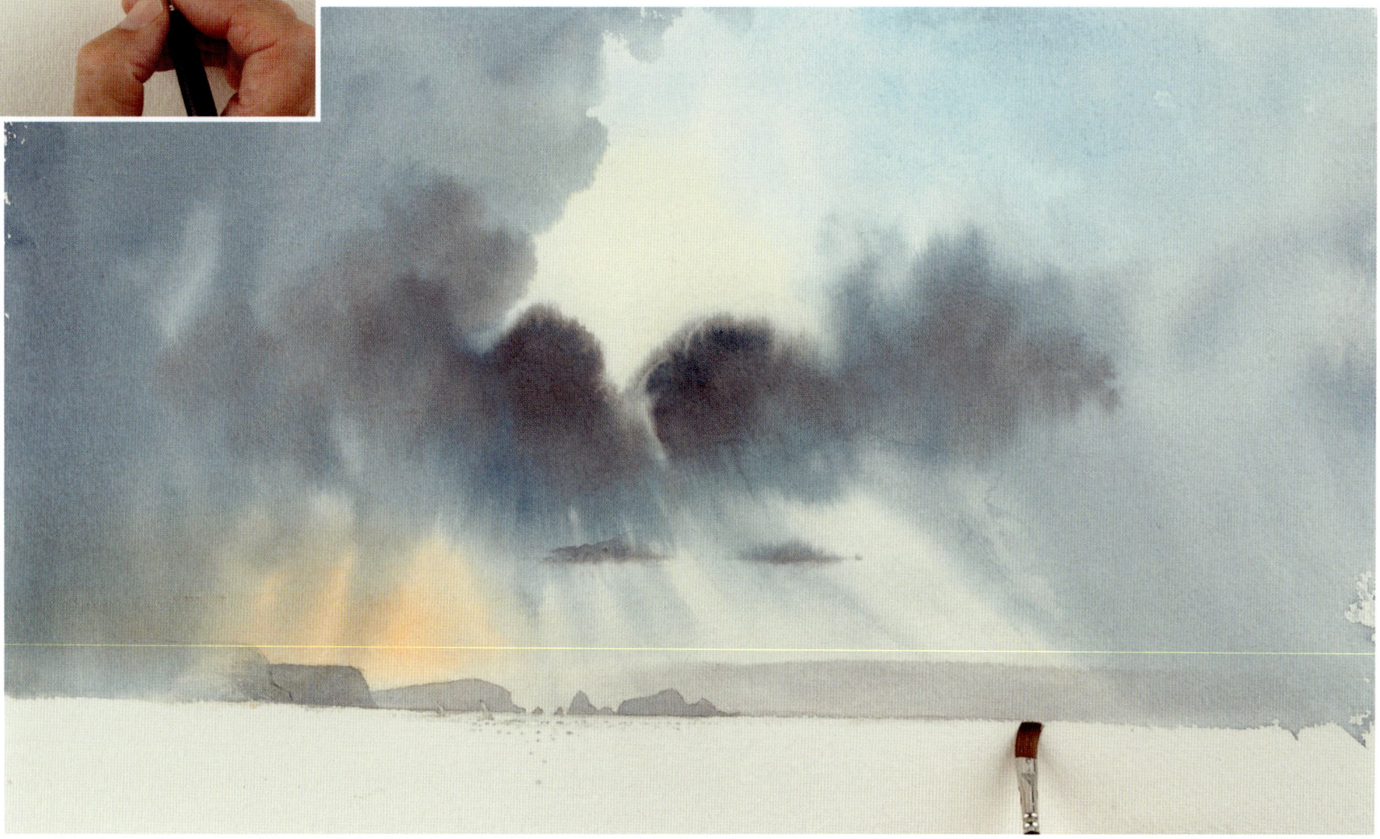

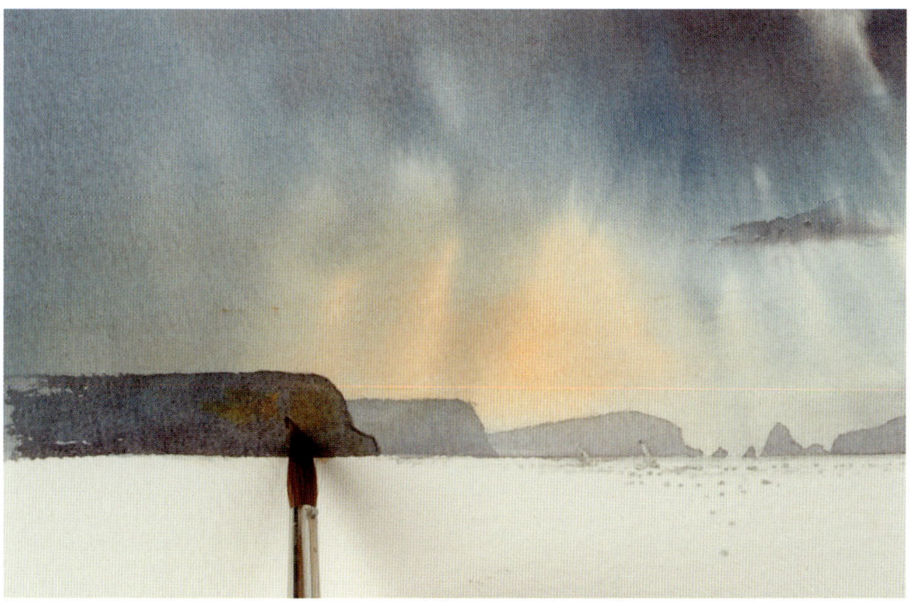

9 Strengthen the nearest part of the headland to bring it forwards, with indigo and cadmium red, then drop in some touches of yellow ochre. Allow to dry.

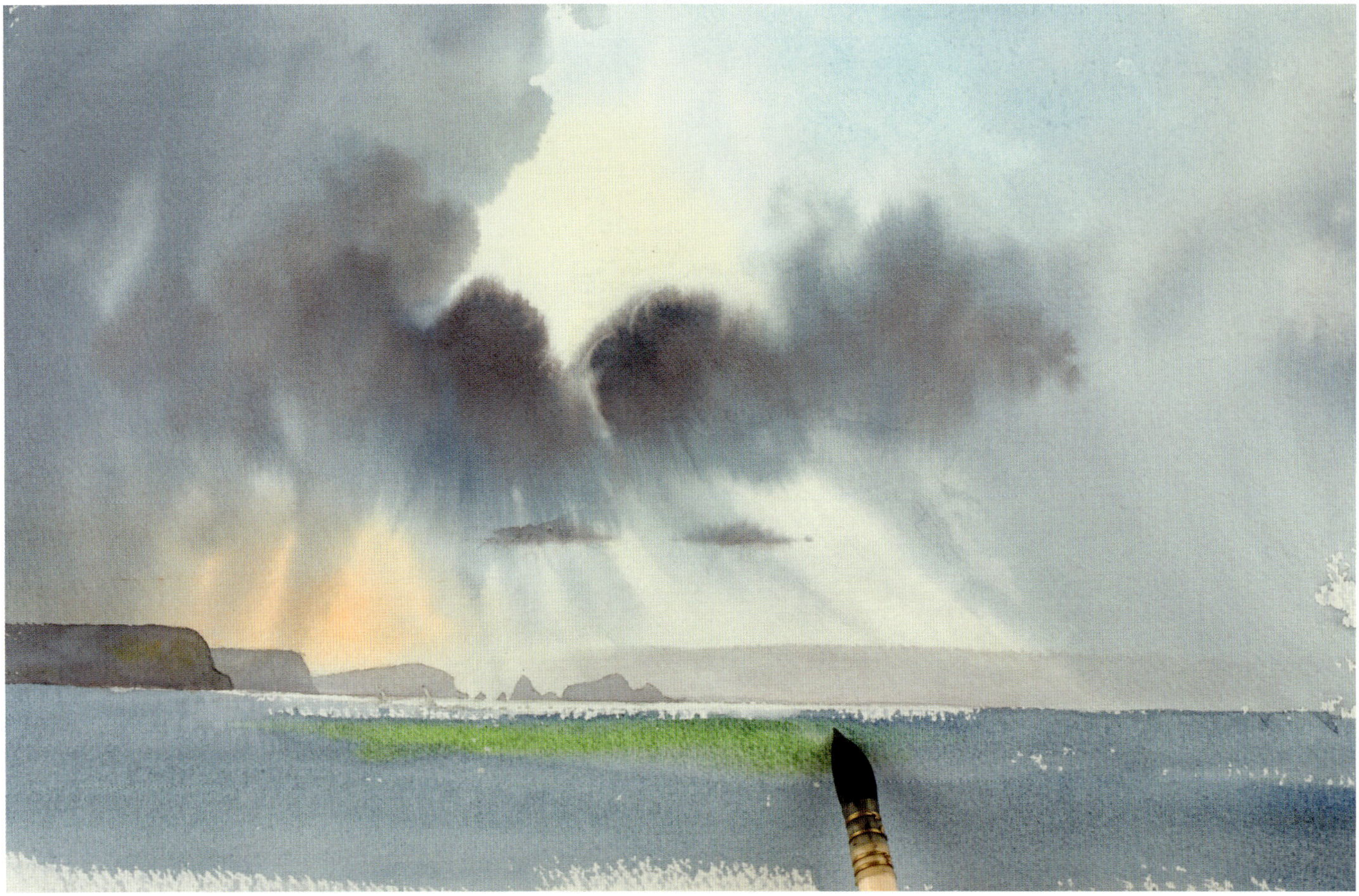

10 Paint the sea using the squirrel mop and a mix of indigo and cadmium red. Sweep the colour across the paper, leaving tiny white bits to suggest sparkles. While this is wet, sweep in cadmium yellow pale below the shafts of sunlight. Allow to dry.

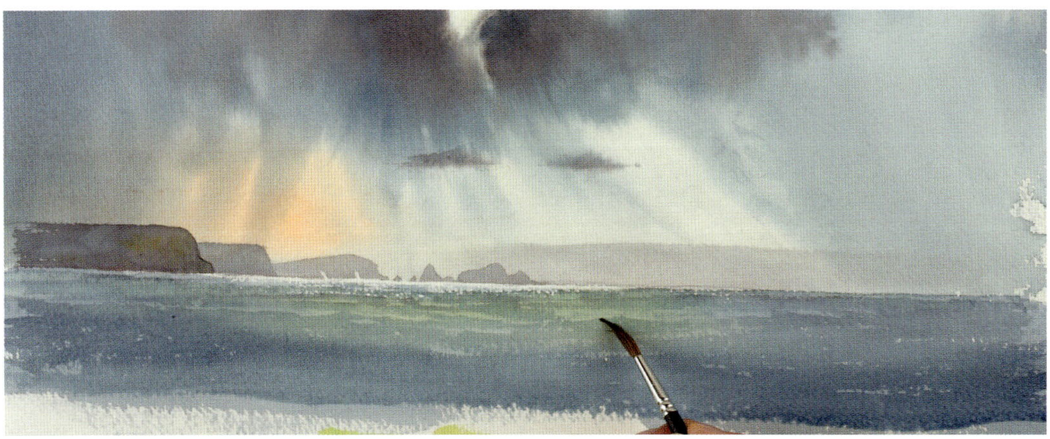

11 Remove the masking fluid and go over any excess white with indigo and cadmium red on the no. 7 brush. Hint at waves and darken the bottom of the painting with the same mix.

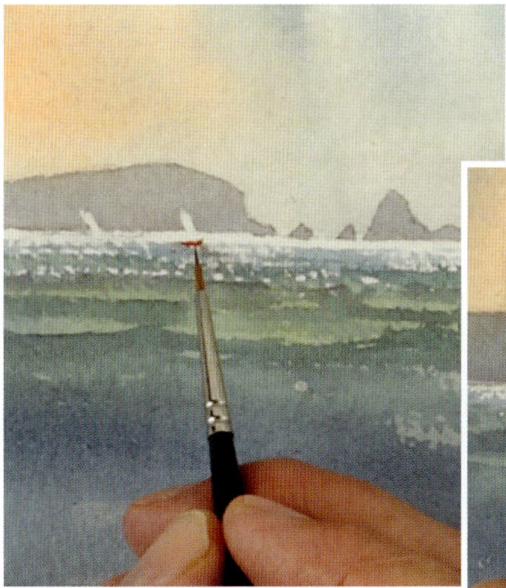

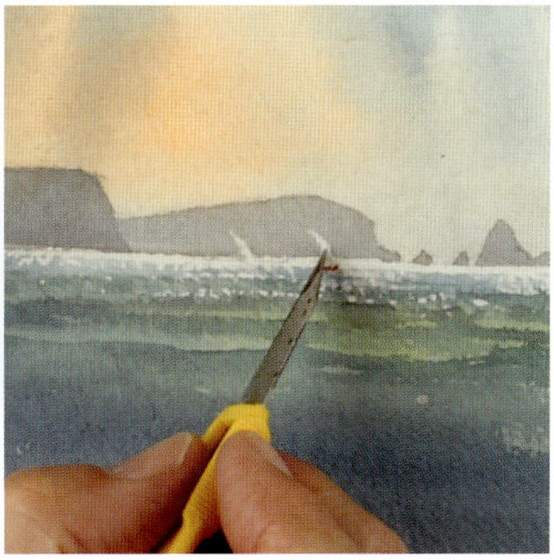

**12** Use the no. 1 rigger to paint one yacht hull in cadmium red, then use a craft knife blade to tidy up the sails and to scratch out ripples in the sea.

*The finished painting.*

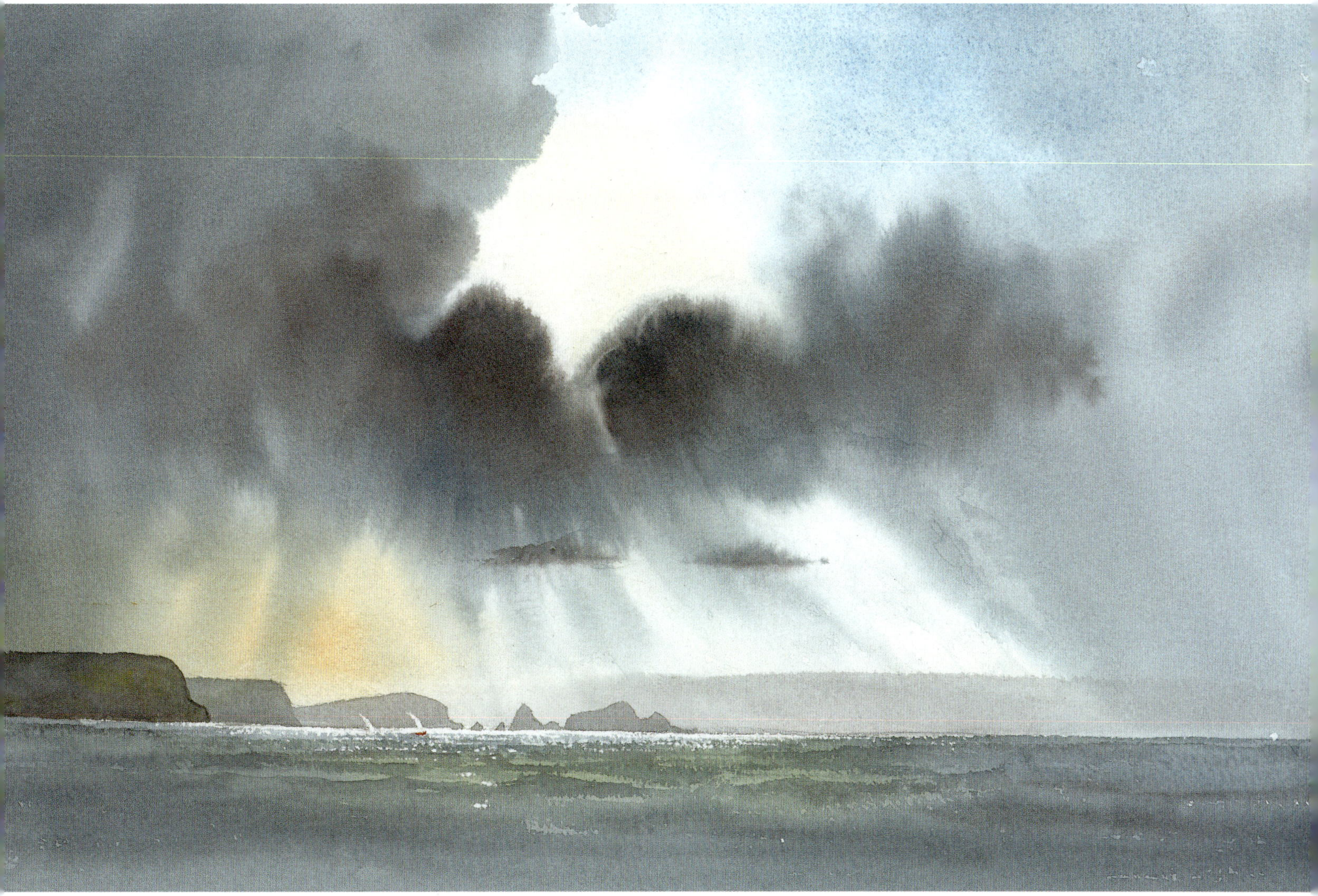

# LIGHT & ATMOSPHERE

Light is a fundamental requirement for our painting, and with consideration it can be one of the most exciting aspects of our work, especially when combined with strong atmosphere. In this section we look at how we see direct light, the riveting power of cast shadows to suggest sunshine, the magic of reflected light, shimmering light, the colour of light and how atmospheric conditions can affect the way we see lighting. The intention is to add something special to your paintings, often with simple little devices.

So often we see dull, lifeless watercolours where the lighting is so flat and boring that however well we have executed the work, it does not stand out from the crowd. With a little thought and know-how, you will find your paintings given a tremendous lift by the techniques shown in the following pages. However, don't try to include them all in one painting, overwhelming the viewer with stunning light effects all over the composition. If everything sparkles, then nothing will stand out as a strong focal point.

Mood or atmosphere is the icing on the landscape cake. It can totally transform a scene and inject a sense of power and drama at the same time. In this section you will see how we can enhance a 'normal' landscape into one conveying the power and beauty of nature's finest moods, how we can use it to lose unwanted detail, or suggest mystery, impending doom, a light, airy afternoon, tranquil moments and much more.

Mood can be especially effective in highlighting a centre of interest or suggesting a narrative. The methods that follow will provide you with the skills to heighten the emotional power of your paintings. You can completely change the mood of the original scene if you wish. Try to get out of the habit of always painting fields green, clouds white, or mud brown – flood the whole composition with a colour mood to suit your idea, even if it conflicts with the colours we normally assume to be correct. Those who fail to see pink mud are truly restricting their imaginative palette.

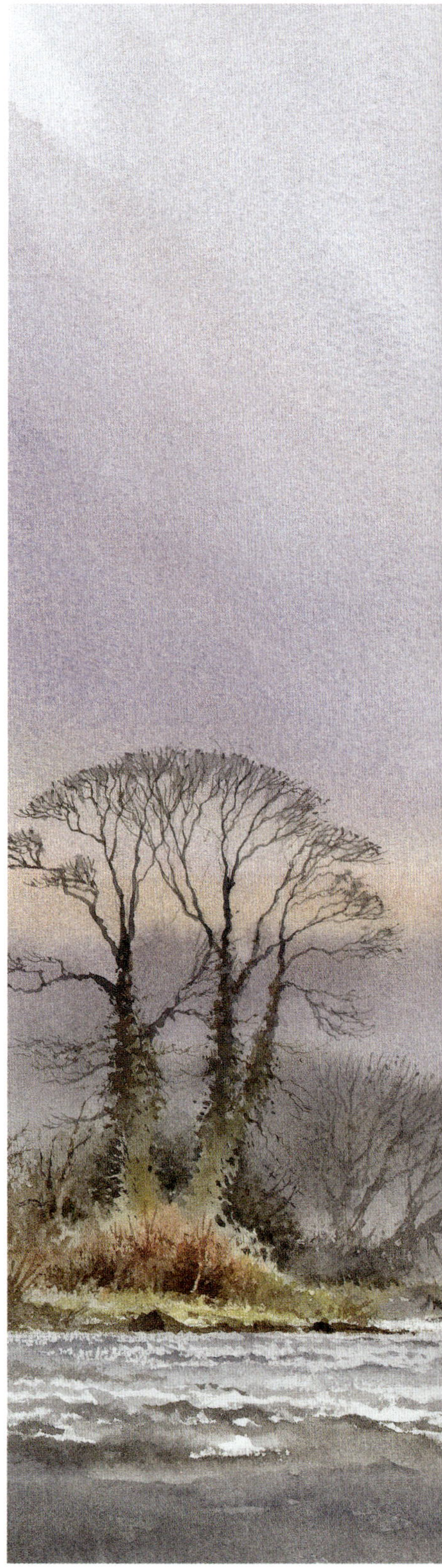

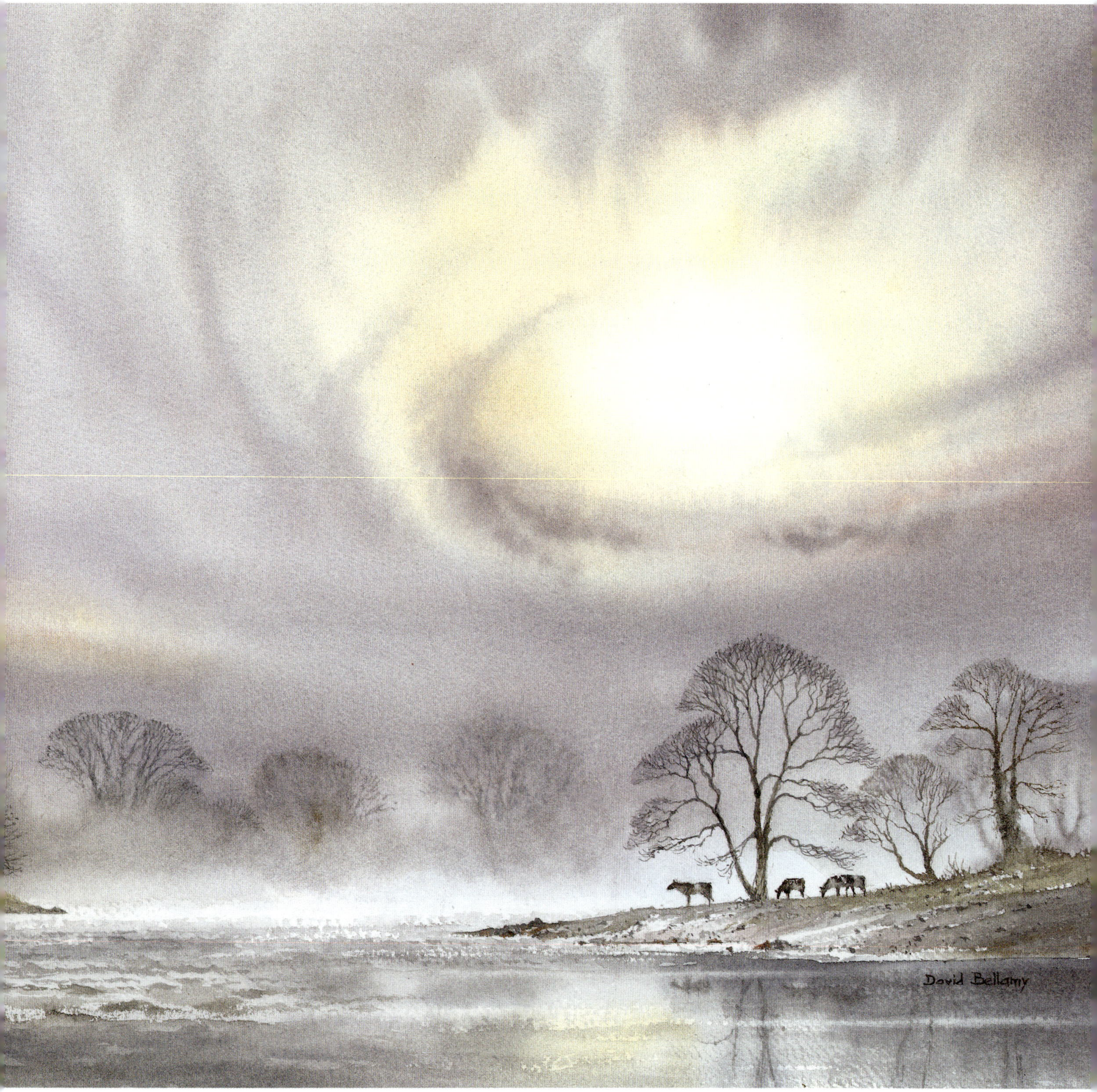
David Bellamy

## WARM AND COOL LIGHT

Colour temperature can be an effective tool in suggesting the time of day, as well as giving an impression of hot or cold weather, and this can affect the whole painting, or just a part. Even with a snowscape you may wish to put across a sense of warm evening light catching snowy features, so a glaze of permanent alizarin crimson over those features might work well. If you want a certain passage in the painting to appear warmer, then paint cool blues, greys or greens next to it and this will intensify the warm colours. Note that some reds, for example, are warmer or cooler than other reds, and so on. Here we look at how to suggest early morning and late evening by the quality of light.

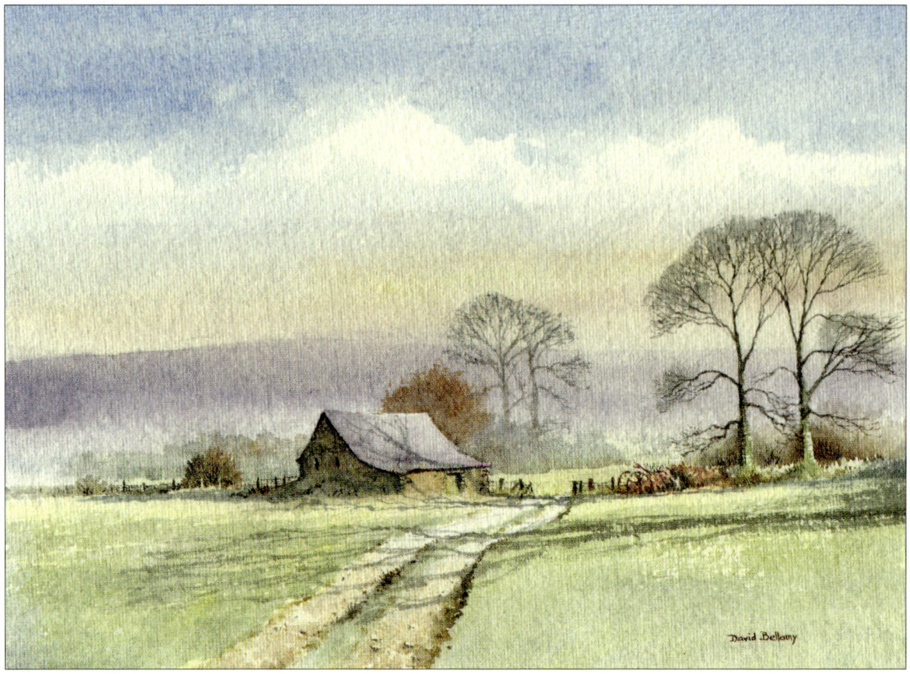

BARN AT TRERICKETT
*20 x 29cm (8 x 11½in)*

*The cool light and long shadows suggest very early morning, as the day has not yet warmed up.*

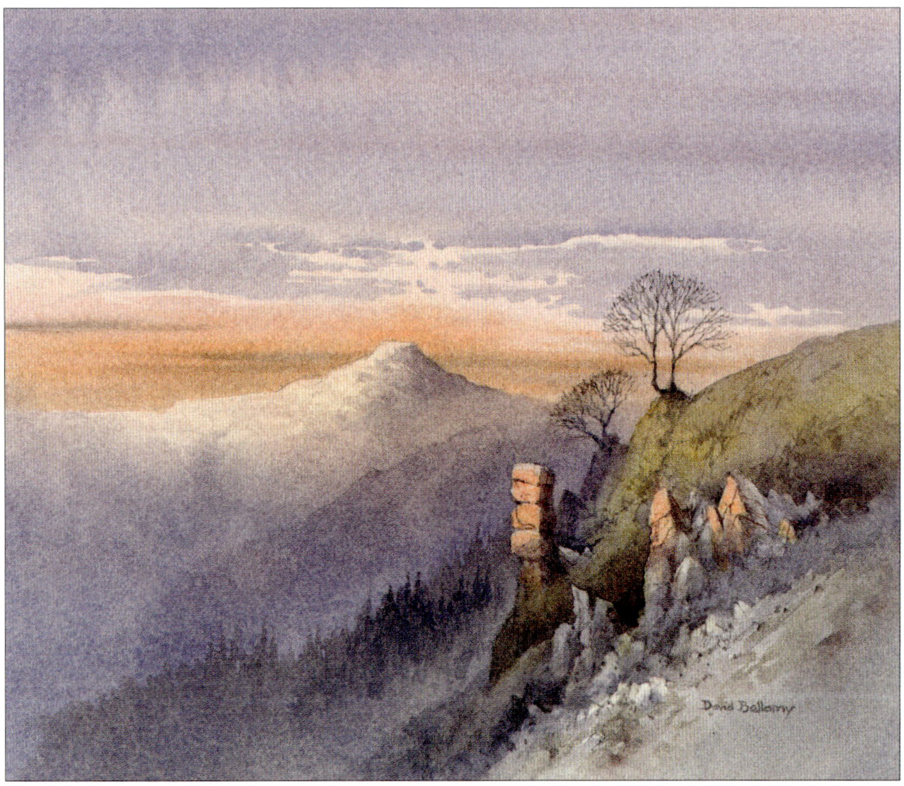

SUGAR LOAF MOUNTAIN IN FADING LIGHT
*18 x 22cm (7 x 8½in)*

*The warm light reflecting on limestone crags gives a strong sense of approaching dusk in this Welsh scene. Creating half-lit features in a painting makes the viewer feel that the sun is sinking low.*

# LAYING GLAZES TO INCREASE LIGHT EFFECTS

A transparent glaze washed across part of the painting that has thoroughly dried can be an impressive method of subduing that passage or highlighting an adjacent one, as well as warming or cooling an area. In these illustrations, the glazes also suggest distance.

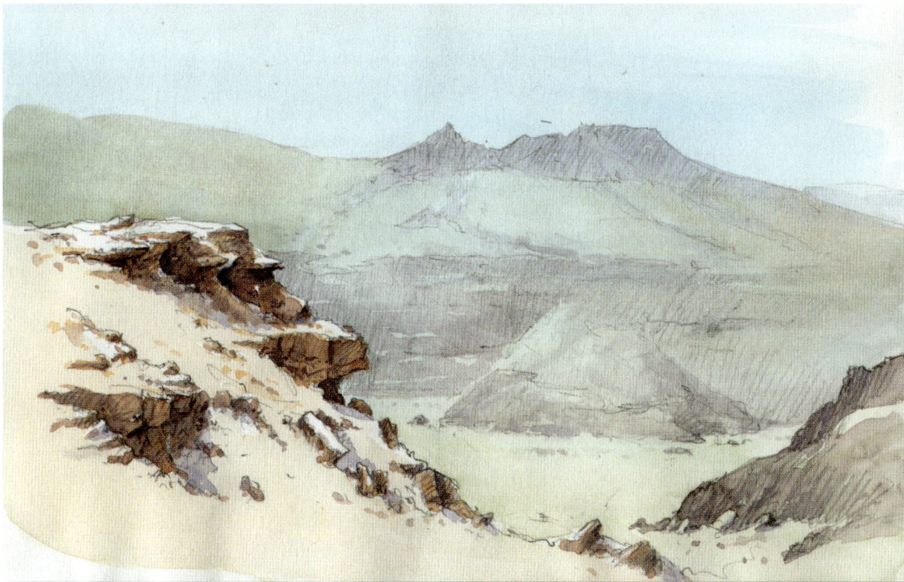

AQABA PASS, GILF KEBIR, EGYPT

*Capturing a sense of intense heat in this watercolour sketch in an A4 (28 x 21cm/11¾ x 8¼in) book was achieved not only by strong contrasts on the foreground rocks, but also by laying a glaze of weak cobalt blue over the background, including the sky. Initially all the background mountain had been painted with the same warm Naples yellow you see in the foreground. There was no wait for the wash to dry as this is one of the hottest places on earth.*

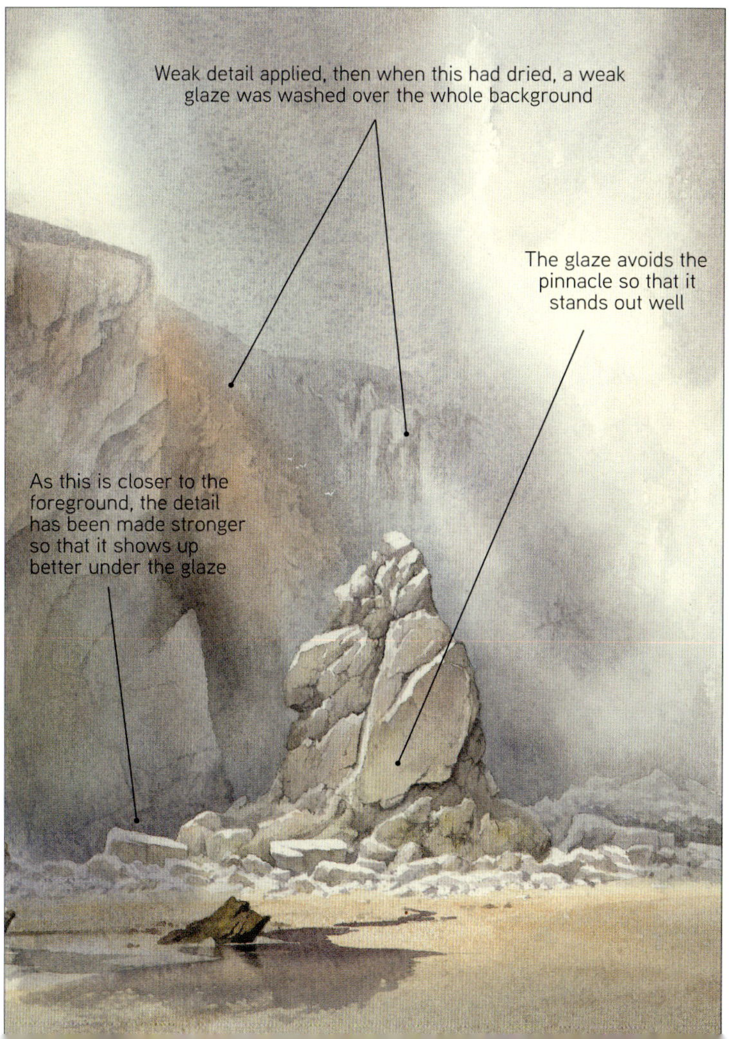


PINNACLE, BULLSLAUGHTER BAY, WALES

*28 x 21cm (11 x 8¼in)*

*The rock pinnacle has been made to stand out by the lack of detail or hard edges in the background cliff. This was achieved by painting in some weak detail, allowing it to dry and then laying a transparent glaze of French ultramarine with a touch of burnt umber right across the background, thus subduing further the suggested detail.*

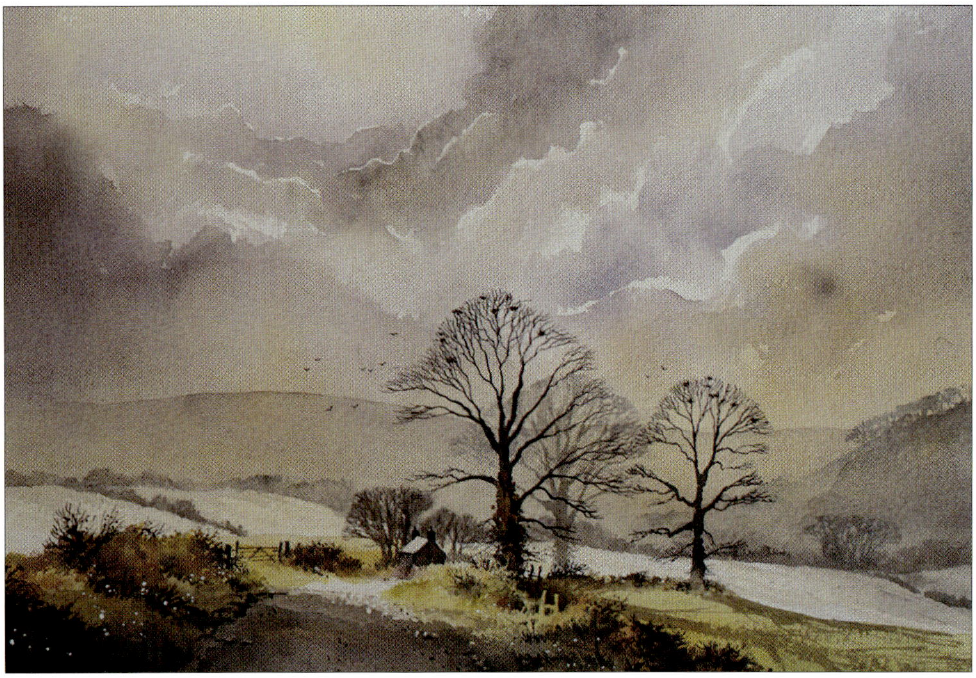

COUNTRY LANE

*20 x 28cm (8 x 11in)*

*The lighter parts of the scene such as the cottage roof and the further part of the lane have been accentuated by leaving those areas as white paper, and the middle-distance fields are off-white. This provides strong contrasts with the closer fields, trees and hedgerows, suggesting a sunny feeling in the middle distance.*

## INTRODUCING MANUFACTURED LIGHT TO INTENSIFY CONTRAST

Many scenes can benefit from altering the strength of tonal contrast to make certain features stand out. Creating a stronger light area by improving or manufacturing a light patch is an excellent technique to highlight a focal point, and both paintings on this page have been improved in this way. Sometimes it simply involves leaving the paper untouched, as with the cottage roof in the upper illustration, and creating strong darks next to that part. Consider your original source material carefully before working on the really critical aspects of the scene, whether you are working from sketches, photographs or out in front of the actual scene. Does it need emphasis or increased contrast? Maybe try a thumbnail or two of that particular spot in the composition. Don't take every scene and paint it exactly as it stands. The light is constantly changing and thus the relationship between all the various features also constantly changes, so this is a superb way in which to exercise your creativity.

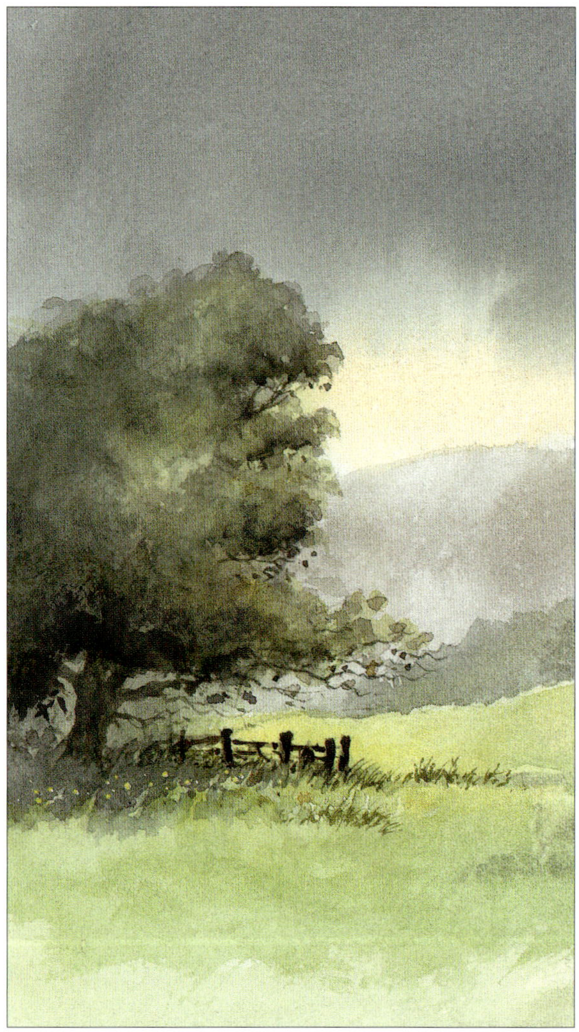

SUMMER TREE

*In this small part of a watercolour painting the background field has been painted with a lovely bright yellow, even though the actual field was a drab green. The yellow lifts the scene, making the fence posts stand out, so don't be afraid to spice up parts of your composition with some manufactured light in this way.*

## USING CAST SHADOWS TO AVOID REPETITION

You will come across many examples of repetitive detail in landscapes, and however exciting each bit of detail may be, the overall effect can appear rather uninteresting if all is included. An excellent way to reduce this repetitive boredom is to wash cast shadows over part of the scene, whether it is a long line of intricate cliff structure, a forest in the middle distance, a mass of buildings, as in the example below, or one of many other instances of elaborate detail.

Pick out the most exciting features that you wish to highlight and work a wash round them, creating both hard and soft edges to the shadow wash if possible. Either make one part stand out strongly by including extra detail, or make some foreground feature stand out in powerful contrast to the background mass.

AMMAN

*I gazed across the rooftops in Amman, Jordan, and saw the whole scene was lit up by strong morning sunshine, every building brilliantly lit. This would make for a rather boring painting, so after drawing the main buildings in, I laid a shadow wash over all but those I wished to stand out, then added some darker shapes in places. The palm trees and minarets were especially useful in creating variety and depth. This technique is excellent for reducing repetition.*

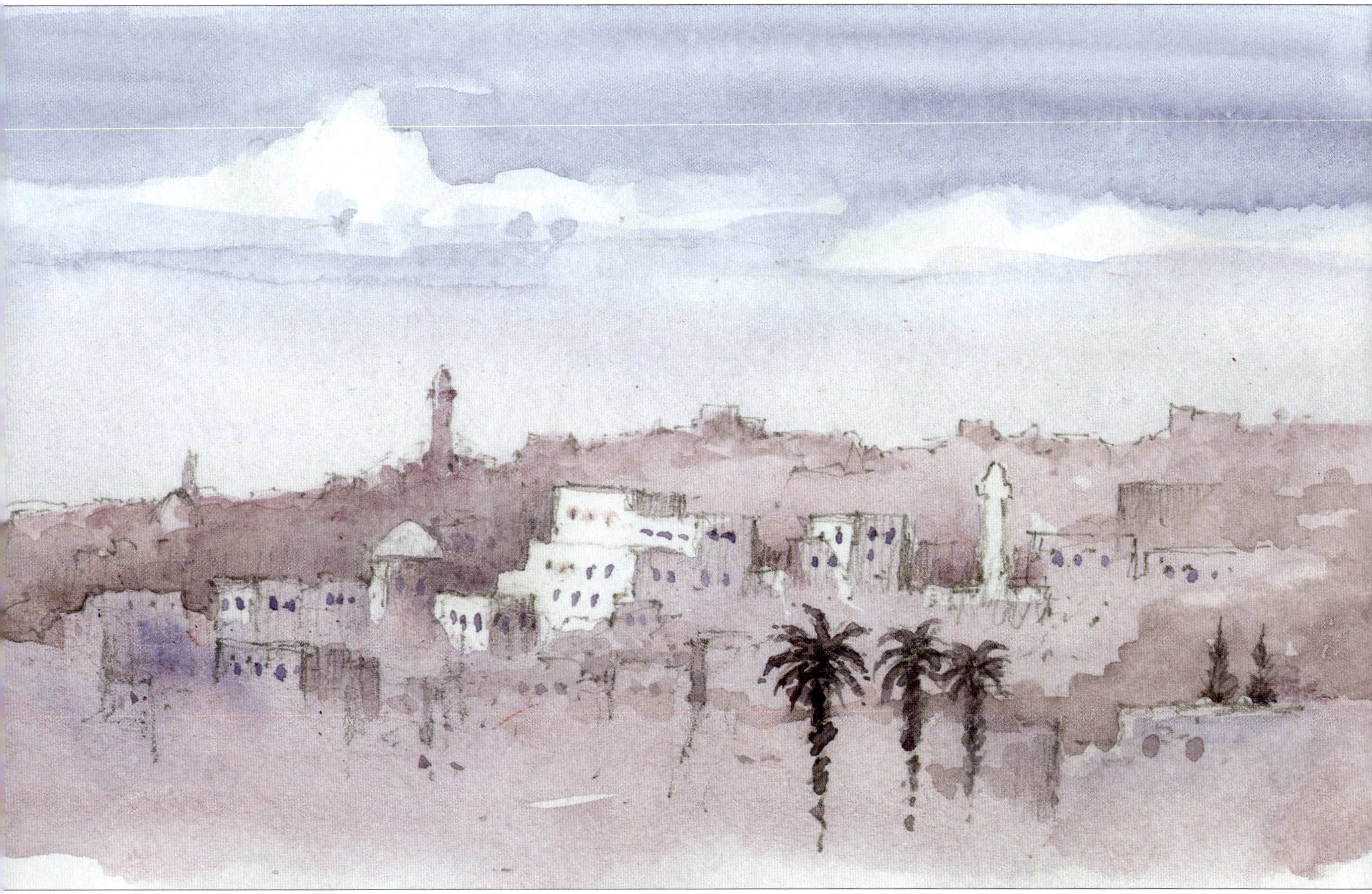

# LIGHT FROM VARIOUS DIRECTIONS

The four images on these pages show the light source coming from different directions, and how this can affect the overall impression. I often change the direction of the light from that shown in the original scene, sometimes quite dramatically, to suit the mood I wish to create. The stone barn illustration at the bottom of this page has been kept deliberately dull to highlight the problem, when in fact I would normally spice it up quite a bit.

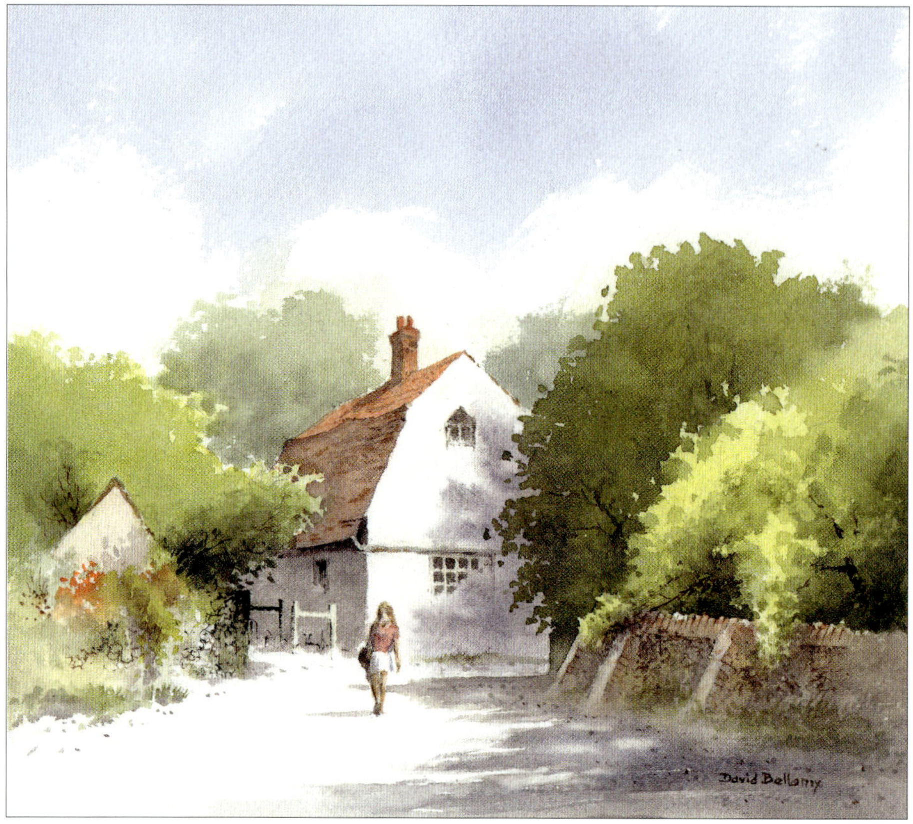


CAMBRIDGESHIRE VILLAGE – SIDE LIT
*20 x 20cm (8 x 8in)*

*Lighting coming from one side can emphasize form and is extremely useful when depicting cast shadows.*

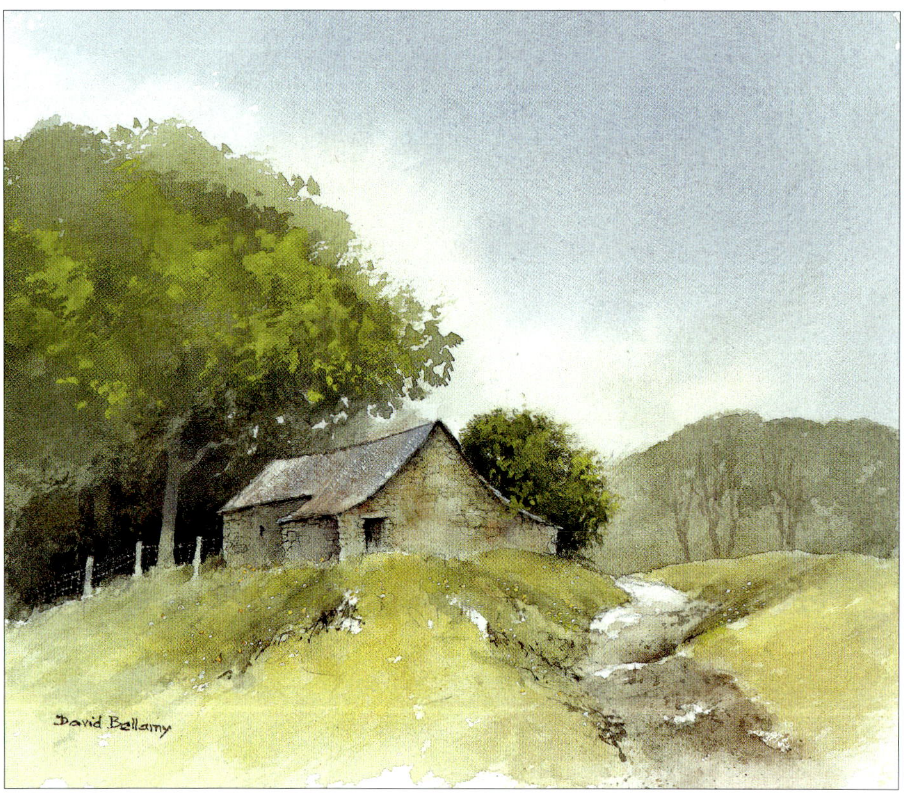


STONE BARN – FRONT LIT
*15 x 18cm (6 x 7in)*

*The light here is not strong but the extreme ends of the barn stood out, as they were against really dark features. However, I had to emphasize the darker left-hand side of the barn as the front lighting simply made the structure look too flat. This can be a problem when sunlight catches the two sides you are viewing, so one should be exaggerated, as in this case.*

### SUMMER LANE – TOP LIT

*16 x 13cm (6¼ x 5in)*

*Around the middle of the day during the warmer months, sunlight is angled from high above the subject. This can create strong highlights on the tops of trees, buildings, vehicles, and so on. Cast shadows are correspondingly minimized as shown in this scene. High back-lit scenes can appear really dramatic.*

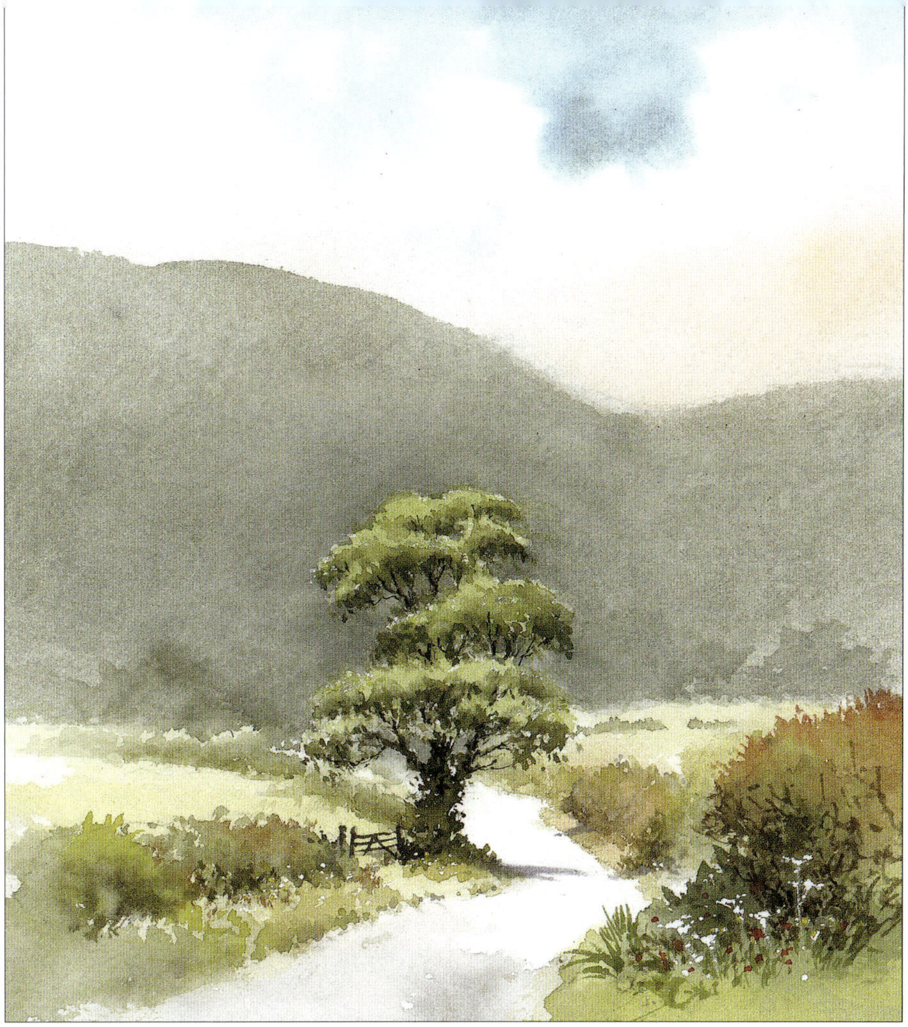

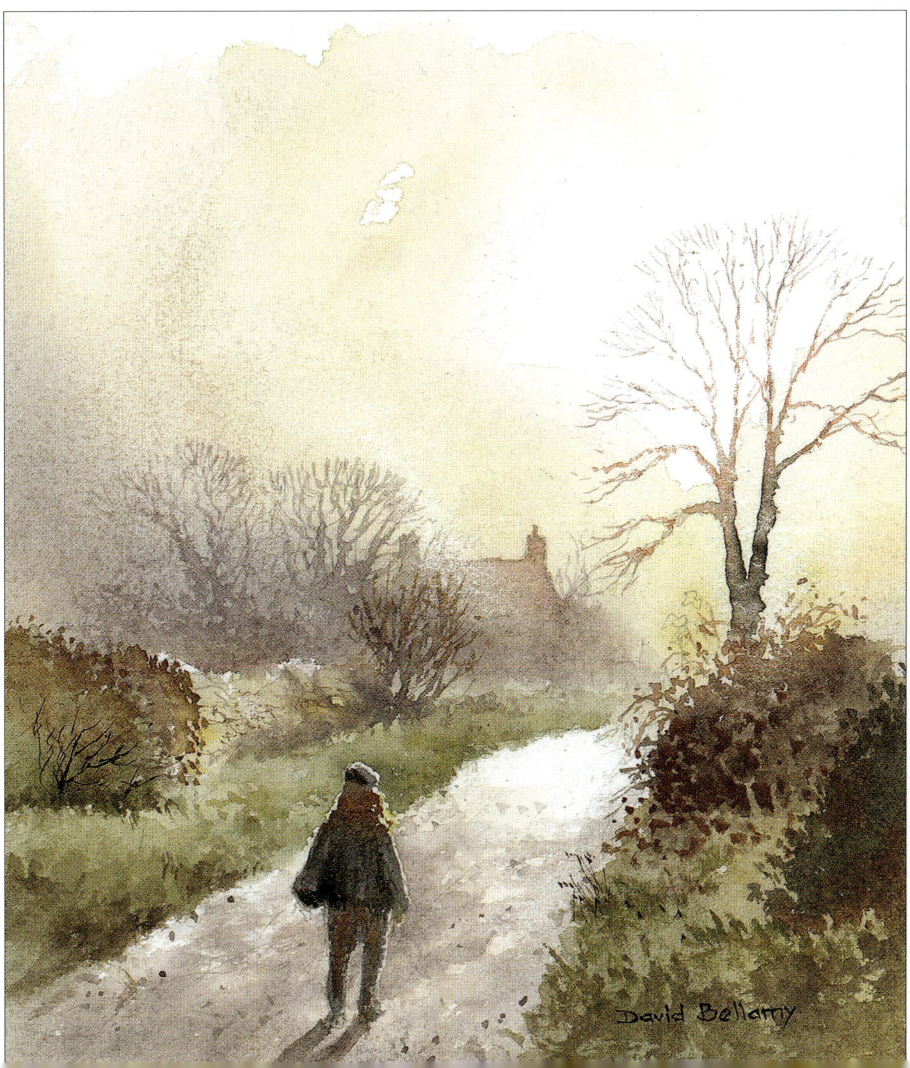


### LANE AT EVENING – BACK LIT

*13 x 12cm (5 x 4¾in)*

*Back-lit views can increase the drama and atmosphere considerably, and can simplify the more distant features, often to the degree that they appear only as silhouettes. Many objects, especially the closer ones, can have light rims around them, as on the figure in this scene.*

# INTENSE SUNLIGHT

Capturing intense sunlight is not too difficult, and as with so much to do with painting, creating a really authentic response relies on careful direct observation. In the first picture we study direct sunlight and how it appears to burn out any feature close to the line of the sun, and at the same time imparts a powerful orangey-red glow to the closest features such as branches. More often, however, you will be concerned with how strong sunlight falls on an object or landscape feature, as in the other two illustrations. Strong contrast between lit and shadow areas is, of course, vital, but also watch out for that shimmering effect you sometimes see where shafts of sunlight fall on parts of the scene, as in the painting opposite, just above the building and slightly to its right. Here the edges have been softened and the contrast between light and shadow is less intense.

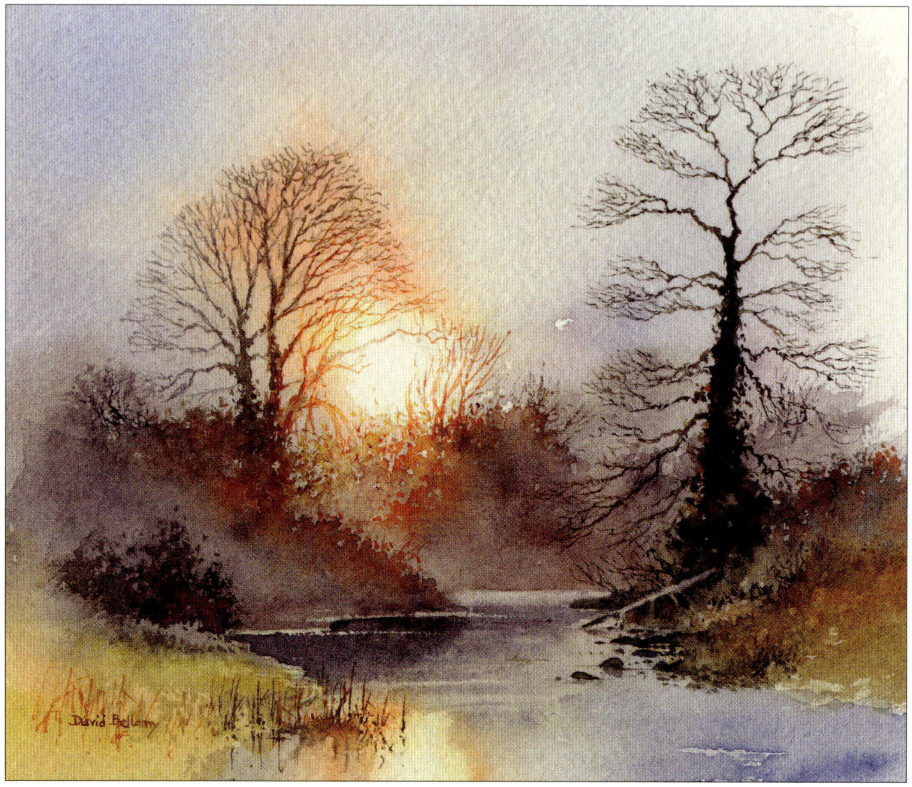

SETTING SUN
*15 x 17cm (6 x 6¾in)*

*The power of the setting sun can bleach out detail in features such as tree branches. Take care looking directly into the sun – unless it is very weak, use dark glasses, preferably grey-tinted rather than with a colour cast. Many of the elements become silhouettes, often with a warm colour cast closer to the sunlit area.*

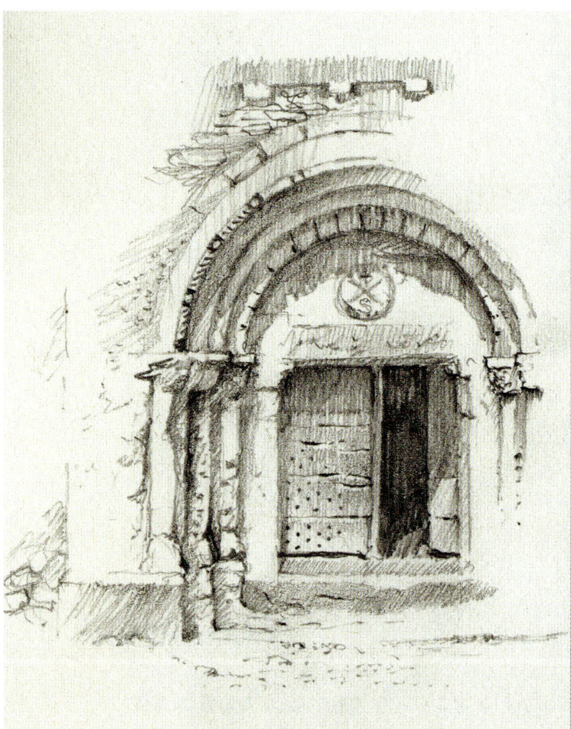

DOORWAY OF EGLISE SAINT-ÉXUPÈRE, ARREAU

*In this pencil sketch I tried to put across the sense of intensely strong sunlight falling on the ancient doorway and heightening the worn nature of the stonework. However, avoid putting too much detail into an area that is catching strong sunlight, as it will detract from the effect.*

**BENEATH MOUNT SINAI**
*32 x 46cm (12½ x 18in)*

*The intense midday sunlight falling on rocks has been accentuated by leaving the tops of the rocks as white paper to provide strong contrasts. The sun is slightly to the left in this painting, and the scene is back lit. Note the reflected light illuminating the white-washed front of the building and on the right-hand side of the rock just to its left. A heat-haze obscures much of the cliff detail in the rear.*

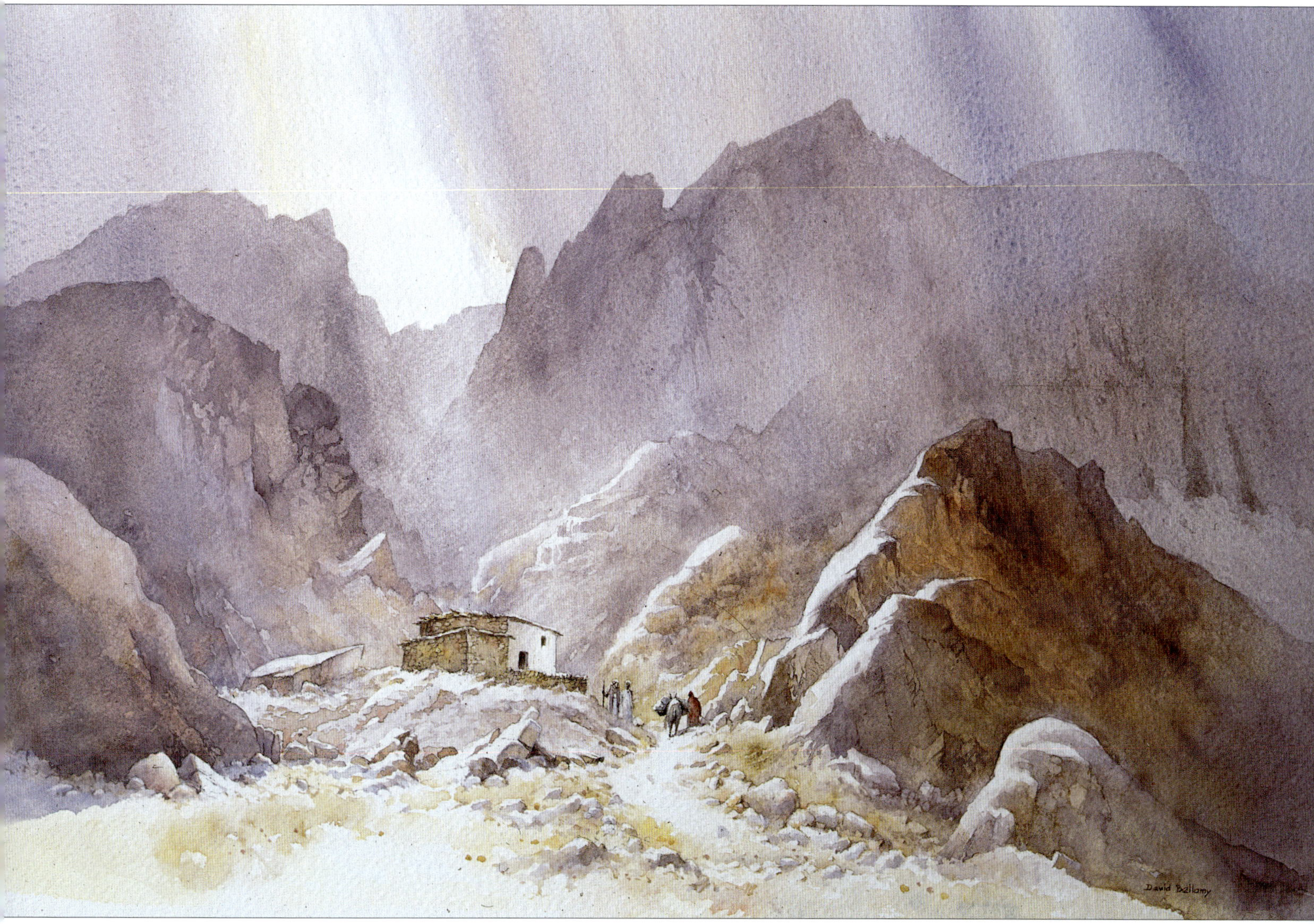

# PAINTING THE SUN

Sometimes it can be really effective to include the sun in your painting. It needs careful placement, and is usually included in scenes depicting very early morning or towards sunset. Avoid placing it slap in the centre of your sky, and to increase its effectiveness you can position it directly over a stretch of water to create a reflection highlight. You may also want to obscure it slightly between tree trunks, behind bare branches, or with atmosphere or part of a cloud. Sometimes a stark circle can appear too intrusive. I also lay a thin transparent glaze across it on occasion, to suggest the sun shining through a thin film of cloud, and this is especially useful if you wish to reduce the contrast.

There are a number of ways of rendering the sun. It is the brightest part of your composition, and your brightest tone in a watercolour painting is the white paper itself (unless you are working on tinted paper), so it is usually best to keep the sun as a white orb. Now and then I paint a weak yellow or red across it, usually only over part of the orb. Often I simply paint the darker sky round the sun, in a negative manner, but masking fluid is an excellent alternative. You can use a coin or a plastic stencil that has a variety of circle sizes, or whatever suitable object comes to hand, to draw the sun with a pencil. You can also lift out a circle from a damp wash by covering a coin with tissue and pressing it into the wash, but this method will not produce such a brilliantly white image as the others.

EVENING LIGHT, LANDSHIPPING

*The sun is visible behind the trees and muted in the evening atmosphere, whereas normally it is the brightest part of the work and so I leave more white paper showing. Here I have used weak cadmium yellow pale with a touch of cadmium red.*

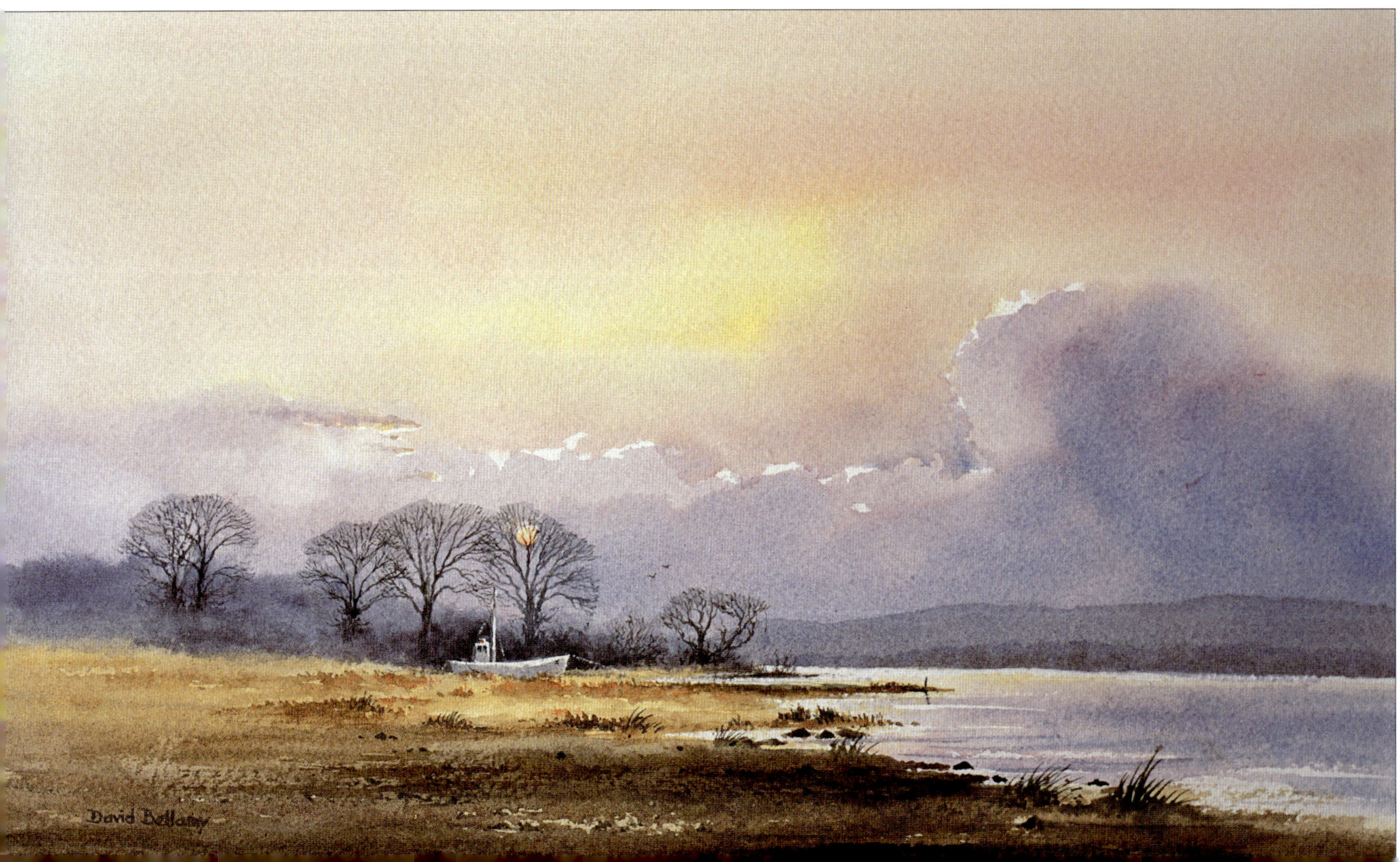

## MAKING THE MOST OF SHADOWS

Cast shadows are by far the most effective way of suggesting a feeling of sunshine in your painting, so make the most of them: exaggerate, extend and enlarge them to your advantage. Shadows falling part way across a cliff or a bridge, for example, are especially exciting. Where you have a lovely white house, by all means push those trees closer in to give yourself an excuse to lay cast shadows over the walls and roof – it will breathe a little magic into your painting.

If you feel the shadow before you is too grey and boring, liven it up with a touch of red into whatever blue you are using. Lay these shadows across your already-painted feature once it has completely dried, and use them to describe the contours, ruts and other variations in the ground. When I am out working before nature, I try to place all the cast shadows at around the same time so that they are consistent – it is surprising how quickly that sun moves round and alters the angle and size of a shadow.

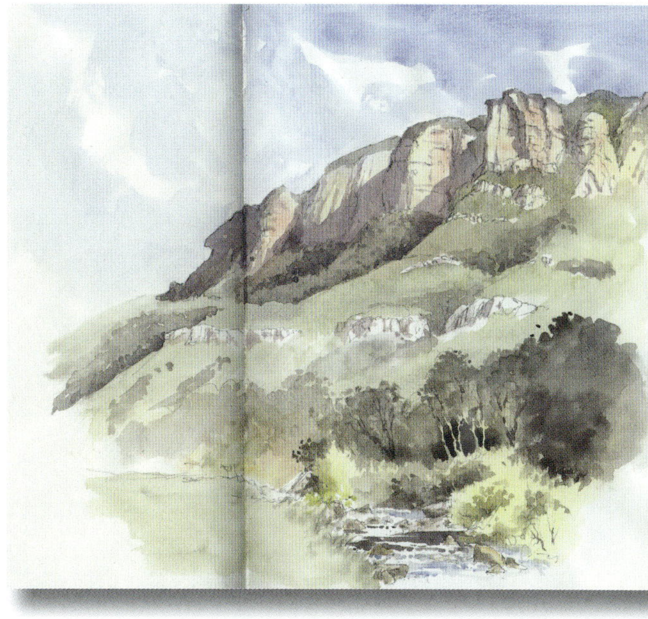

CLIFFS IN NATAL, SOUTH AFRICA

*Throwing shadows across cliffs, bridges or buildings is a lovely way of creating variety within a feature, and I watch out for the effect whenever the opportunity arises. I sketched these cliffs at 6:15am and had no need to exaggerate the shadows, which I sometimes have to.*

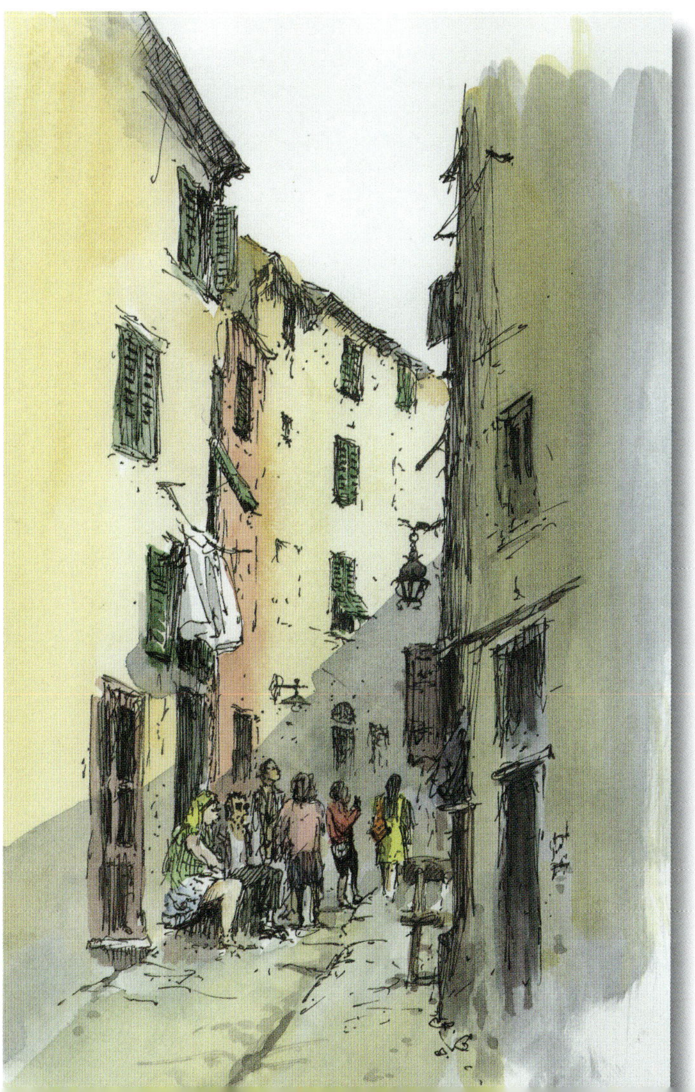

ALLEY IN PORTOVENERE, ITALY

*An ink and watercolour sketch done on the spot in an A4 (28 x 21cm/11¾ x 8¼in) sketchbook. I loved the way the alley turned slightly to the right as it went away. The shadow area makes the sunlit side look even warmer and sunnier. My only concern with this sketch is that I have made the closest figure slightly too large in proportion to the others. This can be a common problem where a number of figures are involved and one is trying to record figures before they get up and move away.*

# REFLECTED LIGHT

Reflected light is that which bounces off a surface that is in strong light, and is a weaker, secondary light. It works best when thrown off a white surface such as a white wall, a cloud, or an iceberg for example, but when strong light bounces off a coloured surface, that colour is also transferred as coloured reflected light. The reflecting surface may not always be visible in a composition. Reflected light can be useful to show up detail of secondary importance or to relieve a rather dull passage, but it also suggests a feeling of authenticity in your work. It is a well-used tool by photographers, and you can easily practise it on still life by holding up a large piece of white card close to the object on to which you wish to project the reflected light, allowing the light source to hit your sheet of card and bounce on to the object. Don't forget, you are in control of where the light bounces, so position it where it is most effective.

**POLAR BEAR**
*32 x 47cm (12½in x 18½in)*

*Apart from a few rocks at sea level, all the rest is ice. There are a number of examples of reflected light in the scene, but the most prominent is the narrow vertical ice buttress just right of centre and directly above the small iceberg floating in the water. You can see how the lightest part of this buttress is at the bottom, nearest to the source of reflected light.*

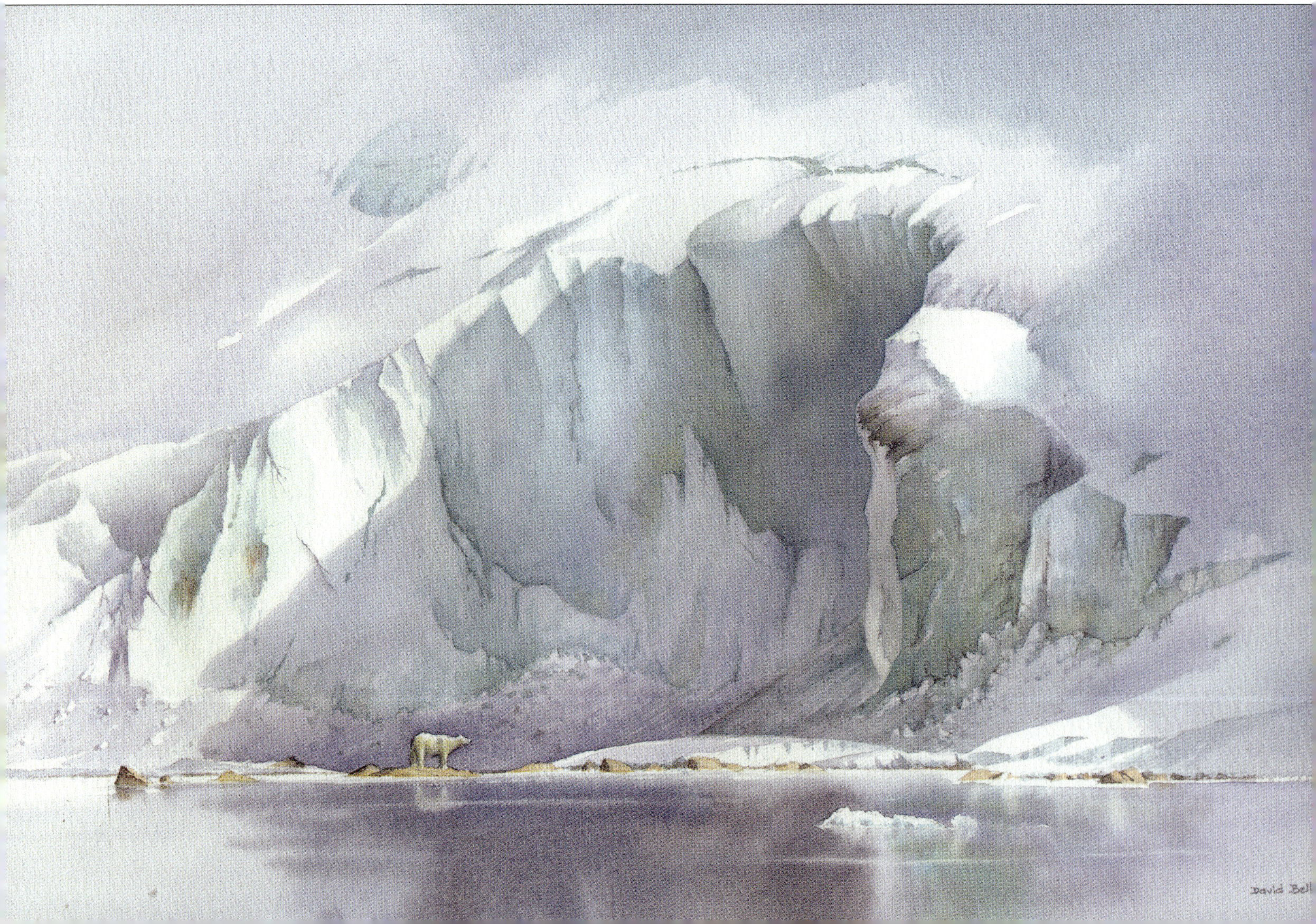

### REFLECTED LIGHT ON ICEBERGS

*Icebergs, like white clouds, are great reflectors of light and this photograph of giant icebergs illustrates well how ice walls in shadow can be lit up brightly in this way.*

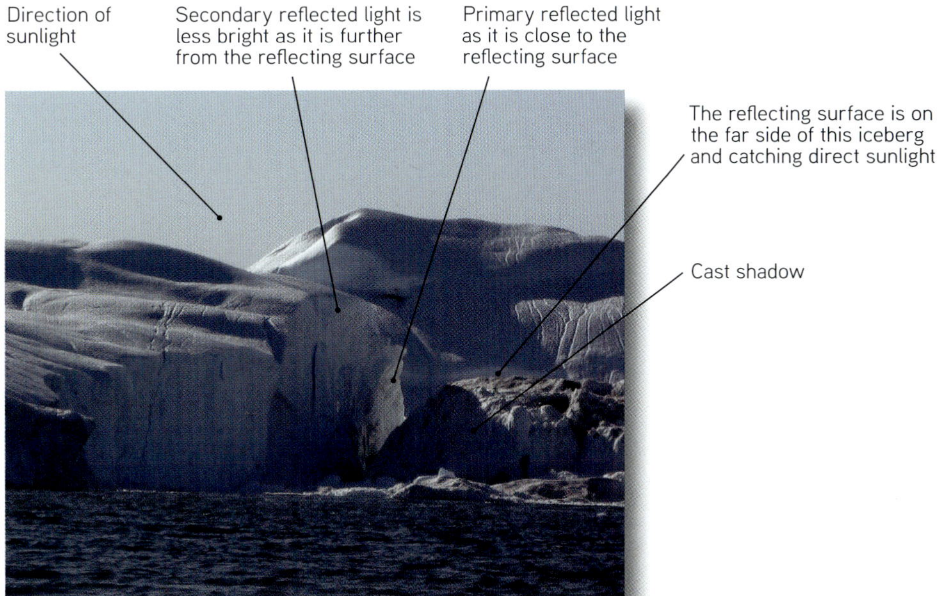


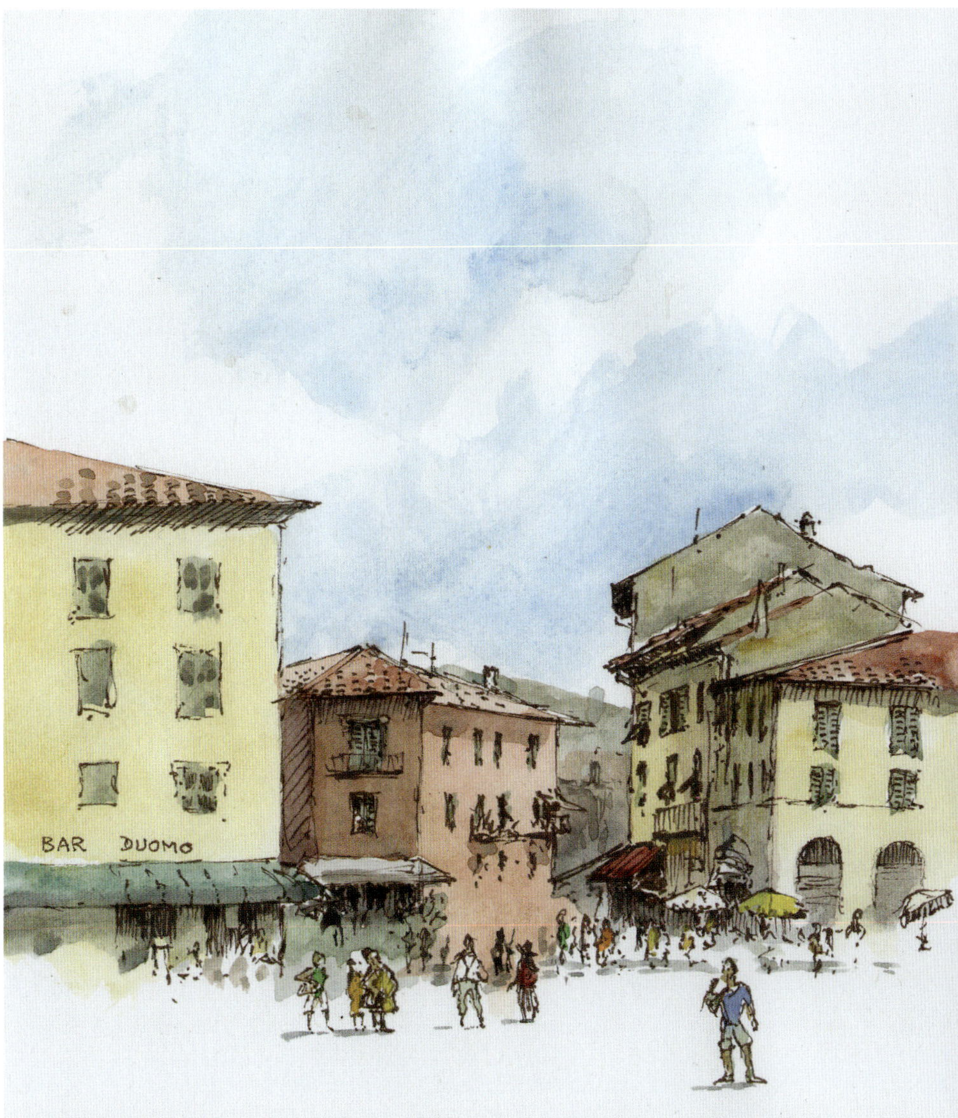


### VIA SANTA MARIA, PISA

*In this pen and watercolour sketch, the light is coming from the top right. Note the strong reflected light on the yellow wall above the deep red canopy. This will have been thrown up by the opposite wall. Note how it graduates into shadow.*

## ACCENTUATING LIGHTING

Both the illustrations on this page were done on the spot, and I was keen to make the light areas stand out, firstly by darkening the skies and trees to highlight the roofs, and secondly by strong definition on the buildings. Introducing powerful contrasts is a superb method of heightening drama.

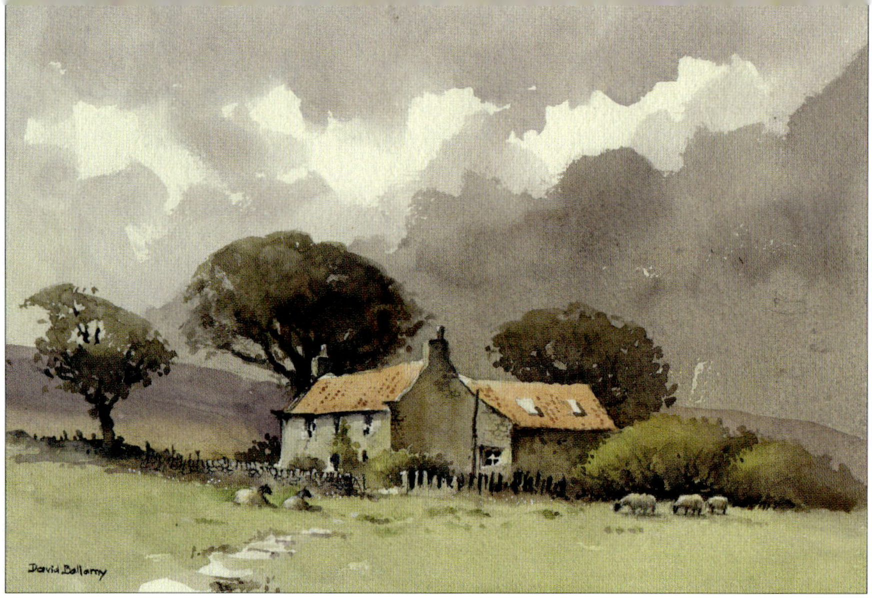


COTTAGE AT GOATHLAND, NORTH YORKSHIRE

*20 x 27cm (8 x 10½in)*

*This was carried out on site as a demonstration and I wanted to illustrate how to accentuate the lighting, taking it from the mundane to the exciting. The dark trees made the tiled roof stand out, and creating a dark sky further highlighted the roof. There are a number of strong tonal contrasts, and I have also employed counterchange on the fence and dry-stone wall, where each moves from light to dark, a powerful technique for creating drama.*

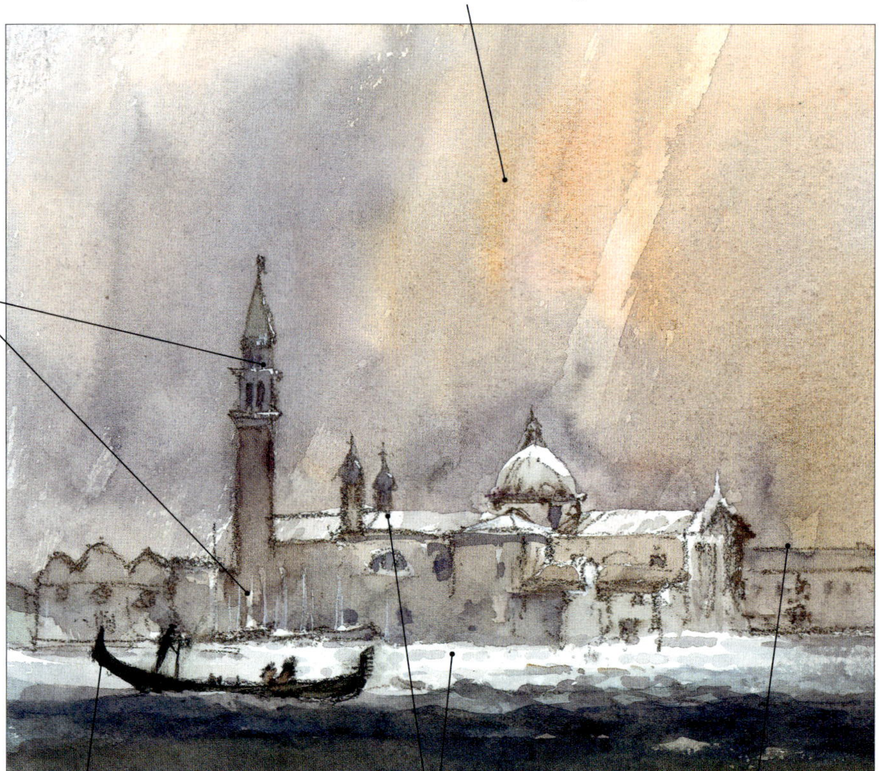


SAN GIORGIO, VENICE

*16 x 22cm (6¼ x 8½in)*

*Quite a crowd gathered around as I did this rapid watercolour sketch while sitting on the quay. I wanted to capture the strong mood and intense light falling on the building and the middle distant water. I drew with a dark brown watercolour pencil, mostly into the wet washes, which is an excellent method when speed is vital, as you don't need to wait for the washes to dry. The extremely strong darks in the foreground really make the white water stand out, adding plenty of drama.*

## TINTED PAPERS

If you wish to create a really strong sense of unity and mood in a watercolour, then try some on tinted papers. The Turner Grey paper is no longer made, but the painting below was done on Blue Lake paper, which is currently available. With tinted papers, any strong highlights have to be introduced with white, and my preference is for white gouache, which has a strong covering power. Both these scenes depict moonlight, which is always most effective over water or snow, and involves less detail and colour than with daylight landscapes. Try to avoid too many highlights. In each case, the actual colour of the paper is that of the light area next to the white of the moon. Tinted papers have a further advantage in that they will encourage you to leave some of the paper untouched.

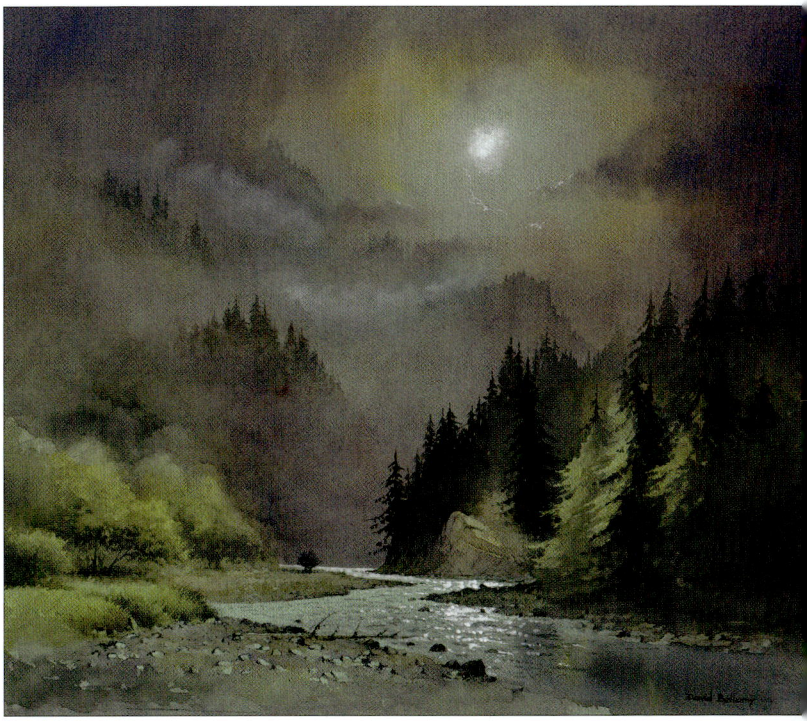

MOONLIGHT ON THE RIVER
*23 x 29cm (9 x 11½in)*

*I still have a few sheets of the old Turner Grey paper and this was used to create an atmospheric moonlight scene of the River Ystwyth in Wales. The highlights were created with white gouache.*

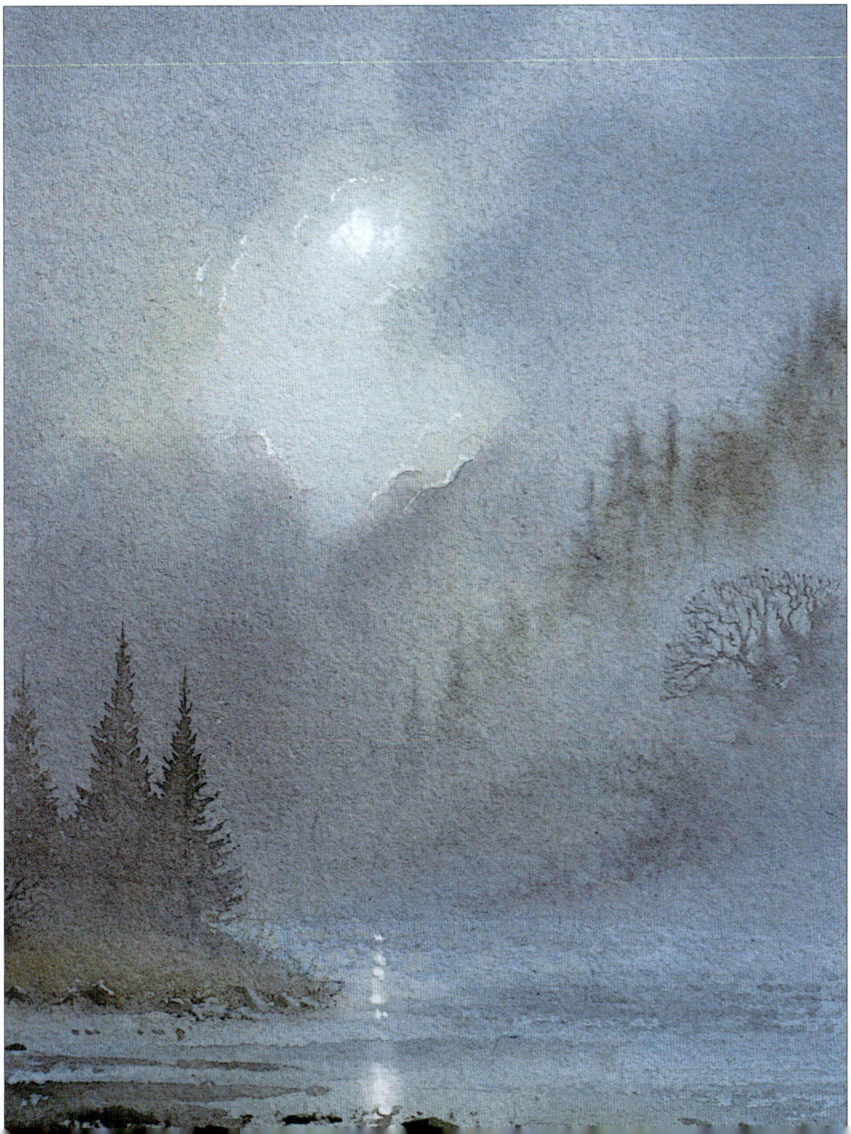

LAKE BY MOONLIGHT

*Another scene carried out on tinted paper. Everything is simplified in moonlight, and it helps if strong highlights are present, in the form of water or snow for example.*

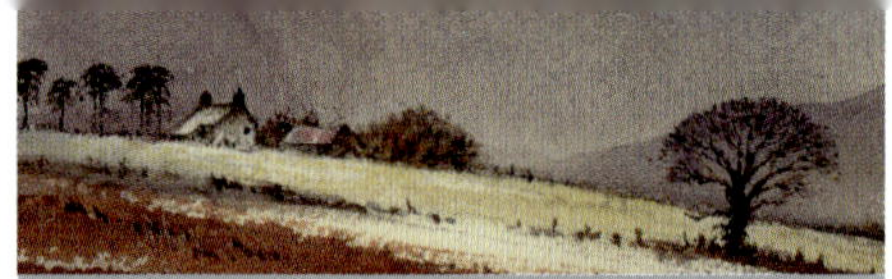

# SUNLIGHT & SHADOW

Capturing a sense of sunlight in a painting can often elude us if we overwork the scene. It is vital to keep the painting fresh by using as few brush strokes as possible, and if you want to emphasize the sunny nature of a scene, nothing works better than cast shadows across simple, clean and uncluttered washes of reasonably bright colours.

**MATERIALS USED**

Saunders Waterford 640gsm (300lb) Rough watercolour paper

Brushes: squirrel mop, no. 10 round, no. 4 round, no. 1 rigger, no. 7 round

Colours: Naples yellow, cerulean blue, yellow ochre, French ultramarine, cadmium red, raw umber, cadmium orange, Winsor blue (red shade), cadmium yellow pale

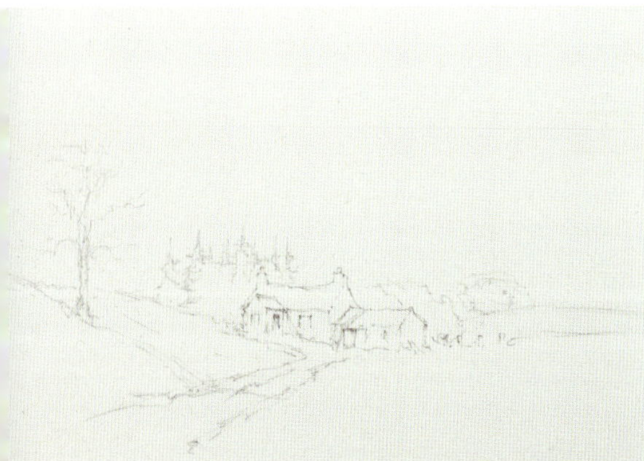

1 Draw the scene with a 6B pencil.

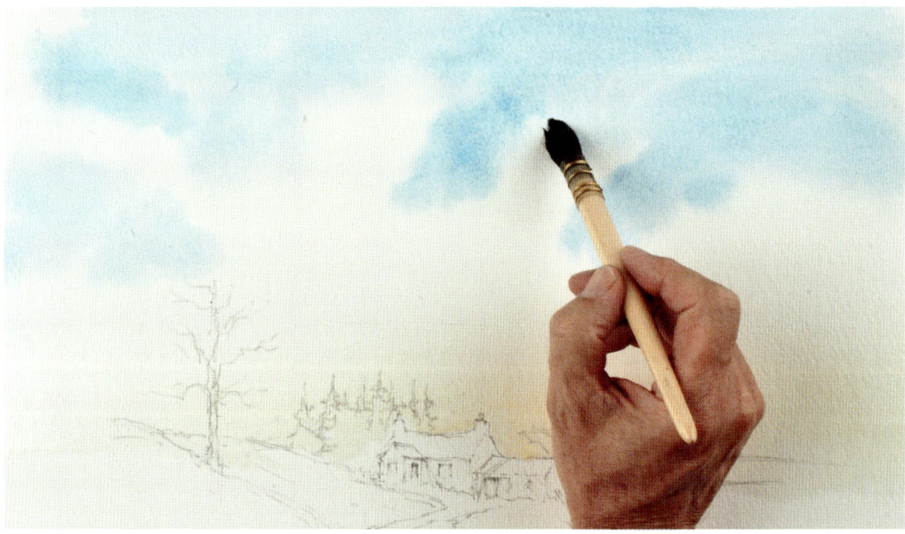

2 Wet the sky area and over the trees with the squirrel mop and drop in Naples yellow in the lower sky and cerulean blue higher up, leaving spaces for clouds.

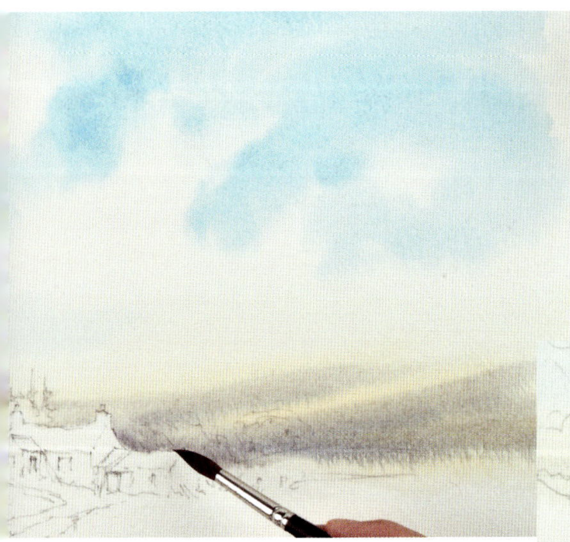

3 Warm up the lower part of the sky with yellow ochre, then strengthen the sky behind the house with French ultramarine and cadmium red on the no. 10 brush, suggesting cloud. Paint the stone of the outbuilding with the same mix, then drop in yellow ochre. Paint the fence area and the track with a pale wash of Naples yellow and leave the painting to dry.

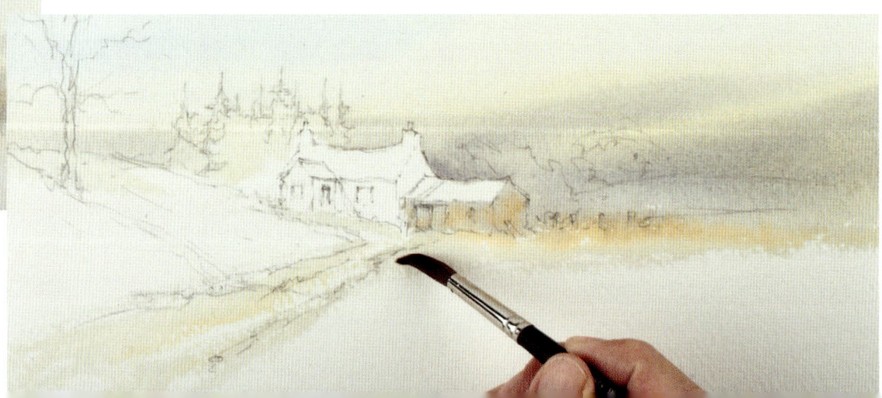

4 Bring out the fence by negative painting, using the no. 10 brush and raw umber to paint the field behind it.

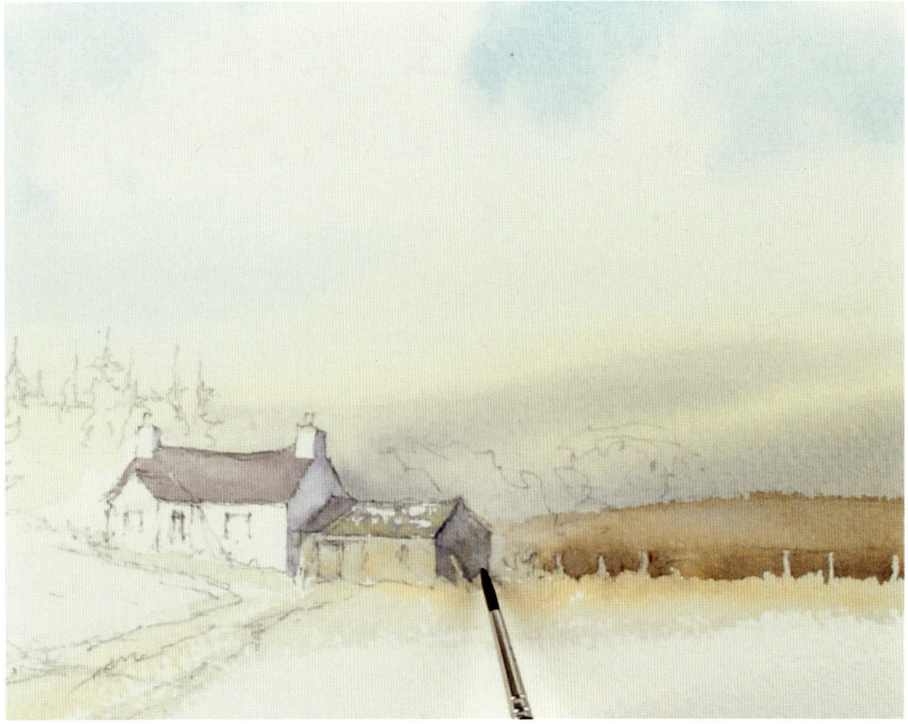

5 Paint the roofs with cadmium red and French ultramarine. Drop a little cadmium yellow pale into the outhouse roof. Allow to dry, then paint the shaded gable ends and the cast shadow on the outbuilding with French ultramarine and cadmium red on the no. 4 brush.

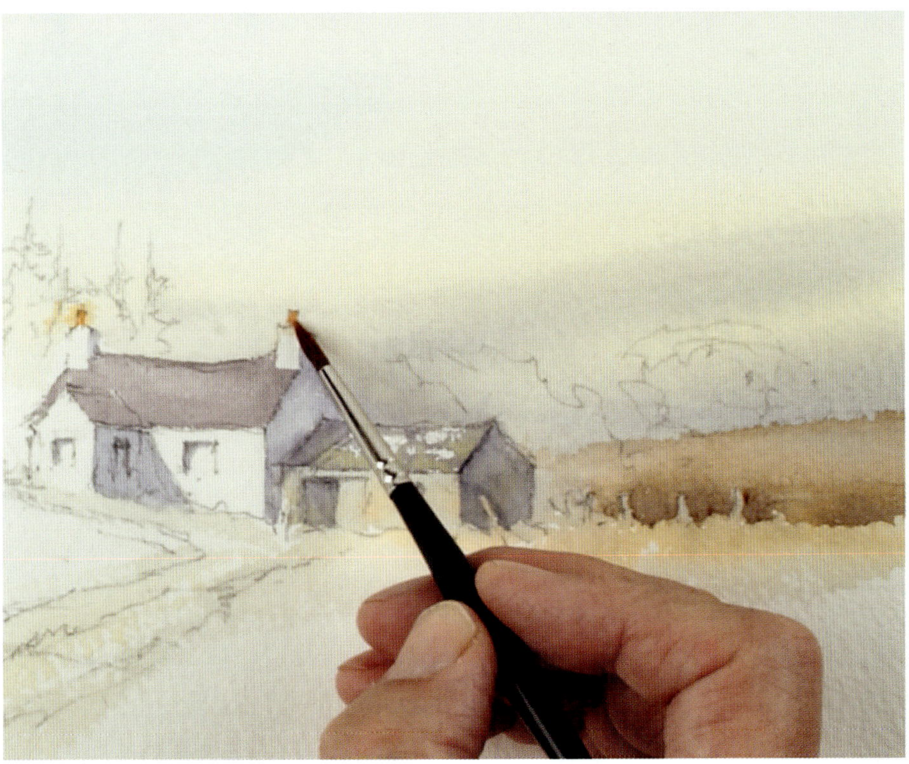

6 Add a little architectural detail with the shadow mix, then paint the chimney pots with cadmium orange. Allow to dry.

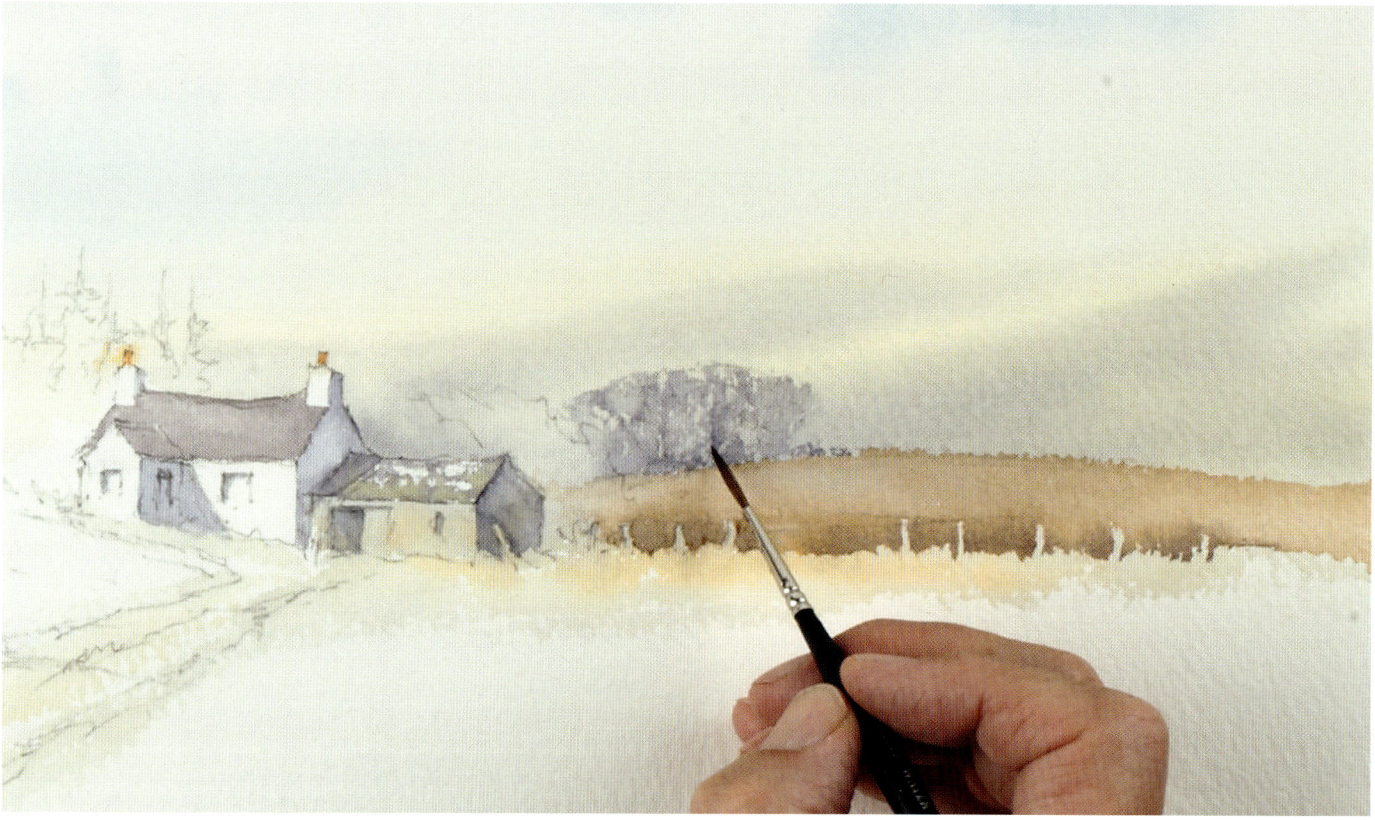

7 Still using the no. 4 brush, dry-brush a mix of French ultramarine and cadmium red to create the distant stand of trees, then use the no. 1 rigger to put in a hint of detail.

8 Paint texture in the ploughed field with the no. 1 rigger and raw umber.

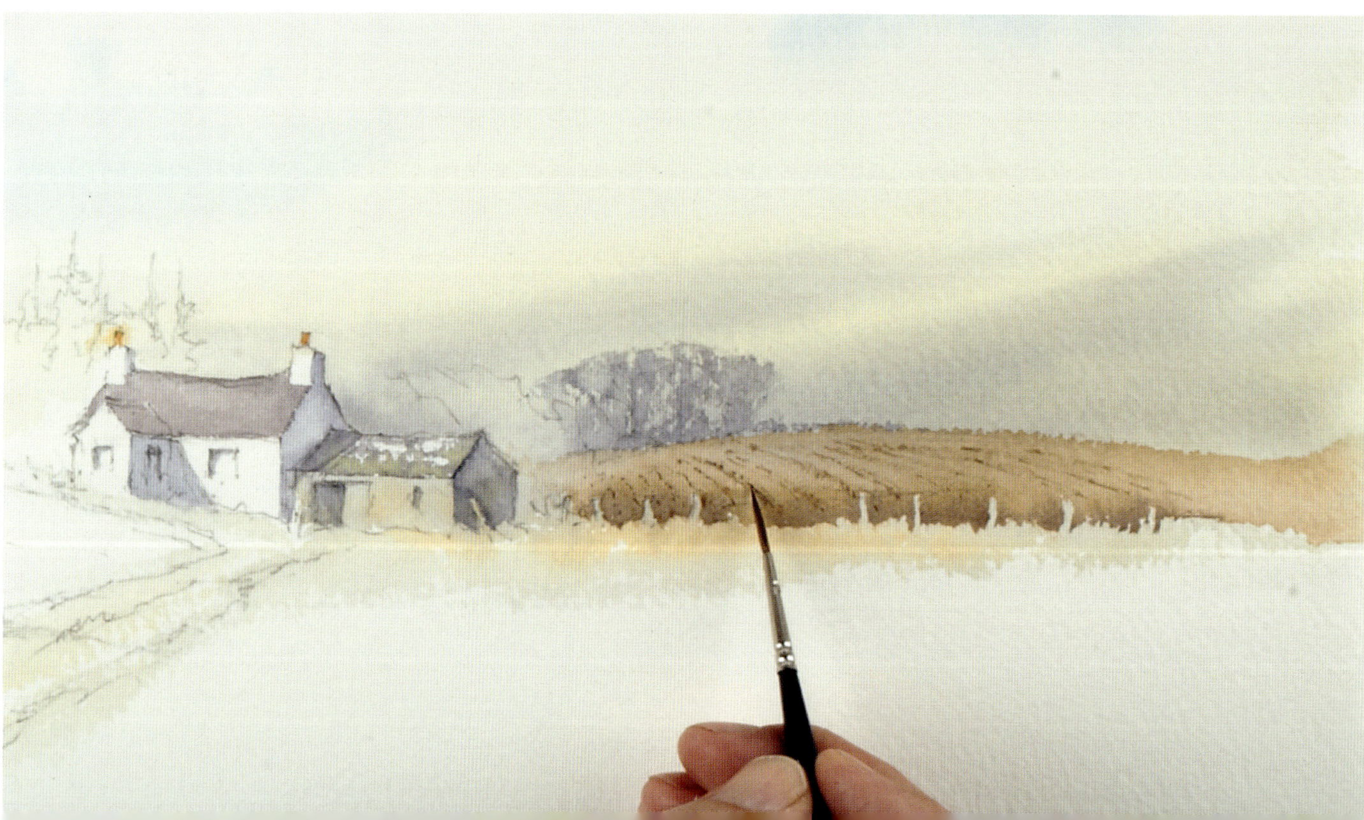

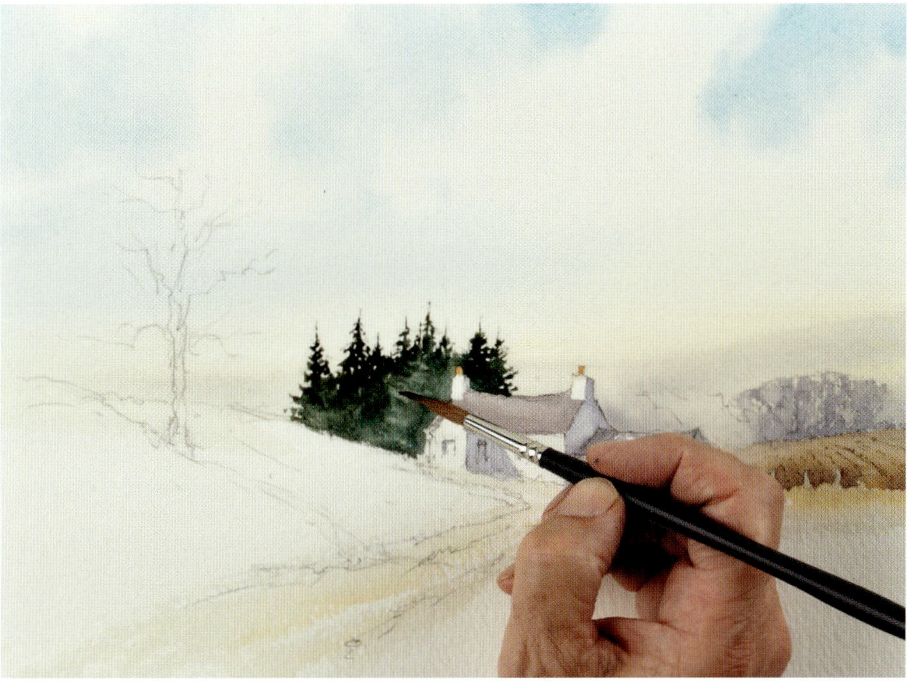

9 Mix Winsor blue (red shade) and raw umber and use the no. 7 brush to paint the conifers behind the house. While this is wet, use a damp brush to lift out some colour to create definition in the mass of trees.

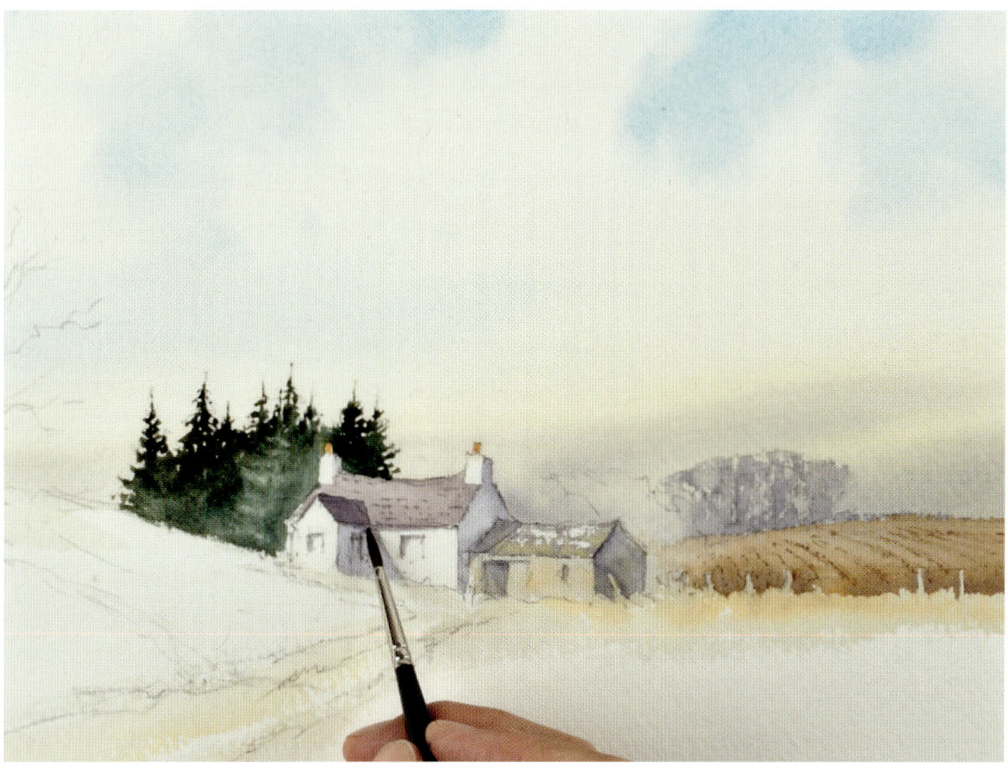

10 Use the no. 4 brush and a mix of cadmium red and French ultramarine to paint the porch roof, and put in a touch of detail on the main roof of the house.

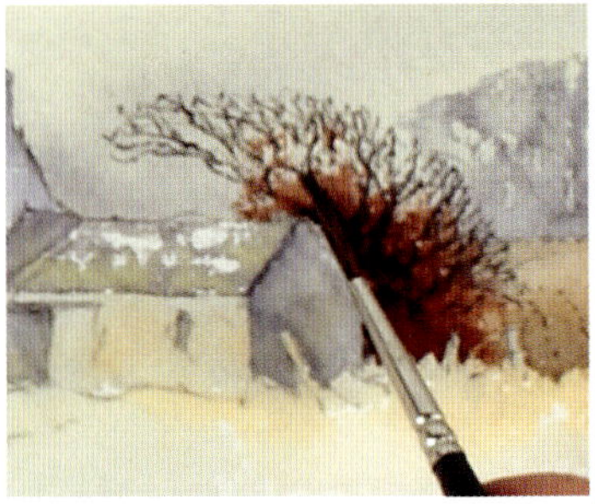

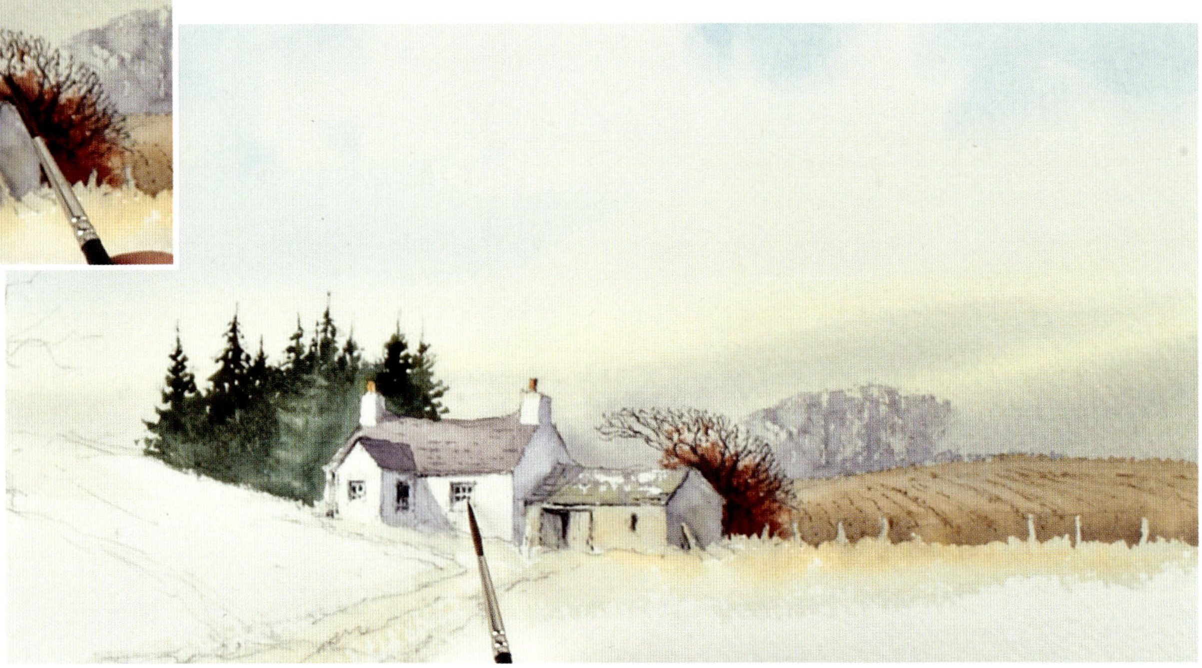

**11** Paint the bush behind the outbuilding with cadmium red and burnt umber, using just burnt umber to darken it in places. Then use the no. 1 rigger and a mix of burnt umber and French ultramarine to paint delicate branchwork protruding from the bush. Use the same mix and brush to paint architectural detail on the house and outbuilding. Bright sunlight creates strong contrasts between the light outside of the buildings and the dark inside.

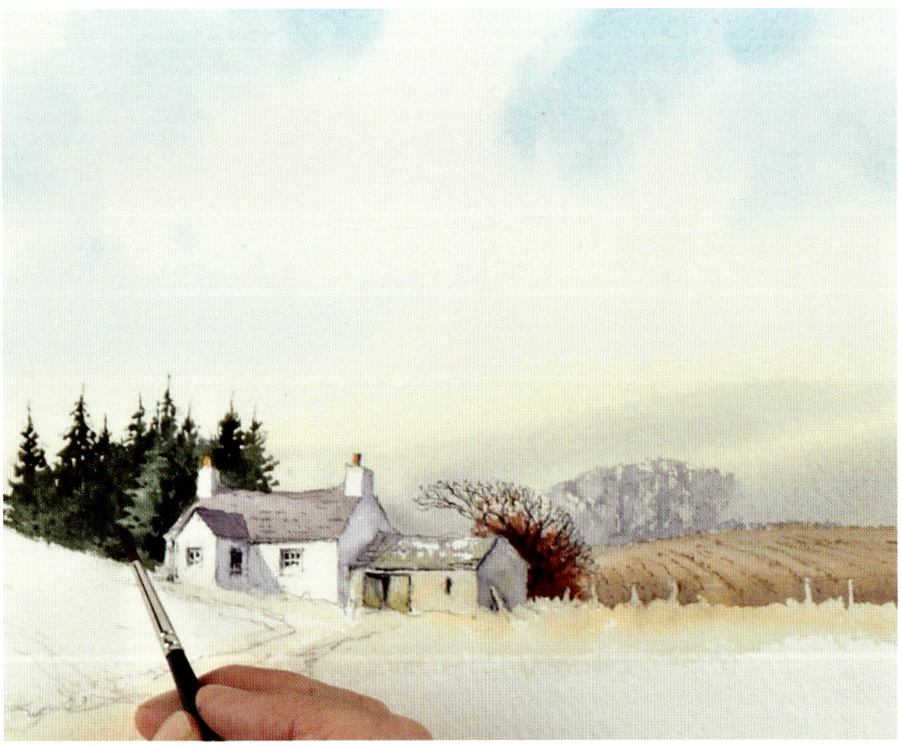

**12** Make the outbuilding door look more rustic with a wash of cadmium yellow pale and a tiny touch of the conifer green – Winsor blue (red shade) and raw umber. With a no. 4 brush and the same green, add detail to the conifers.

13 Use the no. 10 brush and a mix of the conifer green with cadmium yellow pale to paint the grassy area on either side of the path. Use a fairly dry brush and leave flecks of white. Make the green stronger at the bottom of the painting, and add cadmium yellow pale on its own for sunlit grass. Add texture to the outbuilding with the no. 1 rigger and a mix of French ultramarine and burnt umber. Paint a shadow on the side of the path with the rigger and a mix of raw umber and French ultramarine.

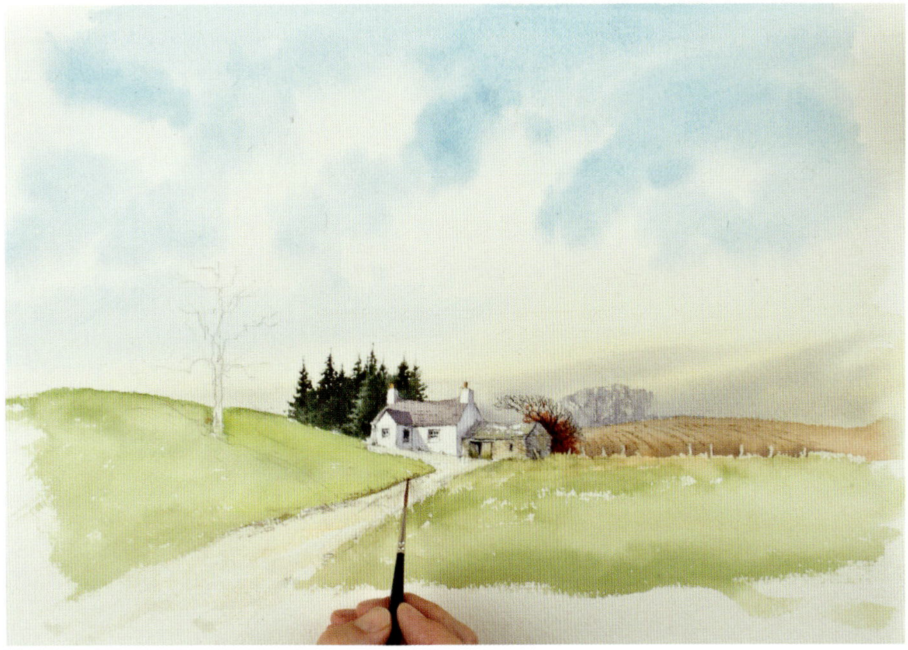

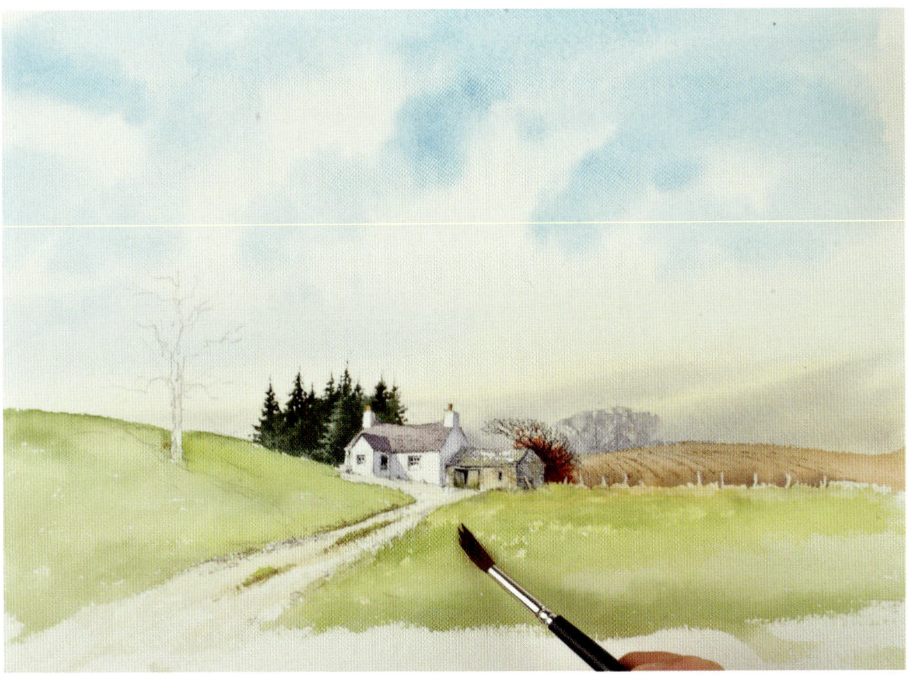

14 Paint a line of grass in the centre of the track with a mix of cadmium yellow pale, Winsor blue (red shade) and raw umber on the no. 1 rigger. Darken the shaded side with Winsor blue (red shade) and raw umber. Change to the no. 10 brush and wash over the grass on either side of the path with cadmium yellow pale with a bit of the darker green mix.

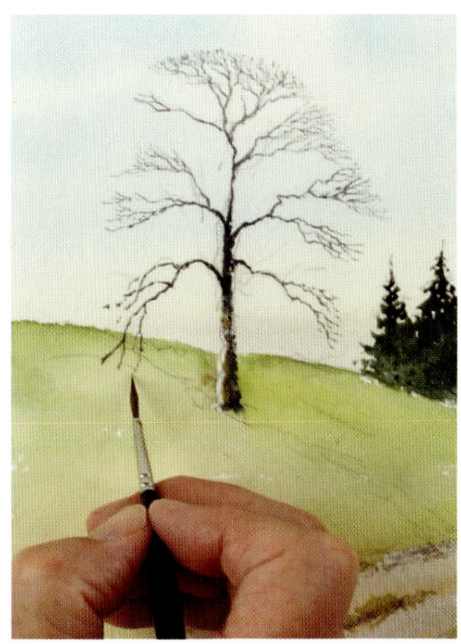

15 Paint the winter tree on the left with French ultramarine and raw umber on the no. 4 brush, then drop in yellow ochre. Change to the no. 1 rigger and paint the branchwork with raw umber and French ultramarine.

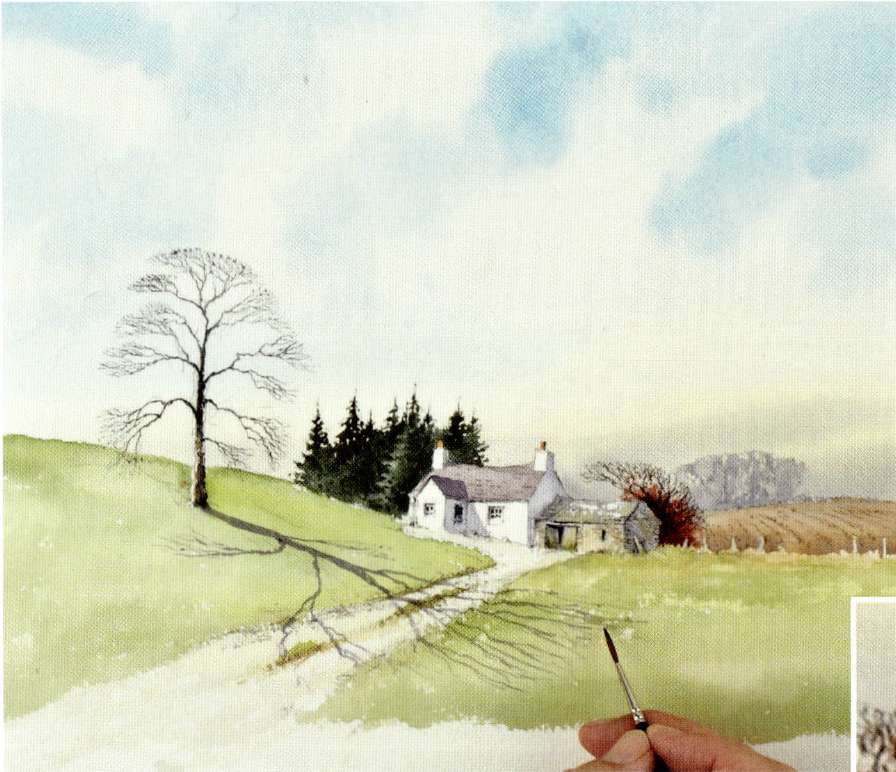

16 Use the no. 4 brush and a mix of French ultramarine and cadmium red to paint the cast shadow from the tree. Change to the no. 1 rigger for the finer parts. When this dried, it appeared too stark, so I weakened the shadow with a damp sponge. To add a little life, put in crows flying above the distant trees with French ultramarine and burnt umber.

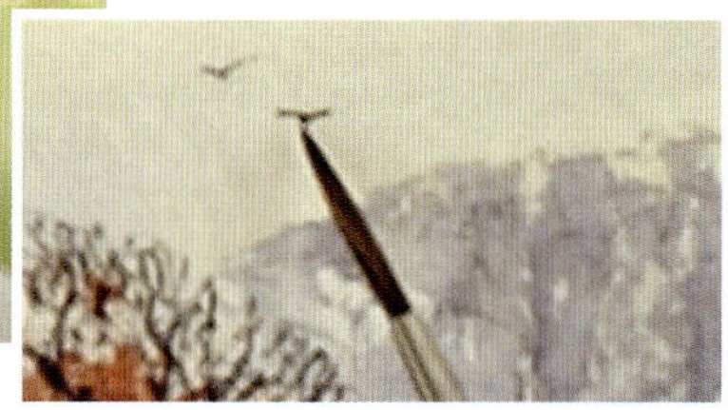

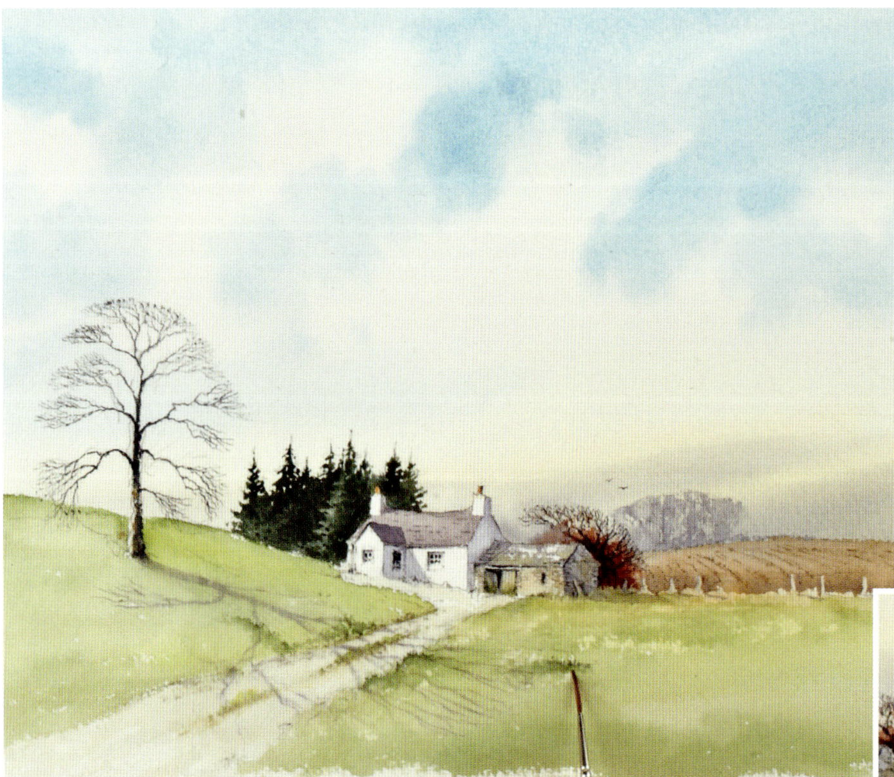

17 Still using the no. 1 rigger, paint clumps of grass to break up the grassy area with raw umber and French ultramarine. Scratch out the wire for the fence using the point of a craft knife blade.

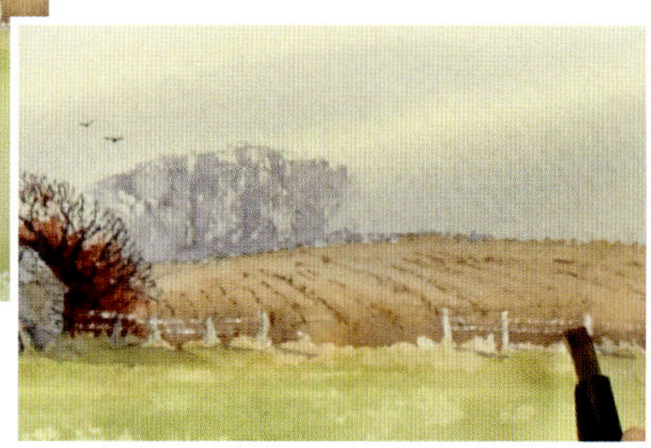

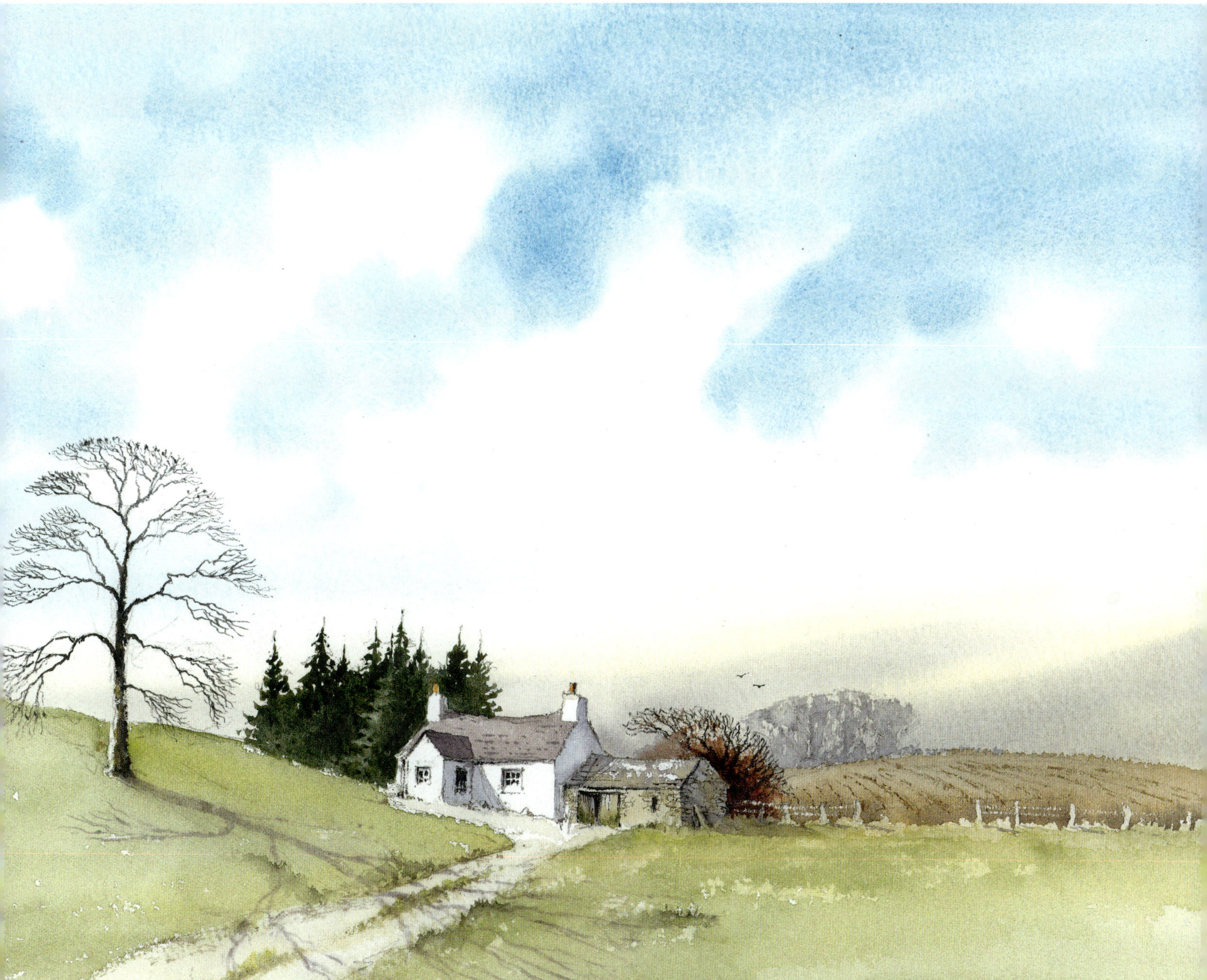

*The finished painting.*

# BASIC METHODS OF CREATING ATMOSPHERE

There are numerous methods of enhancing or creating a moody scene, and here we will look at some of the most powerful ways of injecting that atmospheric quality into your landscapes. The first thing you should consider is whether the mood should be light, and airy, or sombre, dark, threatening, tranquil, restless, perhaps even sinister – in fact whatever you feel most fits your subject and the manner in which you wish to portray it. Then see if any ideas for moody treatment in this book and others appeal to you.

## Unity of colours

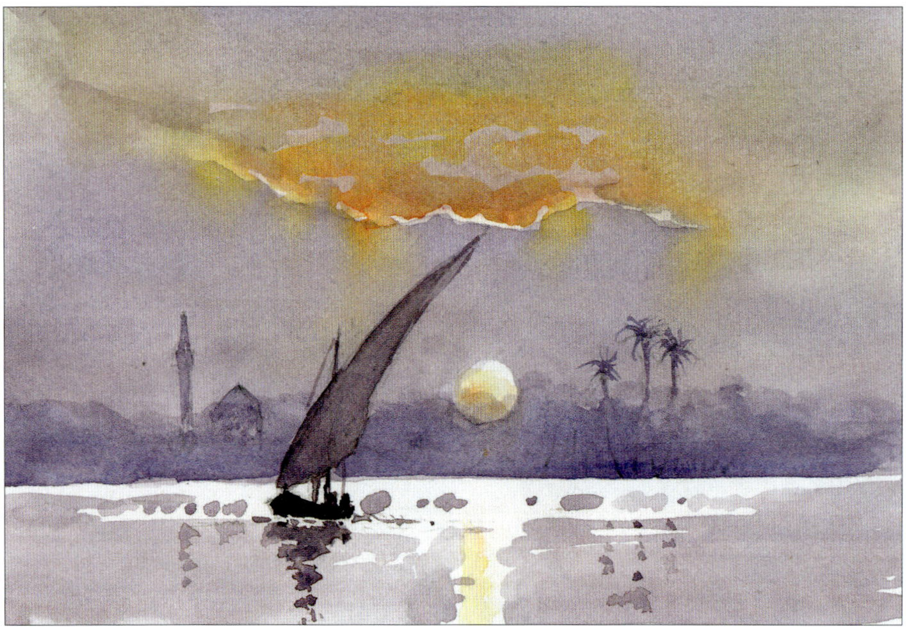

SETTING SUN, LUXOR, EGYPT

*With the sun sinking fast, I had no time to mess about. Unity of colours and a limited palette are vital to creating a sense of mood, and this rapid sketch on cartridge paper is mainly a work of French ultramarine mixed with cadmium red, leaving the highlights as untouched paper. For the warmer part of the sky, I used cadmium orange, plus a touch in the sun, and also a few splashes of Naples yellow. The orange was crudely applied at the last minute, and I should have softened off the lower half of the sun, but sketching a scene like this, however crude, will give you excellent experience at rendering atmosphere.*

## Creating a light, airy mood

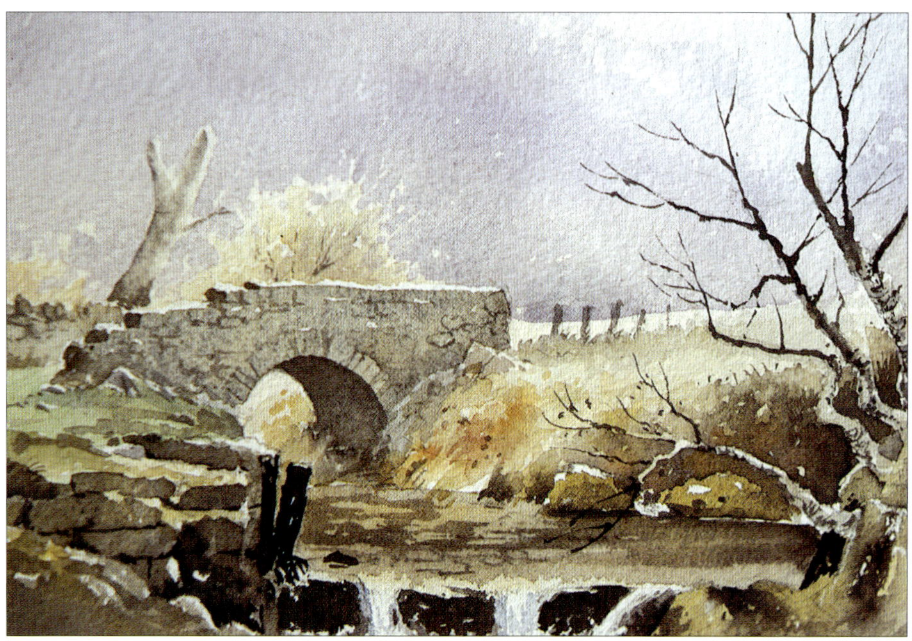

STONE BRIDGE

*Here dark foreground features set against a high-key background suggest a lovely sunny, airy atmosphere, further emphasized by flecks of white paper appearing in many places, and especially the top of the bridge parapet.*

## Sombre mood

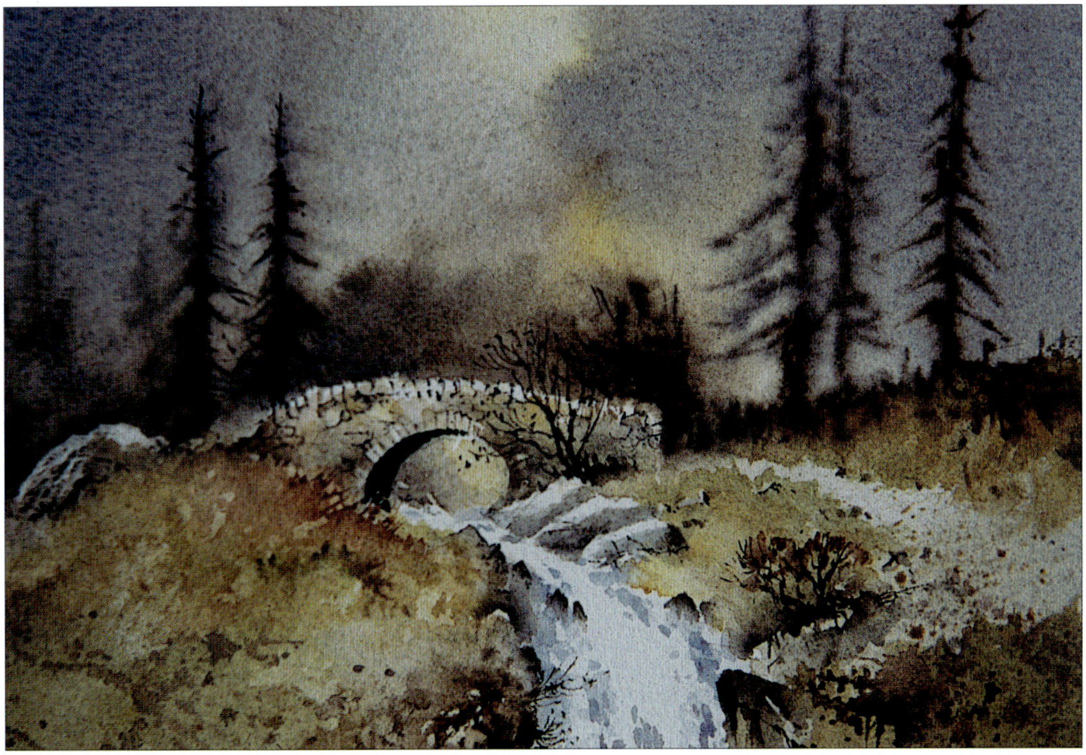

WOODLAND BRIDGE

*This small work shows the value of hard and soft edges: the background has been kept soft, thus throwing the emphasis on to the focal point – the bridge, with its hard edges. This stands out strongly against the dark, wet-in-wet woodland. I used masking fluid to retain the whites on the bridge detail.*

## Suggesting detail

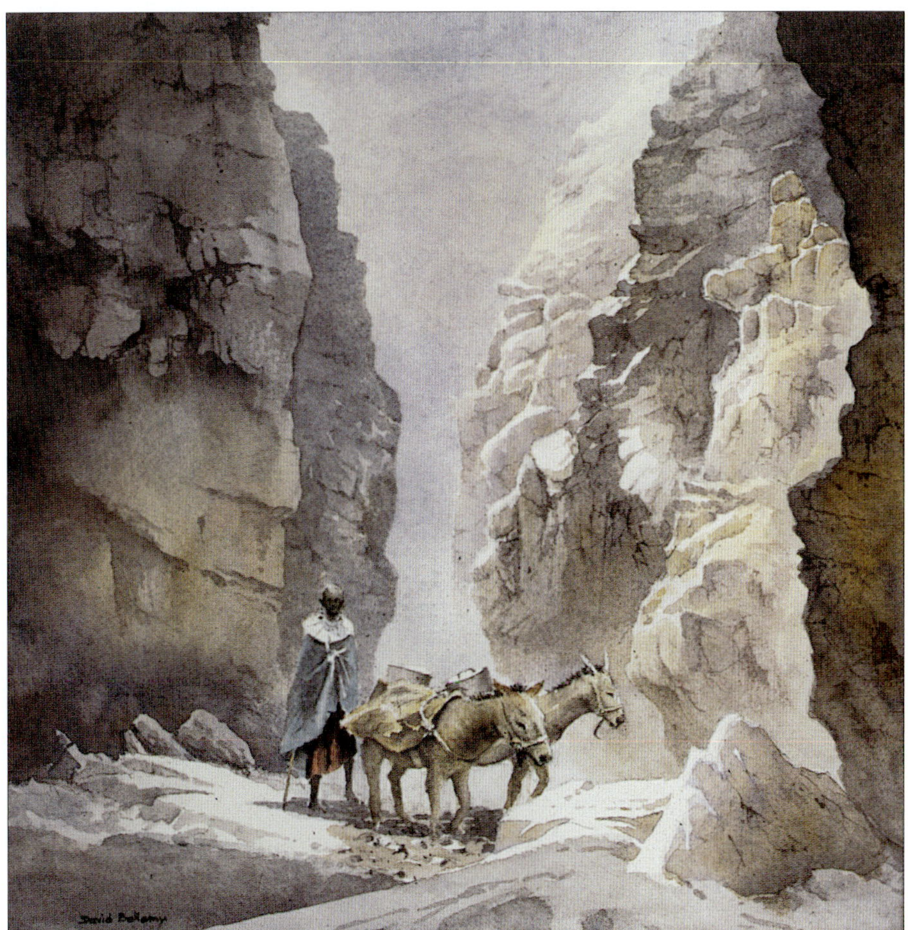


MAASAI GIRL

*Iambeini was out collecting water in the Olkarien Gorge, Tanzania, with her donkeys when we met her. She was shy about posing, but seemed to enjoy the encounter once she became used to us. There was much intricate rock detail in the background cliffs, which I have subdued in places and completely lost in others, especially around the figure and her donkeys.*

# USING ATMOSPHERE TO SUGGEST SPACE AND DISTANCE

In any landscape the most powerful tool at your disposal for creating a sense of space and distance is that of atmospheric or aerial perspective. While cool colours recede, you can still paint fairly warm colours in the distance provided you have warmer colours or stronger darks in the foreground. You can see how the effect of strong tones and more highly-defined detail in the foreground of the Amsterdam watercolour create the sense of depth when just using one colour.

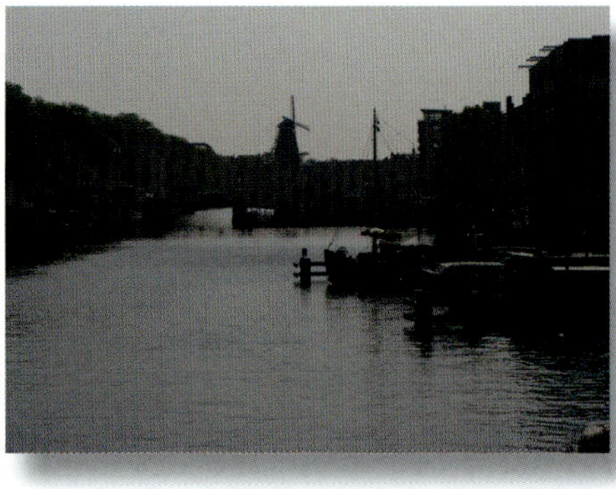

*This photograph of a windmill in Amsterdam reveals very little colour, which often occurs in back-lit scenes, and is the subject of the accompanying sketch.*

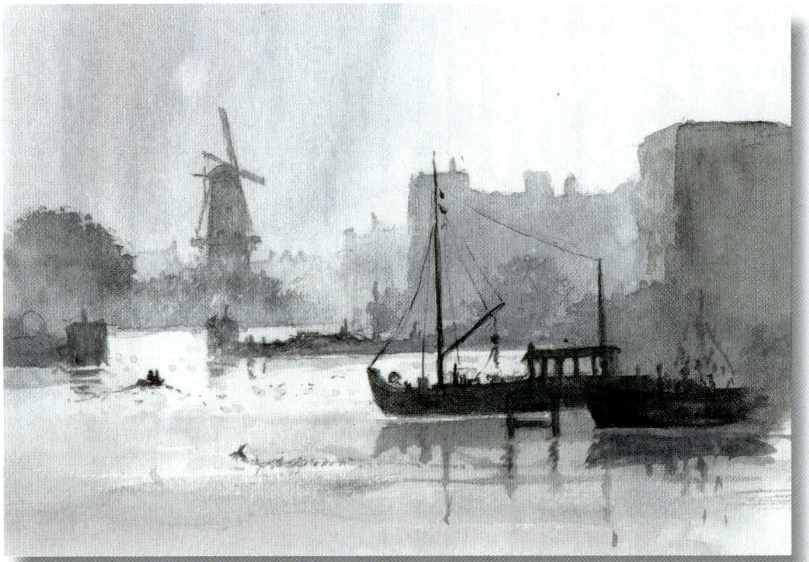

**WINDMILL IN AMSTERDAM**

*A watercolour sketch of the scene in the photograph, carried out in an A4 (28 x 21cm/11¾ x 8¼in) sketchbook of cartridge paper. As there was so little colour in the back-lit scene, I decided to carry this out in monochrome, an ideal way of suggesting mood and unity in a scene. It is much simplified and I have altered the positions of one or two features. The rowing boat went past as I sketched, a few minutes after I had taken the photograph.*

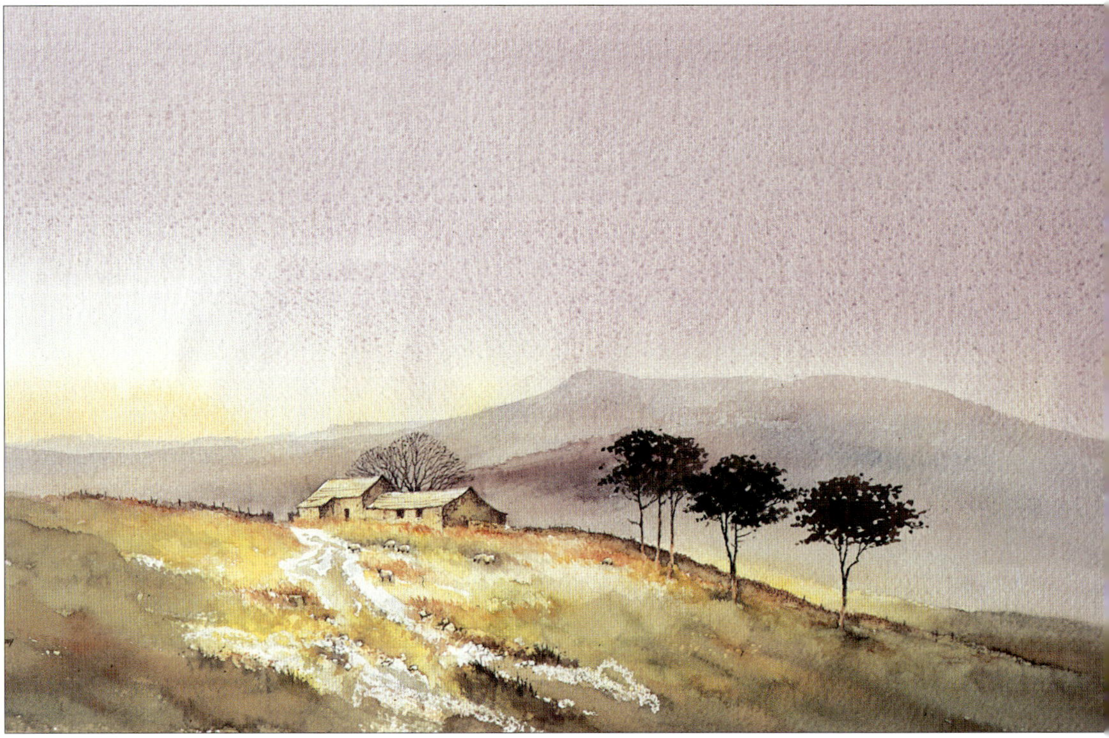

**PENNINE BARNS**

*28 x 47cm (11 x 18½in)*

*The atmospheric perspective in this watercolour is enhanced by the soft, cool colours in the distance. These contrast with the warmer foreground colours. Note how the left-hand wall diminishes and loses much detail as it recedes into the distance on the far left.*

# HAZE AND LIGHT MIST

If you are painting in hot, desert-type scenery, you may not get mists or fog, but a heat haze is equally effective at reducing background detail. Utilizing a light haze in a watercolour is something I do fairly often, otherwise everything stands out in such stark detail that features tend to look as though they are running into each other. I am particularly fond of the light sea mist that invades beaches at low level, as in the Solva painting below. Long beaches with high cliffs are especially good places to find the phenomenon.

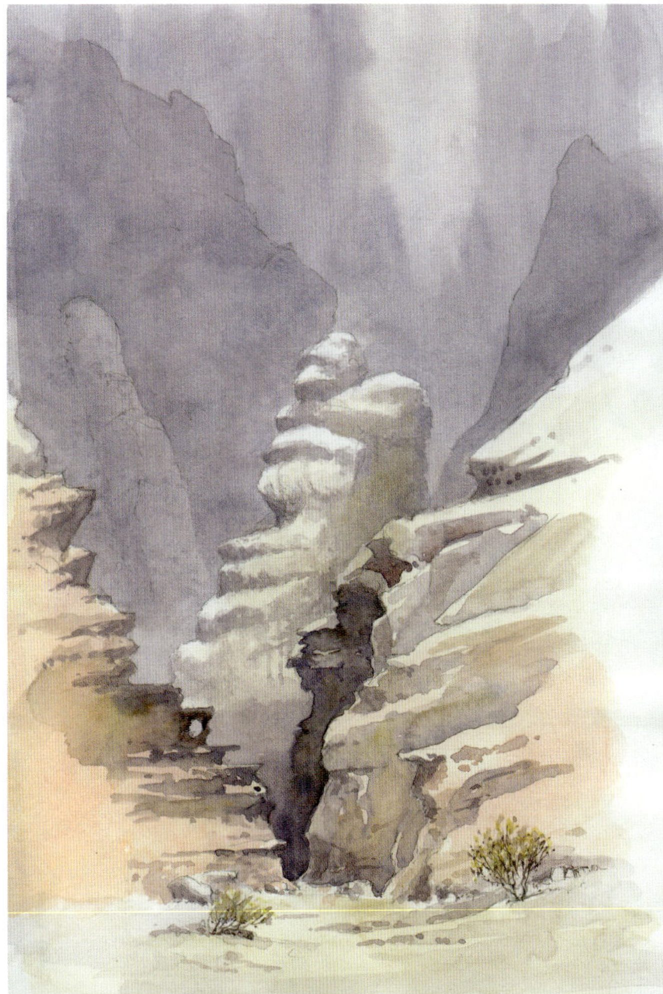

KHAZAREH CANYON, JORDAN

*This is a watercolour sketch done on an A4 (28 x 21cm/11¾ x 8¼in) cartridge sketchbook. Background haze is suggested by soft edges and a single blue-grey colour set against the warm reds in the foreground. This dried so quickly in the intense heat that the hard background edges to the washes had to be sponged off with a soft, natural sponge when I returned to the tent later. The sponge is an excellent tool for creating mist.*

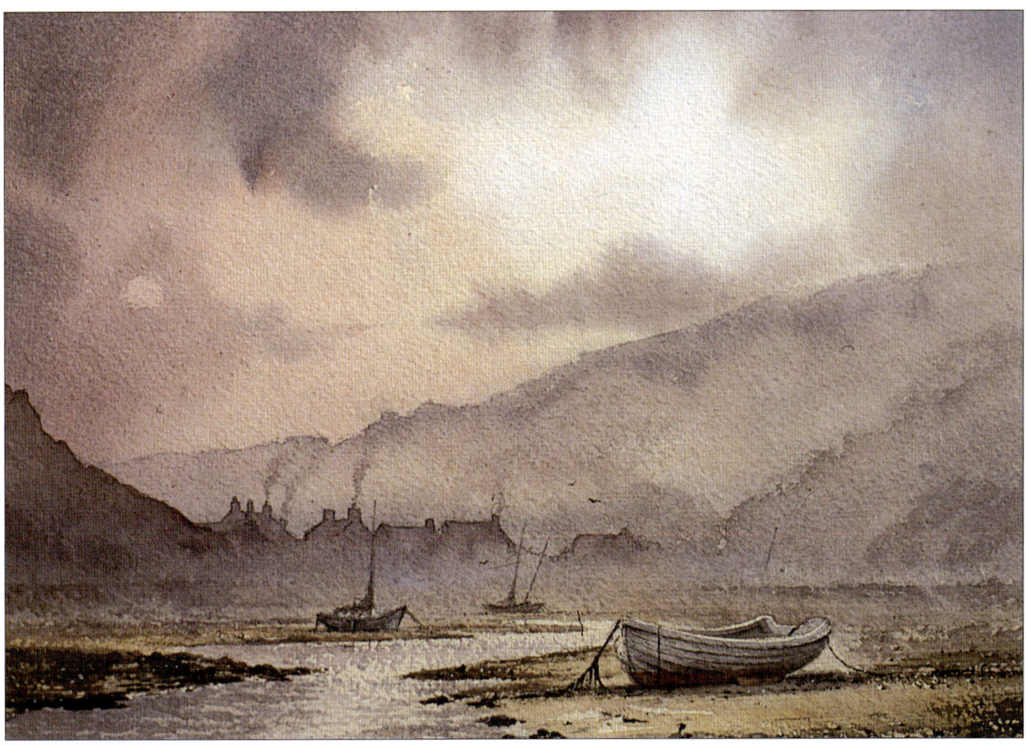

EARLY MORNING, SOLVA

*21 x 31cm (8¼ x 12¼in)*

*The feeling of low-lying mist in this Welsh scene is created by showing only the tops of the cottages, and by the stronger detail on the boats that are closer to the viewer. Light mist can be extremely attractive when combined with sunlight filtering through and perhaps sparkling on the water.*

# FOG

The best method of depicting fog is the wet-in-wet technique. With strong detail and sharp edges on foreground features, the foggy effect can be emphasized. The secret is to flood the paper with a fluid wash over the area where you wish to create fog, then allow it to start drying. I mix all my washes before starting this process, otherwise the first wash may dry too much before I am ready. The second application of colour, which in the example below would be the fainter background trees and the dark area that defines the roofs, must be a strong mixture with no excess water. Only experience will show you exactly how damp it should be, and how long to wait before applying this second wash. You can test the wetness of the first wash with small dabs of the second colour and check if it is giving you the desired effect, then go for it once it is just right.

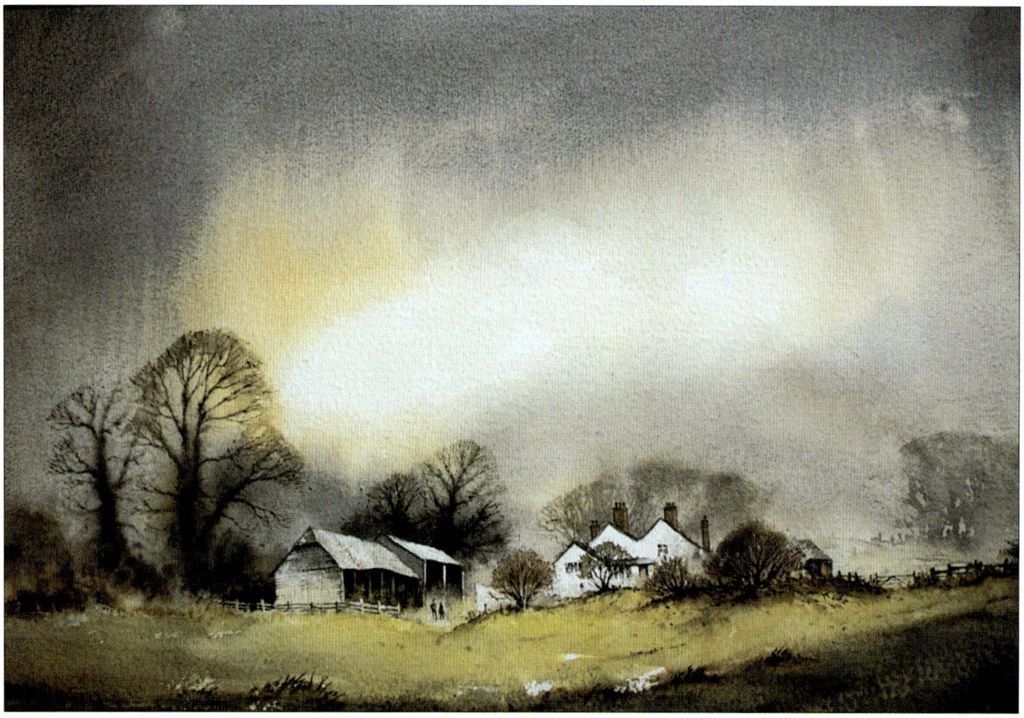

FARM ON THE NORTH DOWNS

*45 x 60cm (17¾ x 23½in)*

*Foggy days can provide interesting and atmospheric compositions. In this scene I was mainly interested in the rustic barns on the left, and when the painting returned from framing, I realised how much better it would have been to have subdued the farmhouse a little to throw more emphasis on to the barns.*

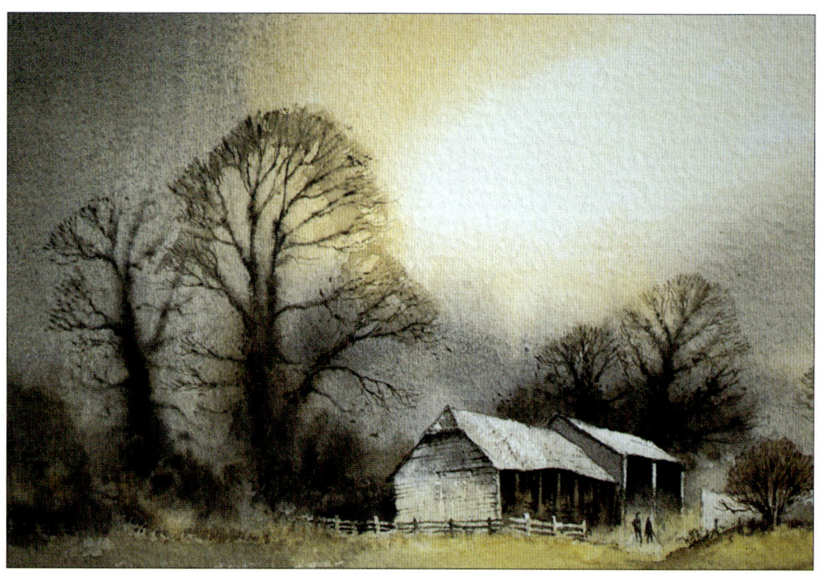

DETAIL OF THE PAINTING

*In this close-up of the barn, the damp light is suggested by the light-toned roof that undulates delightfully. I graduated the gable end of the building, a method that adds interest without cluttering up a passage, and subdued the urge to paint in too many boards. Note the counterchange on the fence, caused by the background tone changing. The backdrop to the scene was achieved with the wet-in-wet application of washes.*

## LOSING PART OF A MOUNTAIN IN CLOUD

Obscuring part of a hill or mountain in cloud is an excellent way of creating atmosphere, breaking up a monotonous ridge, or providing more emphasis to an adjacent crag or summit that is left clear of cloud. The effect can be achieved in a number of ways. A common problem occurs at the completion of a painting when you realise that the continuous sharp-edged ridge would work better had it been broken up with a puff of cloud or mist. I often sponge out part of the ridge with a soft sponge and clean water, shielding any important parts with a sheet of paper.

The most usual method of creating a mist-shrouded summit is shown here. Part of the mountain was washed with clean water, which was also taken across the adjacent sky, and then the mountain colour was drifted into the wet area to create a soft transition. You may find that you need to redefine an edge by pulling out colour with a large, damp, round brush while the paper is damp.

A third method is to paint in the summit, crag or feature that you wish to obscure, but do it faintly and perhaps leave out part of it. When this is dry, lay clean water over it and the adjacent sky – go well beyond where you think the water will reach – and then apply a weak wash of the colour for the cloud or mist. This will act as a glaze, allowing the painted feature to show through, but less distinctly than the rest of the mountain.

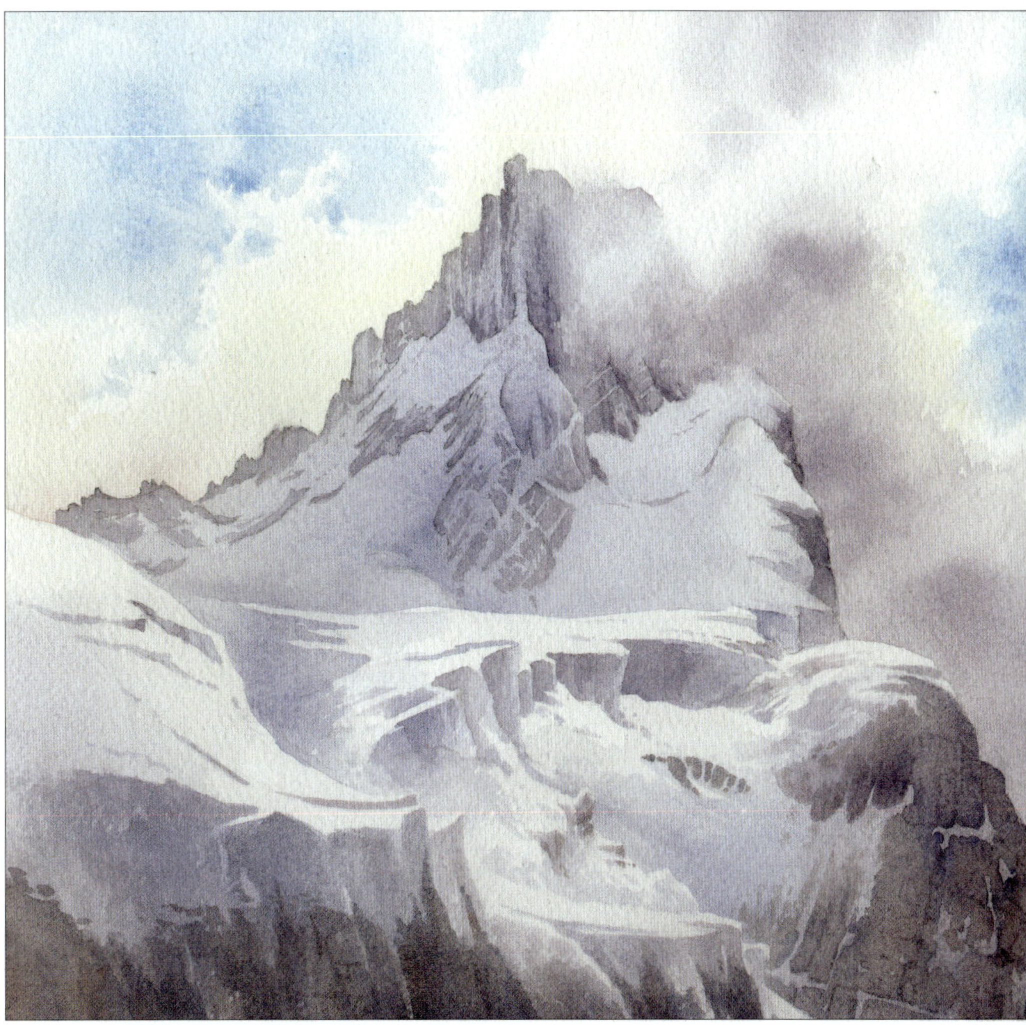

CUMBRE PRINCIPALE, CHILE
*28 x 35cm (11 x 13¾in)*

*Often a painting is improved by leaving out certain details, and this is a useful device where a mountain is too dominant or shows too much detail. In this watercolour, the summit is partly obscured by cloud. This effect was achieved by wetting the area to be obscured, plus the adjacent sky, then drifting the mountain colour into the area. It often helps to take out some wisps of colour with a damp round brush, and this can suggest movement and variation in the cloud or mist.*

## CREATING MIST AMONG CRAGS

When painting a complicated scene like this gully, it is best to break it down into several stages and not feel overwhelmed by sheer detail. Misty backgrounds will lack colour variety, so tonal variations applied wet in wet are best, bringing in warmer colours only closer to the foreground. Simplify as much as you can, including the main features only.

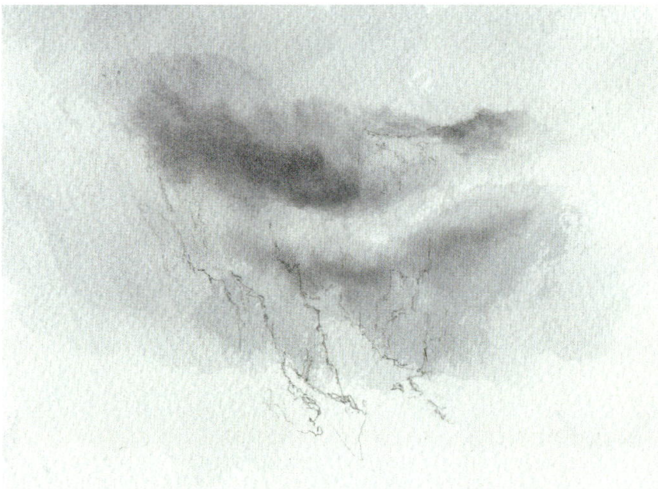

1 I applied a wash of Payne's gray with a touch of burnt umber over the background and running into the sky, then almost immediately a darker mixture to suggest the background crags and to define the wraith of mist, working wet in wet into the first wash.

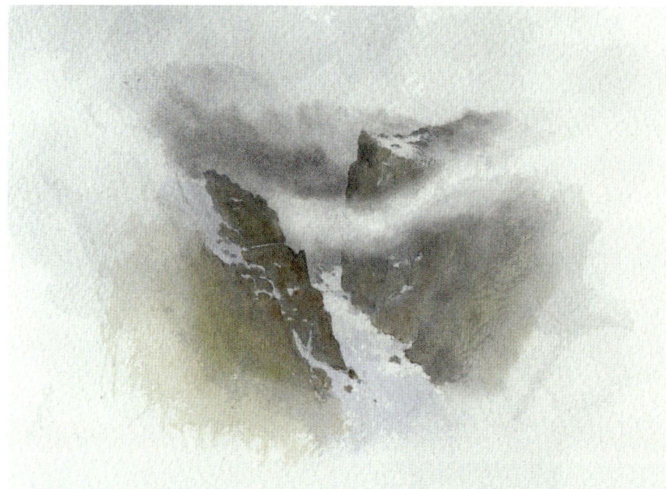

2 When the paper had dried, I painted in the main crags, dropping some yellow ochre in while they were still wet, and leaving the snow areas untouched. I also dropped in a touch of light red to give the central cliff a bit of a lift. Then I applied some cobalt blue over the snow areas, leaving some of the paper untouched to appear as white.

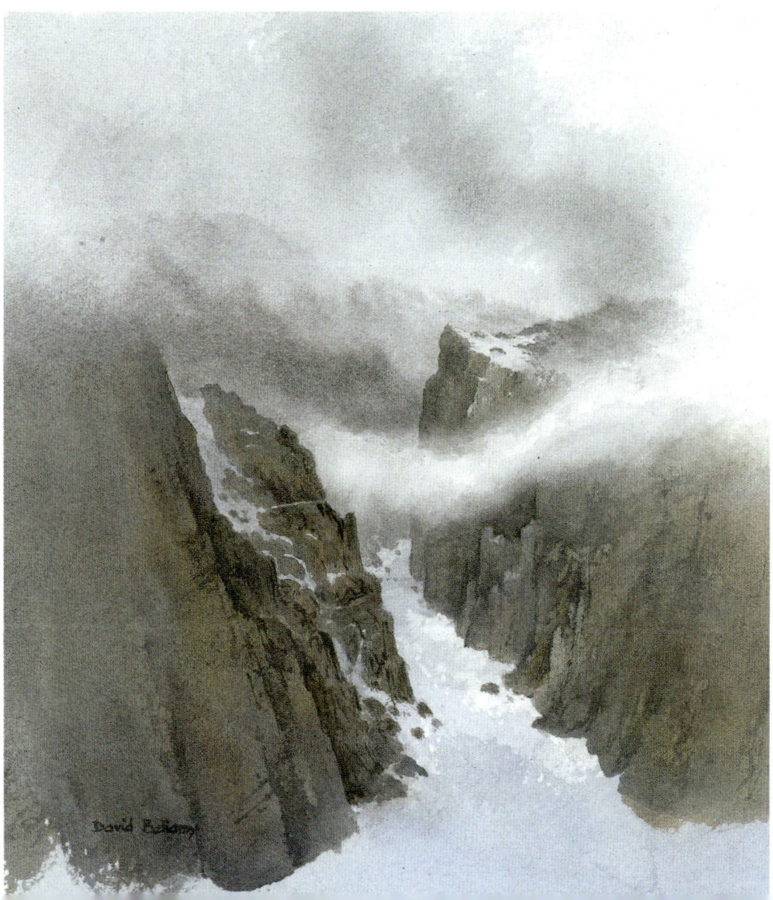

3 I wet the paper above the left-hand cliff and laid a wash into it to suggest the soft transition. I then wet the top right area and added a little more tone, again to create this softness that is so vital in suggesting mist-clad crags. Before completing the piece some further details were added to define gullies and fractures.

## MIST AND SUNLIGHT PATCHES

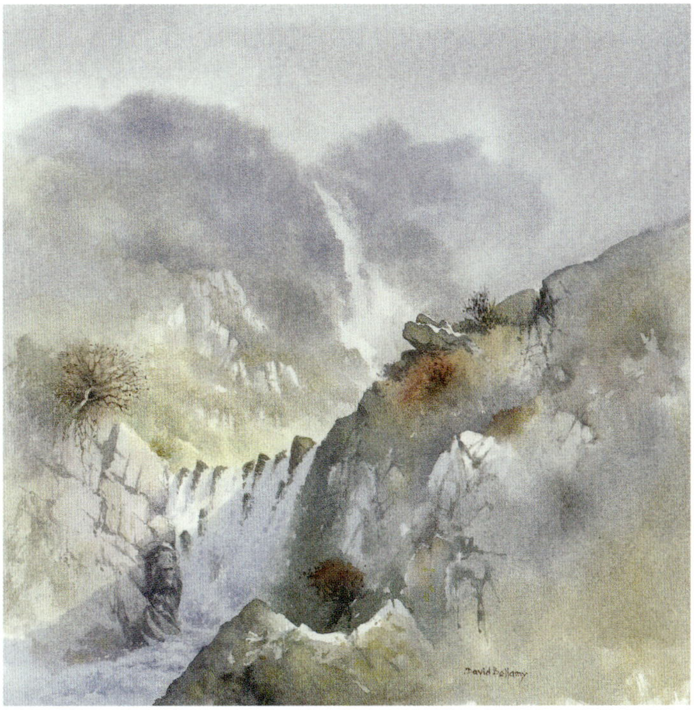

**HELVELLYN GILL, LAKE DISTRICT**
*22 x 20cm (8½ x 8in)*

*Strong foreground definition, a light, misty background plus a hint of weak sunlight can combine to improve a scene. This is a method I often introduce to change an otherwise ordinary landscape into one of intense mood and mystery.*

*I always do at least one thumbnail sketch to indicate where the main features will appear, how and where they will be lit, where the mist will be, and most importantly, how much will be revealed in that misty background. Only when I am happy with the arrangement do I begin work on the watercolour.*

*In this painting the background directly above the waterfall was painted first, on dry paper, leaving the light rocks absolutely white. When this was dry, I applied a weak wash of ultramarine and cadmium red over the background, avoiding the white cascade, coming down over the already defined rocks, slightly muting them, and adding some cadmium yellow pale just above the falls. Taking a stronger mixture of the same colours, I then defined the darker background cliff wet in wet, again avoiding the cascade. When all this was dry, I painted in the waterfall and all the foreground, leaving the shadow of ultramarine and cadmium red until the very end.*

## SMOKE AND STEAM

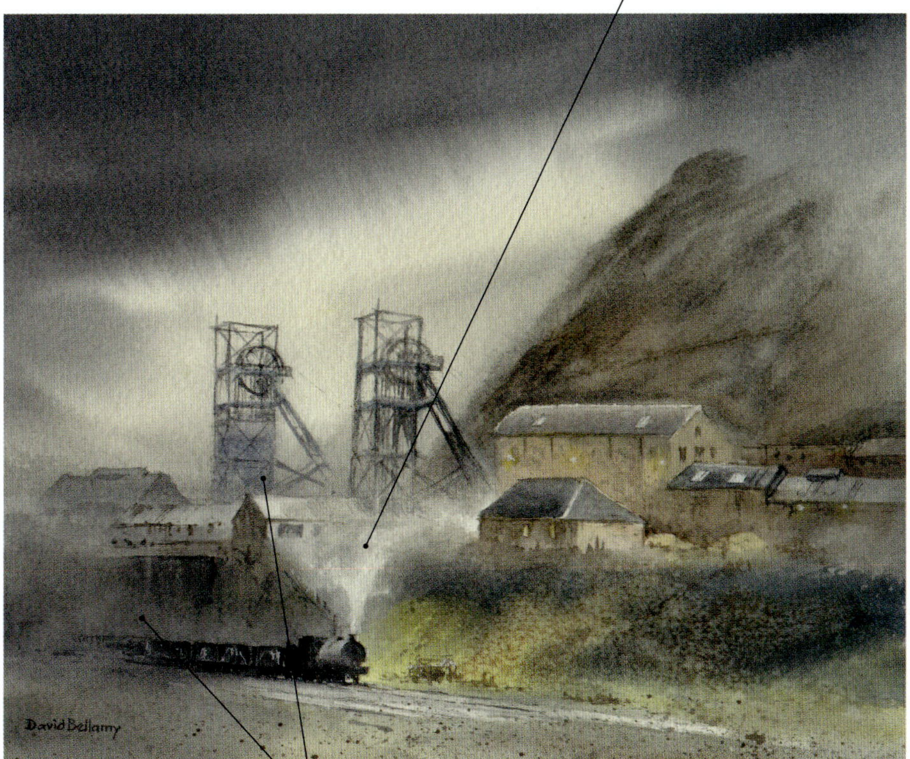


**STEAM AT MARKHAM COLLIERY**
*18 x 21cm (7 x 8¼in)*

*Man-made smoke and steam can be effective in losing detail where it becomes overwhelming, or where you may wish to make a certain feature stand out. It is also a great device when you are not sure what is actually happening at some point in the painting. This works especially well with industrial subjects.*

# AN ALTERNATIVE METHOD OF CREATING ATMOSPHERE

Layering is a useful alternative to the wet-in-wet technique, especially where you may wish to suggest a weak, but reasonably sharply defined background feature. It is simply a series of layers, or glazes, laid over an already painted area, and is invaluable in suggesting an ethereal mood.

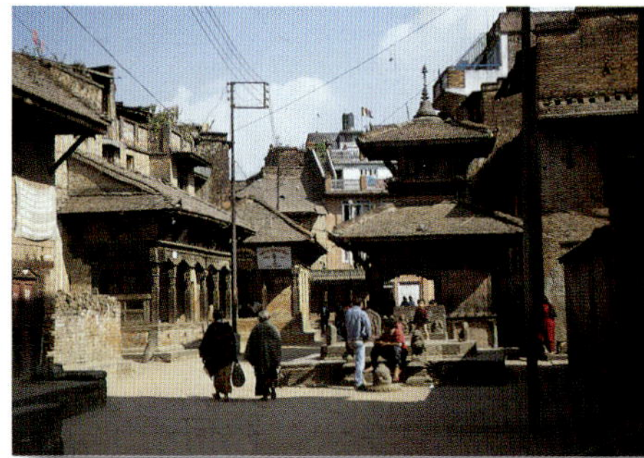

*In this photograph of Bhaktapur in Nepal, there is far too much detail in the actual scene, especially in the background, and in the painting I wanted to introduce a sense of atmosphere.*

**BHAKTAPUR IN EARLY MORNING LIGHT**

*25 x 32cm (10 x 12½in)*

*I began by laying in the shapes of the background buildings with weak blue-grey washes, with a hint of detail in the bottom centre and the left-hand side above the sloping roof. When these were dry, I laid a weak, transparent layer of French ultramarine with a touch of permanent alizarin crimson over the already painted areas. Next, the building above the four figures in saris was rendered and the tall far-right one. I repeated the layer of transparent weak colour over these additions, to further emphasize the atmospheric mist. Much stronger detail was then introduced to the foreground buildings and the main figures were painted, with the cast shadows providing a strong feeling of directional sunlight. In addition to suggesting mist, this glazing technique is ideal for conveying unity to an area of the painting.*

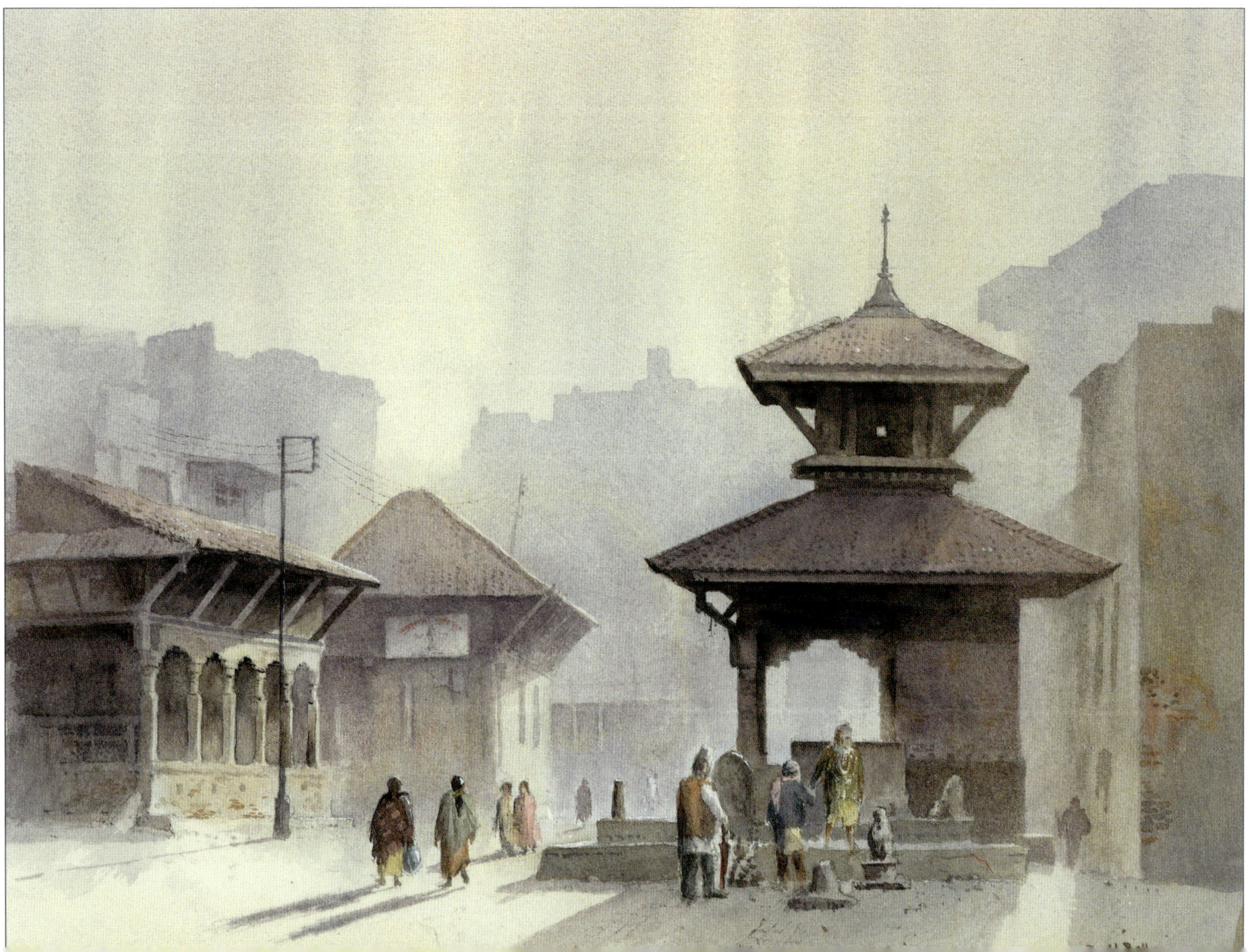

# RAIN SQUALLS

The glaze technique shown in these stages can create an exciting illusion of a rain squall, but try it out on your old 'failed' paintings first to gain confidence.

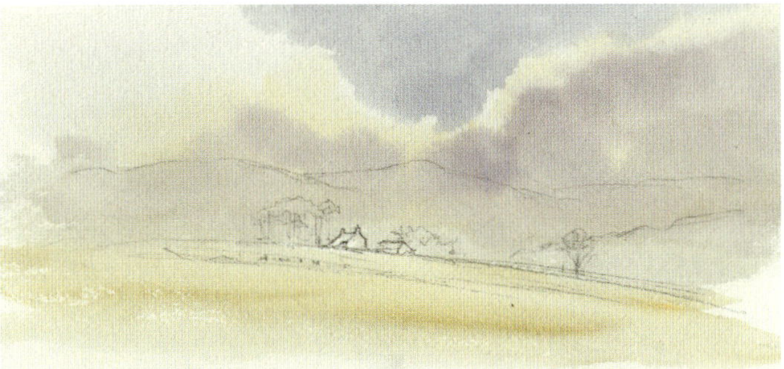

1 I painted a weak wash of Naples yellow over the lower sky and hills, with yellow ochre in the foreground area. To suggest the shadow side of the clouds, I applied a wash of cobalt blue and perylene red into parts of the Naples yellow while it remained wet, so that the edges were soft. Then, before allowing the paper to dry, I brushed some cobalt blue with a weak touch of burnt sienna into the centre part of the sky.

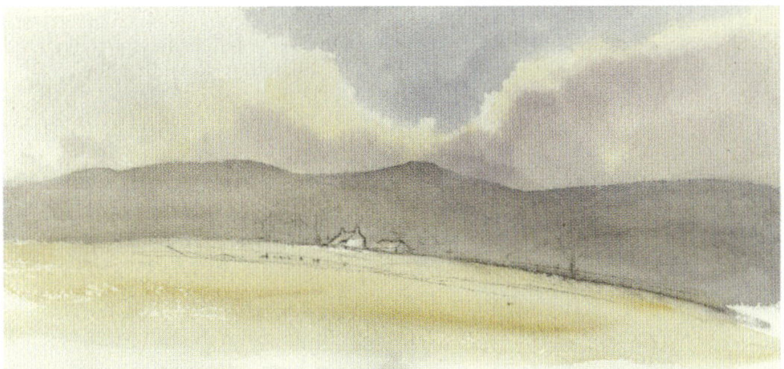

2 On dry paper I laid a wash of French ultramarine and burnt sienna to describe the hills.

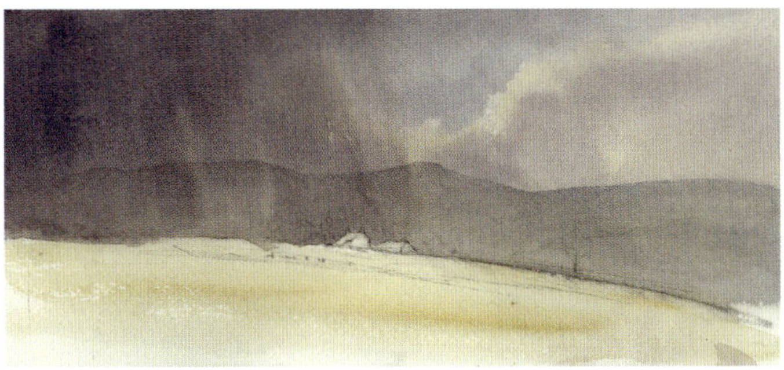

3 Once again I let the paper dry completely before continuing. I then wet the sky and hills and dropped a strong mix of French ultramarine and cadmium red into the left-hand side, bringing it down over the hills. I kept the board at a fairly steep and slightly diagonal angle to allow the wash to run down over the hills, like rain sweeping across the landscape.

4 I painted in the farm detail and trees, mainly with raw umber and French ultramarine, then the foreground with burnt umber and cadmium red. Practise this technique on scrap paper until you feel confident with it.

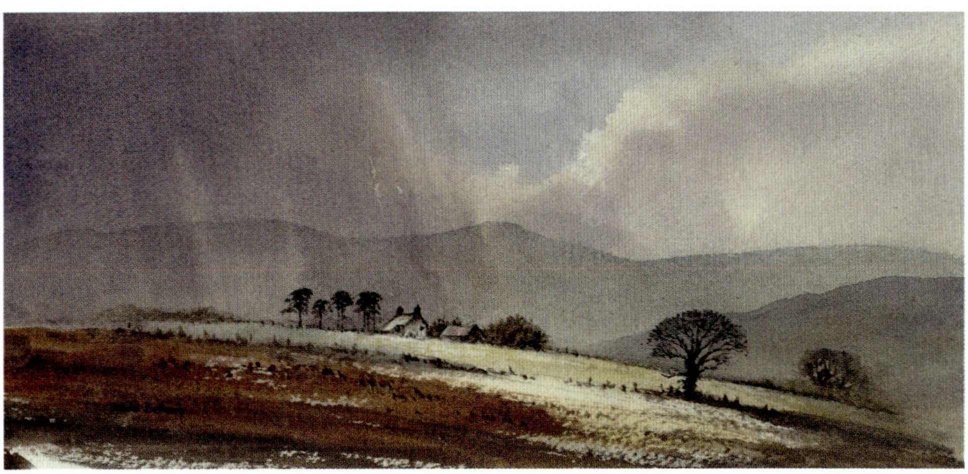

# FALLING RAIN

Being too literal can destroy the effect in many paintings, and with falling rain it is vital not to overstate the impression with strident vertical strokes. A few light strokes against a dark patch is often quite enough to suggest rain. Likewise, limit the number of ripples caused by raindrops falling on to a puddle.

### RAIN

*It is the easiest thing in the world to overwork falling rain. There are a number of ways of depicting this, apart from that of the glaze method shown earlier for the distant rain squall. Here we look at how to tackle falling rain close up, but always remember to economise with the amount of detail.*

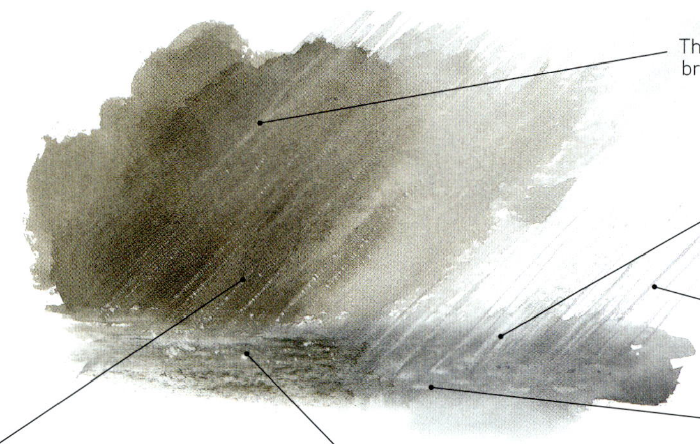


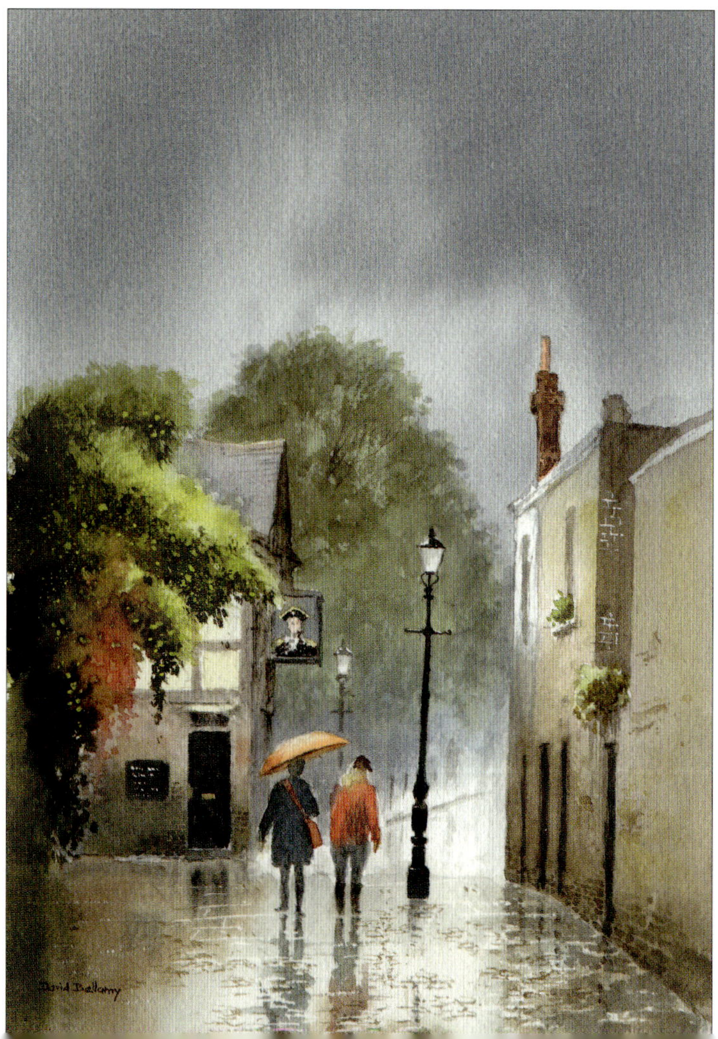

**COBBLED LANE, HACKNEY**
*24 x 15cm (9½ x 6in)*

*There is no better way to suggest a damp day than to create reflections on pavements, ideally breaking them up, as in this small watercolour, with slivers of light and the inundations of the partly cobbled street. An umbrella instantly shouts 'rain', even if you do not actually describe the rainfall, as here, and a hazy blue-grey background provides dim, distant shapes seen through light rain or drizzle.*

# COLOUR EMPHASIS AND MOOD

When you are considering what sort of mood to apply to a moorland or mountain painting, it is important to think about your choice of colours and how the overall colour effect will influence the viewer's response. At this point I decide whether the overall impression is to be warm or cool, and if I intend to use tinted paper, the tint will have a strong bearing on this. In the painting below I chose de Wint paper because I wanted a warm mood. Note how the slight shadows on the front of the castle have been achieved not with a cool blue, but a warm red. Don't always go for what may seem to be the obvious colour choice.

LAUGHARNE CASTLE

*20 x 28cm (8 x 11in)*

*This watercolour was painted on biscuit-coloured de Wint paper, which is no longer available. The moody sensation has been created by the two dominating colours: the light ochre on the castle, which was aided by the tint of the paper, with echoes on parts of the sky and ground, and the murky purple clouds billowing in the background. The colours have been heightened in places with dabs of cadmium red on the castle, cadmium yellow pale on the flat surface of the ground, and Winsor blue on the boats.*

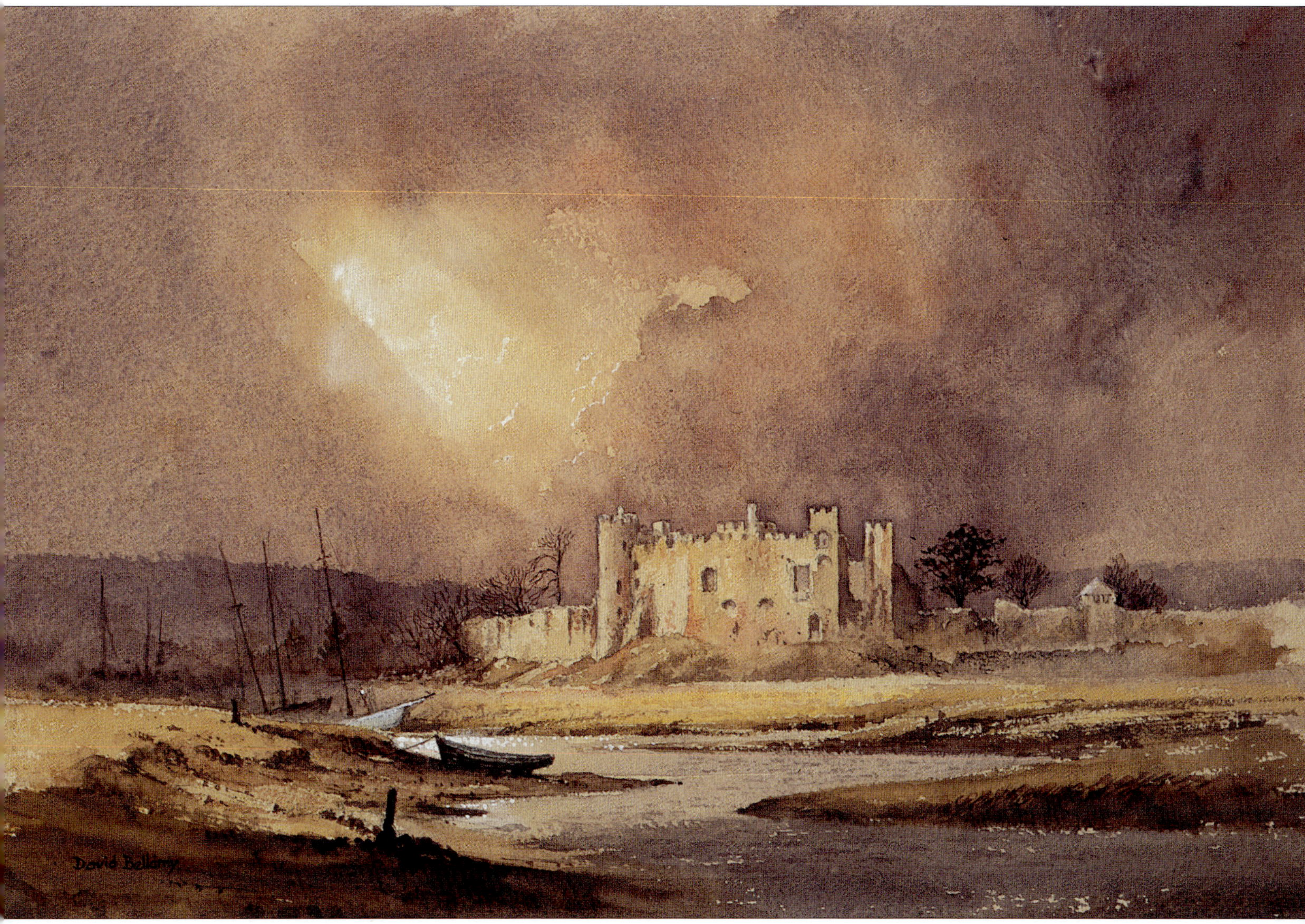

## CREATING TRANQUIL MOODS

While wind, storms and dramatic scenes rely on diagonals and vertical emphasis, to convey a sense of peace and tranquillity, we need the emphasis to be on a more horizontal composition.

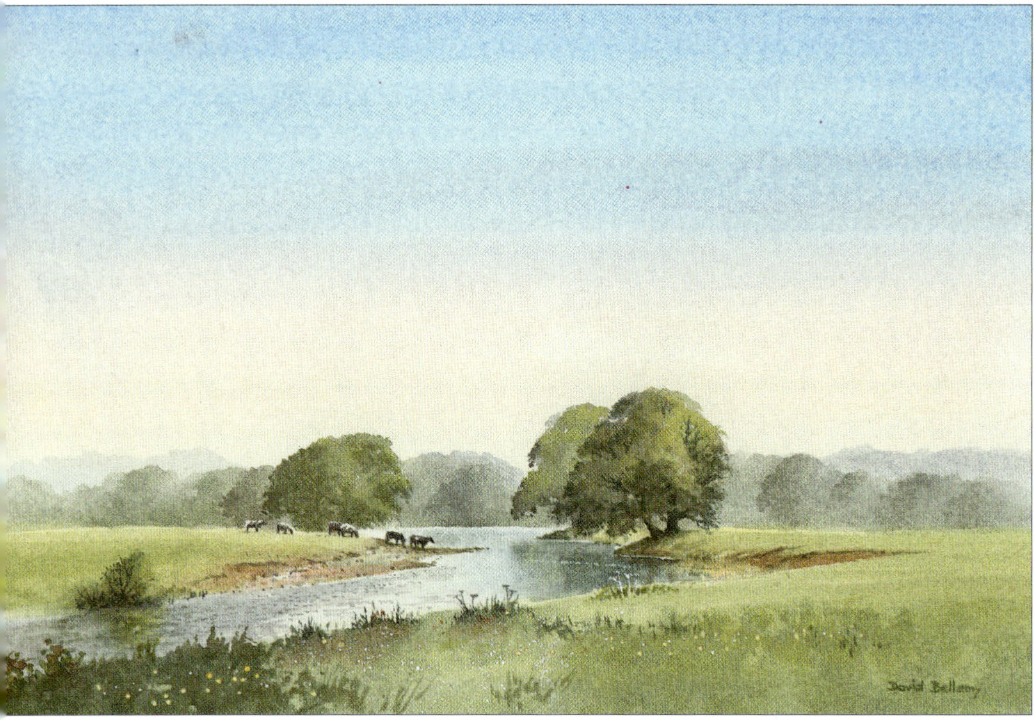

**RIVER WYE IN SUMMER**
*20 x 29cm (8 x 11½in)*

*To suggest a tranquil mood, it is hard to beat a placid river with reflections, and the cow is normally one of the most calm-inducing of animals. In this small watercolour I have combined these two elements and kept the whole scene devoid of strident verticals.*

**OCTOBER EVENING**
*13 x 21cm (5 x 8¼in)*

*Here I have conveyed the warmth of a peaceful autumn evening where a rusting old farm implement lies in the undergrowth – another way of introducing a sense of tranquillity and escape from a hectic world.*

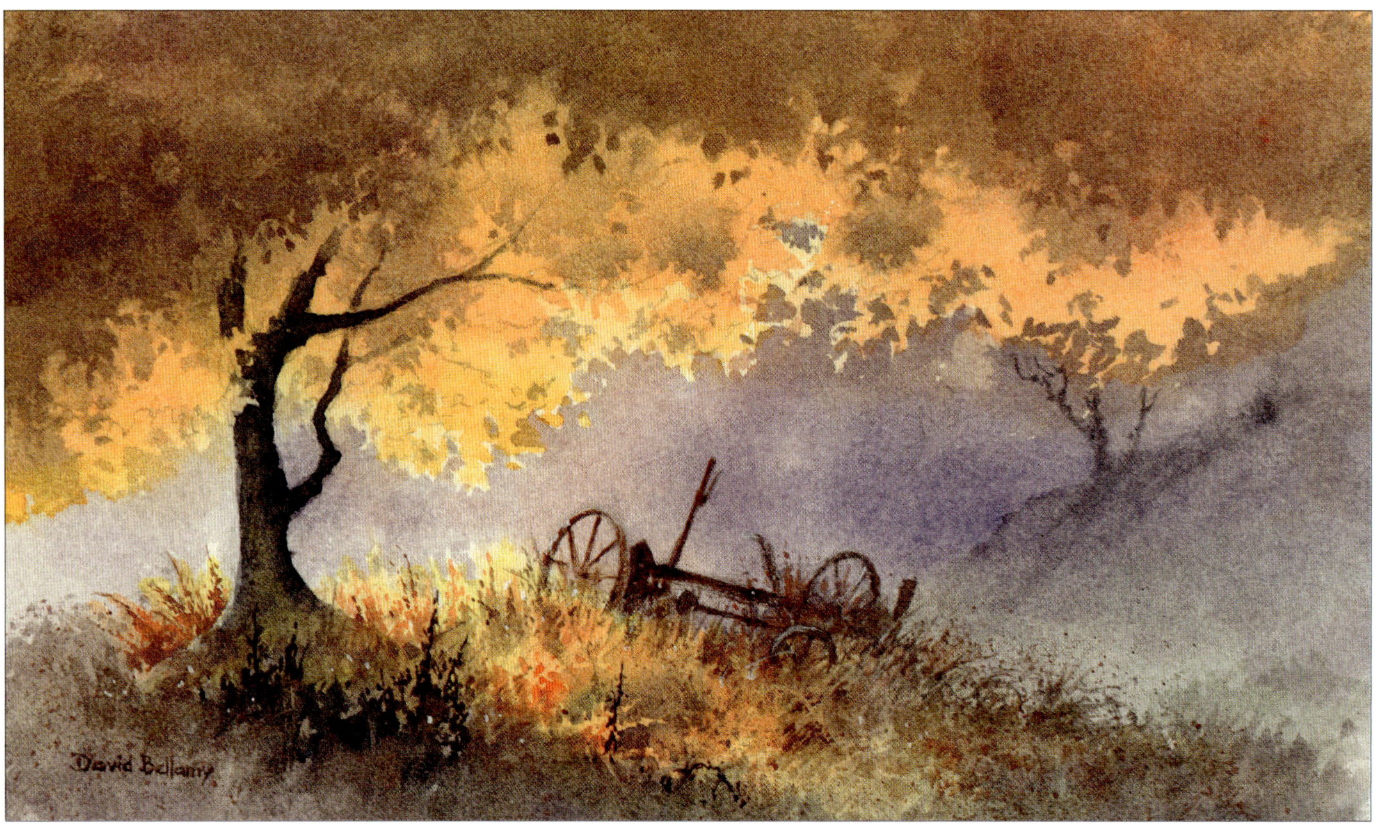

## VILLAGE ATMOSPHERE

In a village or town, although you are perhaps painting a scene with much less depth than a wide landscape, you still need to lose background detail and suggest a sense of space and depth. This can be achieved by losing most of the detail on features that are positioned behind other objects, whether buildings, vehicles or people, regardless of how clearly you can see the scene.

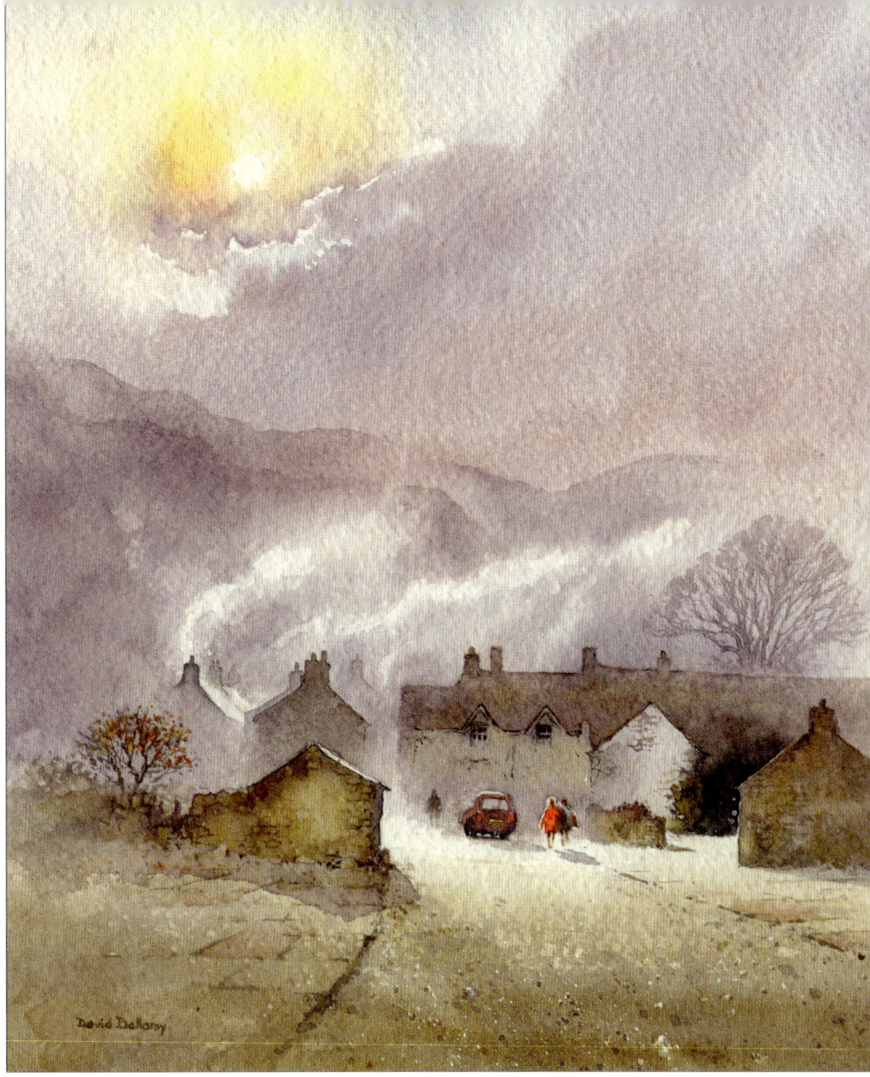


MORNING LIGHT, BRADWELL
*27 x 22cm (10½ x 8½in)*
*With back lighting, the halo effect round the figures where the sunlight catches them can really bring them to life. Blonde or light-coloured hair can be especially scintillating against the light. By contrast the figure in shadow is quite subdued, so it pays to think carefully before you place any figures in a composition, particularly if you want them to stand out.*

## THE ADVANTAGES OF DUST, DIRT AND SAND

Dust stirred up into the air can be an effective means of losing detail and providing a hazy, mysterious background. Trucks driven across the desert or along a dusty track are generally followed by clouds of dust, so make use of this effect whenever you can, as it can also imply movement.

MOROCCAN HORSEMEN
*19 x 19cm (7½ x 7½in)*
*Dust is an extremely useful commodity for losing detail, especially in the case of riders, and here it helps to convey a sense of movement in the horse's legs.*

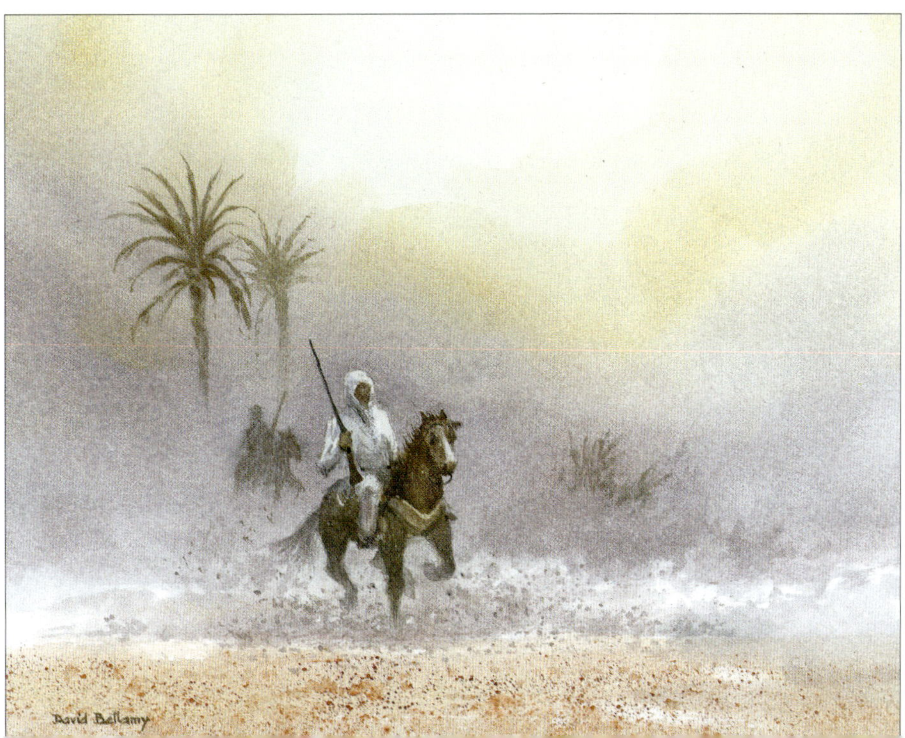

# MOORLANDS & MOUNTAINS

The more uncultivated landscapes of mountain and moor have, down the years, held great fascination as subject matter for landscape painters. In the early days they were seen as places of terror and mystery, the haunts of bandits and the like, and attracting dramatic descriptions such as 'the horrid graces of wilderness' as Lord Shaftesbury put it in 1709. He was actually eulogizing on the beauty of raw nature.

In this section we are not just concerned with the savage places, but chiefly the outstanding scenery encompassed within the mountain and moorland environment. Much of the techniques and examples are applicable to lowland landscapes, of course, but in the mountains you are far more likely to find rustic subjects such as ancient dwellings, rutted cart-tracks (yes, even ruts can have tremendous visual appeal) and colourful characters, and where better to find waterfalls and tumbling, rocky streams that are delightful companions as you seek that ideal subject?

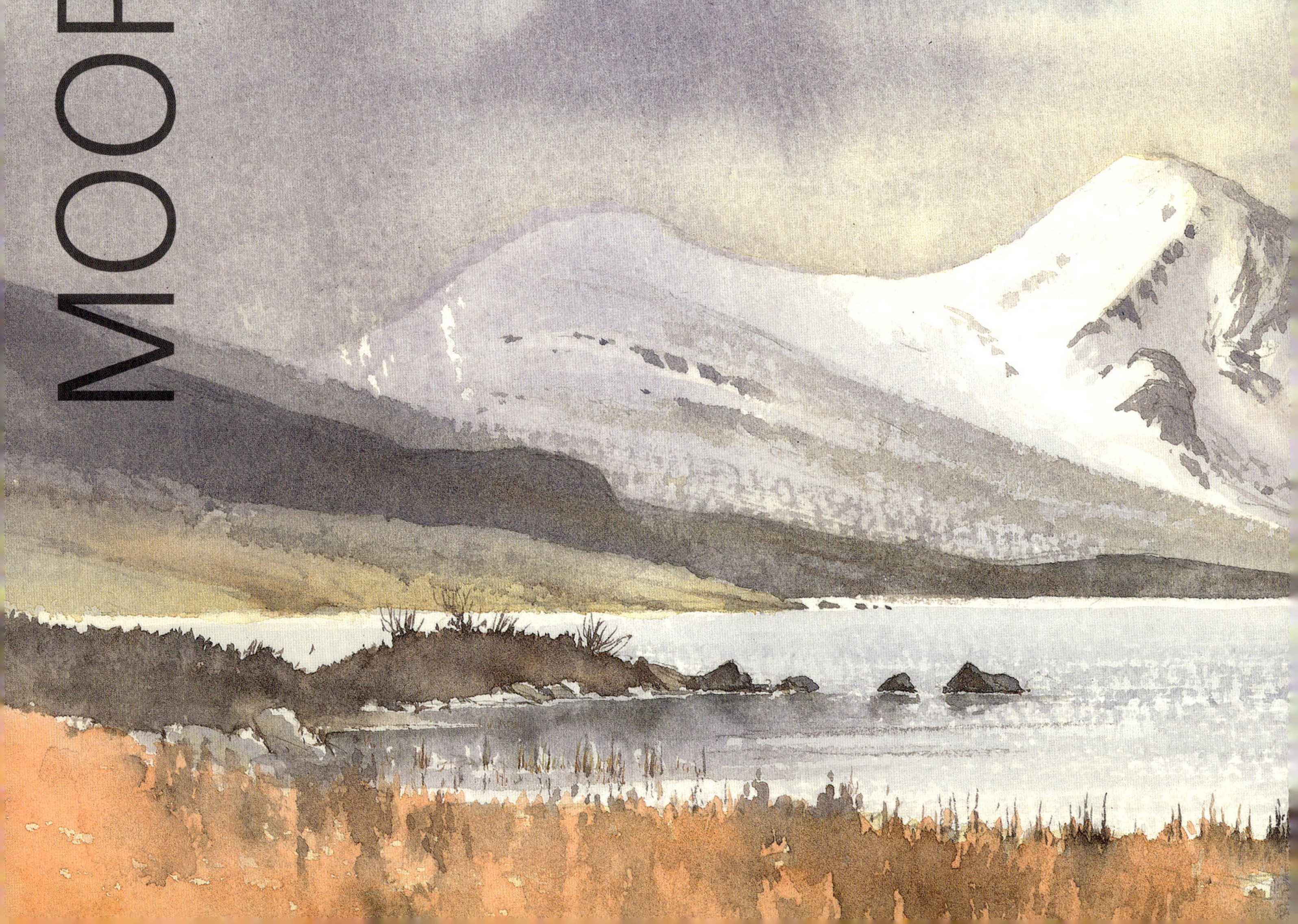

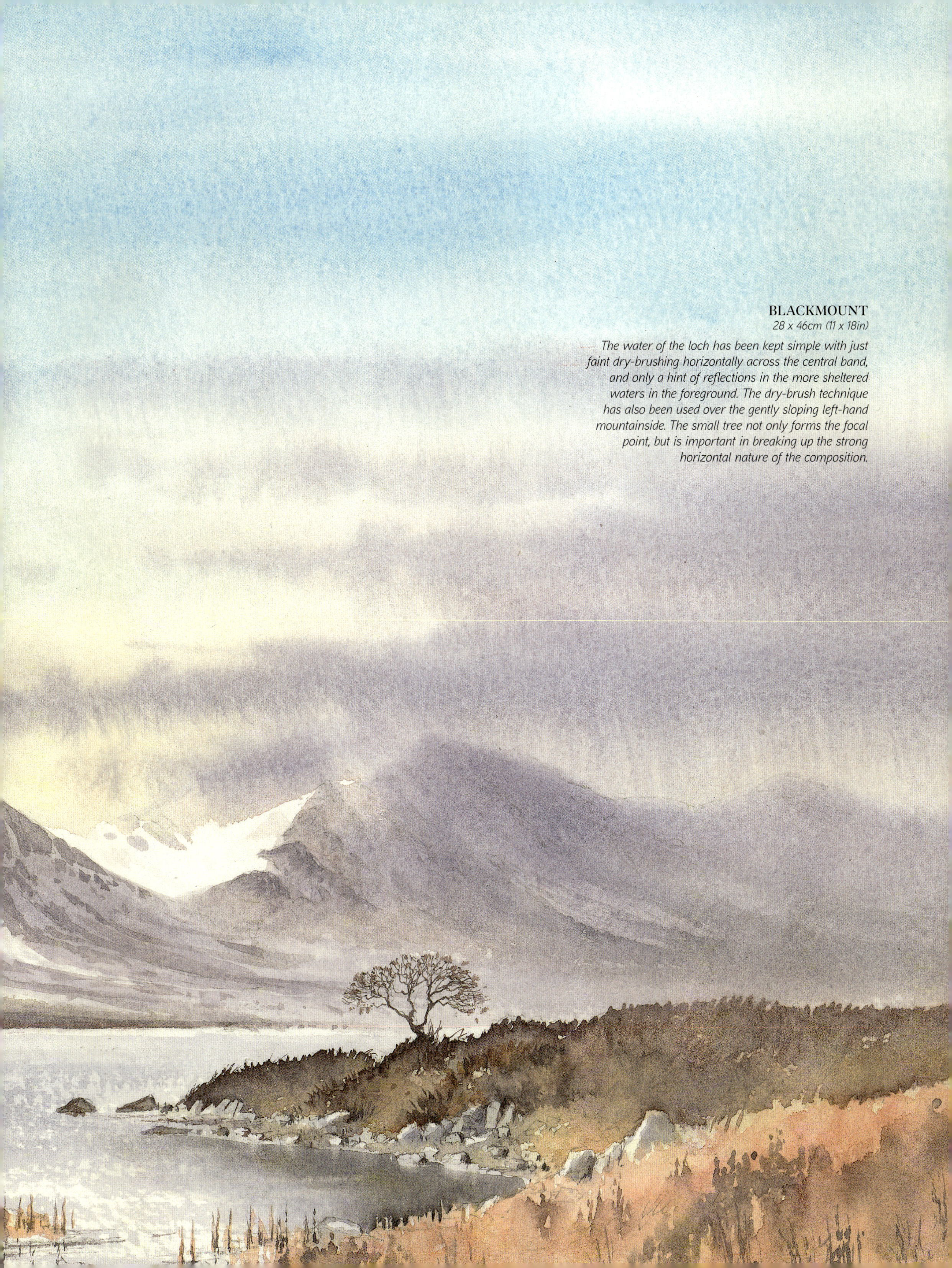

BLACKMOUNT

*28 x 46cm (11 x 18in)*

*The water of the loch has been kept simple with just faint dry-brushing horizontally across the central band, and only a hint of reflections in the more sheltered waters in the foreground. The dry-brush technique has also been used over the gently sloping left-hand mountainside. The small tree not only forms the focal point, but is important in breaking up the strong horizontal nature of the composition.*

# Trees

Trees are often shown as a centre of interest, or as a supporting feature. They can also provide a sense of calm and shelter in an otherwise savage mountain landscape. Whether they are seen as an individual specimen or as a mass running down a mountainside, keep them simple and avoid trying to include every leaf and branch. Trees are also excellent when used to break up long horizontal or diagonal lines, such as the far shore of a lake.

## FIVE COMMON MOUNTAIN TREES

Many different species of trees adorn mountains and moorlands, but these five are especially useful. They can be added to wild landscapes to enhance the composition, or as a centre of interest. These examples can be introduced individually or in groups.

### THORN TREE

*These small trees, with their contorted, often interlocking branches, are so useful to balance a composition, relieve the monotony of a dry-stone wall, or to support another feature as a centre of interest. I also like to use them to break up long ridge lines. With winter trees, the rigger brush is unparalleled for delineating the fine branches. As it is easy to have too much water or paint on the brush, test it on scrap paper first, twirling it across the surface to find the right strength and consistency of paint, and to achieve a fine point.*

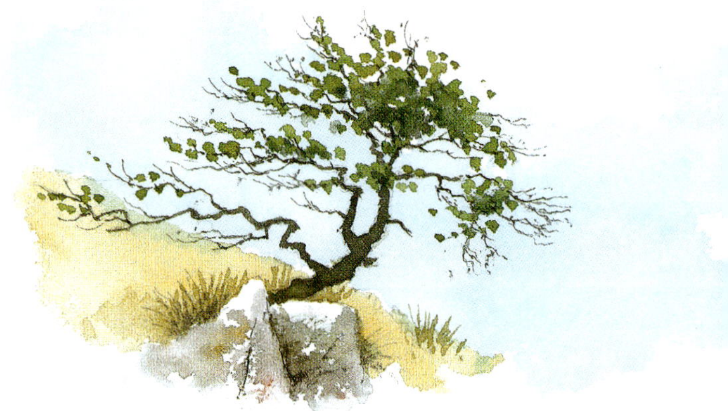

### LARCH IN WINTER

*The larch is a distinctive tree, with branches sweeping down to curve back upwards at the tip. In winter they provide a violent splash of orange, especially when caught in sunlight. A tall larch to one side of the foreground can provide an excellent framework to a focal point, while a stand of several of them makes a splendid centre of interest.*

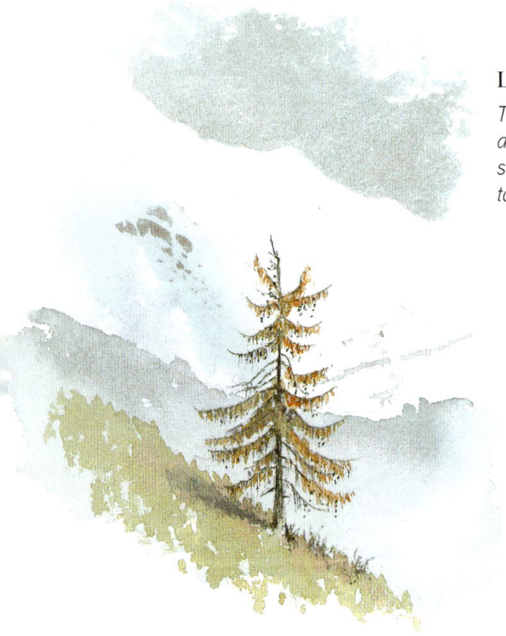

### ROWAN TREE OR MOUNTAIN ASH

*These can often be seen growing out of cliffs or rocks, and are useful to accompany waterfalls and crags, or to punctuate bare mountain slopes where they grow at quite high altitude. In September their bright red berries flourish and can be used to add a splash of colour to a scene.*

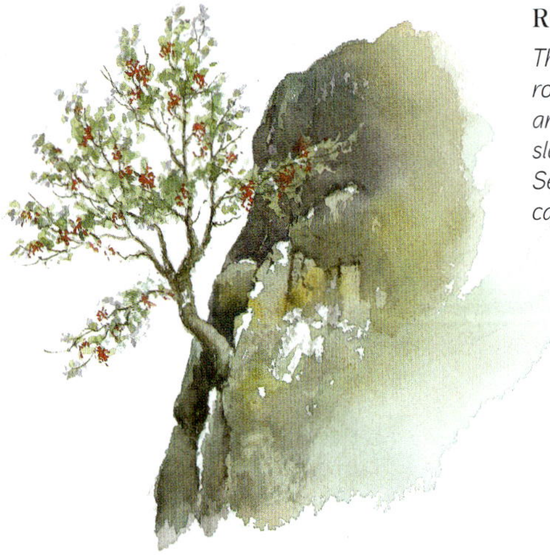

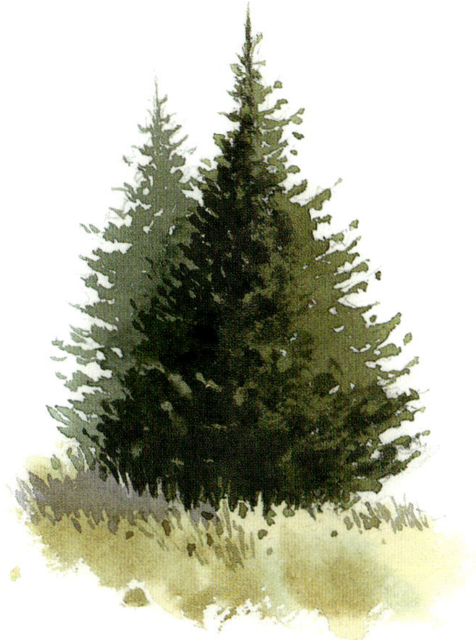

**CONIFERS**

*Conifers are usually seen as a mass, but it's worth picking out one or two specimens at the edges of the mass and giving them a little more shape. They can vary considerably in size and shape, and are useful to support or highlight other features in a scene. The specimen shown here is a Norway spruce.*

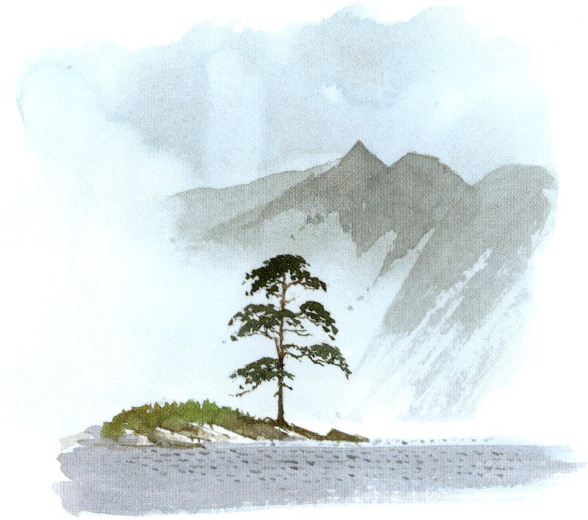

**SCOTS PINE**

*Alone or in stands, these tall, graceful trees work extremely well as a focal point in many scenes, their trunks quite orange at times. Mature specimens often only show branches near the top.*

## MASSED TREES

Large areas of mountainsides are often cloaked in masses of conifers. These areas need not be as daunting as you might think. Usually the underlying ridges and gullies are betrayed by the rise and fall of the lines of conifers and we can use this to advantage. Where such a ridge runs down, the trees can be given a little more prominence, such as a slightly darker row. You can soften the darker wash at the bottom to join the main mass. You only need one or two of these ridges of trees, or perhaps three on a particularly large area. These can be further enhanced by mist, sunlight or shadow, which are especially effective for breaking up large tree masses. Dropping other colours into the wash while it is wet also works well with autumnal colours. These masses can also be broken up with one or two prominent crags rising out of the mass. Normally the rocks on such crags are lighter in tone than the surrounding conifers. A refinement on this would be to deliberately highlight a handful of pine trees at the top of the crag.

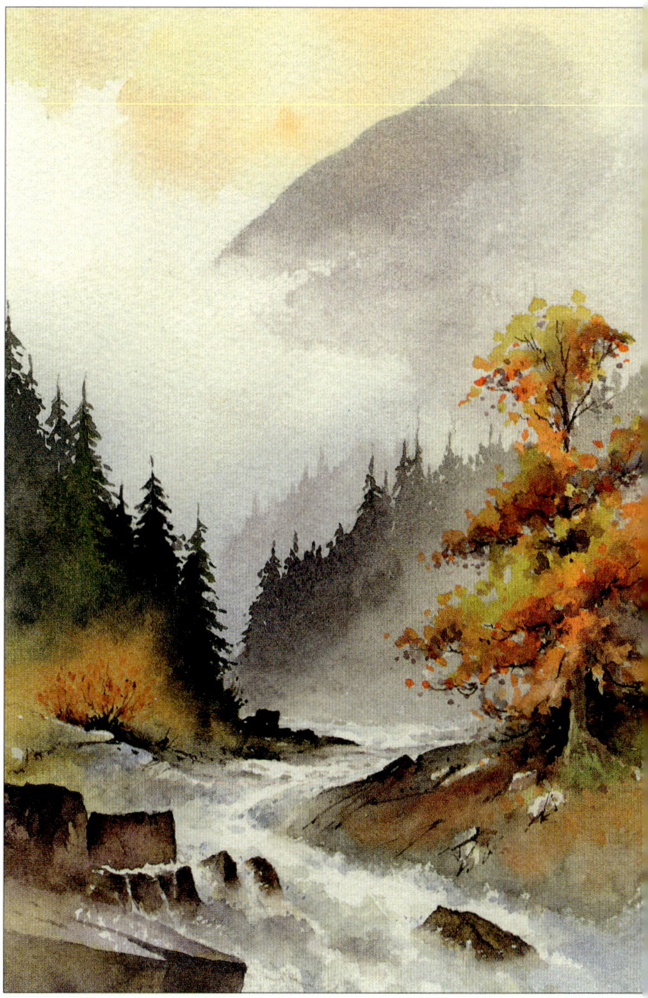

**STREAM IN THE DOLOMITES**
*23 x 16.5cm (9 x 6½in)*

*By creating a sense of atmosphere I have lost much of the tree detail beyond the tall tree on the right. The massed conifers have been rendered in a mainly flat wash with only slight graduation in the closer masses. Note how vital it is to ensure you apply the right strength of tone to suggest recession. Sometimes, if I wish to emphasize the sense of atmosphere further, I will lay a transparent glaze across the background, including the sky and both tree-lined ridges descending from the top right, before painting the dark trees coming down on the left.*

# Water

Water can bring life to your landscapes and in the mountains and moors we are lucky in having such a variety of tumbling water courses that include waterfalls, minor cascades, sparkling streams bubbling over a rocky water course and deep pools, sometimes crystal clear and sometimes dark and sombre.

## REFLECTIONS

Reflections can be depicted either by the wet-into-wet technique or by layering colours one on top of the other once the bottom one has dried. Most of the time I use the former, as in the Moorland Cascade painting, opposite. This involves laying the initial wash and waiting for it to reach a state of optimum dampness before it dries completely, before applying the reflection colour which must be barely damp, otherwise too much water will cause a runback to form when you drop it into the already-laid wash. As outlined opposite, this often needs adjustment.

The layering technique simply involves laying a wash representing the shape, tone and colour of the reflection, letting it dry, then overlaying a transparent wash over the area covered by the water. Sometimes more than one wash is needed to describe a variety of reflections within the area before the final overlaid wash is applied.

REFLECTIONS IN A LAKE
*25.5 x 40.5cm (10 x 16in)*
*The sparkle effect is easier to achieve if you use Rough paper, but resist the temptation to put it all over a large area of water. Here the light horizontal slivers were lifted out with a damp flat brush, and this helps to break up the reflections.*

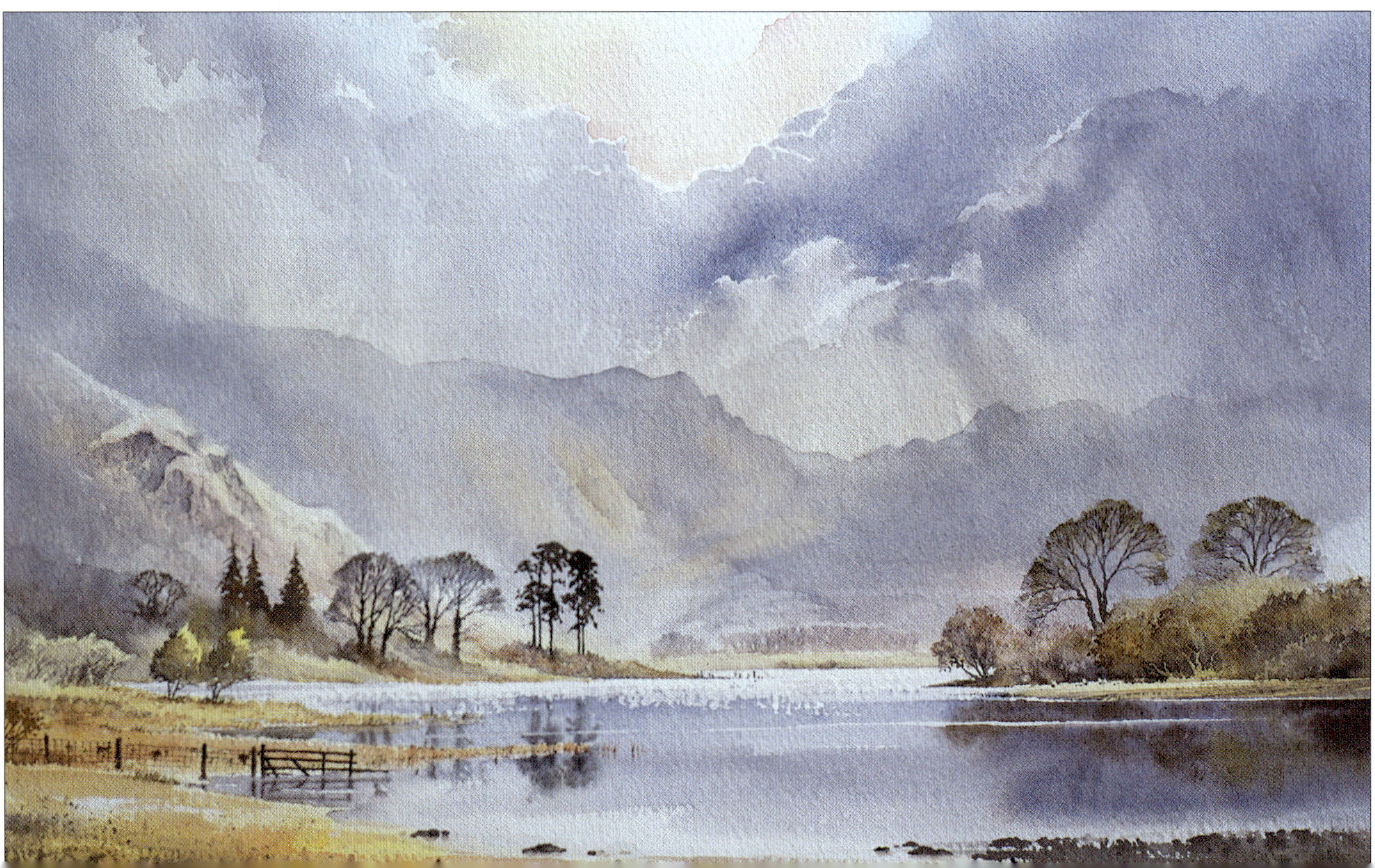

**MOORLAND CASCADE**
*18 x 28cm (7 x 11in)*

*Moorland cascades and pools make a delightful composition. Sometimes I add a thorn or rowan tree beside the cascade, but here it has sufficient interest with rocks and tumbling water. The contrast of hard-edged, dark rocks against the lighter water works well to highlight the water. The foreground reflections were achieved with the wet-into-wet method by dropping in the dark reflections while the pool was still damp. As so often happens, the reflections spread out too far and I had to curb them with a damp brush which I had dipped in clean water and then wiped on a paper tissue.*

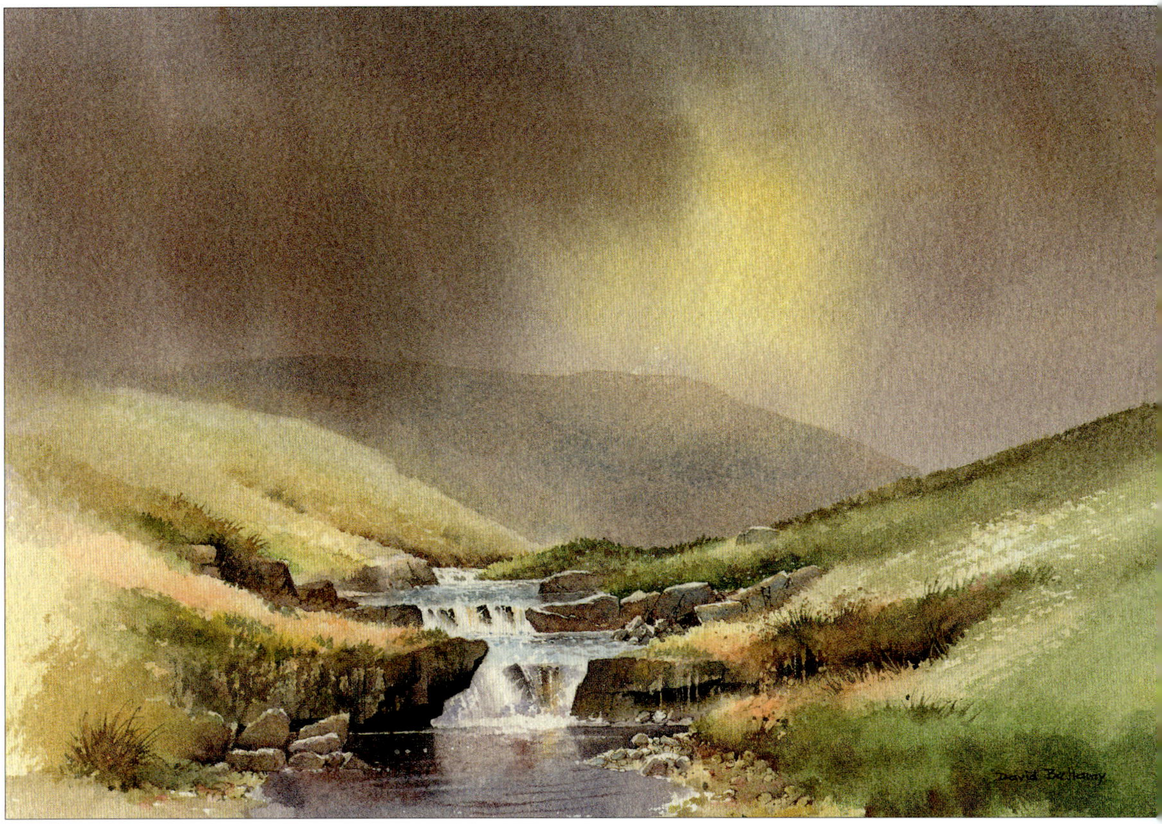

## TACKLING DIFFERENT TYPES OF WATER

The stretch of water you are painting might have several different types of water: sparkling, placid, rippled or cascading, and bringing them together can be a problem.

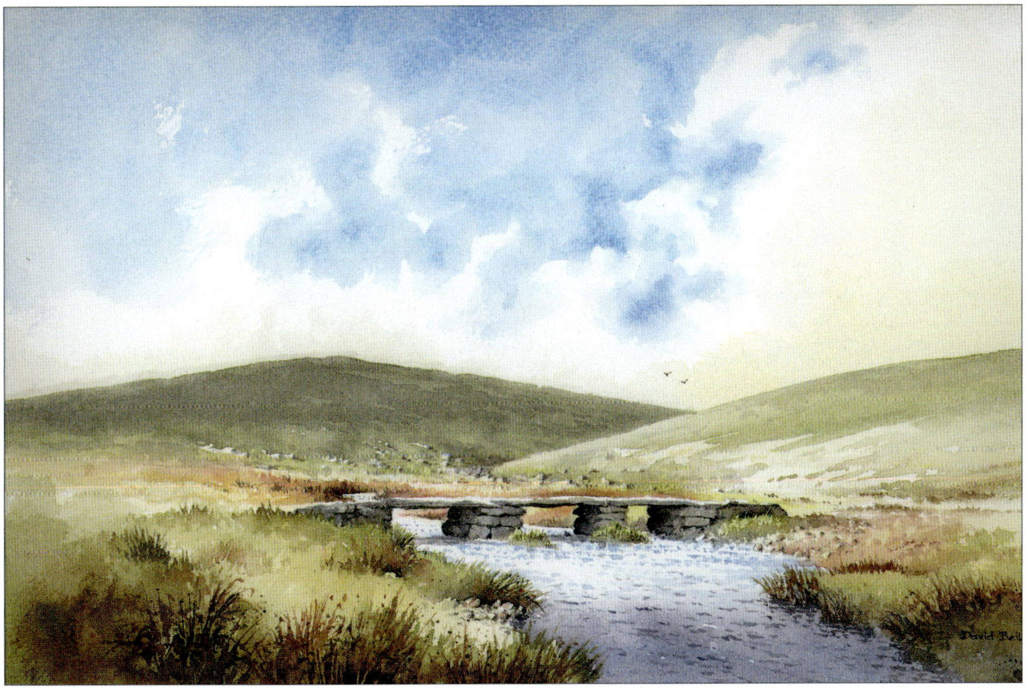

**TEIGNHEAD CLAPPER BRIDGE**
*20 x 30.5cm (8 x 12in)*

*Here I have dabbed cobalt blue over white paper directly below the bridge, to represent the sparkling water – this could alternatively be done using the dry-brush technique. When this was dry, I wet the lower part of the stream with clean water, taking it up over the bottom of the sparkling area, and then washed in a mix of cobalt blue and cadmium red, letting it drift up softly towards the sparkling water. Finally, with a stronger mixture of the same colours, I dabbed in the ripples when the wash was dry.*

### GLEN NEVIS

*23 x 30.5in (9 x 12in)*

*The actual water has been kept simple with dry-brush applications of colour to suggest strong backlighting falling on the water. The colour becomes stronger in tone as it gets closer, becoming darker in the foreground as it swings to the left and away from the light. I achieved this by using horizontal flicks of the brush with more liquid paint.*

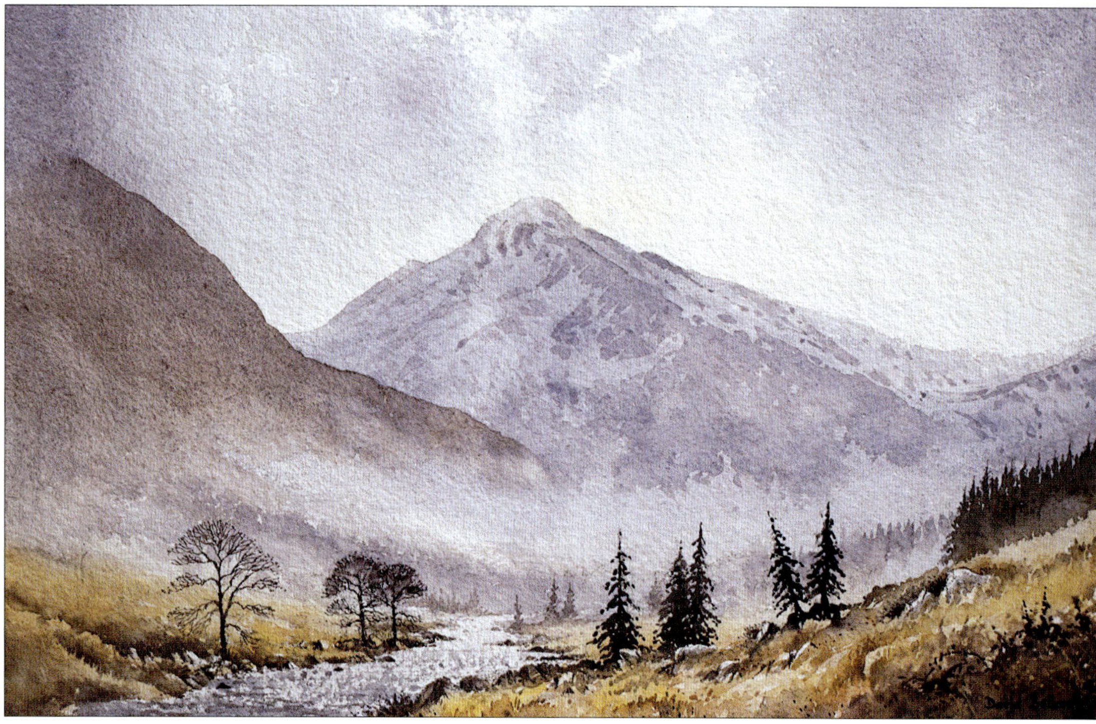

### TUMBLING CASCADE

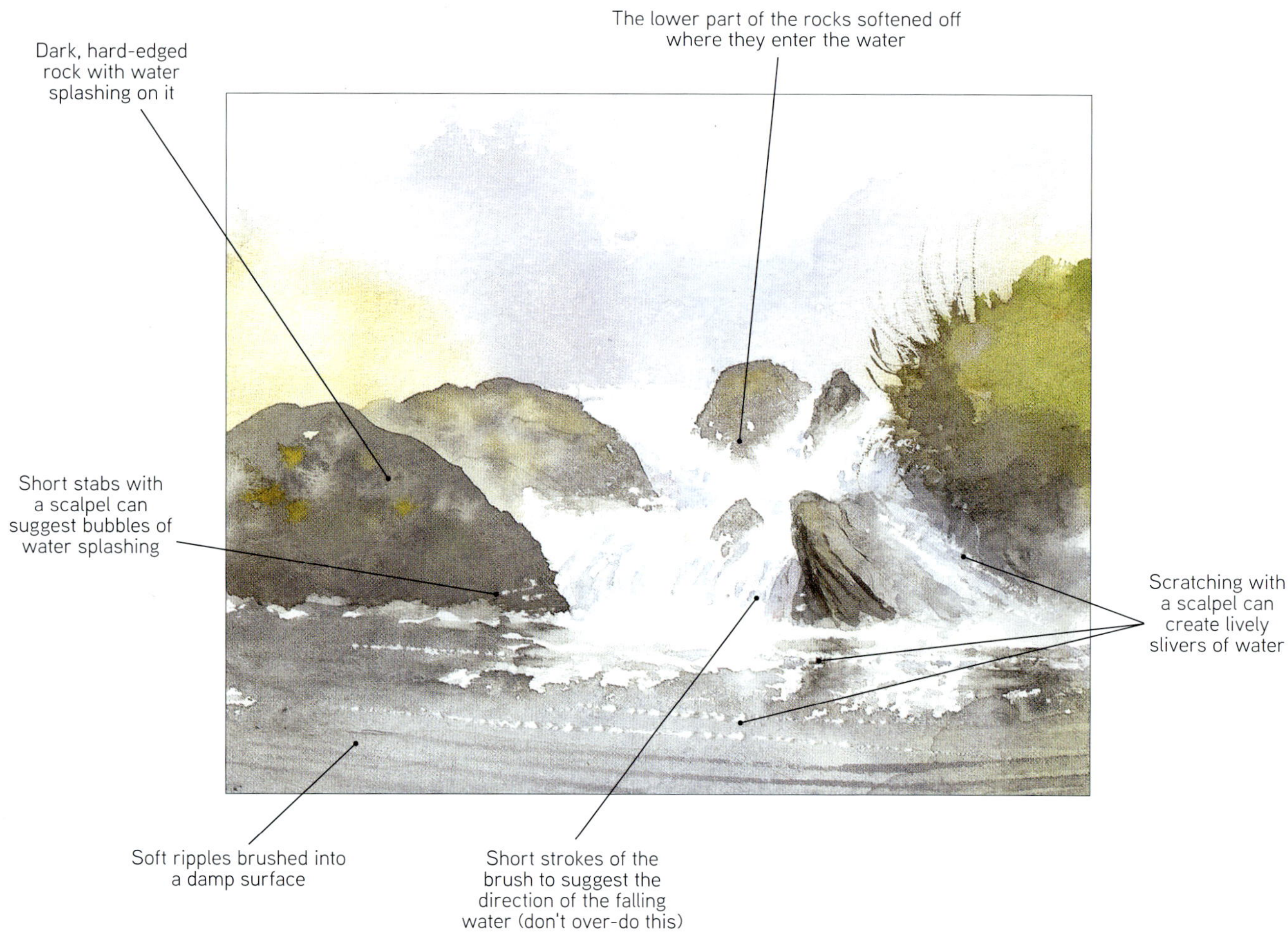

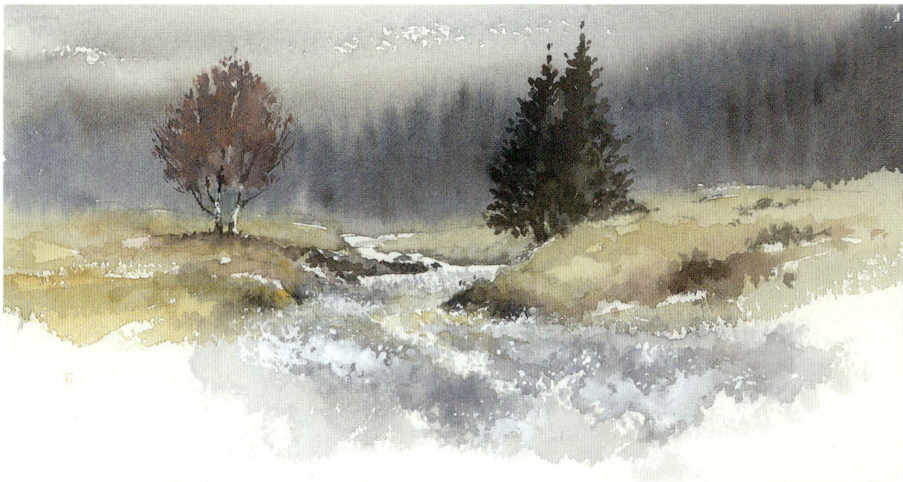

STREAM IN SPATE

*Painting water that is crashing, roaring and cascading in spate is quite a challenge, needing circular, dabbing motions with a round brush. One way to improve your chances of success is to paint in the darker tones in this vigorous, dabbing manner, leaving untouched spaces here and there, and when this is dry, apply white gouache with the side of the brush to create the lighter swirls. Just above the crests of these swirls, dab in a few white blobs to suggest drops of water as I have done in this small painting.*

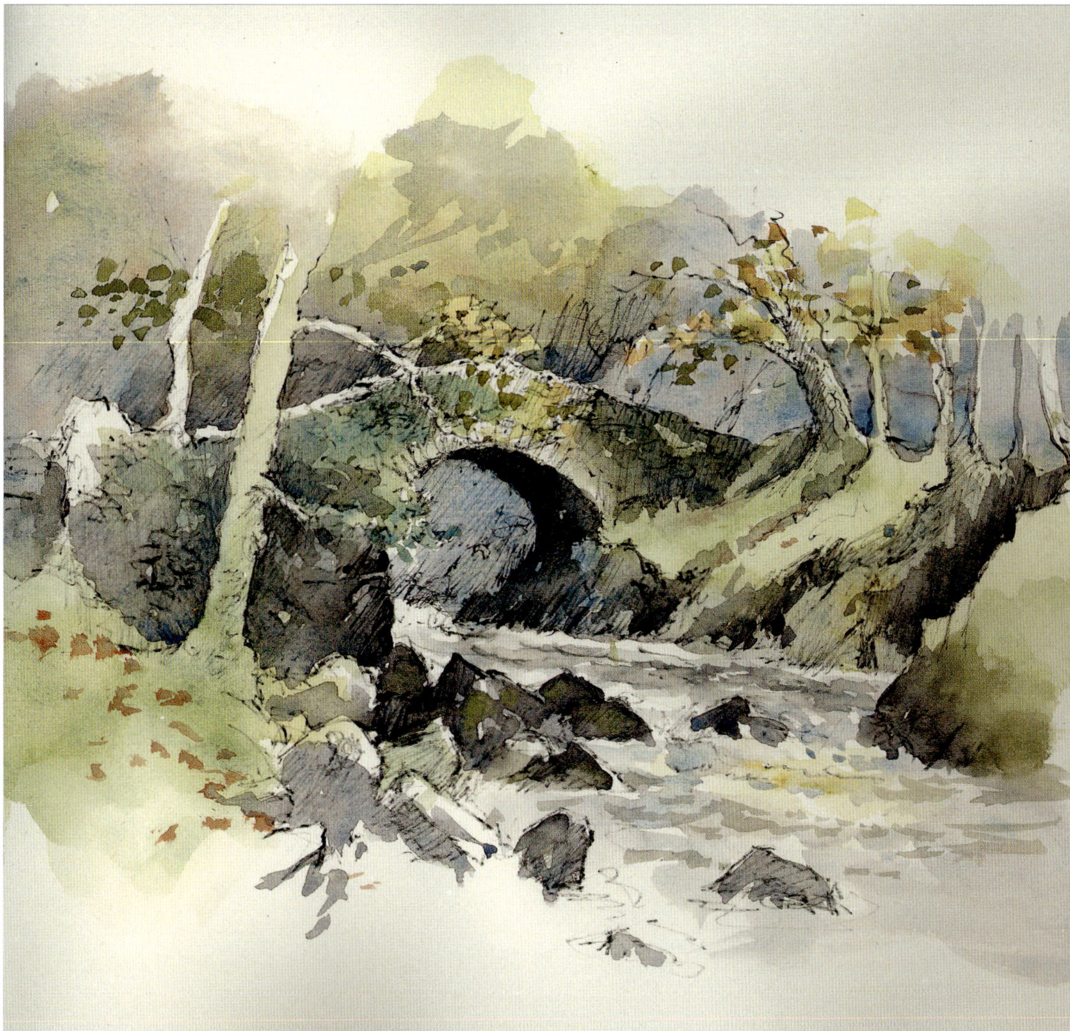

BRIDGE ON THE RIVER ARTRO

*In this watercolour sketch the water has been kept simple with short, vigorous brushstrokes, retaining much white paper to show it up against the dark rocks. Note the yellow ochre dropped in on the bottom right where the colour of peat affects the water.*

# Rocks and crags

As a painter you cannot take mountains seriously without tackling rocks. These can take many forms, some shapely, others simply a crumbling mess. It pays to concentrate on the more handsome specimens that appeal to you, and although sometimes you have to include ones that are less appealing, you can subdue these and highlight an adjacent passage. Before you start painting rocks, consider the colour – is the area you are about to work on just one colour or is it variegated? Look for the main shadows, then the fracture lines, and with crags and cliffs, the fault structure. Is the main line of fault vertical, horizontal or diagonal in varying degrees? Usually you will see a tendency for the fracture lines to run in one of these directions, and translating this on to your painting can give your work a sense of authenticity.

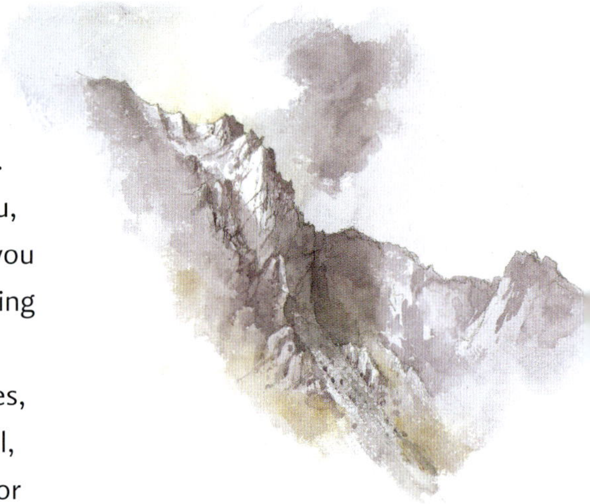

SUNLIT CRAGS

*When painting rock scenery, take note of the main fault lines as well as the overall structure. Often there is a strong bias in these fractures: horizontal, diagonal or vertical. In these crags we see a definite diagonal emphasis from bottom left to top right. Try to avoid putting in every fracture line, however strong they may appear. Pick out the main ones and leave some of the face devoid of too much detail. In this watercolour sketch I have resisted the urge to depict detail on the more distant cliffs in order to suggest that they are further away.*

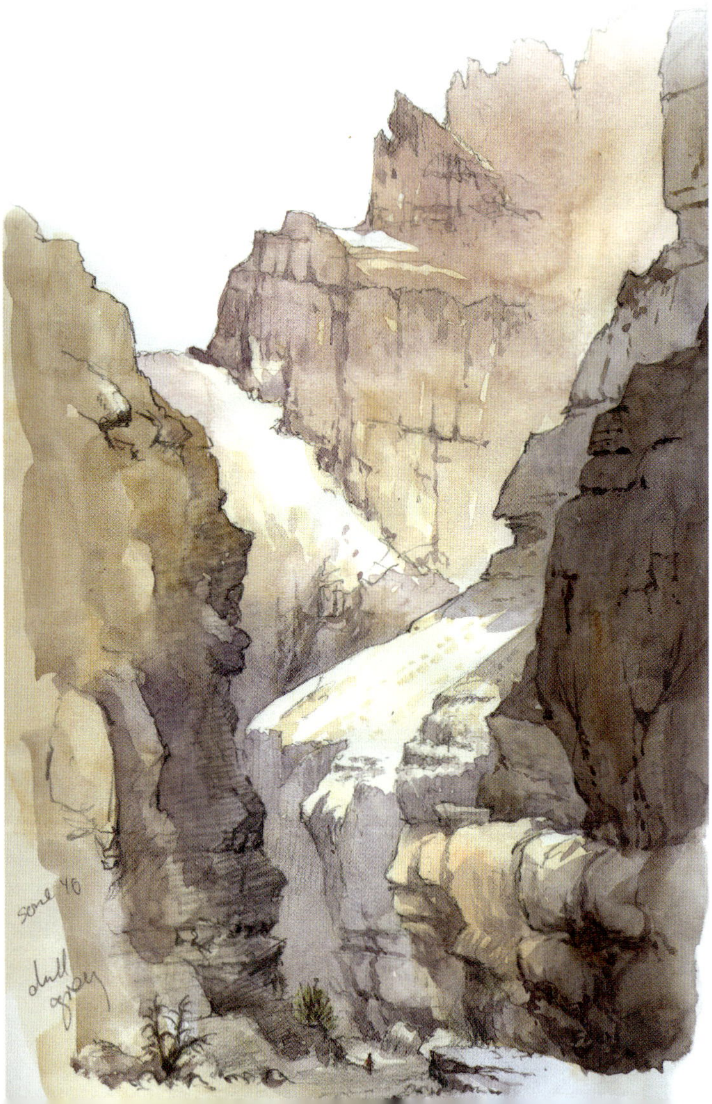

TACKLING A ROCKY GORGE

*The intense sunlight catching the high cliffs fails to penetrate to the bottom of this sublime scene in Wadi Nakhar in Oman, and often the temptation is to make the lower parts too dark. In places like this, watch for strong reflected light creating subtle highlights on rock faces. Where the gorge disappears round a bend, I have kept the cliffs devoid of detail, while making the closer face much stronger in tone. Initially I intended the word 'face' to mean 'rock face', but I see there is also a profile of a human face at that point, one of three in the sketch. I included Jenny at the bottom as she provides a marvellous idea of the immense scale of this place.*

## MAKING ROCKS GROW OUT OF THE GROUND

There is a danger that rocks will look as though they are plonked on top of the ground, rather than being embedded in it. This can be avoided using the method described below.

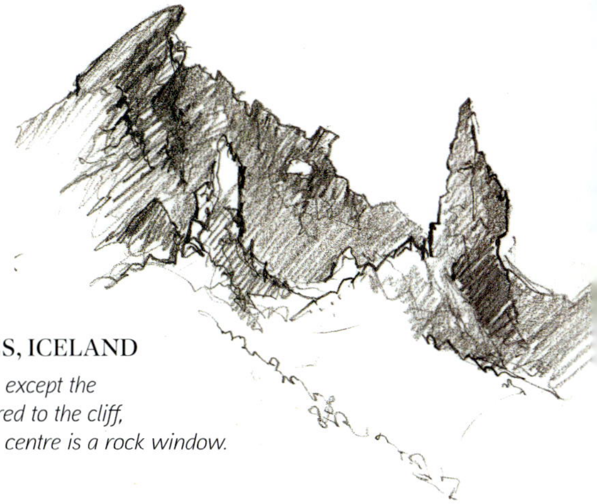

VOLCANIC ROCK PINNACLES, ICELAND

*All the edges are hard in this sketch, except the bottom ones where the rock is secured to the cliff, thus giving a sense of solidity. In the centre is a rock window.*

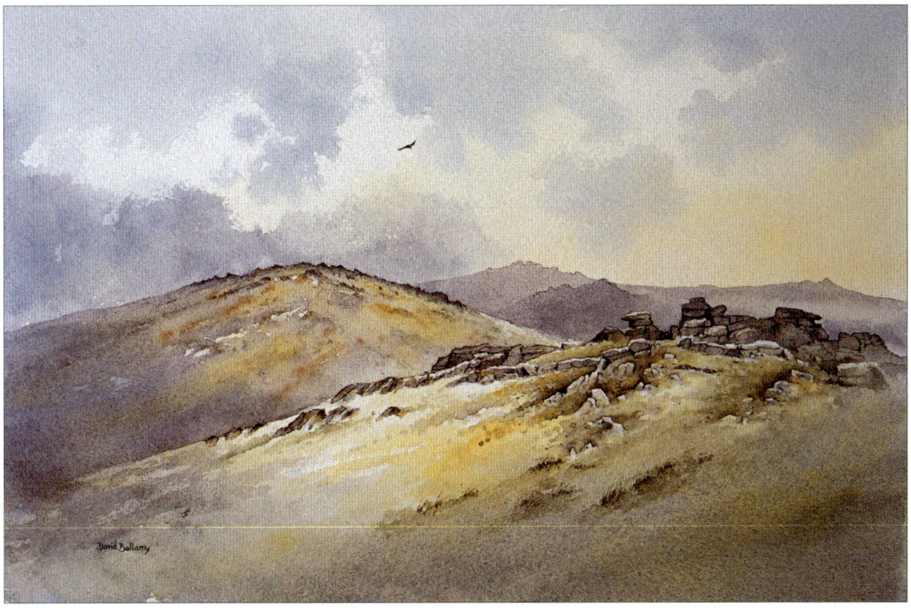

DARTMOOR TORS

*20 x 30.5cm (8 x 12in)*

*These granite tors and their satellite boulders look as though they are growing out of the ground. This is achieved by avoiding a strong bottom line to the rock and either drifting some of the ground colour up into the tor, or bringing it down into the ground below.*

## BOULDERS AND LOOSE ROCKS

Boulder fields and scree can be daunting to render as there are so many individual shapes. Much simplification can be achieved by reducing the number of those shapes, losing edges, just suggesting some definition and leaving quiet areas. It also helps to break up the monotony of massed boulders with bushes, an occasional tree, a fallen trunk, or even an animal. One device I often employ is to lay a transparent shadow across part of the boulder field – French ultramarine and cadmium red works well. It is also a good idea to highlight one or two boulders, thus varying the emphasis.

FOREGROUND ROCKS AND BOULDERS

*Note how in this Alpine scene dark vegetation and ground has been used to highlight the tops of the boulders, while the bottoms are faded into the ground unless there are other rocks in front. Some are rounded, some angular, and a fallen tree provides a little relief from the mass of rock shapes. If you wish to vary the boulders further, then dropping colour such as yellow ochre or cadmium red into them while they are still wet gives a convincing appearance.*

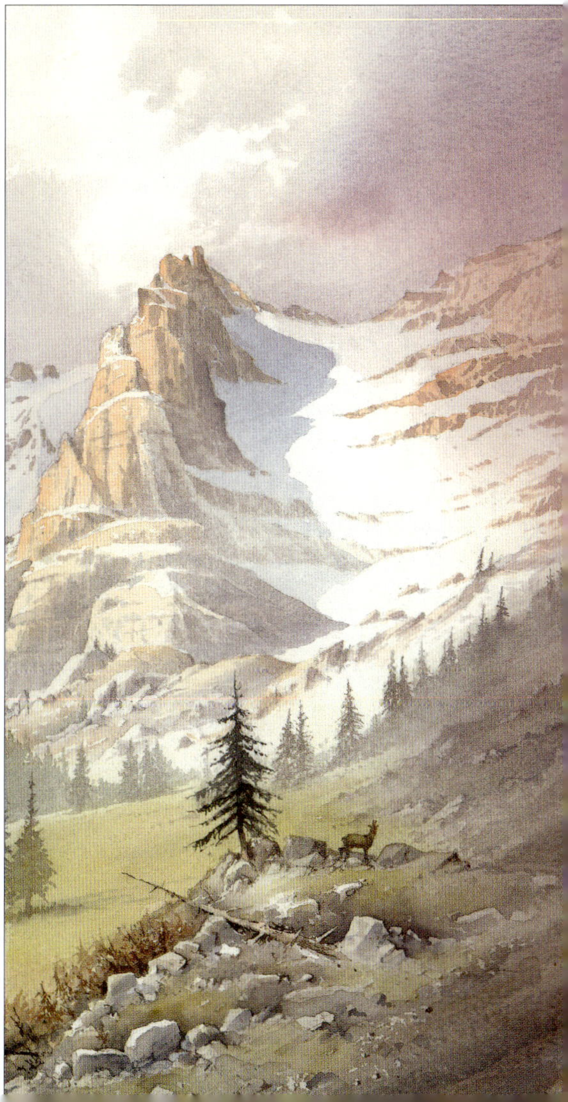

# Moorland scenes

Moors can range from pleasant valleys to dreary, high, mist-clad acres of peat-hags, with some hills rising to almost mountainous proportions, capped by rocky tors and outcrops. Out on the high moors you occasionally come across little gems, perhaps a stone packhorse bridge over a tumbling stream, or some shapely crags rising above the surface of a heathery slope. Here we will look at how even the more mundane parts of the moor can be livened up, starting with a simple rendition of a moorland scene using broad washes in three easy stages.

## KING'S TOR

1 Firstly I laid a weak wash of cadmium yellow pale over the sky, bringing it down over most of the paper. When the paper was dry, I applied the distant ridge using a fairly weak mixture of French ultramarine and Indian red, and softened the wash off at the bottom.

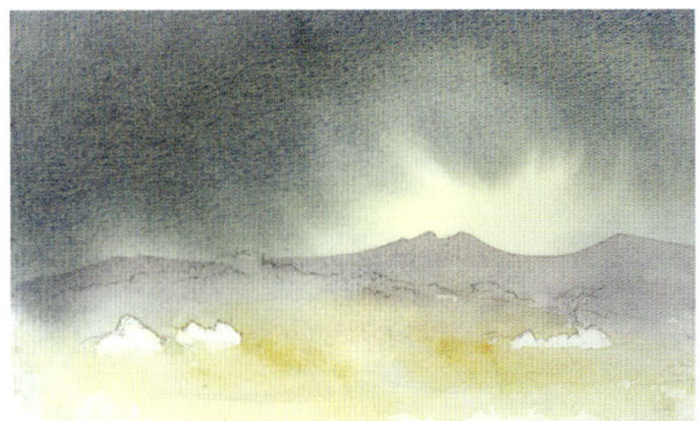

2 Once the paper had dried completely, I re-wet the whole surface and dropped in a strong mix of burnt umber and French ultramarine over the sky, allowing it to run down over part of the distant ridge to suggest a rain squall. I added yellow ochre to the lower part of the wash in the foreground.

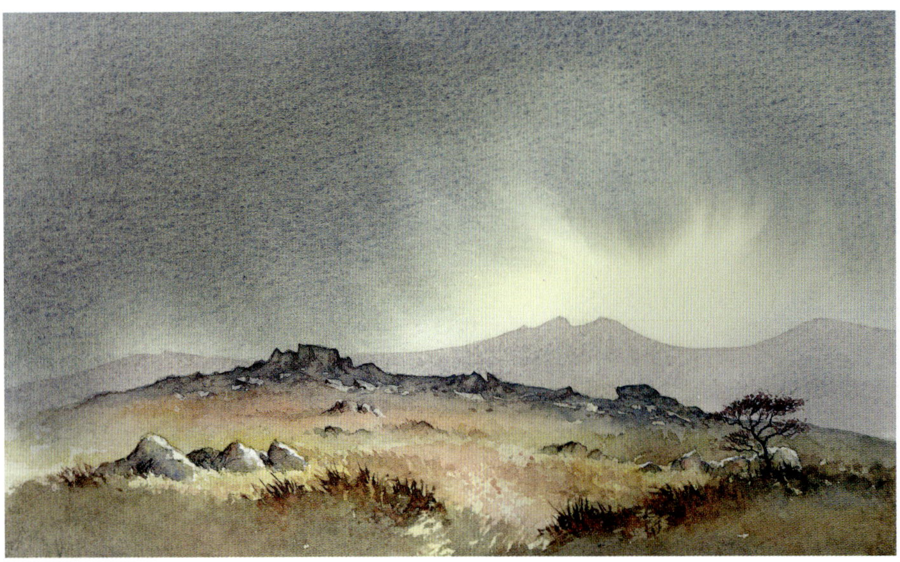

3 For the main tor I painted a wash of stronger French ultramarine and Indian red, dropping in a little yellow ochre, then some light red below the rocks, blending it all in. Then I painted the foreground rocks, while the thorn tree was rendered with a rigger. The dark grasses were applied using a mixture of French ultramarine and burnt umber. Some Indian red was dropped in.

## CREATING MOORLAND TEXTURES WITH WAX RESIST

One superb method of suggesting rough textures or intermittent snow on the ground, is by using a candle or wax crayon to create a resist. Wax repels watercolour washes and on Rough paper the textural effect will be even more pronounced. Lay the wax on first, then apply the wash over the top. While you will not get highly accurate detail with this technique, it gives spontaneity and an uninhibited appearance. If you want to suggest snow, use white or off-white wax, but otherwise any colour can be used. Try this out on scrap paper first before you commit to it in your full watercolour painting.

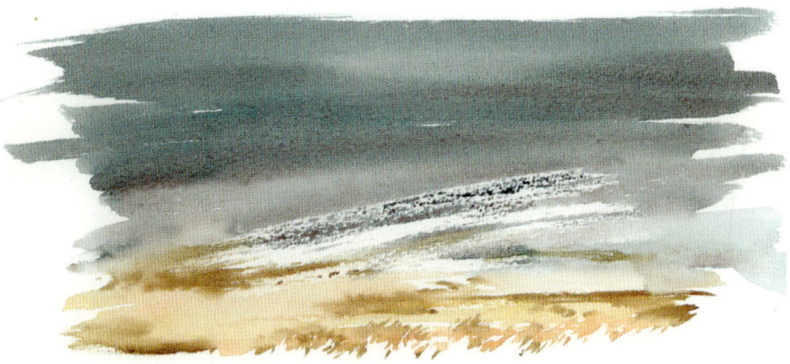

1 To suggest of a moor partly covered in snow, I dragged a candle across the paper in a shallow diagonal for the slope, then applied a wash of blue-grey across it. Part way into the candle wax area, I introduced some yellow ochre and brought this down to the foreground area. The wax resists the watercolour to create the required effect.

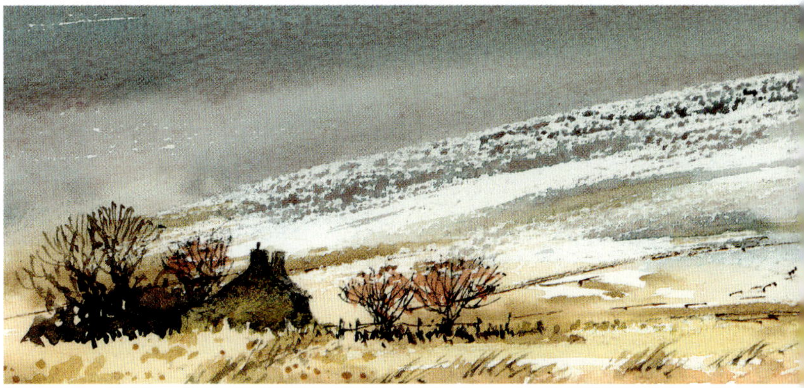

2 The cottage and trees have been added to complete the scene. Naturally, when laying on the candle wax, I avoided the area where these features were to appear.

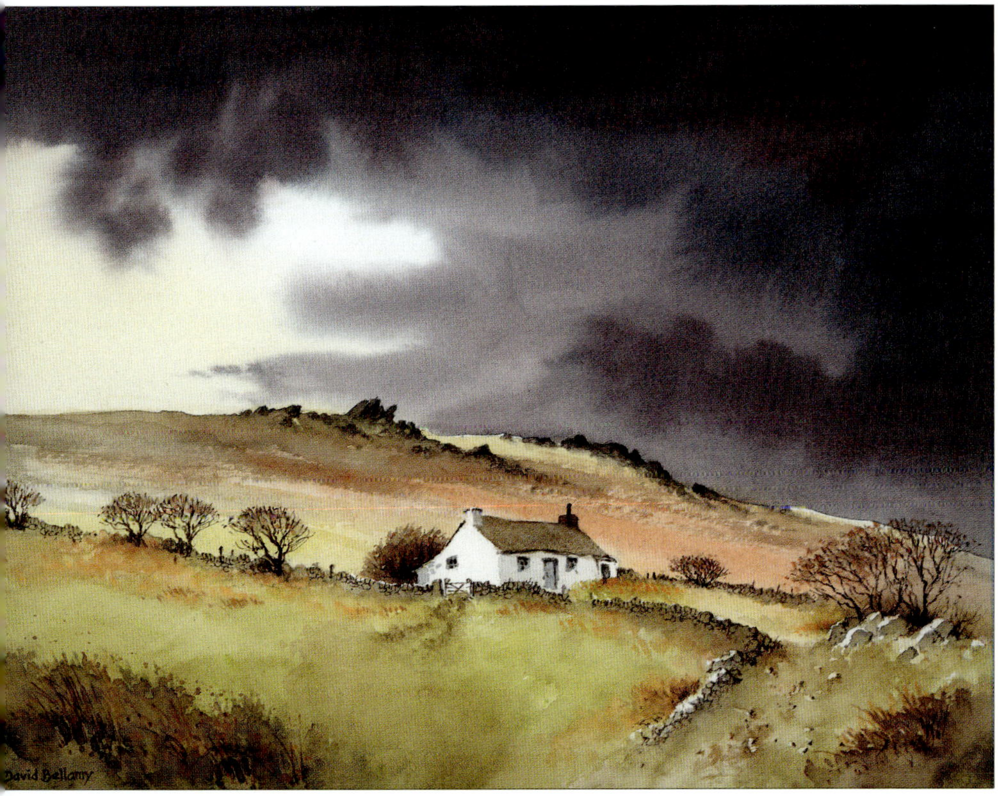

**MOOD AND COLOUR**
*20 x 30.5cm (8 x 12in)*

*Emphasizing strong colours can bring a painting to life. In this painting, the various diagonal washes of light red, yellow ochre and cadmium yellow pale across the background slope overlap. After applying a mix of light red and French ultramarine to the crags, I brought a slightly weaker version of this mix down diagonally over part of the yellow ochre and light red in a rapid, dry-brush fashion, suggesting rough ground.*

*The moody sky was begun with a fluid wash of Naples yellow across the left-hand half, followed immediately by a medium-tone wash of Indian red and French ultramarine over the right-hand sky, taking it across the top to the left. Without pause, I then applied a stronger version of the same colours to form the darkest clouds that dropped into the Naples yellow on the left. Unusually, the sky was done after I had painted yellow ochre on the moor and allowed it to dry. The crags were painted after the sky had dried.*

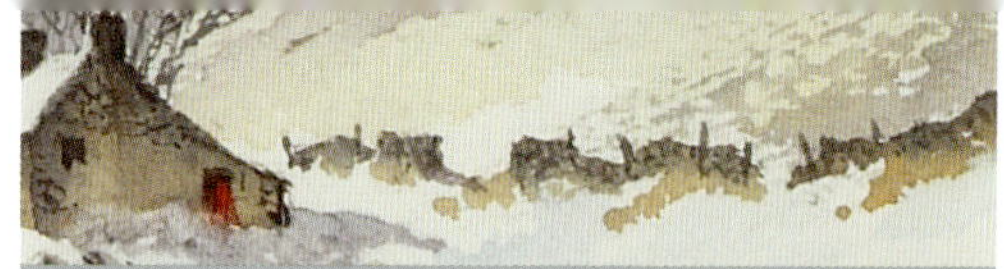

# CHAPEL LE DALE

When painting a snow scene like this one in Chapel le Dale, Yorkshire, try to introduce some warm colours to avoid an overall cold result. This can be done in the sky, reflections, vegetation or in a building. In this demonstration I show how to add warm reds and yellows to a winter moorland landscape.

**MATERIALS USED**

Saunders Waterford High White, 300gsm (140lb) Not watercolour paper

Brushes: squirrel mop, no. 7 and no. 4 round, no. 1 rigger, no. 1 round and 6mm (¼in) flat

Colours: Naples yellow, cadmium yellow pale, cadmium red, French ultramarine, cobalt blue, yellow ochre, burnt umber

Paper tissue

1 Draw the scene.

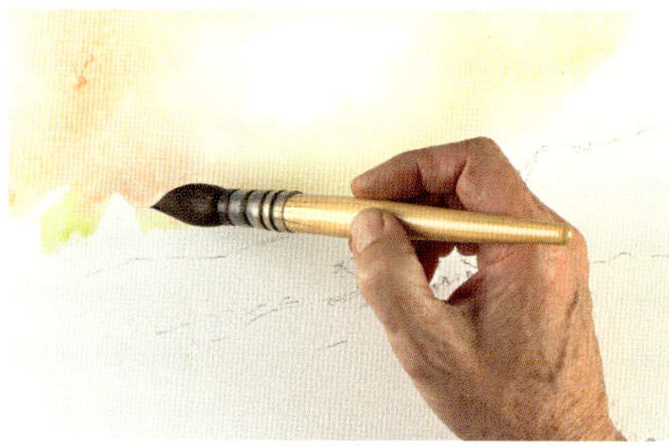

2 Use the squirrel mop to paint a touch of Naples yellow around a central white space in the sky, then while this is wet, drop in cadmium yellow pale, then cadmium red.

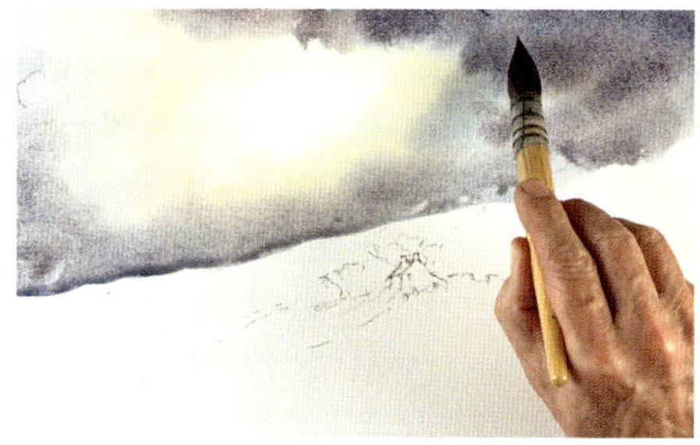

3 Drop in ultramarine around the edges of the sky, then a mix of ultramarine and cadmium red, and then a stronger mix of the same colours at the very edges of the sky.

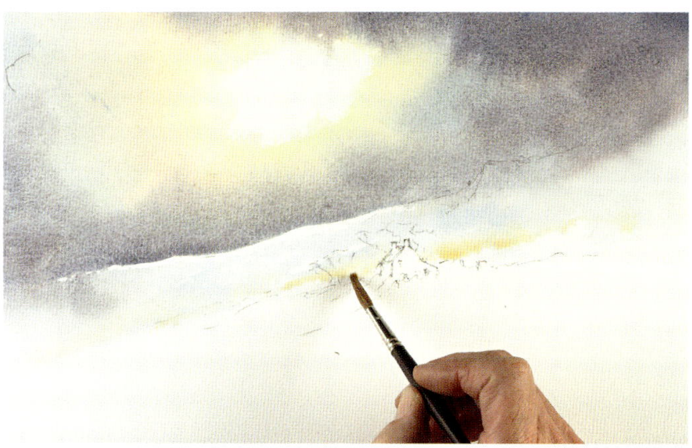

4 Change to the no. 7 round brush to soften the cloud colour into the dry white area. Then use a clean brush with water to bring the cloud colour down into the snowy area on the far left. Use a dry brush to paint a wash of cobalt blue across the distant snow, leaving highlights white, then add yellow ochre and allow to dry.

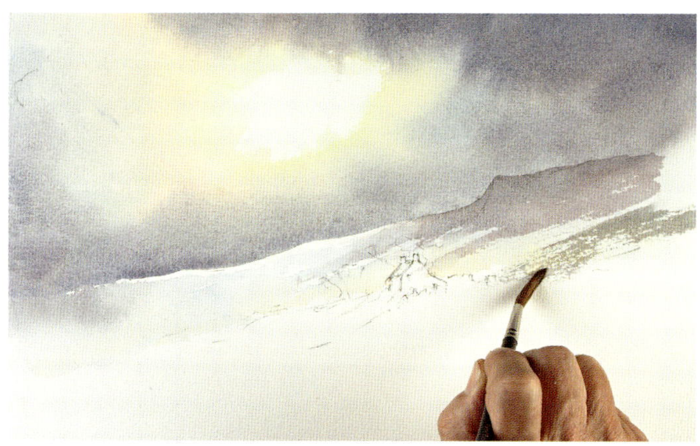

5 Paint the distant moorland with a mix of ultramarine and cadmium red, then use a mix of burnt umber and ultramarine with the dry-brush technique to paint the partly snow-covered area further forwards.

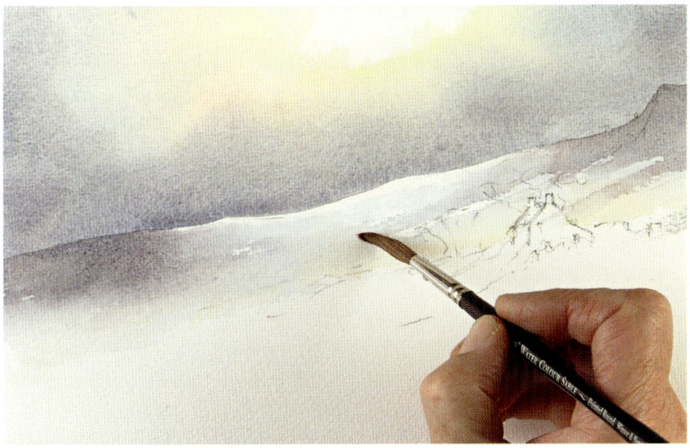

6 Wet the far left-hand side with clean water, then bring ultramarine and cadmium red across to emphasize the light in the centre. Feather the darker area off with clean water towards the centre.

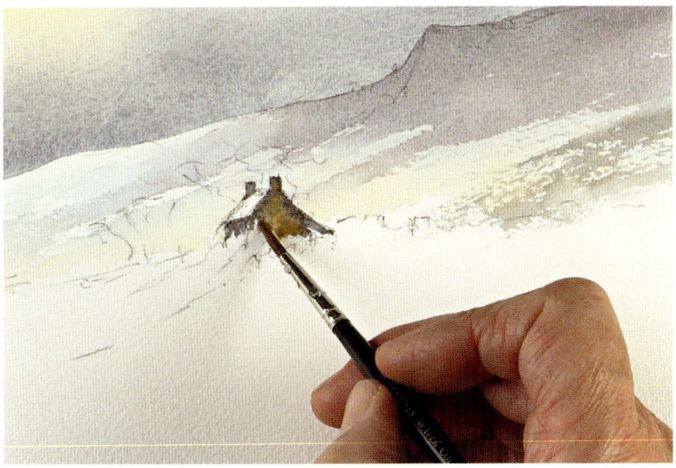

7 Use the no. 4 round with a weak mix of ultramarine and burnt umber to paint the building. Drop in yellow ochre lower down and this will spread upwards, creating texture. Allow to dry.

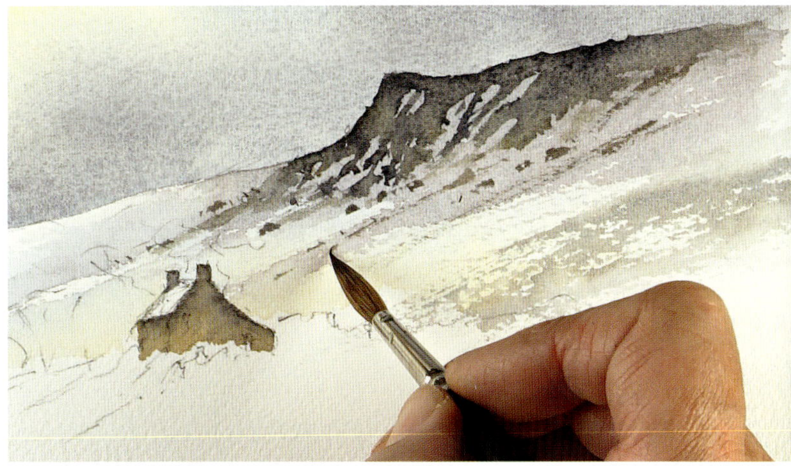

8 Use the point of the no. 7 brush and a mix of ultramarine and burnt umber to paint the strong darks on the crag, suggesting the structure. Drop in yellow ochre while still wet. Drag a mixture of ultramarine and cadmium red down from the crag to link it with the house and create texture.

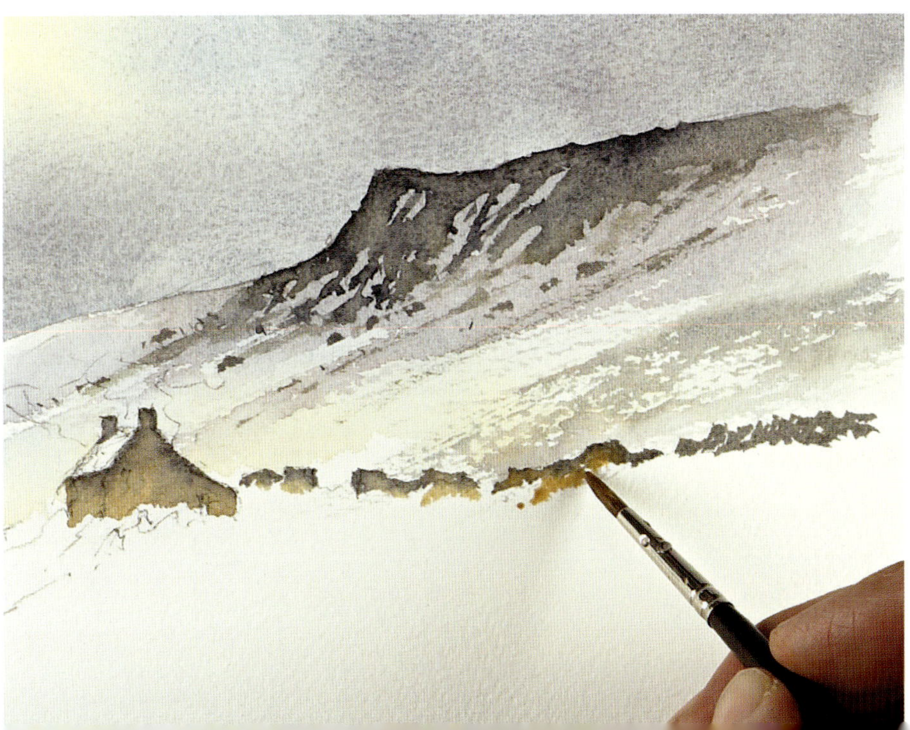

9 Use the point of the no. 7 brush and a mix of ultramarine and burnt umber to paint the intermittent dry-stone wall, then change to the no. 4 round and drop in yellow ochre beneath the wall, suggesting grasses.

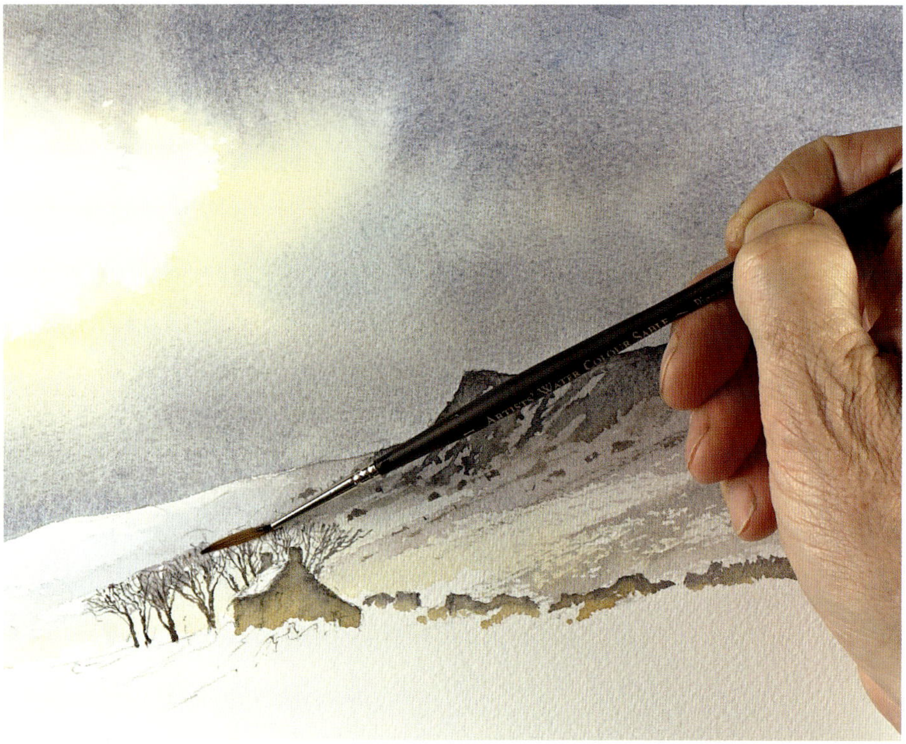

10 Paint the trees around the house with the no. 1 rigger and the ultramarine and burnt umber mix, working from the bottom upwards. Then pick up a mix of ultramarine and cadmium red and use the side of the brush to create the mass of twigwork, this time working downwards from the top of the trees.

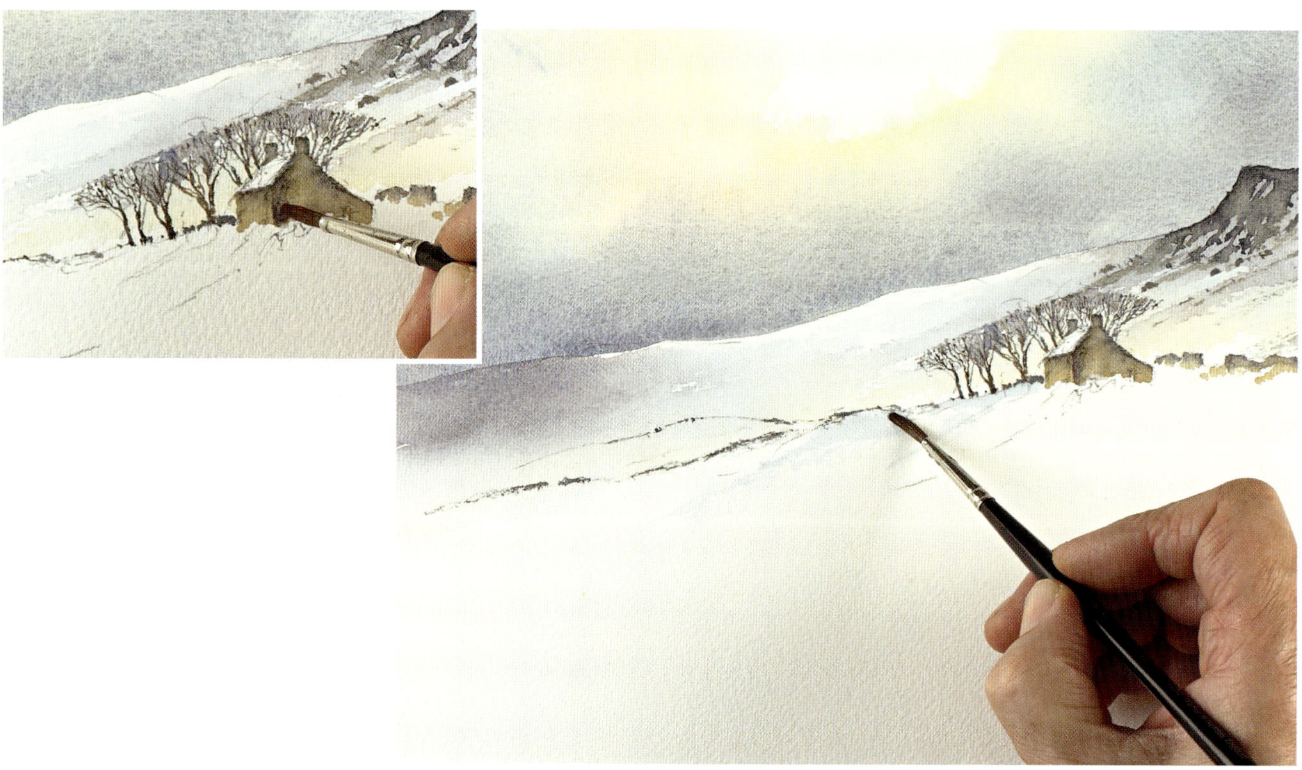

11 Use the same brush and mix to paint the continuation of the dry-stone wall, and another wall coming to meet it. Then use the no. 4 brush to paint the shadow on the house with ultramarine and cadmium red, to define the corner. Fade off the colour to the right with clean water. Paint snow shadows with a thin wash of cobalt blue, suggesting the undulating land.

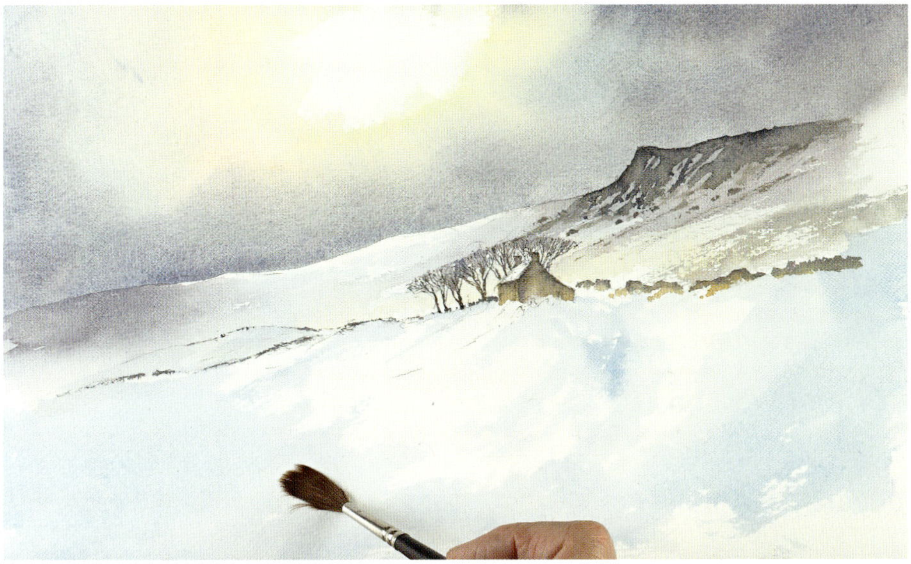

12 Create a lead-in to the scene by suggesting a snow-covered track leading to the house, using the same brush and wash. Add ultramarine to the wash and soften the track with clean water. Continue describing the snowy land, changing to the no. 7 brush and painting darker shadows at the edges of the scene, reflecting the dark-edged sky. Allow to dry.

13 Use the no. 1 round brush and a dark mix of ultramarine and burnt umber to paint the posts by the wall and to hint at stonework. Paint the details of the house in the same way, then drop in cadmium red for the door while the dark colour is wet. Paint cast shadows from the house with ultramarine and cadmium red.

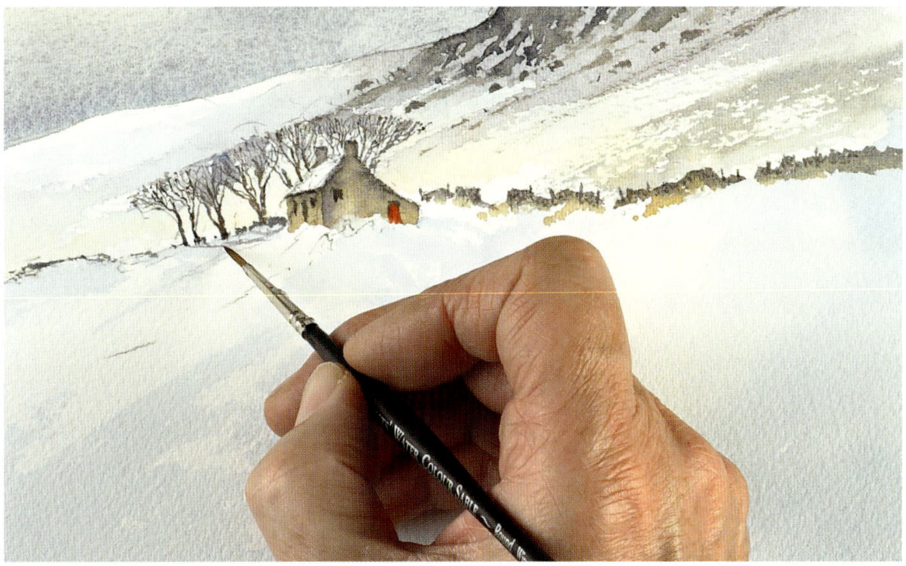

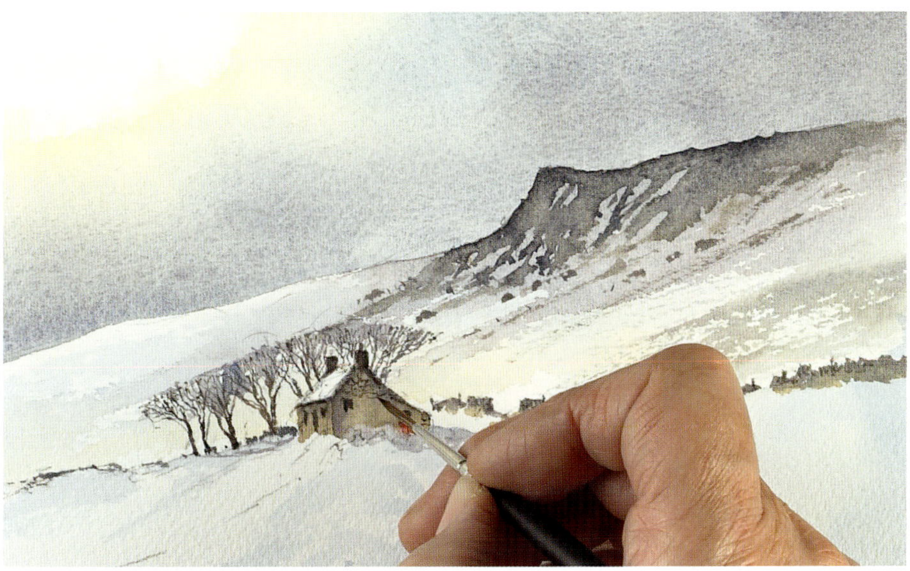

14 Strengthen the chimneys with ultramarine and burnt umber, then use the no. 1 rigger to suggest the stonework of the house.

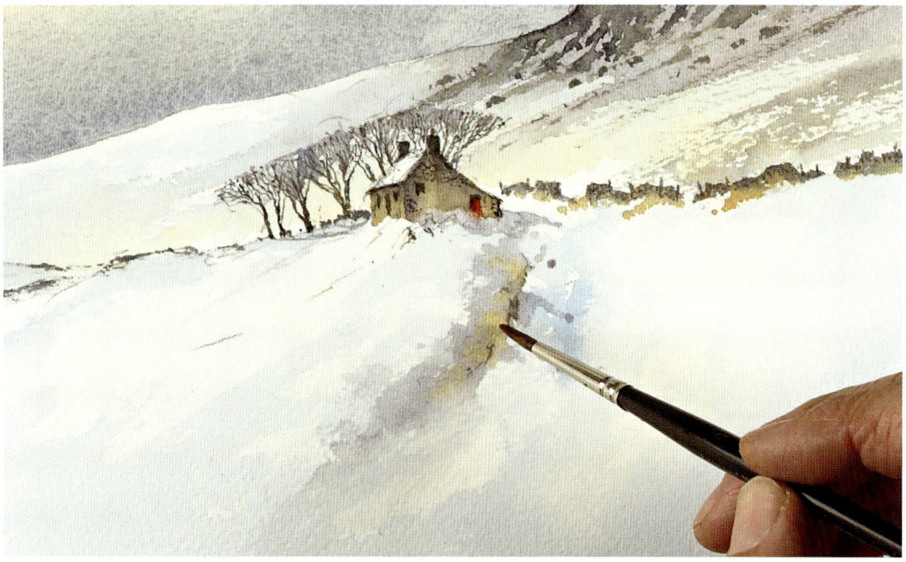

**15** Darken the shadow on the bank beside the track with the no. 4 brush and ultramarine and cadmium red. Use the side of the brush to create a ragged effect, then drop in a touch of yellow ochre.

**16** Define the snowy ridge of the roof by darkening the background behind it with ultramarine and cadmium red.

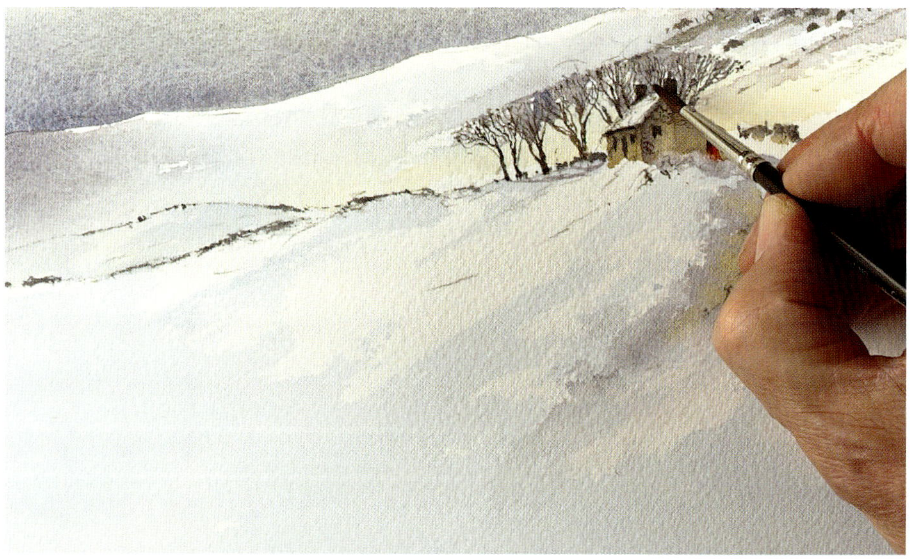

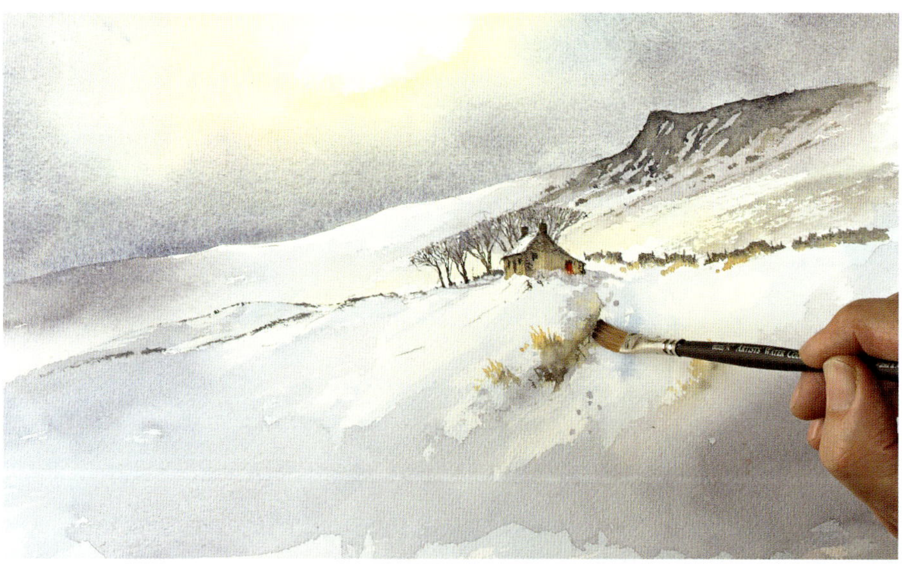

**17** Darken the left-hand and right-hand sides of the snow with ultramarine and cadmium red on the no. 7 brush to emphasize the lighter area of the focal point, then use the no. 1 rigger and yellow ochre to suggest grasses. Darken them in places with burnt umber and ultramarine. Use the edge of the 6mm (¼in) flat brush and clean water to soften the track.

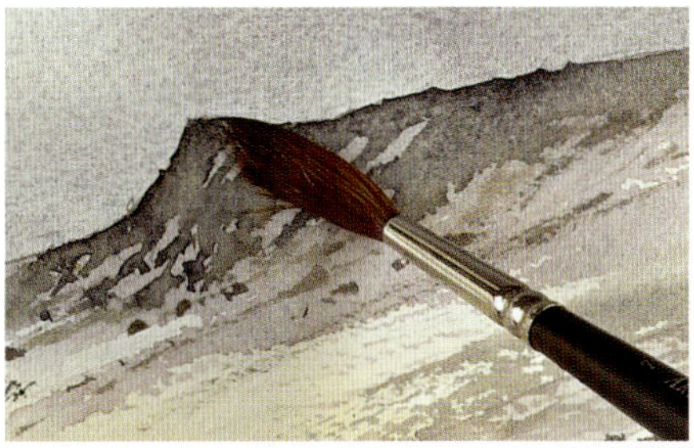

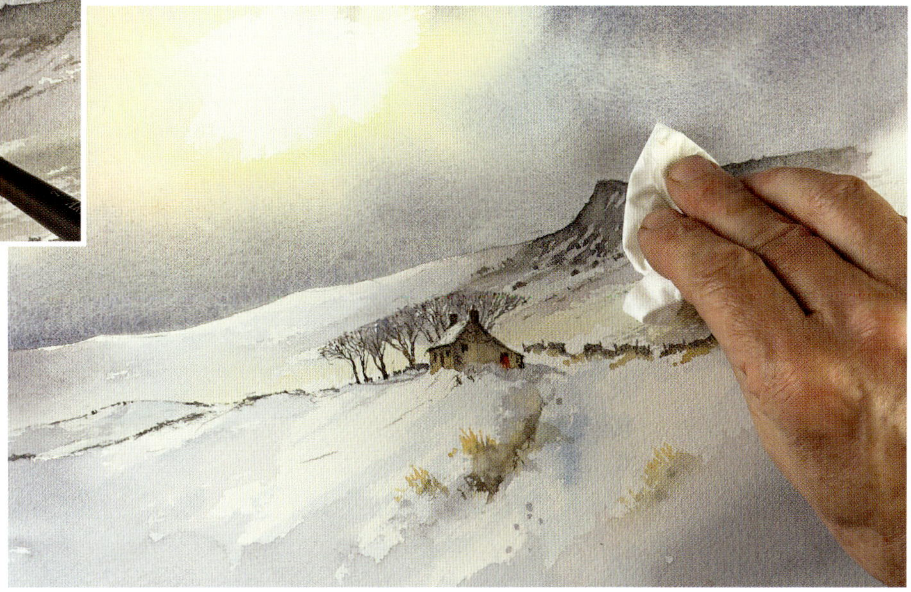

**18** Use the no. 7 brush to float clean water over the distant crag, then dab it with a paper tissue to soften it a little.

*The finished painting. At the final stage, I erased the pencil lines to keep the white clean.*

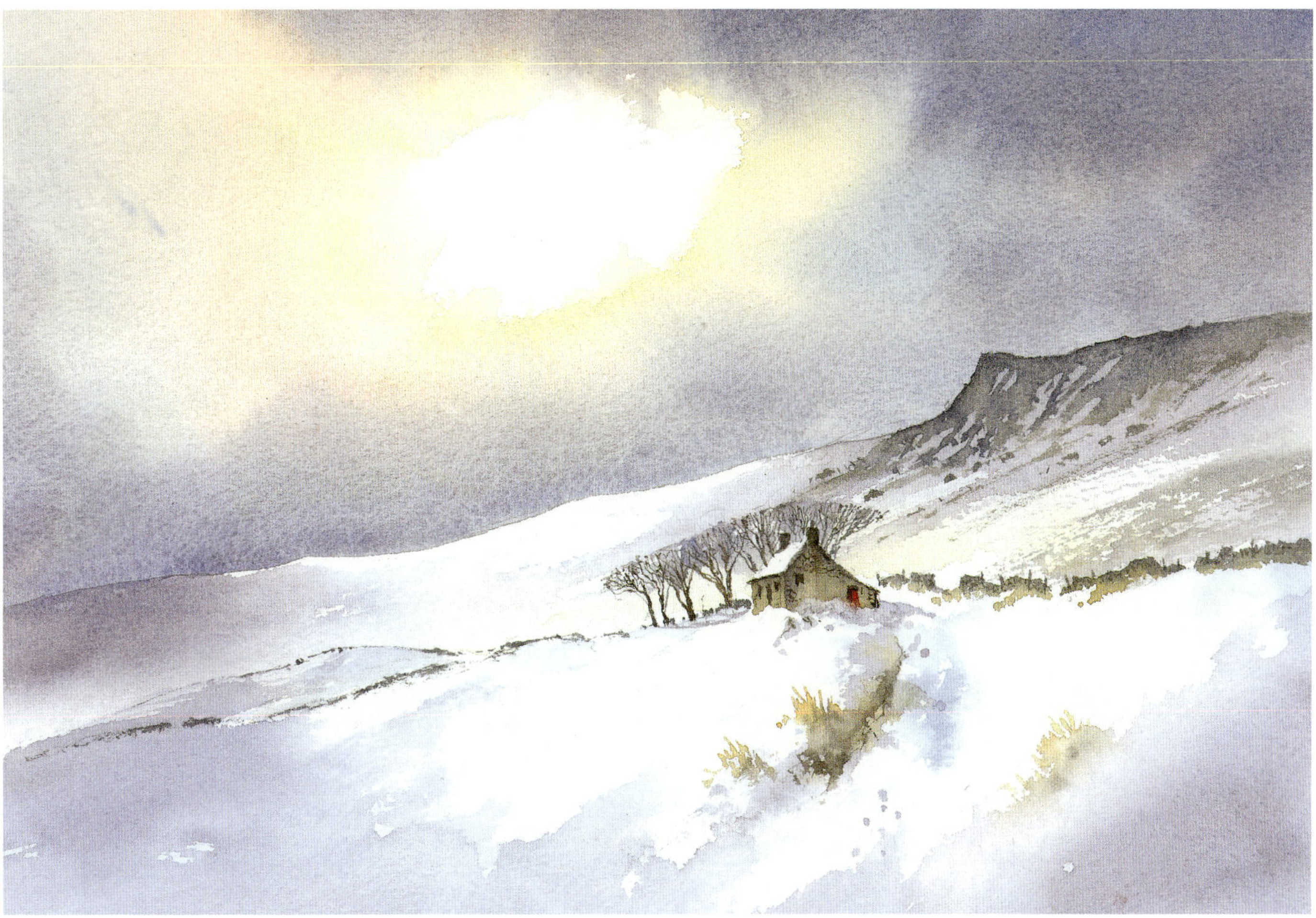

# Mountain scenes

Mountains can be painted with you nowhere near the subject. In this chapter we take a closer look at them, as well as paint them in the distance. Often, even climbing just a few hundred metres up a path will offer you a much improved perspective, and give you a more intimate relationship with rocks and crags. If you are painting a portrait of a particular mountain, often the optimum viewpoint is around halfway up the opposite mountain.

I cannot emphasize enough how important it is to move around to seek out the best angle to paint your subject. Ask yourself questions such as, 'Should I move further away from the shepherd's hut to give it a greater sense of isolation, or is it more important to show up the textures on the stone wall?'; 'Do I want to emphasize the savagery of this place by including only boulders and crags in the foreground, or would a softer approach with trees suit it better?'; 'Is this viewpoint dramatic enough or should I move closer to the abyss to highlight the sublime nature of the place?' Whatever your choice, make sure you at least photograph each of the possibilities so that you have a record of them all.

BEN CHALLIUM, SCOTLAND

*This watercolour sketch, done on the spot, shows a classic mountain composition viewed from the valley, with the peak in the distance and a stream leading into the composition. Part of the mountain is highlighted by sunshine on a ridge that leads upwards towards the top left, then turns back towards the summit. A foreground boulder adds interest here, but slightly altering the tree might help improve matters. If it was extended a little higher, it would break up the long diagonals coming down from the middle right-hand side. Nearly all diagonal slopes in the sketch meet at the foot of the mountain and this would be an excellent place to position a strong centre of interest, such as a small tree or crag, strengthened with tone and colour to make it stand out. A figure or a deer could also work. I would also improve the stream, possibly by including a deep pool with reflections.*

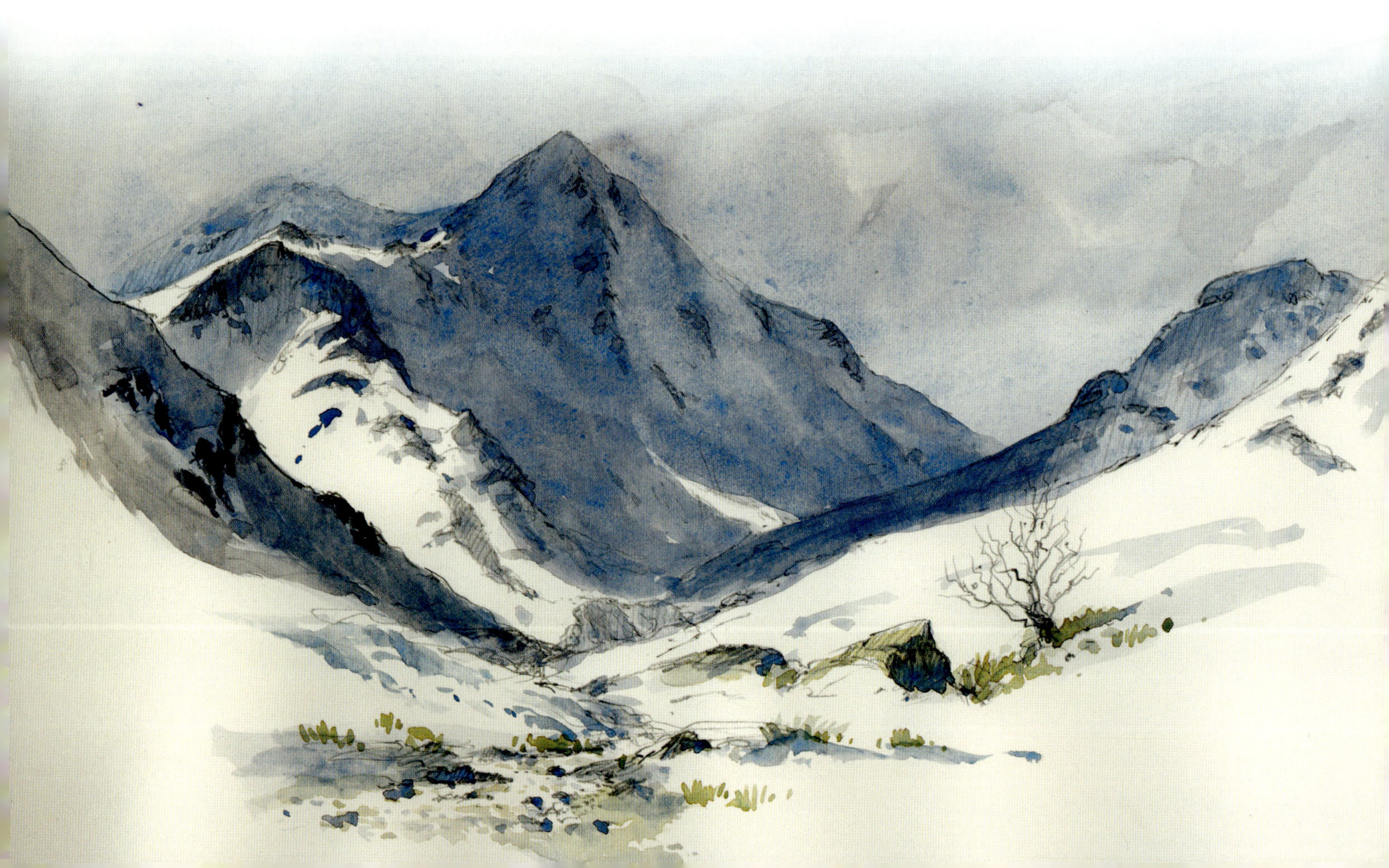

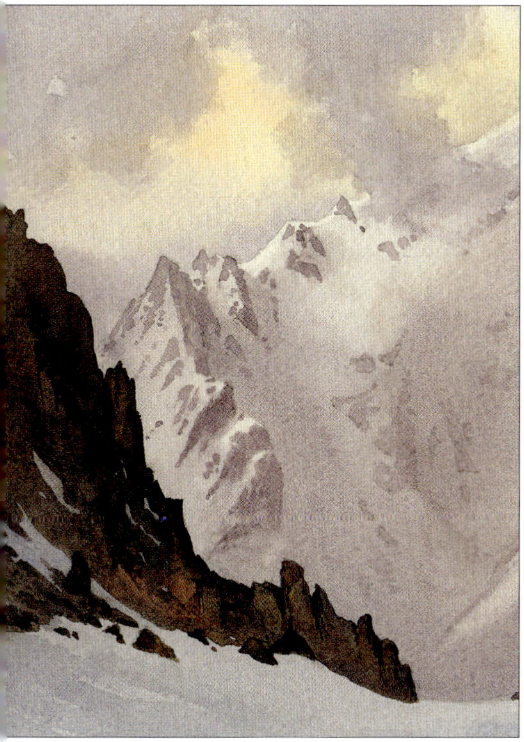

# MOUNTAIN PERSPECTIVE

Nowhere is the sense of space and distance more obvious than in the high mountains, as demonstrated in the scene shown below.

AERIAL PERSPECTIVE

*In this scene the distant crags and ridge appear to be much further away because of the lighter tones and lack of strong detail compared with the foreground crags. I also dropped a splash of orange into the lower rocks while they were wet. Warm colours like orange help to suggest that the feature is closer to the viewer.*

### Suggesting depth

- Warm colours (red, orange and so on) in the foreground
- Cool colours (blues, greys, greens) in the distance
- Stronger, darker tones close to the viewer
- Lighter tones further away
- Stronger detail in the foreground
- Hardly any detail in the distance
- Larger objects (e.g., trees, clouds, people) closer to the viewer
- Roads, tracks, streams and walls narrowing as they recede.

## High level perspective and composition

In normal landscape painting, the height of the viewpoint often does not matter, but in the mountains it can be critical, as seen here. Two of these watercolours of the Cuillin Ridge on Skye, one of the Western Isles of Scotland, show poor composition which detracts from the result in numerous ways.

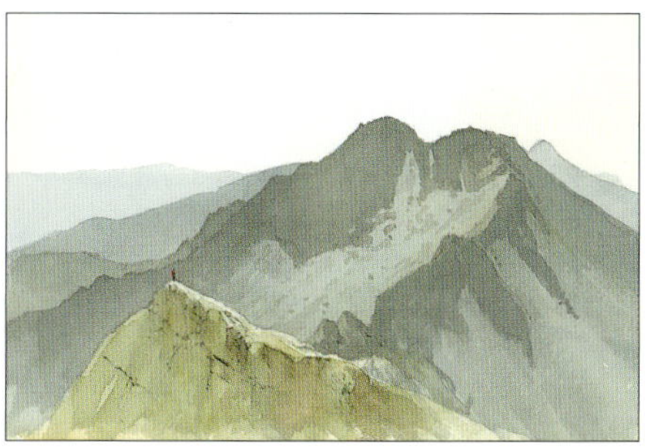

CUILLIN RIDGE 1

*At high level, the height that the artist works from can be critical, as well as the angle. In this first view of the mountain Sgurr Thormaid, the focal point is too far to the left and quite low in the picture: not the ideal composition.*

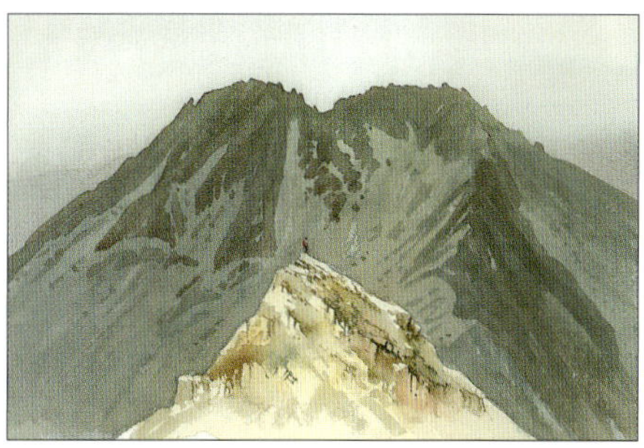

CUILLIN RIDGE 2

*Here I have moved further left along the ridge to bring the peak forming the focal point into the centre, but as well as being too central the absolute peak is directly below the notch in the distant twin summits. Coincidences like this should be avoided if possible. Although my lower viewpoint has increased the height of Sgurr Thormaid, the composition still needs adjustment.*

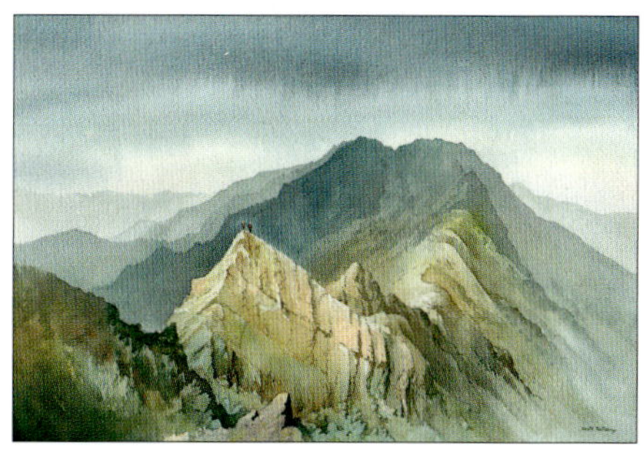

CUILLIN RIDGE 3

*30.5 x 40.5cm (12 x 16in)*

*This is my final composition, which I feel works best. It shows the handsome line of the main Cuillin Ridge dipping and curving, with Sgurr Thormaid standing out warm-coloured against a cooler, duller background. Showing more of the peak has added to the drama, and I felt it was wise to give the climber a companion. Although lower than nearby peaks, Thormaid has a shape and ruggedness that make it a fine centre of interest, but of course all this would be to little avail if it were not for the strong light on the peak.*

# RENDERING MOUNTAIN SLOPES

The sides of mountains are so varied, covered in massed conifers in lower parts, cliffs, crags and boulder fields, scree, mixed bushes and scrub, gullies, gorges, ridges and of course snow slopes. We have covered examples of these elsewhere, but here I want to tackle that bane of all mountain painters: the bald, uninteresting rounded mountainside, and turn it into something more appealing.

**DETAIL OF LOCH PITYOULISH PAINTING (SHOWN OPPOSITE)**

*The numbering indicates the order of working.*

1. A weak wash of French ultramarine and cadmium red over the whole mountainside, visible at this point

2. This more level area catches the light, so I dropped some weak aureolin into the French ultramarine/cadmium red wash while it was still wet

6. Strongest tones applied again with French ultramarine and burnt umber

5. Weaker details as the features recede

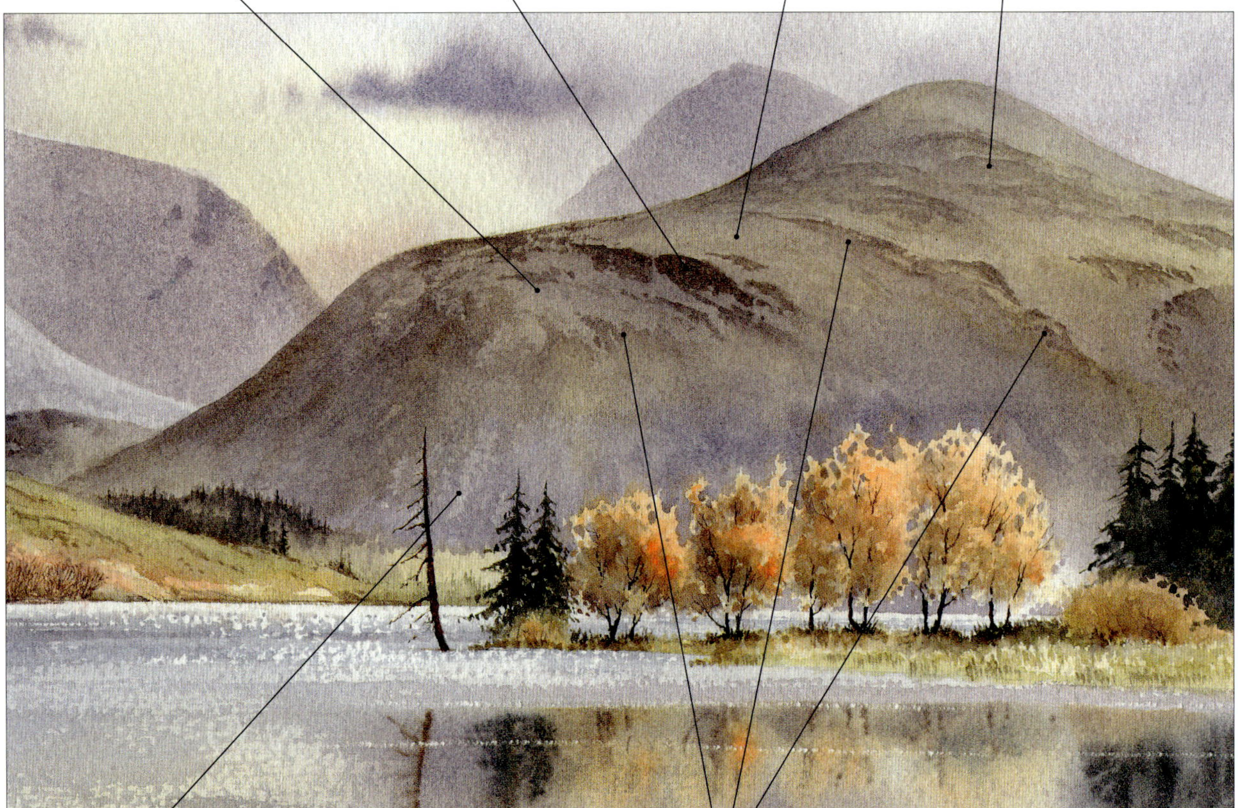

4. At this point I got rid of any excess water on the brush and used almost vertical strokes to create the dry-brush effect

3. Medium-toned applications of French ultramarine plus burnt umber to suggest rocks running down towards the trees, without any detail. This was done on a dry surface

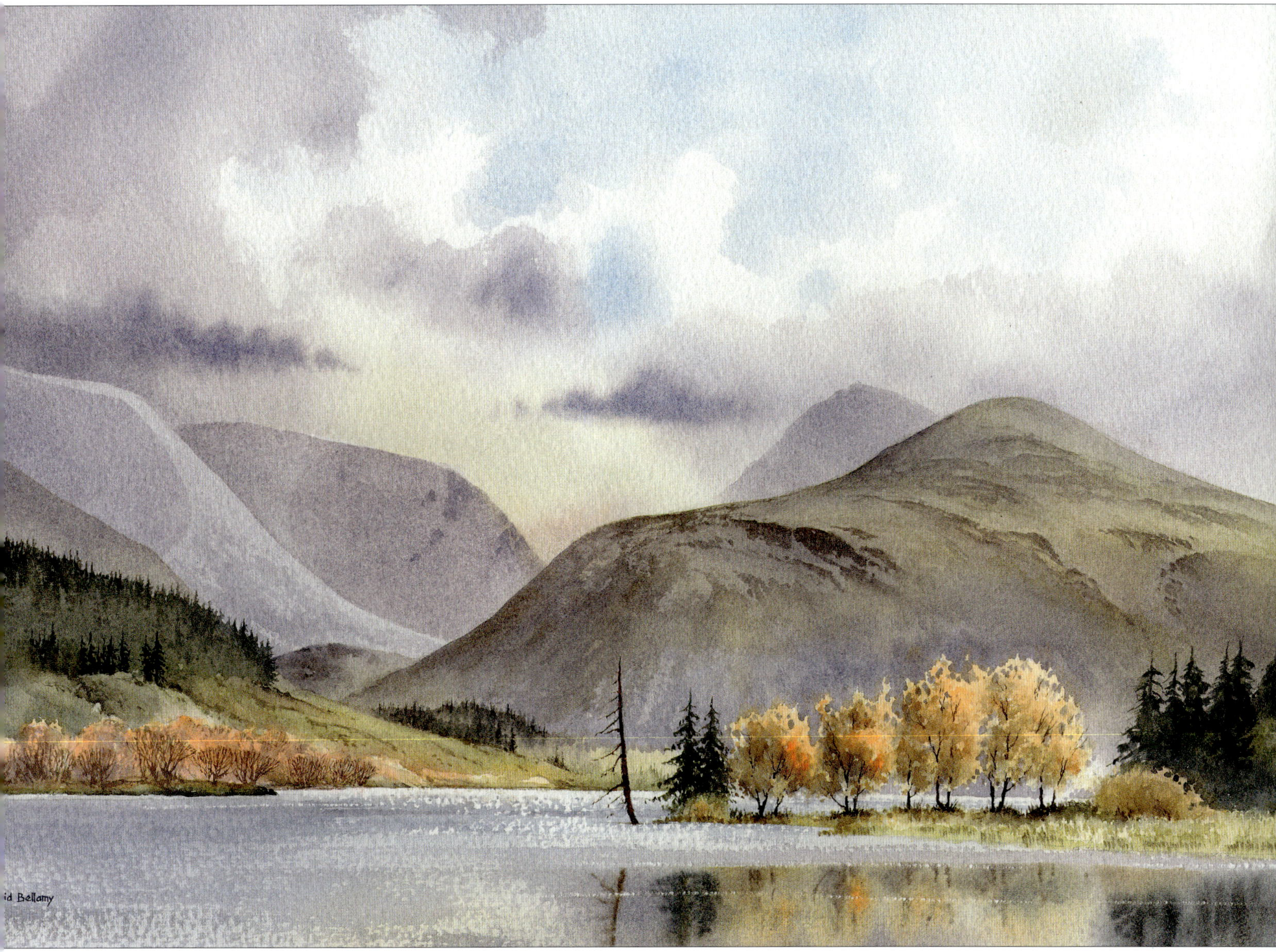


**LOCH PITYOULISH**
*28 x 40.5cm (11 x 16in)*

*In this view of Loch Pityoulish in the Cairngorms in Scotland, the large bulk of the hillside rising directly on the far side of the loch is typical of this range of mountains – rounded and lacking in dramatic outlines. Creating interesting textures on such slopes is important, but should not be overdone as this passage needs to support the focal point – the trees – rather than compete.*

*The matter was complicated by the birch trees being so much lighter than the background. I began by painting the autumn colours in cadmium orange with some yellow ochre. When this was dry, I brought a mixture of French ultramarine and cadmium red down over the hillside, stopping at the tops of the trees, defining their ragged edges. While the wash was wet, I dropped a hint of aureolin into the upper half and allowed it to dry. Then, with varying strengths of French ultramarine and burnt umber, I painted the rock masses, making them less intense higher up where the mountain receded into the distance. The same mixture was then brought down over the lower slopes, mainly with downward strokes of the brush to suggest the slope direction. This is most evident where I have allowed the brush to become thirsty, creating a dry-brush effect behind the dead pine in the centre. The lower area of the hillside needed to be fairly devoid of detail to avoid cluttering up the immediate background to the trees.*

*I laid the dry-brush application over the further part of the water and softened the bottom band with a wet brush so that there would be a lack of definition between the sparkling wind-rippled water and the smoother, sheltered surface. The latter was brushed in with a fluid wash of French ultramarine and cadmium red, and the reflected colour was dropped in wet into wet, more subdued than the actual trees. Once this wash had dried, I scratched over the area with a scalpel using horizontal strokes.*

# USING FIGURES TO CREATE A SENSE OF SCALE

Figures can intrude in a painting, especially if not handled sensitively, and it is a good idea to ask yourself why you wish to include them, and where they will have most effect. If shown in the immediate foreground they become the main subject of the painting, with the mountain simply as a backdrop. Further back they give a much better sense of scale to the mountain. Two or three figures is usually enough – the only time I have painted a large group is when depicting a mountain rescue incident or army patrol. Are your figures to be shepherds, farmers, walkers, climbers, hunters or what? All these people dress for their particular pursuit and colour has an important influence on how they are seen.

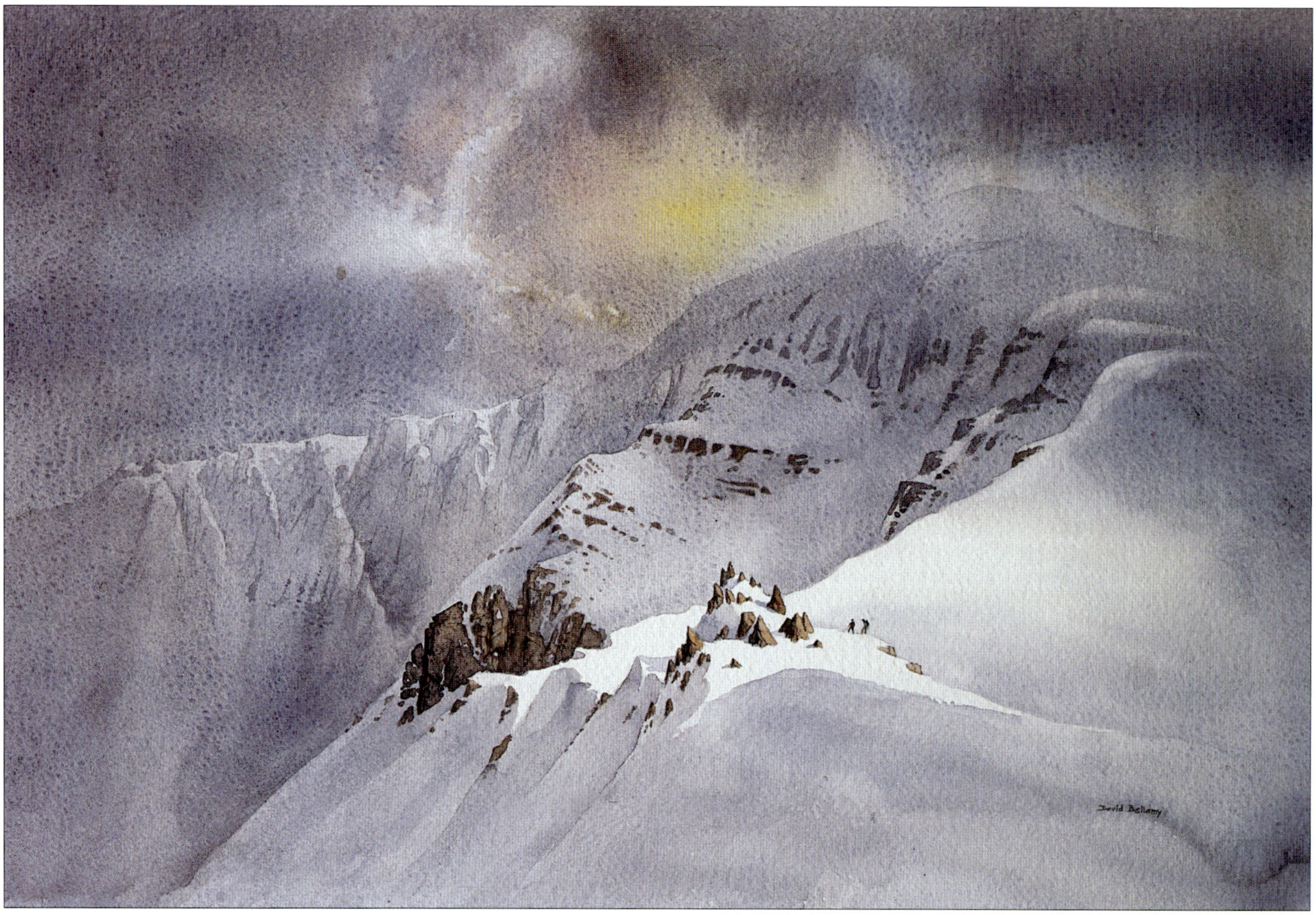

**MOUNTAIN VIEW WITH FIGURES**
*28 x 46cm (11 x 18in)*

*This painting shows the north face of Carnedd Dafydd, in Snowdonia, Wales. Without the tiny figures, this composition would lose its sense of scale, as well as the centre of interest. There is nothing else in this painting to give any idea of the size of the mountain – no trees, no houses, no cars, nothing that will give us a clue. By changing the size of figures in a mountain painting, you can effectively suggest a larger or smaller peak, but you need to place them in the middle distance to give a reasonably true sense of height.*

# PAINTING SNOW AND ICE

Snow can graphically bring out the stark delineations of rocks and crags, but depending on the light, can lose many less obvious features. Photographs of snow scenes can be extremely deceptive in flat lighting, when all subtle tones are lost. Sunshine on snow slopes tends to be harsh, so I wear neutral-tinted sunglasses. If your eyes are not comfortable with the light, it drastically affects your tonal judgement.

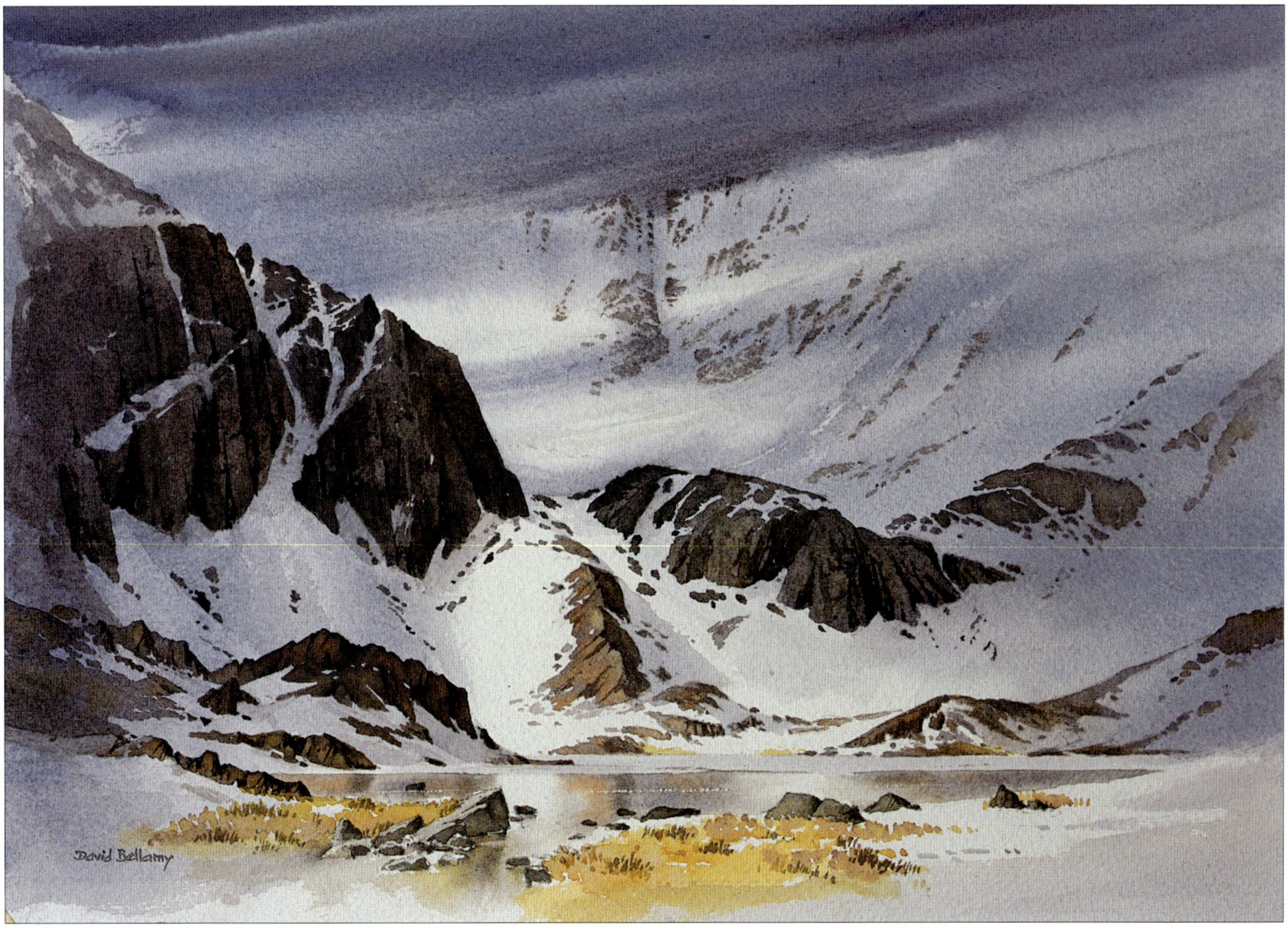


THE WELL OF THE MOON
*23 x 30.5cm (9 x 12in)*

*One of the dangers in painting snow-covered mountains is in seeing only black and white. This is especially true on gloomy days, without sunlight to bring colours to life. Look hard for colours in rock. In this painting of Ffynnon Lloer – The Well of the Moon – in North Wales, the important rocks have had cadmium red dropped into their basic colour while still wet, warming them up considerably. Light red and yellow ochre are two other colours that are excellent for this purpose. The shadows are important in suggesting the snow slopes and providing relief from the contrast of white snow and dark rock. They were achieved with French ultramarine and cadmium red.*

*Note how snow lies in cracks and gullies and shows up the rocks and crags. The effect of strong winds blowing cloud streamers across the upper reaches has been achieved with horizontal brush strokes with a mop brush, and completed before the closer cliffs and crags were painted.*

*The ice on the tarn was achieved by the wet into wet technique. Firstly I floated clear water over the area, then after allowing it to begin drying, I dropped in the vague reflections with appropriate colours. To achieve the feeling of ice, avoid pin-sharp reflections and use downward strokes of the brush into a damp surface. If any colour drifts too far across, simply pull it out with a damp, clean brush.*

# GLACIERS

Ice-falls on glaciers provide dramatic scenes, and it is in the crevasses and breaches in the ice that you will find the most vivid and exciting blues, greens, yellows and so on. As the ice formations are constantly changing, you are not bound to copy each shape faithfully, so there is considerable opportunity to arrange your composition to suit your needs.

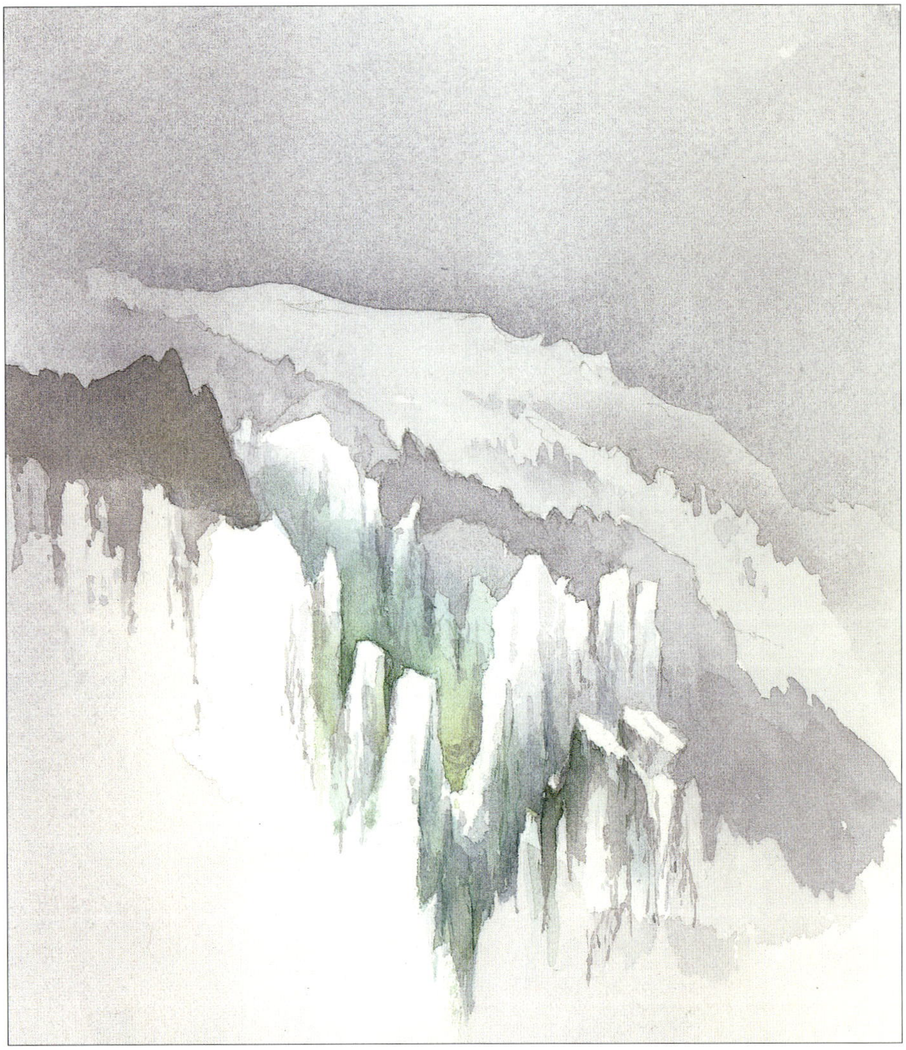

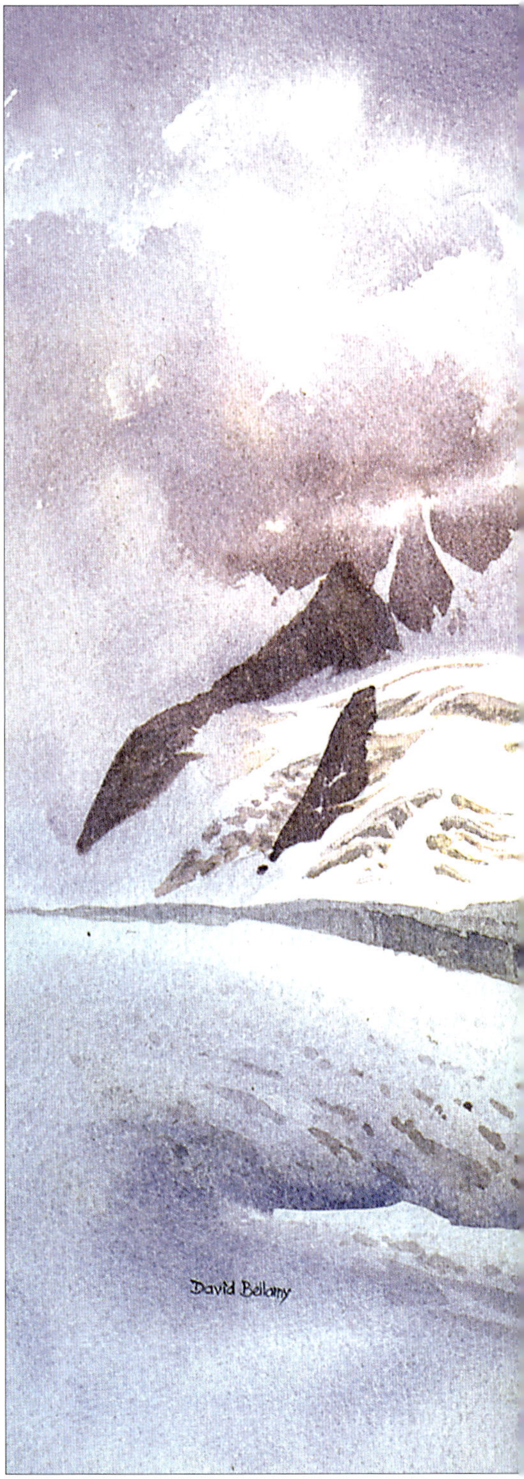


**GLACIER STUDY**

*This small colour study of the edge of the Russells Glacier in Greenland illustrates the varied tones and colours that can be seen in glaciers. The amount and strength of colour in ice can often be astonishing and it is worth moving around to see where it is most intense. These strong colours work well in supporting a focal point, and while a figure would be excellent to suggest scale, only a madman would climb among this array of unstable ice towers.*

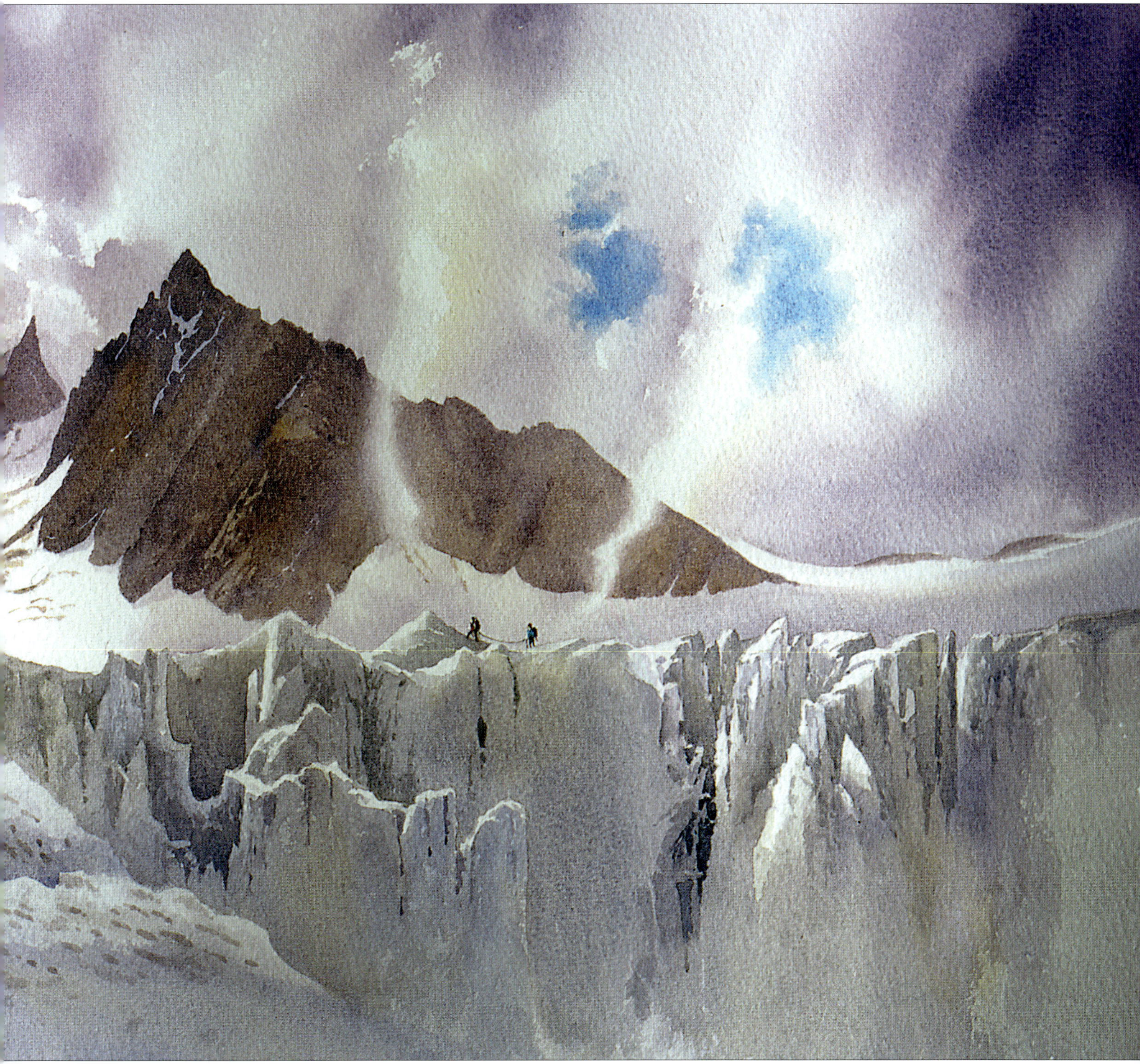

BEC ROUGE AND THE GLACIER DU TOUR

*28 x 46cm (11 x 18in)*

*So intense was the sunlight on snow and ice in this scene from the French Alps, that I could not do without my glacier goggles – they are a neutral colour to avoid a colour cast which can seriously affect the finished result. Although I didn't put a lot of colour into the ice here, I did lay some cadmium yellow pale into the shadow areas of the crevasse walls in places. The tops of the ridges and seracs (ice columns) have been left as white paper. On the gentler slopes on the left are a series of hollows in the hard ice, although they look like footprints. I laid these on before slightly subduing them with a shadow overlaid with a wash of French ultramarine and cadmium red. The ice forms have been considerably simplified, especially in the immediate foreground, and the figures give some idea of the size of the chasm.*

# MOUNTAINS FROM THE VALLEY

In this scene the mountain forms a distant backdrop, so it is important to avoid too much detail there. You will learn to render a series of ridges cloaked in massed conifers, together with the associated reflections in the lake.

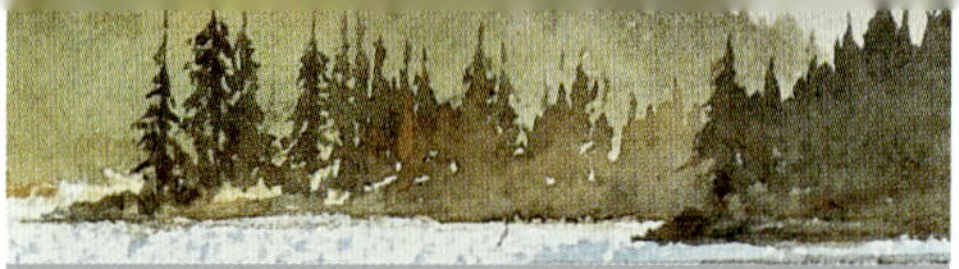

**MATERIALS USED**

Saunders Waterford 640gsm (300lb) Not watercolour paper

Brushes: squirrel mop, 13mm (½in) flat, no. 7 round, 6mm (¼in) flat, no. 4, no. 10 and no. 8 round, no. 1 rigger and no. 1 round

Colours: cobalt blue, permanent alizarin crimson, cadmium red, yellow ochre, raw umber, new gamboge, cadmium orange, burnt umber

Paper tissue

Sponge

Scalpel

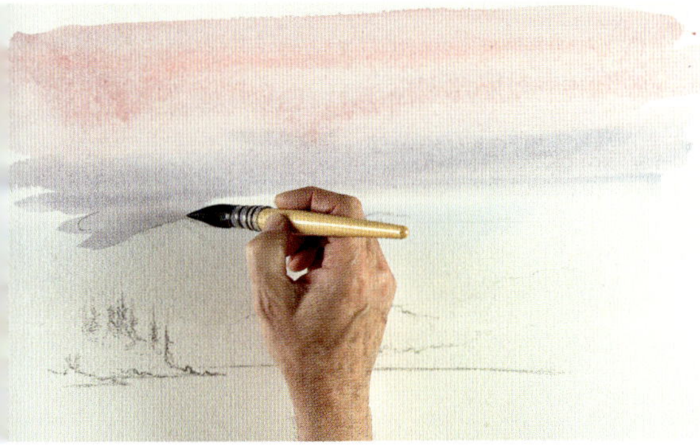

1 Draw the scene. Wet the sky and mountains with a squirrel mop and clean water and paint a pale wash of cobalt blue over the mountains. Allow to dry. Sweep a wash of alizarin crimson across the sky in horizontal strokes. Drop in a mix of cobalt blue and alizarin crimson at the bottom, working round the peaks to highlight the snow.

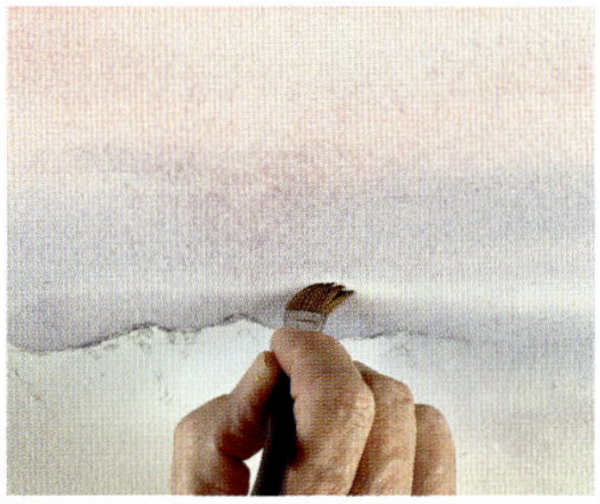

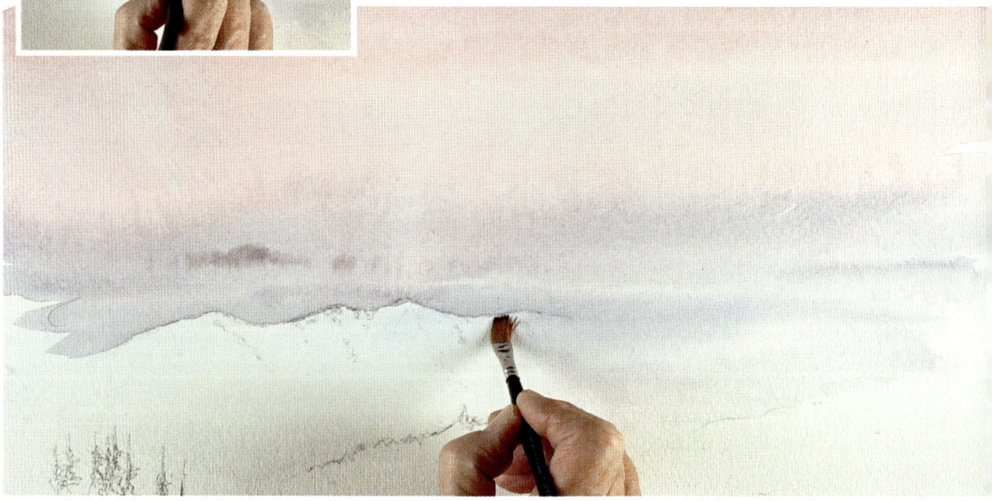

2 While this is wet, lift out some slivers of light with the 13mm (½in) flat brush, wetted and blotted on a paper tissue. Use the no. 7 brush and a mix of cadmium red and cobalt blue to drop in clouds wet into wet. Allow to dry. Use the 6mm (¼in) flat brush and clean water to soften the edge of the mountain to fade it into the cloud.

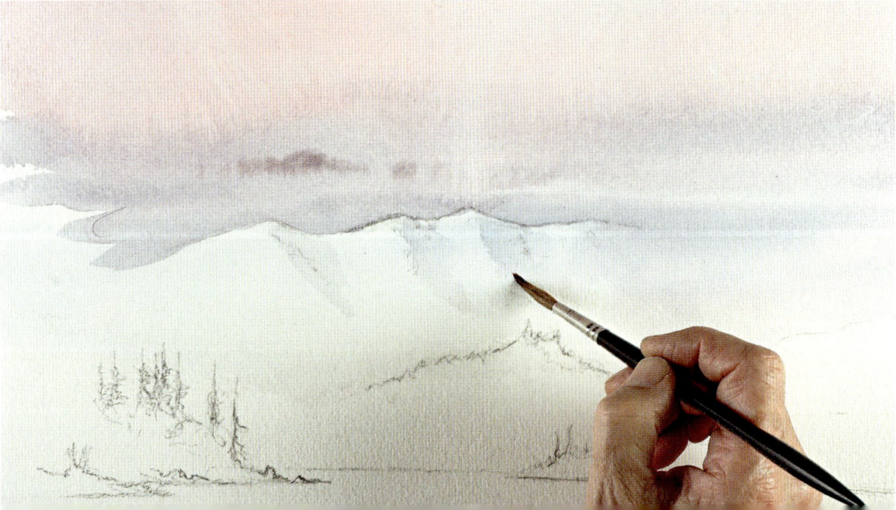

3 Create undulations in the distant peaks to highlight ridges running down the mountain, using the no. 7 brush and a weak wash of cobalt blue with a touch of alizarin crimson.

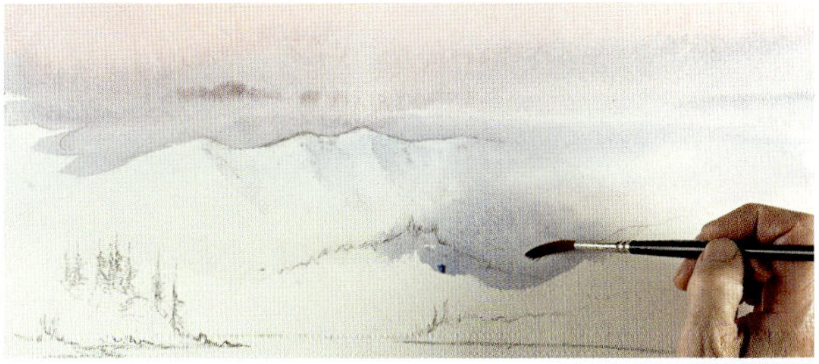

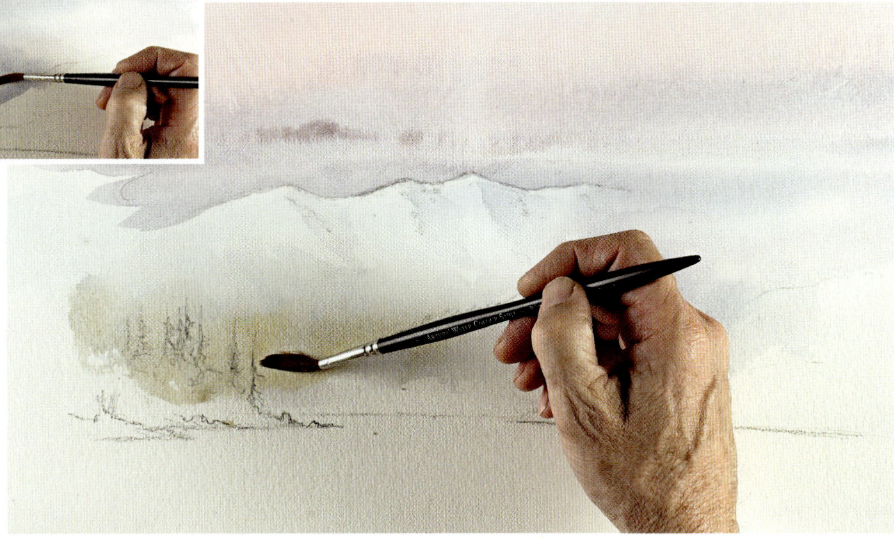

4 Run water over the right-hand side of the middle distance and drop in a stronger mix of cobalt blue and alizarin crimson. Soften the edges with clean water. Paint shadow on the left-hand side in the same way, then drop in yellow ochre as the mountain reaches the ground. Allow to dry.

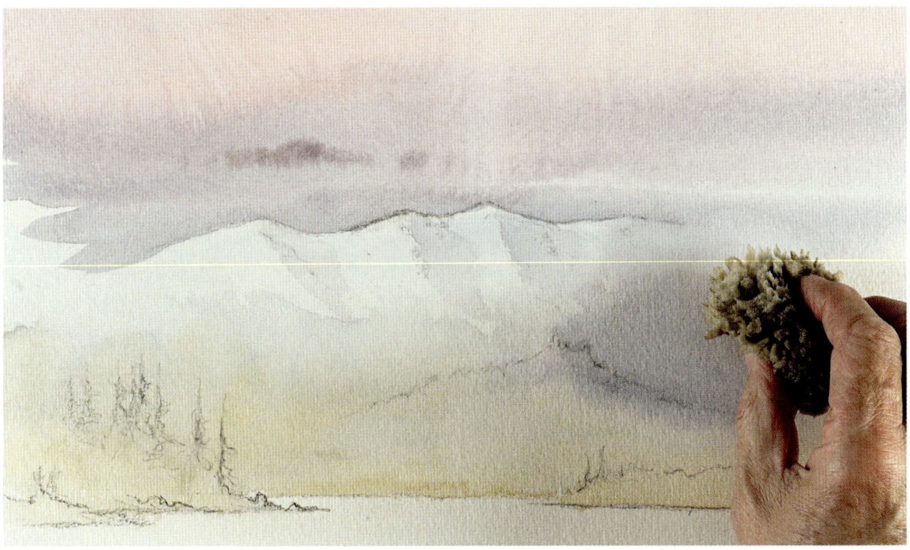

5 Get rid of any unwanted hard edges that have formed using a sponge and clean water to soften them. Allow to dry.

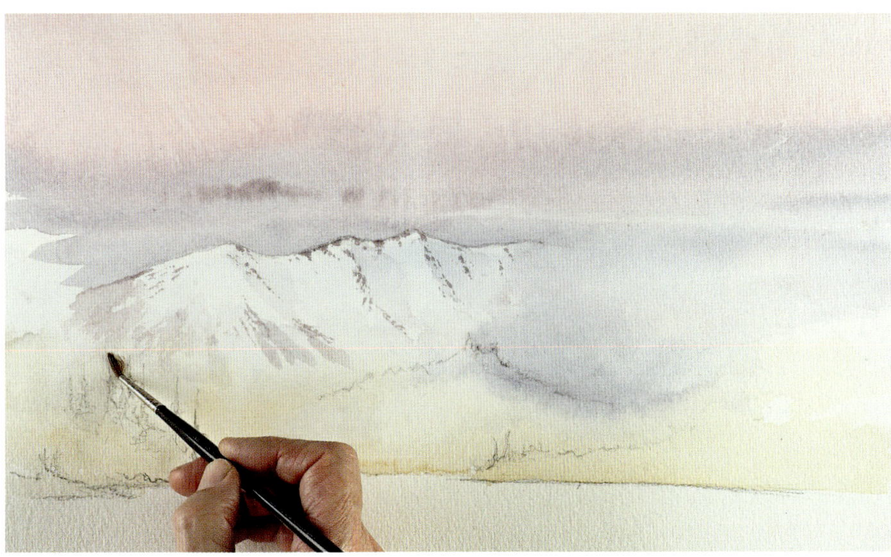

6 Use the no. 4 brush and a mix of cadmium red and cobalt blue to paint the details of crags sticking out of the snow on the mountain tops. Use a weaker mix and the brush on its side to create texture on the lower slopes.

7 Dab in yellow ochre wet into wet. Wait until this is just damp, and paint in gullies with raw umber, cobalt blue and alizarin crimson. Here we are creating the illusion that the lower part of the mountain is much nearer to us. Soften off at the bottom with clean water.

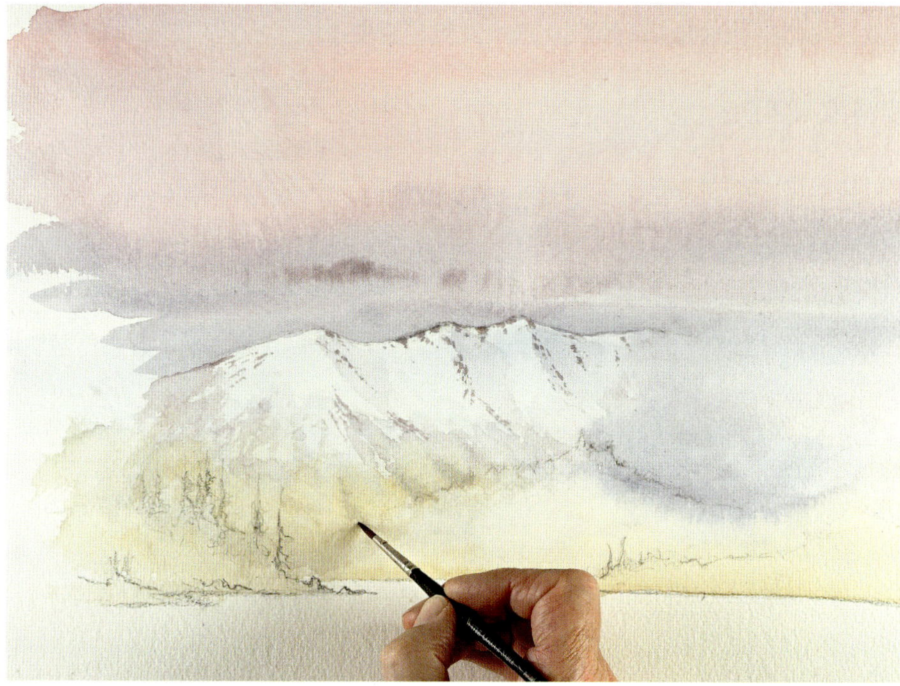

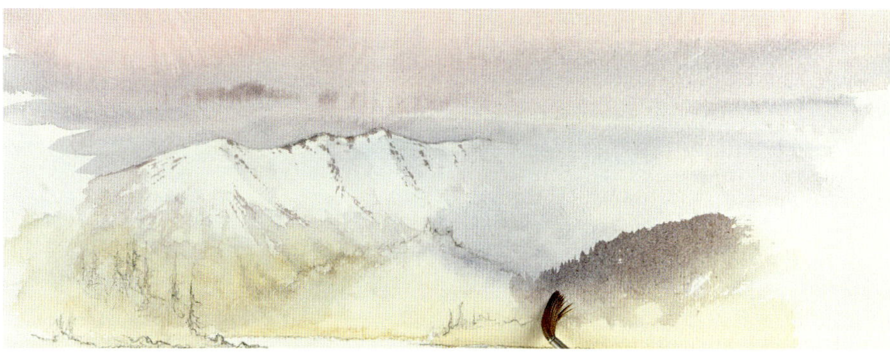

8 Create another ridge in the distance with a mix of cobalt blue and cadmium red, using the shape of the brush to suggest treetops. Soften at the bottom with clean water and allow to dry.

9 Use a no. 7 brush with a good point and a mix of cobalt blue and new gamboge to create massed conifers in the middle distance. Darken with raw umber in places and continue, then drop in cadmium orange to break the monotony and to suggest larches. Paint round the crag.

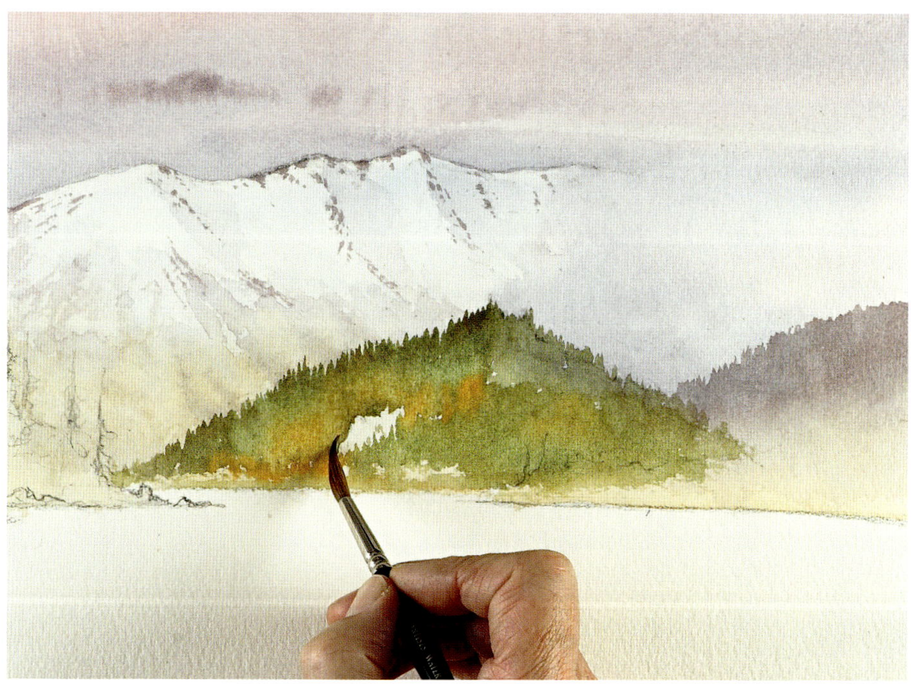

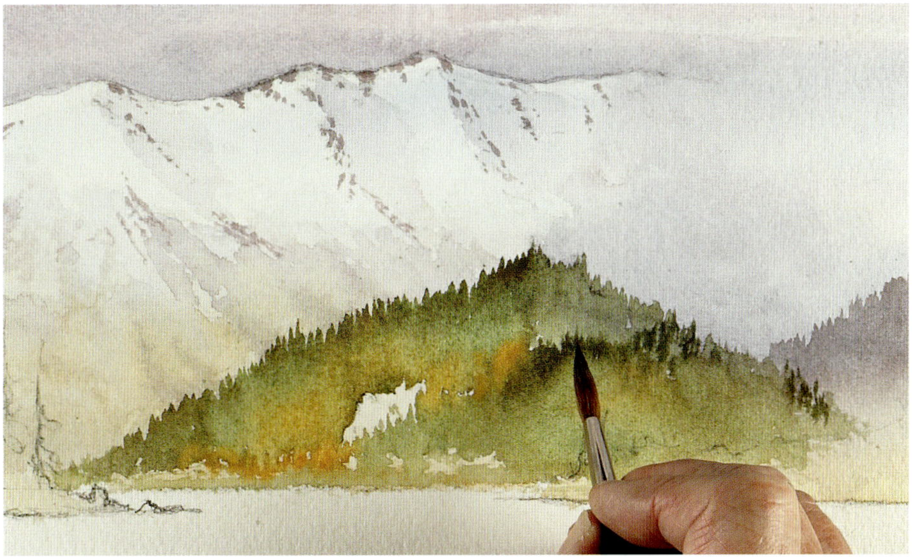

10 Mix cobalt blue and raw umber and paint a darker ridge of conifers.

11 Paint the fracture lines in the crag with the point of the brush and a mix of burnt umber and cobalt blue. Drop in more cadmium orange. Add shade to the lower part of the crag with the no. 4 brush and a mix of cobalt blue and burnt umber. Allow to dry.

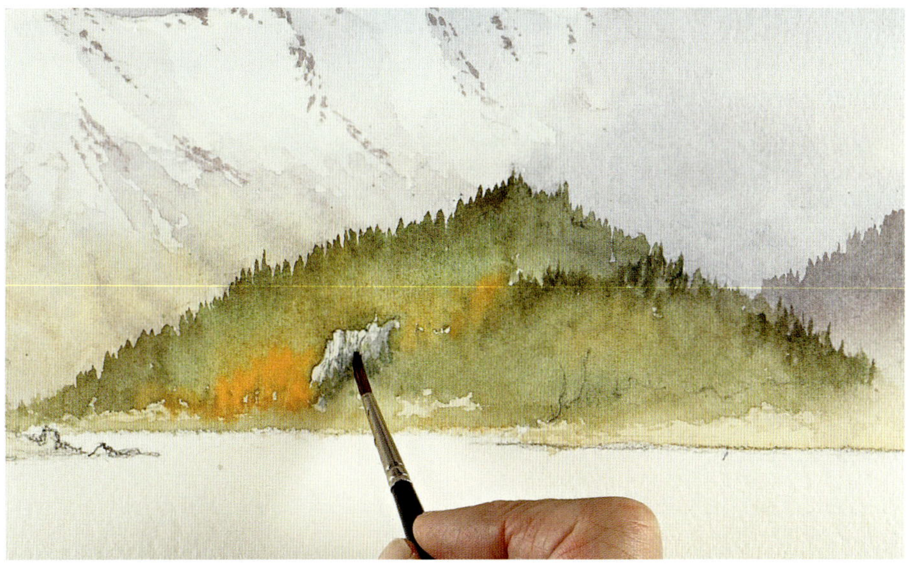

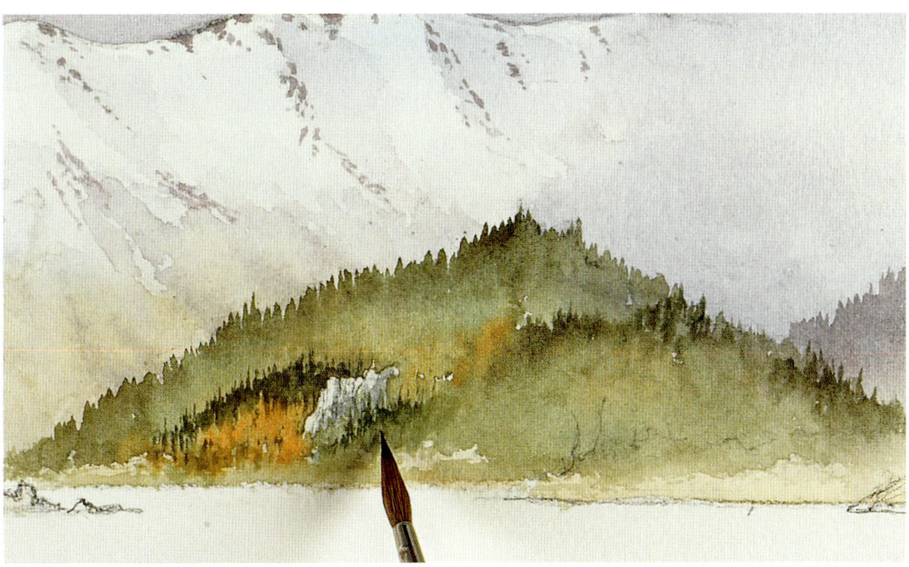

12 Make the larches stand out by painting a dark mix of cobalt blue and raw umber behind them, then paint more dark trees beneath the crag, and soften them in with clean water.

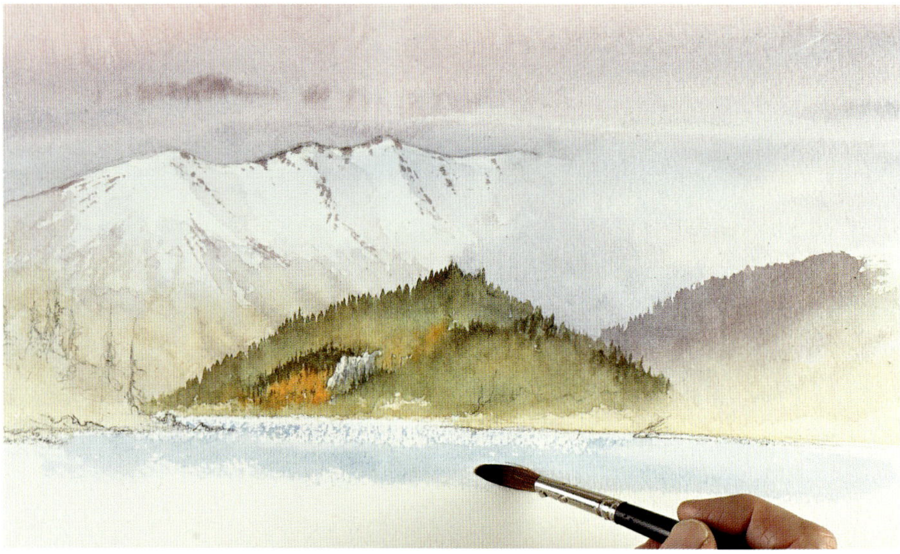

13 Use the no. 10 brush and the dry-brush technique to paint cobalt blue over the water by the far shore. Soften this at the bottom to create a soft transition between the ruffled and the smooth water.

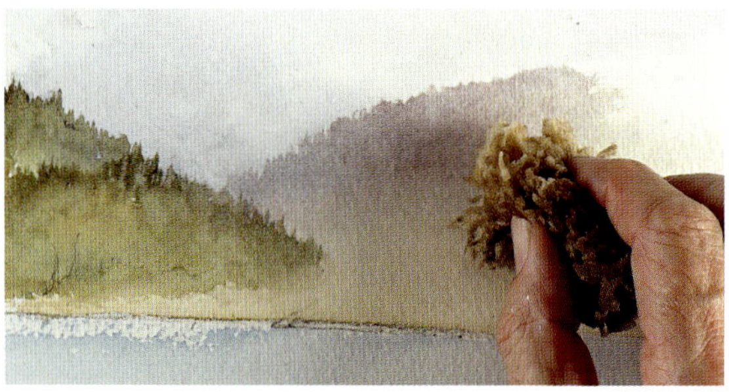

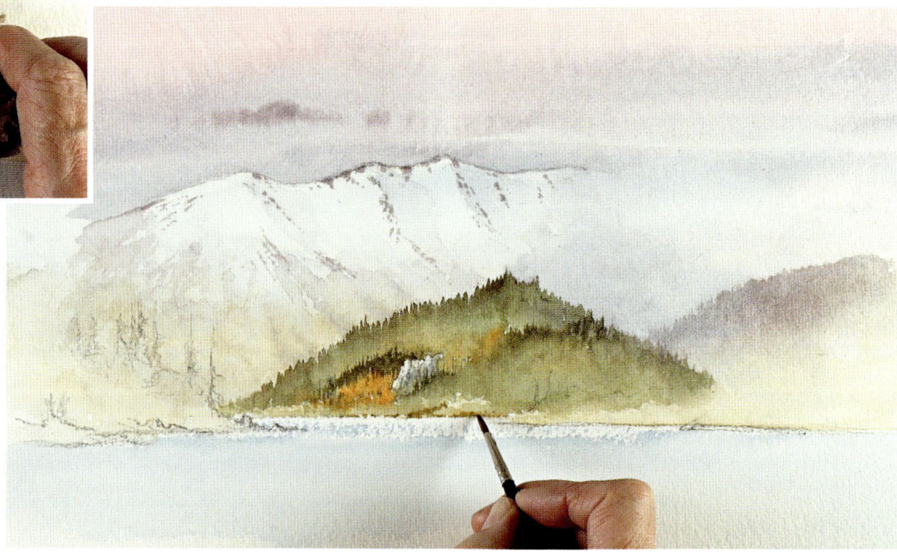

14 Push the ridge on the right further into the distance by fading it with a sponge and clean water. Take the no. 4 brush and a mix of raw umber and a little cobalt blue and sharpen the far shoreline.

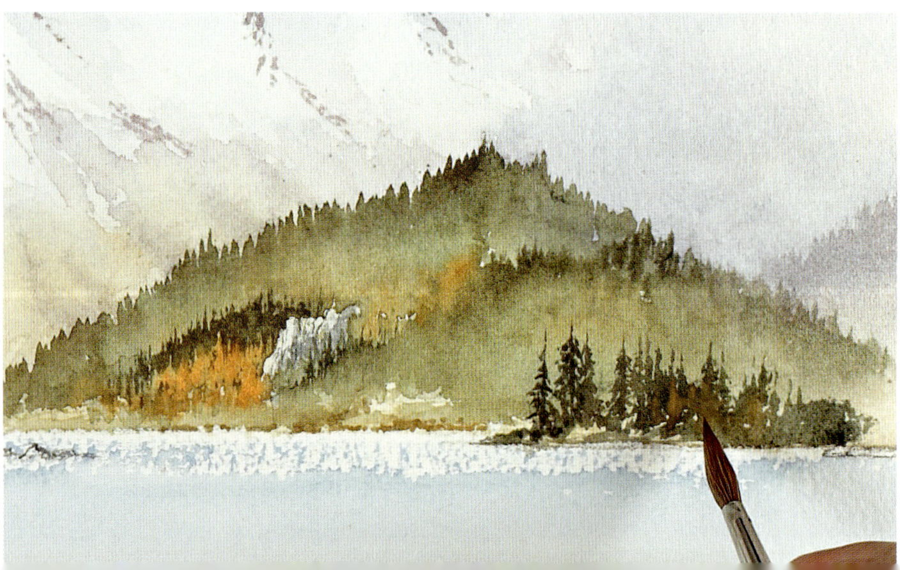

15 Paint trees with raw umber and cobalt blue, and drop in yellow ochre.

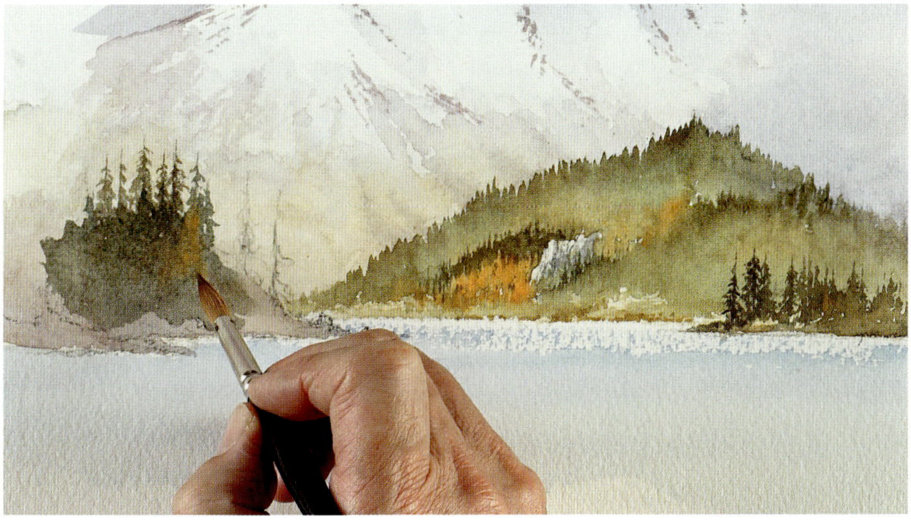

16 Paint the area on the left of the shoreline with cadmium red and cobalt blue. Allow to dry. Use the point of the no. 8 round to paint conifers with raw umber and cobalt blue. Drop in yellow ochre.

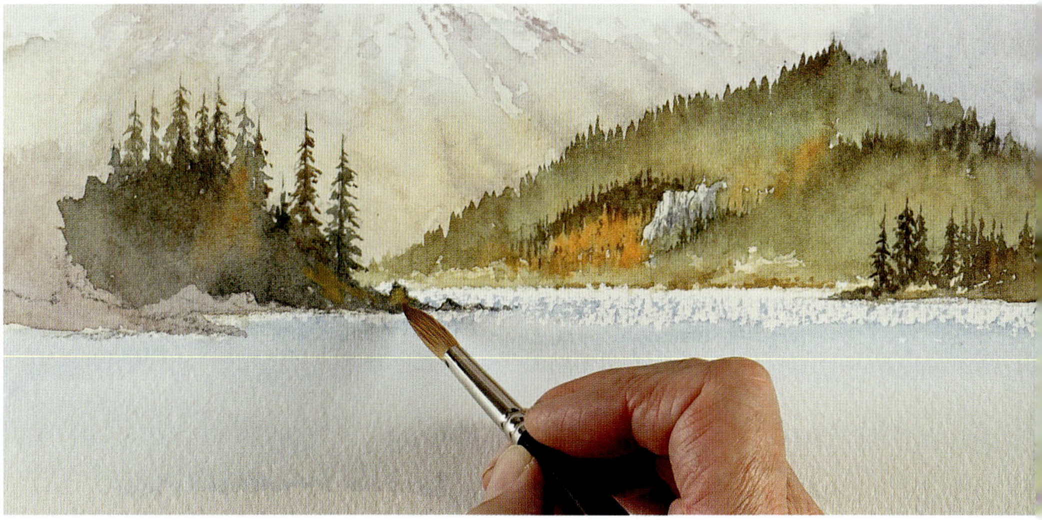

17 Paint rocks with the same mix, making them sharp and strong against the light background, then drop in cadmium orange while they are wet.

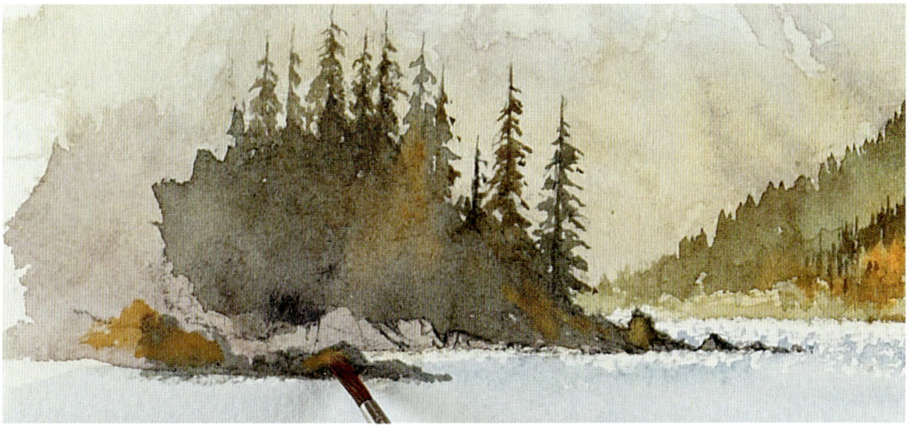

18 Use the no. 1 rigger with a mix of cobalt blue and burnt umber to paint the fracture lines on the rocks and to darken behind them. Change to the no. 4 round and paint a darker line of rocks with cobalt blue and raw umber, then drop in yellow ochre and allow to dry.

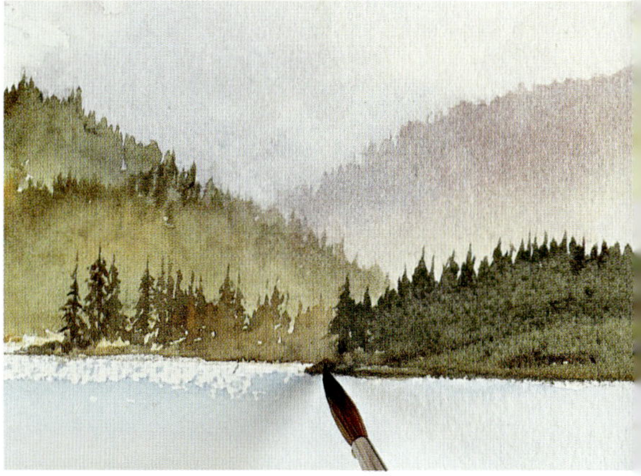

19 Use the no. 7 brush and raw umber with cobalt blue to paint trees on the right, then mix burnt umber and cobalt blue to paint rocks beneath the trees.

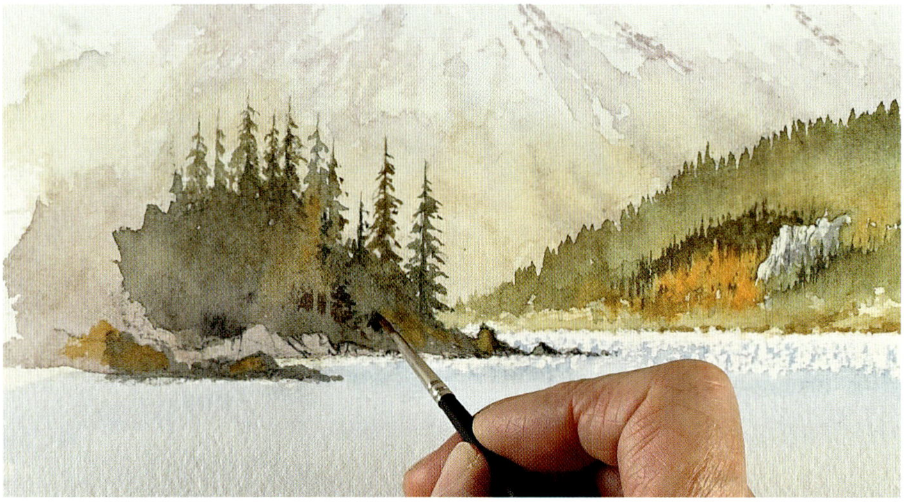

20 Change to the no. 1 round brush and do some negative painting in the trees on the left with cobalt blue and burnt umber. Hint at tree trunks. This is the focal point so needs to draw the eye.

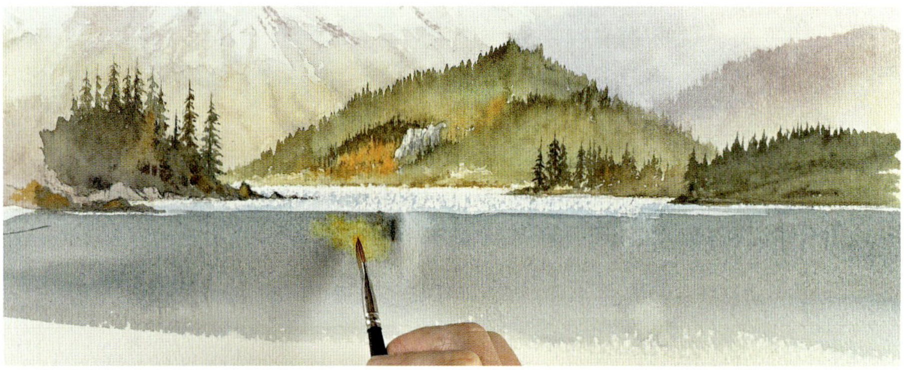

21 Wash cobalt blue and burnt umber across the lake with the squirrel mop. Lift out a little of the colour with the 6mm (¼in) flat brush, to suggest a reflection of the crag. Drop in raw umber and cobalt blue reflections, then cadmium orange with the no. 7 round brush.

22 Paint tree reflections while the area is wet with cobalt blue and raw umber. Vary the mix to suit the trees that are being reflected. Paint some of the green in the orange reflection.

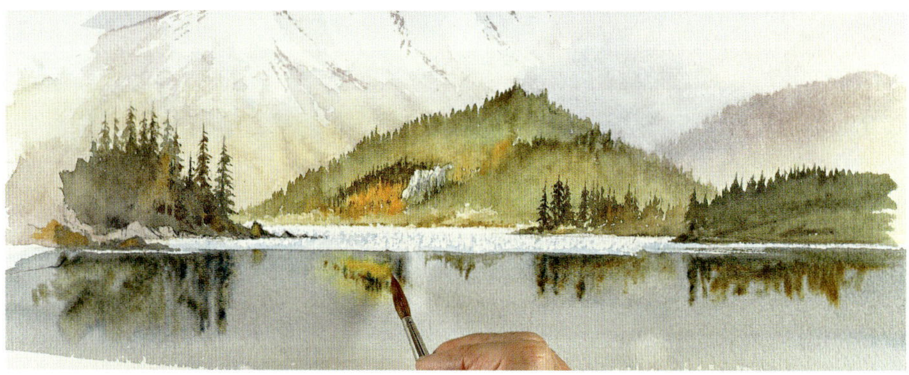

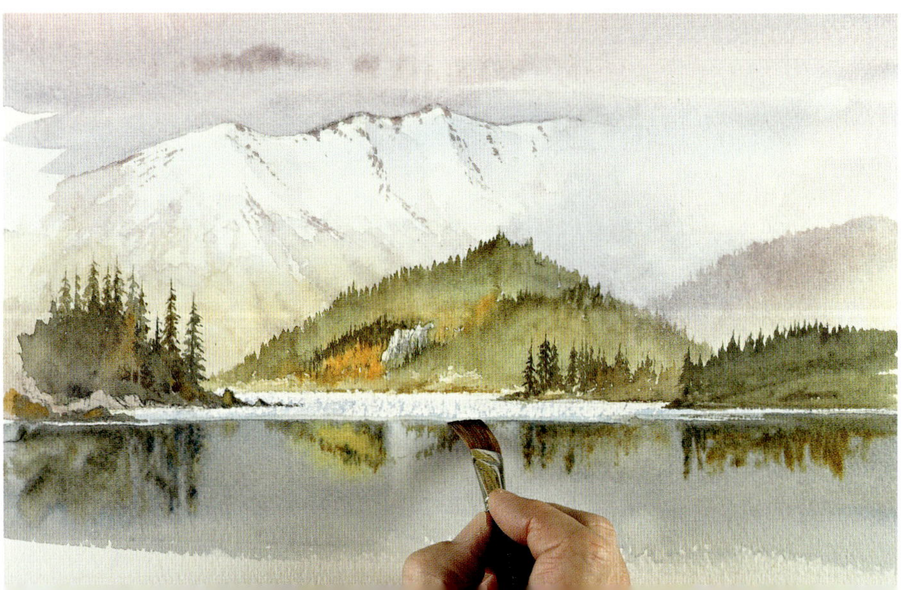

23 Soften the transition between the smooth and the ruffled water with the 13mm (½in) flat brush and clean water.

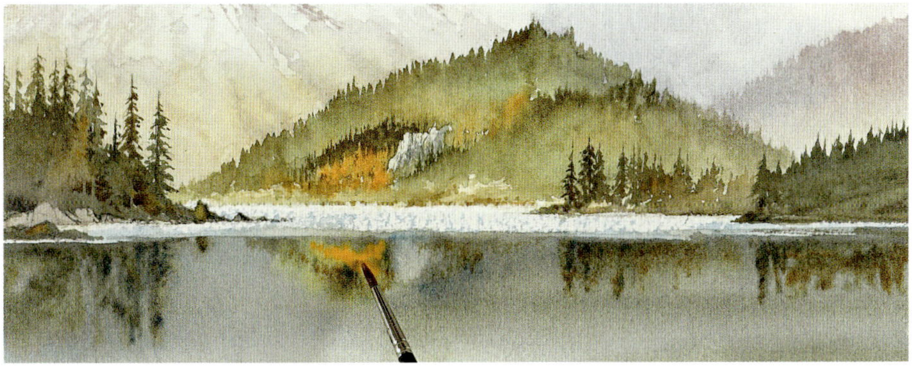

24 Continue working on the reflections while the area is wet. Paint a reflection of the green hill with the no. 7 brush and cobalt blue with raw umber, then intensify the reflection of the larches with the no. 4 brush and cadmium orange. Allow to dry.

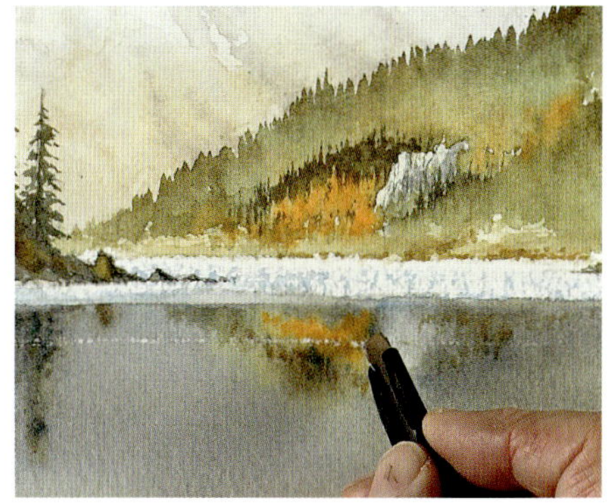

25 Scratch out ripples across the reflections using a scalpel.

*The finished painting.*

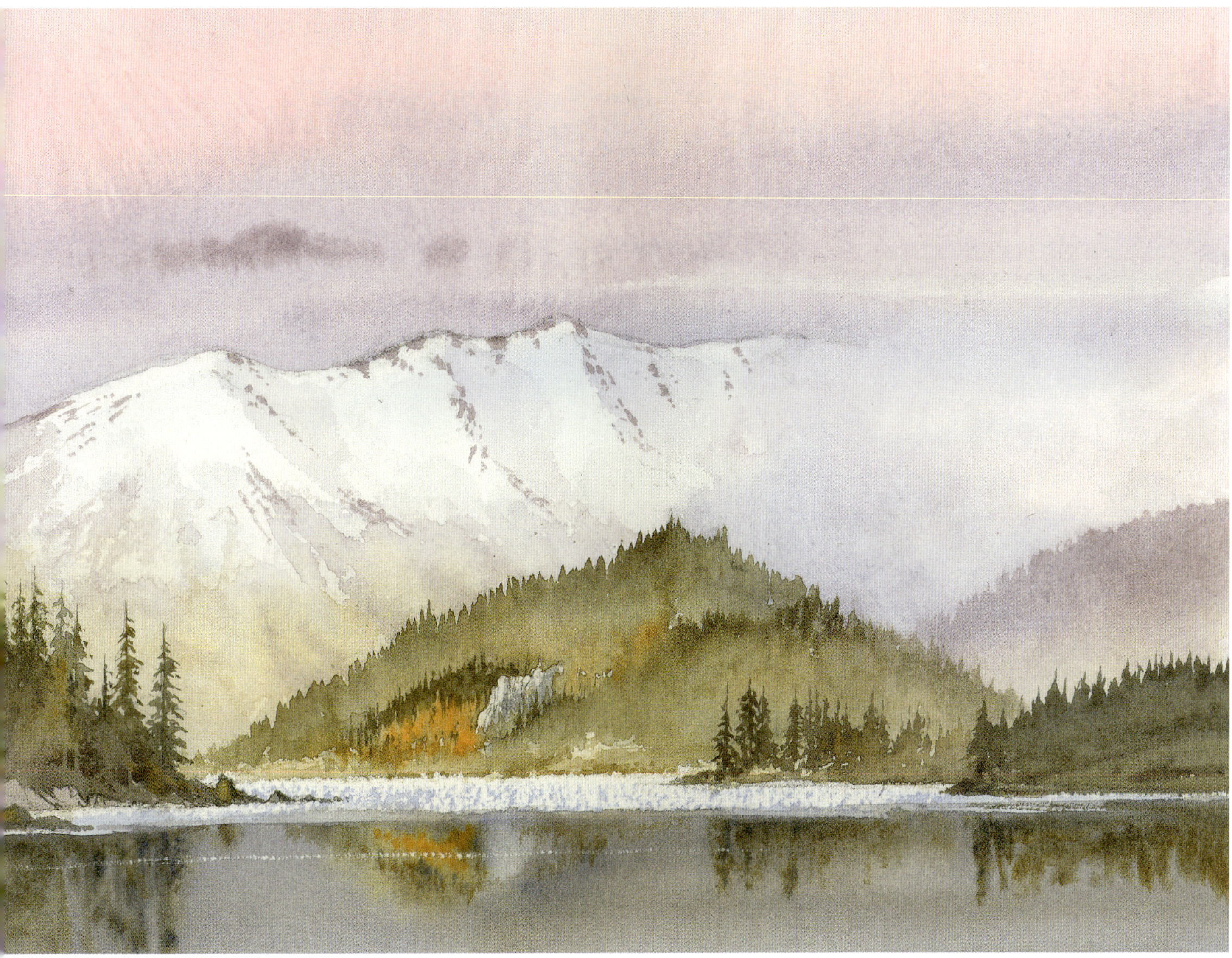

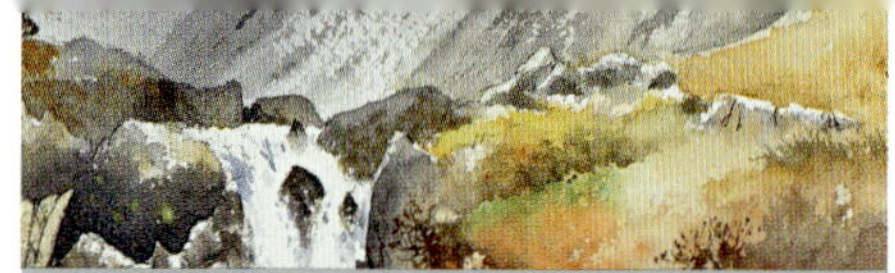

# MOUNTAIN CASCADE

The combination of rocks and tumbling water provides a fascinating centre of interest, and this is accentuated by strong detail and tonal contrasts, bright colours, a lead-in and a backdrop that gives further emphasis to the falls.

## MATERIALS USED

Saunders Waterford 640gsm (300lb) Rough watercolour paper

Brushes: squirrel mop, no. 12, no. 10, no. 7 and no. 4 round, no. 1 rigger and 6mm (¼in) flat

Colours: Naples yellow, French ultramarine, burnt umber, raw umber, yellow ochre, burnt sienna, cadmium yellow pale, cadmium red, perylene maroon, viridian

Water spray

Scrap paper

Sponge

Scalpel

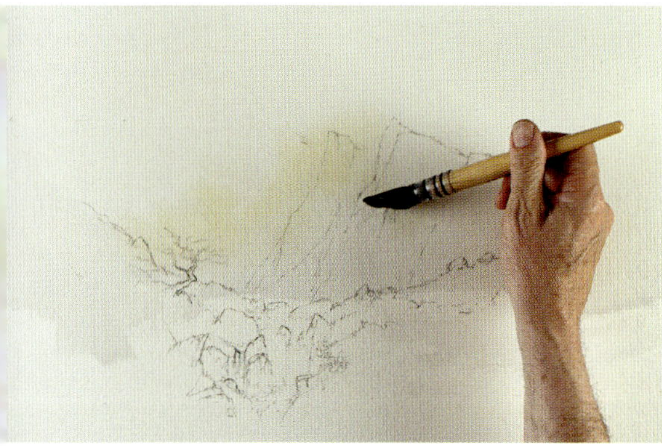

1 Draw the scene. Apply water to the sky and mountains using the squirrel mop, then drop in a little Naples yellow.

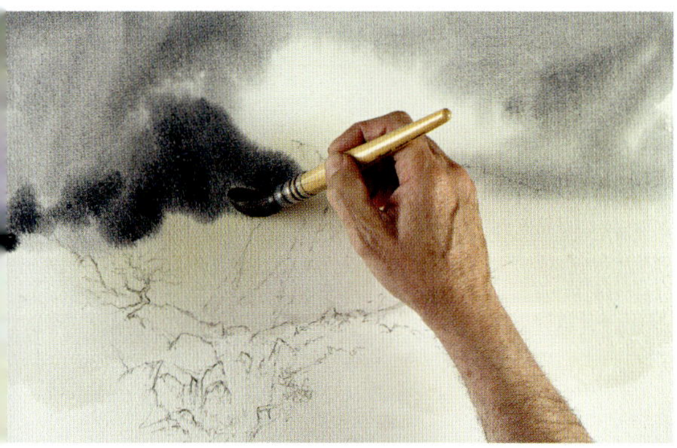

2 Paint the dark cloudy areas of the sky with ultramarine and burnt umber, and put in the rising peak on the left with a stronger mix of the same colours, all while the paper is wet.

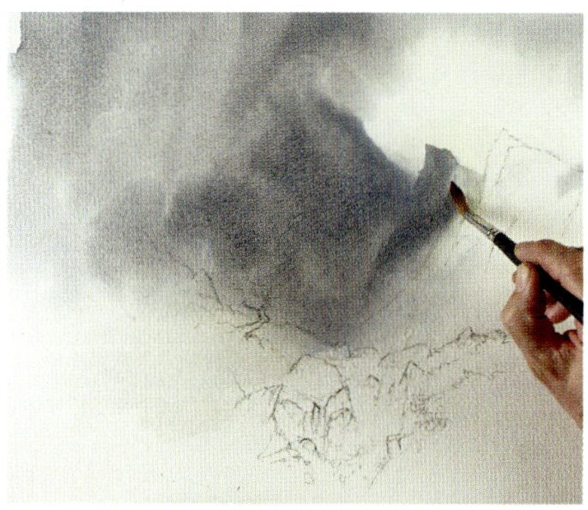

3 Define the edge of the peak by lifting out colour with a clean, damp, no. 12 brush. Paint the next peak with a no. 10 round and the same mix, and drop in raw umber wet into wet. Allow to dry.

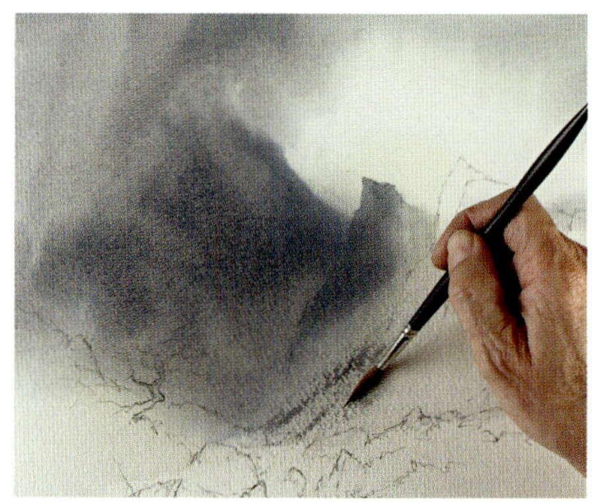

4 Use the no. 7 brush fairly dry, on its side, with a mix of burnt umber and ultramarine to create the scree coming down the mountain with the dry-brush technique. Allow to dry.

5 Paint the middle peak, creating a strong, hard edge and using the point of the brush and the same mix to create structure. Add a little raw umber and water as you come forwards.

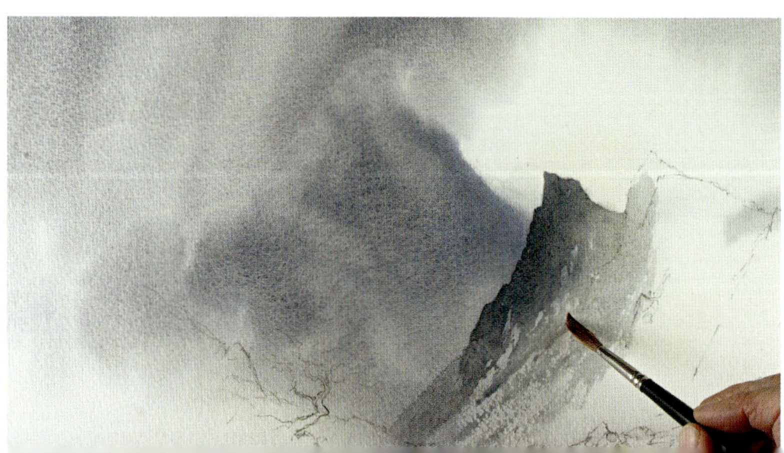

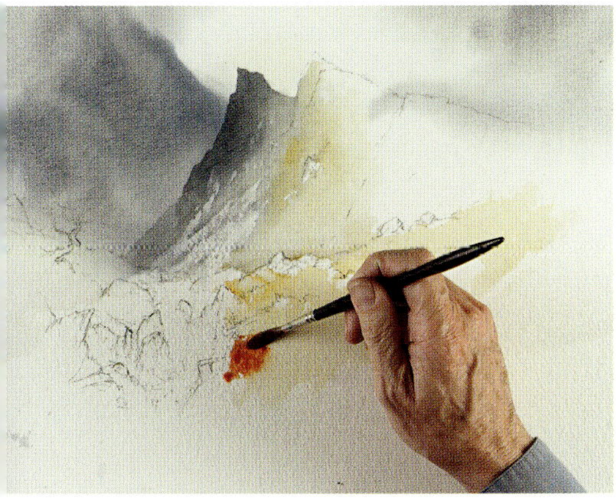

6 Bring in yellow ochre further forwards, and drop in a little burnt sienna to suggest warm-coloured earth to lift the scene.

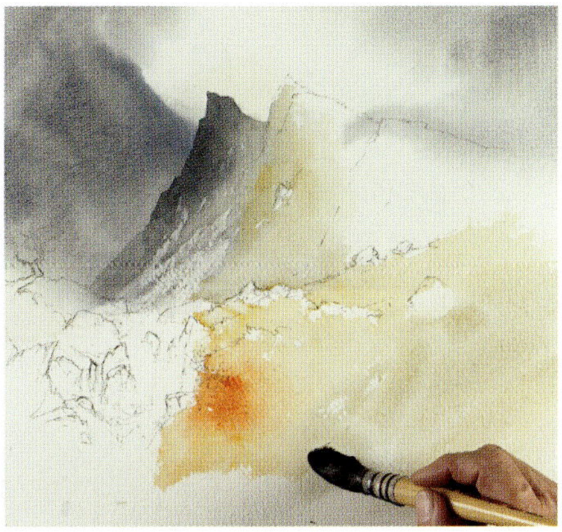

7 Use the squirrel mop to extend the yellow ochre wash across the right-hand foreground.

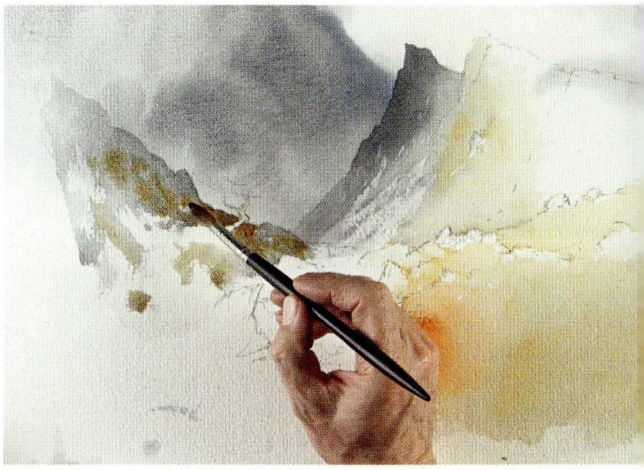

8 Change to the no. 10 round brush to paint the sloping crags on the left, working negatively around the trunk of the thorn bush. Drop in raw umber wet into wet.

9 Use the brush on its side to create a textural finish for the rock with raw umber and a touch of ultramarine, then change to the no. 4 brush and drop in yellow ochre.

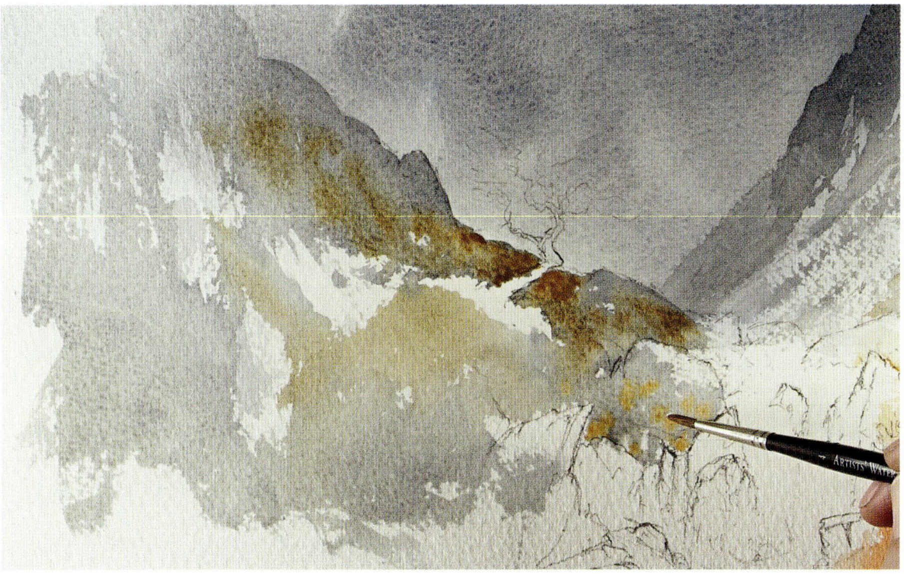

10 Paint the rock beside the cascade with a mix of raw umber and ultramarine. Spray the rocky area around the cascade with water to create textural effects. Allow to dry.

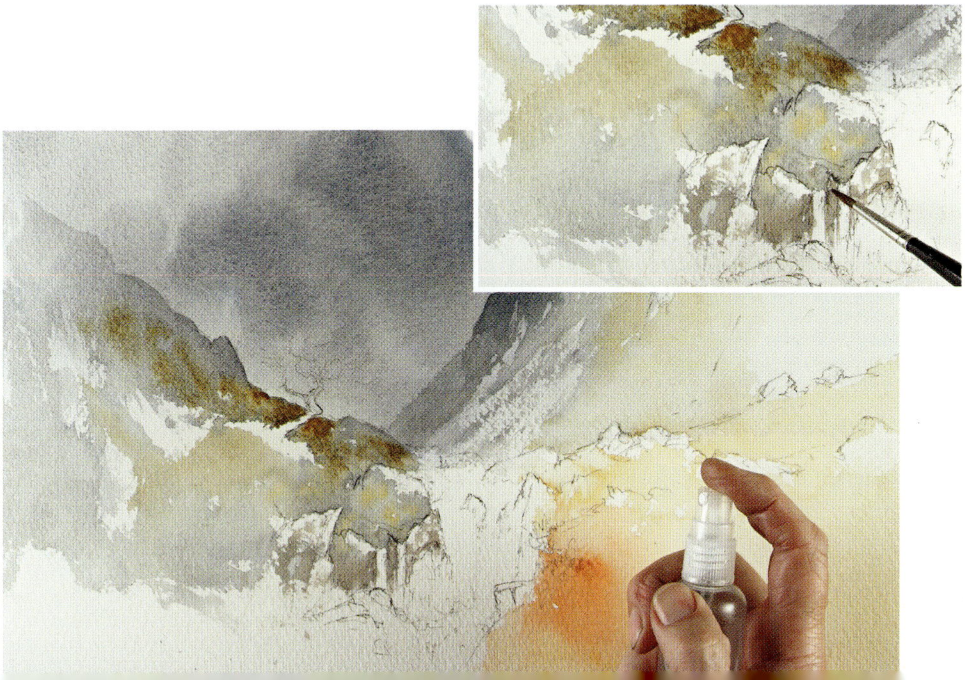

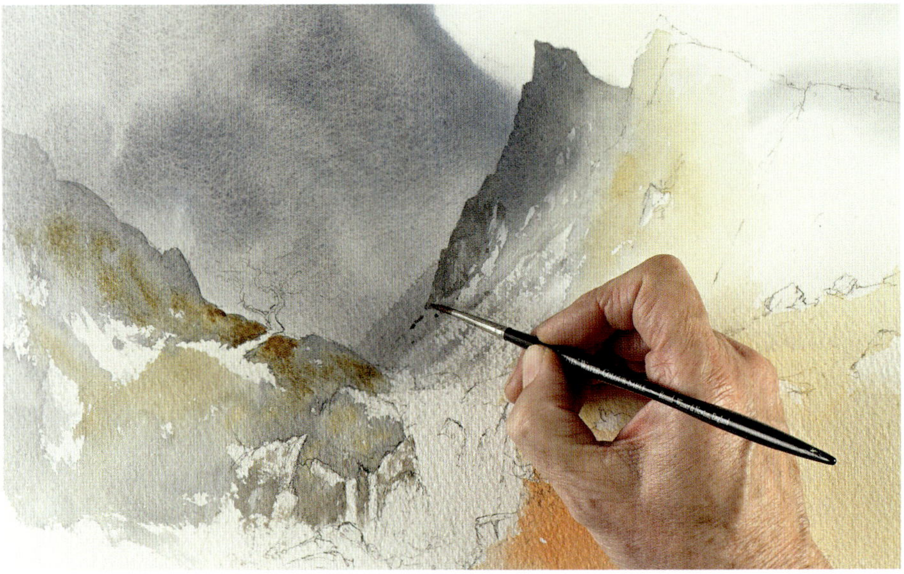

11 Tidy and strengthen the edge of the middle peak with the no. 4 brush, using a mix of ultramarine and burnt umber.

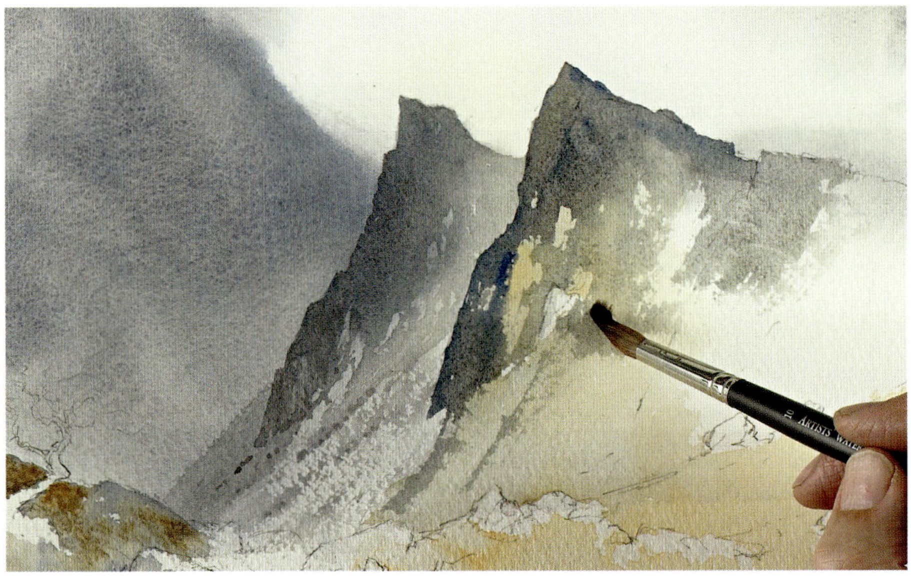

12 Change to the no. 7 brush to paint more of the mountain.

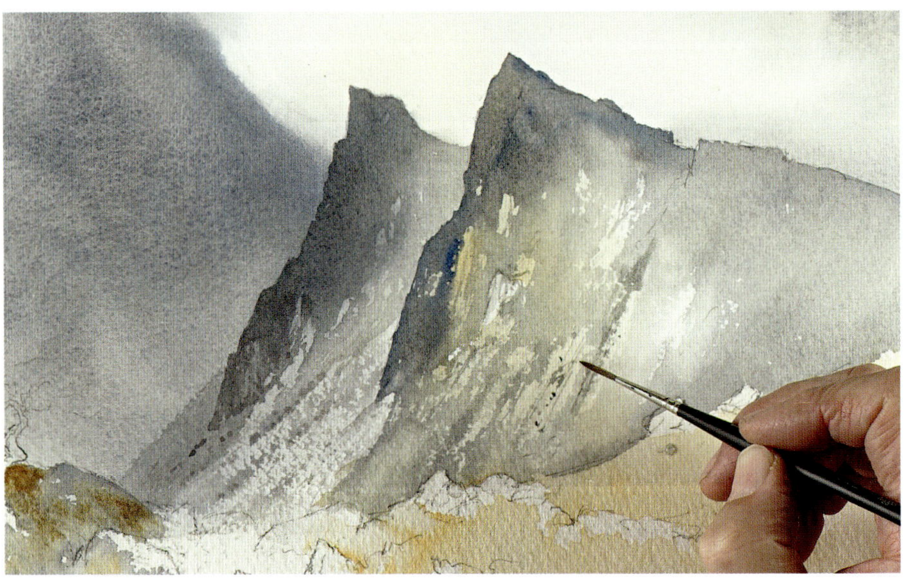

13 Use the no. 1 rigger and a mix of ultramarine and burnt sienna to paint fracture lines on the mountain. Allow to dry.

14 Paint the boulders above the cascade with the no. 7 brush and the same mix, then drop in yellow ochre wet into wet.

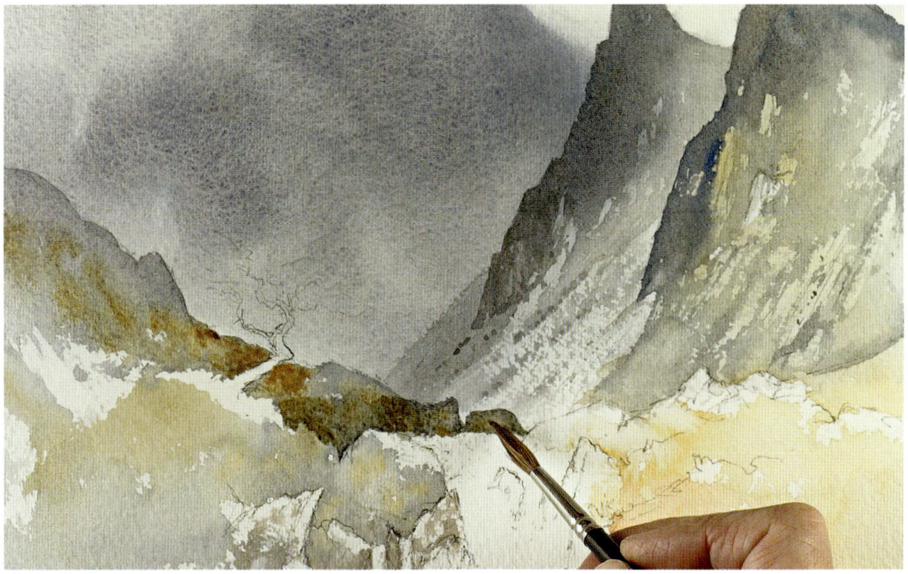

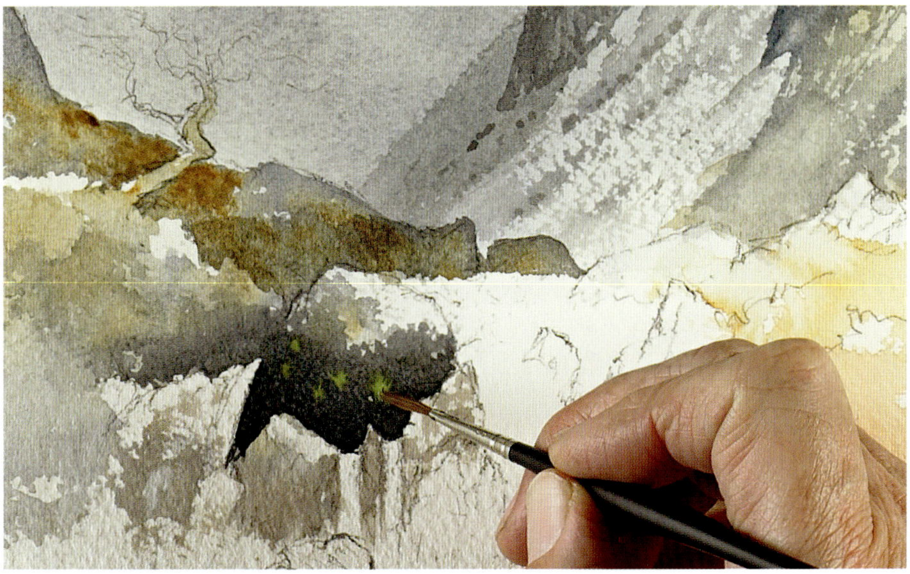

15 Strengthen the boulder with ultramarine and burnt umber, then paint the trunk of the thorn bush with raw umber. Spray this area again to create speckles. Use the no. 1 rigger and cadmium yellow pale to paint dots of lichen on the boulder.

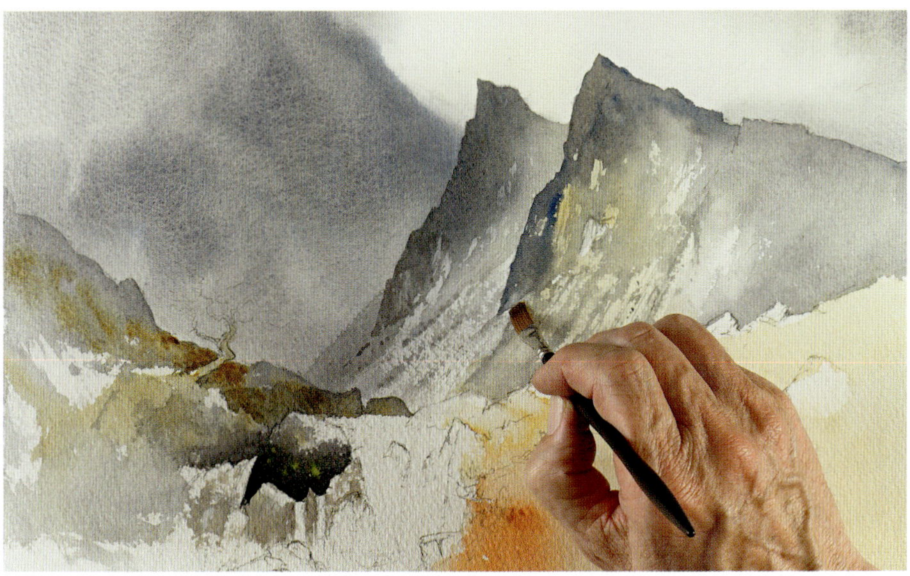

16 Soften some of the hard edges of the peaks with the 6mm (¼in) flat brush and clean water.

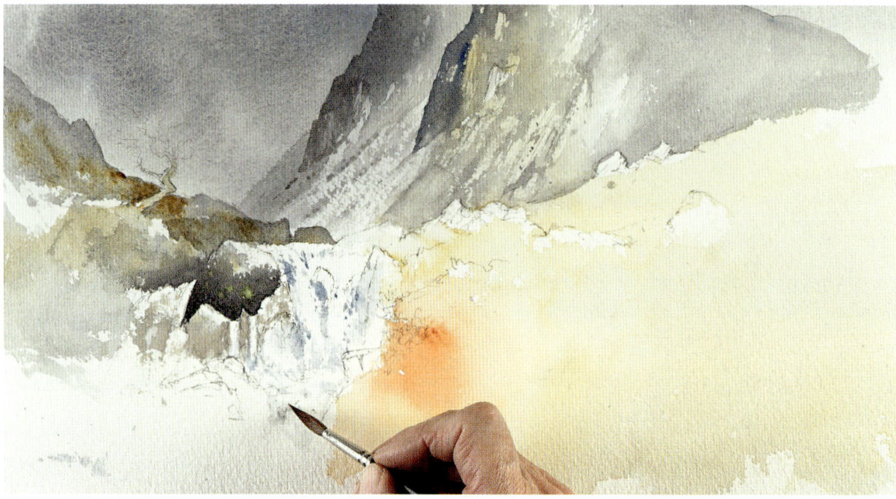

17 Paint the shaded areas of the waterfall using the no. 7 brush and ultramarine. Leave some of the paper white, especially where the water is aerated lower down.

18 Use the tip of the no. 7 brush to paint the sharp rocky edges on the left-hand side of the scene with burnt umber and ultramarine. Drop in yellow ochre.

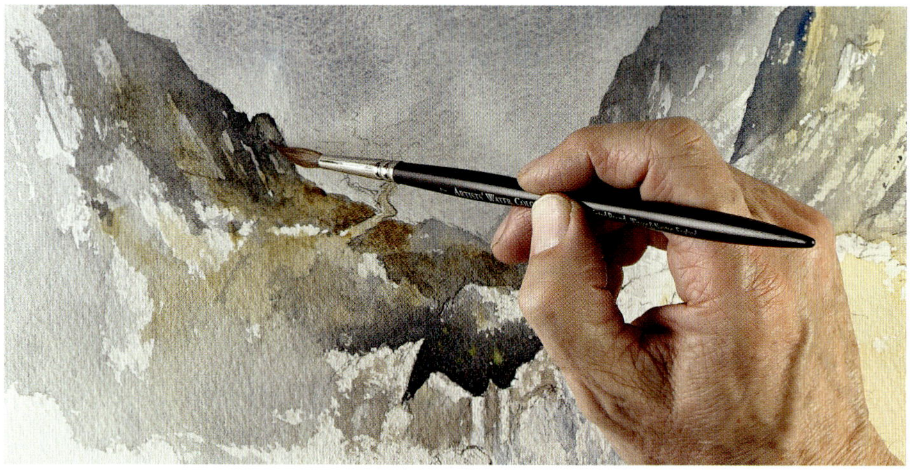

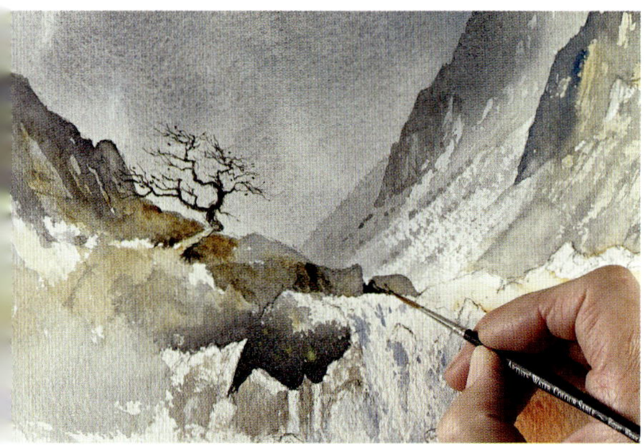

19 Use the no. 1 rigger and ultramarine and burnt umber to paint the thorn bush. Allow to dry. Reinforce the darker area behind the trunk with negative painting, then paint shadows and streaks in the rock with the same brush and mix.

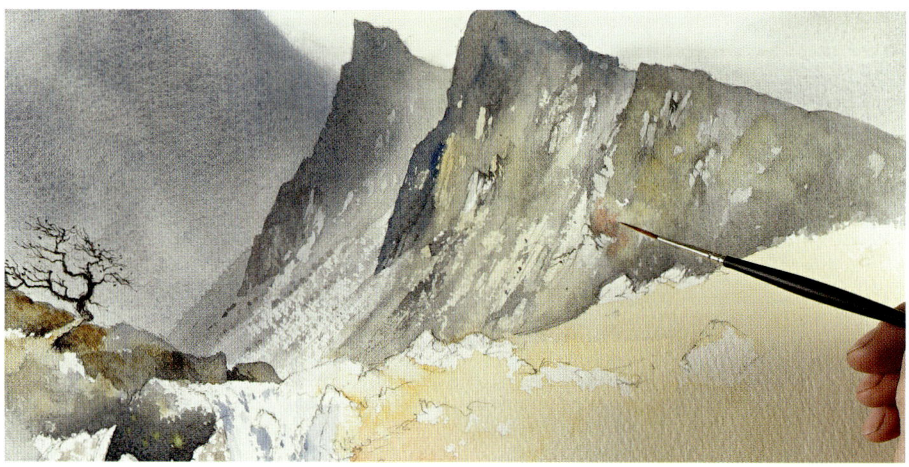

20 Use the point of the rigger to suggest fractures in the mountainside as it slopes into the corrie – the shape sculpted out by a glacier – and other features of the rock face. Soften in places with clean water and use the rigger almost dry and on its side to create texture. Drop yellow ochre, then cadmium red into the wet wash.

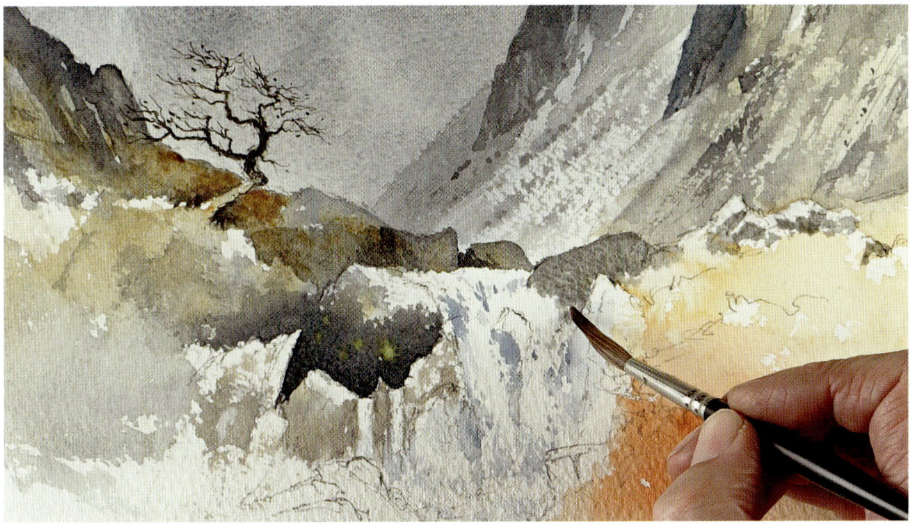

21 Paint rocks near the white water with the no. 7 brush and burnt umber and ultramarine.

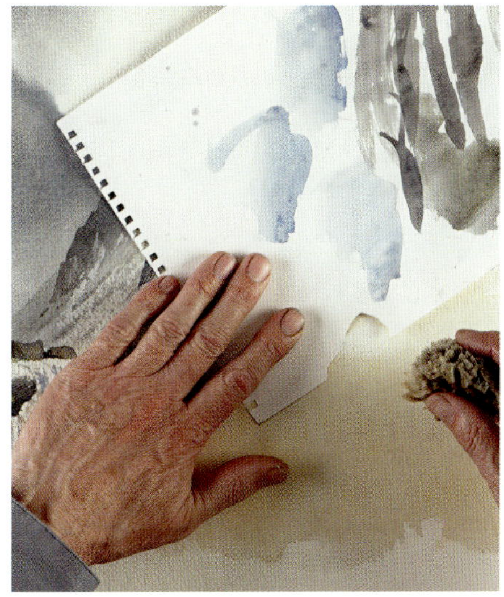

22 Make a stencil by tearing a piece of scrap paper and use it with a sponge to lift out colour from the yellow ochre area on the right to create a new rock.

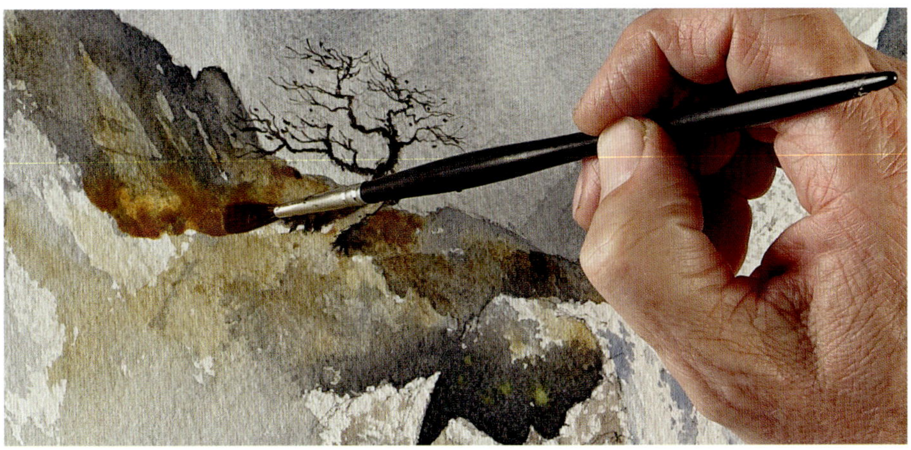

23 Paint raw umber on the rocks around the waterfall and thorn bush with the no. 4 brush.

24 Paint rocks in and around the cascade with ultramarine and burnt umber, leaving speckles of white to suggest water bubbling up.

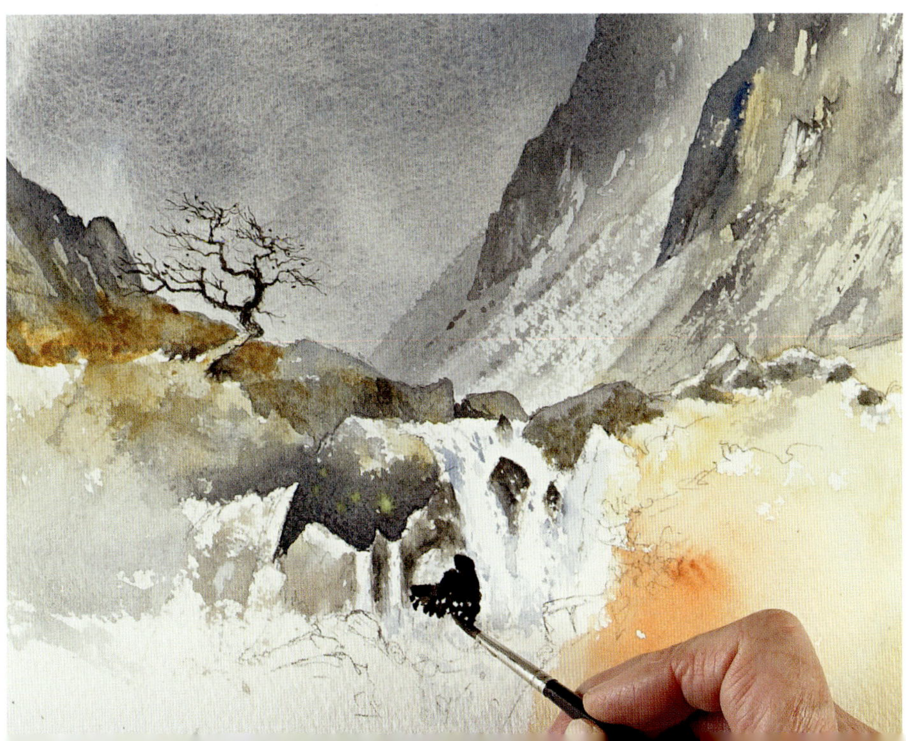

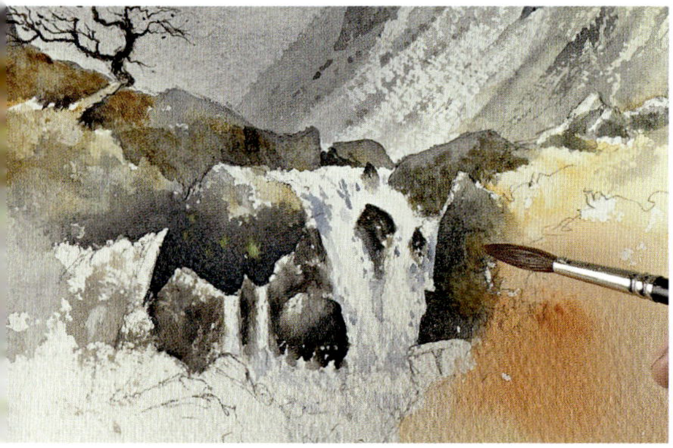

25 Paint the rock to the right of the cascade with the no. 7 brush and burnt umber and ultramarine, then drop in yellow ochre.

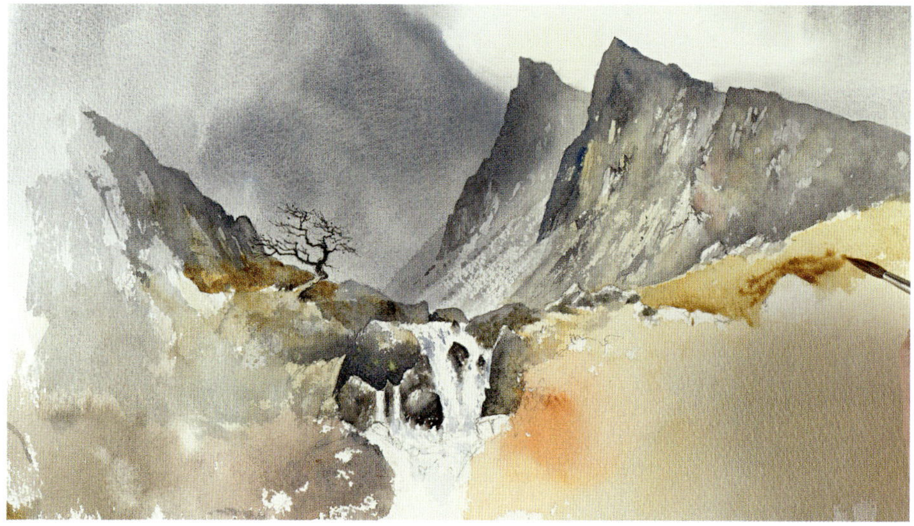

26 Fill in the area to the left of the cascade with a wash of raw umber, then paint perylene maroon and ultramarine just below this, and raw umber at the bottom left of the scene. Apply a wash of yellow ochre and then raw umber around the stencilled rock.

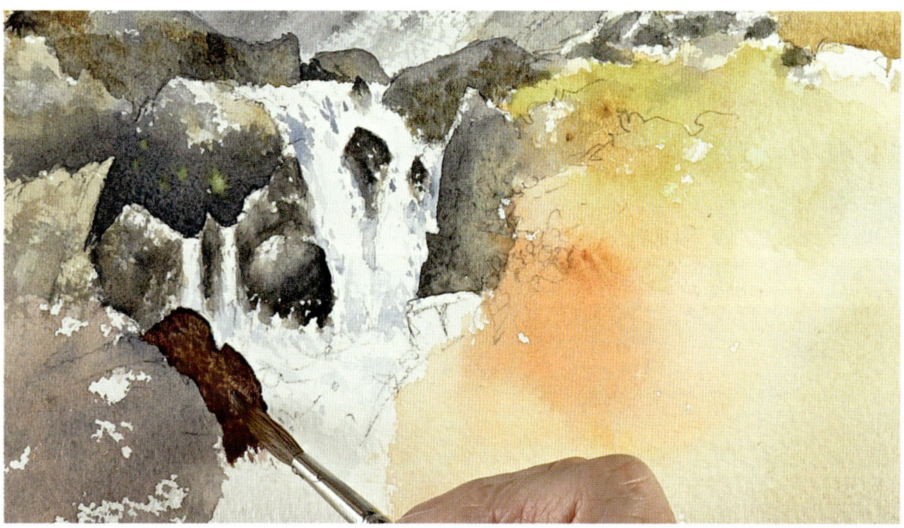

27 Wash in more raw umber and then cadmium yellow pale to create brightness to the right of the cascade, which is the focal point. Paint a rock with perylene maroon, and drop in yellow ochre.

28 Use a very pale mix of perylene maroon and ultramarine to paint the rocks on the right, leaving white highlights at the top, then drop in yellow ochre.

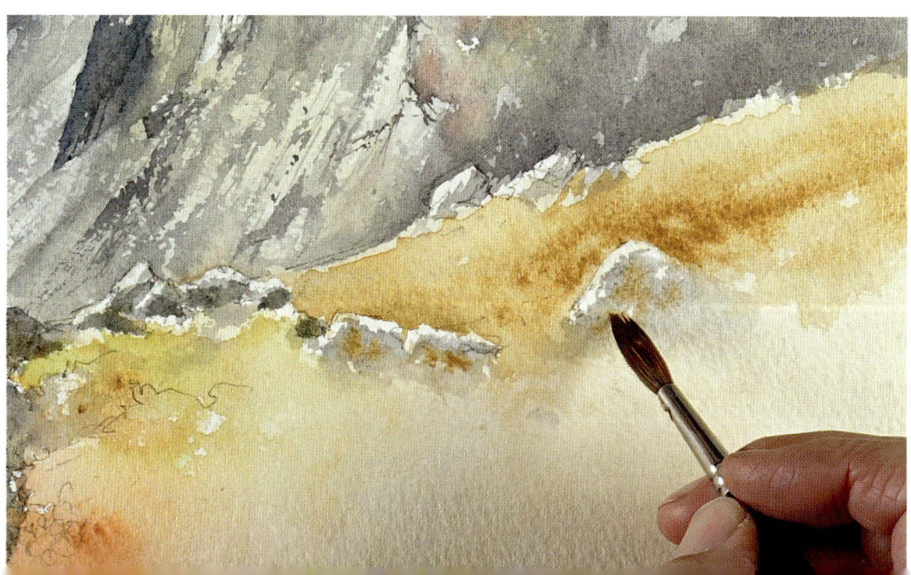

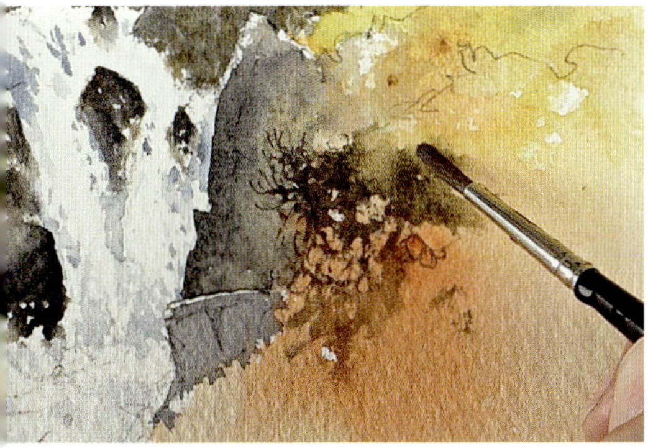

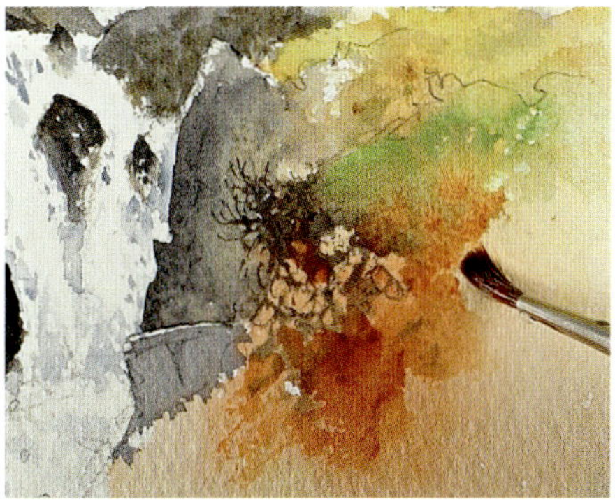

30 Mix viridian with cadmium yellow pale and drop in green around the thorn bush, then burnt sienna to imply undergrowth.

29 Paint the heather to the right of the cascade with the no. 1 rigger and burnt umber and ultramarine, then add tone with the no. 4 brush.

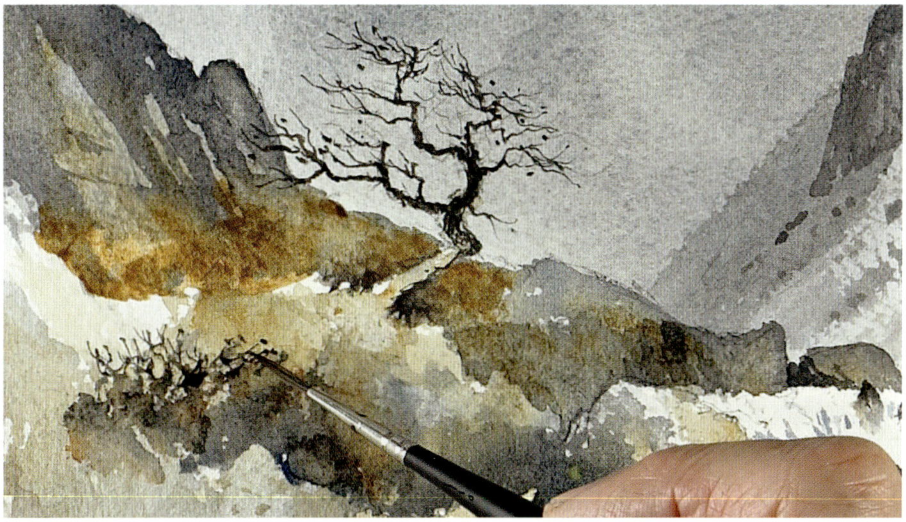

31 Paint rock shapes with burnt umber and ultramarine, then use the no. 1 rigger to create the effect of heather around the rocks.

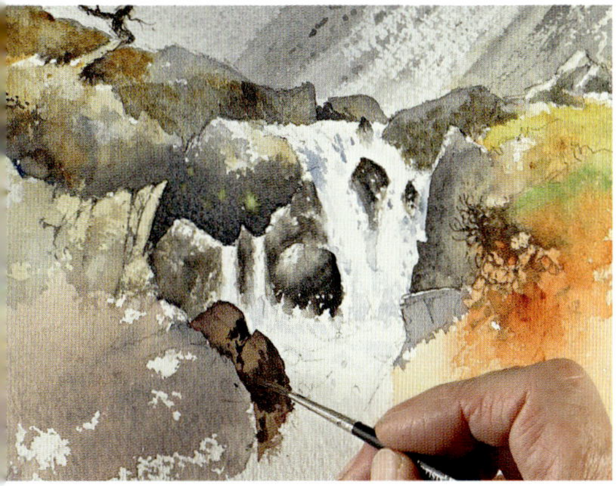

32 Create fracture lines and other rock details with the same brush and mix.

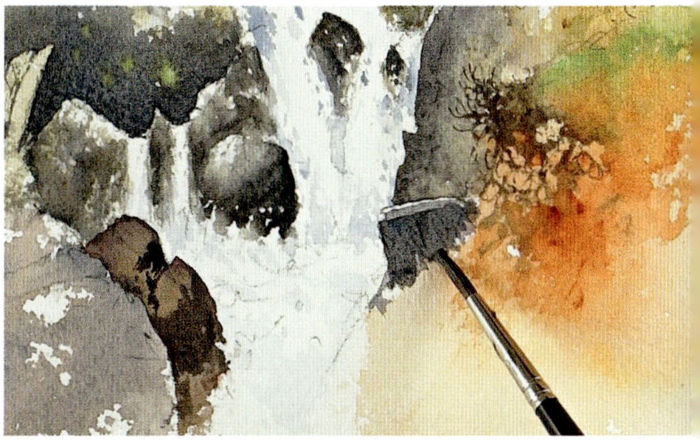

33 Add shadow to the side of the grey rock beside the cascade with ultramarine and burnt umber.

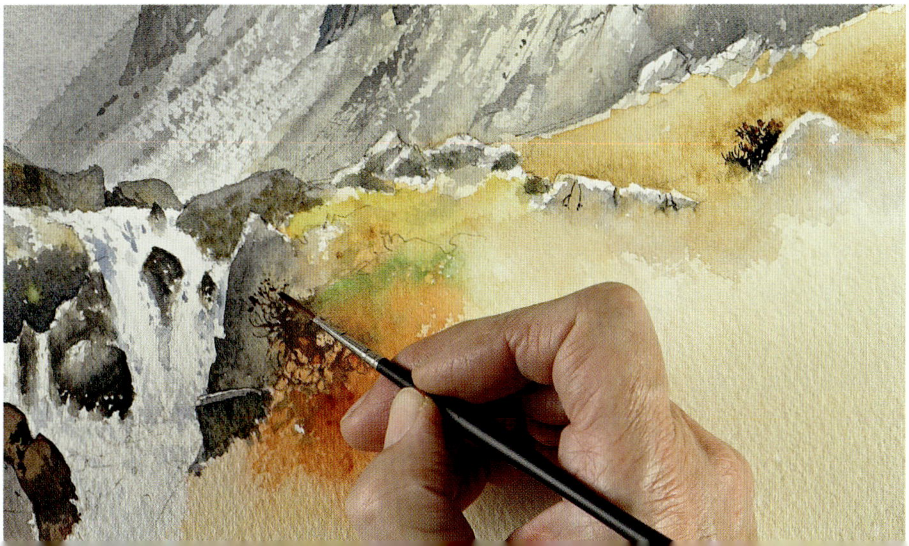

34 Still using the no. 1 rigger and the same mix, paint the heather to the left of the white rock that was stencilled, then drop in perylene maroon to this and the heather beside the cascade.

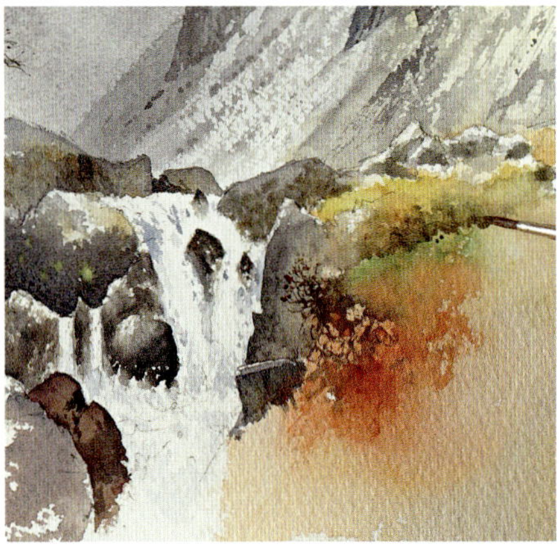

35 Use the no. 4 brush and a mix of raw umber and ultramarine to paint a darker area behind the bright green grass to highlight it.

36 Change to the no. 1 rigger to paint grasses beneath the right-hand rocks with the same mix, then with the no. 4 brush, paint yellow ochre below the grasses and drop in perylene maroon.

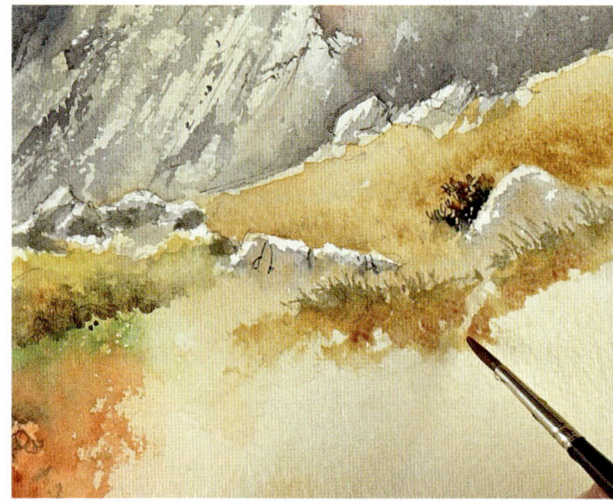

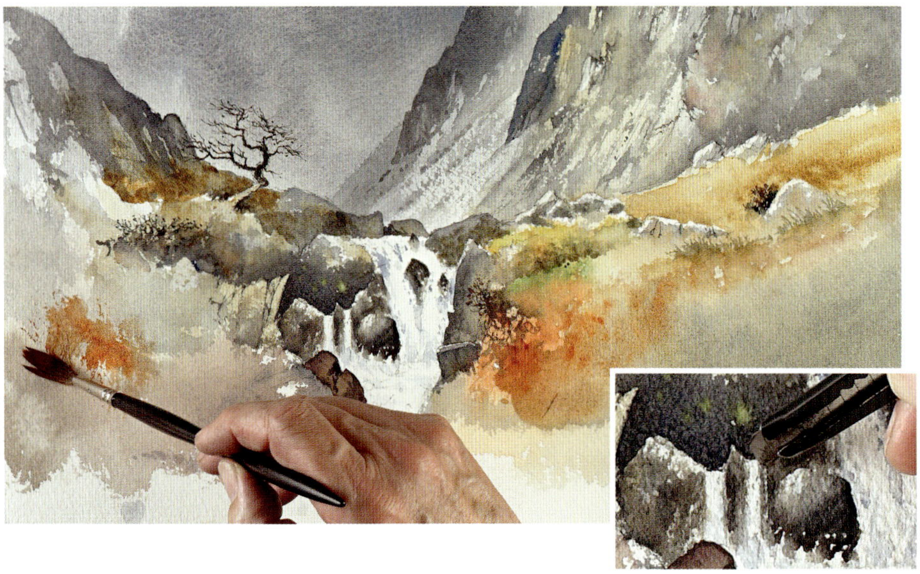

37 Wet the painting at the bottom and use the no. 7 brush and burnt umber and ultramarine to grey the lower part of the right-hand side. Drop in burnt sienna wet into wet, and paint some on the left-hand side to balance it. Paint more of the burnt umber and ultramarine mix to subdue any areas that are too light, and allow to dry. Use the scalpel blade to scratch out drips of water against the dark rock.

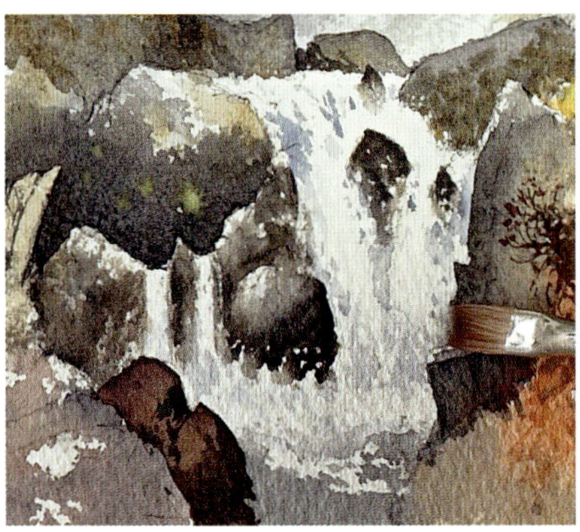

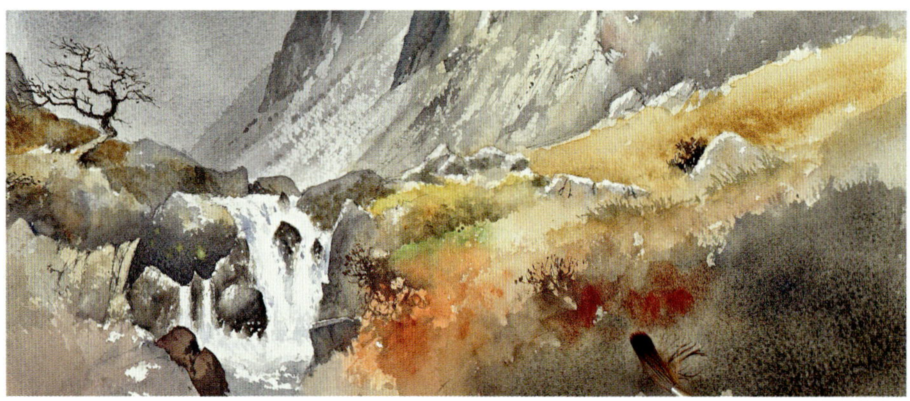

38 Paint a little ultramarine and burnt umber at the bottom of the waterfall with the no. 7 brush, then use the 6mm (¼in) flat brush with clean water to soften the rock to the right, creating the effect of misty spray.

39 Paint heather on the right with the no. 1 rigger and ultramarine and burnt umber, then use the no. 4 brush to add tone around it. Darken the bottom right-hand side of the painting with the no. 7 brush and a bluer mix of the same colours, then drop in perylene maroon.

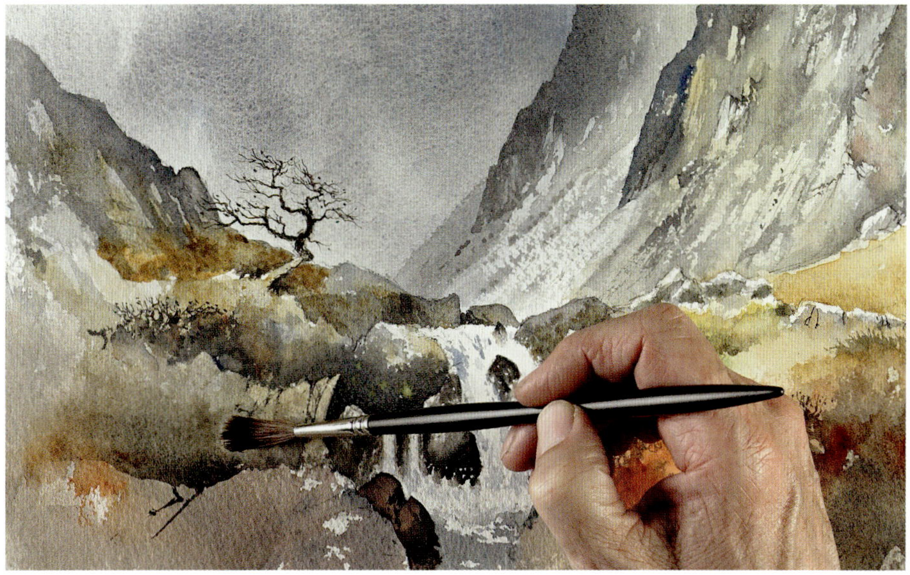

**40** Use the no. 7 brush and ultramarine and burnt umber to suggest rock shapes on the left of the painting. Change to the no. 1 rigger to add fractures to various rocks.

*The finished painting.*

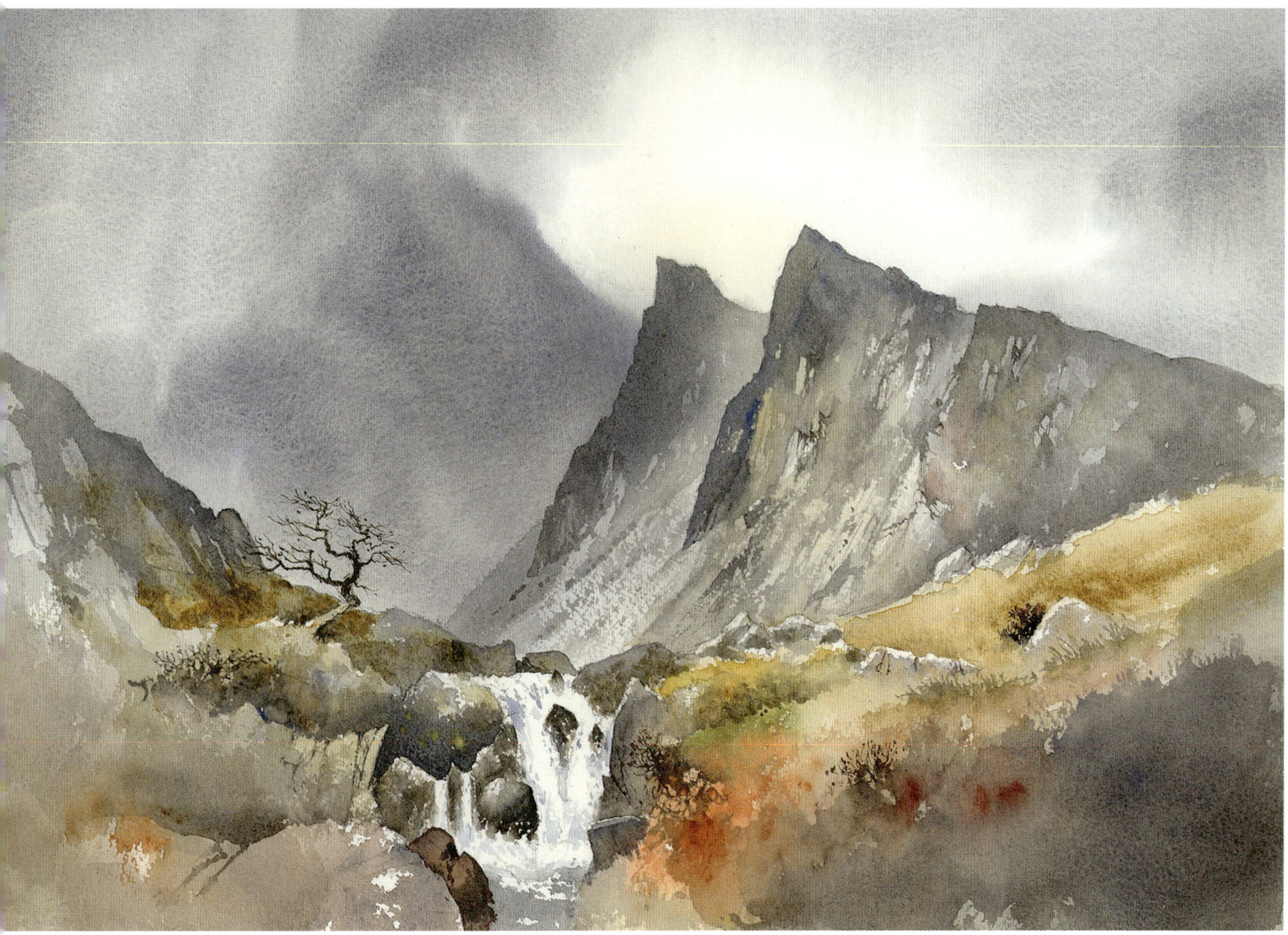

# SEAS & SHORELINES

Painting by the sea has always been a popular activity for both the occasional painter and the professional. Sitting on the beach sketching, working up a simple drawing at a quayside café, or painting on the deck of a cruise ship makes a pleasurable part of a summer holiday for some, while to others it is a year-round activity in all seasons. The combination of painting and enjoying the sea environment is especially therapeutic. It has never been so easy to collect images of your own to work from, so I urge you to go forth with a sketchbook and pencil, alongside a camera or smartphone and capture those fascinating scenes on the coast.

Before you go outside, however, this section guides you in how to tackle the various types of subject found on the coast, so that you gain experience and confidence in drawing and painting before having to undertake these terrifying pleasures. Don't feel you need to create crashing waves, intricate boat designs, complicated harbour scenes or confusing cliff structures, as there are simple alternatives to each of these. You are encouraged to begin with the easy approach and gradually build up your expertise until you are working on more complicated scenes.

Whether you paint in a realistic fashion, or prefer the kind where it is not really necessary to attach that mast to the boat, you will find a wealth

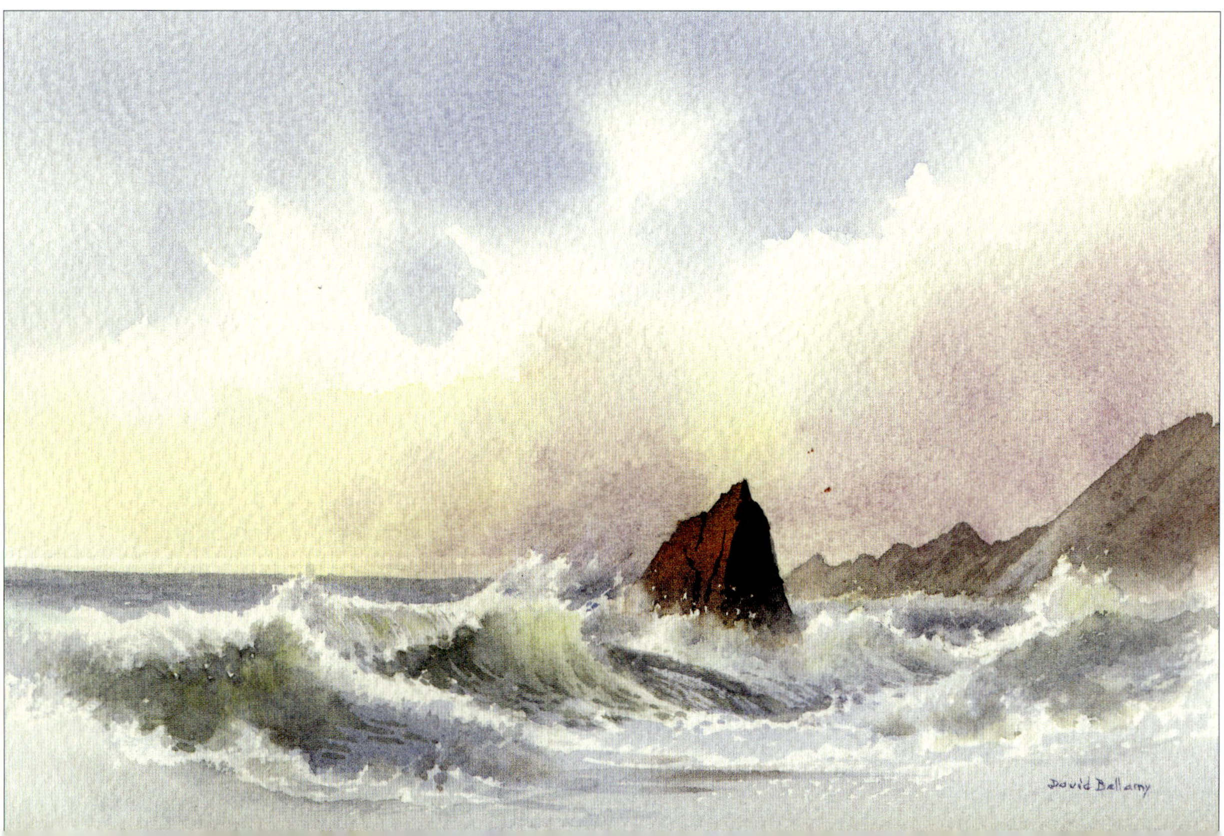


BREAKING WAVE
*18 x 25.5cm (7 x 10in)*

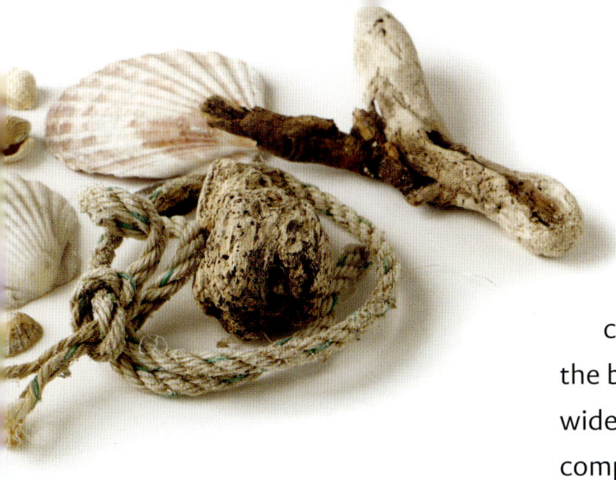

of techniques and ideas in the following pages. My own work in watercolour tends towards the more traditional methods of working, but with the development of so many additives and exciting new approaches, I have brought in techniques such as collage, monoprinting, textural effects and additives that will push the boundaries of your watercolour painting. You will come across a wide selection of skies and moods which you can transfer to your own compositions. In later chapters you will find out how you can improve your compositions, get the best out of your photographs, and introduce figures and seabirds into your work.

Don't despair if things go wrong – with perseverance you will find your work progressing even without you realizing. You paint because it gives you pleasure, and the aim of this section is to encourage you to enjoy the experience of capturing the fascinating world of sea and shoreline.

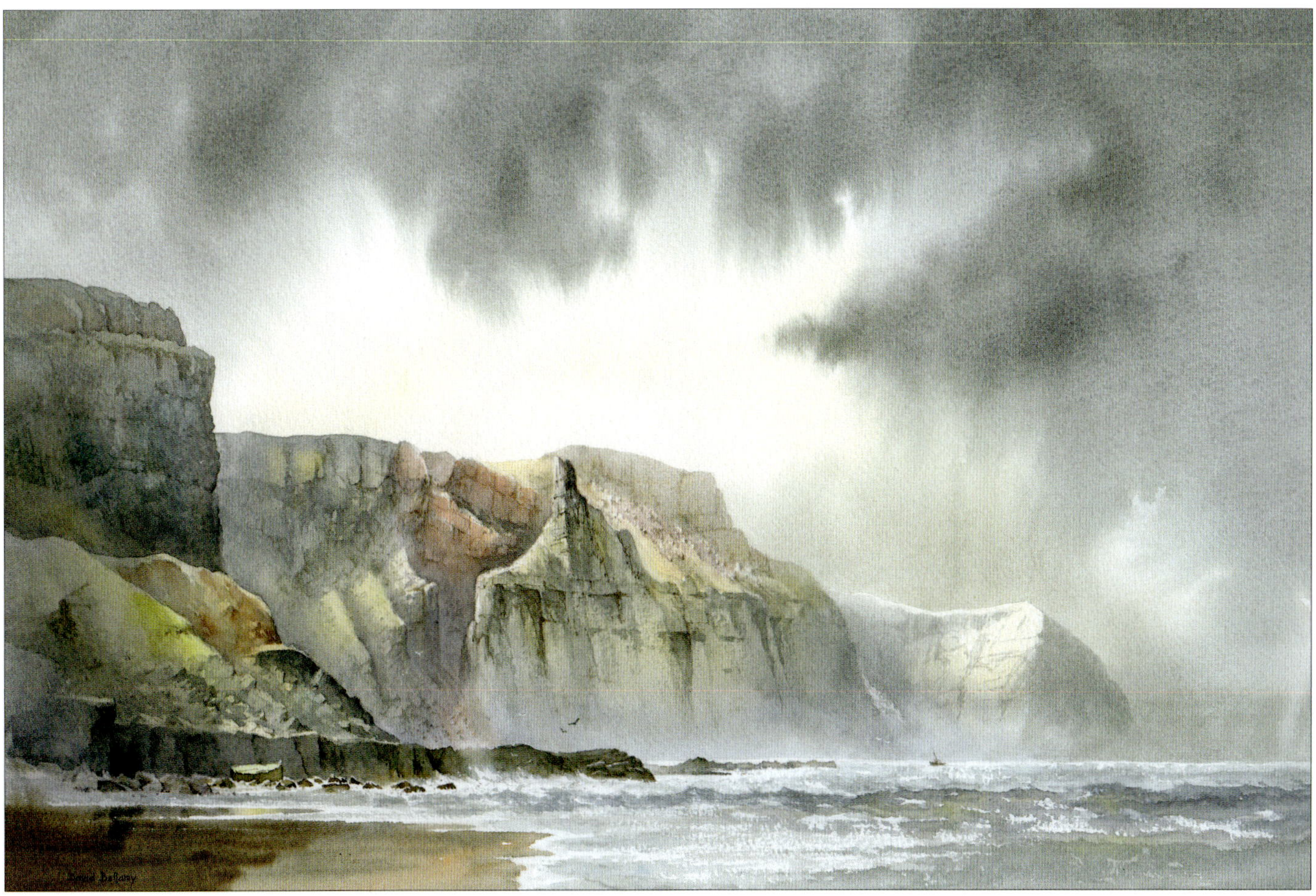

HAROLDSTON CHINS
*30.5 x 45.5cm (12 x 18in)*
*The cliffs are at their most interesting where they are crumbling away, and thus providing a focal point in this watercolour.*

# Coastal features

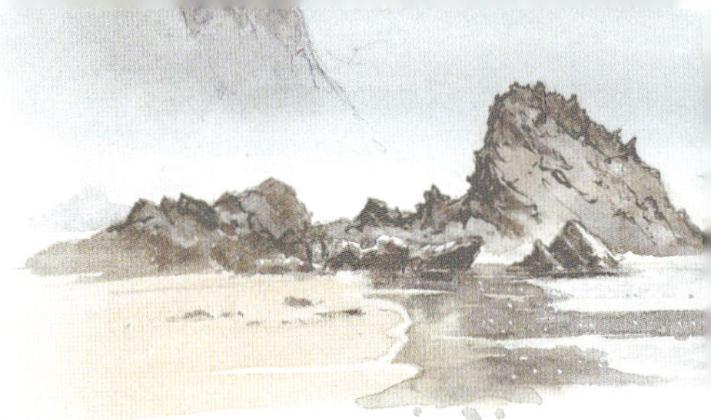

**The best way of learning to paint coastal features is to go out and work directly from nature. This can be daunting without some prior experience and many folk are not easily able to get out. This chapter is therefore aimed at introducing you to the problems and delights of working on these fascinating subjects to give you the confidence to start.**

Practise as much as you can, even if you have only ten minutes before you need to start cooking the evening meal. Being ready and organized for these spare moments can make a great difference, and you really don't need several hours of spare time to push your watercolour knowledge a little further. Keep a few pencils and a cartridge sketchbook handy for these moments and simply draw the objects around you, perhaps extending this to drawing model boats or laying simple washes of watercolour, and experimenting.

I often cover my drawings and sketches with copious notes and diagrams as in the sketch of the cod-liver oil factory below, which was a rushed affair enhanced later at base with some tonal work in pencil. Subjects like this building (below) make for an easier introduction to landscape work for the beginner because you have a definite structure before you, and it is much simpler to render than an amorphous collection of rocks, seaweed and marine detritus. That can come later when you feel more confident.

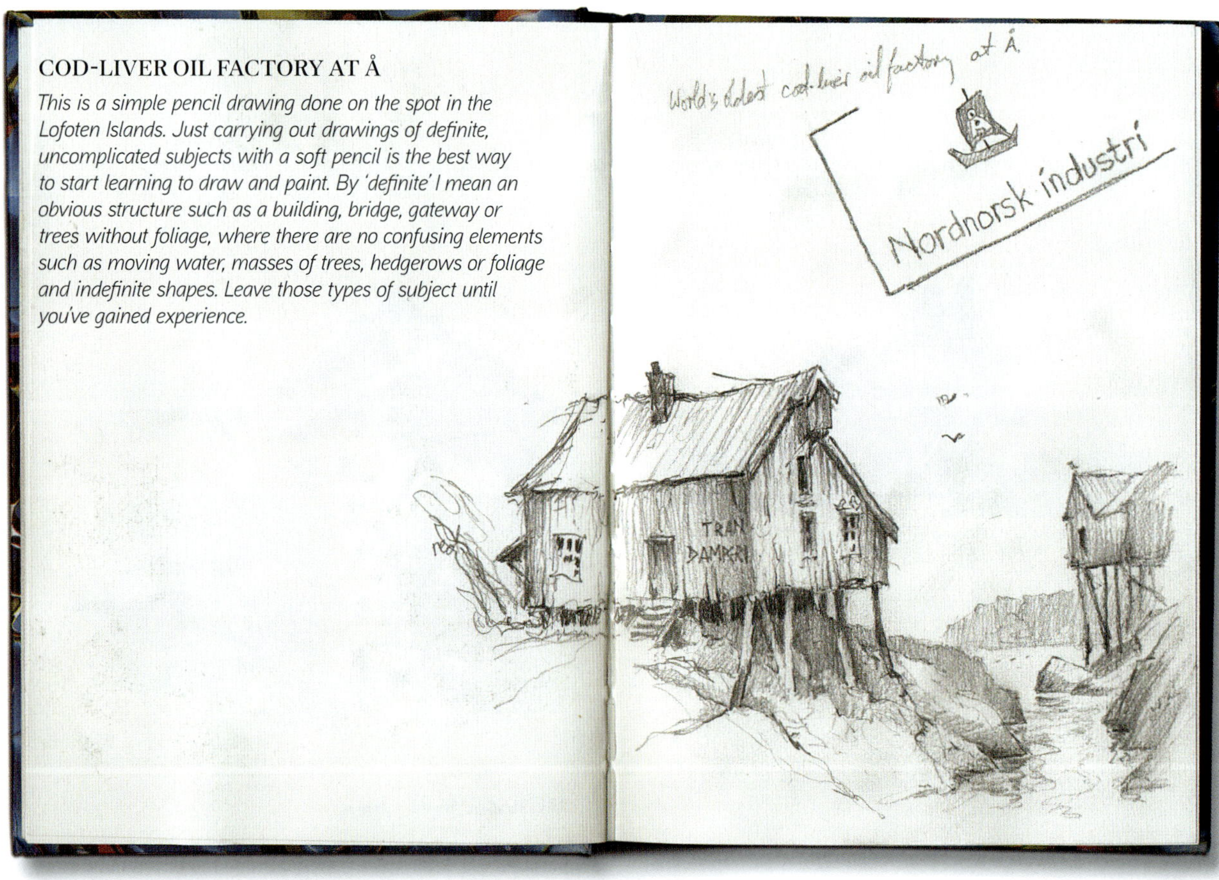


**COD-LIVER OIL FACTORY AT Å**

*This is a simple pencil drawing done on the spot in the Lofoten Islands. Just carrying out drawings of definite, uncomplicated subjects with a soft pencil is the best way to start learning to draw and paint. By 'definite' I mean an obvious structure such as a building, bridge, gateway or trees without foliage, where there are no confusing elements such as moving water, masses of trees, hedgerows or foliage and indefinite shapes. Leave those types of subject until you've gained experience.*

# PAINTING CLIFFS

The secret to painting cliffs is to study them with a view to picking out the most prominent lines of fractures and shadow areas, how you are going to emphasize the main colours, where you will suggest most detail, and how the overall cliff is affected by tones.

Don't try to include everything, as that will make you feel overwhelmed. Begin with a light pencil drawing, seeking out the main shapes and deciding where you will put the emphasis. If there are strong gullies and fracture lines, pick out the most interesting of these and lightly delineate the most exciting bits of detail.

Next, think about all the colours you need to paint the cliff. Prepare those mixtures plus any colours you may wish to drop into wet washes. Forget about the shadows for the moment. Begin applying colour washes, starting with the lightest colours. With watercolours we need to begin light and gradually work in the darker colours, laying these over the lighter ones in places. Drop in any additional colours – perhaps where you see a change in the rock colour – then allow the whole to dry. Now you can paint in the shadows. Wait for these to dry, then draw in the fracture lines with a fine brush or rigger, applying greater pressure to the brush where you need a wider fracture line. Introduce any rock detail into the cliff with a medium-size brush such as a no. 6 or 8 round.

Note that cliffs tend to be darker in tone lower down, where they get washed regularly by the sea, and you are likely to need to introduce darker tones in this area. You can do this by laying a wash of clear water over the bottom half of the cliff, and then applying the darker colour to this lower area. Do not take it right up to the top of your wash of clear water, as the intention is to achieve a soft edge to the darker area.

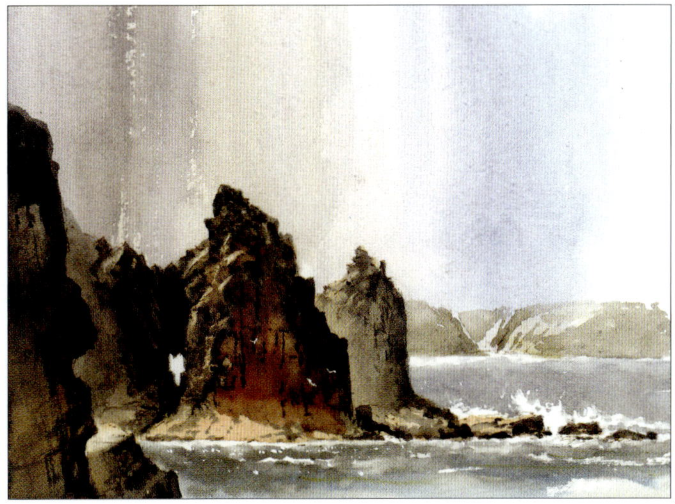

**TOWER POINT**
*18 x 21.5cm (7 x 8½in)*

*Cliffs are complicated structures to render, but here I deliberately chose a backlit subject so that much of the detail was lost in shadow. Flecks of sunlight highlighted parts of the rocks and this slowly changed as I sketched. I've scrambled in and out of these towers at times so have a fairly intimate knowledge of the place and have thus been able to work out that the right-hand tower is separate from the rest, so I accentuated the space by lightening the right-hand tower and darkening the right-hand edge of the left-hand tower.*

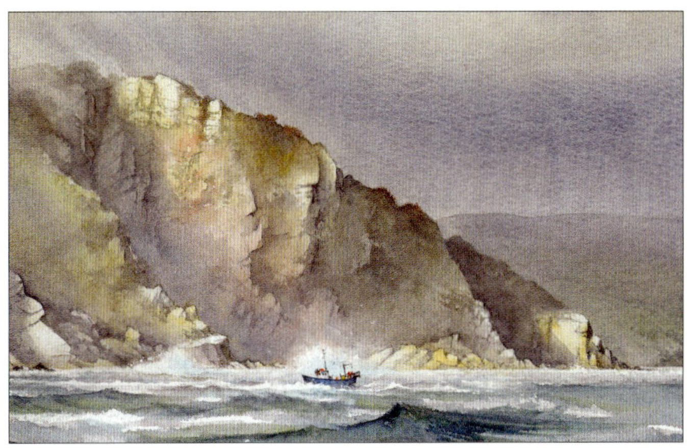

**RENDERING CLIFF DETAIL**

*This is only part of a huge imperial-sized watercolour and illustrates well my three approaches to painting complicated cliff scenery. Firstly strong detail can be seen at the top left and high above the boat. There is more subdued detail directly above the boat, and no detail at all in much of the area above the diagonal rib of rocks extending forwards from the prow of the boat, and also the area to the stern, above the jumble of rocks.*

## USEFUL COLOUR MIXTURES

The colour mixtures shown to the right are effective for basic sea greys. They range from light to dark, warm to cool, and I often use two of the mixtures in the same sea scene, with a cool mixture in the distance and a warmer, stronger band closer to the foreground.

Additionally, while the wash is wet, I commonly drop in other colours such as cadmium yellow light, yellow ochre or phthalo blue. These grey mixtures are far from exhaustive and can be achieved with a variety of colours.

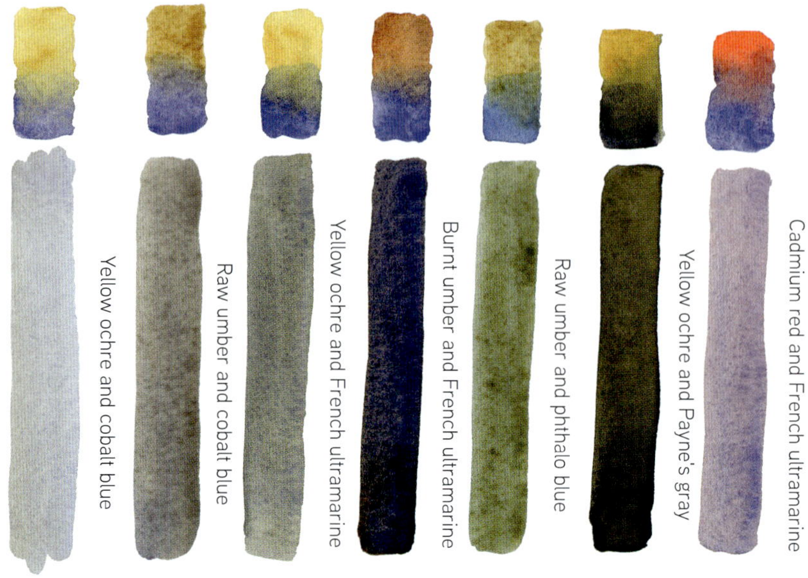


## PAINTING BEACHES, SURF AND ROCKS

The combination of beaches, surf and rocks can provide the artist with delightful compositions. Watch for variations in tone and colour on the sand – I often lay a wash of Naples yellow or yellow ochre and, when that has dried, overlay a colour. I use permanent alizarin crimson or another red if I feel it needs warming up – sometimes over part, sometimes whole – or a darker colour if I need a cast shadow. This can be done wet-into-wet, but it's simpler to begin by overlaying the wash on dry paper.

Note how parts of the beach are more interesting when they are wet and therefore darker. These are excellent places to emphasize the definition between beach and surf. Try to avoid having a strong, sharp surf-line all the way across a composition as this will intrude: break it up by losing it in places, or soften it off with a damp brush. You can do this while the paint is still wet or leave it until the paper is completely dry.

With surf, keep it simple. Don't try to include every nuance of tonal detail. Resist the temptation to include every mini-wave you can see. Gain your experience on gentle waves to start with, working up to massive breakers later, as described further into the book. The painting Dunraven Bay opposite is a good example of what to look for in a less complicated line of surf. As with the beach, it's interesting to drop in a different colour to provide a little variation in the water. Beach pools and rivulets running into the sea can add interest and break up monotonous passages, and I often introduce these from other sketches, even if they are not actually present.

Rocks tend to be a little easier than moving surf, but need care. Don't feel you have to cover every square centimetre with detail or fractures, and it is helpful to indicate a slight change in colour in places: colour changes are usually gradual, fracture lines tend to be stark. It's good to have fracture lines disappearing into shadow areas in places. There are many examples of various types and shapes of rock in this book, with a variety of treatments, so copy some of the examples that appeal to you.

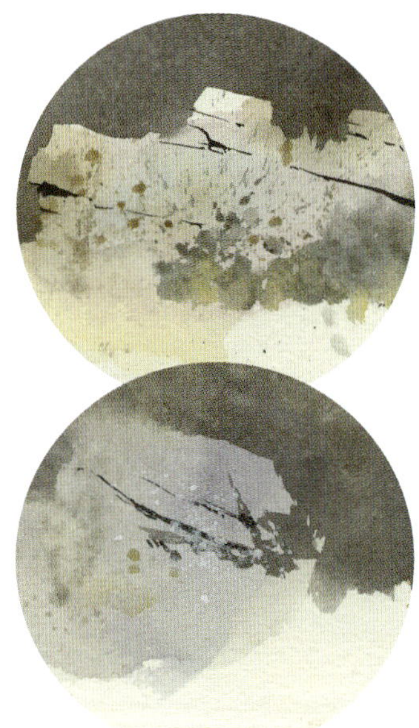

**ROCK FRACTURES**

*Rocks vary considerably in character. Here I have illustrated fracture lines using a rigger, applying different pressures on the brush to create thicker and thinner fracture lines as I require them.*

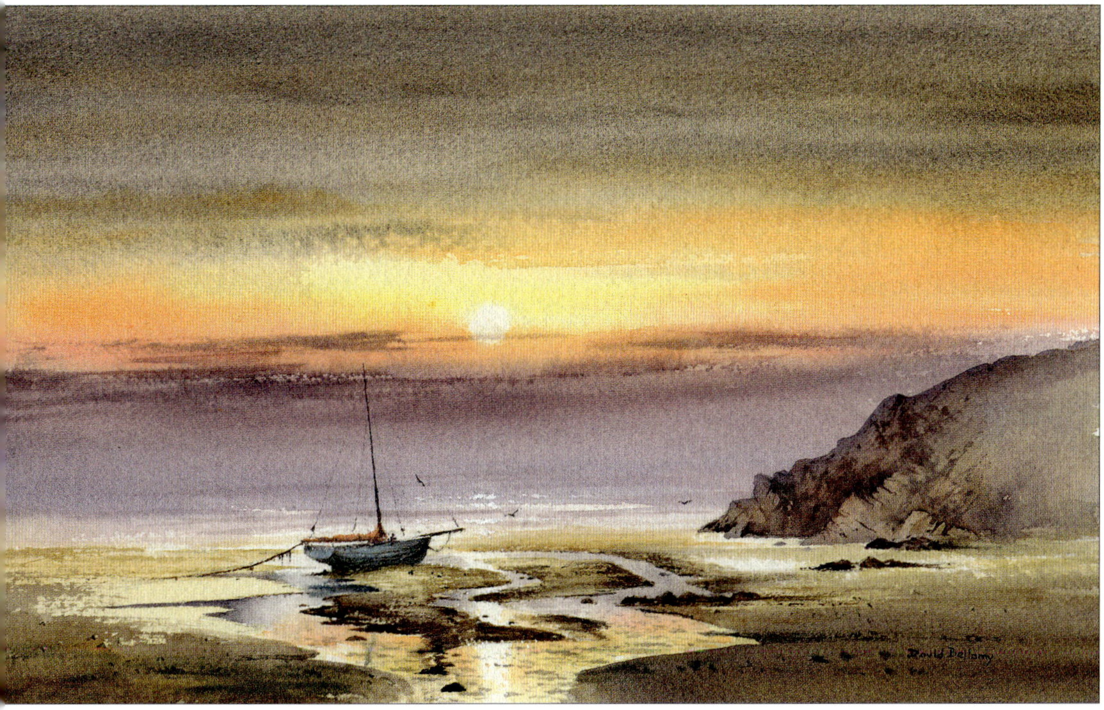

BOAT AT SUNSET

*18 x 28cm (7 x 11in)*

*I like to make the most of pools and rivulets on the beach. They can add interest, act as a lead-in, or support a focal point such as a rock or – as in this case – a shapely boat.*

DUNRAVEN BAY

*15 x 23cm (6 x 9in)*

*Painting the sea can be extremely complicated, so we need to break it down into manageable chunks. In this watercolour of the beach at Dunraven Bay, the sea has been kept fairly simple: the distant water has been painted with a weak mixture of French ultramarine and cadmium red, and this is considerably strengthened as it gets closer, especially where it defines the crest of the white breaking wave. When the sea wash had dried, I dabbed in small flecks of the same mixture to suggest the rippled surface. Where the beach is wet, the sand is darker, again defining the edge of the surf. I have deliberately softened off the edges of both the wave-tops and the surf in places to suggest a more natural look.*

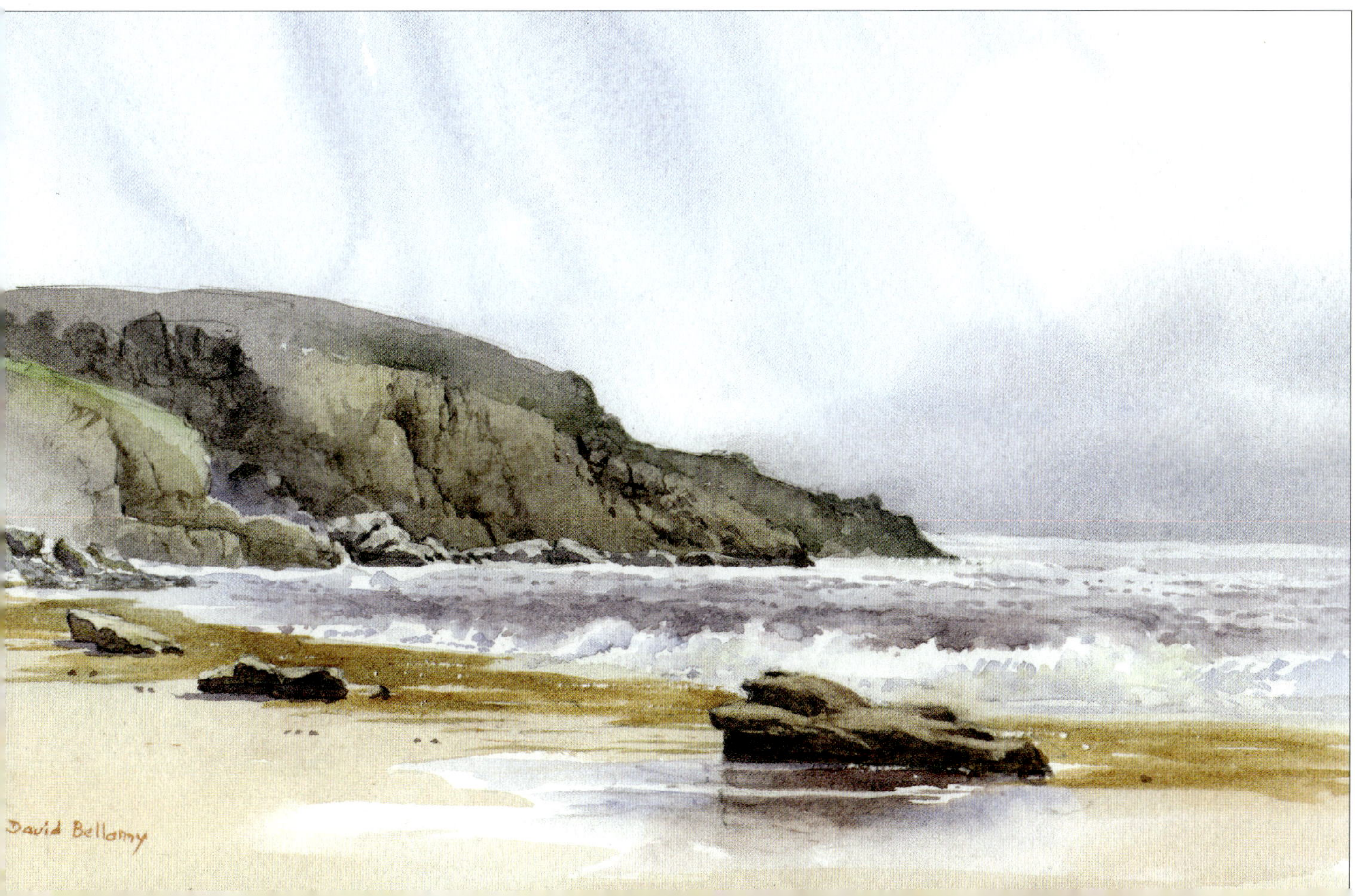

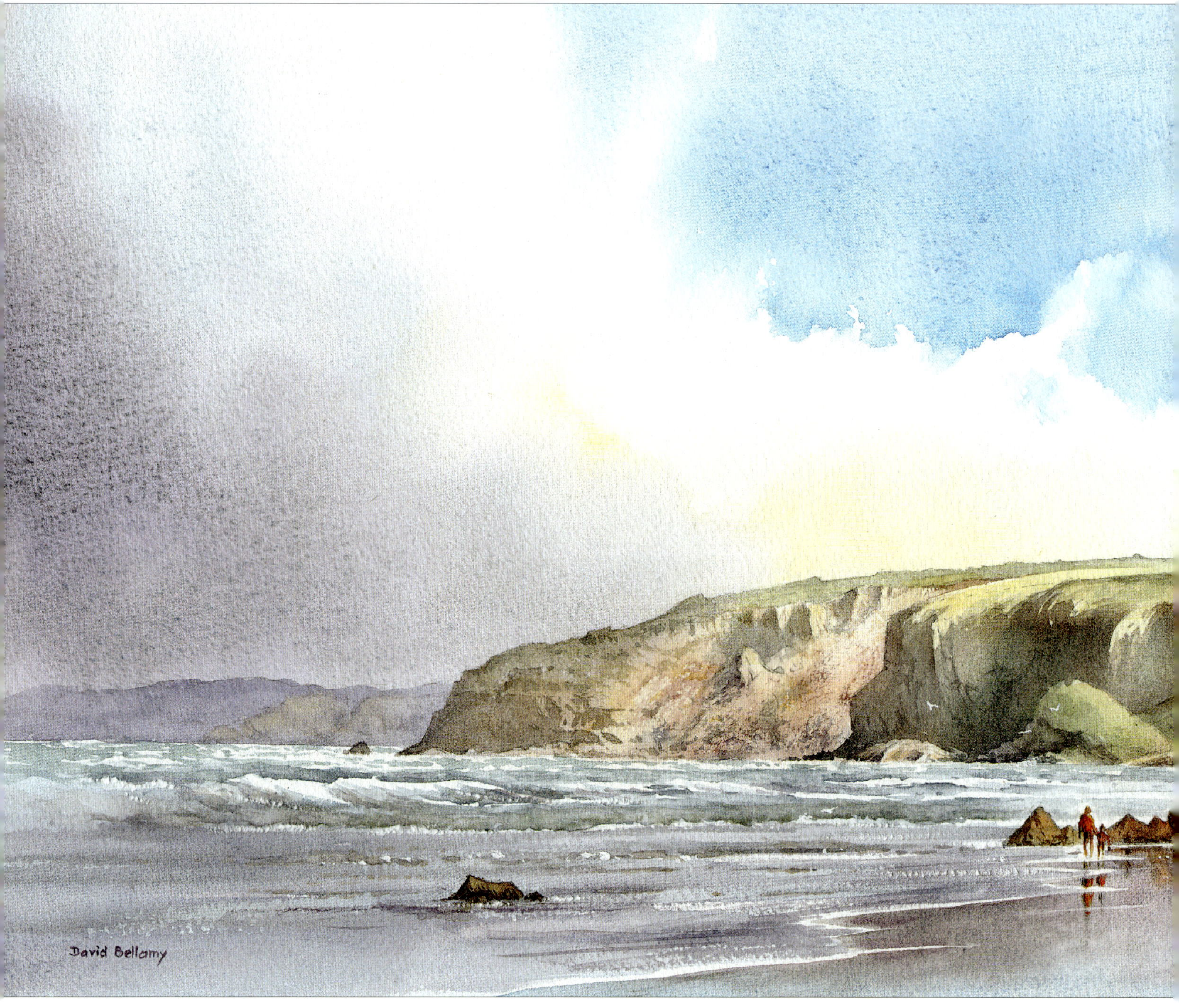

BROAD HAVEN REFLECTIONS

*28 x 43cm (11 x 17in)*

*Although I carried out an original sketch I also spent some time waiting for people (often with their dogs) to come wading through the wet surface of the beach; I then photographed them and did quick pencil sketches, concentrating on the figures and their reflections. I did this from a distance to avoid causing any concerns. The reflections were achieved by laying a wash of cobalt blue and cadmium red between surf and sand, and dropping in the rock and figure colours wet into wet.*

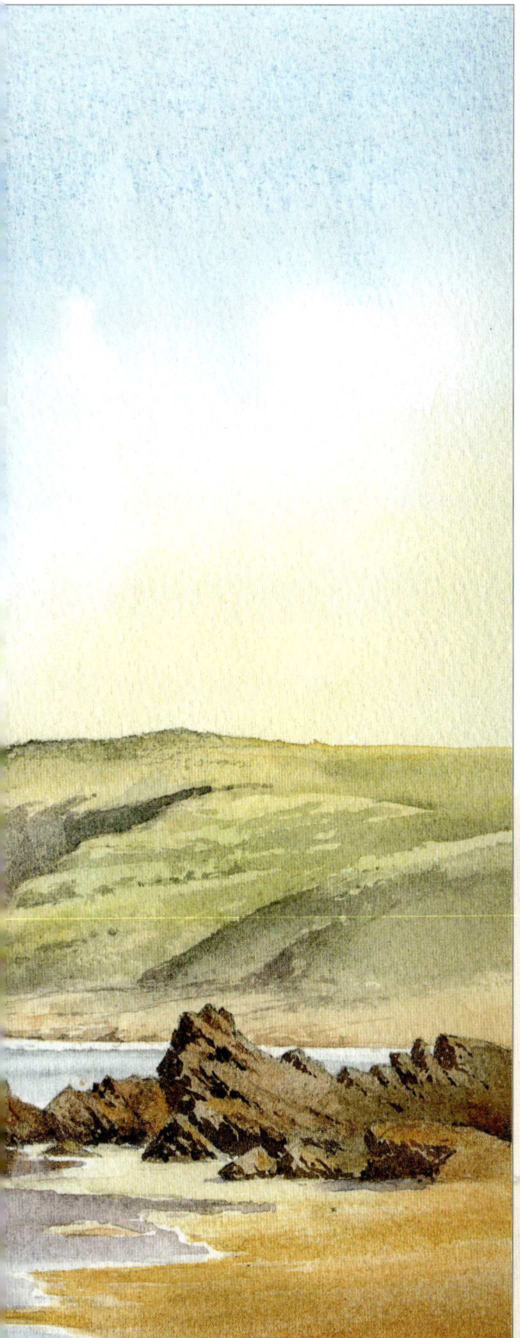

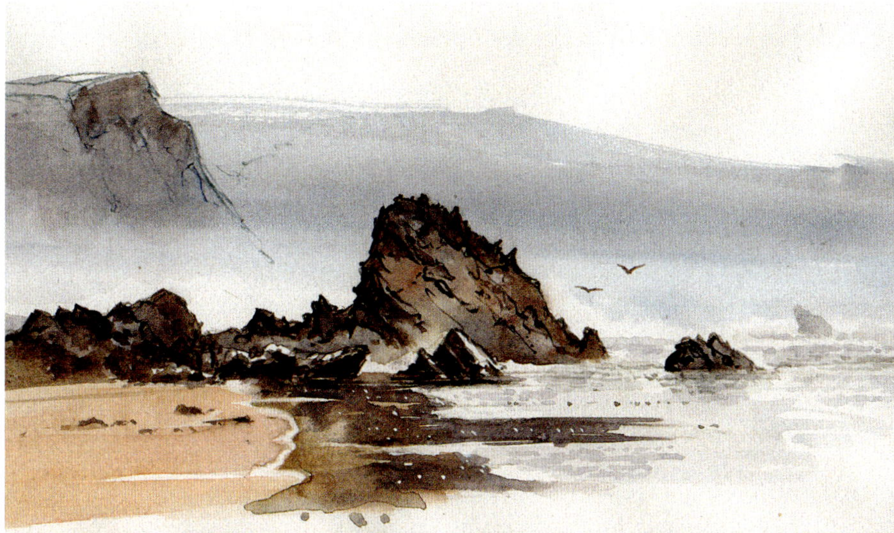

## INTRODUCING WATERCOLOUR PENCILS INTO A SKETCH

*Although a faint sea mist subdued much of the distant lower cliff in the sketch above, I have accentuated it to improve the atmospheric effect. I used normal watercolour washes but drew into the wet washes with dark watercolour pencils such as black and blue-grey. I prefer the Prismalo watercolour pencils for this technique as they have a harder core which tends to stay sharper for a longer time. There are two enormous benefits from this system: I can work faster as I don't have to wait for the washes to dry, and if it rains, I just carry on – rain may wipe out most of the colour washes but often improves the watercolour pencil effects.*

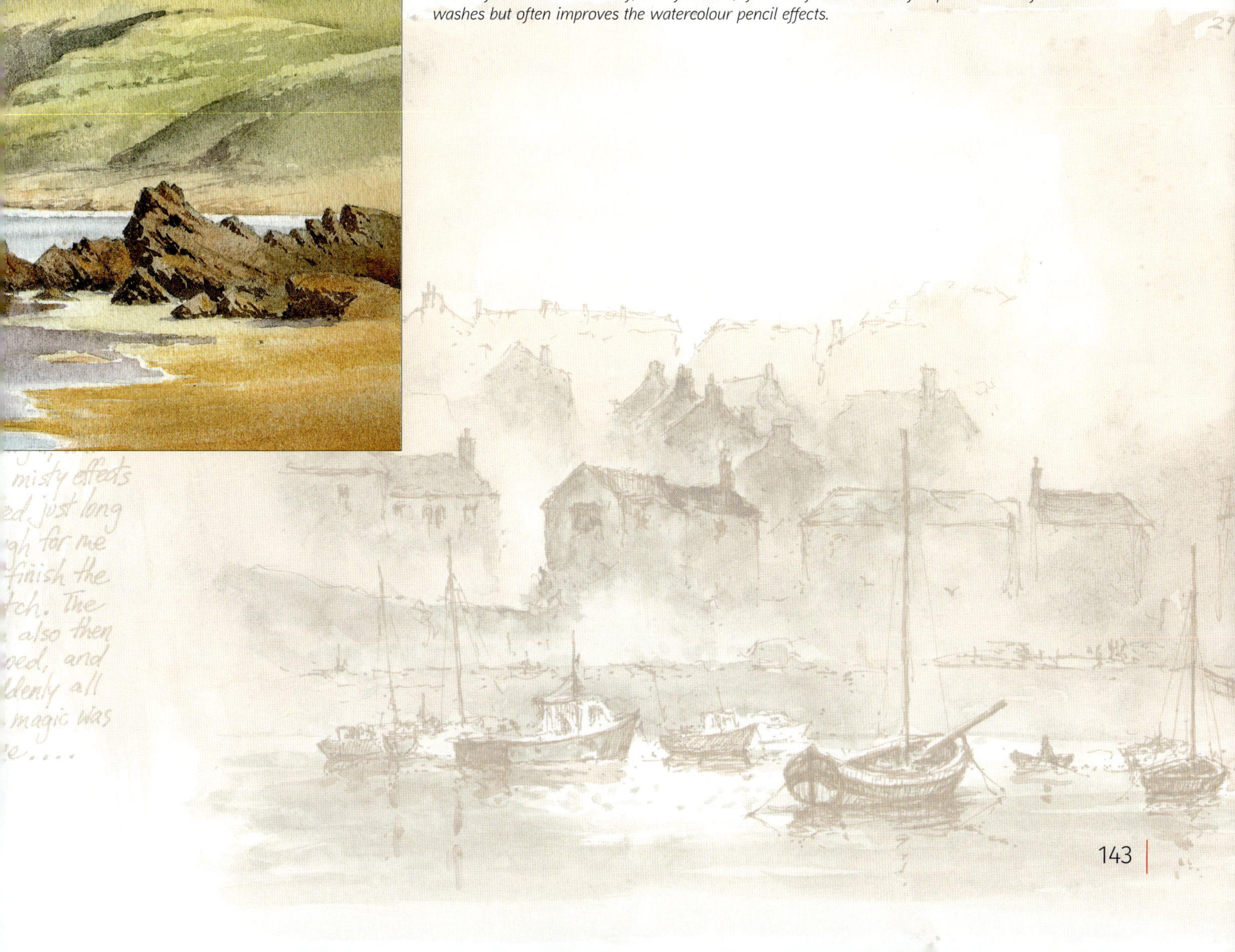

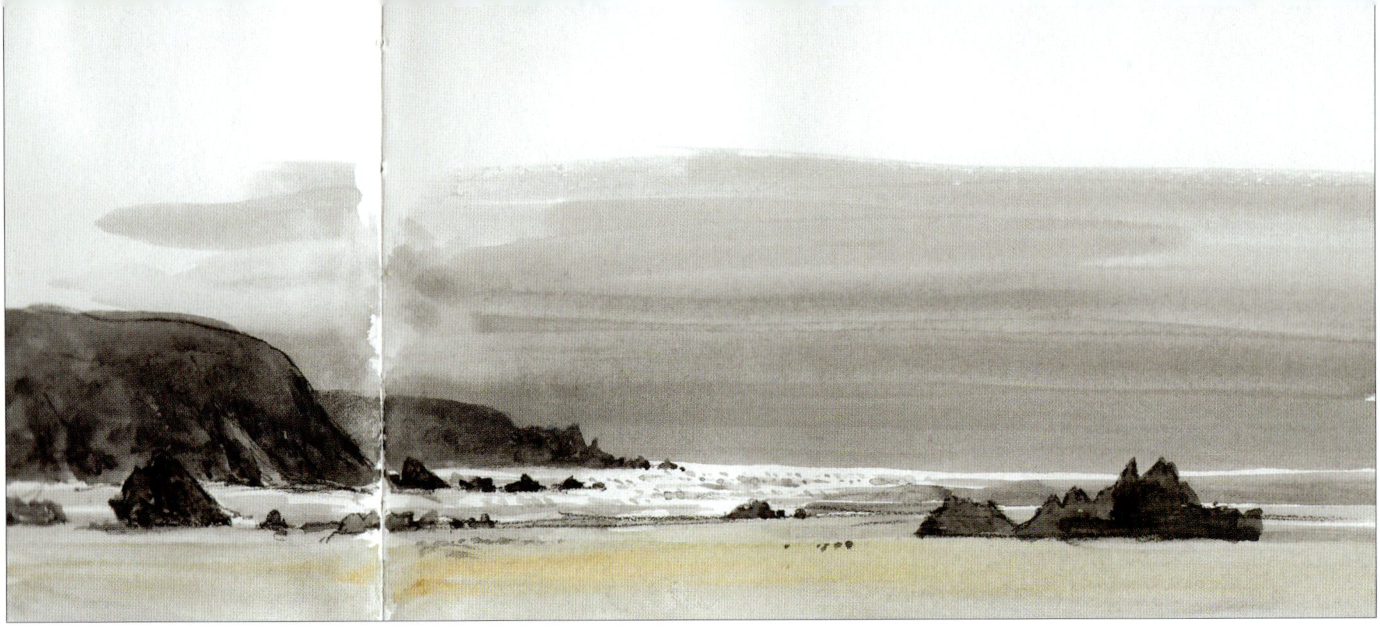

### GENTLE SURF

*Often there are not any distinctive waves, as in this simple watercolour sketch on cartridge paper. Here the small waves have been suggested by horizontal strokes of a no. 10 round brush plus a few little blobs to impart a sense of movement and sparkle, leaving white streaks with a horizontal emphasis.*

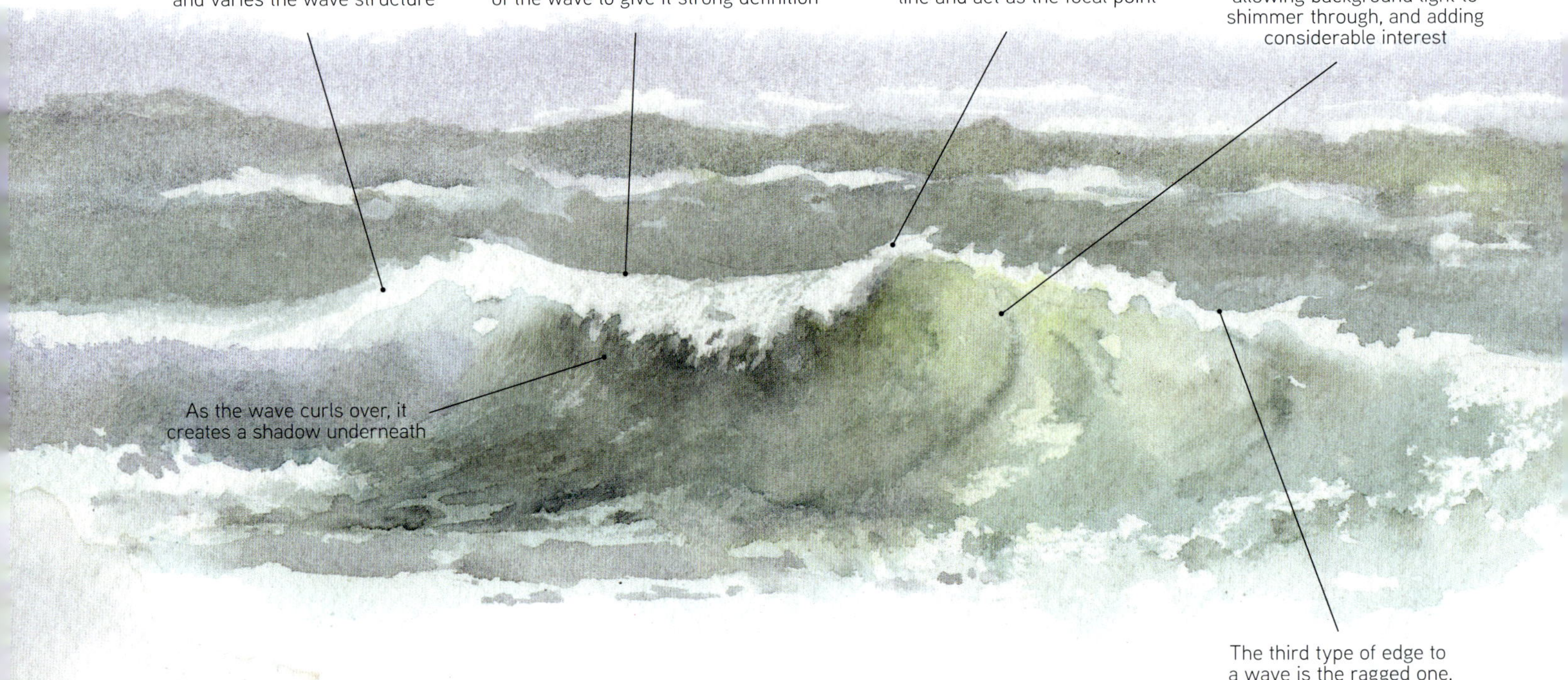


### WAVE STRUCTURE

*This shows the basic structure of a breaking wave. Wave structures can vary considerably and it is helpful to carry out many studies of different types of waves while you are on the spot. Don't rely entirely on the camera. This is a fairly typical wave as it breaks. As it curls over, a shadow is created beneath the crest, which at this point usually stands out prominently against the background. At the same time, as the wave extends upwards, the wall of water becomes thinner, enabling a translucent light to pass through, often quite bright when lit from behind.*

# PAINTING WAVES

Waves vary from minor ripples to monstrous walls of water. We begin with a gentle surf sketch (see opposite, top) which can introduce an air of tranquillity to a scene. We then move on to analyse the structure of a more complicated wave as it breaks onto the beach (see opposite, bottom). This kind of wave can act as the focal point for the whole composition and can have endless variations in colour, size, shape and tone. Work from these examples so that by the time it comes to sketching them directly on the spot you are better placed to render the structure of many kinds of wave.

In strong winds the waves not only seem larger, but often spindrift is blown sideways over the top of the wave as you will see in the example of *Windy Day, Barafundle Bay* (see below). As this is more complicated, you may wish to postpone working on this type of wave for now and come back to it when you are more adept at the techniques involved.

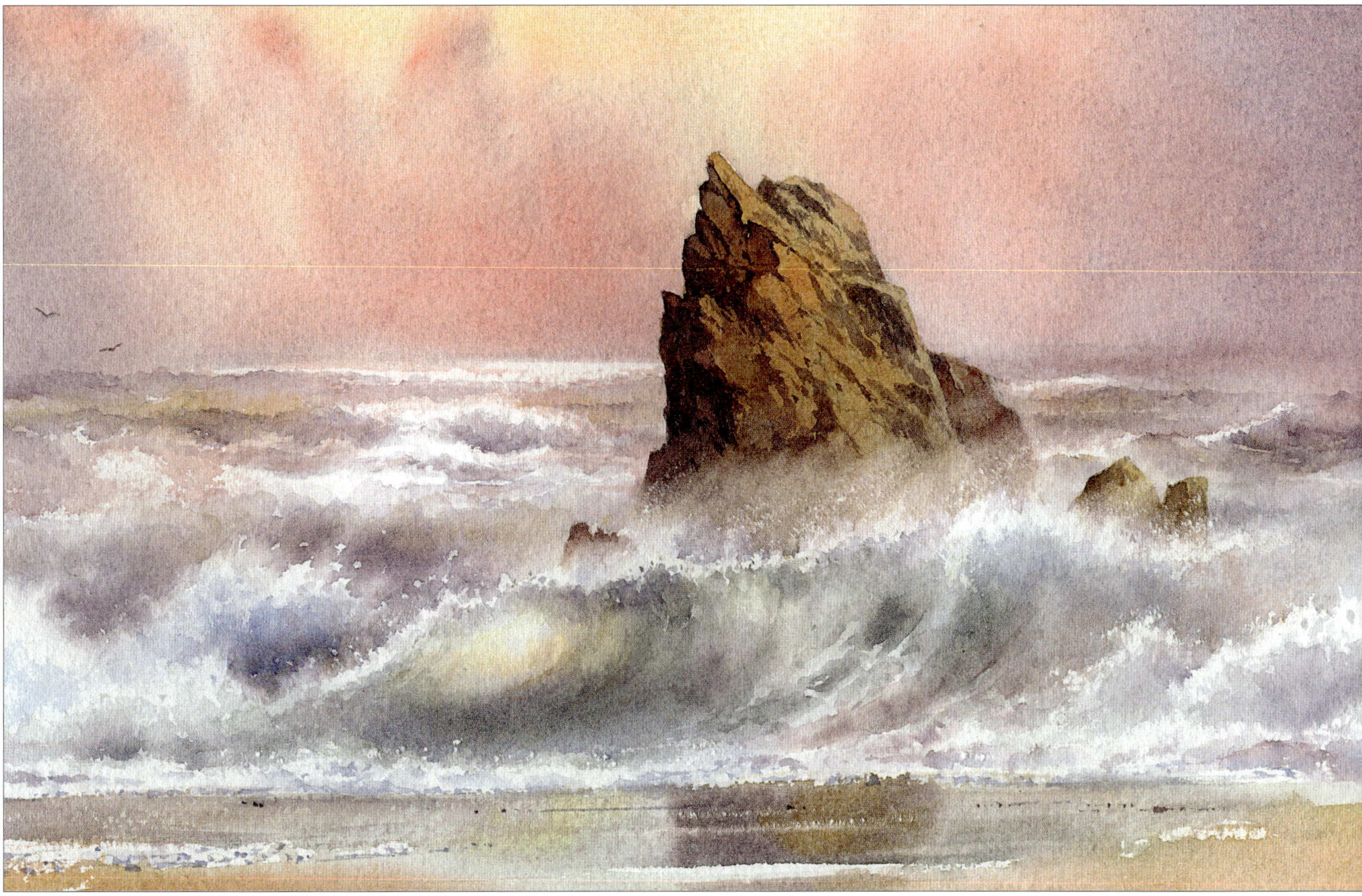

**DETAIL FROM WINDY DAY, BARAFUNDLE BAY**

*This concentrates on the central part of the painting where the wind is catching the crest of the wave and hurling spray to the right. This effect was achieved by pulling out colour diagonally upwards from the crest of the wave using a 12mm (½in) flat brush. When the area directly above the wave had dried, I scratched out suggestions of blown spray with a scalpel.*

## INTERACTION OF ROCKS AND SEA

This is one of my favourite subjects, especially when wild Atlantic breakers are hammering the coastline. Water draining off a large rock can be a complicated – but evocative – subject.

Avoid putting in every minor rivulet cascading down the rock, and instead concentrate on the outstanding ones, noting where they fall into a shadow area. At these points I lay on a weak shadow colour with French ultramarine or cobalt blue, sometimes touching in a little permanent alizarin crimson in order to pick out these details.

Always ensure that you have plenty of white cascading water present, by leaving that part of the paper untouched: these areas form the highlights. The next stage is to introduce the dark wet rocks, in each case softening off their bottom edges where they disappear into the water. Finally, note foaming water at the bottom of the mass of rock, and where the edge gets lost in places.

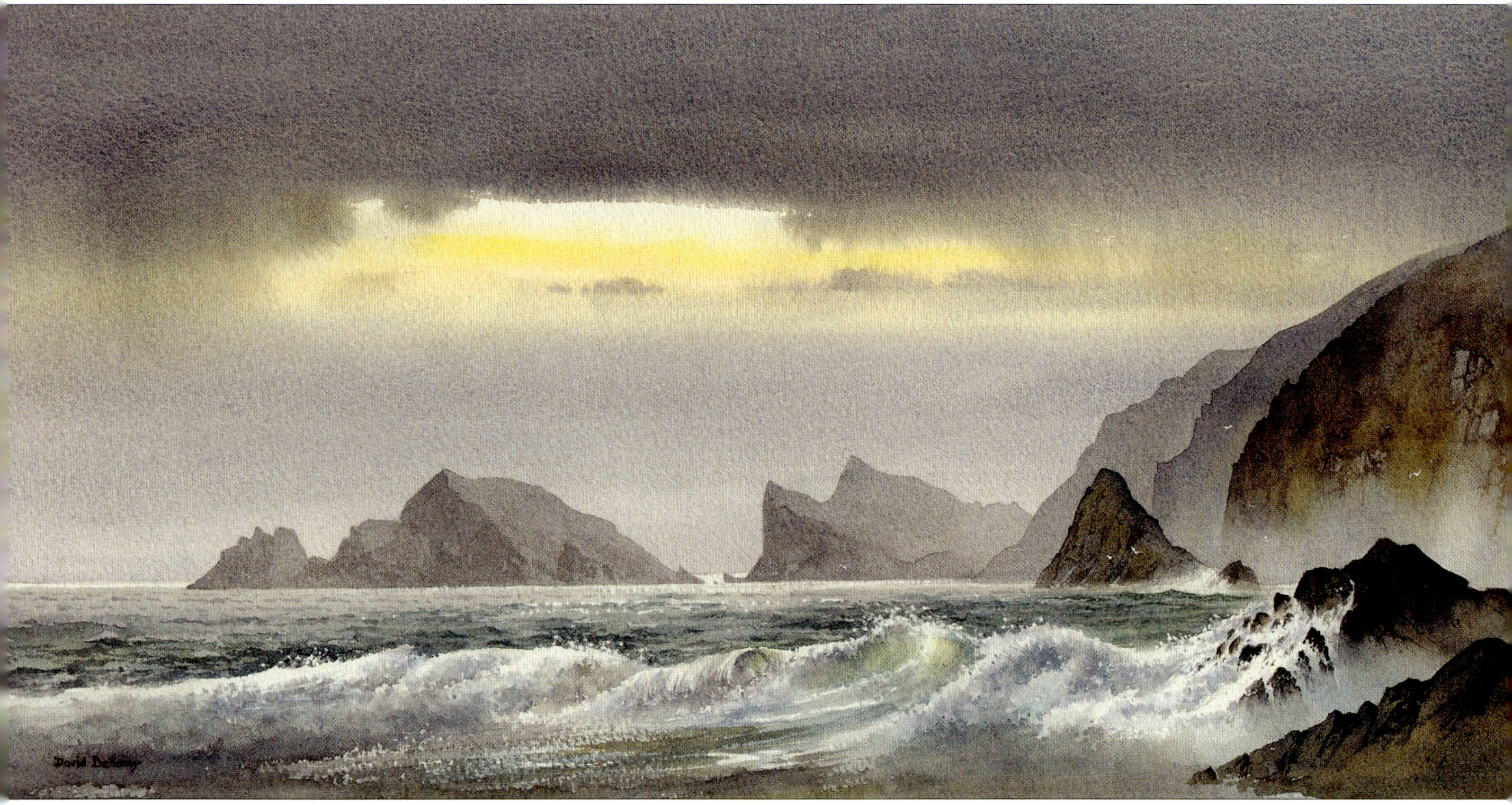

**ROCKY ANVILS**
*23 x 46cm (9 x 18in)*

*The sparkling white spots below the great rocky anvils were achieved by using masking fluid immediately after completing the drawing. I spotted this on with a small brush, taking care to clean the brush off well with warm soapy water afterwards, as masking fluid can quickly ruin brushes. When the fluid was dry, I painted over it with a light blue-grey wash.*

*For the water draining off the foreground rocks, I first painted in the light blue-grey shadowy part of the falling water, leaving the tops mainly as untouched white paper. When this had dried, I described the strong dark rocks with a mixture of burnt umber and French ultramarine.*

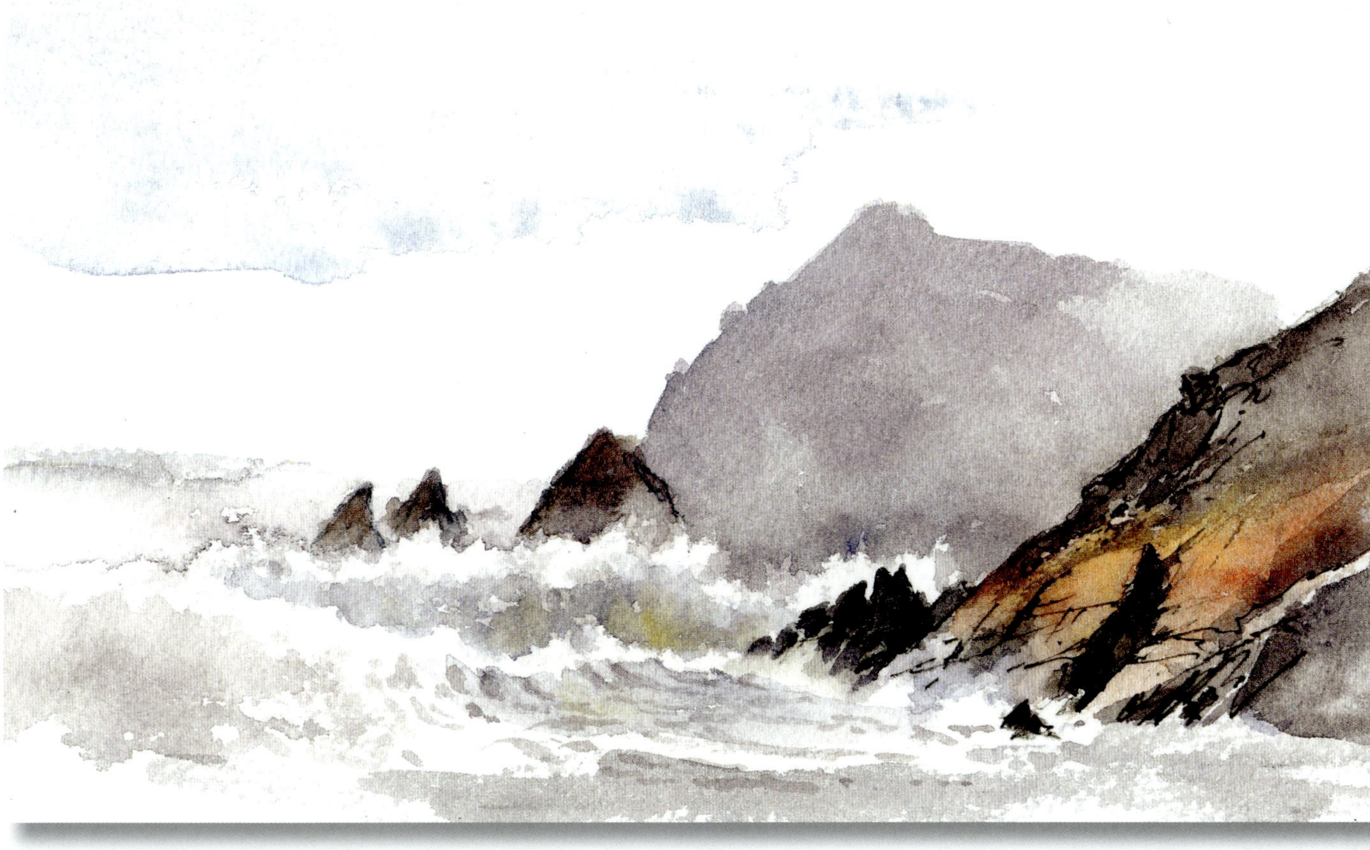

BOISTEROUS SURF, WESTDALE BAY

*18 x 21.5cm (7 x 8½in)*

*In this watercolour sketch, the water was more complicated than in* Rocky Anvils *opposite, but even so I have simplified it considerably from the actual scene. Much of the wave-top area has been described using the side of a round brush in semi-circular sweeps to suggest the choppiness. See how dropping a touch of yellow ochre into the wet sea wash below the central triangular rock has enhanced the wave, and the darkest jagged rocks are emphasized by the white splash behind them.*

INTERACTION OF ROCKS AND SEA

*For this sketch I used a 4B pencil and to achieve the soft-edged splashes I pulled out the graphite with a fine pencil-eraser. Careful observation of the way the sea hits the rocks is vital. The repetitive nature of the waves helps you to observe time after time how best to render the various actions and movements. Videoing the action can be helpful.*

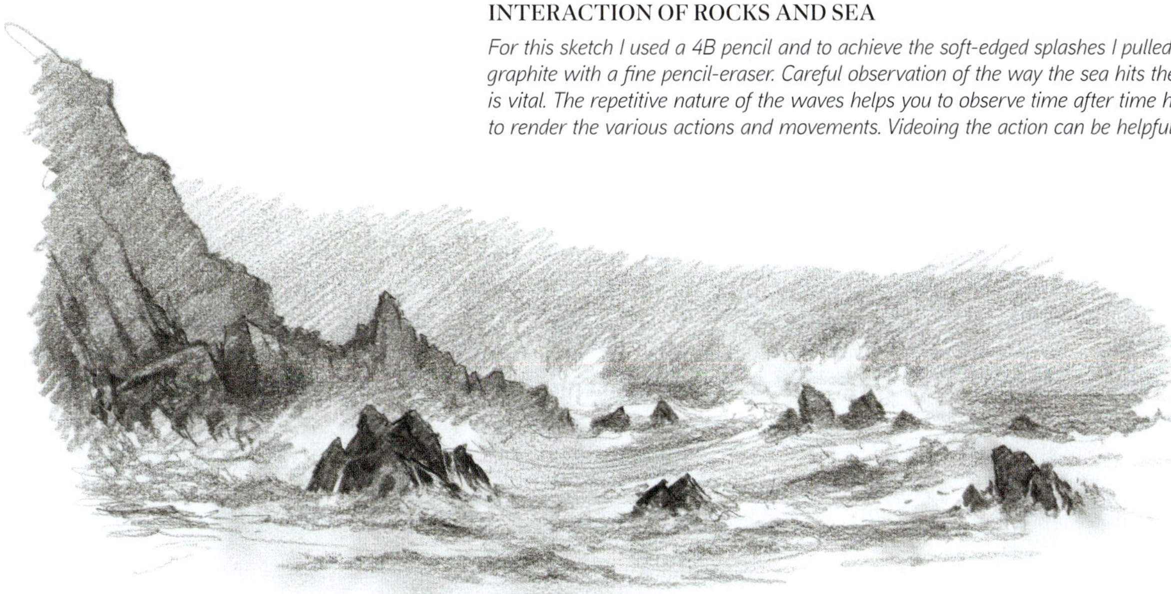

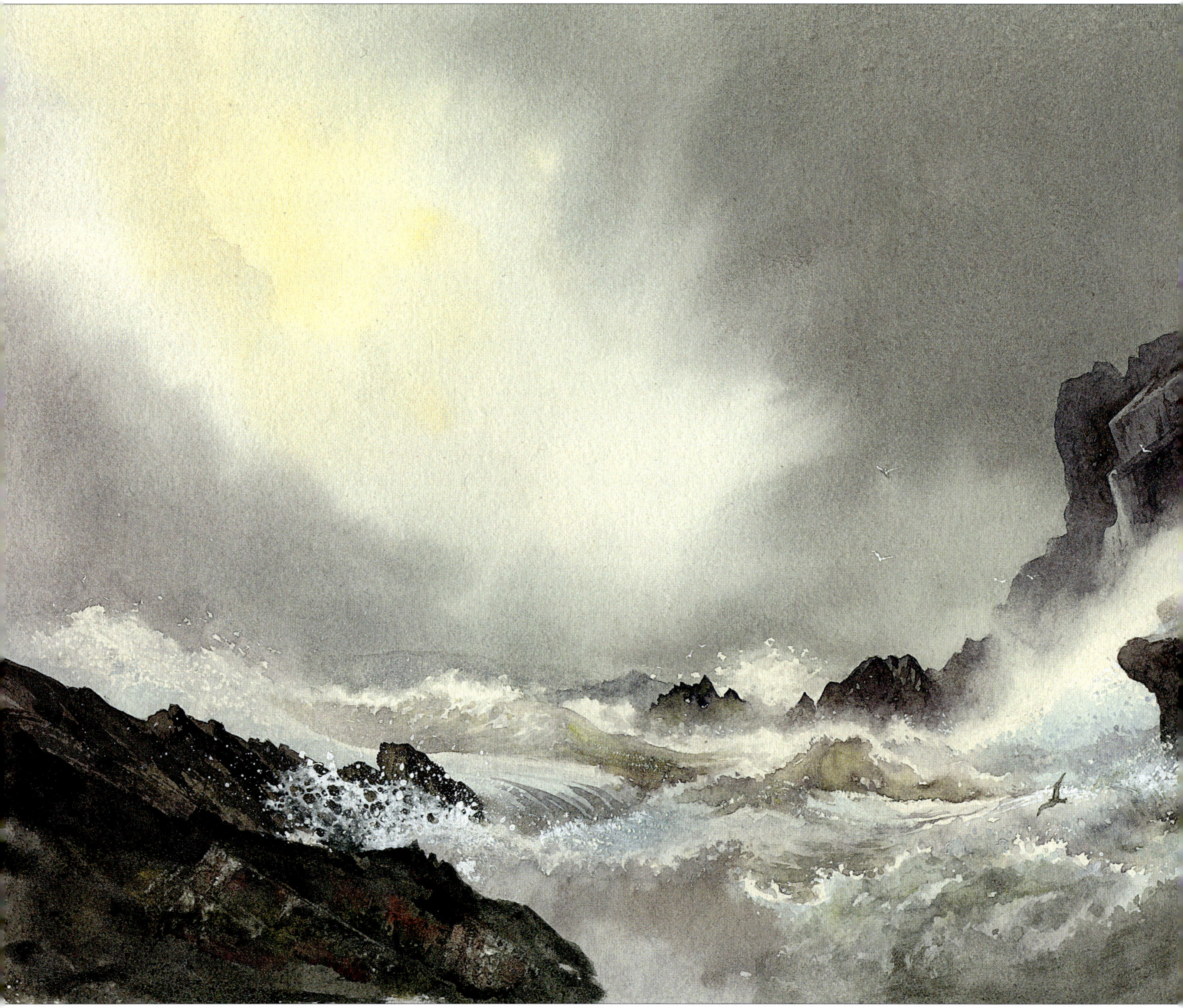

**STORMY COASTLINE**

*30.5 x 40.5cm (12 x 16in) 300gsm (140lb) Rough paper*

*Creating whites in turbulent seas can be a challenge, but there are several ways of achieving this, as shown in this watercolour carried out on Saunders Waterford Rough paper. On the left I produced a splash by dabbing a sponge in white gouache and applying it to a dark background. Here and there I have stabbed and scratched with a scalpel to suggest white foam – this is most evident below the right-hand rocks to the right of the gull. The white areas were left as the white paper by working around them with colour.*

## Capturing the whites

Where rocks and sea meet there is generally a lot of white surf, spray and splashes, and these can be tackled in numerous ways. In some of these examples I have included a variety of techniques to achieve these whites, as they can add so much life and movement to a scene. Try them all and see which ones suit you best: masking fluid, scratching with a scalpel, white gouache or acrylic, negatively painting round a white object and leaving the paper white, or even rubbing a candle across the water to act as a resist. This latter method is more of a hit and miss affair, but can be effective.

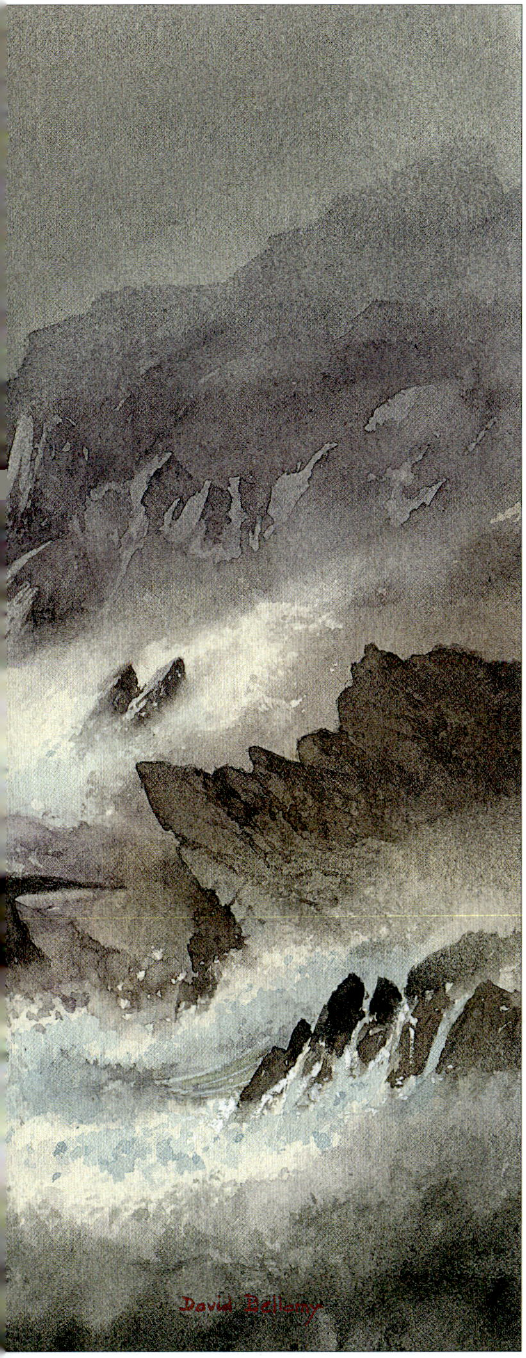


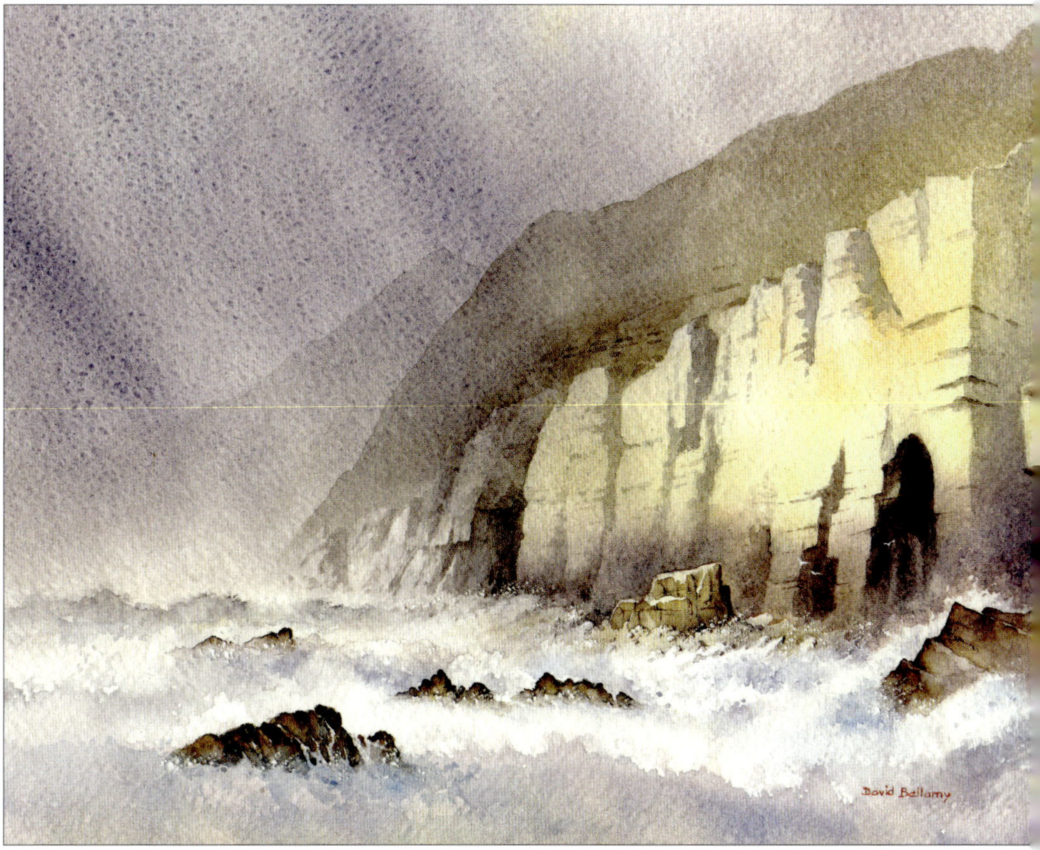


WAVE-LASHED CLIFFS
*23 x 28cm (9 x 11in) 300gsm (140lb) Rough paper*

*The darker tone of the lower part of the cliffs helps to accentuate the white foaming surf as it crashes against the rocks, and the final stage of this painting was to scratch out splashes at the top of the surf with a scalpel, mainly using a diagonal stroke to suggest movement towards the cliffs. Some of these strokes half-obliterate rock detail effectively. The textures were enhanced by using a Saunders Waterford Rough watercolour paper surface.*

# DRAWING AND PAINTING BOATS

Boats can cause a lot of teeth-gnashing, especially if you are trying to draw an example with voluptuous curves, as you often see in the Mediterranean. If you are not happy including boats, but they are vital to the scene, then keep them simple – the further away they are, the better! Draw them broadside-on, which is the simplest profile. Break them up with figures working in front of them or with draped nets, tarpaulins or other marine clutter.

Usually in a harbour scene there are different types of boats, so go for the easier ones and move them into positions where you can lose certain parts of the vessel. You can lose detail in boats through judicious positioning and effective use of light and shadow. There are further ways of tackling boats in the chapter A day by the sea, when you are actually confronted by them.

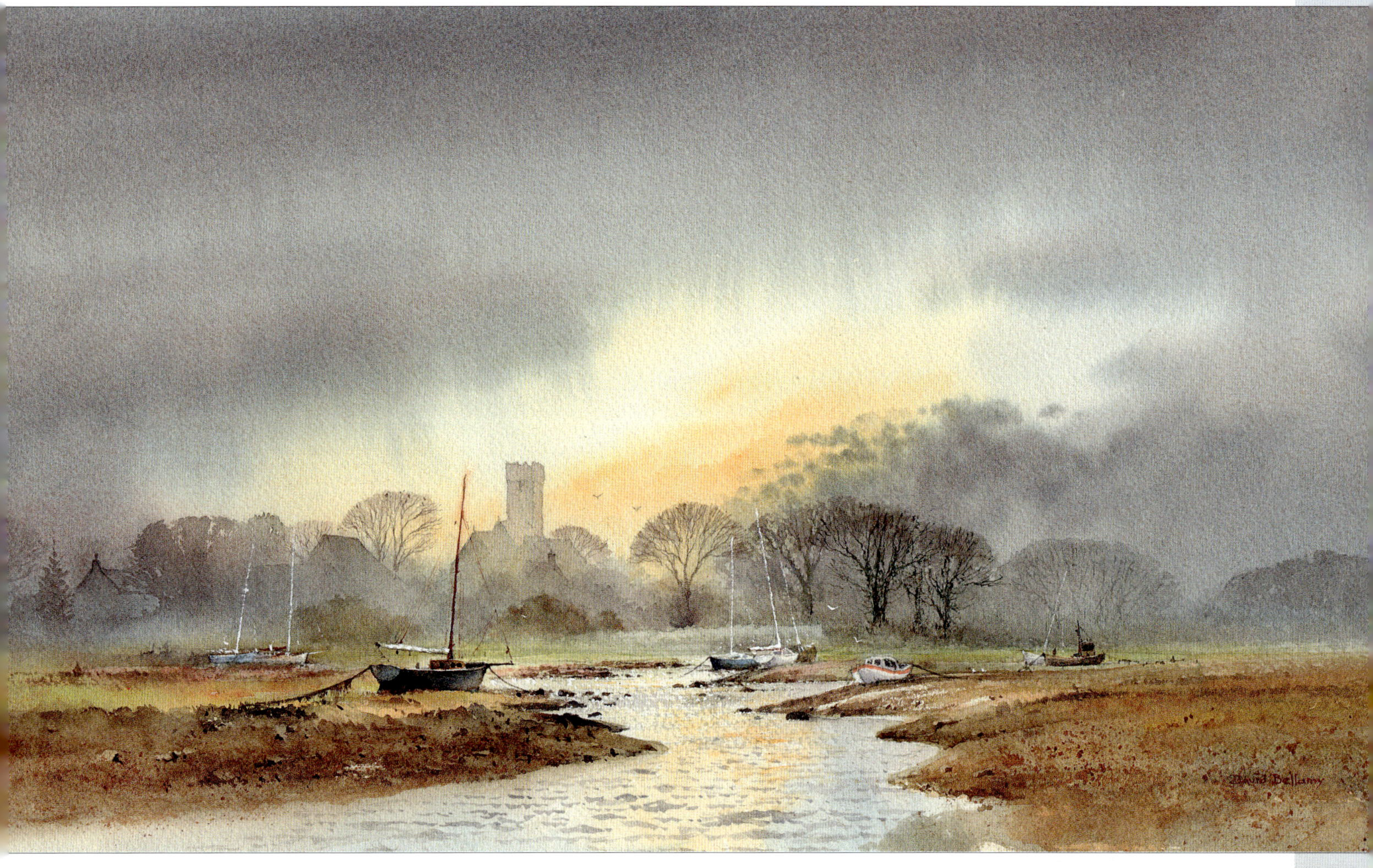


APRIL EVENING, ANGLE

*20 x 43cm (8 x 17in)*

*These boats are fairly easy to draw when they are broadside-on. Where you have several boats, it pays to overlap some otherwise the composition may well appear contrived. Note the reflected light on the forward part of the hull of the closest vessel.*

## Drawing boats using a box

This is a relatively complex approach, useful for boats lying on one side. The secret is to work out the important lines and angles first. There is no need to draw a complete box structure, and as you gain experience, you will need less of the construction process. Make sure the construction lines are faint and easily erased.

1 The rudder line is important as it indicates the angle at which the boat lies, and also the line of the mast and other verticals, such as those of a cabin. Hold a pencil vertically against the rudder line to assess the initial angle.

2 Add the mast, making sure that it is parallel to the rudder.

3 Draw line B–C at 90° to the rudder line and estimate its width by comparing it with the height of the boat.

4 Establish the parallel horizontal construction lines and the boat's length.

5 Points D and E are approximately halfway along the boat and show where the hull would appear if it was straight along. However, as the hull normally curves outwards at this point, points F and G are approximations of where the hull would actually appear.

### TIP

Cabins can have a forward, backward or sideways rake, but just as with the mast, the line of the rudder will help you to assess this.

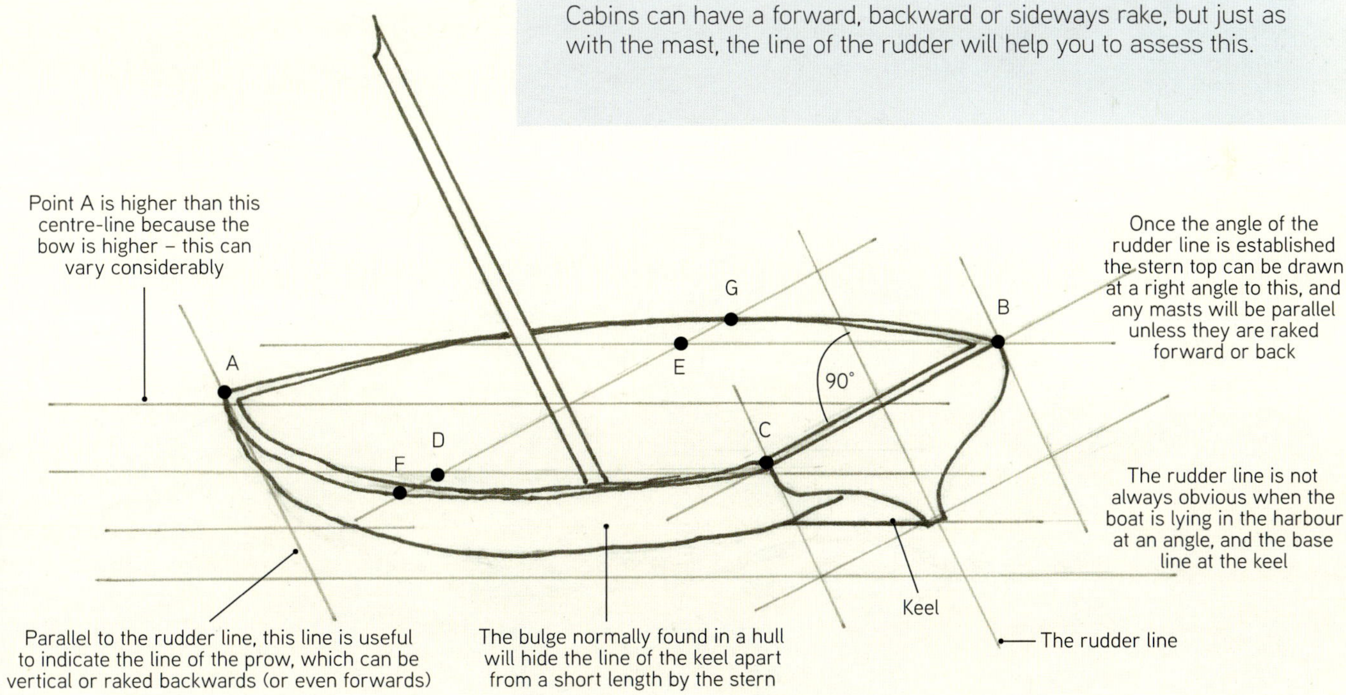

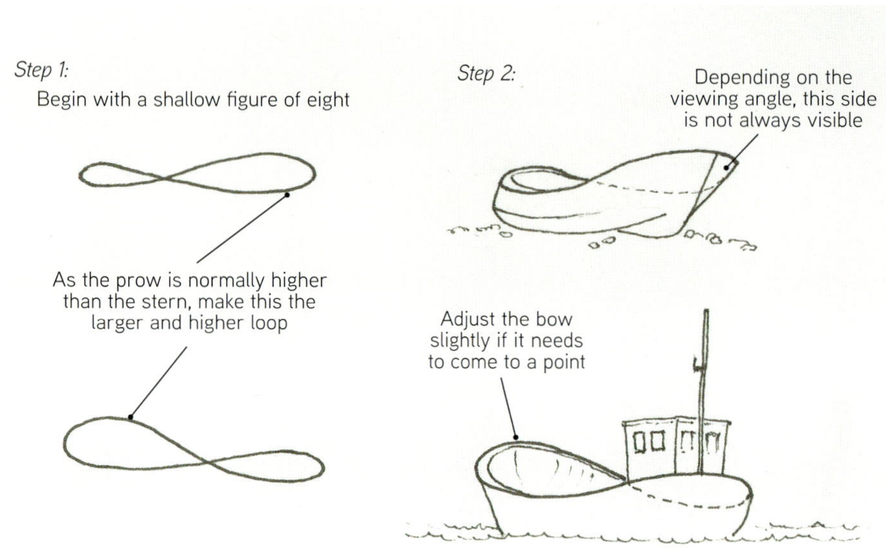


## Drawing boats using a figure of eight

This method is useful in some cases but is rather limited and does not suit all boats. It can be a useful guide when trying to render the graceful curves of small boats.

The stern can easily be changed from the round version shown in this example, to one with a square end.

## Drawing boats using a model

Working from a model boat which has fairly authentic lines can be an excellent way to practise drawing boats. You can place the model on a pile of books, adding to the pile or removing books as you need to change the viewing height, as well as moving the model around for different viewing angles. Illuminating it with a desk lamp from a variety of positions is also effective.

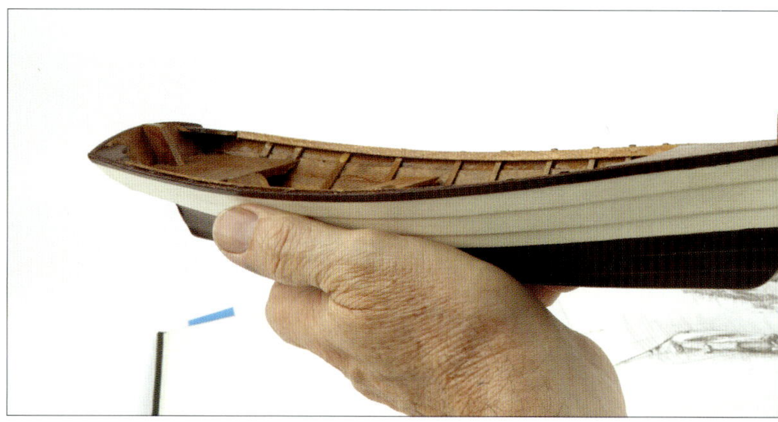

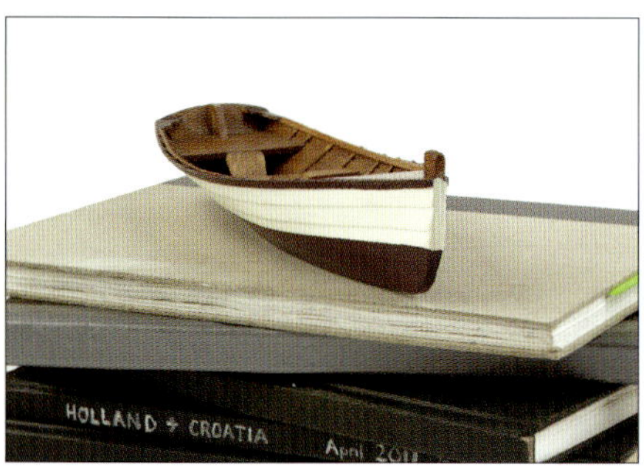


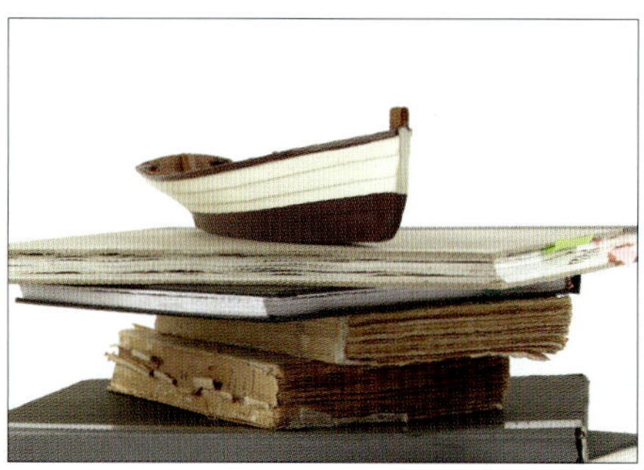

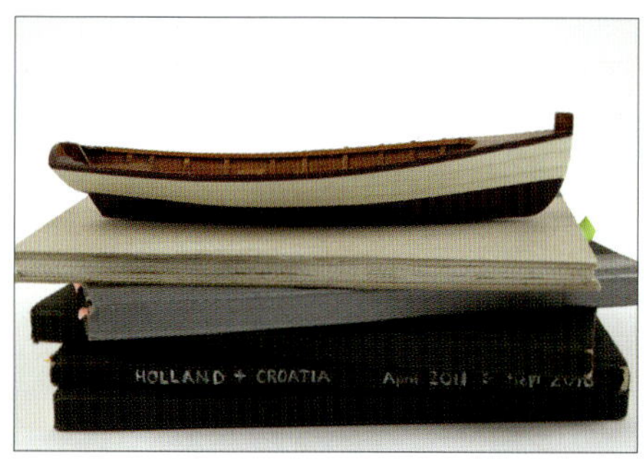


*So long as the model has faithful curving lines, it will give you excellent practice as you can move it around to different angles as well as raise or lower it for a new vertical perspective.*

### Rigging and sails using French curves

Don't forget the ropes and chains, as these can add handsome curves in a composition dominated by straight harbour walls and buildings, and can also be used as a lead-in to the focal point. French curves, which are plastic templates that describe various curves, are ideal for this.

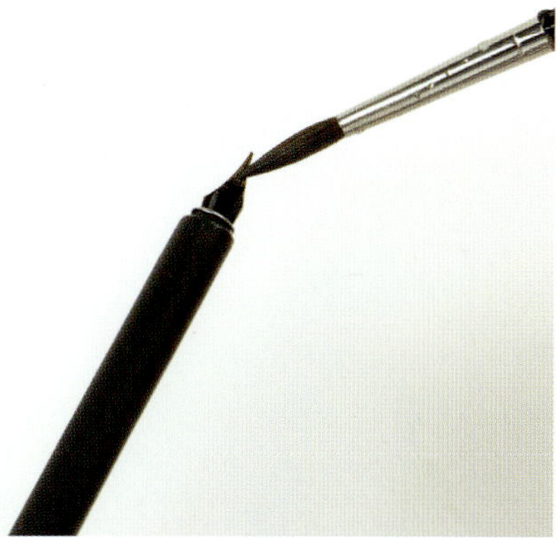

1 With the bulk of the boat drawn, load a no. 6 brush with a dark mix – burnt umber and indigo in this example – and draw it across the dip pen nib.

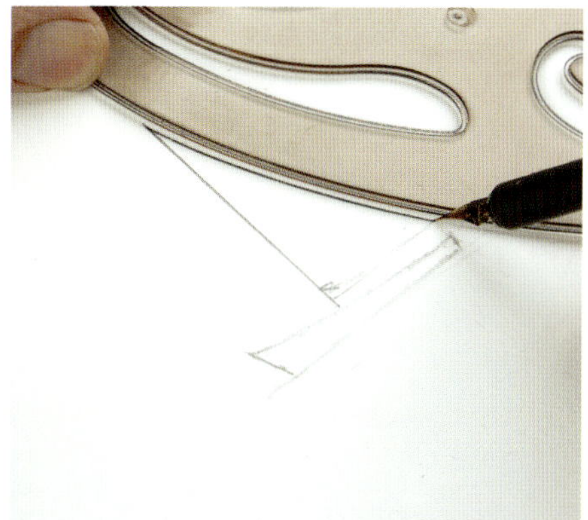

2 Place the French curve in place on the surface, and draw down the side of it, then lift the curve away. This is effective when there are several lines of rigging blown into parallel curves by the wind.

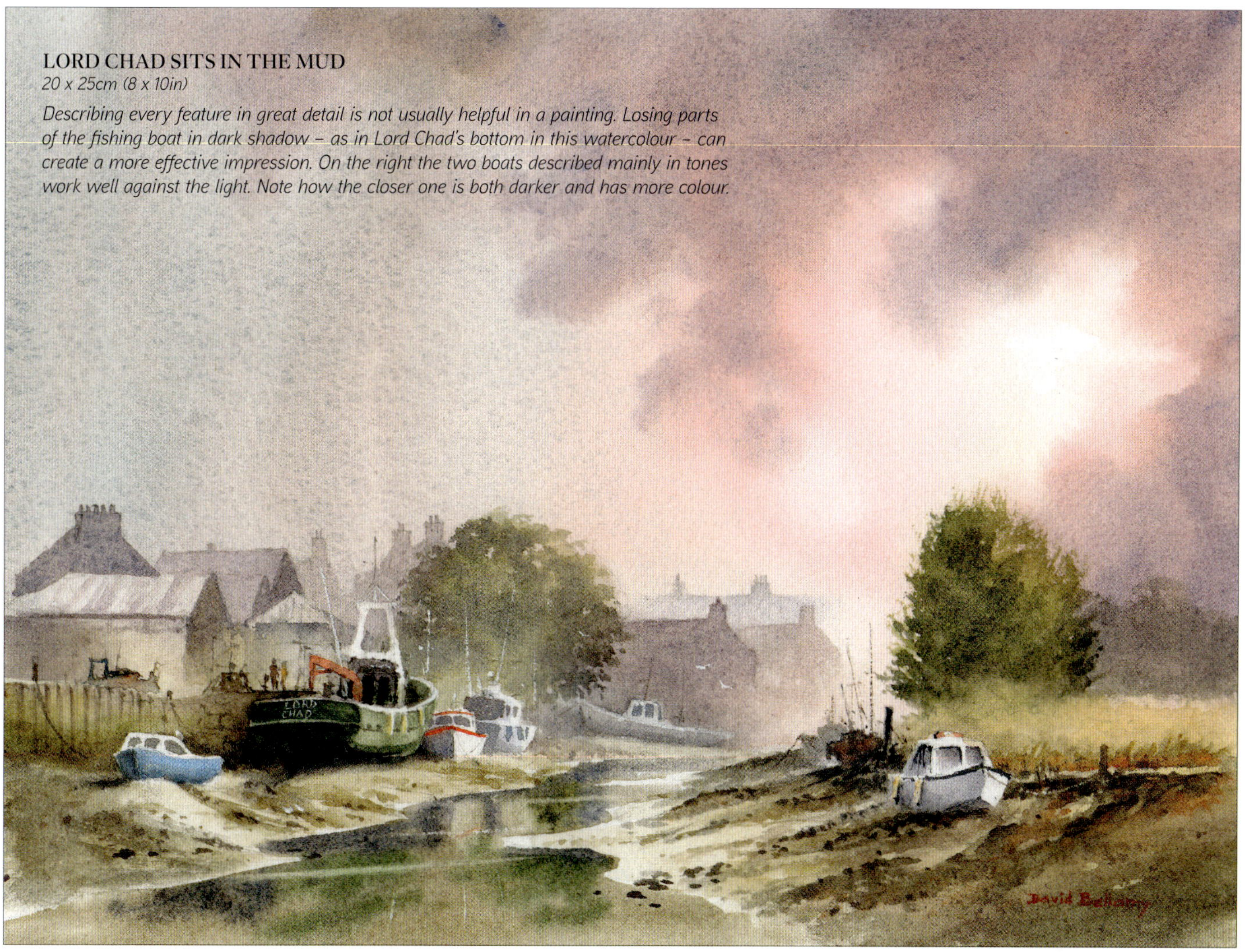


LORD CHAD SITS IN THE MUD

*20 x 25cm (8 x 10in)*

*Describing every feature in great detail is not usually helpful in a painting. Losing parts of the fishing boat in dark shadow – as in Lord Chad's bottom in this watercolour – can create a more effective impression. On the right the two boats described mainly in tones work well against the light. Note how the closer one is both darker and has more colour.*

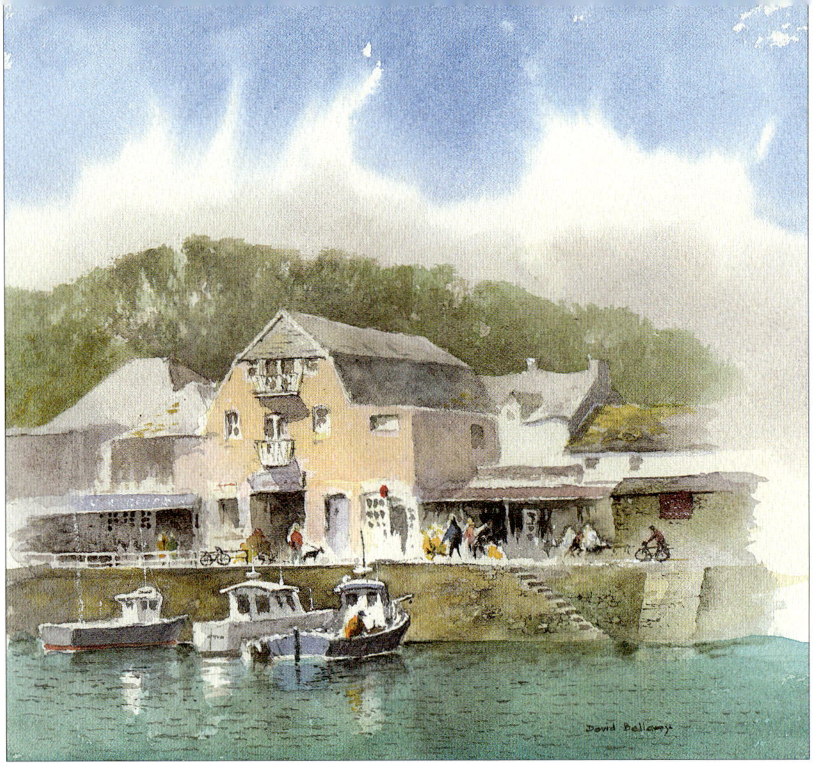

**PADSTOW HARBOUR**

*20 x 20cm (8 x 8in) 300gsm (140lb) Not surface*

*This was an alfresco demonstration for a course where I was keen to emphasize the sense of strong sunshine by featuring many white areas juxtaposed against darker shadows on boats and buildings. As there was quite a lot of detail involved I painted on Saunders Waterford Not. The reflections are minimal as there was a slight breeze, and these were achieved by working in the darker parts negatively around the white cabin reflections, and then painting in the darker hull and rudder post reflections. I generally prefer to work in reflections with the wet into wet method, but show this as an alternative example.*

## PAINTING HARBOURS

It is easy to overwork harbour scenes, as there is usually so much happening. Try to reduce excess detail by simplifying parts of the scene, perhaps bringing in smoke, haze or mist, or strong backlighting to induce mood. Concentrate on one area where there is a strong focal point, and add figures to support it. Figures can be suggested rather than carefully described, and they can be used to hide architectural or marine detail. Suggest reflections instead of painting crystal-clear mirror images that can overwhelm the eye. When we view a scene our eye is selective about what it takes in – peripheral vision indicates that something is present just beyond where we are focussing our gaze, but it is vague. To include all this as strong information that can be viewed easily is too much – we need quiet, uncluttered parts in our paintings.

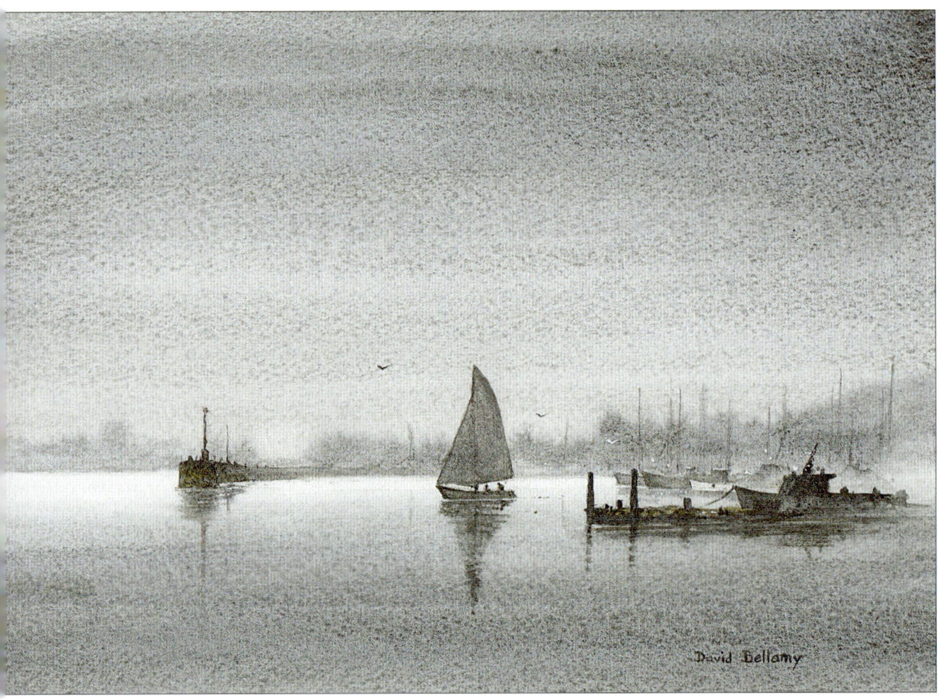

**EVENING MIST, TORQUAY**

*18 x 28cm (7 x 11in)*

*The mist was welcome, as it obliterated much of the background detail. The suggestion of the soft-edged background detail was done with the wet into wet technique, firstly by laying on the sky wash and then, after waiting a minute or two, applying a stronger mixture of the same colour to indicate vague buildings and vessels. When the stronger detail was painted onto dry paper later, this provided a strong sense of depth to the work. The reflections were painted again wet into wet once the sea wash had begun to dry. Often you will need to adjust shapes to conform to reality, and you can do this immediately with a slightly damp brush without any paint to take out part of an edge.*

## BOATS AT LOW TIDE

*18 x 25cm (7 x 10in)*

*Harbours at low tide offer you great opportunities for taking advantage of water channels, chains, ropes, buoys and similar details to use creatively. Pools of water or channels as in this scene can provide reflections, act as a lead-in or break up large expanses of mud, and you can happily position them where it suits you best.*

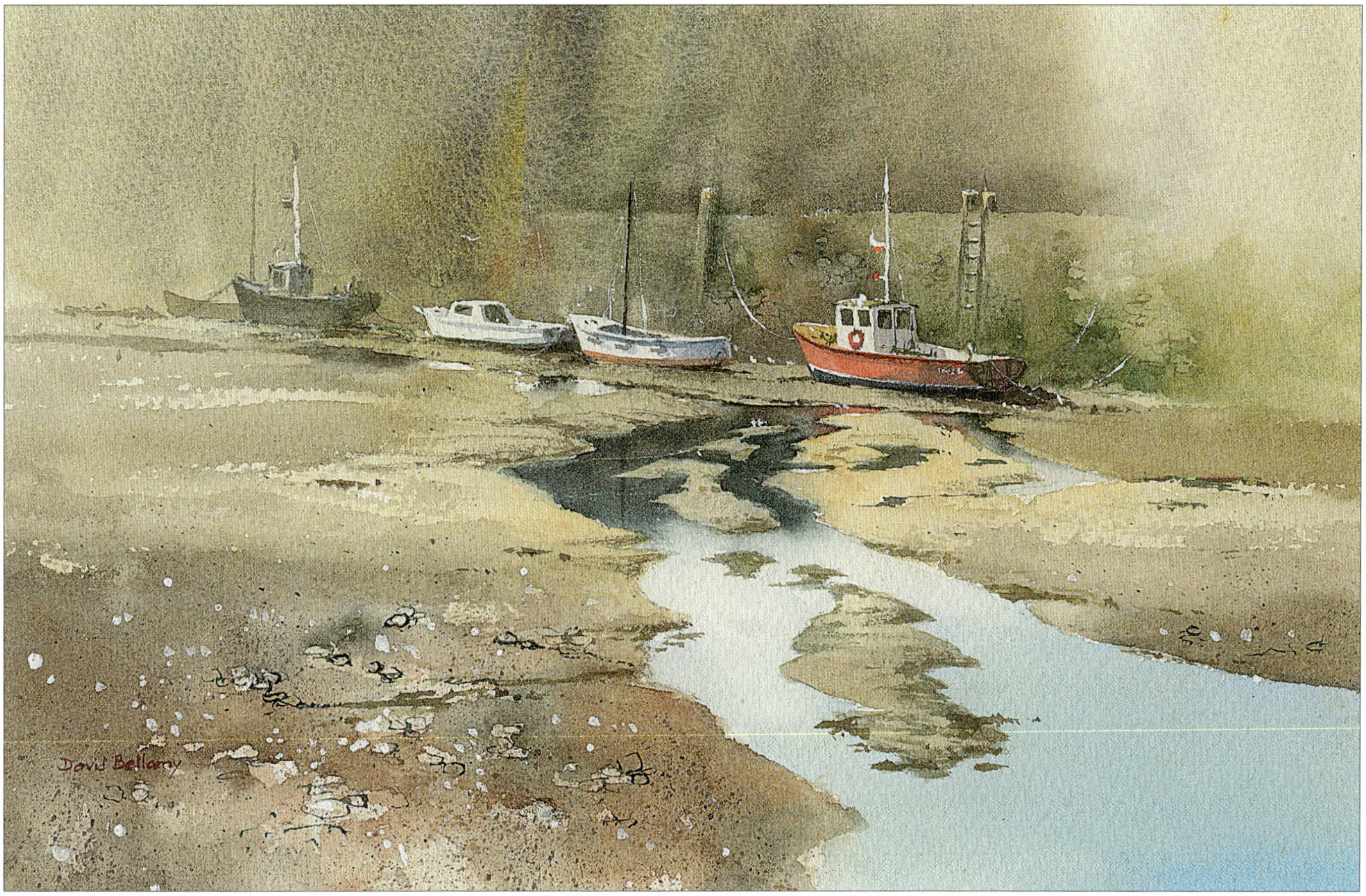


## HARBOUR DETRITUS AT HASTINGS

*Where lobster pots, fish boxes, plastic drums, ropes, nets, buoys and even a rusty caterpillar tractor litter the place, as in this sketch, it can help to turn it into an abstract or semi-abstract passage within the overall composition. In this way you can be extremely creative with your shapes and colours, and it's worth trying out various combinations on scrap paper beforehand. I thoroughly enjoyed working on this heap of 'rubbish'.*

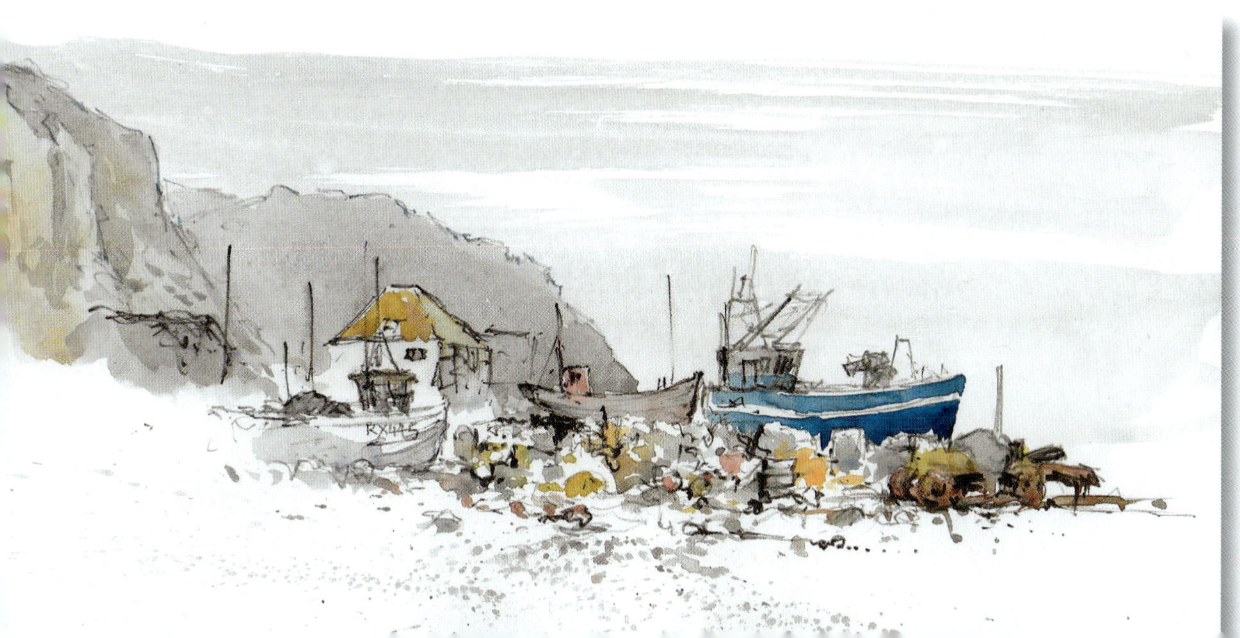

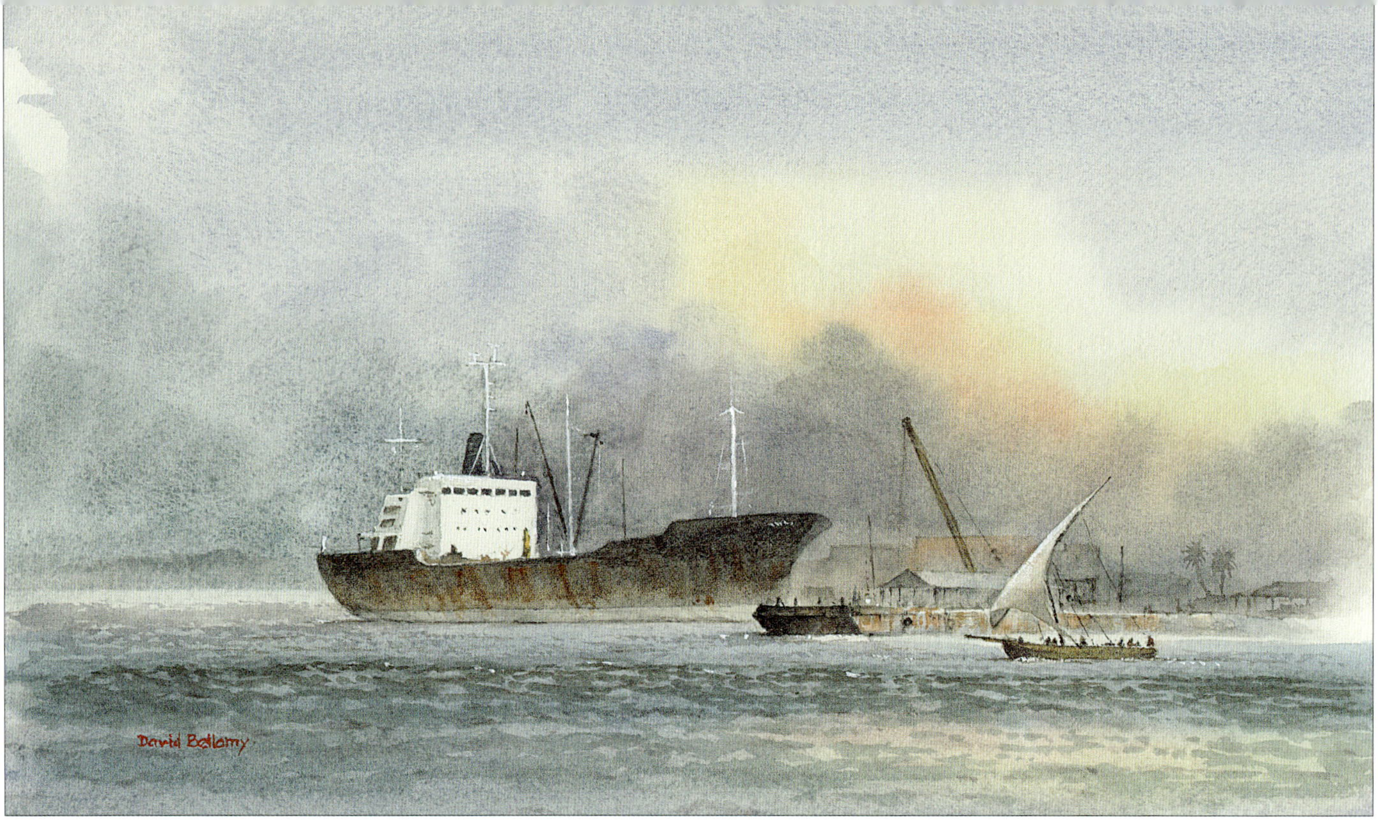


ZANZIBAR BERTH

*18 x 28cm (7 x 11in) 640gsm (300lb) Not paper*

*It is especially important to get the perspective right with large ships, and the same principles apply here as when drawing a building.*

*Here the eye level is only slightly above the waterline, so as the hull recedes towards the stern of the vessel the line of the decks goes down towards the left, each meeting at a vanishing point well off the left-hand edge of the painting. Conversely, the front top of the superstructure recedes towards the right, so this goes down to another vanishing point (not shown) away to the right of the painting.*

*The small dhow on the right is several hundred metres closer than the ship, but is still dwarfed in comparison: positioning a smaller object near a large one will enhance to sense of size of the former.*

## LINEAR PERSPECTIVE AND SCALE

In a harbour, it is hard to avoid the effects of linear perspective, and often it is right on top of you, which tends to accentuate the problems. While it is vital to have a fair idea of how the perspective is affected by your viewing position, it is not worth losing sleep over the matter.

Firstly establish your eye level: this is usually around two-thirds of the way up a door, depending on your height. The eye level changes if you climb up or down steps or a slope, or sit down.

The main thing to remember is that any horizontal lines that appear above your eye level will run downwards as they get further away from you, and those below your eye level run upwards as they run away from you, so it is important to work out the nearest point of those lines before you begin drawing.

These lines eventually meet at a vanishing point on your eye level line, often way off the paper. To work out the angle of the slope of a feature (such as the line of a roof, or a ship's deck), hold your pencil horizontally at arm's length, with one eye closed and the pencil appearing to 'rest' on one end of the line you are interested in drawing. This is a rough guide but will give you a fair idea of which way the line is falling, and the degree of the angle at which it is falling. This is useful to compare with other similar lines which might be higher or lower. The further away the line gets from your eye line, the more acute the angle becomes. My main example here is that of a large ship, but the same rules apply to buildings.

It is also useful to consider how scale affects the scene. Including a small object will make the larger one so much bigger, and it is also good to slightly overlap these if possible, though it is not vital.

## ZANZIBAR BERTH PERSPECTIVE DIAGRAM

*This shows the two-point perspective applied to the painting of the large ship, and is equally applicable to buildings. As you can see, the actual vanishing point, which is always found on the eye level, occurs well off to the left of the painting.*

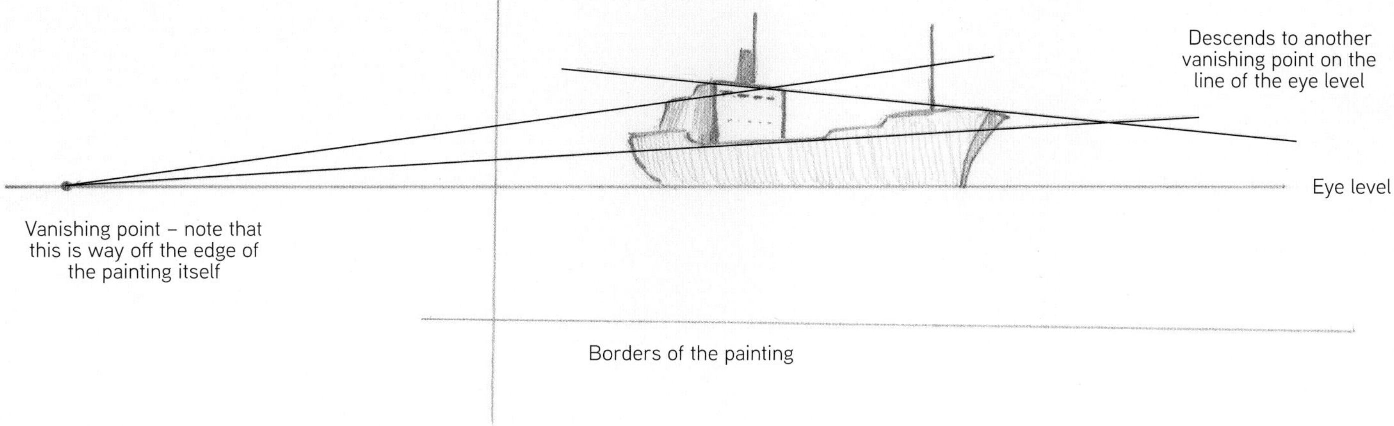


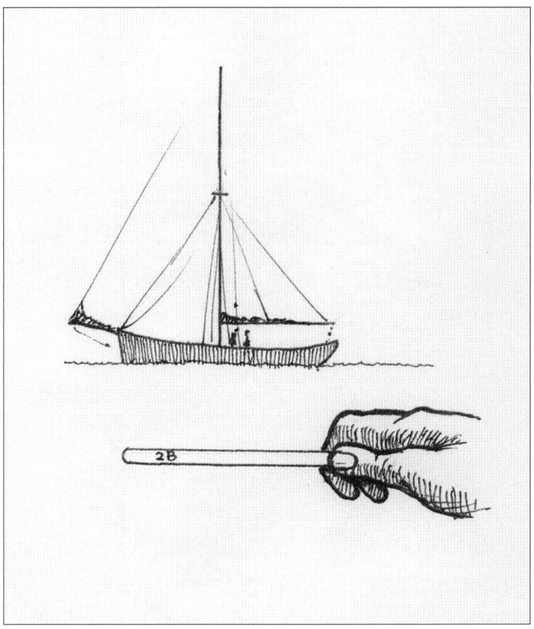


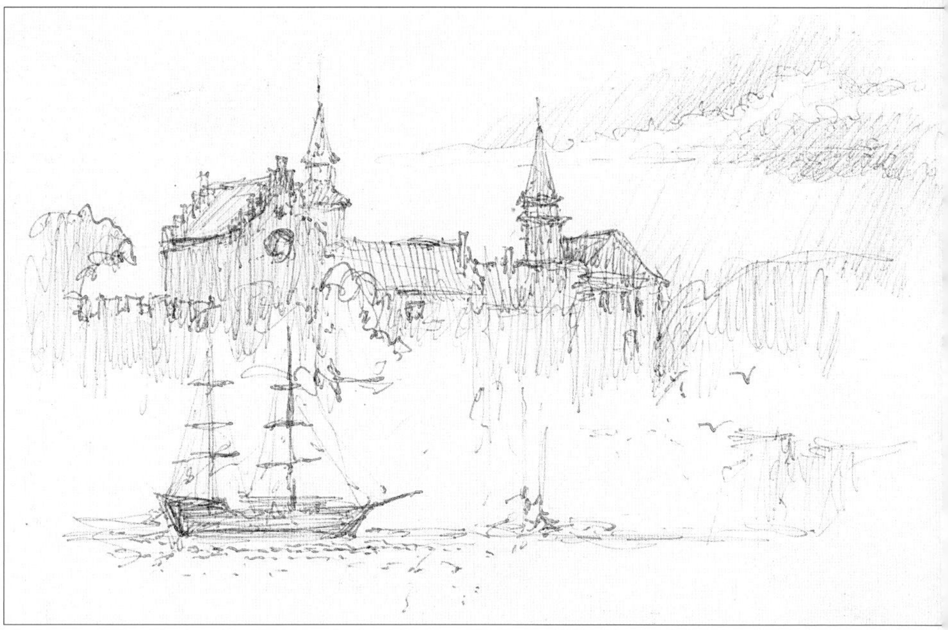

## COMPARING SIZES OF FEATURES

*Measure the length of a vessel with a pencil held at arm's length and one eye closed. Here, the top of the pencil corresponds to the bow and the stern is indicated by the tip of the thumbnail. Holding the pencil thus, turn it 90° to check how many boat-lengths equal the height of the mast – almost one and a half times here.*

## OSLO HARBOUR SKETCH

*This is a sketch done in ink on the back of a menu while eating out by the quayside. The lines of the two roofs on the outside of both spires descend as they recede to the left in each case. The closer you are to the building, the more acute the angle of descent becomes.*

*As it is impractical to go around with sketchbooks several feet long, not to mention set squares and T-squares, trying to fathom out these angles of perspective using vanishing points that would normally extend way over the page of a normal sketchbook, we need to use careful observation to record these subtle angles. A pencil held horizontally at arm's length with one eye closed will give you a fair idea of which way the feature line is angled, and also the approximate degree of that angle. It is not absolutely precise, but will serve you well in this often perplexing situation.*

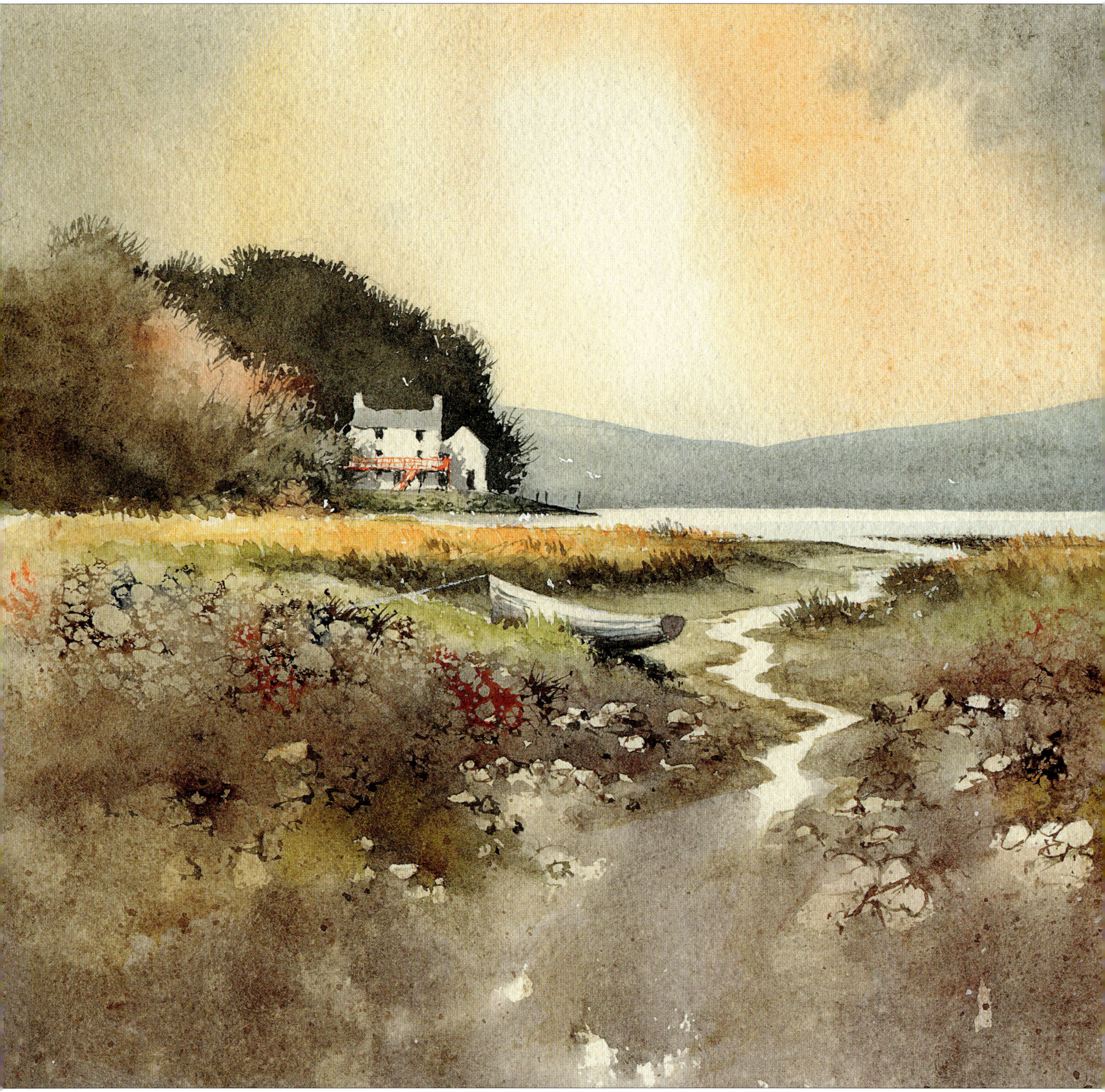

# Composition for seascapes

To help you achieve a sound composition from your sketch or photograph, do one or more small studio sketches in pencil, trying a slightly different layout of the scene each time, with a variety of positions for the focal point. This focal point is vital to success and is normally placed around one-third of the way into the painting, both vertically and horizontally, thus giving you four optimum positions. However, being precise in all this is not vital. Normally one focal point is best, but you will probably need subsidiary ones to enhance the balance of the overall layout. Think about creating a lead-in such as a path, river, wall, a rope linking a boat, or whatever seems appropriate, leading the viewer from the foreground into the general position of the centre of interest. Other features such as trees, bushes, fences, marine objects such as lobster pots or nets, colourful buoys, seabirds and people can all support the focal point if positioned close by, so don't hesitate to move these to your advantage.

DYLAN'S BOATHOUSE
*23 x 28cm (9 x 11in)*
*In this watercolour I decided to make more of the foreground with its lead-in of a small creek with a boat. The focal point is the building where I have given it the strongest tonal contrasts, and is positioned about one-third down the paper and almost one-third from the left side. The emphasis on the horizontals accentuates the haunting quality of the estuary.*

# DEVICES TO GIVE YOUR PAINTINGS 'ZIP'

Painting a scene exactly as it appears before you is fine, but at some stage you will wish to put something of yourself into the painting. This is essential to produce a work of art rather than just a simple copy of what is in front of you, and the next few pages will illustrate how to stamp your own creativity and expression onto your painting. You will see how to create emphasis on cliff scenery in a subtle way, which can alter a view without really making the change so drastic that it no longer looks like the original scene. In addition we look at how to use the atmosphere to change a scene by obscuring features and emphasizing others. These devices will enable you to give your work more power without actually introducing any drastic changes to the scene.

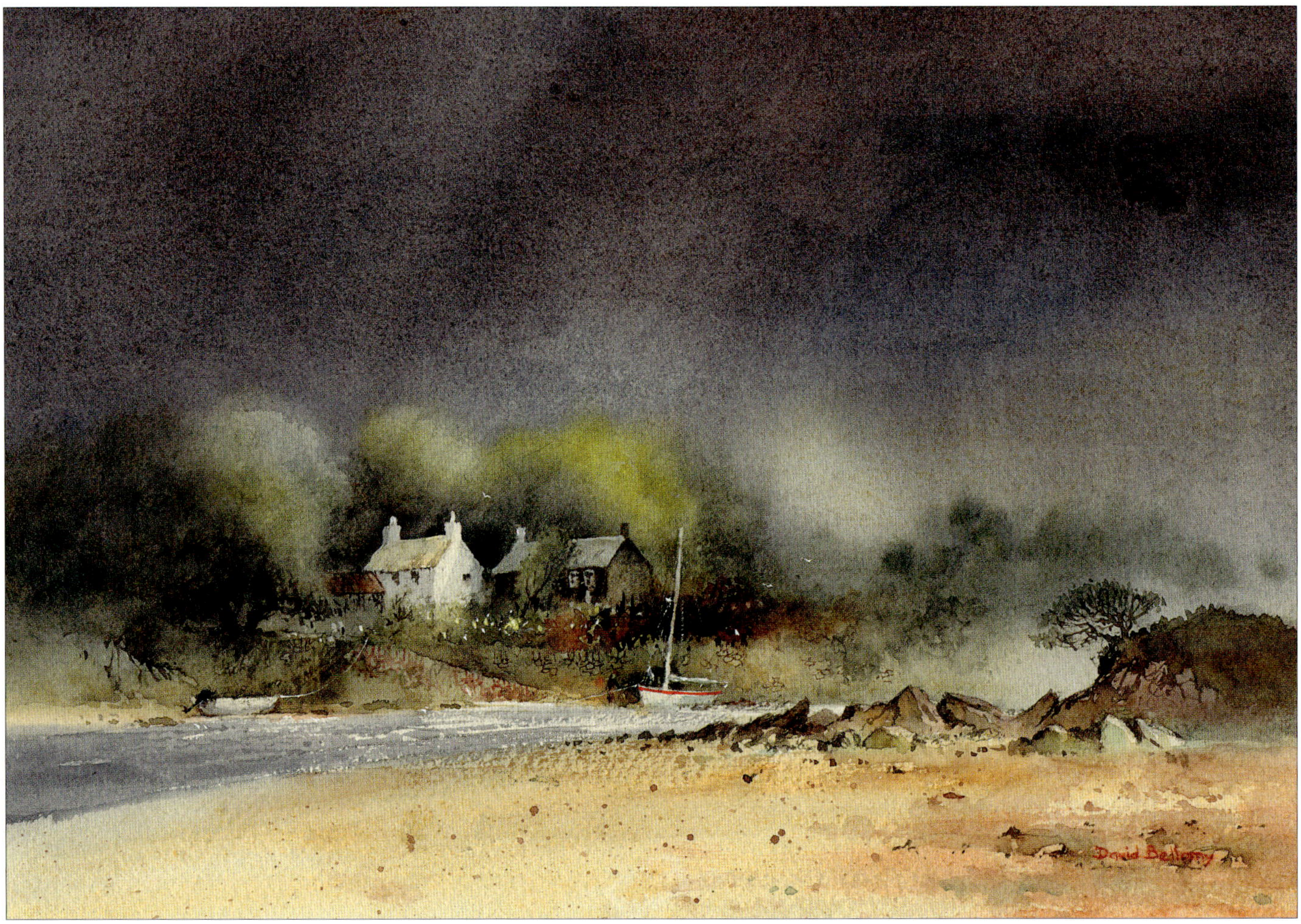

MOODY DAY, SANDY HAVEN

*18 x 25cm (7 x 10in)*

*The atmosphere has been outrageously exaggerated, as it was a fine, sunny day when I visited the spot. I began by laying masking fluid over the buildings and boats, and then applied the main washes, working wet into wet with the various colours. Colour was pulled out of the upper part of the trees to suggest the lighter foliage. I enlivened the scene by applying a few dots of white gouache in front of the houses. Note that the actual scene has hardly been changed, only the atmosphere.*

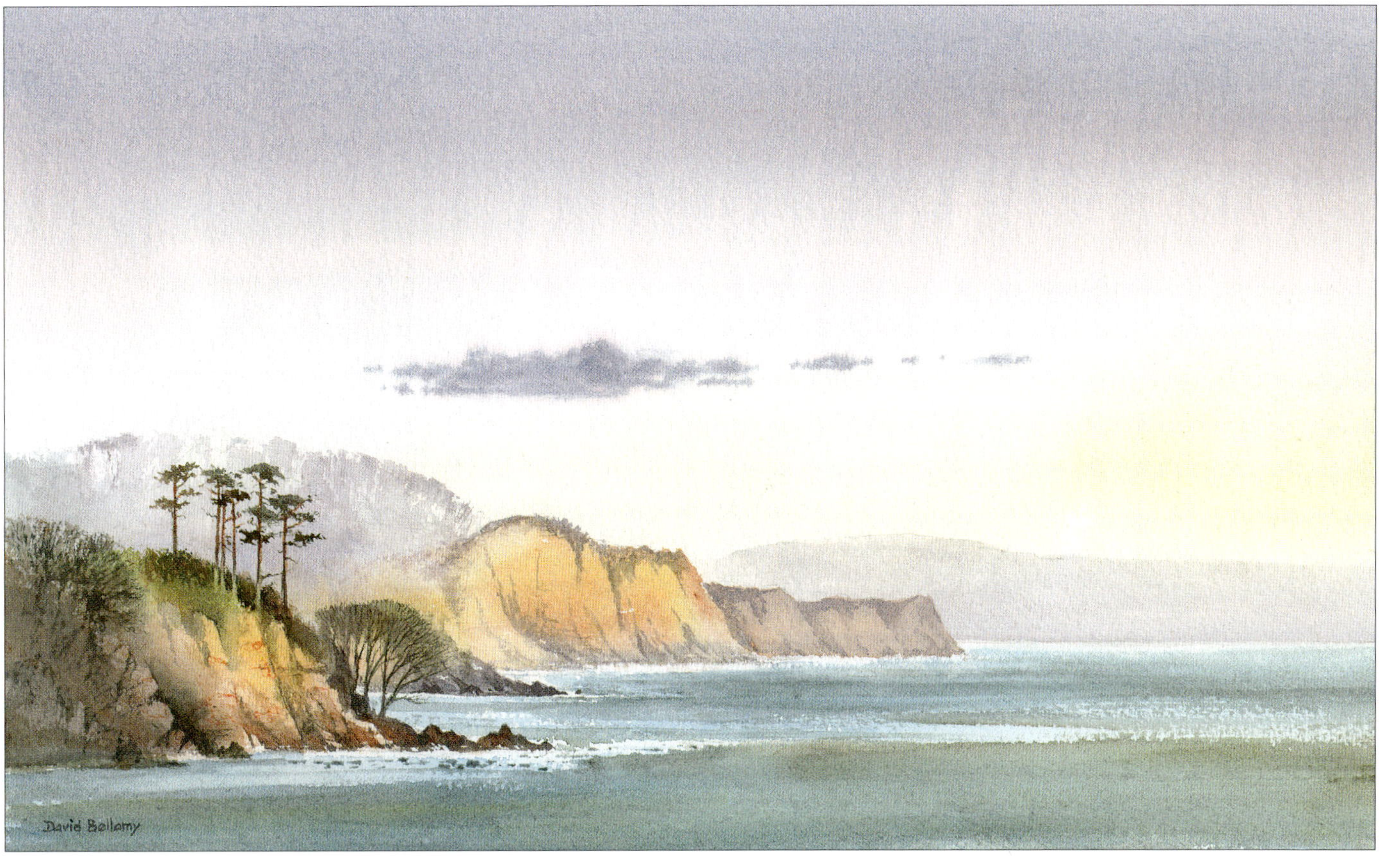


BABBACOMBE BAY

*23 x 35.5cm (9 x 14in)*

*Although this is a beautiful subject, it did need a few subtle changes to enhance the effect. The line of cliffs was the same colour and tone all the way along, so my first alteration was to introduce some shadow on the further parts, and at the same time leave out much of the cliff vegetation which tended to intrude. With the centre of interest in the bottom left I suggested white foaming sea against dark rocks, and to make the trees stand out I deliberately lost all detail in the further tree mass to the rear, simply suggesting them with a wash of French ultramarine and cadmium red. Finally I reduced the strength of the contrasts at the extreme left cliffs by glazing over the area with a dark shadow. Strong contrasts at the edge of a composition tend to draw the eye out of the picture.*

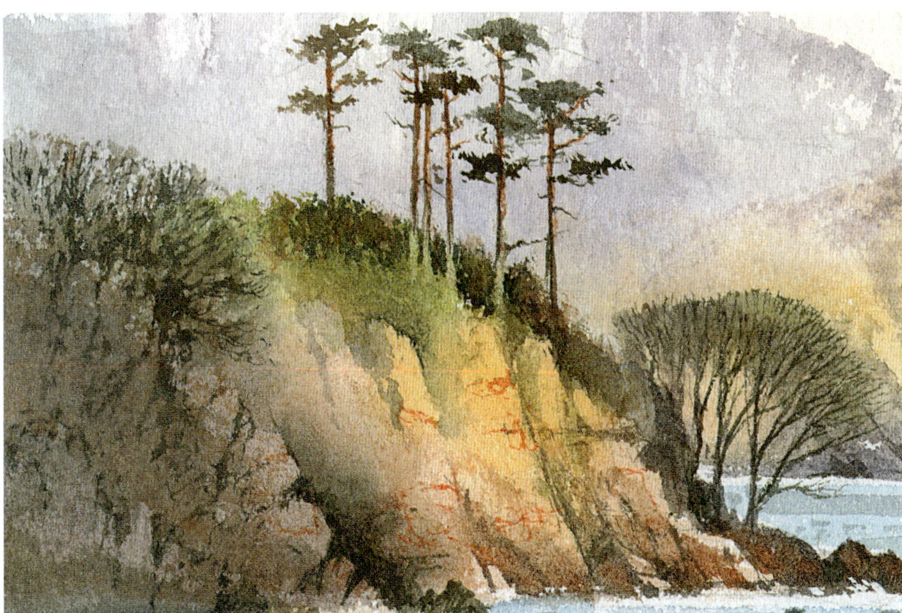

*This close-up of the cliffs shows the area around the centre of interest.*

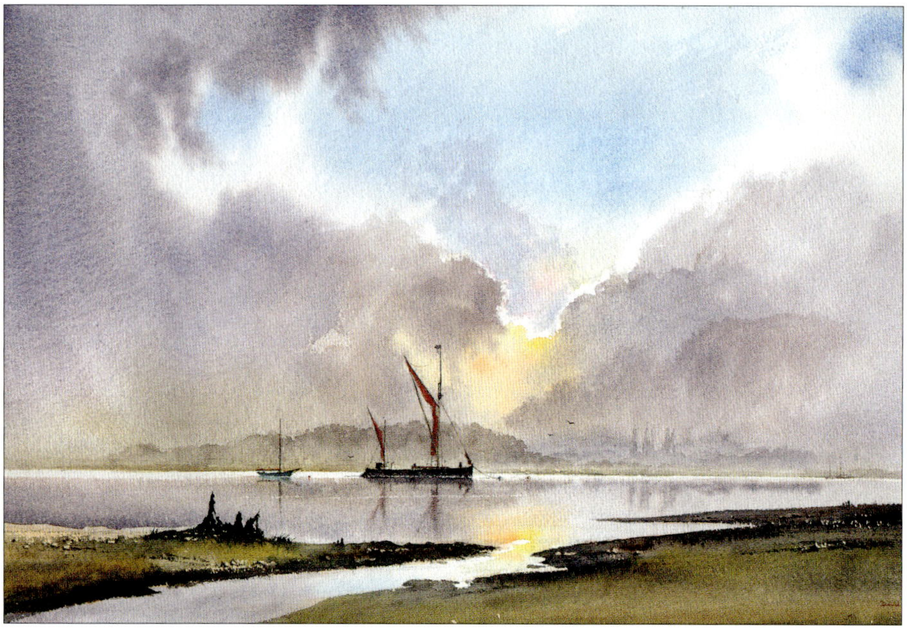

**BLACKWATER MOORING**
*30.5 x 51cm (12 x 20in)*

*This was an overcast day with a cloudburst imminent, but I wanted to suggest a pleasant, sunny afternoon. I chose to paint this on Waterford Rough to help suggest ragged cloud edges and foreground textures. I started by lifting the sky from its dismal gloom with cobalt blue and a mixture of French ultramarine and cadmium red, splashing in strong new gamboge just above the prow of the vessel to liven it up. The Stygian background was replaced with a mass of trees using French ultramarine and cadmium red, with a touch of yellow ochre. Breaking up the foregrounds of horizontal shorelines with mooring posts, mini-creeks, weed-draped rocks and the like can add interest and avoid monotony.*

## PERSONALIZING THE SCENE

We shall now take this theme of improving a scene to our advantage a little further with a number of more pronounced changes, yet still keeping the scene reasonably faithful to the original. Locations are changing all the time, from the natural elements, sunlight, seasonal changes, new buildings, a new coat of paint on a door or wall, the arrival of a new boat, or simply a change in the state of the tide, which can drastically alter the water level and reveal or hide interesting features formerly visible or invisible. As a consequence, if we revisit a spot, we may find it looks quite different.

With the green rock tower illustration (see below) the simplification of detail around it was necessary to make the feature stand out – a vital compositional device – whereas the emphasis on the water splashes was a personal decision, as that was how I wished to add interest to the work. My changes in the Blackwater Mooring painting are mainly personal reflections on how I wanted the scene to appear.

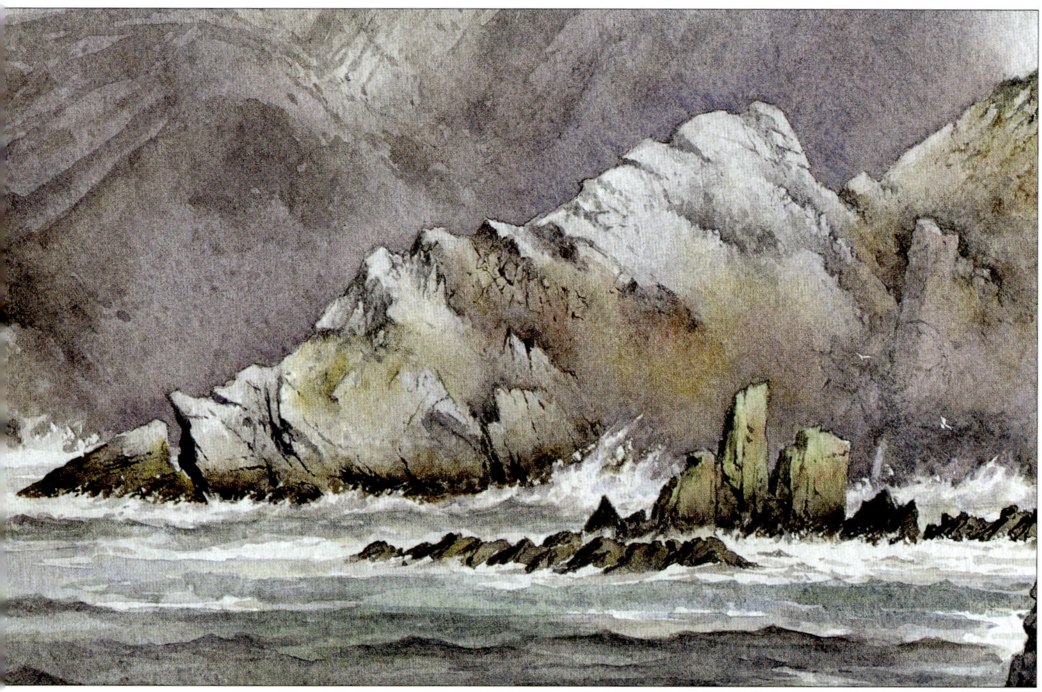

**DETAIL FROM ROCK TOWER**

*This tower stands in front of complicated cliff architecture, and so to highlight it I left the cliff directly behind it devoid of detail – compare that part with the rest of the cliff. Further emphasis was achieved by juxtaposing dark rocks at the bottom of the tower against white splashes of surf. Adding in the splashes was a personal choice, as the sea was not nearly so boisterous.*

# EMPHASIZING THE CENTRE OF INTEREST

The most powerful way of making a centre of interest stand out is to highlight it with the strongest tonal contrasts available: the white of your paper set against your darkest tone. This does need care at times, though, when you have a more distant focal point and therefore need to suggest a sense of space in the painting, in which case your stronger tones might need to be in the foreground. If there is little detail in the foreground dark areas while quite a bit of detail in the distant centre of interest, then this should work. Bright colours around or beside the focal point also help to indicate its importance, and I sometimes flood the rest of the composition with a dull glaze, keeping this away from the focal point so that, like a theatre spotlight, it shows up that feature.

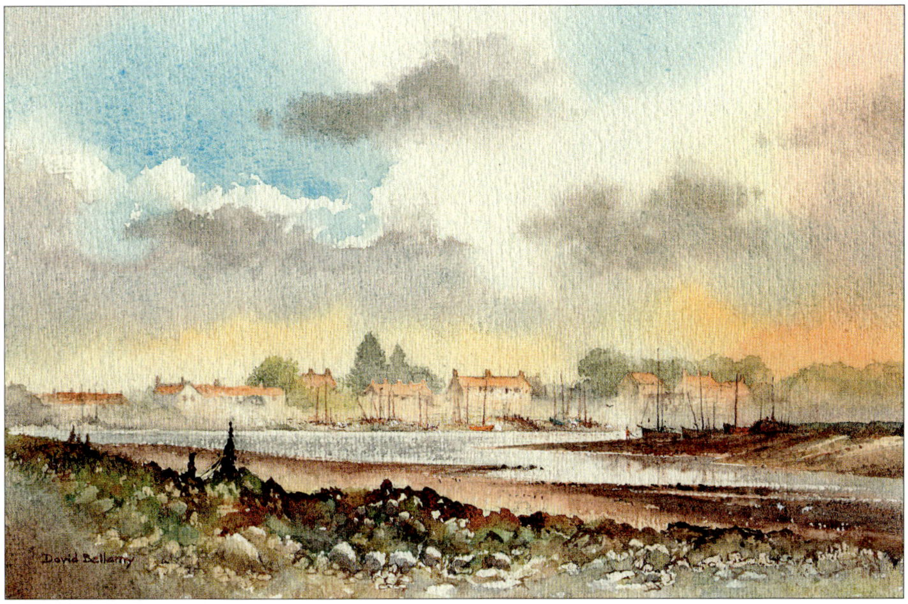

BURNHAM OVERY STAITHE
*20 x 28cm (8 x 11in)*

*Here the focal point is a clutch of dark boats on the distant right. I highlighted them by keeping the far buildings faint, yet allowed their red roofs to show through and thus draw the eye towards the boats. These were rendered dark and sharp-edged, and while still wet I dropped a little red into some of them.*

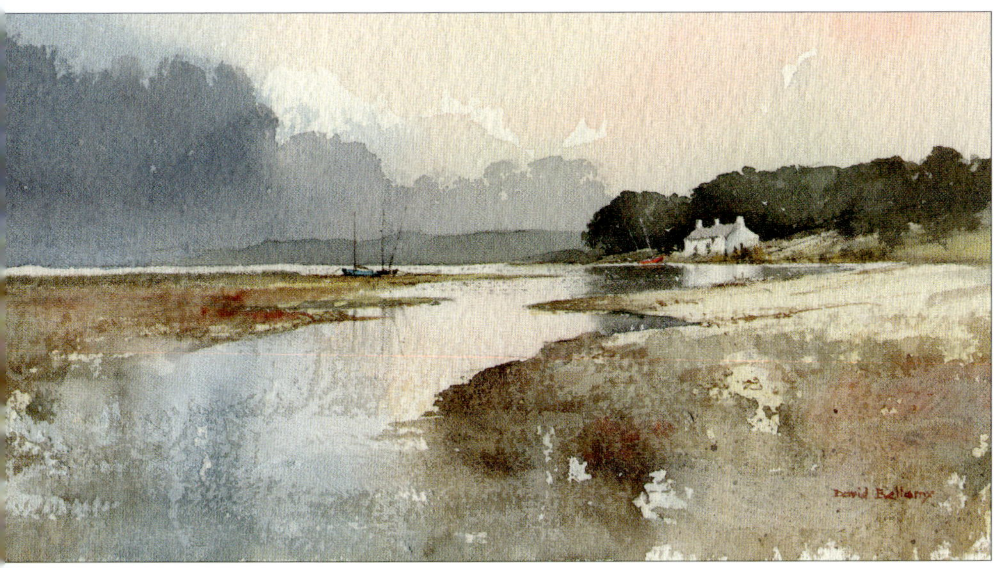

NEVERN ESTUARY
*11.5 x 23cm (4½ x 9in)*

*Note that in this small composition the centre of interest has been highlighted in several ways: the lead-in of the River Nevern, the white building set against dark trees, the red boat moored outside and a few gulls circling nearby. The more central boats provide both a balance to the composition and break up the horizontal lines. The foreground was created by laying on a thin smear of Daniel Smith watercolour ground with a painting knife and leaving it overnight to dry before starting to paint. The work was done on an off-cut of Waterford 640gsm (300lb) Rough paper, as I like to use a stiffer paper when applying the watercolour ground.*

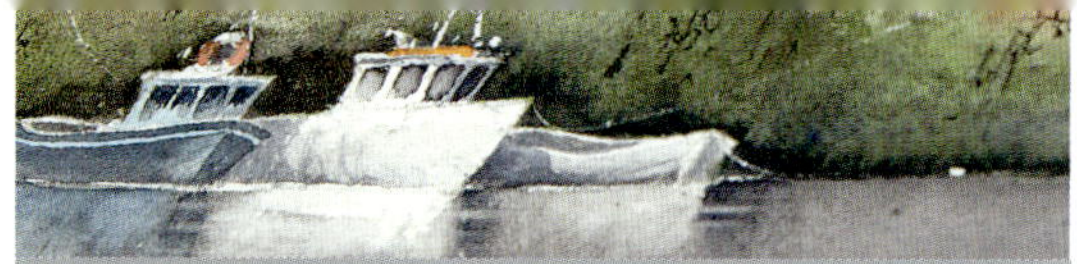

# CRAIL HARBOUR

The lovely old harbour at Crail has much to offer the artist, but whichever way you look the view is rather complicated. My aim here was to create a sunny aspect, with the background buildings reduced in detail with a hazy approach. The lower buildings, with their crow-stepped gables (where steps run up alongside the ends of the roof), make for an attractive focal point.

## MATERIALS USED

Saunders Waterford 640gsm (300lb) Rough watercolour paper

Brushes: Synthetic no. 10 mixing brush; large squirrel mop; no. 8 round; no. 3 round; no. 10 round; no. 6 round; no. 1 rigger; 6mm (¼in) flat synthetic; no. 1 round

Colours: Nickel titanate yellow; quinacridone gold; sodalite genuine; French ultramarine; yellow ochre; transparent red oxide; permanent orange; burnt umber; green apatite genuine; cadmium red medium hue; moonglow; light red; phthalocyanine blue

4B pencil

Masking fluid and old rigger brush

White gouache

Scalpel

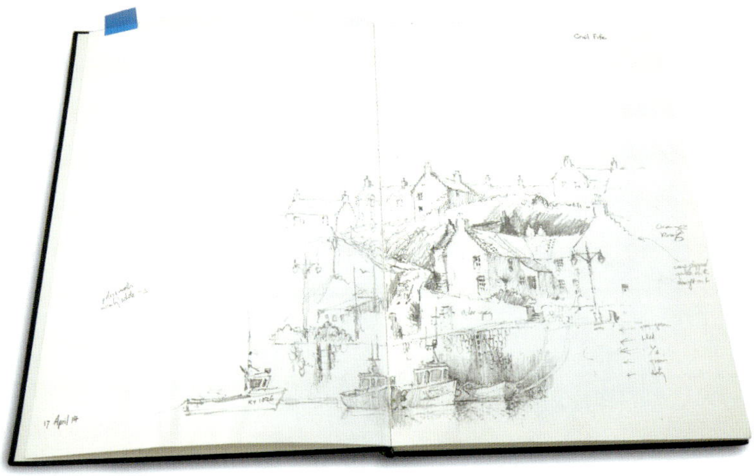

*The initial sketch*

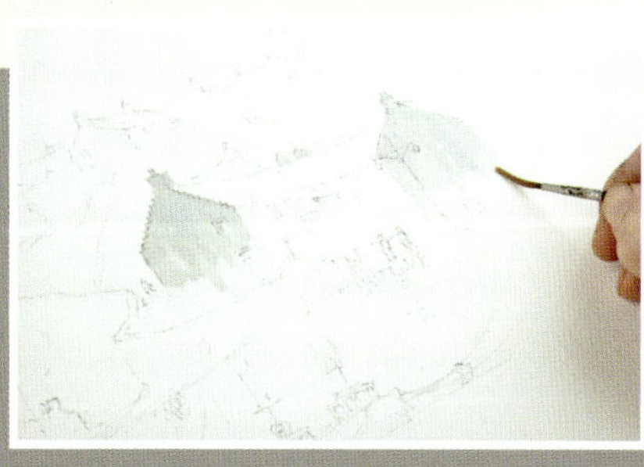

**1** Referring to your photographs and initial sketch, use a 4B pencil to draw out the scene. In terms of composition, I want to subdue the distant background and the large area of brickwork, while bringing the group of buildings on the right into focus. I also want to introduce some figures to avoid the picture looking ghostly. You'll notice I have brought the lobster pots on the left-hand side more into the picture, in front of the left-hand building. I add the figures at the end, once the rest of the composition is in place, as they will always draw the eye to the focal point. When you come to the crow steps (see above), describe a faint line to guide you, then draw in the steps. Apply the masking fluid in the areas shown, using the old rigger brush (see inset).

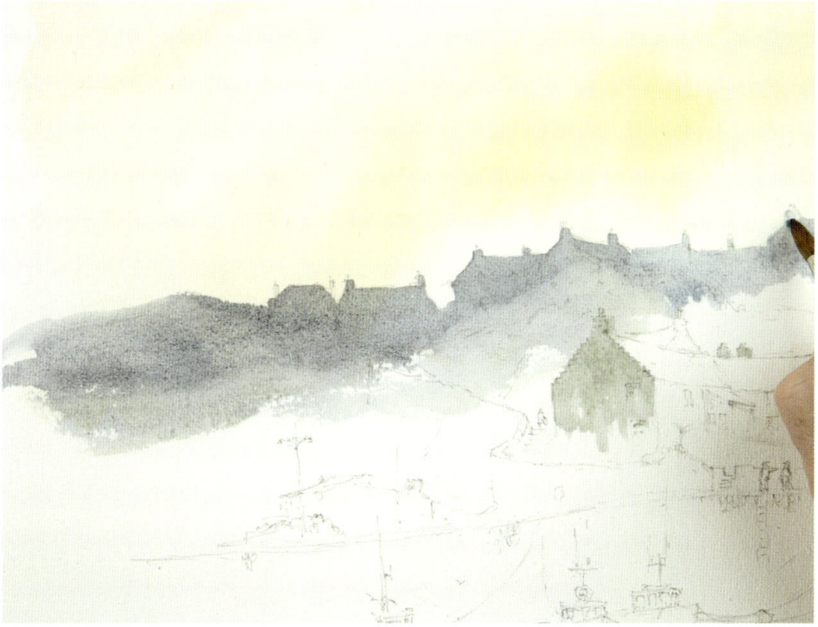

2 Use the large squirrel mop with clean water to wet the sky. Add in some nickel titanate yellow near the horizon, then add quinacridone gold to vary the sky. While the sky dries, prepare a dark blue-grey mix of sodalite genuine and French ultramarine. Once the sky is completely dry, paint along the ridge line. Working from left to right, use the side of the no. 8 brush to apply the blue-grey mix across the left-hand side. Change to the point of the brush for the buildings.

3 Working quickly, change to the no. 3 round and touch in the chimney pots while the paint remains wet. Add some quinacridone gold and yellow ochre wet into wet underneath the blue-grey area, working right the way across the painting. Use quinacridone gold particularly around the central figure on the steps – this will help draw the eye later.

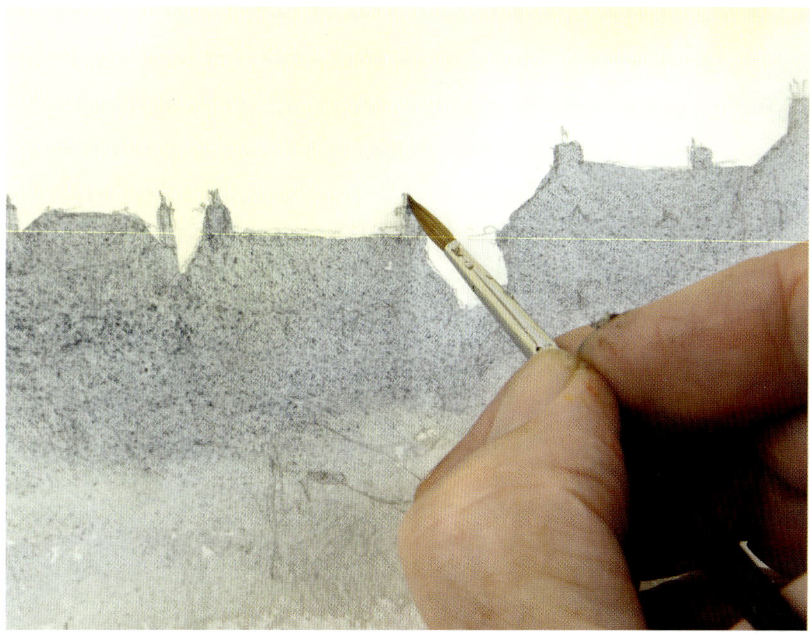

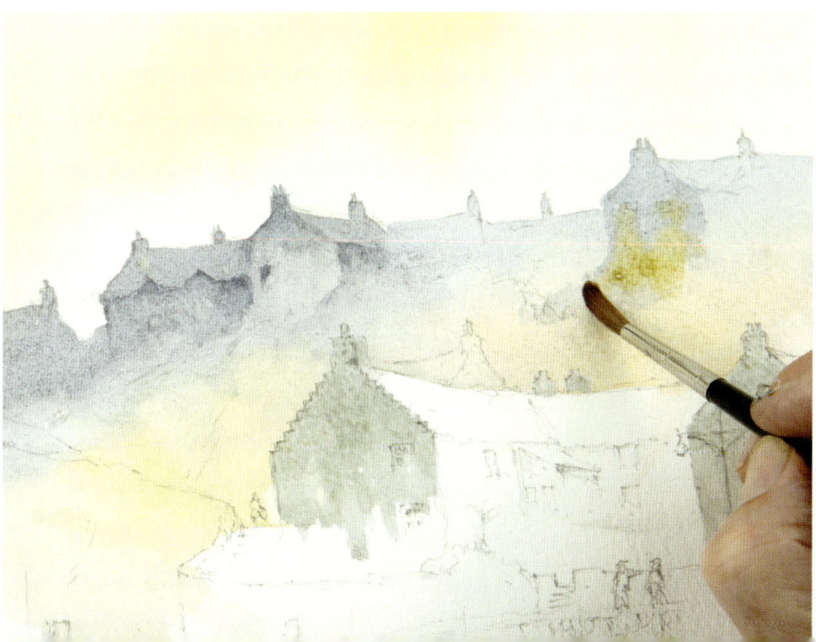

4 Using the same blue-grey mix, develop a few areas on the closer background houses with the no. 6 brush. Avoid over-detailing the area, but add some visual interest. Use a lot of water on the brush to reduce the strength of the wash. Drop in a little yellow ochre on the right-hand background buildings for warmth.

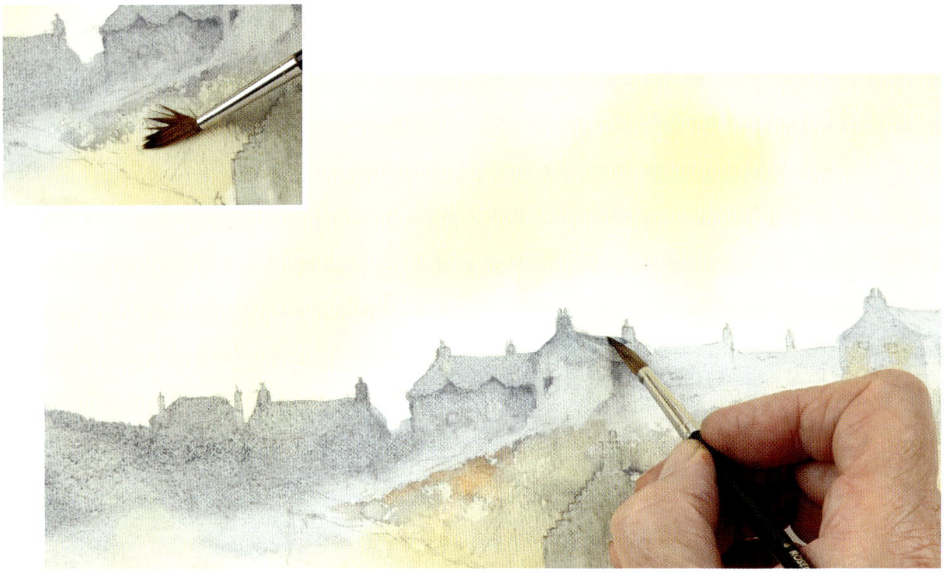

5 Add dilute yellow ochre, using the side of the brush to create a slightly ragged edge behind the main buildings (see inset). This will create faint textural appearance to the area. Slightly warm the central area with dilute transparent red oxide, dropping it into the wet yellow ochre. If necessary, add further tonal touches, and refine the edges of the distant buildings once the paint has dried.

6 Still using the blue-grey mix of French ultramarine and sodalite genuine, begin to build up the houses in the midground with the no. 6 round brush. Drop in some transparent red oxide for warmth. Add the shadows of the central steps in the same way.

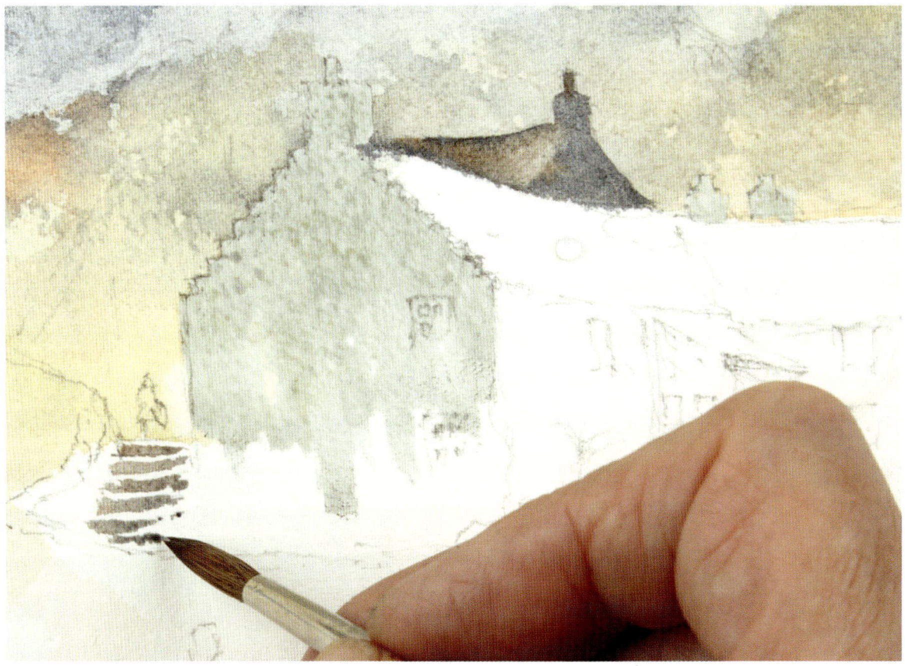

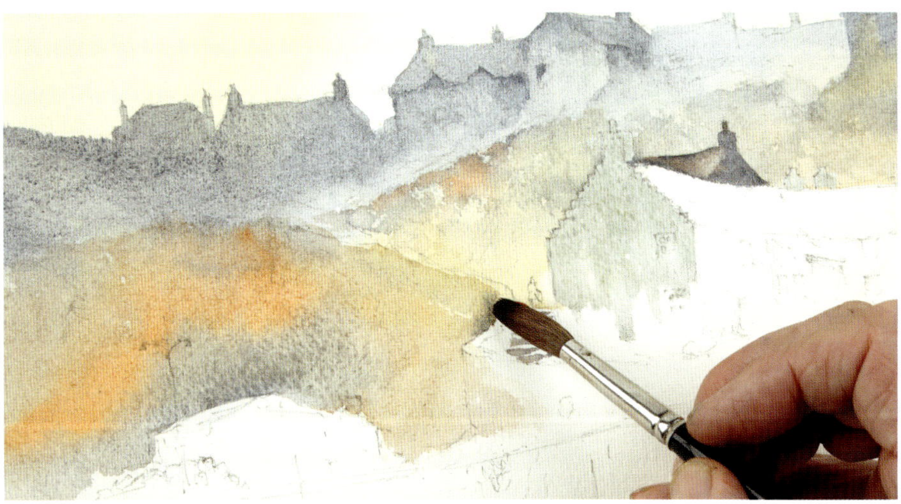

7 Change to the no. 10 round brush and add a variegated wash over the rocks on the left-hand side with the blue-grey mix and transparent red oxide. Leave some clean paper at the top of the wall, and emphasize the contrast by adding a little more blue-grey beside it. This gives the impression that the top of the wall is catching the sunlight.

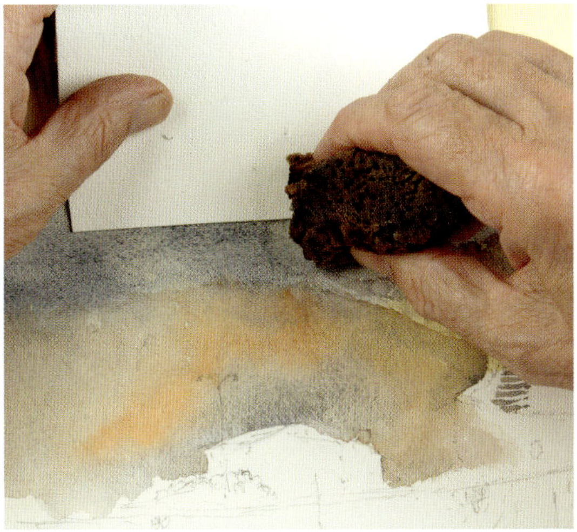

8 With a spare piece of paper to protect the top part of the building, use a damp sponge to lift out some of the blue-grey paint on the left-hand side to bring in a little more light here.

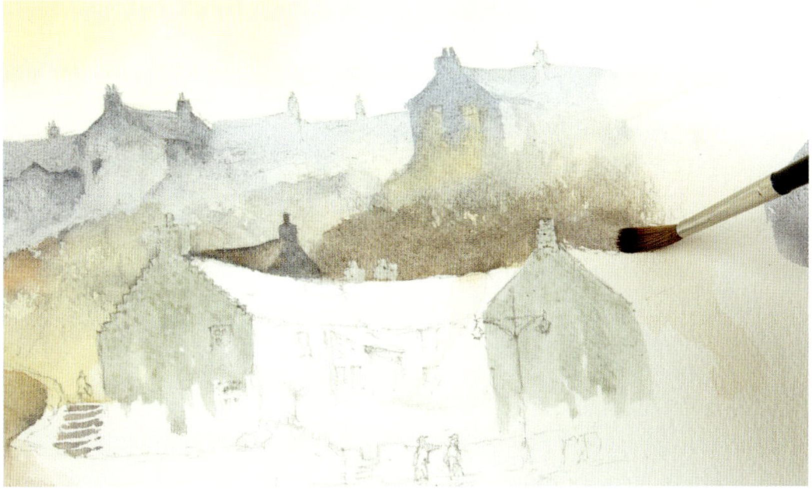

9 Develop the area behind the main buildings, softening the dark area (if necessary) by lifting it with a damp brush; and darkening the area behind the chimneys with a dark mix made by combining a little of the blue-grey mix (French ultramarine and sodalite genuine) with transparent red oxide.

10 Make a deeper grey by adding just a touch of French ultramarine to sodalite genuine. Rewet the sky with clean water using the large squirrel mop, then add the deeper grey mix wet into wet. Leave a central area of light. Tip the paper up slightly to encourage the wash to drift downwards. Use the no. 10 round brush to prevent any lines forming, by breaking any pooling and drawing away excess wash.

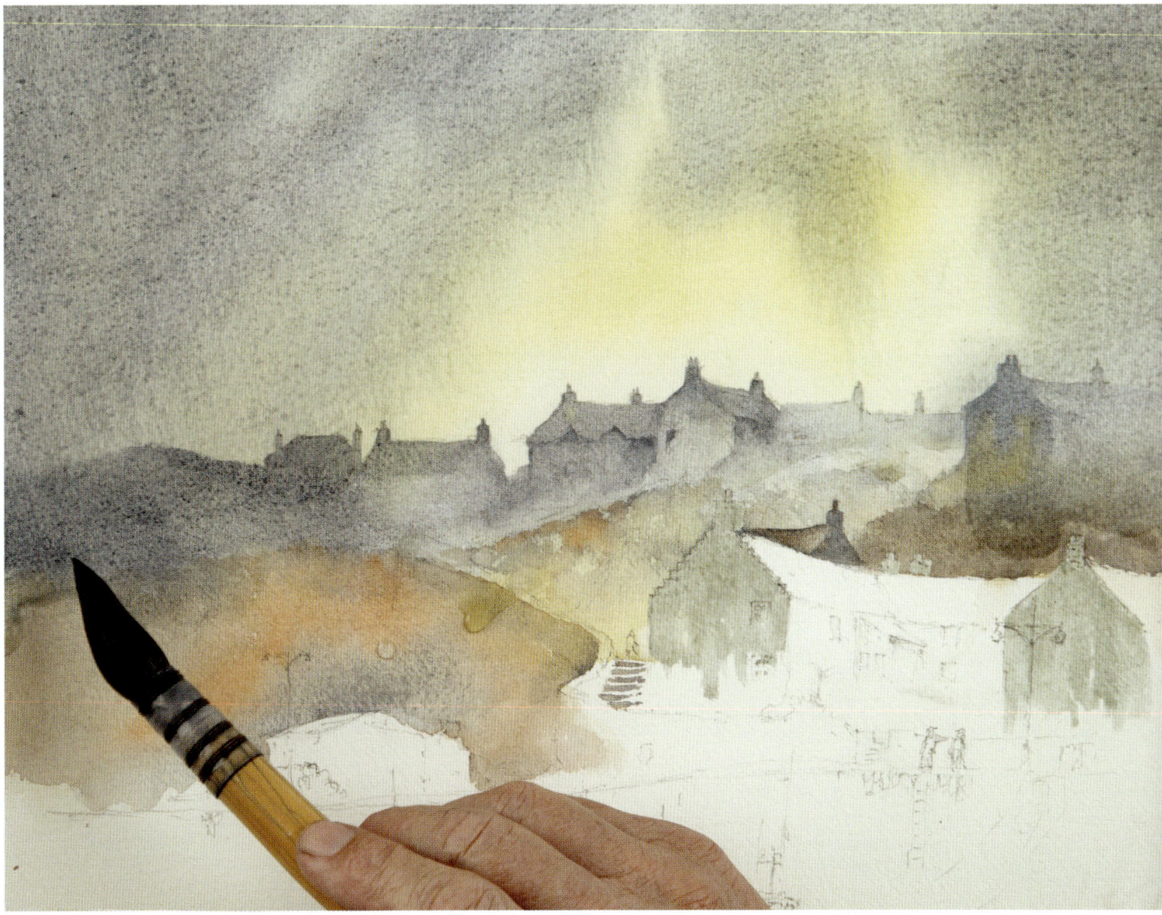

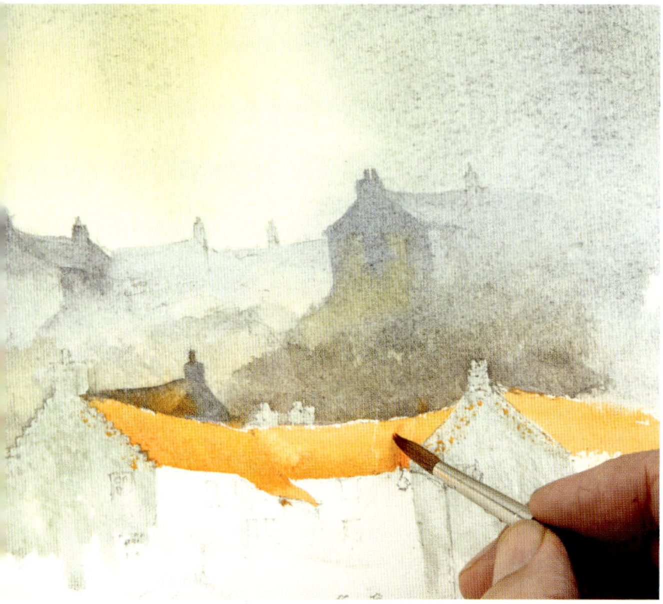

11 Lay the painting flat again. Using the no. 6 brush, paint the rooftops of the main buildings with permanent orange. Add transparent red oxide wet into wet for shadow near the bottom.

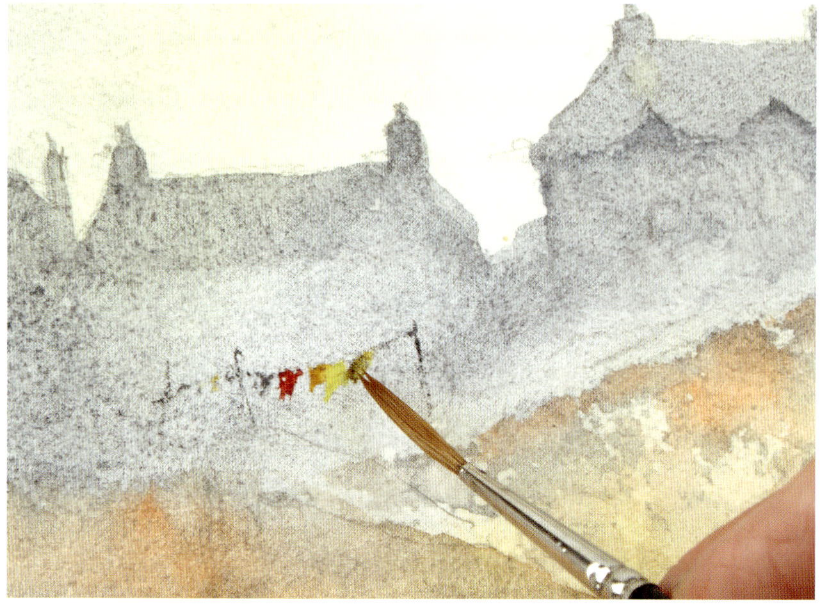

12 Once the painting has dried completely, use the no. 1 rigger with a mix of burnt umber and French ultramarine to add a clothesline above the red rock area. Add some clothes on the line using simple shapes, and bright colours to help them stand out.

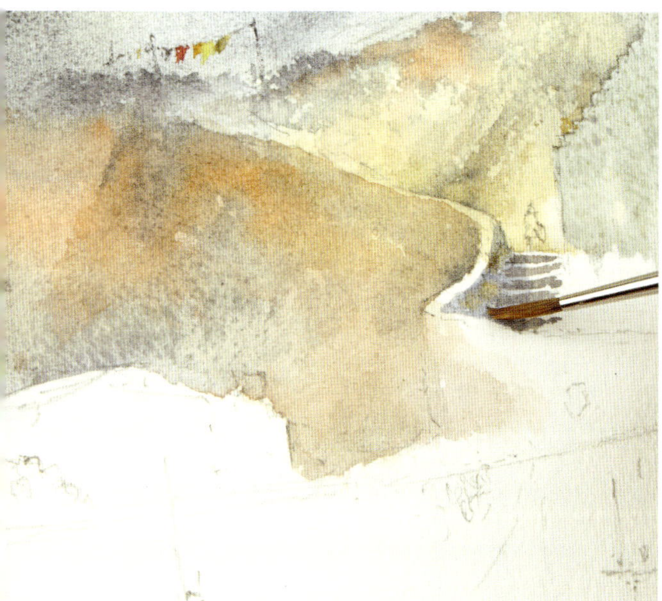

13 Using the no. 3 round brush, add tiny touches of the drab mixes on your palette on the foreground area of the red rocks and near the figure. Develop the wall with the same dull mixes, adding shadow, then drop in a hint of sunlight on the top with yellow ochre.

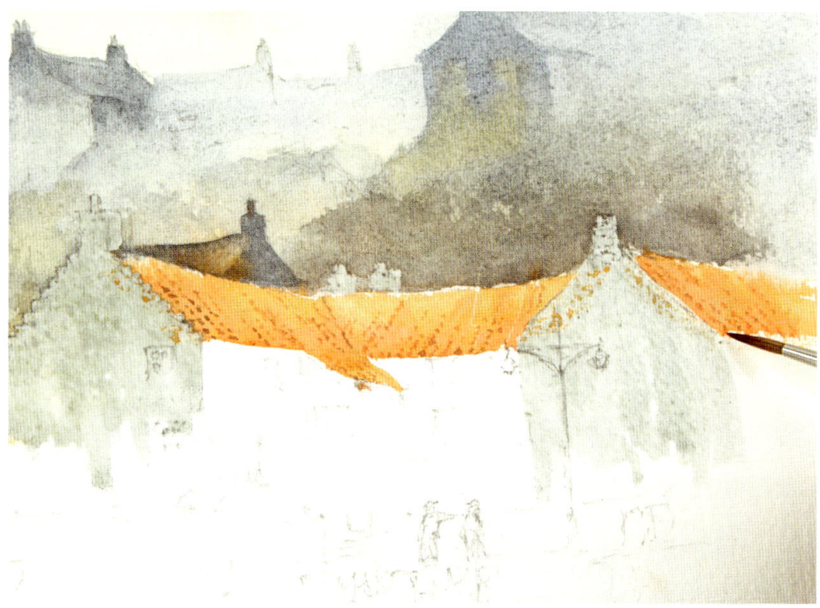

14 Still using the no. 3 brush, suggest the roof tiles with a mix of transparent red oxide and burnt umber. Work with the slope of the roof, adding parallel broken lines of colour. If any marks are too hard and obvious, touch them lightly with a finger to soften the effect. Allow to dry completely.

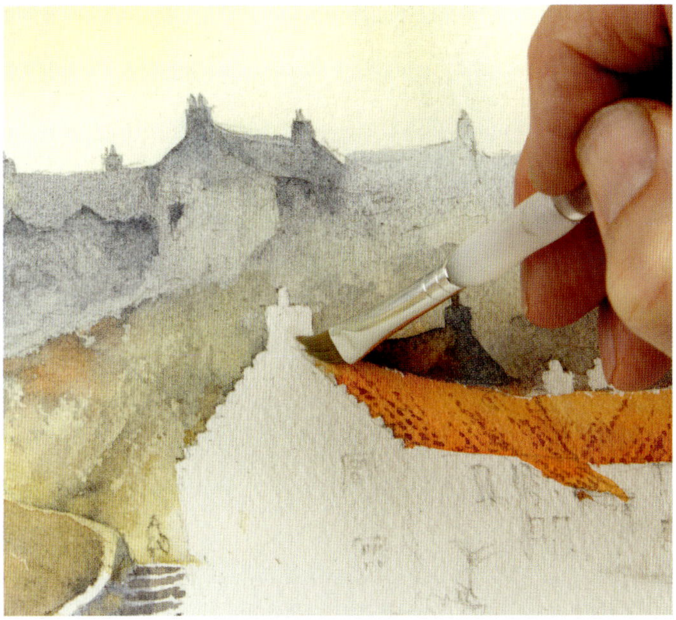

15 Use a clean finger to gently rub away the masking fluid, then dampen with the 6mm ($\frac{1}{4}$in) flat synthetic brush, and gently agitate the crisp edges left by the masking fluid, softening them subtly into the painting.

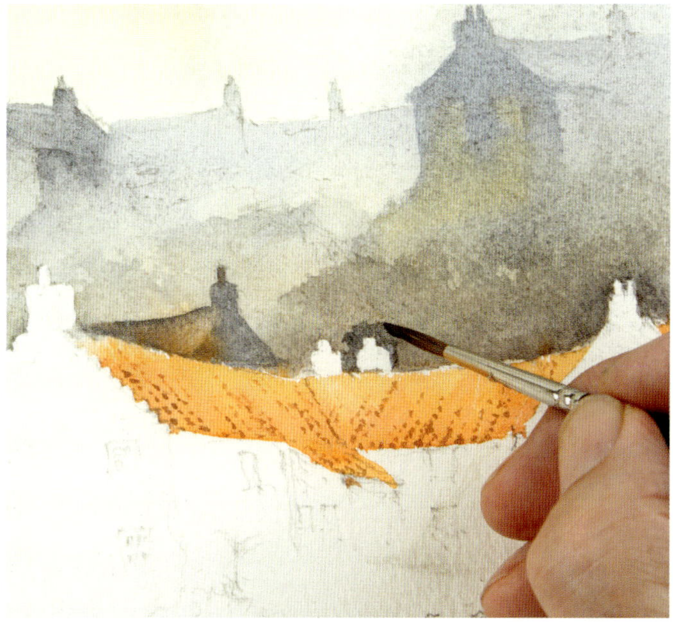

16 Change to the no. 1 rigger and tidy any loose edges on the rooftop with the blue-grey mix of sodalite genuine and French ultramarine. Soften the colour into the surroundings to avoid a hard line on the background.

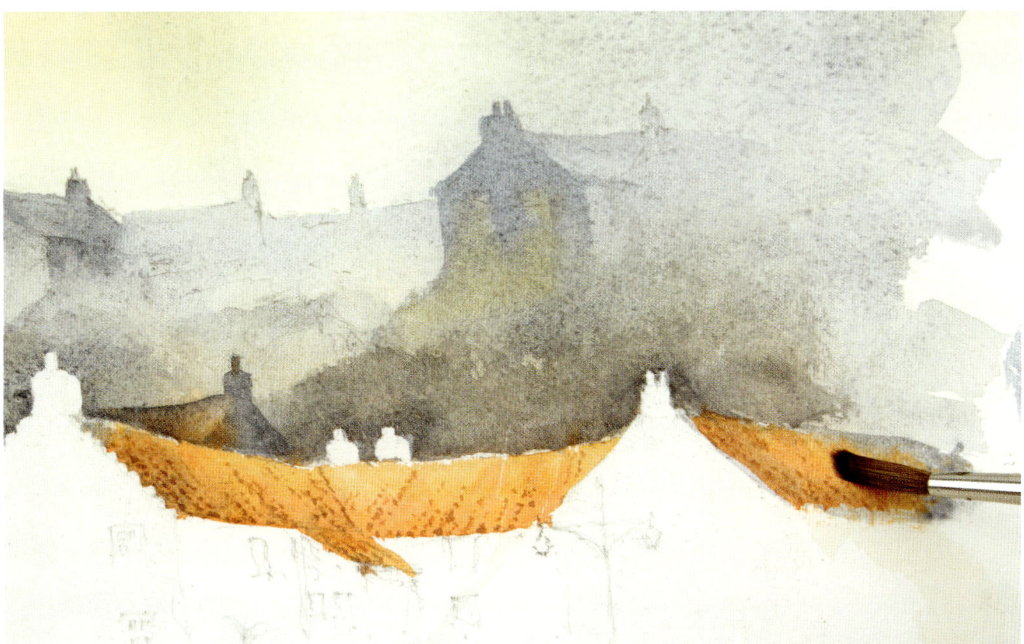

17 The light is coming in from left to right, so I wanted to add a subtle shadow to the roofs in the shade. Use the blue-grey mix, fairly dilute, to add the shadows. On the right-hand side, near the edge of the painting, use a slightly stronger mix. This will ensure that the colour is not too strident, which would lead the eye out of the painting.

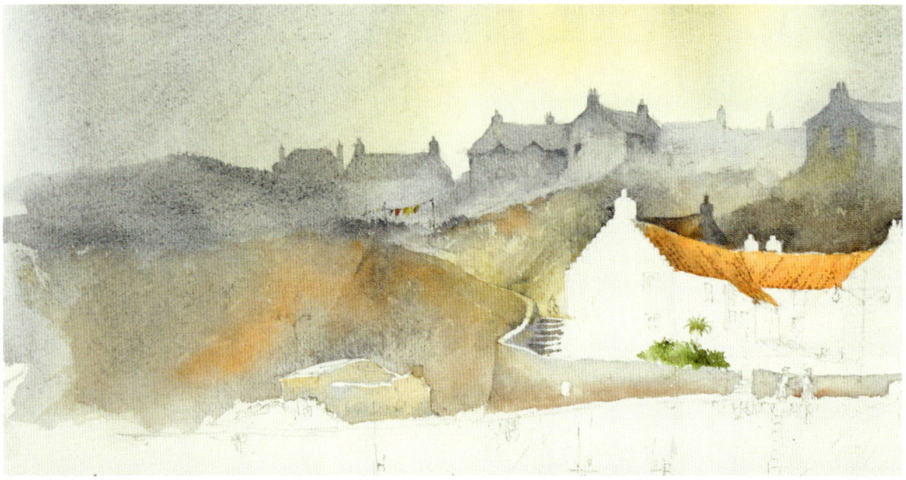

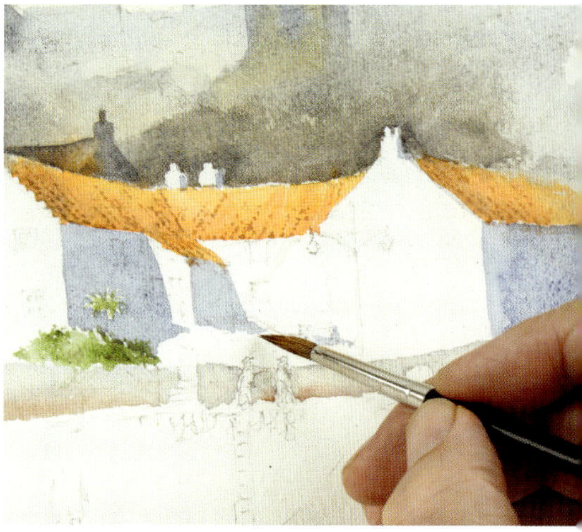

18 Using the no. 1 round brush, paint the palm tree and greenery in front of the main building with green apatite genuine, then add dilute blue-grey mix behind the lobster pots on the left-hand side. Drop in touches of dilute yellow ochre and phthalocyanine blue to push some light into the area. Still leaving a white rim where the top of the wall is catching the sunlight, do the same on the central foreground area. Add some transparent red oxide wet into wet near the base of the wall.

19 Add shadow to the foreground buildings using the no. 6 brush and French ultramarine. Use the tip of the brush to work carefully around and into the details.

20 Use the no. 3 round to develop the lobster pots with the blue-grey mix (sodalite genuine and French ultramarine), and transparent red oxide. Add some striking impact with touches of cerulean blue.

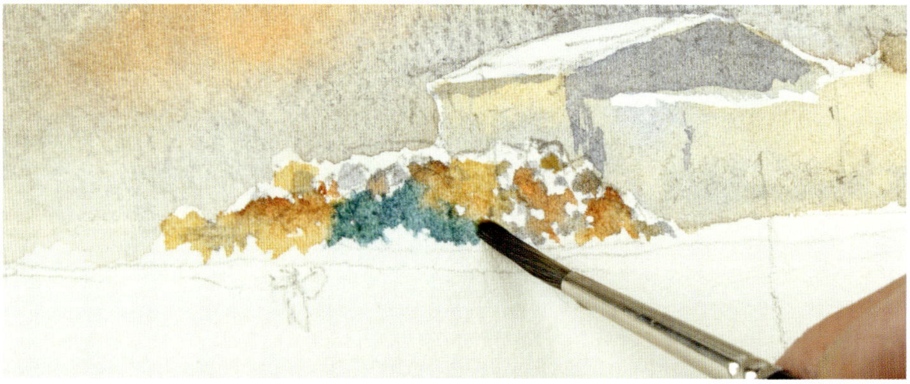

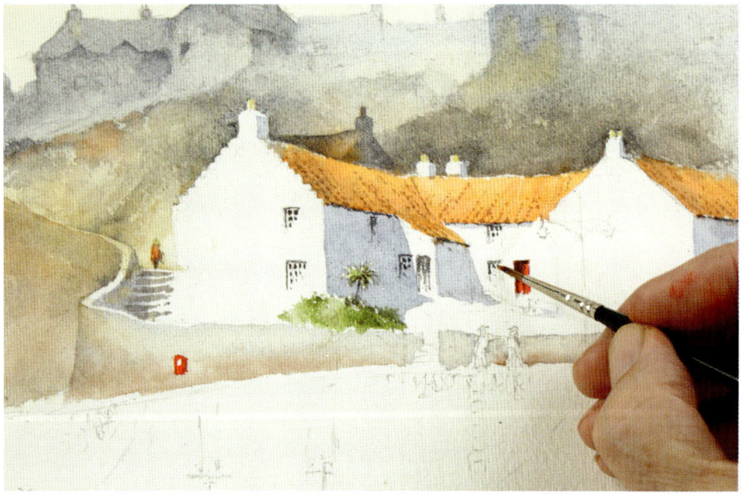

21 Use the no. 1 round to paint the lifebuoy and front door with cadmium red medium hue; and sunlight on the chimney pots with nickel titanate yellow. Paint the central figure, using the same yellow for her hair, transparent red oxide for her coat, and moonglow for her legs. Work carefully, allowing the colours to mix a little wet into wet, but not so much as to become indistinguishable. Use a deep mix of French ultramarine and burnt umber to paint in the window panes on the main building. Add some shadow under the eaves, too.

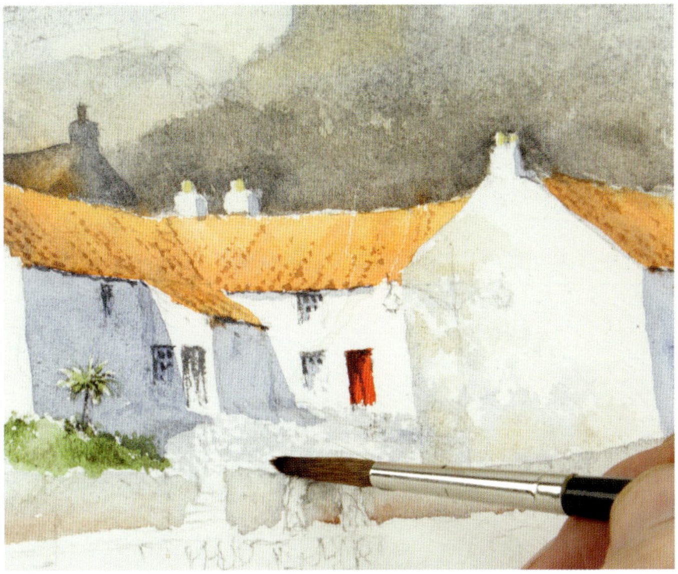

22 Still using the no. 1 round brush, add tiny touches of French ultramarine to suggest the positions of the corners of the walls. Change to the no. 6 round brush and use dilute touches of blue-grey (French ultramarine and sodalite genuine) and yellow ochre to create a mottled effect on the wall and courtyard area.

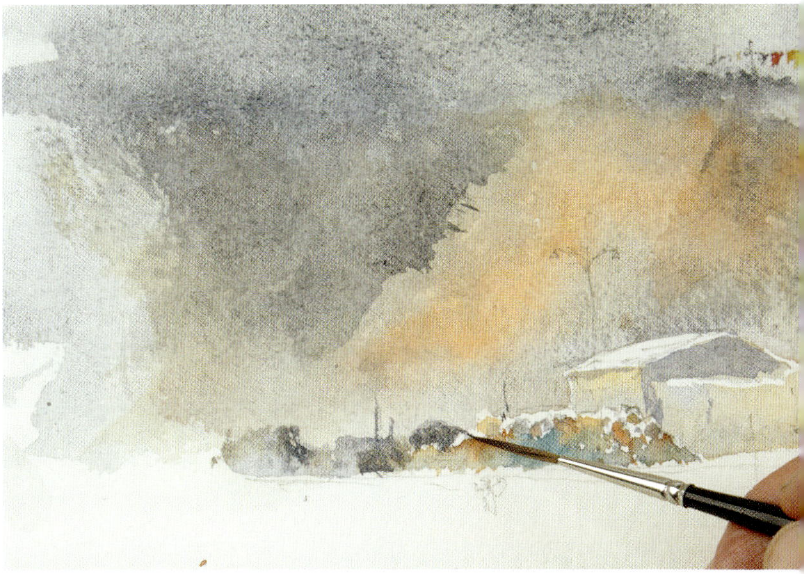

23 Develop the rocks on the left-hand side, adding colour to the dark area around and behind them. Use the blue-grey mix of French ultramarine and sodalite genuine, and the no. 6 brush. Change to the no. 1 rigger and use the same mix to add some detritus near to the lobster pots, hinting at a few posts and similar shapes.

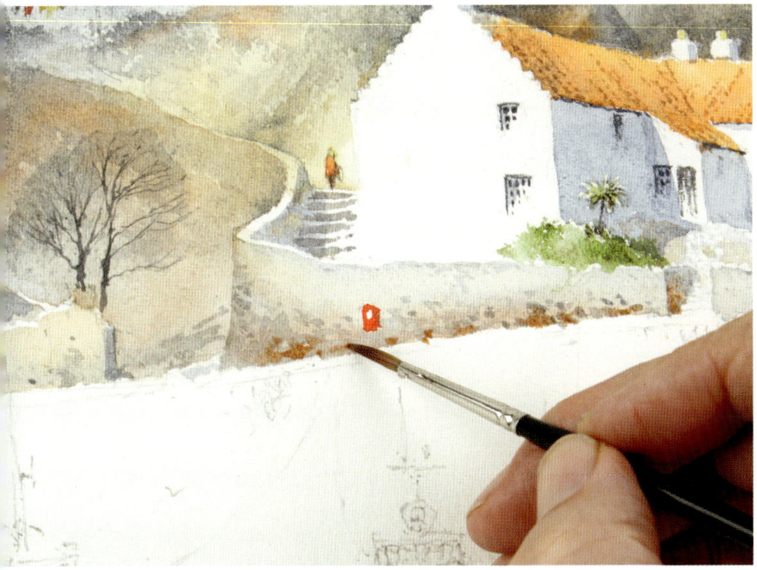

24 Still using the rigger and the blue-grey mix, add the trunk and main branches of a tree. Dilute the mix and use the side of the no. 3 brush to add foliage. Work along the foreground wall, using the tip of the same brush to add blue-grey touches that suggest stonework. Vary the effect by adding light red into the wet paint.

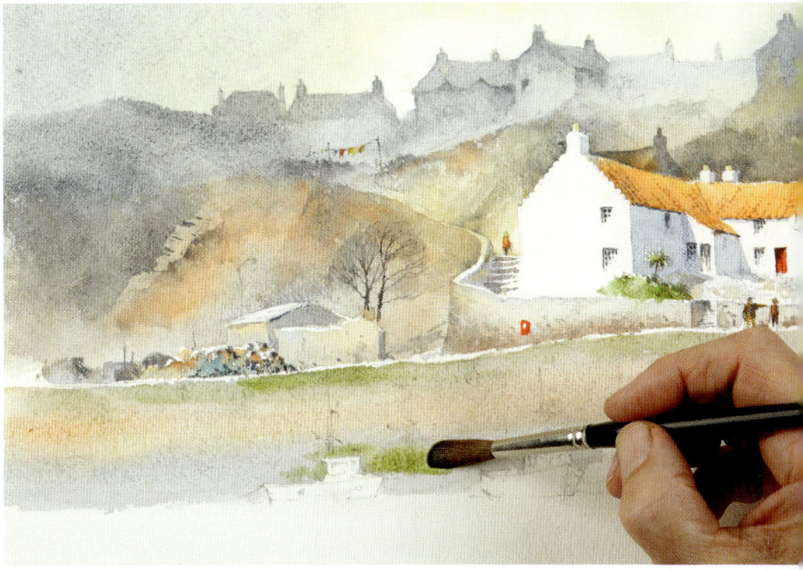

25 Paint the sea wall using a combination of yellow ochre and the blue-grey. Use the no. 10 brush with long horizontal strokes, working carefully around the boats. Add dilute light red wet into wet, followed by green apatite genuine. Use less water with the green.

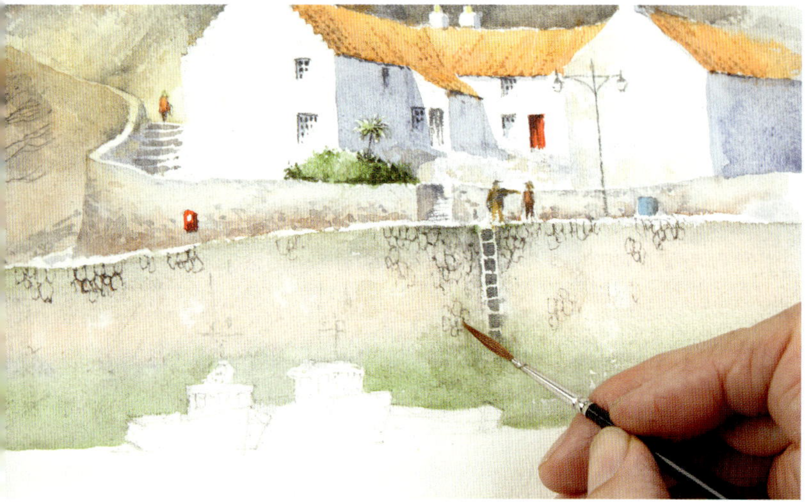

26 Tighten up the green area by the focal buildings with the no. 1 round brush and a mix of French ultramarine and burnt umber. Develop and detail the lamppost, life belt, rubbish bin and ladder with the same colour. Using the rigger with burnt umber, paint the stonework. Vary the pressure you apply, and the amount of paint on the brush. More pressure leads to stronger marks and wider lines; less pressure the opposite. Don't try to paint every brick – instead focus on critical areas. You want to evoke the overall effect, rather than take up building as a second job!

27 Change to the no. 6 round brush and glaze the sea wall with a dilute grey-green mix (apatite genuine mixed with French ultramarine and sodalite genuine). Add touches of transparent red oxide and yellow ochre wet into wet. Add some powerful darks to the base of the wall to help push the rest of the painting backwards. Use a dark mix of French ultramarine and burnt umber, applying it with the no. 6 brush and softening it in to avoid hard lines.

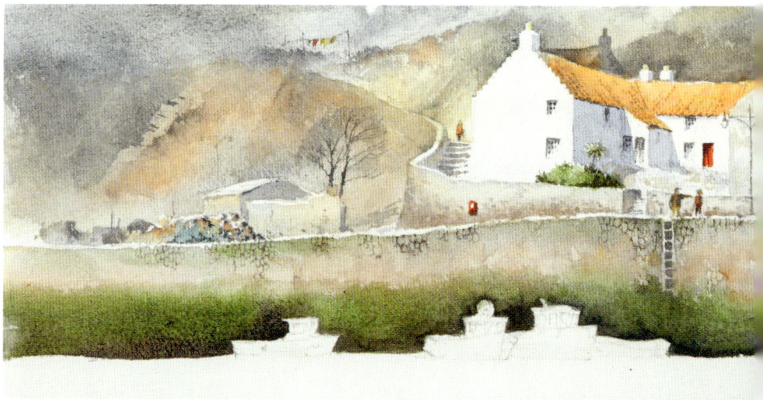

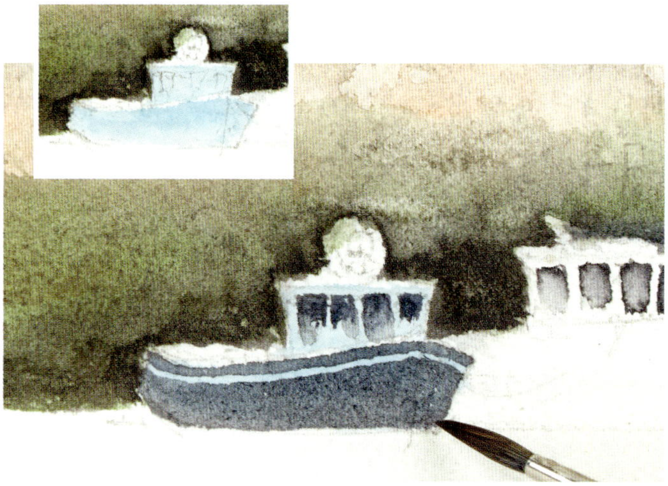

28 Paint the central boat with phthalocyanine blue (see inset), and the windows with the dark mix using the no. 3 round. Once the central boat is dry, overlay the dark mix (French ultramarine and sodalite genuine), leaving a fine line of the lighter blue showing through.

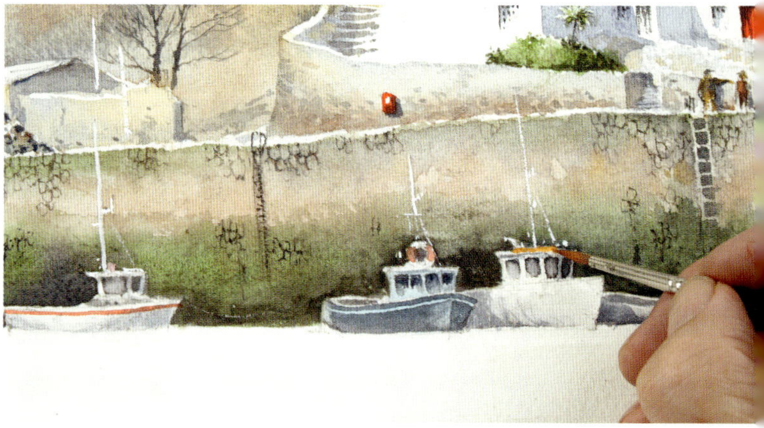

29 The boats are an opportunity to introduce bold, bright colours in the foreground. Lift out some paint with the 6mm (¼in) synthetic flat brush to help suggest the shape of the hull. In addition to the dark mix, add phthalocyanine blue, cadmium red medium hue, and permanent orange to bring in some bold marks; and French ultramarine to subdue the white while keeping the shadows vibrant. Use the no. 1 rigger to paint the masts and other uprights with white gouache.

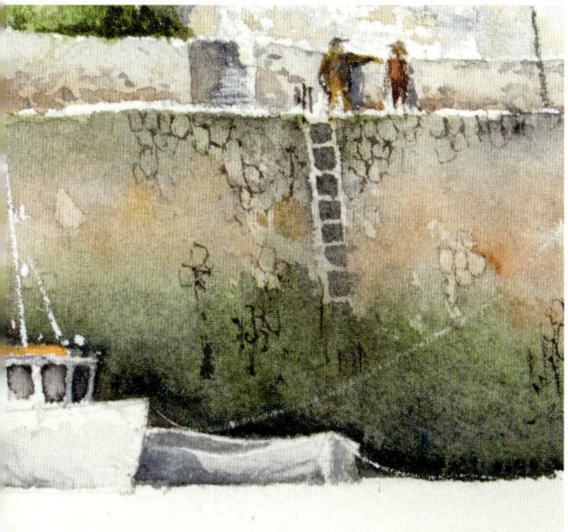

30 Use the tip of a scalpel to scratch out some ropes from the boats to the harbour.

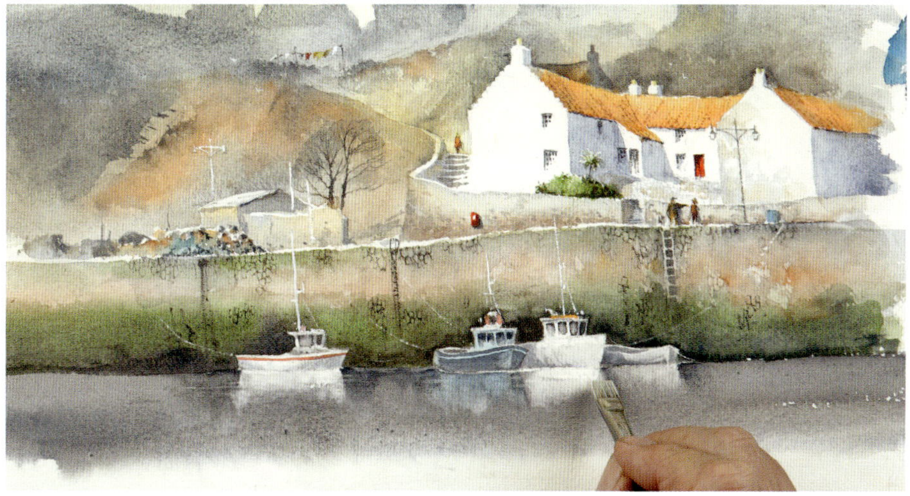

31 Wet the sea area and apply a mix of French ultramarine with a little burnt umber, using the no. 10 round brush. Leave gaps to serve as reflections beneath the white-hulled boats, and soften the edges with a damp brush. Add a little subtle phthalocyanine blue beneath the blue boat and soften in the same way.

*The finished painting.*

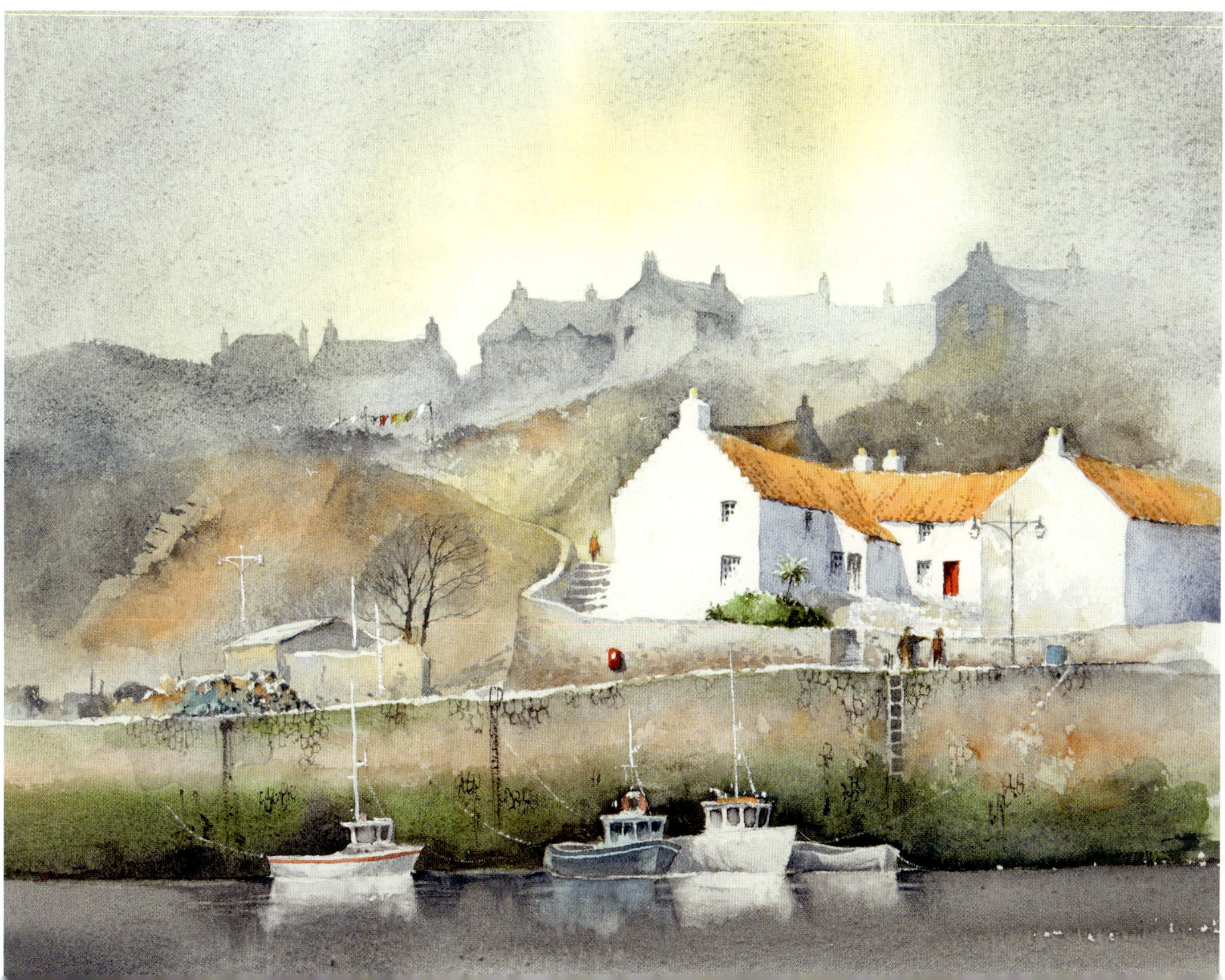

# Figures and birds

Introducing figures and some wildlife in the forms of seabirds into your coastal paintings will greatly enhance your work.

Take every opportunity to sketch people, particularly those working or taking part in some activity, perhaps working on a boat or mending nets as in the sketch of two figures at Hastings. It is even more effective if you have them relating to each other in some way, chasing each other through the surf or tending to children, for example, or perhaps hauling a boat out of the water together.

The sketches of *Turbulent Launching* began with rapid, gestural strokes of the pencil, the detail added at a more leisurely pace once the main action of the figure had been captured. Information such as wetsuits and life-vests can be drawn onto a separate page if necessary, but you should concentrate on the action: it is vital that you capture the dynamic poses the figures are in. Don't be daunted by the prospect as you soon become more adept at capturing such images. Build up a reservoir of sketched figures: some that are fairly close-up and some in the distance, as with the massed bathers (below), which are little more than dots; and of course those figures in between.

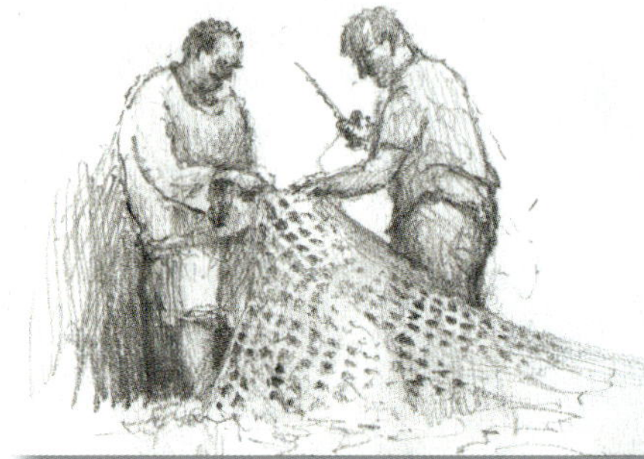

*Seek out working people to add to your collection and try to sketch them in different positions so that you have a reservoir of figure sketches which you can choose to include in a painting.*

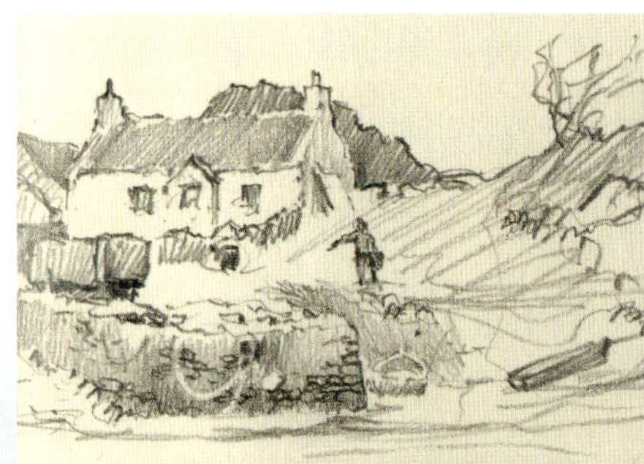

*By observing figures in action you can make them look more authentic. Here the outstretched arm suggests a heavy bucket being carried.*

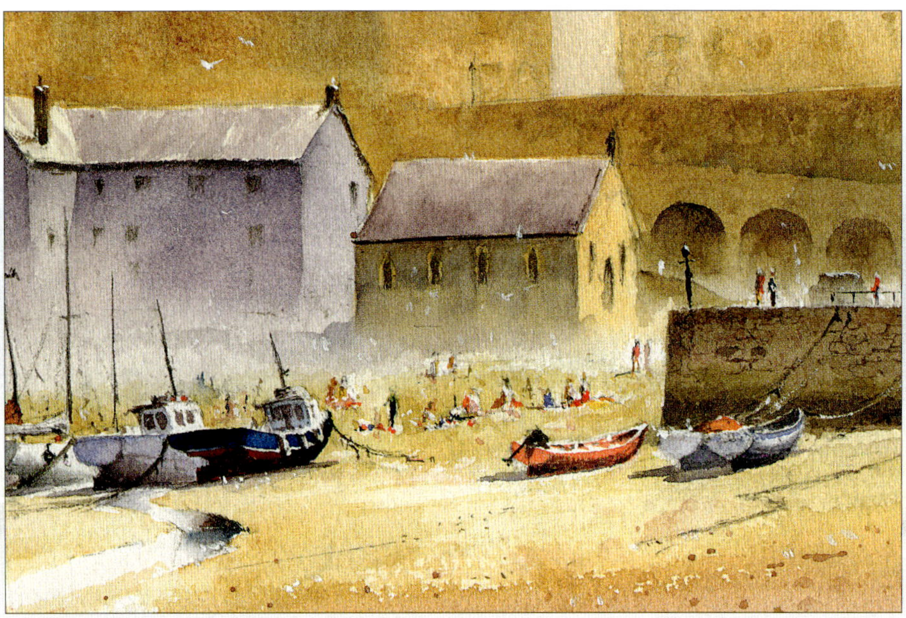

*Rendering distant figures on a beach calls for careful placement and a simple approach to avoid over-working. Suggest them rather than working on detailed individual figures, and allow them to run into each other within a group.*

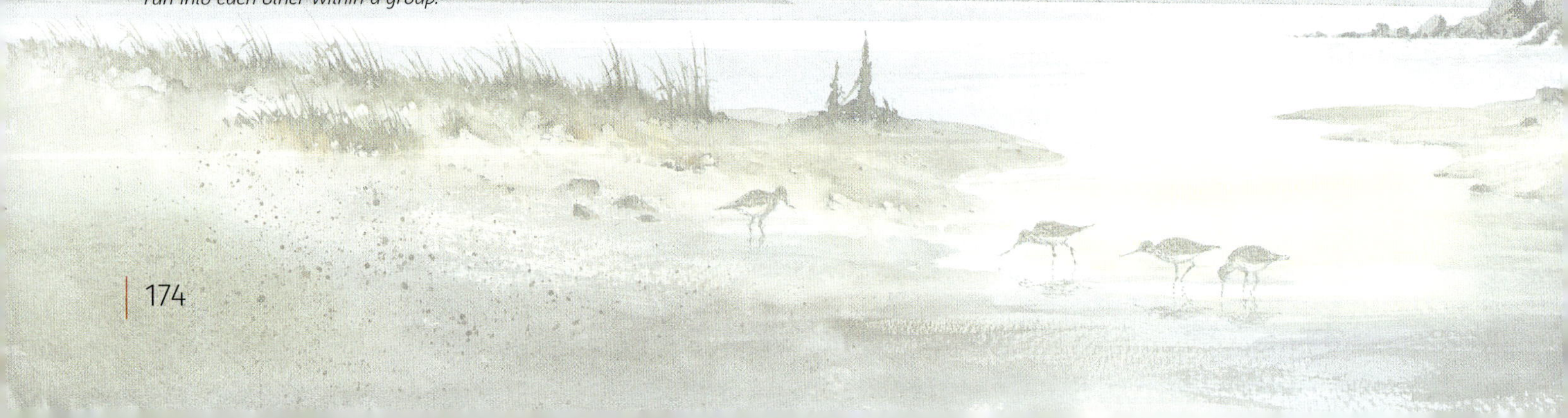

### TURBULENT LAUNCHING

*20 x 30.5cm (8 x 12in)*

*Finding myself in the midst of a regatta being launched, I took the opportunity to carry out a number of sketches of people in action (see below), which I much prefer to folk just hanging around. In the finished painting, the ragged effects on sea and sky suggest a windy day as the two figures battle to get their craft into the animated surf.*

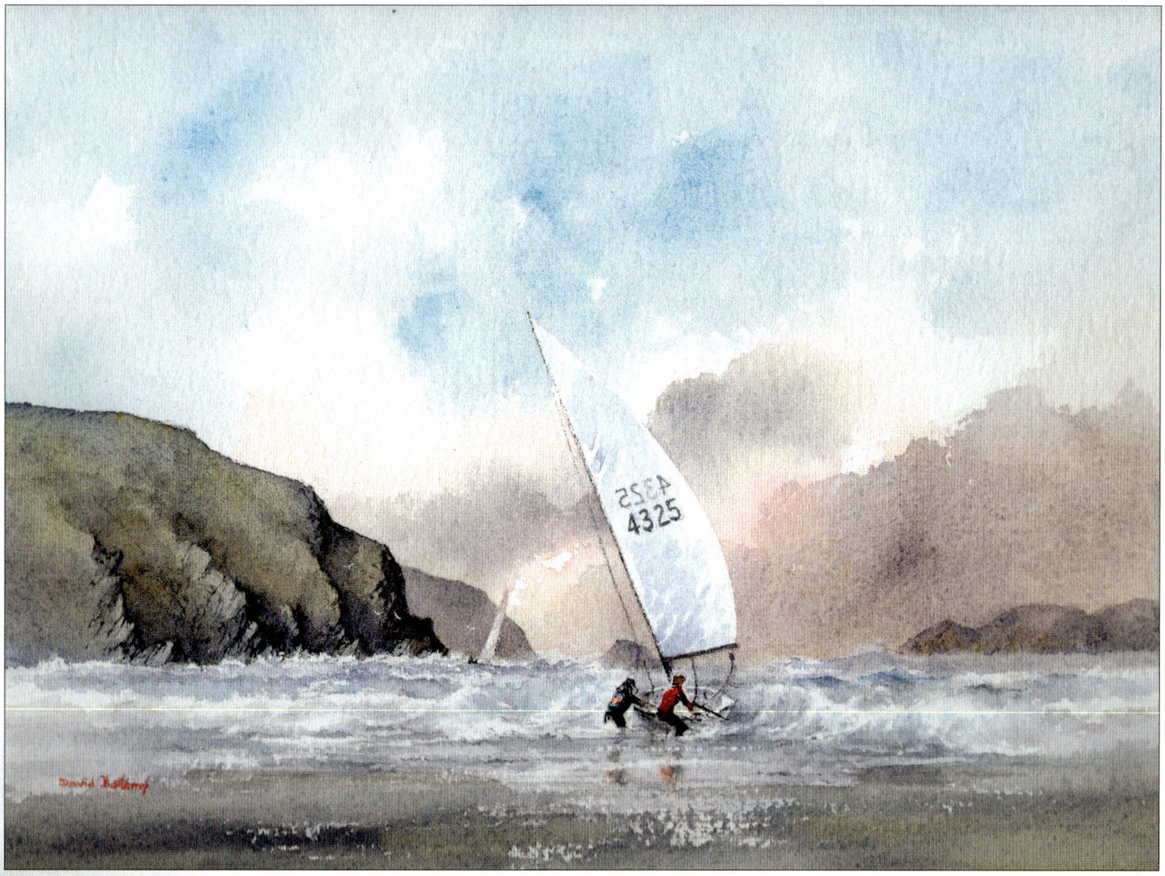


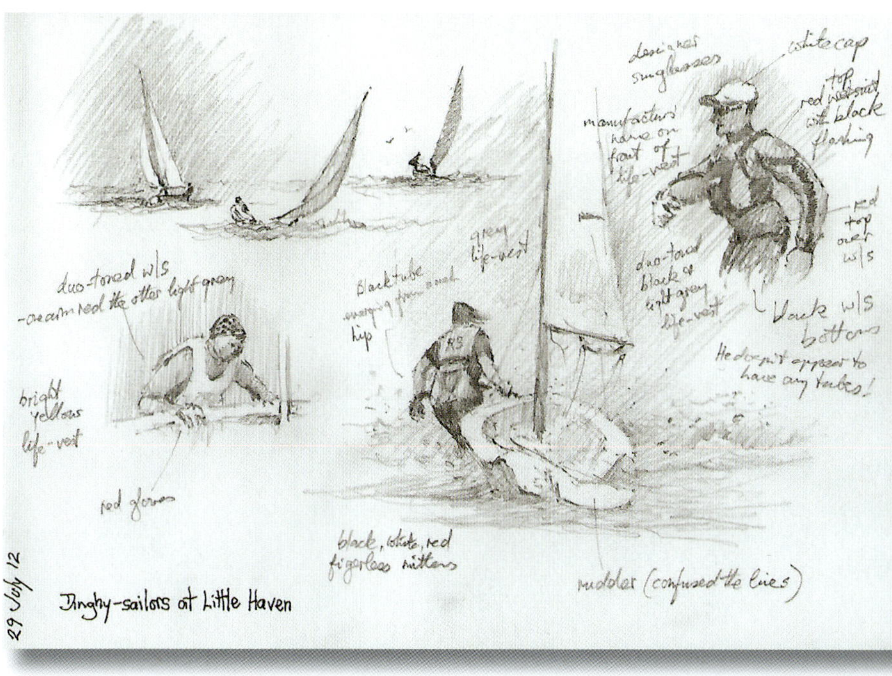

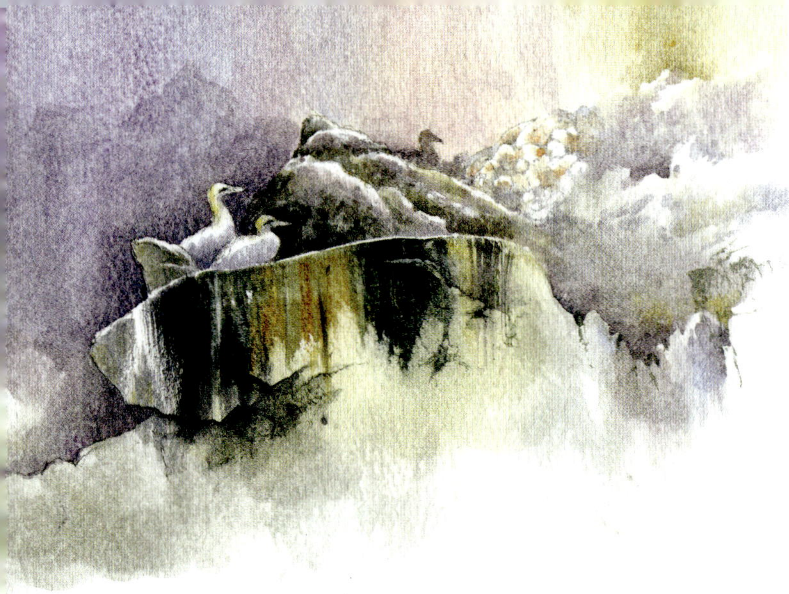

GANNETS RESTING

*15 x 18cm (6 x 7in) 300gsm (140lb) Not paper*

*I originally sketched these gannets from a boat bobbing about under the dramatic black cliffs of Grassholm Island. As they were sitting still and are distinctive , they did not present a great problem. With the large rock on which they sat I took a piece of watercolour paper about 5cm (2in) square and dipped one end of an edge into yellow ochre and the other end into indigo and then scraped it down vertically from the top of the rock, needing to repeat this three times to cover the whole rock. The technique worked well on the Not surface. Afterwards, with a fine, damp 12mm (½in) brush I tidied up the top of the rock where it catches the sunlight, and also pulled out a short horizontal highlight near the right-hand end to add interest.*

## SEABIRDS

While it does suggest a sense of life in a coastal scene, adding a few quick v-shaped marks in the sky may leave some artists unsatisfied. You may wish to make more of the wildlife aspect, especially in natural locations such as cliffs, rocks, estuaries or surf-line.

Common seagulls are fairly easy as they are happy to pose for some time, allowing you to sketch and photograph them on boats, rocks, chimney-pots and so on. Cormorants hang out on rocks close to the shore where you may find a pair of binoculars mounted on a tripod more effective for recording detail. For gannets, puffins, razorbills and guillemots, all of which make superb focal points on a wild coastline, you usually need to take a boat out to an island to find them, which opens up all sorts of exciting possibilities. Puffins in particular are far from timid and may come extremely close. Their antics often seem crazy and always endearing, and they are just about the easiest bird to paint and create a likeness. Guillemots and razorbills tend to stand statuesquely on rocks and cliff ledges for ages, so they too are easy to render. It helps to have optical assistance. Gannets are distinctive and when they are not hurtling through the air, they can make superb subjects as they sit in groups.

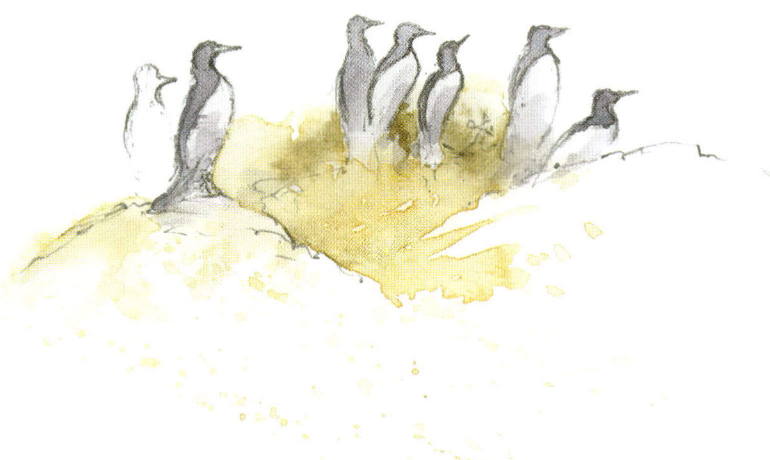

GUILLEMOTS

*Guillemots love to stand around and chat on ledges and rocks, and while like this they are relatively easy to sketch, although you will probably need a pair of binoculars or a spotter scope to record any detail.*

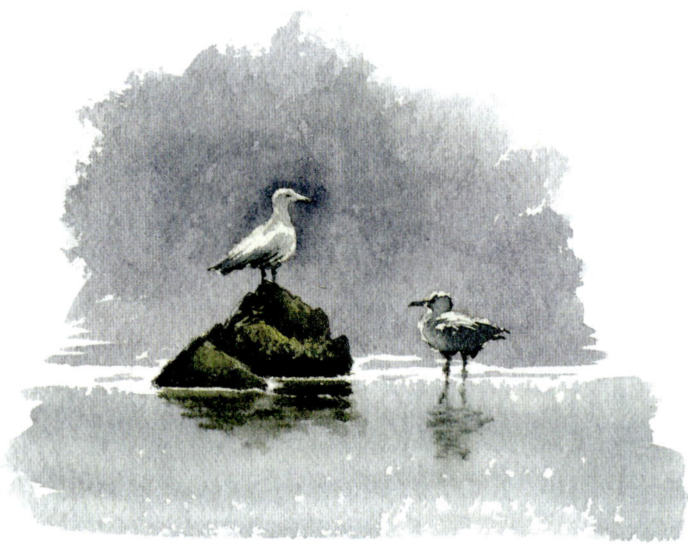

GULLS POSING

*Seagulls are great posers and happily stand for ages on the beach, on top of boats, chimneys and the like, and you can often get close to sketch, but keep your sandwiches out of sight!*

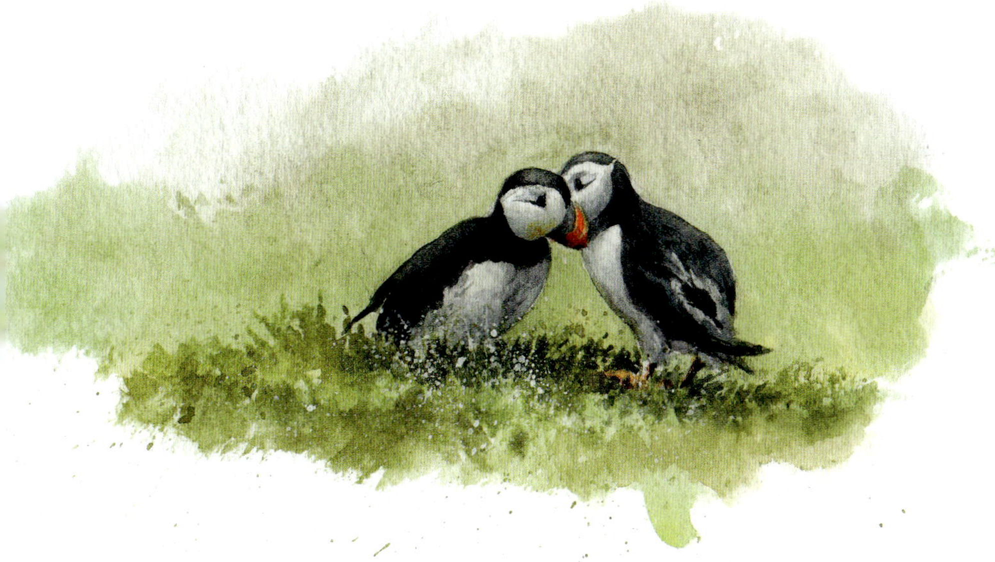

**PUFFIN SECRETS**
*10 x 18cm (4 x 7in)*
*Whenever I visit Skomer Island in late spring the puffins always leave me speechless with their antics as they almost run between your feet. If you love sketching bird behaviour, this is the place to be, and they are just about the easiest bird from which to attain a likeness.*

## Birds in flight

Generally the best places to view birds in flight are the tops of cliffs, and sometimes you will find them hovering against a strong wind, which is an ideal situation to sketch. Find those places where they regularly fly past so that you can draw the bird's features in stages – in reality using several different birds to create the one image, as it is almost impossible to capture all the detail in one pass.

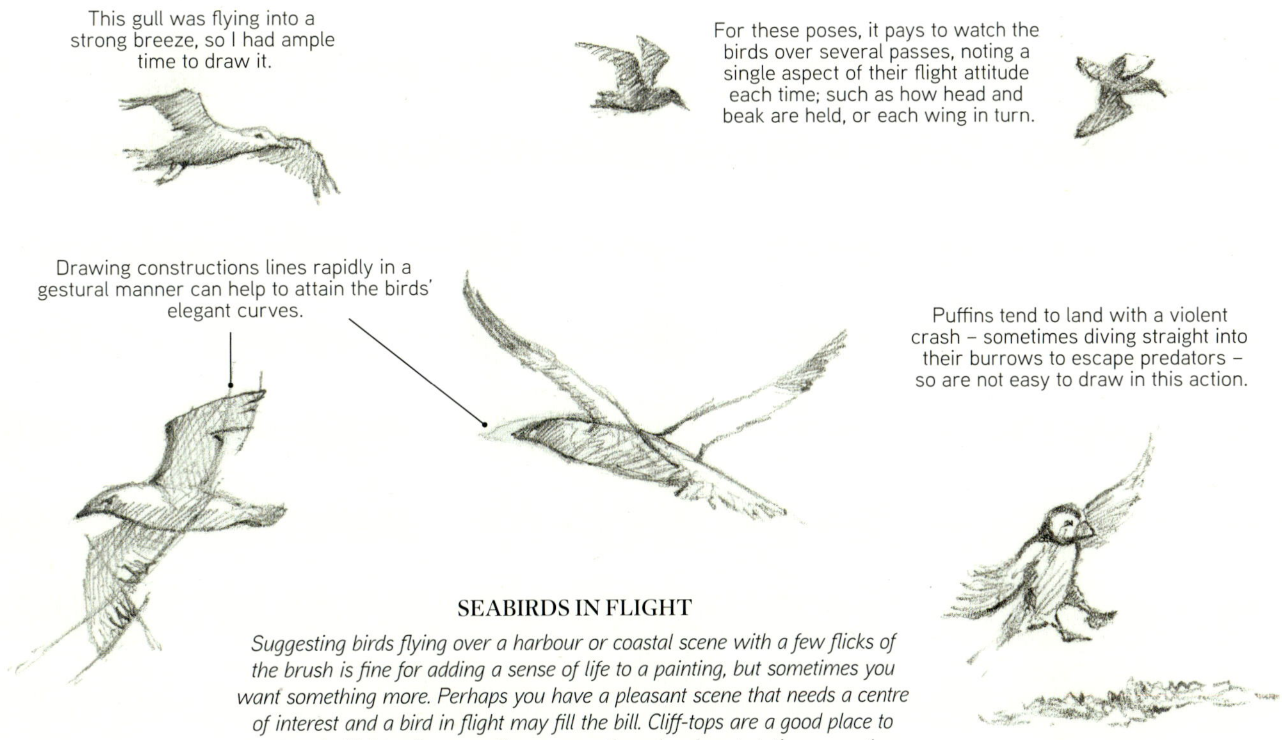


**SEABIRDS IN FLIGHT**
*Suggesting birds flying over a harbour or coastal scene with a few flicks of the brush is fine for adding a sense of life to a painting, but sometimes you want something more. Perhaps you have a pleasant scene that needs a centre of interest and a bird in flight may fill the bill. Cliff-tops are a good place to capture in-flight action as gulls can sometimes be almost stationary as they hold themselves against a strong breeze. In the lower two birds (centre and left) I have included construction lines to aid accuracy.*

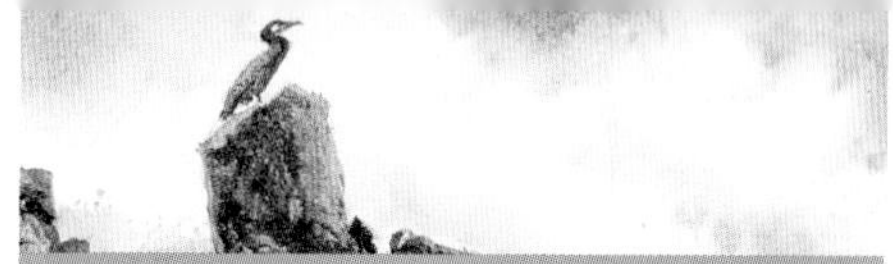

# LONELY CORMORANT

This demonstration has a cormorant as the focal point; it is all about rocks and a boisterous sea set against a moody backdrop. When deciding on the subject, I chose one sketch of cormorants and one of rocks in a different location, bringing it all together in a studio sketch before working on the final painting.

Many people have trouble painting rocks, so here I introduce an alternative approach in the form of collage using thin oriental papers, which contain quite prominent fibres, applied with PVA glue. When using this technique I prefer to paint on heavier papers of 425gsm (200lb) or 640gsm (300lb) weight.

**MATERIALS USED**

Saunders Waterford 425gsm (200lb) HP watercolour paper

Brushes: No. 14 round; no. 10 round; large squirrel mop; 12mm (½in) flat synthetic; no. 4 round; no. 1 rigger; old mixing brush

Colours: French ultramarine; cadmium red medium hue; nickel titanate yellow; lavender; burnt umber; phthalocyanine blue; quinacridone sienna

3B pencil and putty eraser

PVA glue and old brush

Scissors and oriental paper

Kitchen paper

Old toothbrush

White gouache

Scalpel

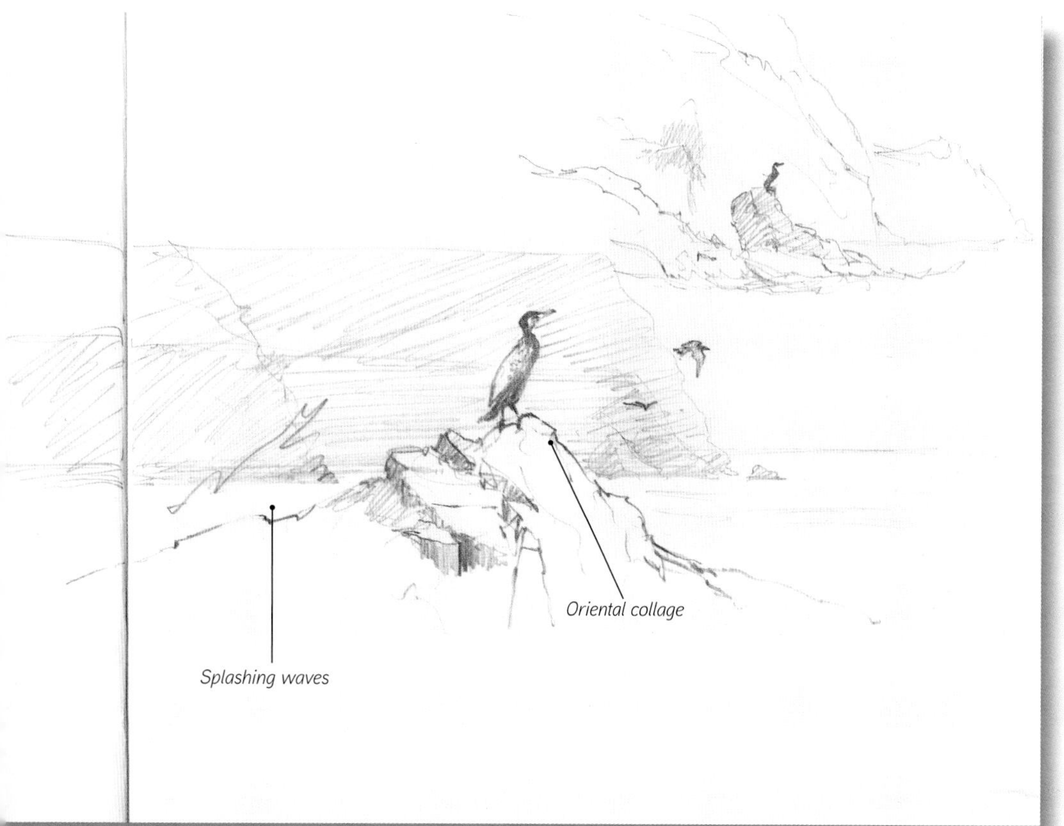


*The initial studio sketch. While I was happy with the bird in the main drawing, I preferred the rock structure of the upper small sketch.*

**1** Using a 3B pencil, refer to your initial sketch while you draw out the scene.

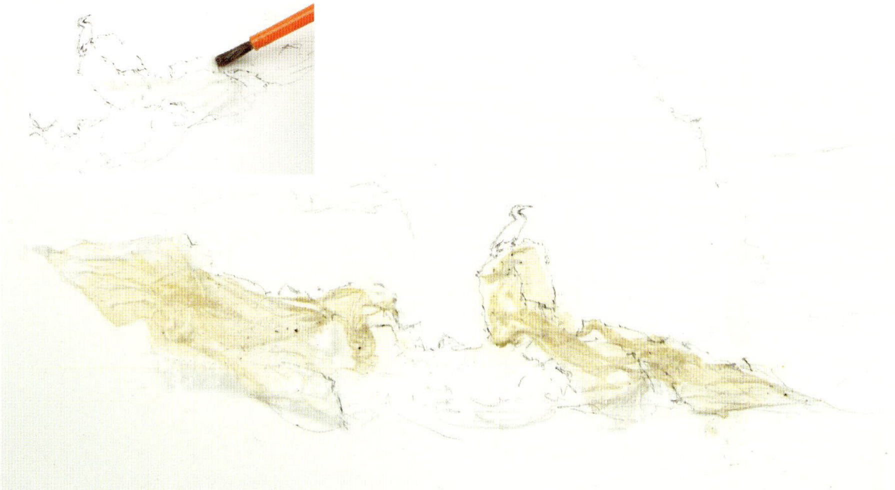

2 Working flat, water down a fair amount of PVA glue, mixing it up with an old brush. Use your scissors to cut some rough shapes from the oriental paper. Tear the pieces to roughly match the shapes of your foreground rocks, cover them with a layer of glue and then place them on the surface. Use your fingers or the brush to position them, aiming to create a rough textural surface (see inset). Work up to the pencil lines of your sketch, but not over – this would create a fuzzy edge, which would look odd on the hard edges of the rock. Build up the foreground rocks gradually – keep the pieces of oriental paper small; if you try to work too large an area at once, you will likely find the paper collapses on itself and becomes unworkable. Allow to dry thoroughly, preferably overnight.

3 Wet the splash area near the centre of the picture, to the right of the cormorant, using clean water and the no. 14 brush, then add a purple mix of French ultramarine and cadmium red medium hue with the no. 10 round brush. Add more of the purple mix wet into wet near the base, aiming to create a soft edge around the splash area.

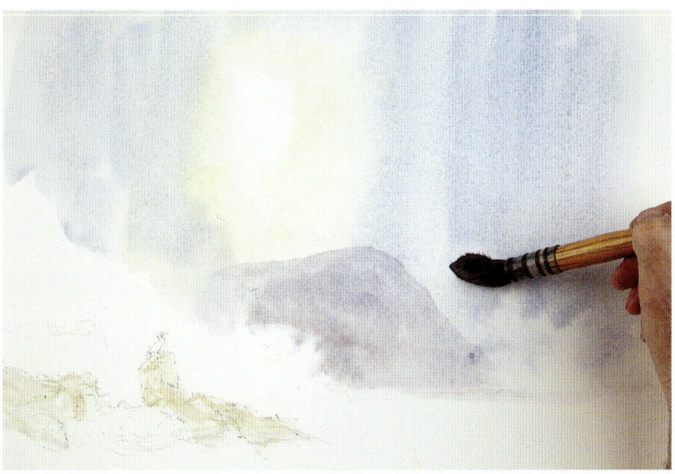

4 Once dry, wet both the whole sky and the rocky area you have painted using clean water and the large squirrel mop. Still using the squirrel mop brush, lay in nickel titanate yellow, leaving a small gap near the top. Pick up lavender on the squirrel mop and lay in vertical strokes to the right- and left-hand sides of the yellow area. Vertical strokes add to the drama. Use an old mixing brush to soften the lower edges of the wet paint, then allow to dry.

5 Change to the no. 10 round. Use a medium-strength grey mix of French ultramarine and burnt umber to paint in the edge of the distant cliff with the side of the brush. Soften the bottom away. To add an area of mist behind the cormorant, wet the base of the midground rocks with the large squirrel mop, then lay in a slightly stronger grey mix of French ultramarine and burnt umber down the left-hand side.

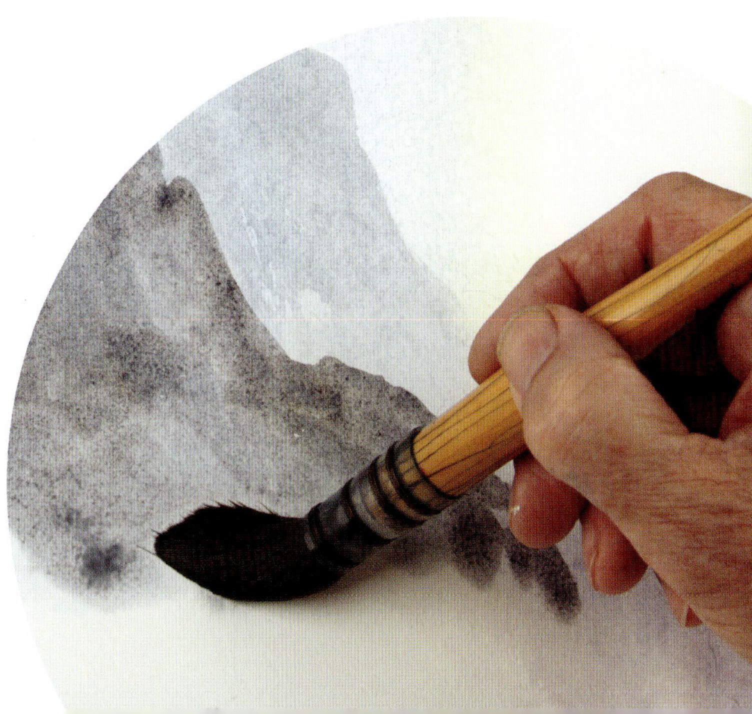

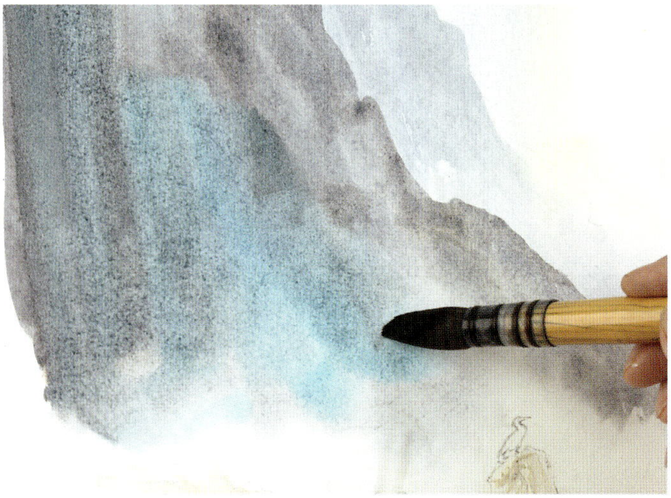

6 Work down into the wet area, then add phthalocyanine blue wet in wet.

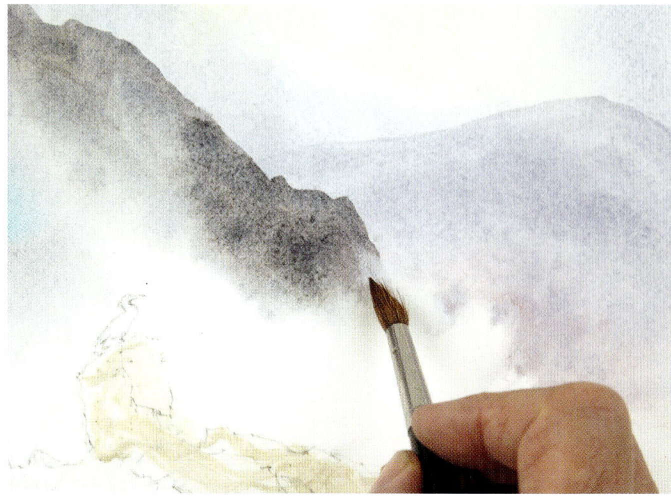

7 Apply more of the stronger grey mix using the no. 10 brush to strengthen the rib of rock on the right-hand side, bringing it down into the mist, then softening it away.

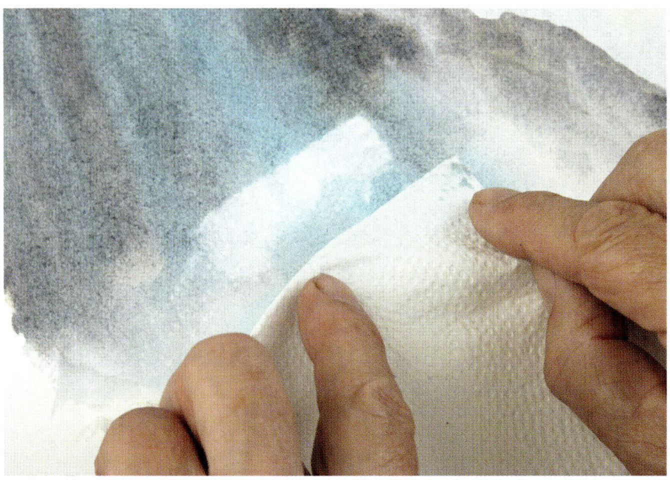

8 Lay some kitchen paper down into the wet paint just above the misty area on the right-hand side, then lift it away to suggest a rocky shelf.

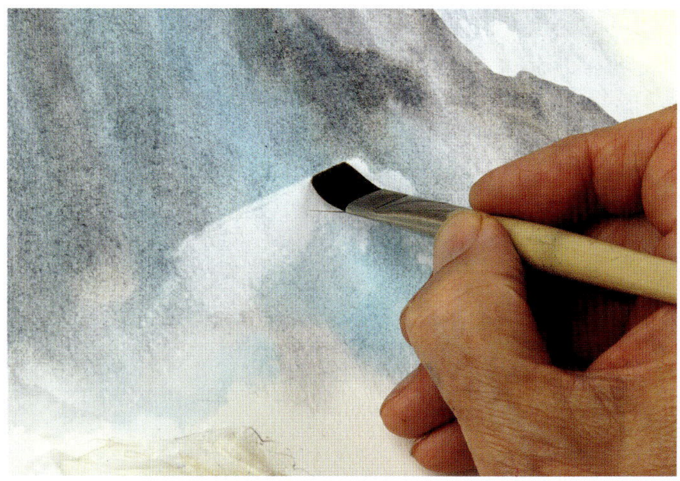

9 Use the damp 'blade' of the 12mm (½in) flat synthetic brush to refine and sharpen the top edge of the lifted-out rocky shelf.

10 Load the no. 1 rigger with the same stronger grey mix of French ultramarine and burnt umber to develop the midground rock face (see inset), creating fracture lines with the point, and general texture with the side of the bristles. Create more texture on the left-hand side using the no. 4 round brush in the same way. Work down to, but not over, the lifted-out area.

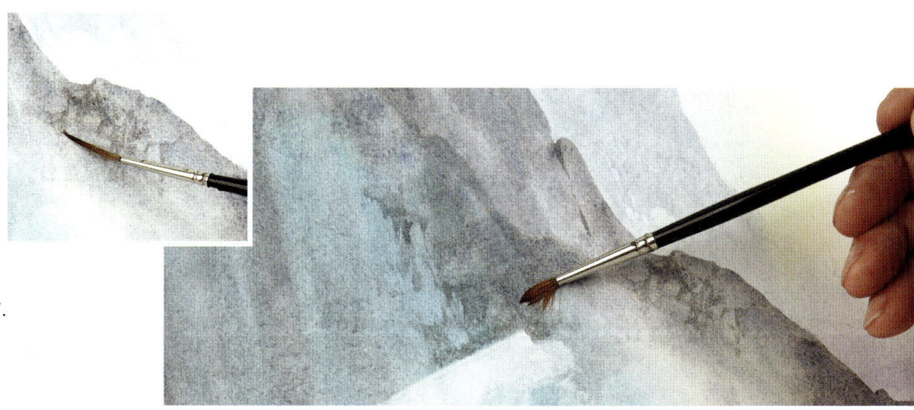

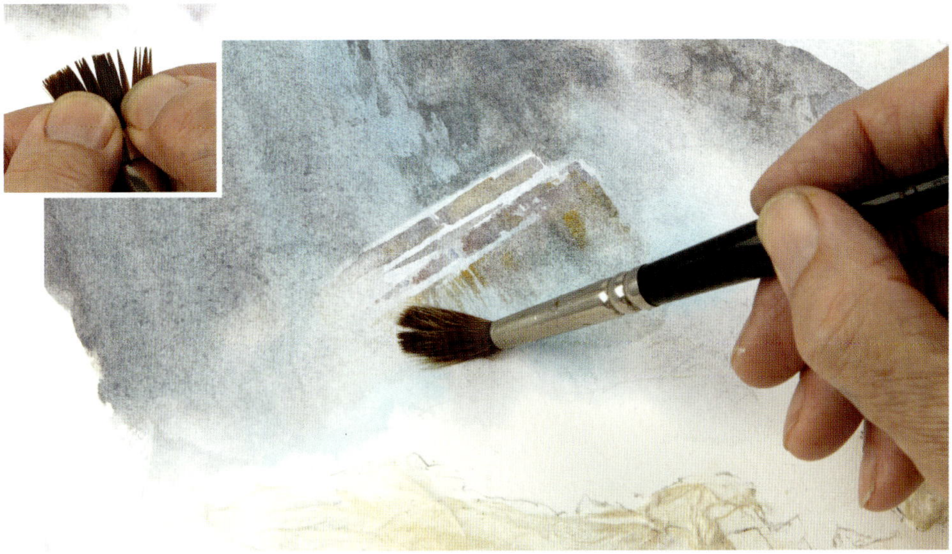

11 Use the 12mm (½in) flat synthetic brush to add short, broken parallel lines of the stronger grey mix of French ultramarine and burnt umber to the shelf of rock. Split the bristles (see inset) and use the brush to add textural colour and detail, adding in touches of yellow ochre, too.

12 Change to the no. 6 brush, and use the same mix of French ultramarine and burnt umber to strengthen the shadow on the right-hand side of the shelf. Once dry, add fracture lines to the shelf using the no. 1 rigger, again with the dark grey mix.

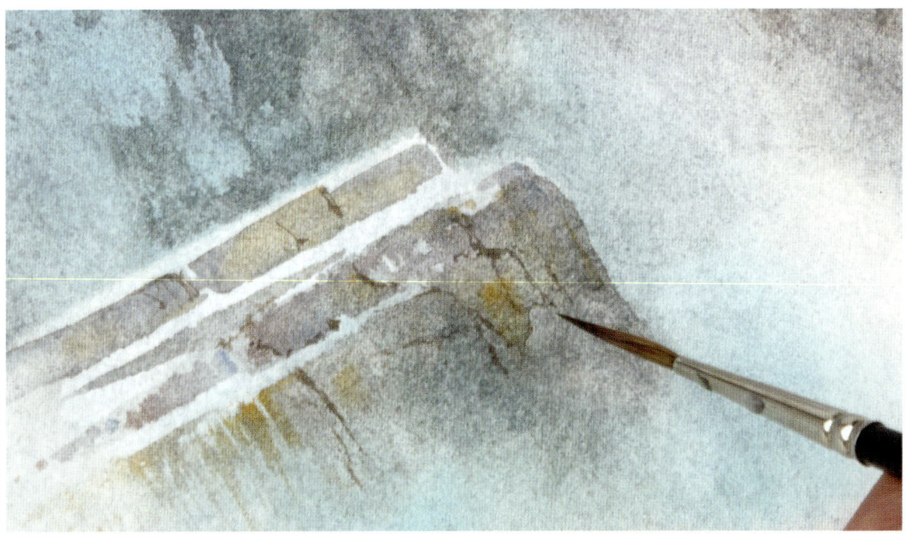

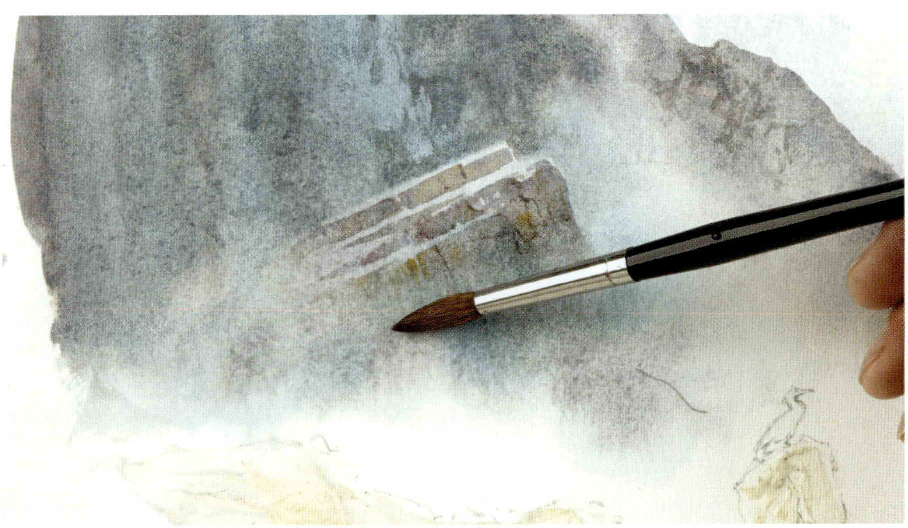

13 Wet the area to the left of the cormorant, and add some more of the stronger mix of French ultramarine and burnt umber, drawing it down into the wet area. This will give the impression that the rocky shelf is emerging from behind the foam.

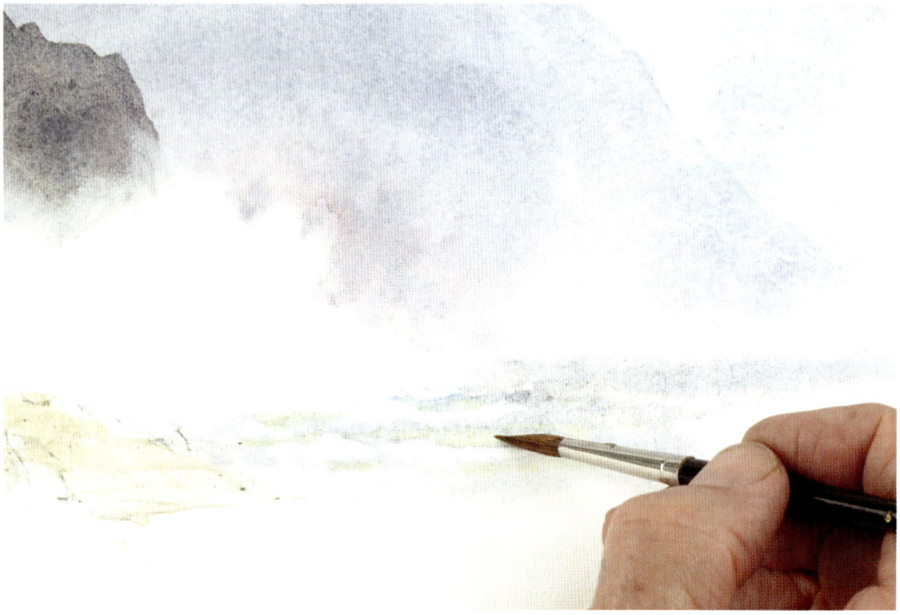

**14** Wet the sea area with a damp sponge. Still using the same stronger grey mix, load a no. 6 round and begin to paint the hazy distant water, using wandering, horizontal touches of the side of the brush. Working wet into wet, add hints of nickel titanate yellow into the sea near the focal point (the cormorant). This will create eye-catching greens and prevents the sea looking dull.

**15** Still using the no. 6 brush, wet the inner part of the splash with clean water, then add some subtle touches of the grey mix (French ultramarine and burnt umber). Add some more grey into the nearby sea, too, and work up to and over the textured rocks beneath the cormorant. Allow the area to dry completely.

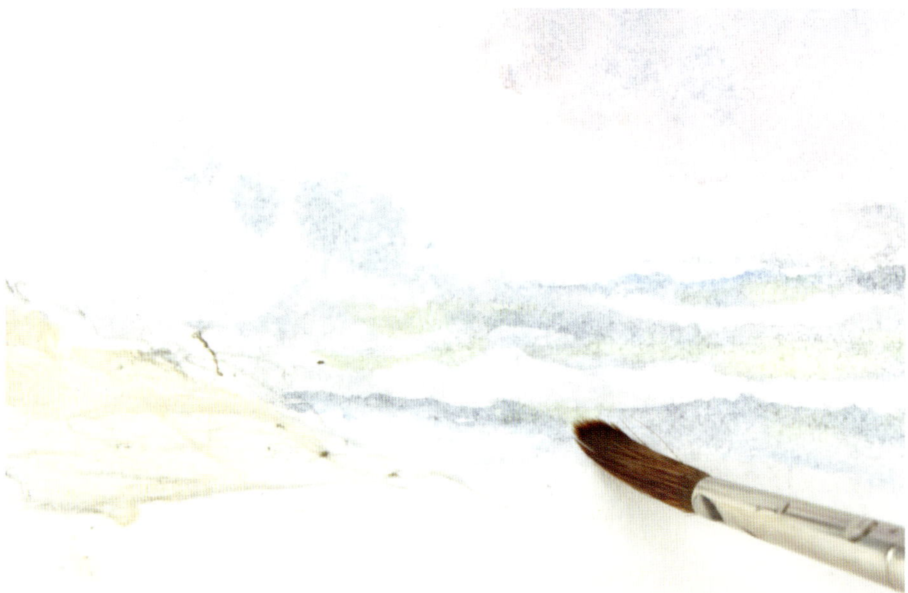

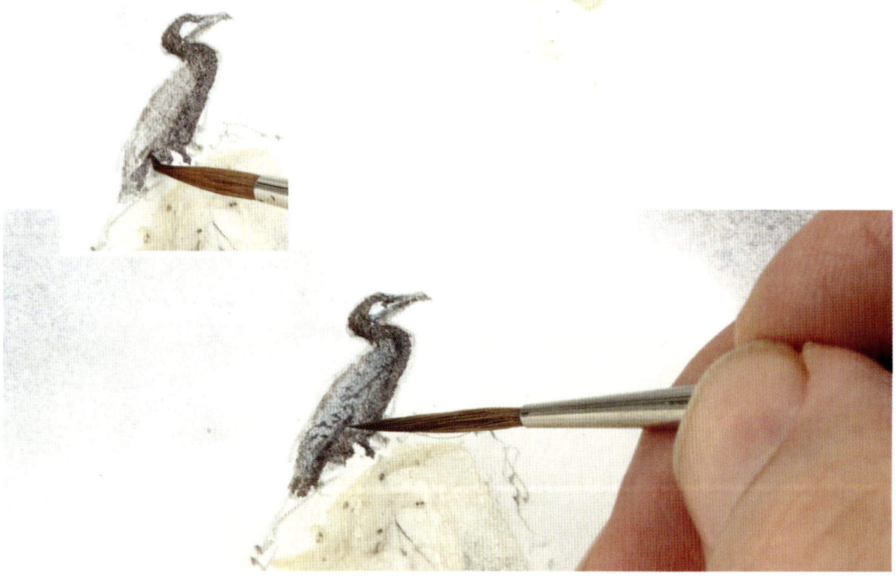

**16** Paint the cormorant with the dark grey mix and the no. 3 round. Use short controlled strokes, and leave gaps for markings and detail (see inset), then wet the brush and soften the colour into the light areas. Touch in some phthalocyanine blue for the sheen on the feathers. Allow to dry, then use the no. 1 rigger to add a few darker flecks to the back in order to suggest some feather texture.

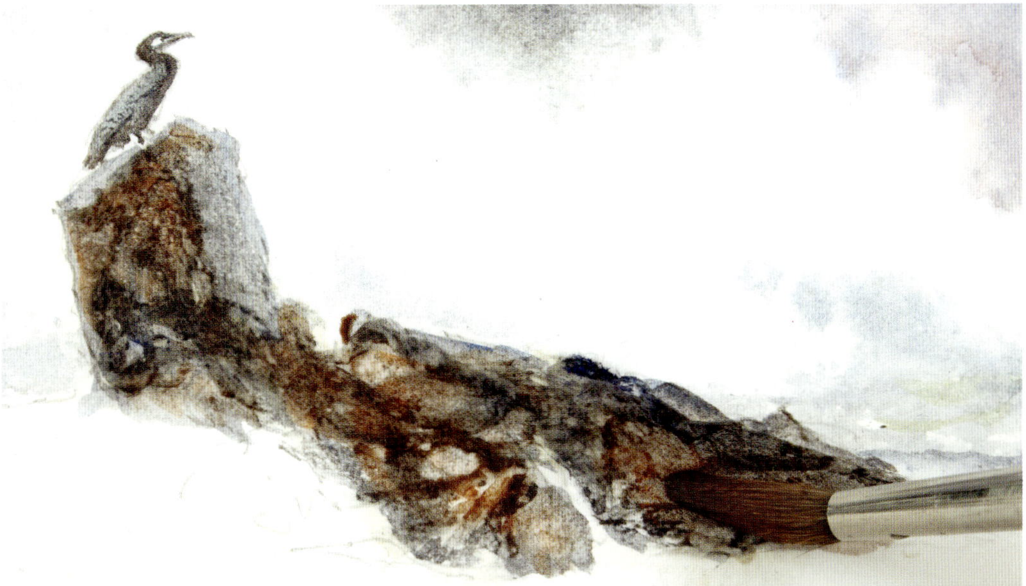

17 To paint the pre-textured rocks beneath the cormorant, use a no. 10 round brush to apply a dark mix of French ultramarine and burnt umber. Use a strong but fairly fluid mix to help it reach the recesses. Add quinacridone sienna for warmth, and to bring the area forward.

18 Paint the other foreground rocks with the same colours and techniques. Use French ultramarine to paint the shadowy midtones of the water draining from the rocks, applying the paint with the no. 3 round brush and using the strokes to indicate the direction of the water.

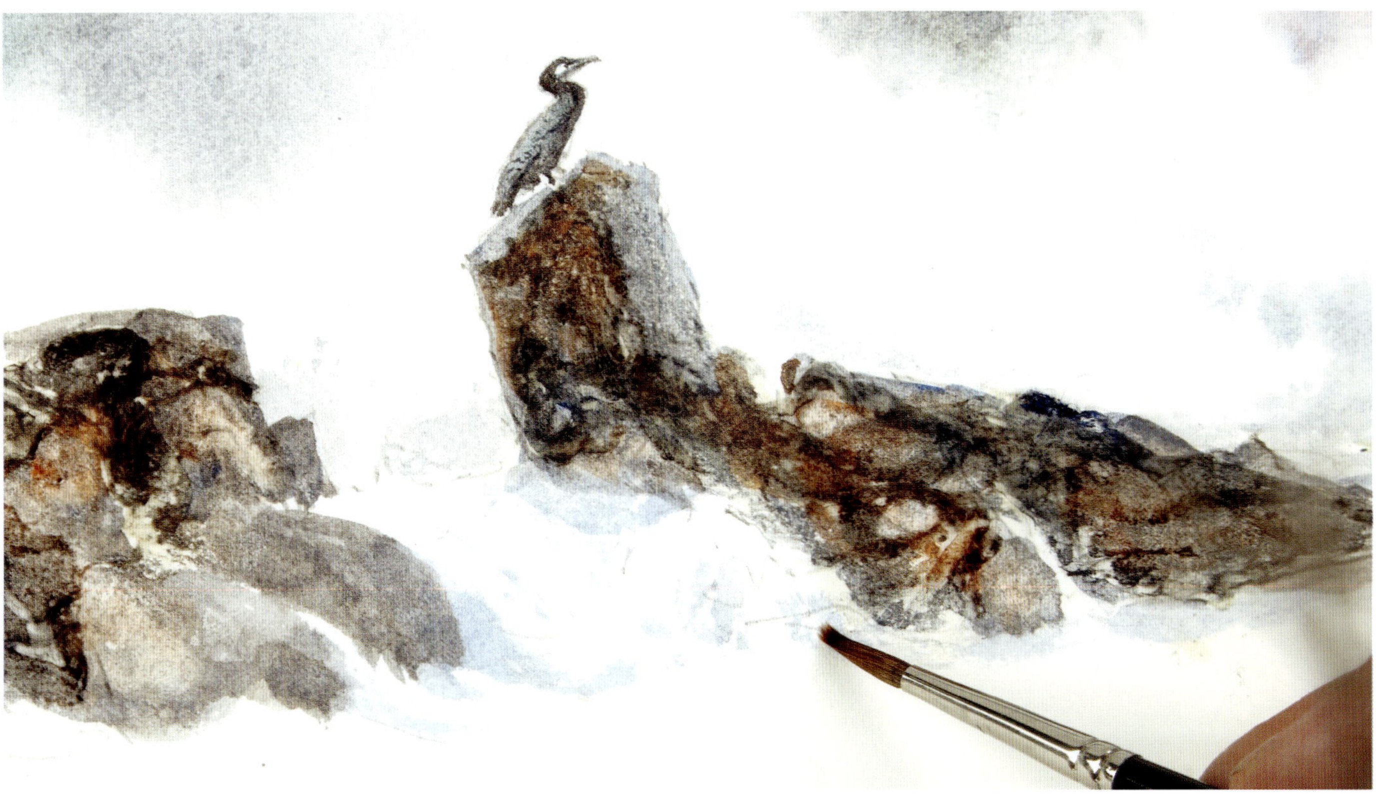

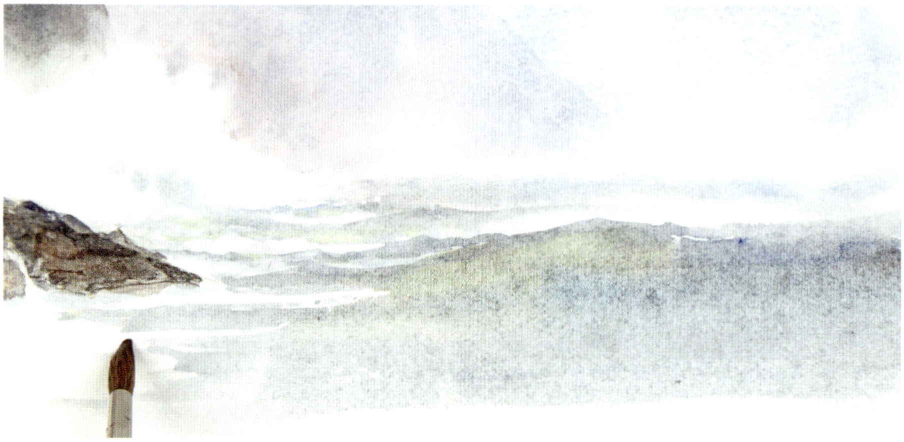

19 Extend the sea into the foreground by building a stronger-toned band of the water with the no. 10 round, using the grey mix (French ultramarine and burnt umber). Add a touch of nickel titanate yellow, and light marks using the grey mix, to add interest to the water.

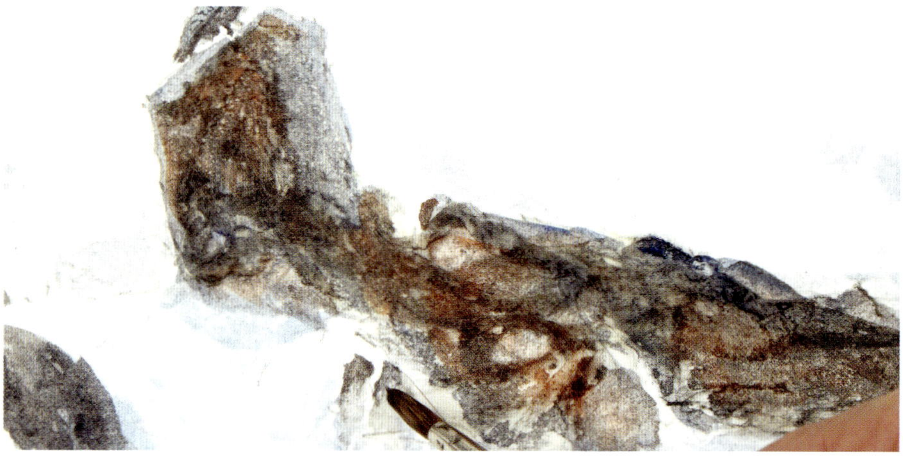

20 Using the tip of the brush, add faint broken marks of the pale grey mix into the pool of foam, strengthening them here and there for depth.

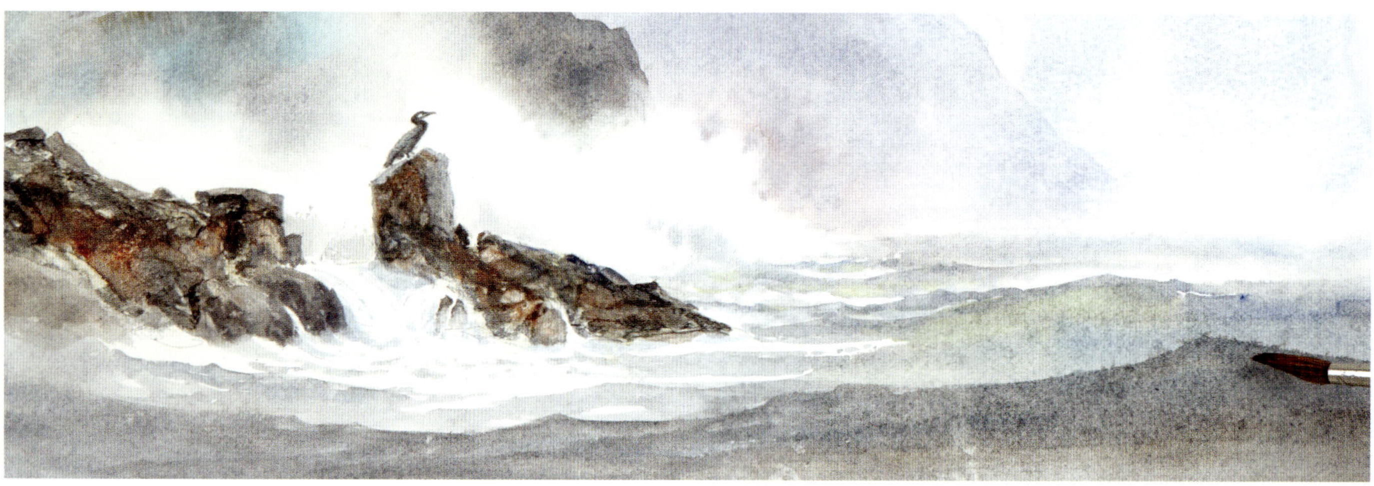

21 Change to the no. 4 brush and use the strong grey mix to add rocks visible within the foam. Keep the tops of the marks hard and clear, and soften them nearer the base, where they disappear into the water. Use the same mix to refine and sharpen the foreground rocks, then change to the no. 10 round brush and paint the sea on the left-hand side with the paler grey mix. Take the water up to the rocks, using broken horizontal strokes. Leave a few gaps of white paper, particularly nearer the central foam, and use darker mixes towards the paper edge. Create a darker band of waves at the border of the picture, suggesting some wave peaks.

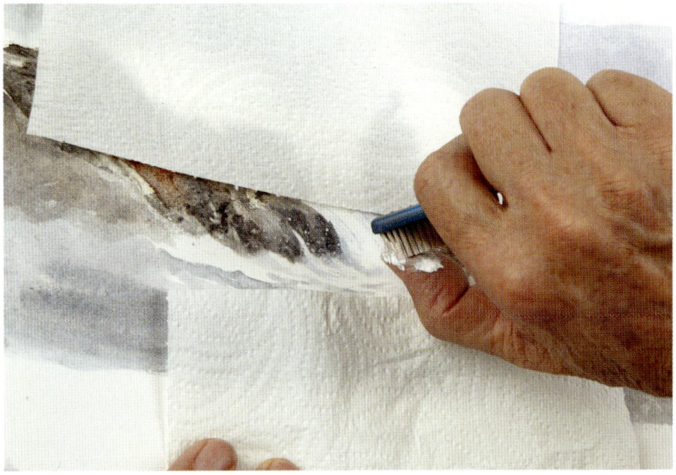

22 Allow to dry, then use an eraser to remove any intrusive pencil marks. Lay kitchen paper to help mask any important areas, then tap your old toothbrush into a pool of slightly diluted white gouache. Hold the toothbrush over the foam area, and gently draw your thumb over the bristles to spatter paint onto the surface.

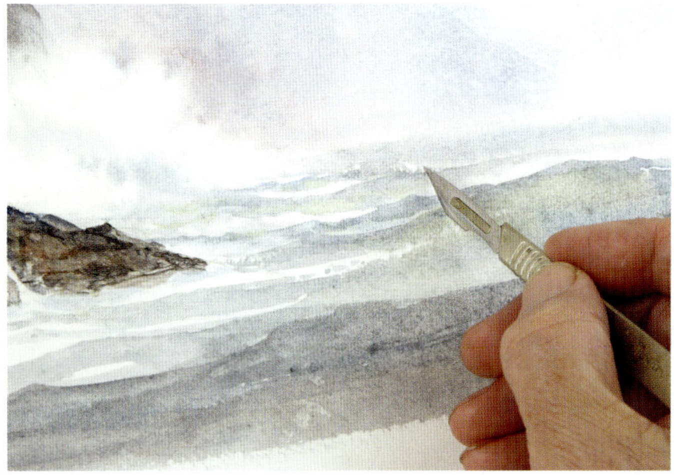

23 Finally, use the point of a scalpel blade to carefully scratch out a few subtle highlights on the sea.

*The finished painting.*

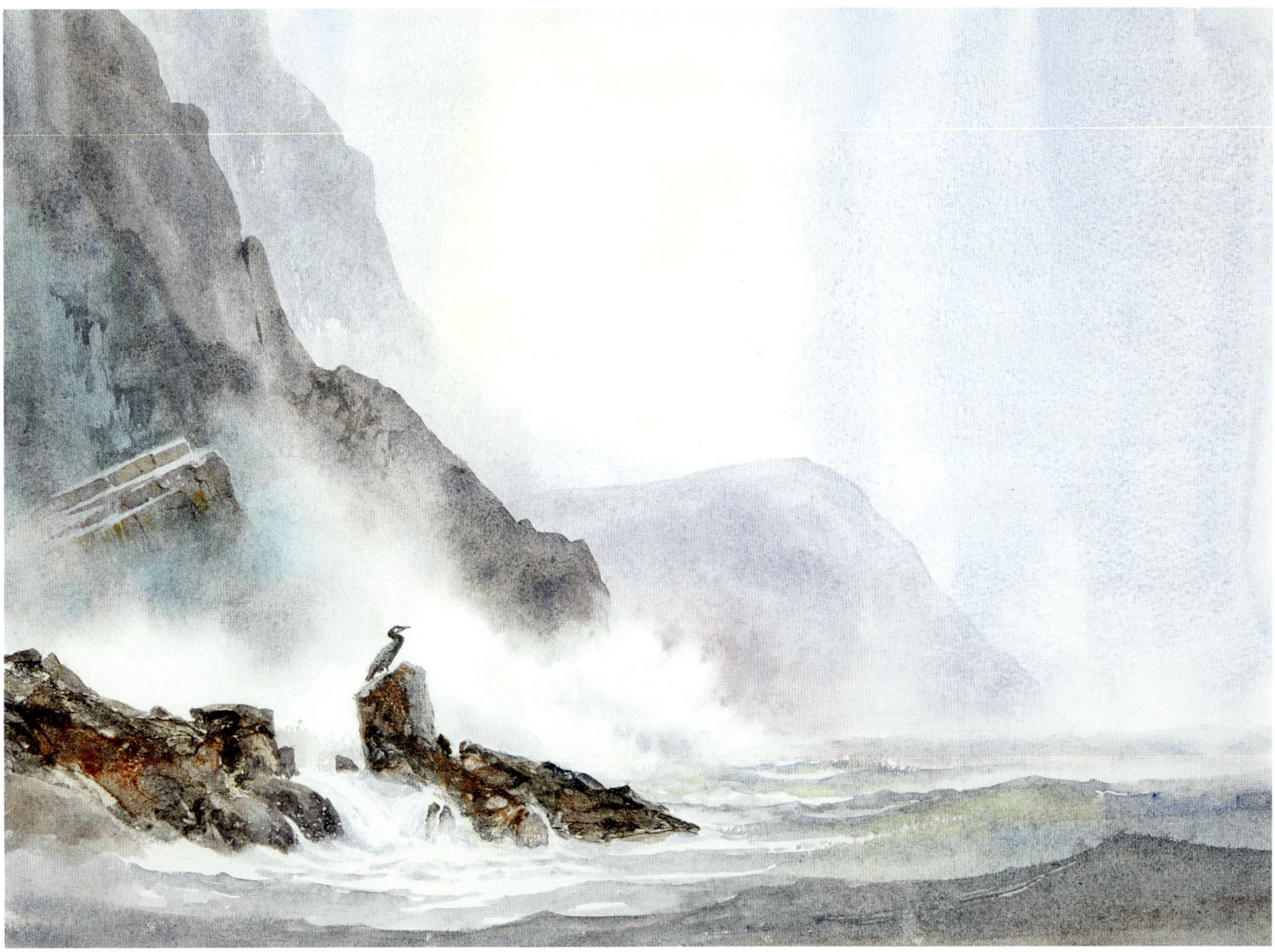

# All at sea

Working from a boat is not for everyone, even just offshore on a fine summer's day, but it does give you an interesting new perspective on the coastline. You see things that you would not otherwise observe, whether on a ferry across the channel, a two-hour boat trip round the bay to watch dolphins, a ten-day cruise, or major expedition to some far-flung coast.

## WORKING FROM A BOAT

I've used all sorts of methods of exploring coastlines, including kayaks, rubber rings and simply treading water in a wetsuit with a water-resistant sketchbook, but there's no way I would call myself a sailor, even when I was being tossed around a small yacht in a wild Arctic storm like a pea in a boiling cauldron.

*Wild Cove, Ramsey Island* was sketched from a powerful boat on the exposed Atlantic side off Pembrokeshire. These short trips can give you some excellent material even when the boat heaves up and down, as in this case. Being well prepared is half the battle, with simple, uncomplicated materials to work with: a full watercolour set and easel would be difficult to control. Take a pad or two of paper with some graphite water-soluble pencils, watercolour pencils and a couple of water brushes. Always having spares on trips like this is sensible, as things can easily fall overboard or get lost. Take a plastic bag for your camera and don't get it out until you know which direction the spray will be coming from (it can still catch you and drench you in seawater), but it's less hazardous if you can find shelter in the lee of the cabin.

On a pleasant day in calm conditions, working with a simple watercolour kit can be effective. Watercolour pencils are an excellent medium for sketching at sea, especially as they are easier to control on a rocking boat. You will probably need to work quickly if you are close to the shore as the perspective changes rapidly. Even if the boat is not under way, it will be moving around with the movement of the sea, so capture the essential features at speed if you can.

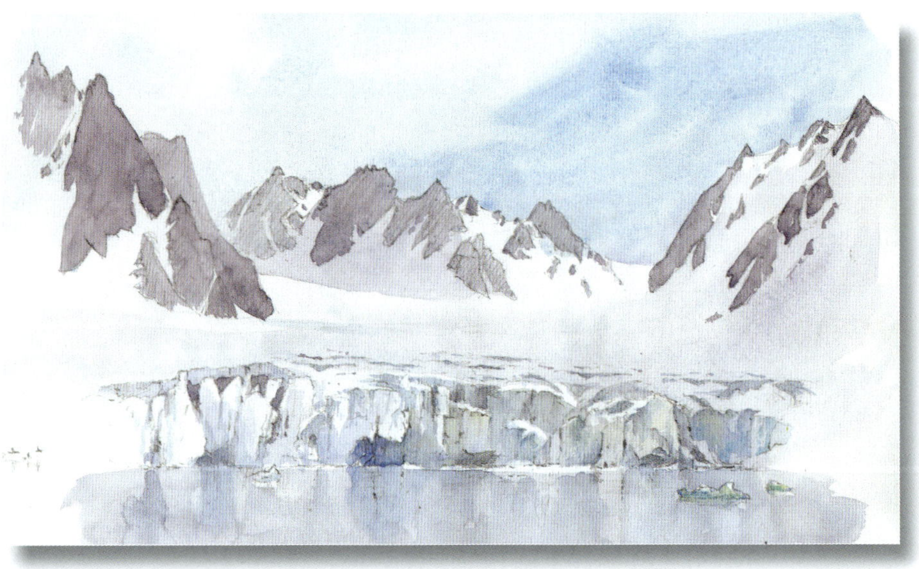

SELLSTROMBREEN GLACIER, SVALBARD

*Our small boat was heading directly for the glacier, which at this point was miles away, so there was plenty of time for me to work up the sketch. As in this case, I often apply pencil hatching to the darker areas, intending either to apply watercolour later, or once the drawing stage is complete. Note the varied colours in the glacier face.*

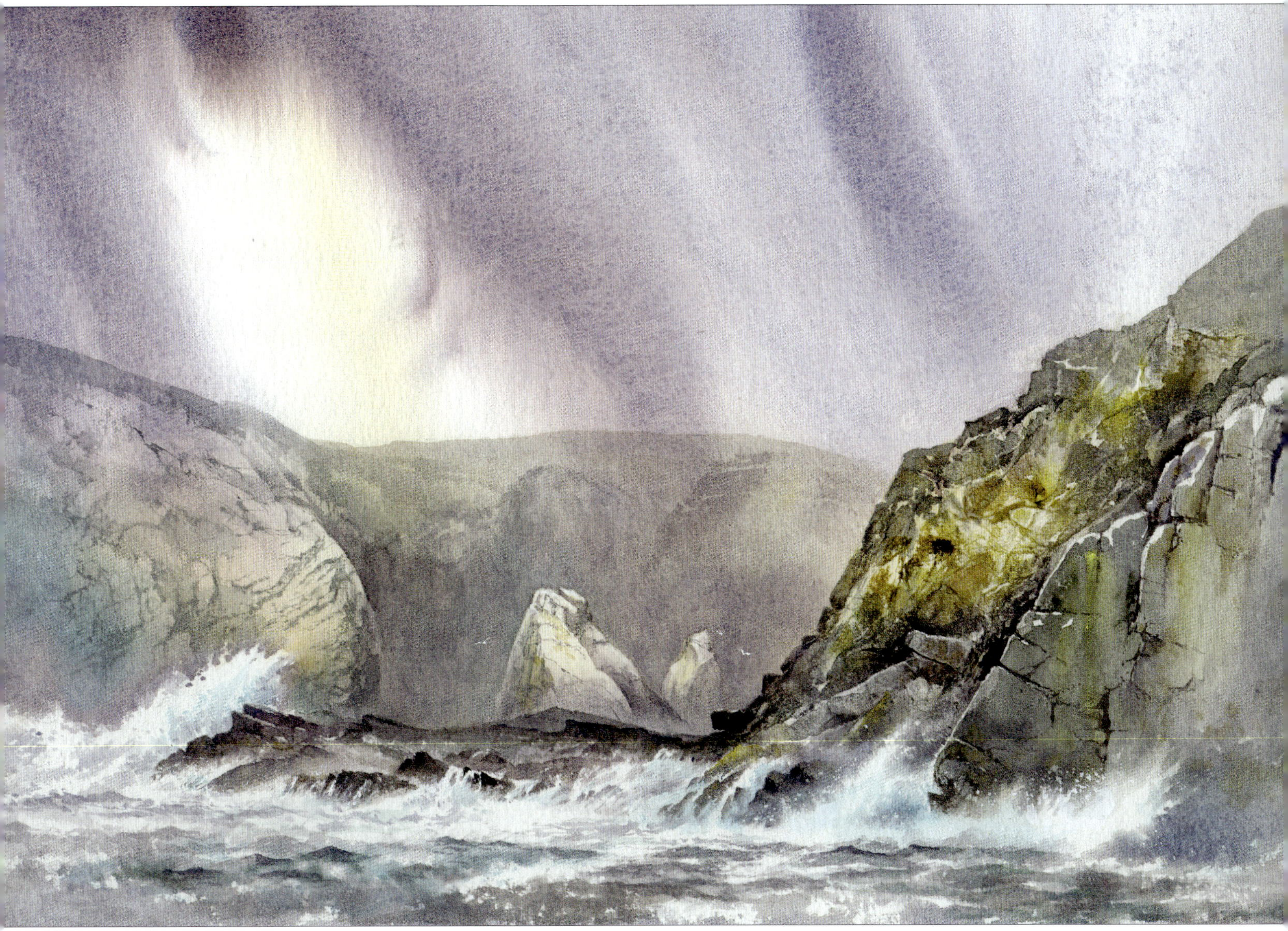

**WILD COVE, RAMSEY ISLAND**

*30.5 x 43cm (12 x 17in)*

*This shoreline of the island is exposed to Atlantic moods which on this day were throwing the craft around, and so not the easiest time for sketching. On the plus side, it does mean that dramatic splashes of water and waves make the composition much more interesting.*

# TACKLING THE COASTLINE FROM THE SEA

Sketching and painting from a little off-shore provides the artist with a totally different perspective of the coastline. It usually allows you to manoeuvre into interesting positions, especially under impressive cliff scenery. However, no matter how expert the skipper is at keeping them on station, boats tend to move around, so you will find the subject constantly changing. You need to work quickly, seeking out the important features. In particular, closely observe the tones and how the surf is interacting with rocks, cliffs and general shorelines. Once you have your main composition down on paper you can either apply colour or make colour notes, but it is the tones that will give shape to the features and thus form the basis of your composition.

Watercolour pencils are extremely versatile on a boat. You need just a few colours, with a number of strong darks such as black, indigo, grey, dark brown and sepia. Wetting the applied colours with a water brush does away with the need for a water container. Once you get home, you can finish off the work if you wish by laying on darker tones. You can, of course, go further, as in the case of the illustration below, where I have rubbed sandpaper across the tip of a white pencil over a re-wetted part of a dark area. This has created some lively white spots of foaming water.

**CLIFF STRUCTURES IN WATERCOLOUR PENCILS**

*This small sketch was carried out with watercolour pencils, beginning with a light grey Prismalo pencil to establish the outlines, and then working in the colours with the Caran d'Ache Museum watercolour pencils which have superb blending qualities. It was completed in the studio to illustrate what can be achieved with these pencils.*

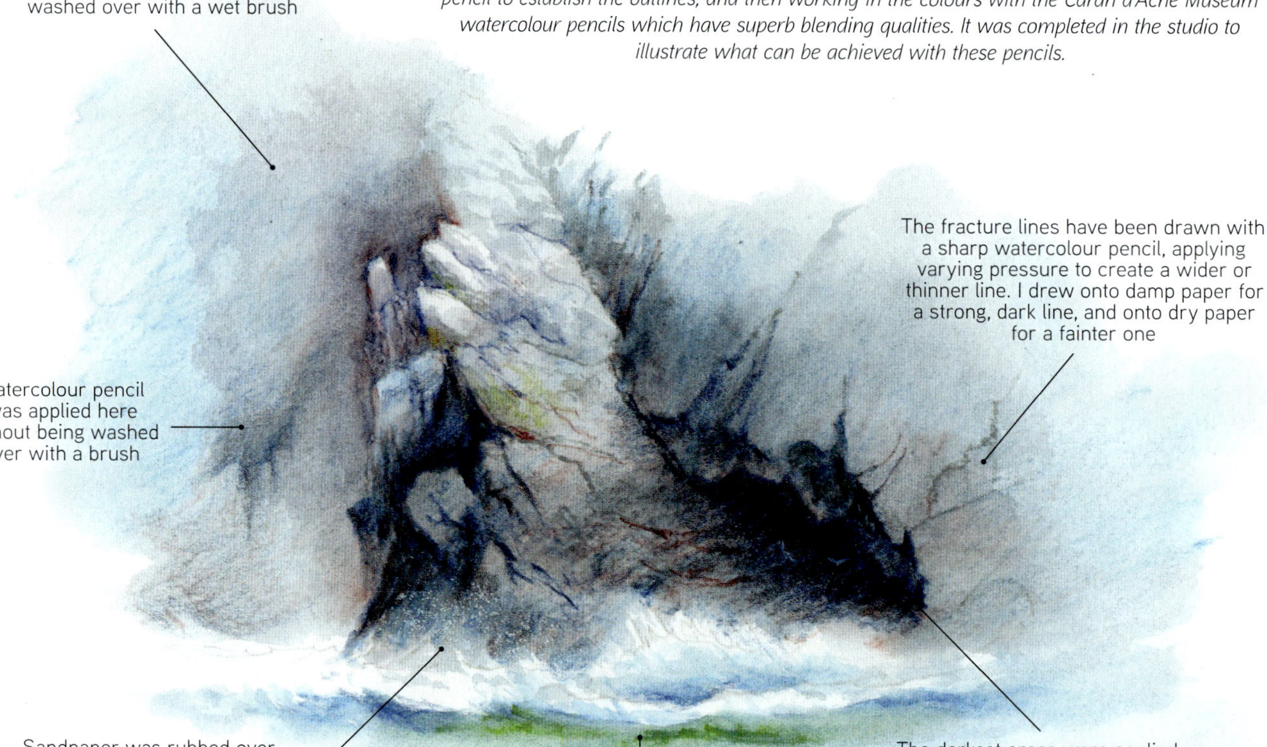

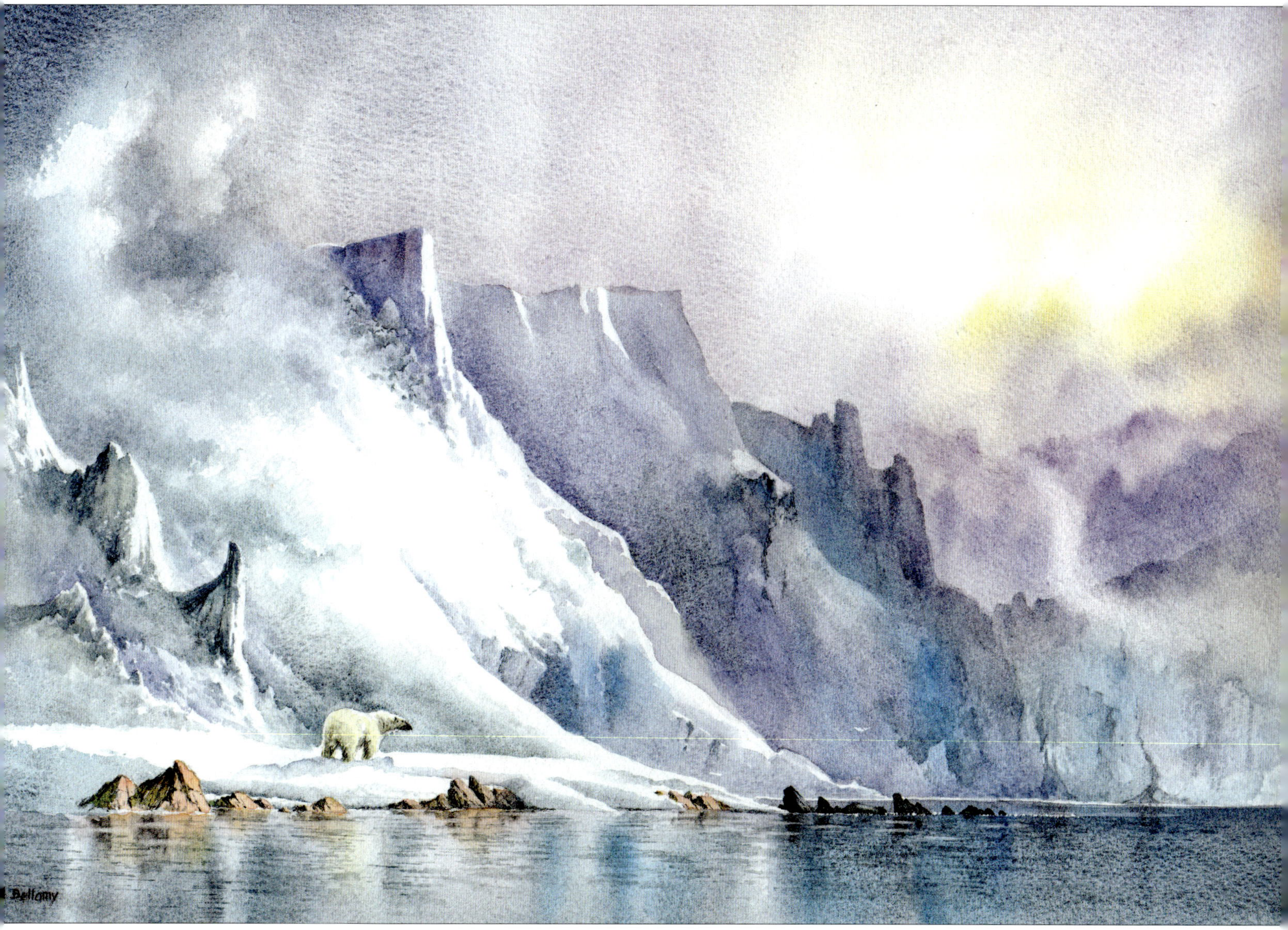


**THE HUNTER**

*32 x 43cm (12½ x 17in)*

*I found this large male bear a little further along the Svalbard coast and decided to place him beneath these dramatic ice cliffs of Smithbreen Glacier where they plunge into the sea. Where fresh ice has calved off the glacier front, the colouring of the ice usually changes, so towards the right and directly above the dark rocks in the water I have brushed in some phthalocyanine blue to suggest this and freshen up that area.*

*The glacier top edge stands stark and sharp, so to reduce this effect I have introduced low clouds on the left by simply running the dark blue cliff-top into a wet passage, while to the right of this I have broken up the dark cliff with some white verticals which suggest buttresses caught in sunlight. The third place where I have broken the line is on the far right where I have pulled out a bending stream of cloud as it moves upwards in front of a lower part of the ice cliffs.*

## PAINTING SEA AND SKY

Just as with landscape paintings, your composition will benefit enormously if you support your focal point – in this case the vessel out at sea – with another feature. Apart from a second craft or the odd oil rig there probably isn't much you can do other than feature an interesting passage of sea next to the vessel, plus maybe a suggestion of stronger colour or tonal value nearby. Generally there is little by way of wreckage floating around as there was in the days of Turner and Bonington, and probably the most you are likely to encounter are sad bits of plastic. However, the odd seabird might be worth including.

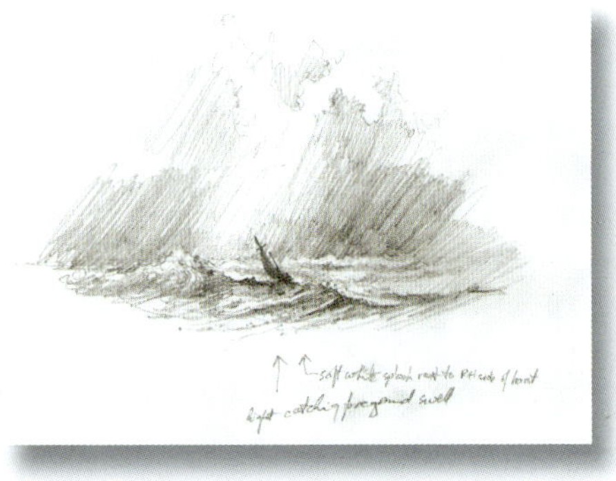

ATLANTIC SWELL STUDIO SKETCH

*Because I intended this painting to include a potent atmosphere I laid the sketch out with strong pencil tones, noting the salient points such as the wave along which the boat appeared to be travelling.*

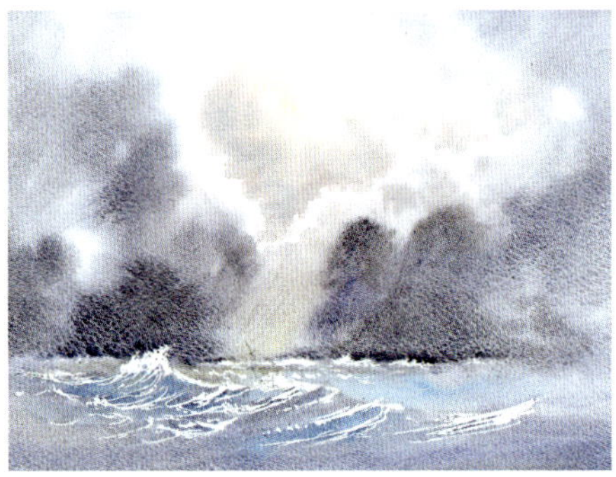

1 I applied masking fluid to the wave highlights and a mixture of French ultramarine and bloodstone genuine over most of the sky and part of the sea, varying it in intensity. Phthalo blue was dropped into the sea in places.

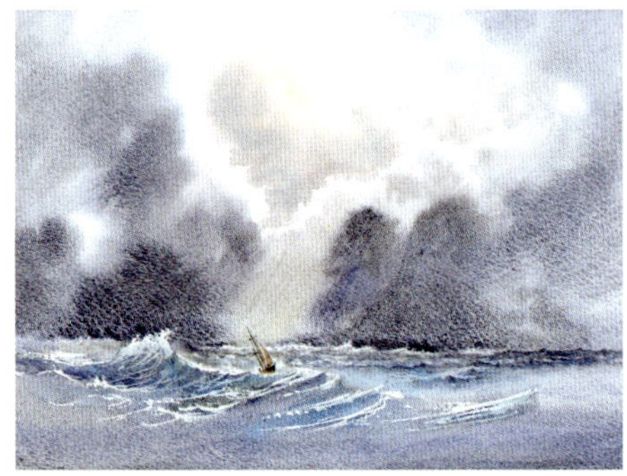

2 I darkened the sea at the right horizon and then the sails with transparent red oxide. A little cadmium yellow light enlivened the sea below the boat. I then painted shadow colour on the left side of the splash and wave.

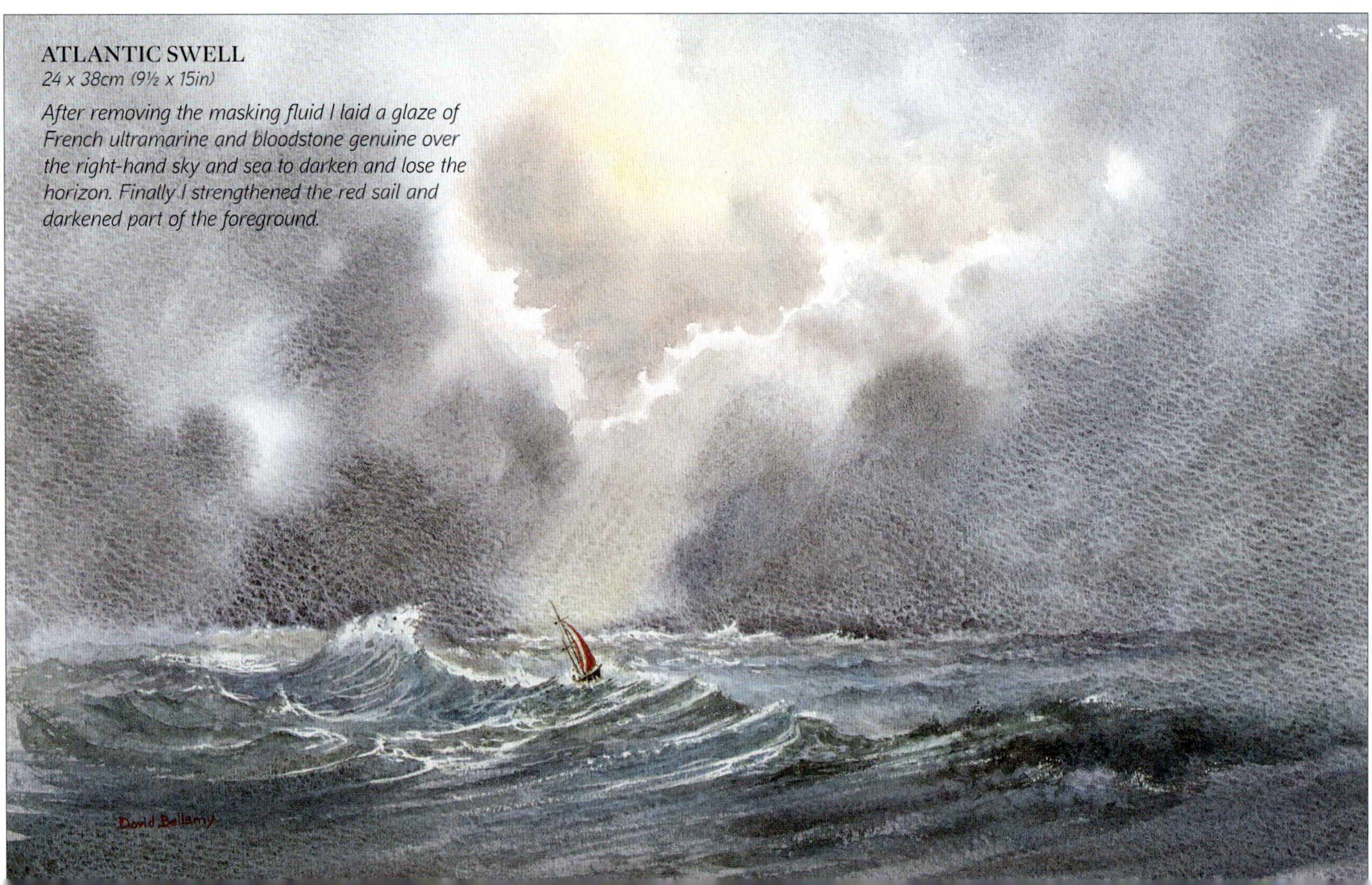


ATLANTIC SWELL

*24 x 38cm (9½ x 15in)*

*After removing the masking fluid I laid a glaze of French ultramarine and bloodstone genuine over the right-hand sky and sea to darken and lose the horizon. Finally I strengthened the red sail and darkened part of the foreground.*

# PAINTING WILD SEAS

Working on the craggy coast of Pembrokeshire has given me countless opportunities for capturing wild seas and I love working in storms. Actually being out at sea in such conditions is a different matter, and best avoided at all costs. The alternative is to witness coastal storms from headlands and cliffs, but take care to avoid being blown off your feet. If I can't find the shelter of a rock, I tend to lie or crouch down to keep the sketchbook and myself in low profile. The wind, however, is relentless and seeks out all your vulnerable spots, so you need loads of elastic bands and bulldog clips. Make sure you grip the sketchbook firmly.

With perseverance you can record the moving sea using the critical observation methods described earlier, and back this up with photographs. Watch out for craft being tossed about offshore in boisterous conditions, and this will give you an idea of how it would appear in more threatening seas.

**LIFEBOAT IN CHALLENGING SEAS**
*28 x 48cm (11 x 19in)*

*The dramatic sky wash was laid on with a large brush loaded with sodalite genuine, while the wave structures were built up gradually with much negative painting to bring out the rough white tops. In places I have dropped in cadmium yellow light and yellow ochre while the initial blue-grey washes were still wet. A great deal of softening off has taken place using a 12mm (½in) flat brush, in particular where the lifeboat appears behind a wall of spray. The actual lifeboat is the Volunteer Spirit from the RNLI reserve fleet, which I was lucky enough to witness roaring through the sea at full tilt.*

Dramatic granulation made in the sky was achieved using sodalite genuine applied with a large brush

This passage was done with a 12mm (½in) flat brush loaded with little water, and the hairs parted with a knife. The paint was applied in the dry-brush manner, but tested first on similar scrap paper

Stab and scratches with a scalpel helped to create white blobs and streaks of aerated water

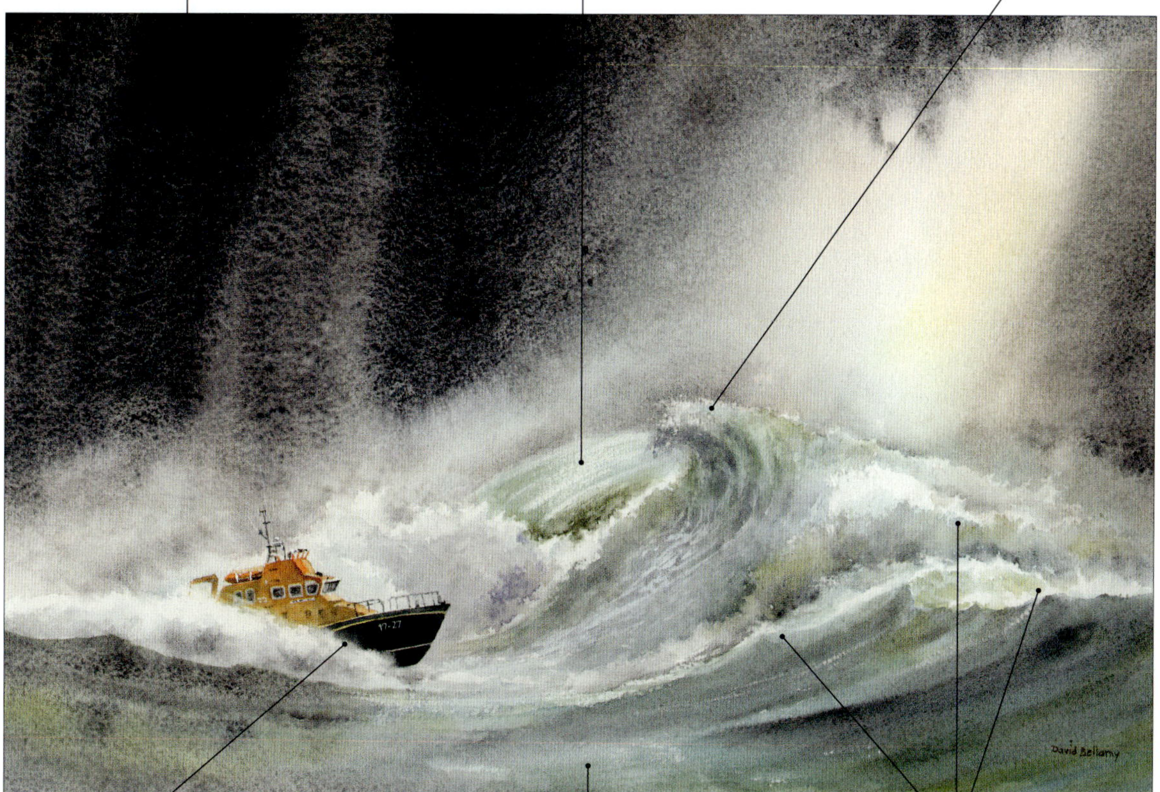

The lifeboat has been positioned in the composition so that it is off-centre and running into the picture. The top edge of the spray that partially hides the boat was softened off with a 12mm (½in) flat brush once the paper was dry

Little foreground detail has been included to ensure the emphasis falls on the boat and wave

The ragged edges to the crests of waves were achieved by scrubbing the side of a no. 8 round brush across the paper and softening it in places

# A day by the sea

By now you should have a fair idea about how to tackle some of the many subjects you are likely to encounter by the sea, and hopefully feel confident about going out to sketch. It is normal to feel a little apprehensive about working with strangers around, especially in crowded harbours in the summer season. If you sit on a stool painting, you will be fair game for the odd onlooker, particularly if you set up an easel and have a large drawing board. You may find it less daunting to begin by taking along just one or two small sketchbooks and a few pencils and do a number of drawings while sitting or standing in less busy spots. People are likely to mistake you for a government snooper making notes – and thus keep well clear of you.

A busy harbour is probably not the best place to start if you are apprehensive, though often you can find an outdoor table at a café from where you can sketch while you sip a cappuccino. People are generally reluctant to approach you while you are sitting in a café. If you get down into the mud of a harbour at low tide, the chances of being engaged are absolutely minimal. Boatyards, estuaries and quiet sections of beaches are where you are more likely to be left in peace, especially when the weather is less than glorious.

The rough sketch of Bunacurry Harbour (see right) was carried out in a few minutes and is the sort of approach you may like to take initially. It is far from one of my best but is extremely effective in providing me with a strong composition from which to work up a painting.

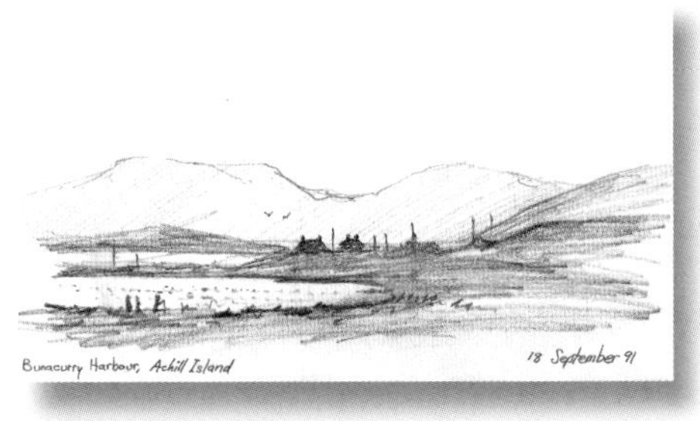


BUNACURRY HARBOUR

*I include this roughly drawn sketch to show not just how simple and quickly rendered it is, but to assure you that it is not vital to draw a complicated and perfect response to a scene. Some of my best paintings have resulted from ridiculous and almost indefinite marks on the paper, sometimes accompanied by a bit of mud. However brief and rough the sketch, you will always be learning from the experience, so enjoy your sketching without being too critical of the results.*

## CRITICAL OBSERVATION METHODS

Because we do much in life which is routine, our subconscious takes over and our brain does not have to consciously analyse every decision we make: changing gears while driving, for example. Similarly, when we are out sketching familiar objects, we tend not to analyse what we are looking at, and therefore fall short of making an accurate recording. We need to get into the habit of critical observation, where you carefully study and analyse the scene before you make any marks on the paper. Opposite are some starting points and tips.

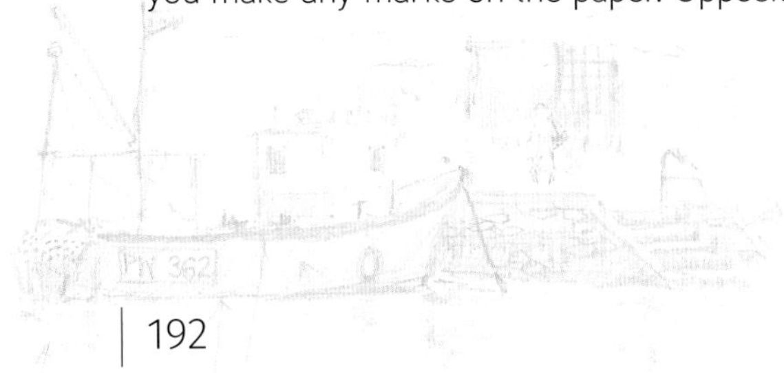

- **Focal point** Determine what is the most interesting and exciting feature in the scene and position it just off-centre on your paper, with ample room around it for extending the surrounding features.
- **Initial line** Pick out a pronounced line on your selected feature: perhaps the roof-line of a building, the base-line of a boat (i.e. the waterline if afloat or the keel if lying in the harbour), or perhaps the horizon line. Start drawing this lightly in pencil. You will probably find that the line may be at an angle and not perfectly horizontal, so hold your pencil at arm's length and close one eye, keeping one end of the pencil appearing to be level with one end of your selected line. This rough guide is not perfect, but will help you gain an idea of how much the line slopes, and therefore ease your perspective concerns. Once your initial line is established, you can draw in adjacent detail such as the chimneys, ends of walls, doors, windows, and so on. Move outwards to include other buildings, vegetation and whatever is around or in front of your subject.
- **Artistic licence** Linear perspective can become complicated in ports and harbours, and you will find that in some places ancient buildings simply do not conform to normal perspective rules and their outlines can appear odd in this respect. I normally exaggerate any deformed perspective as it adds character to the subject.
- **Comparisons** Compare everything before you, not just in size or height, but the tones, how reflected light is affecting the various adjacent features, and where you see counterchange (where an object appears light where it is set against a dark background and darker where it is set against a bright sky). Carefully study the colours before you – can you see subtle colours, such as reflected colours, appearing in part of the scene that were not obvious at first?

Noting these can enhance your finished work. Many of these observation methods can be done without your sketchbook, while you are simply waiting around, and it is helpful to train yourself in this way at every opportunity.

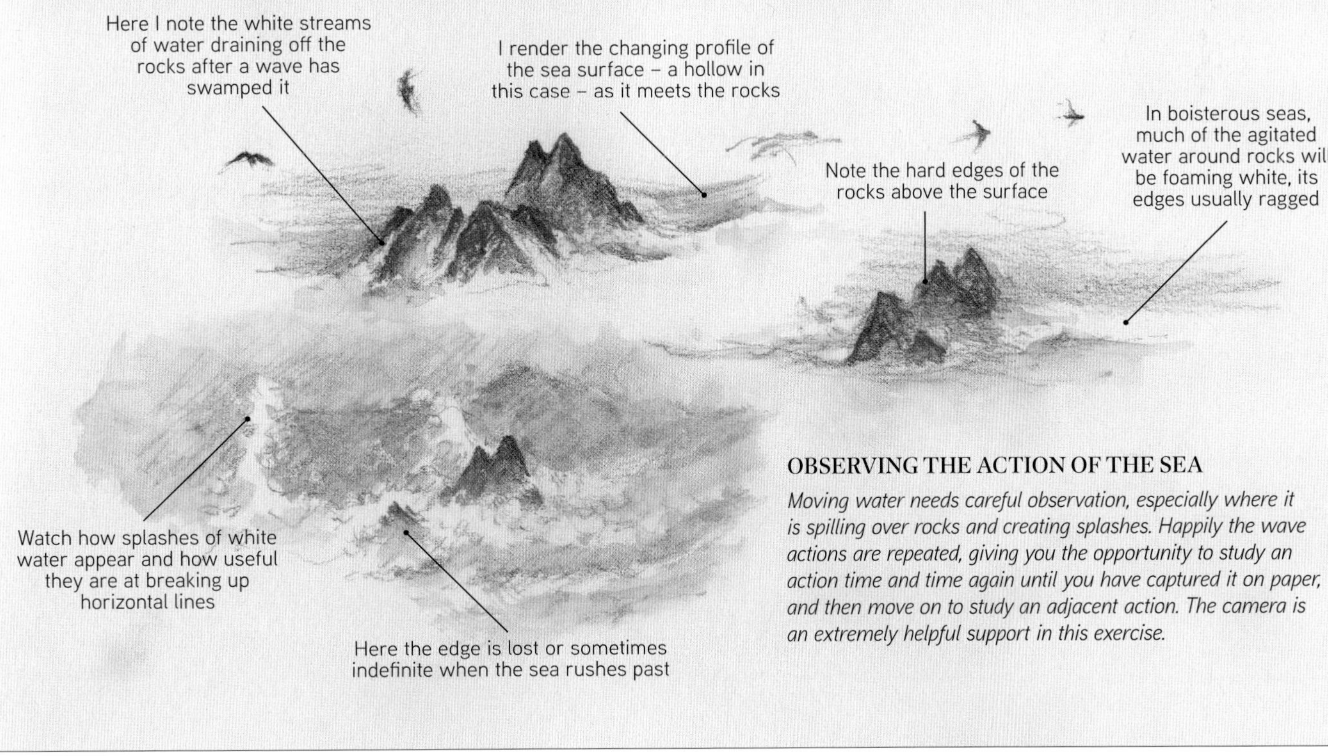


OBSERVING THE ACTION OF THE SEA

*Moving water needs careful observation, especially where it is spilling over rocks and creating splashes. Happily the wave actions are repeated, giving you the opportunity to study an action time and time again until you have captured it on paper, and then move on to study an adjacent action. The camera is an extremely helpful support in this exercise.*

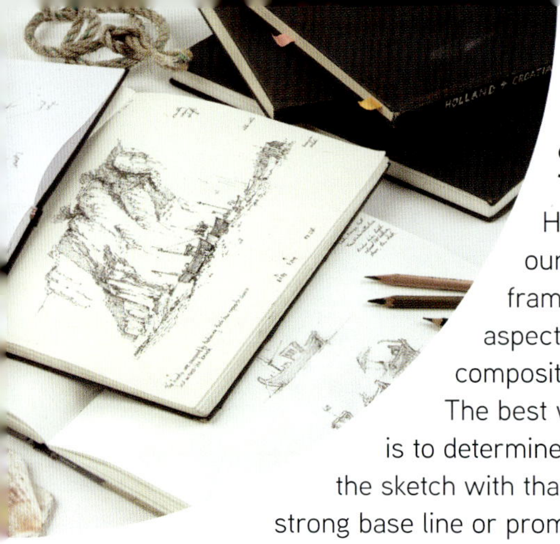

# SKETCHING METHODS

Having discussed how observation is critical to our response to a subject, and how it gives us a framework on how to render the more complicated aspects, here we look at how to tackle the overall composition. Where do we start?

The best way, when looking at a scene for the first time, is to determine which feature interests you most and begin the sketch with that centre of interest. Start the drawing with a strong base line or prominent line on the feature, and work from there. Study the overall composition for a few moments to ensure you can fit it all onto your paper, then start drawing lightly. Consider which features will support your focal point, what may act as a lead-in towards this feature, and which parts of the scene you should emphasize, and which to play down. Keep things simple to start. You don't have to put every window in a building or every boat in a harbour, and you can happily substitute that ugly blasted oak in the middle with the more handsome specimen you can see off-picture to the left.

Sketching in watercolour is a step further, of course, but a very rewarding one, because it is also a major step in improving your general watercolour painting. People tend not to be so tight while sketching in the medium as they are indoors when confronted with a large sheet of watercolour paper. I regularly work on good-quality cartridge paper for fast watercolour sketches, as the smooth paper helps to dry them quickly, but it takes time to learn to control washes on smooth paper. If you work with a wall or boat behind you, it may help you feel more secure, as painting with watercolours tends to attract more interest than just pencil work in a small sketchbook. Work quickly and don't worry about mistakes. Make notes in pencil or ink on the sketch and treat it like a working document. This approach can liberate you from feeling you have to create a perfect composition.

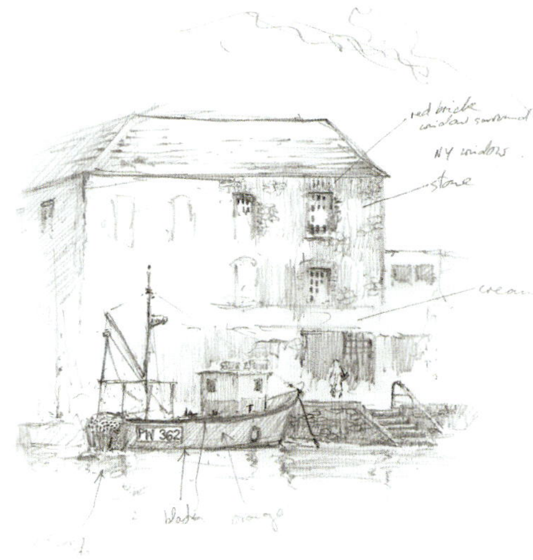

**MEVAGISSEY HARBOUR**

*Sketching in a harbour full of complicated boat and architectural shapes is a challenge, but you can simplify things by leaving out unnecessary detail. Here the fishing boat is the focal point and it has been rendered in detail, but directly behind it the building structure has been played down, even though I could see many features. To include them would cause visual confusion where they would meet the boat superstructure, masts and rigging, as well as over-work the composition. I briefly outlined some of the windows, while drawing one or two in detail. If they are all the same, it is not necessary to sketch all of them, and anyway I am unlikely to include them all in a painting. The stonework has been rendered only here and there – it's more effective to let the eye of the viewer put in the rest of the details. Note that I write in the colours if I am working in monochrome and need this information.*

**SUNLIT HEADLAND**

*A fair wind was blowing as I sat with my back to a rock, so the light kept changing. I enjoy these days because I can pick my moment when the light is in the optimum position. Watch the scene for a while before sketching and work quickly once you have decided on the lighting as it catches your centre of interest, which in this case is the far headland. I could have left out the right-hand half of the sketch and this would have made an excellent composition, but the whole scene was so lovely that I couldn't resist including the lot. Sometimes in cases like this where the distant headland is light, you may need to strengthen the tonal value of the adjacent sky area.*

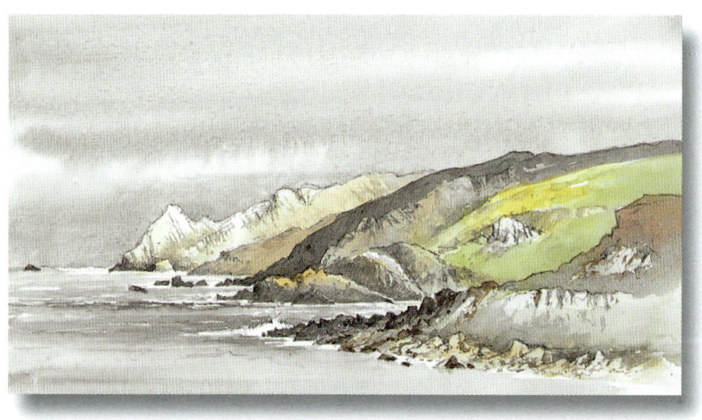

## Painting in low light

Working at night-time or in low light is perfectly possible in harbour areas especially, and has the advantage that much detail is lost and the scene already incorporates a sense of mood. Colours are more subdued, and you may well find this easier to work effectively. I carry a head-torch with me, which means my hands are free to work. There are usually fewer people around to pester you. Tinted paper is an effective tool in creating these scenes and those produced by the Two Rivers company are particularly good for nocturnes as they are fairly dark tints.

Don't try to include every highlight – concentrate on two or three at the most, with one as the main focal point. You may need to slightly exaggerate the colours at this point. Naples yellow is excellent for light patches, especially on tinted papers, as it is opaque and works well with touches of white gouache, which are vital to bring out the highlights on non-white papers.

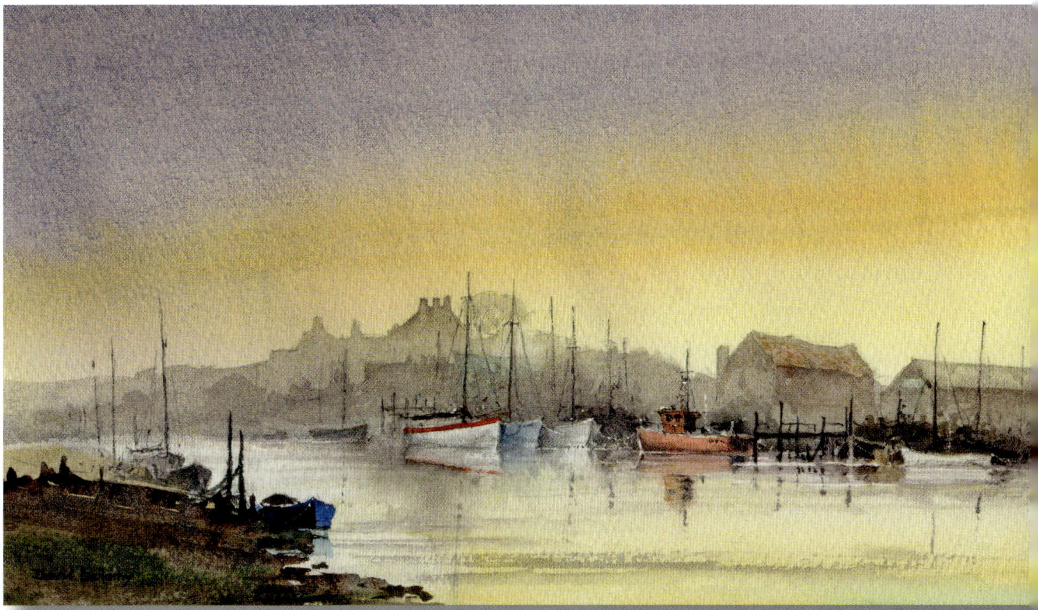

EVENING AT WALBERSWICK

*Low light left a potent mood over the place, almost ghostly with hardly anyone around as I worked quickly before the light faded. Note that while the light comes from the left, the blue boat in the foreground has its shadow on the left-hand side, because of the shadow of the bank. Details on the buildings were barely discernible.*

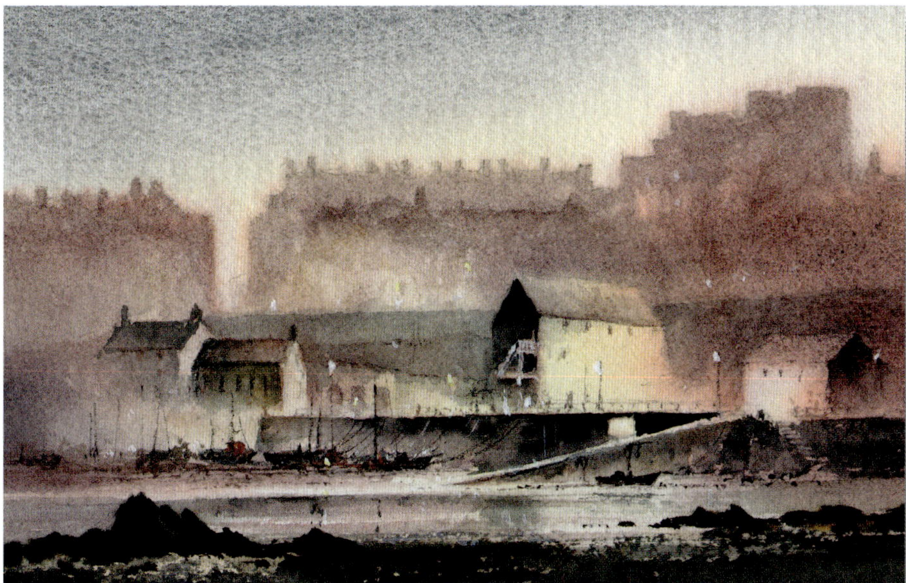

TWILIGHT AT TENBY

*Twilight can be a fascinating time to sketch as it automatically reduces the amount of detail before you and almost forces you to create a moody scene.*

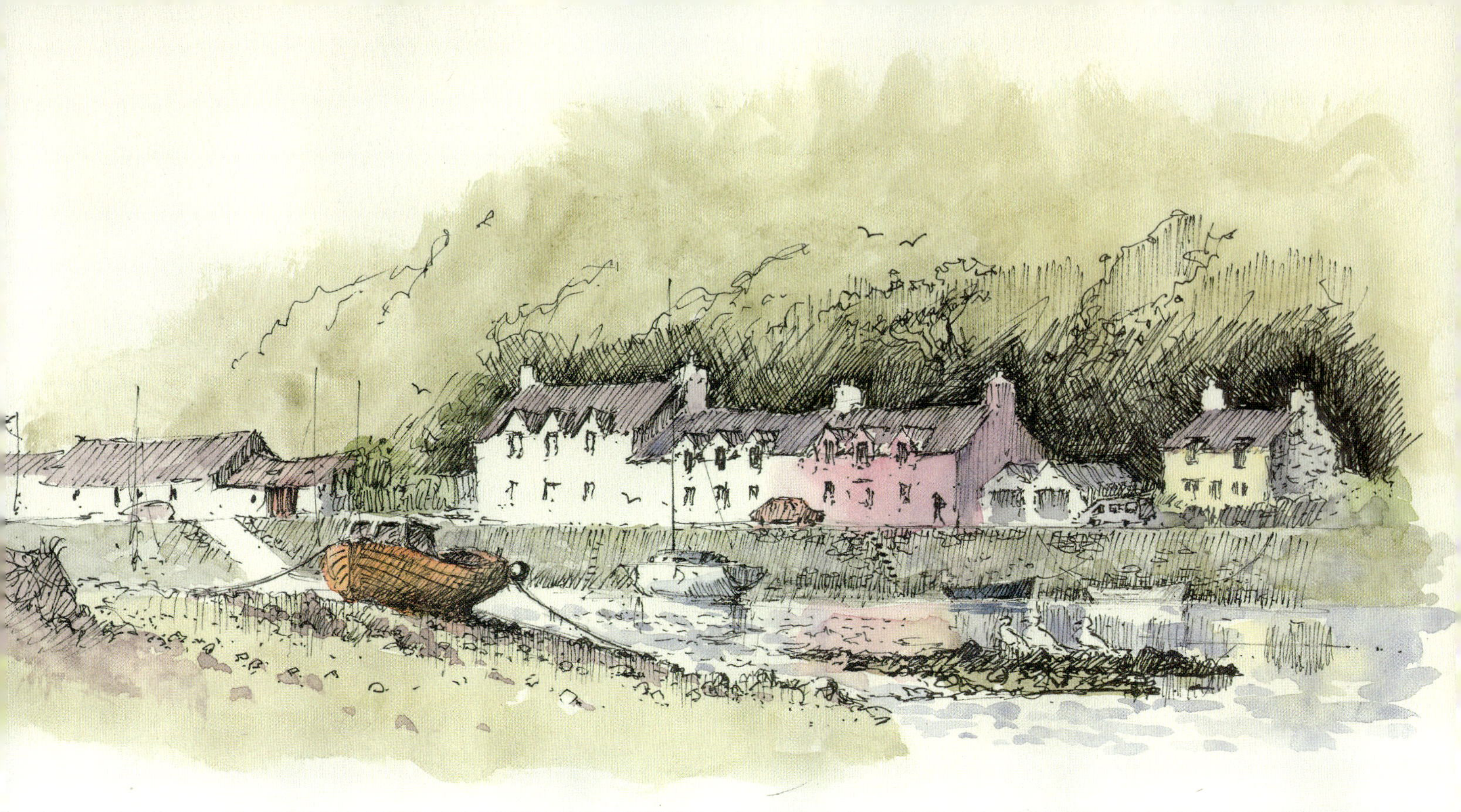

## PEN AND WASH SKETCHING

Modern pens come in a variety of types, line sizes and colours, and while it is hard to beat the style and varied line quality of the traditional dip pens, new developments are creating interesting possibilities. If you wish to work outdoors, of course, the bugbear of having to carry a bottle of ink around with you has always been inhibiting, so it is worth keeping an eye out for other pen types. In addition to the normal type of pen you may find brush-pens invaluable, especially as these can happily work on Rough paper – most metal tip or fibre-tip pens work best on smooth paper, such as Hot-pressed watercolour paper or cartridge paper. I enjoy drawing with a wide range of pens and these pages show a few examples of working you may like to try.

You can approach pen and wash work in a number of ways. If you are not so confident about your drawing skills, carry out an outline drawing lightly in pencil first, then ink it in. You then have a choice of either leaving it like that and continuing to the painting stage – which is how I have tackled the *Kildavnet Castle* sketch (see opposite, top), or you can apply tonal areas with the pen by hatching or cross-hatching as you see in the *Fishguard Harbour* sketch above. If you opt for a hatching method, creating dark areas with the pen, then all you need to do at the painting stage is apply washes of watercolour, ignoring the need to create varied tones at that stage. However, if you simply carry out a line drawing in pen without hatching, then you will need to apply watercolour in the normal manner, including stronger tones with your washes.

**FISHGUARD HARBOUR**

*Pen and wash is an excellent medium for drawing harbour scenes, and an effective way to rescue a watercolour that lacks direction. In this particular sketch I have hatched in the dark areas with repeated lines of the pen to create the tones, so the subsequent washes need only be light applications, with no need for dark tones of colour.*

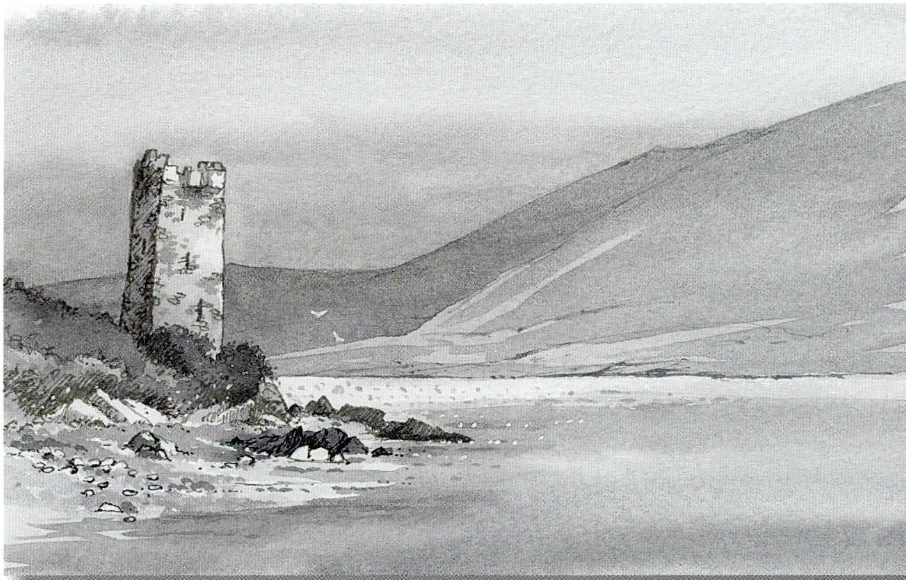

## KILDAVNET CASTLE

*In the past, while working with pen and wash I used to render distant objects and clouds with a broken line, but now you have the option of drawing these with a grey pen and then using a black one for the foreground as I have done in this sketch. The grey pen I used was the excellent Derwent Graphik line maker. Derwent also offers a sepia pen in the same range. The washes were applied with indigo plus a touch of perylene red. Working in this way you can create a sense of depth in your composition more easily.*

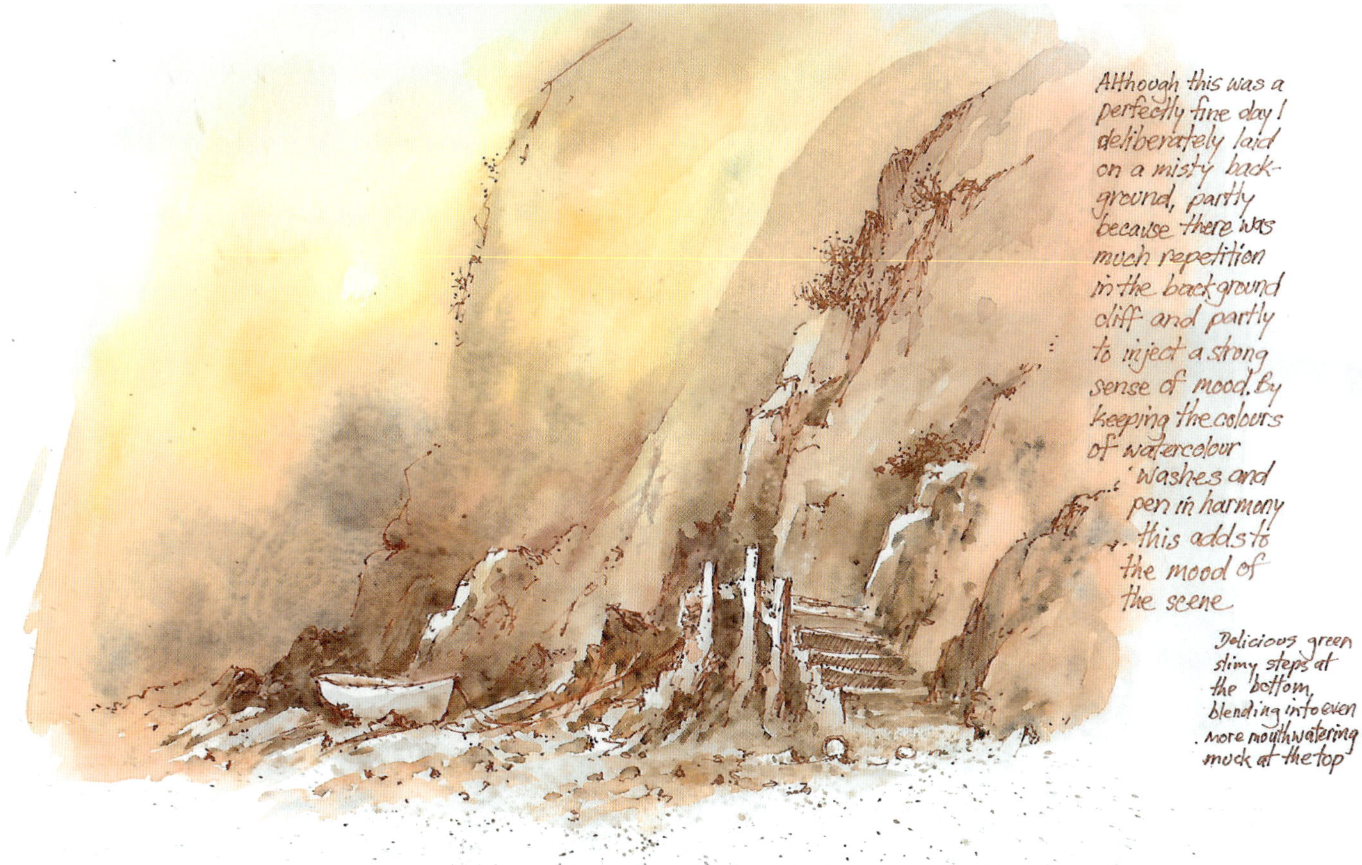


## LONELY COVE

*This sketch was carried out initially with a sanguine pen, then a limited range of colours was painted on, restricting them to Naples yellow, yellow ochre, light red and burnt umber, with a slight touch of cobalt blue added to the burnt umber in places. In this way I achieved a harmonious result, resisting the temptation to render the deliciously slimy green steps and mouth-watering muck in their true colours. Unlike the* Fishguard Harbour *sketch opposite, I have achieved most of the darker areas with stronger watercolour tones.*

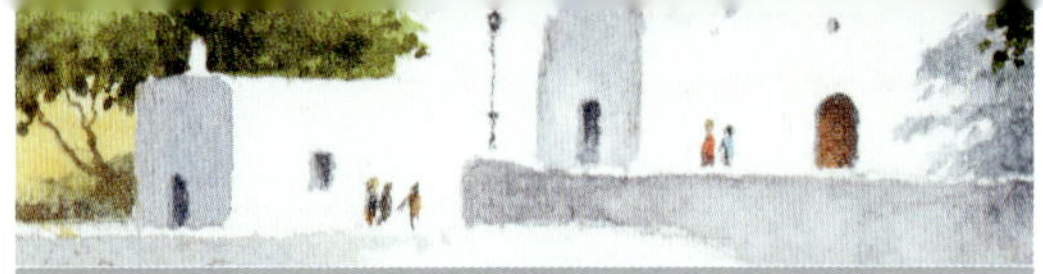

# MYKONOS HARBOUR

After considering my initial sketch of the church (see below), I wanted to make more of the side where the shadows cast from the trees emphasized the strong sunlight. I also wanted to make the background more appealing, and to add a boat both to support the focal point and to break up the shoreline. I drew a studio sketch partly based on the original one, adding detail from photographs and a sketch of the boat.

**MATERIALS USED**

Saunders Waterford 425gsm (200lb) Not watercolour paper, high white

Brushes: Large squirrel mop, no. 6 round, 12mm (½in) flat synthetic, no. 10 round, no. 4 round, no. 3 round, no. 1 round, 6mm (¼in) synthetic flat

Colours: Lavender, cerulean blue, raw umber, French ultramarine, cadmium red medium hue, green apatite genuine, quinacridone gold, lemon yellow, moonglow, quinacridone red, quinacridone sienna, yellow ochre, burnt sienna, burnt umber

3B pencil

Kitchen paper

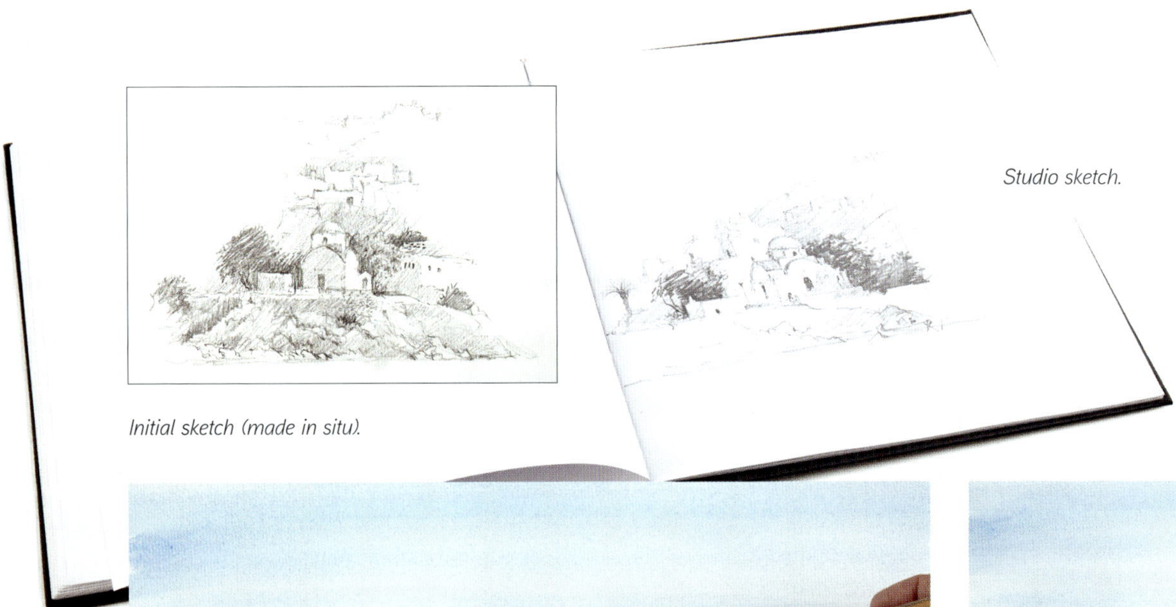

*Studio sketch.*

*Initial sketch (made in situ).*

1 Using a 3B pencil, draw out the scene. Wet the whole sky with clean water, using the large squirrel mop. Work over the top of the mountains, but carefully around the buildings. Change to the no. 6 brush if it helps you work round the buildings. Using the mop brush, lay in a wash of a sky mix of lavender and cerulean blue.

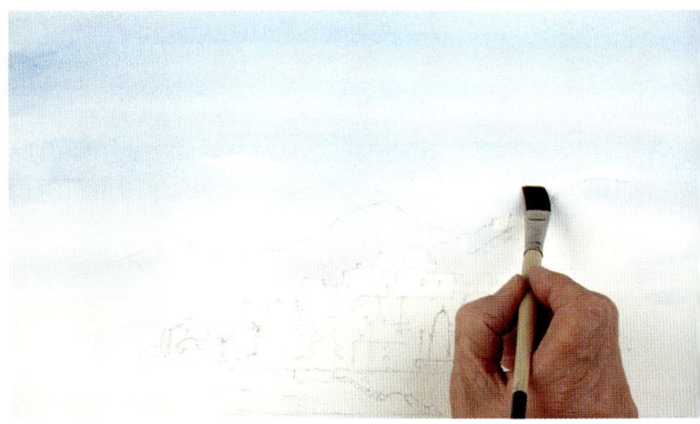

2 Change to the 12mm (½in) flat synthetic brush. Wet it, then squeeze out the water to leave just a little dampness. Allow the sky to dry to the point that the sheen is starting to disappear, then use the blade of the brush to lift out a couple of small, subtle clouds at the level of the mountain tops. Allow to dry completely before continuing.

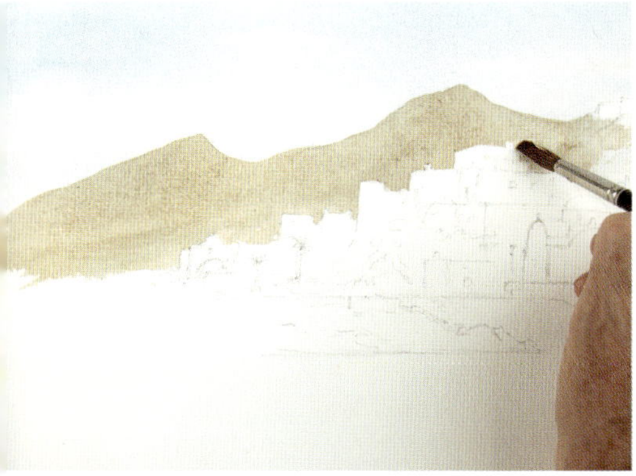

3 Place the background mountains with a dilute wash of raw umber. Use the no. 10 round brush to apply the paint, working carefully around the buildings.

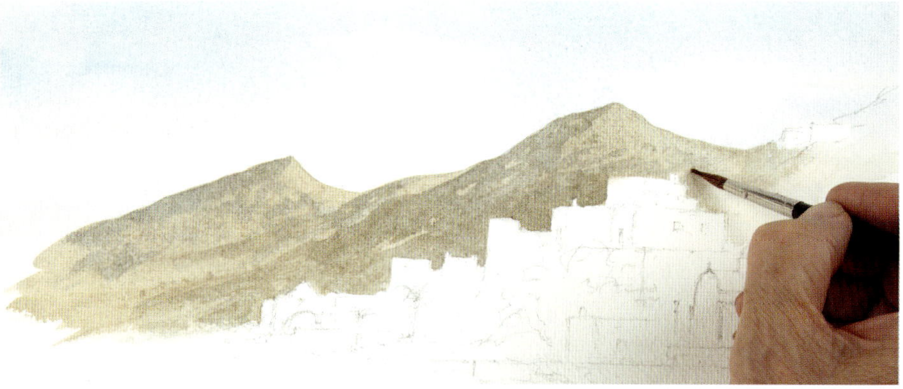

4 Add a touch of raw umber to French ultramarine, and use the no. 6 round brush to glaze the mountains in places to establish the texture and shadow areas. The light is coming from the right-hand side, so place most of the shadows on the left-hand side of the mountains.

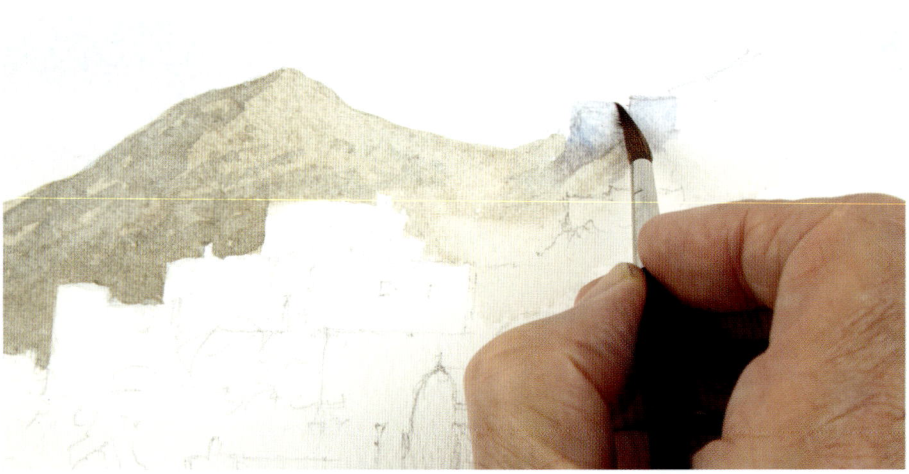

5 Add cadmium red medium hue to your sky mix (lavender and cerulean blue), and use the no. 6 round brush to begin to paint the shaded sides of the buildings on the ridge. Extend the paint down the mountainside as cast shadows.

6 Apply the same colour to the shaded sides of the remaining buildings. To suggest reflected light coming from nearby buildings or the ground, clean the brush and use the damp point to draw out a little of the wet paint from the bottom of the shaded shape.

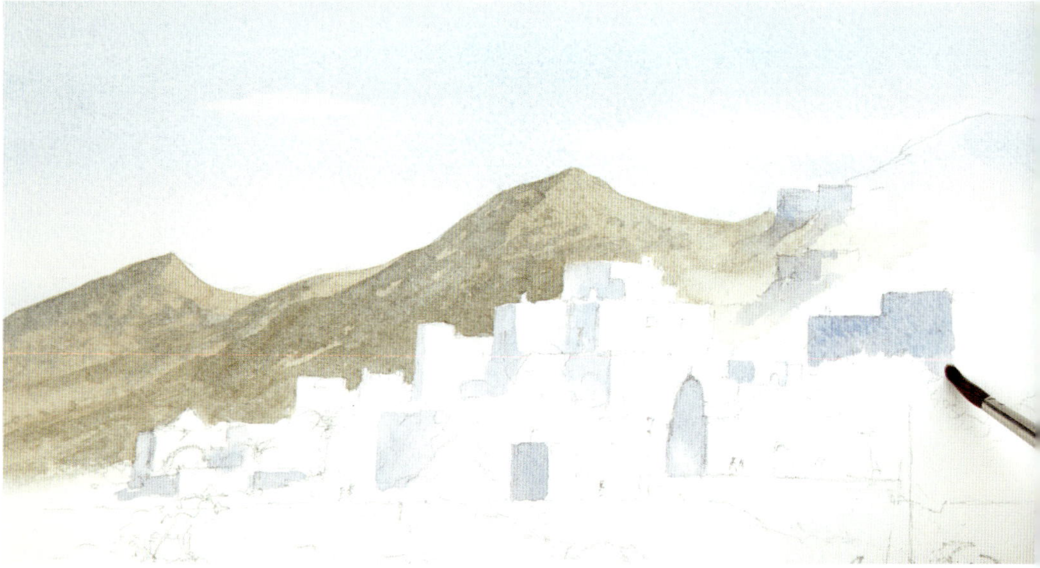

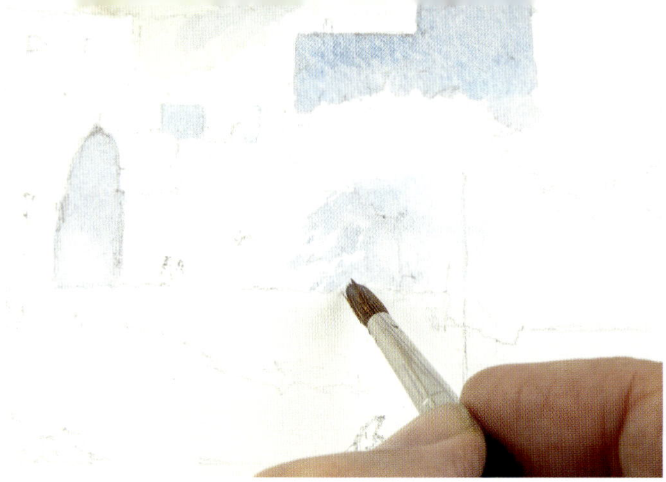

7 The trees will also cast shadow. Use the side of the no. 4 brush to make a slightly dappled shape to the lower left of the tree, developing the texture with the tip.

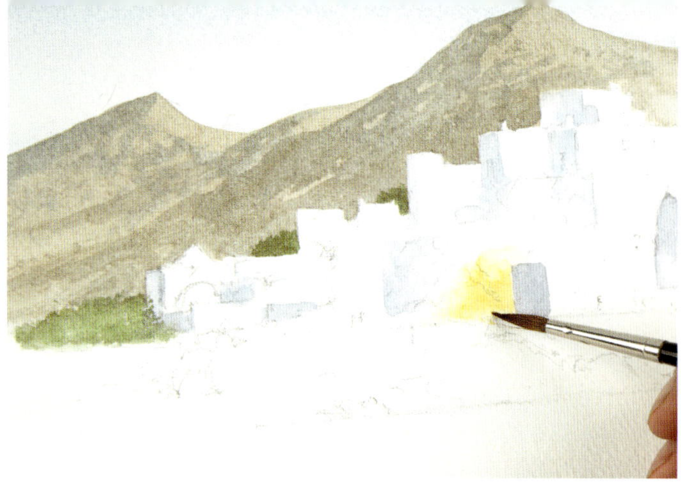

8 Still using the no. 4 round brush, mix raw umber with green apatite genuine and use this green mix to paint the trees in and amongst the buildings. Add some hints of quinacridone gold below the tree in the centre with the no. 6 round brush.

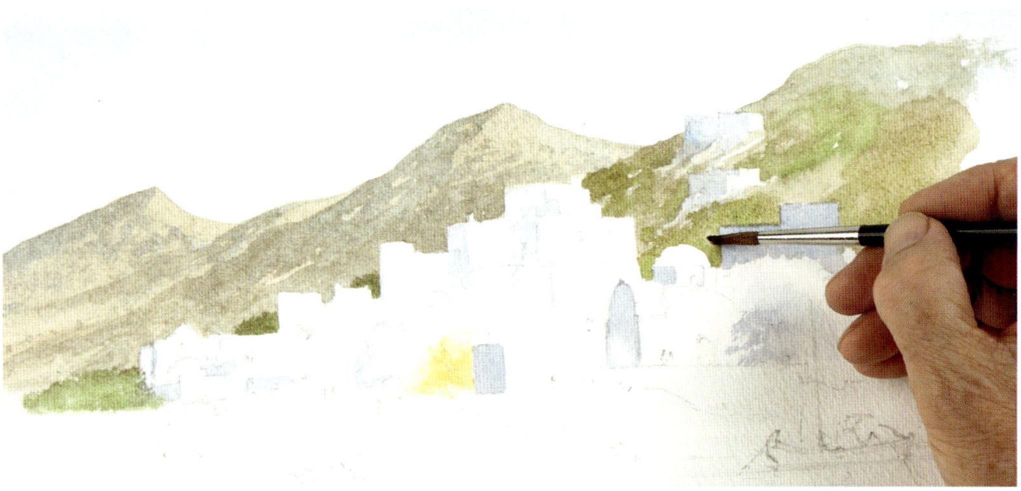

9 Working down the ridge of the mountain on the right, add touches of raw umber to fill in the area, providing some definition to the edge of the buildings. Add some touches of green apatite genuine wet into wet.

10 Mix lemon yellow with green apatite genuine for a fresh green, and use stippling marks to suggest sunlit foliage on the central tree.

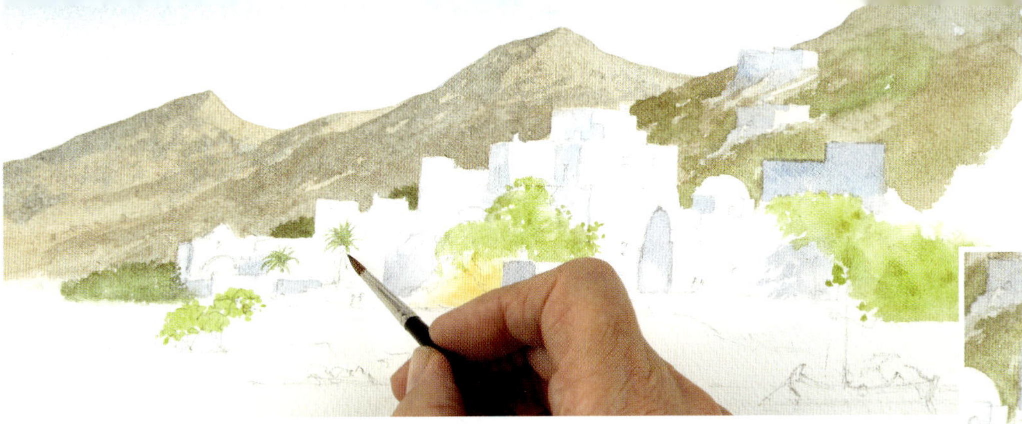

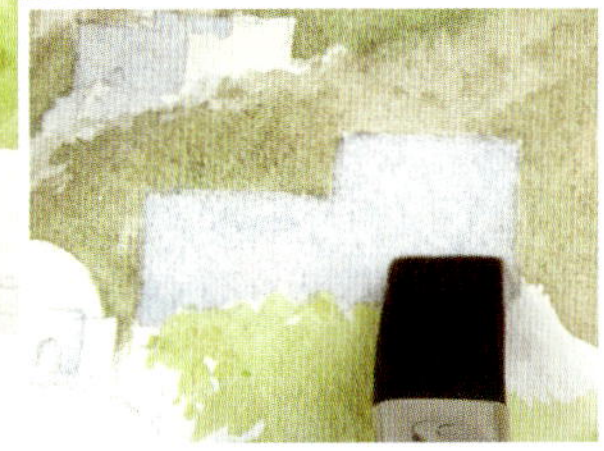

11 Do the same for the tree on the right-hand side and the small trees in the foreground, then paint the palm trees with green apatite genuine, applying the paint carefully with the point of the no. 3 round brush. As you work, you may spot some parts that unbalance the tones. You can glaze these to darken them, or use the 12mm (½in) synthetic flat brush and kitchen paper to lift out a little paint in order to lighten them (see inset).

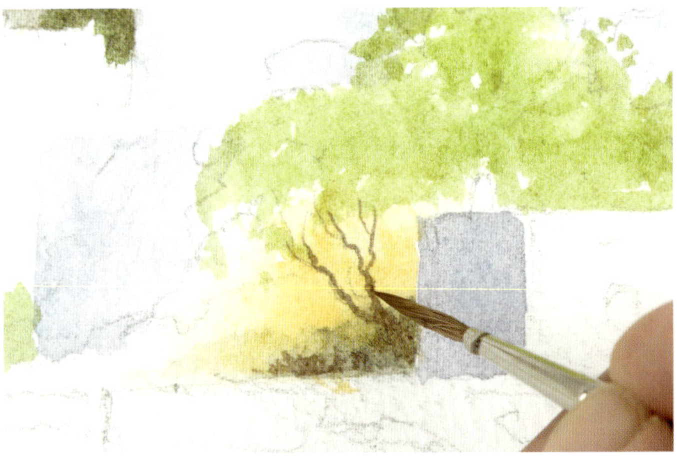

12 Add some contrasting dark tones near the light central area, using a mix of French ultramarine and burnt umber with the no. 3 round brush. While it is still wet, use the no. 1 rigger to draw the mix up to create the trunks of the trees.

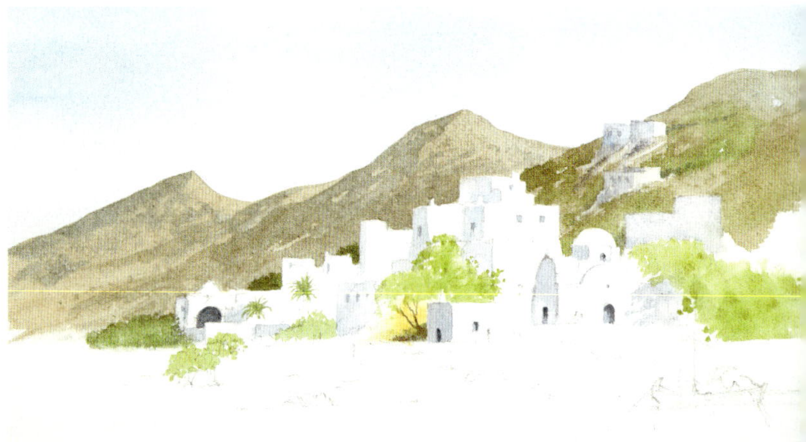

13 Change back to the no. 3 round brush. Add selective glazes of the greyed sky mix (lavender and cerulean blue with a touch of cadmium red medium hue) to the side of the distant building, in order to make it stand out a little more against the other building. Use the same brush and mix to add in the windows and doors across the buildings. Reinforce some of the closer apertures with moonglow.

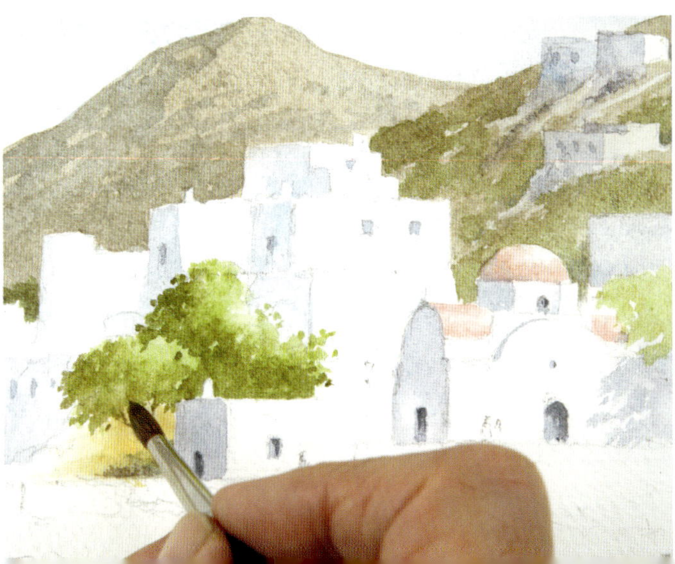

14 Change to the no. 6 round brush. Paint the dome and roof on the church using quinacridone red with a hint of yellow ochre. Reinforce the colour in areas, and add moonglow while wet for shadows. Using a mix of raw umber and green apatite genuine, start to add deeper shadows to the trees. Use a stippling motion towards the edges of the foliage.

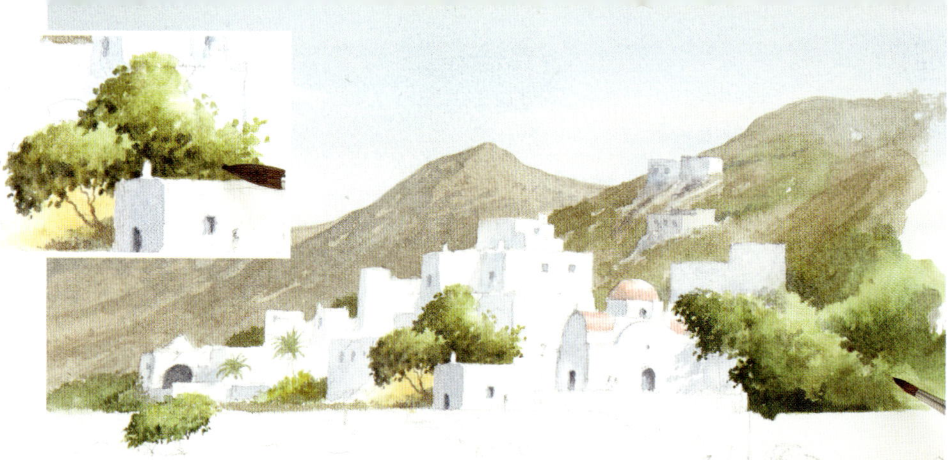

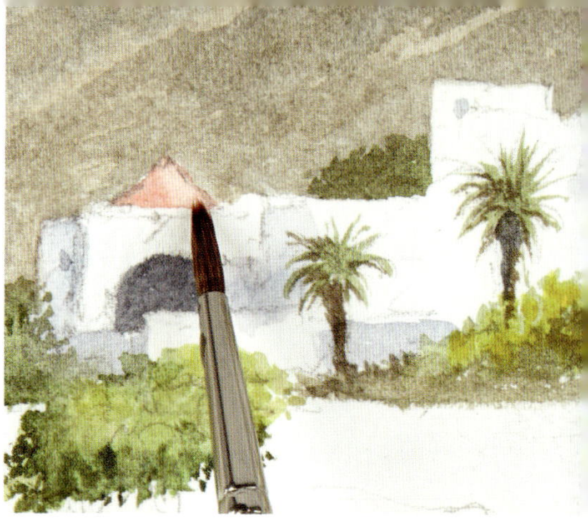

15 Add French ultramarine to the mix, and add the very dark shadows in the same way (see inset). Still using the no. 6 round, build up the foliage across the painting using the same brush and mixes.

16 Change to the no. 4 round and use a dark mix of raw umber and French ultramarine to paint in the trunks of the palm trees and the dark, shaded fronds, then use a pink mix of quinacridone red and yellow ochre to paint the roof of the nearby building.

17 Take a step back and look for any small areas or features that need to be adjusted – either knocking back intruding areas with lifting out, or strengthening too-weak areas with a few additional details or glazes. Here, I have added a few windows to the building behind the church; glazed French ultramarine over the shaded building near the palm trees; and added a small lamp post with the no. 3 round brush and a dark mix of French ultramarine and burnt umber.

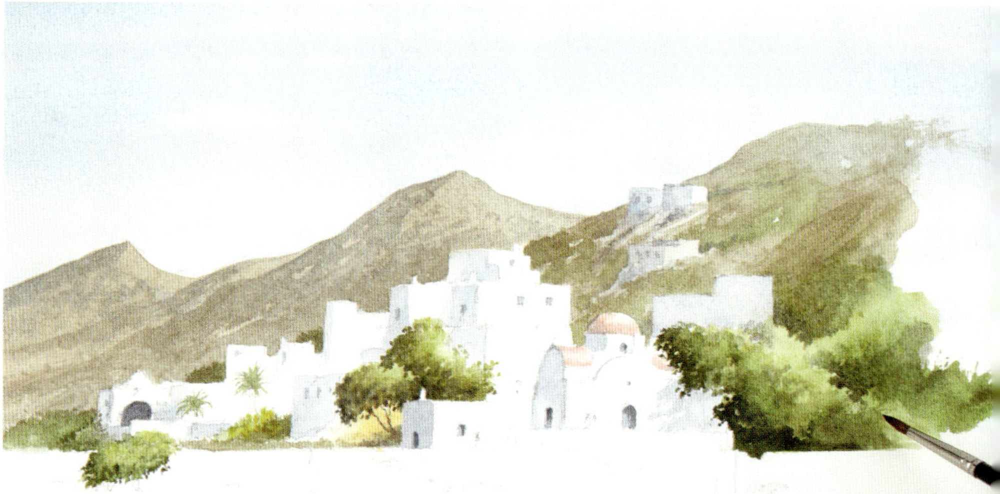

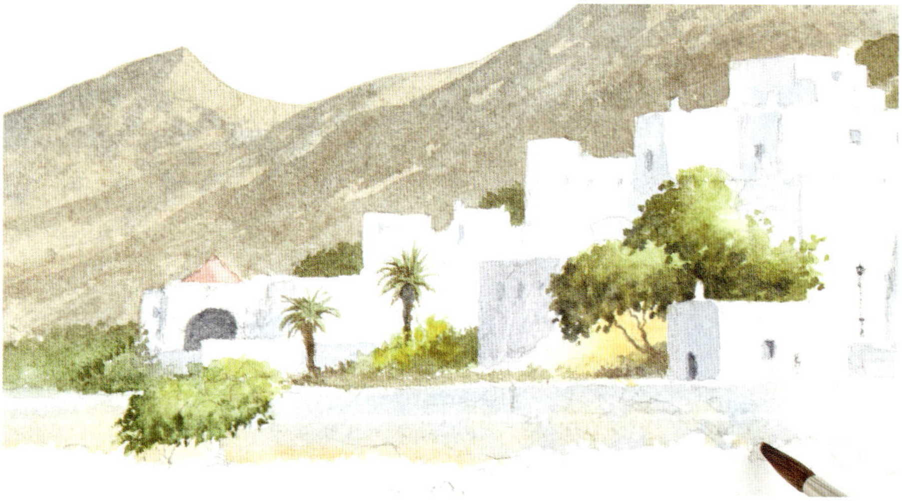

18 Begin to develop the sea wall using the sky mix of lavender and French ultramarine, applying the paint using the no. 6 round. Add some yellow ochre wet into wet.

19 Using the no. 1 round brush, pick out the figures in front of the church using some of the brighter colours on your palette for their tops, and moonglow for darker areas.

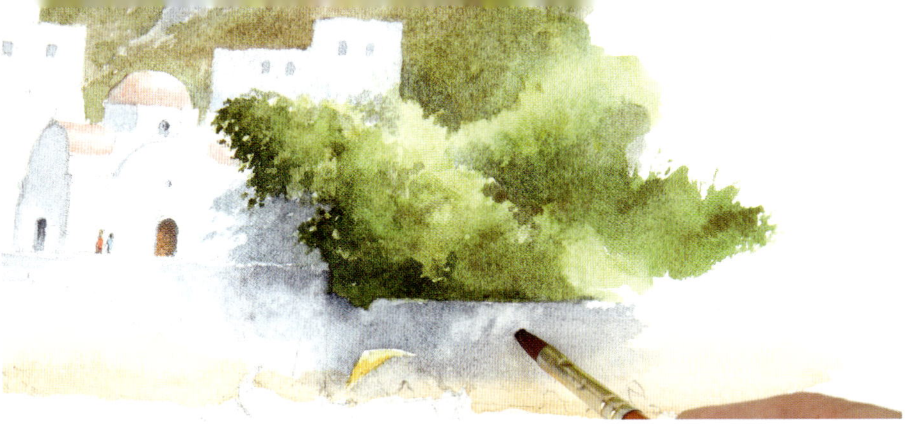

20 Add the parasol with a mix of lemon yellow and quinacridone gold, then lay in the beach with yellow ochre and the no. 10 brush, then develop the shadows around the trees on the right-hand side with a mix of French ultramarine and moonglow. Lift a little of the paint out for highlights on the wall using the 6mm (¼in) synthetic flat brush.

21 Using the same mix of French ultramarine and moonglow, add the cross on the church and trunks to the trees on the lower left-hand side using the no. 1 rigger.

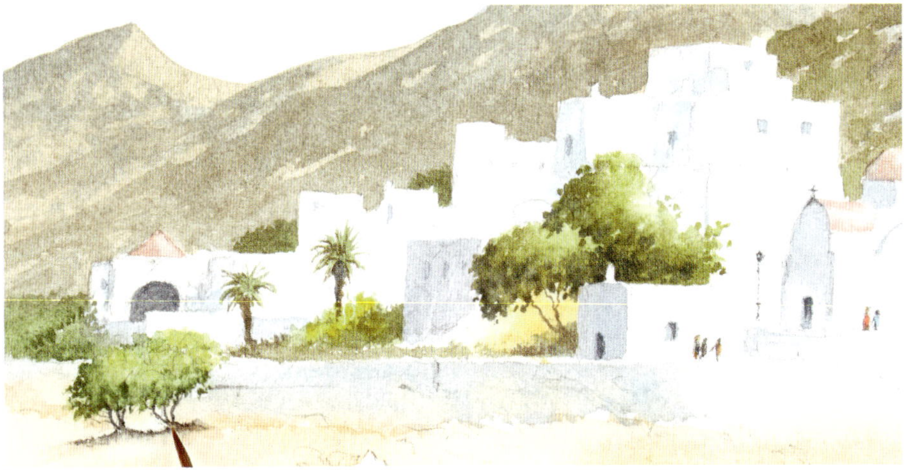

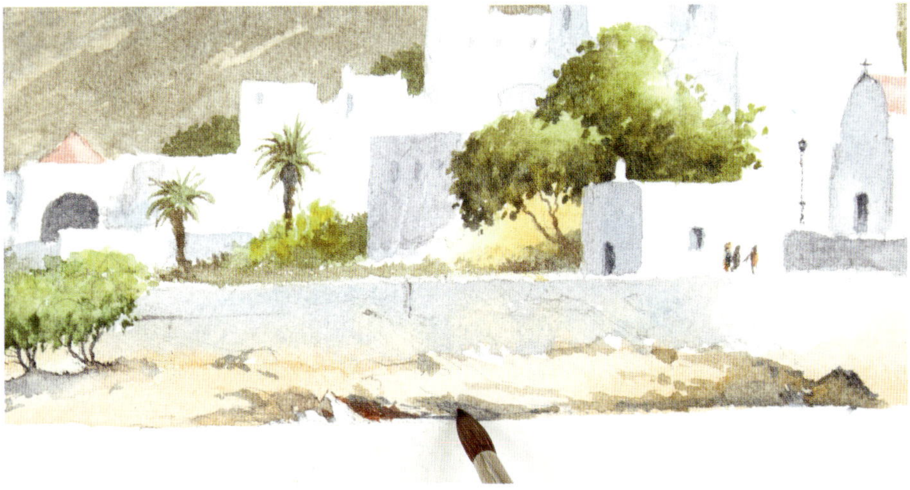

22 Change to a no. 6 round brush and paint the rocky foreshore using French ultramarine, raw umber and a few touches of yellow ochre.

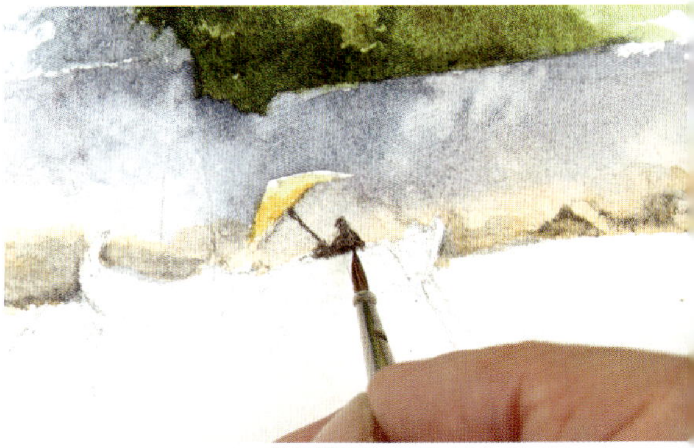

23 Using the no. 1 round brush, begin to detail the boat. Use a dark mix of French ultramarine and burnt sienna for the parasol stand and figure beneath, then switch to quinacridone sienna for other details.

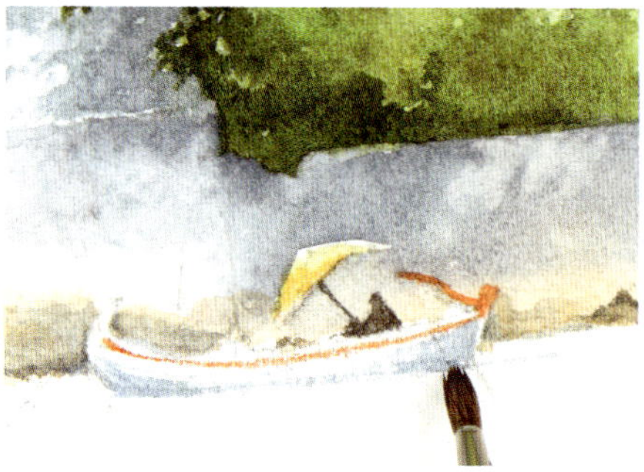

24 Add shadow to the hull of the boat using the no. 4 round brush and French ultramarine, softening the colour in towards the centre.

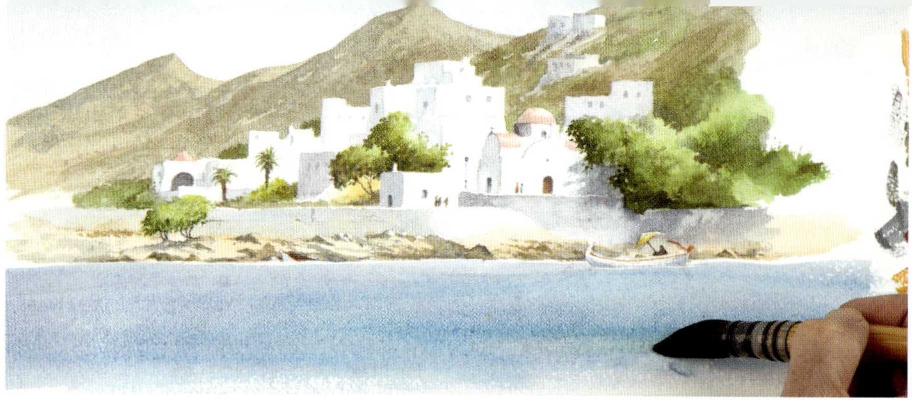

25 Before starting the sea, I have added some further detail to the rocky foreshore with the no. 1 round brush and the dark mix of French ultramarine and burnt sienna. Using the squirrel hair mop brush, lay in broad horizontal strokes of French ultramarine, then add phthalo blue wet into wet.

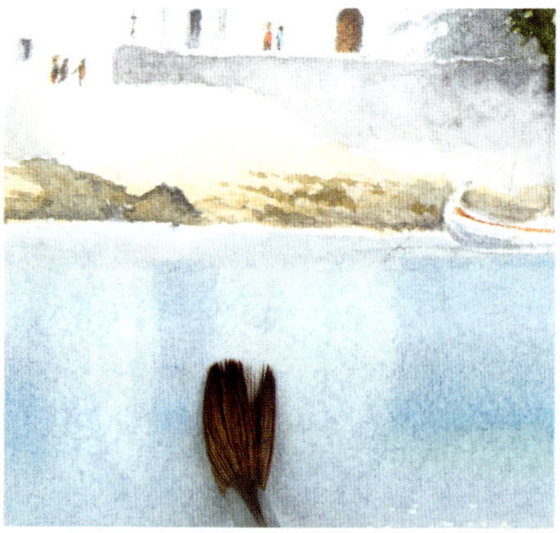

26 While the paint is wet, use a damp no. 10 brush to lift out reflections of the central buildings, drawing the brush down the water.

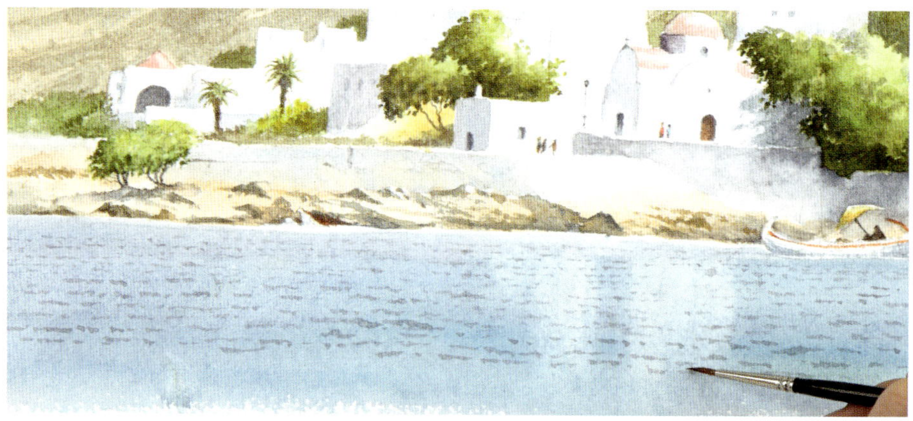

27 Allow the sea area to dry. Using a no. 1 round brush and moonglow, add ripples across the sea, starting from the top and centre.

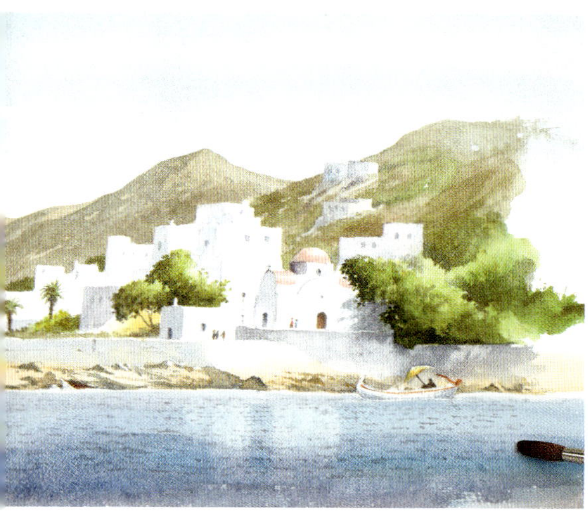

28 Add cadmium red medium hue to French ultramarine and use the resulting rich mix to glaze the lower part of the sea, using broad strokes of the no. 10 round brush.

29 Clean and rinse the no. 10 round brush and wet the sky area, leaving the clouds dry. Add slightly diluted cerulean blue into the wet area with horizontal strokes. Use a wet brush to draw the wet paint down into the valleys between the hilltops.

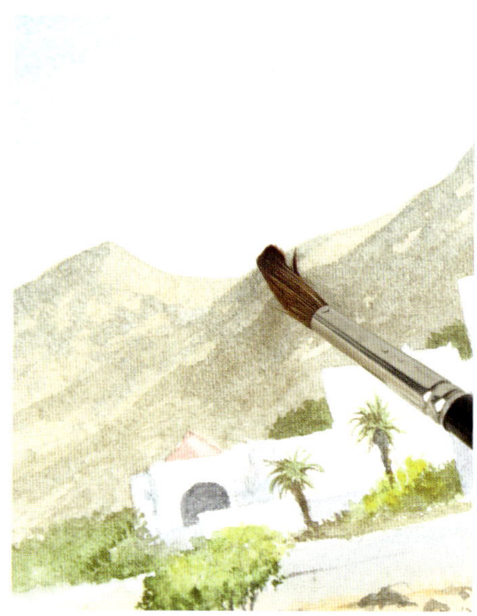

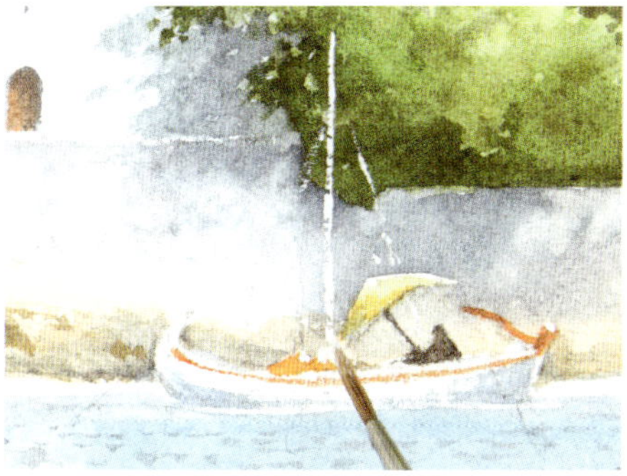

30 Add some cargo to the boat using permanent orange and the no. 1 round brush, then change to the no. 1 rigger and add a mast and rigging with white gouache.

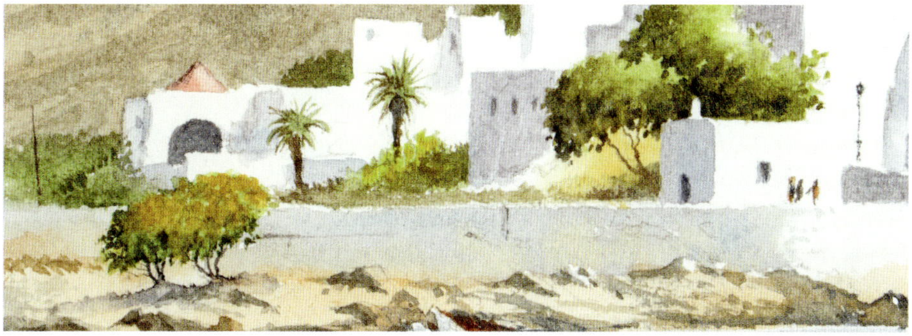

31 To finish, make any final tweaks you feel necessary. I have strengthened the shadows on the central buildings, and warmed the trees on the lower left-hand side, to help differentiate them from each other.

*The finished painting*

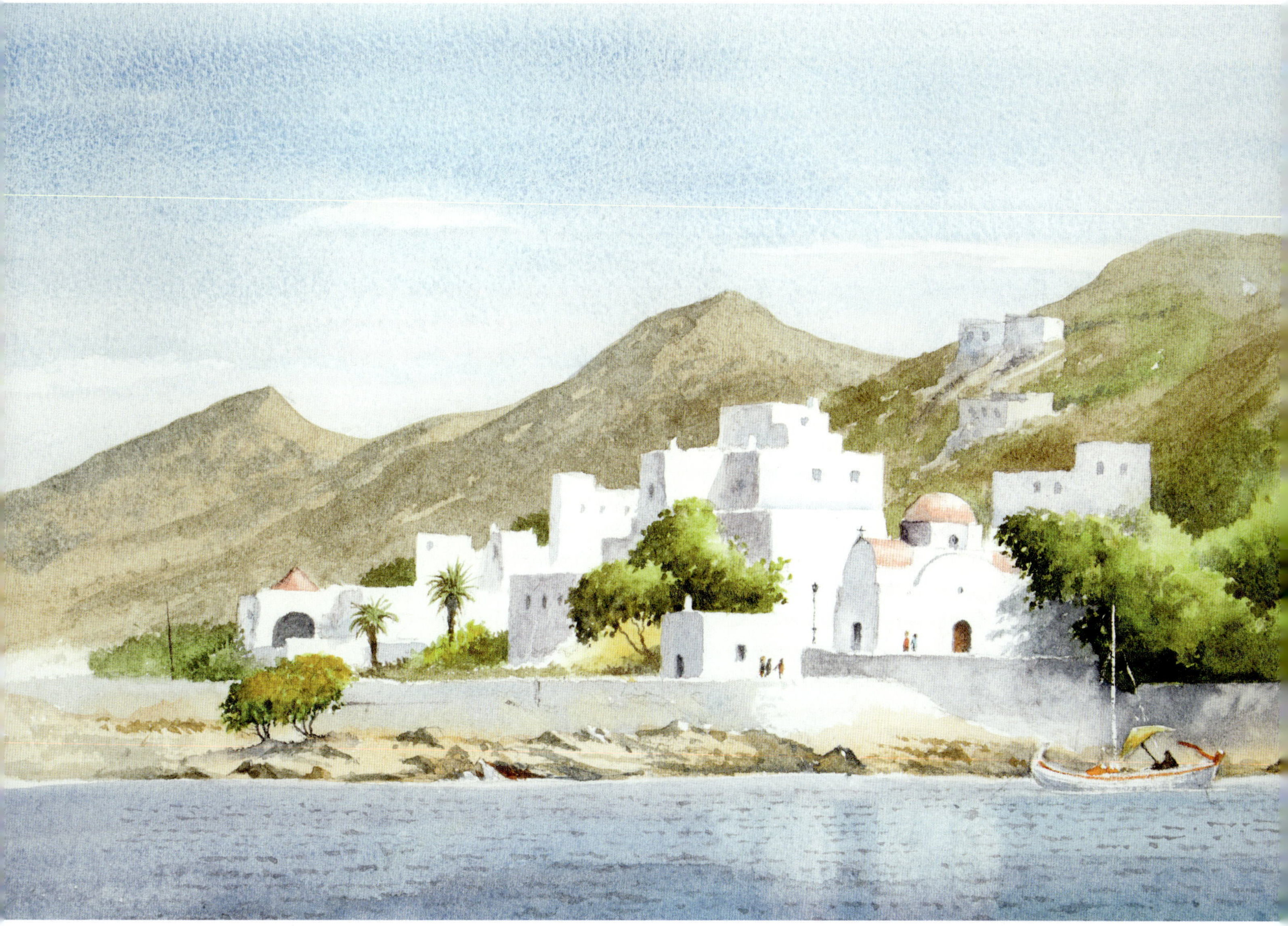

# SEASONS

Living in the UK, we landscape artists are blessed not only with a wide variety of landscapes, but with changing seasons which add further variation to those scenes. One of the joys of the outdoor artist is visiting the same scene at different times of year and finding that that dramatic snow-bound mountain is now a rich green bathed in sunlight. While summer days can make for pleasurable outings in search of landscapes to paint, many artists find it a difficult time of year with all that overwhelming greenery, and often superb subjects are hidden behind massed foliage or riotous vegetation. In the following pages I will try to help you overcome these irritations and make the most of the warmer days.

During winter there is normally a greater variety of colour and winter trees take on a different, at times romantic, beauty in their naked splendour. Winter light is strikingly different from that of summer, giving the artist more opportunities for dramatic mood and heightened accentuation of a motif. Landscapes transformed under snow offer an excellent opportunity to study the reflections of light and colour. The landscape environment is one of enormous complexity, and deep snow simplifies this for us.

Working outdoors in the coldest weather has never been universally popular. Of the French Impressionists, who took great pains to work directly from nature, only Monet, Pissarro and Sisley did any substantial work in the snow. Monet in particular was a hardy soul who painted outdoors in the harshest of winters, and was sometimes spotted working at his easel in deep snow, clothed in three overcoats and gloves, with a heater at his feet. We now have far more efficient winter clothing and aids to working outdoors in less than ideal weather, but I'm not suggesting that you subject yourself to the bleakest conditions in which to paint or sketch. There are now easier ways of capturing the coldest of winter scenes.

This section takes you from painting hot summer days, through the misty, colourful scenery of autumn, to making the most of winter when all is laid bare, and on into the snow-covered countryside with its quiet beauty and new challenges. Finally there is a chapter on springtime with its promise of longer days and fresh colours. The seasons, both in topographical detail and weather effects, can at times merge into each other, to give us even in winter some warm, sunny moods amidst raw, snow-bound landscapes, making it an absolute joy to be out recording the scenes in sketch or photographic form. I shall show you how to capture these moments, making full use of the lighting – for sometimes the scene is more about atmosphere and lighting than about a topographical feature – and how to respond to the original material in your painting at home.

Whether you can't wait to get out sketching in wild snow flurries, prefer to paint while picnicking in a summer meadow, or choose to paint autumn scenes from the comfort of your home, you should find much to inspire and help you in the following pages.

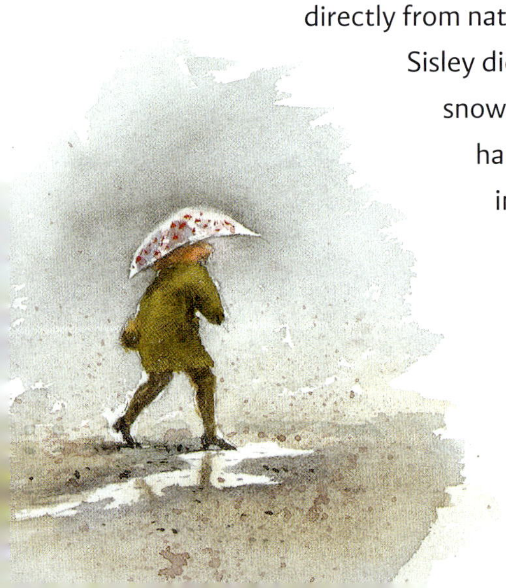

## AN CEARCALLACH, SCOTTISH HIGHLANDS

*30.5 x 38cm (12 x 15in), 640gsm (300lb) Rough paper*

*In this Highland scene, sunlight enhances the warm late autumn colours and evening mist adds a hint of mystery to the background. The summer midges have gone, the air is still, and the gentle evening sunlight makes it a pleasure to be out painting as winter approaches.*

*The yellow-orange tints were achieved with various mixtures of gamboge and cadmium orange and the wine-red massed birch twigs with permanent alizarin crimson. The foreground was accentuated with light red. This is a time when you can happily run riot with your reds.*

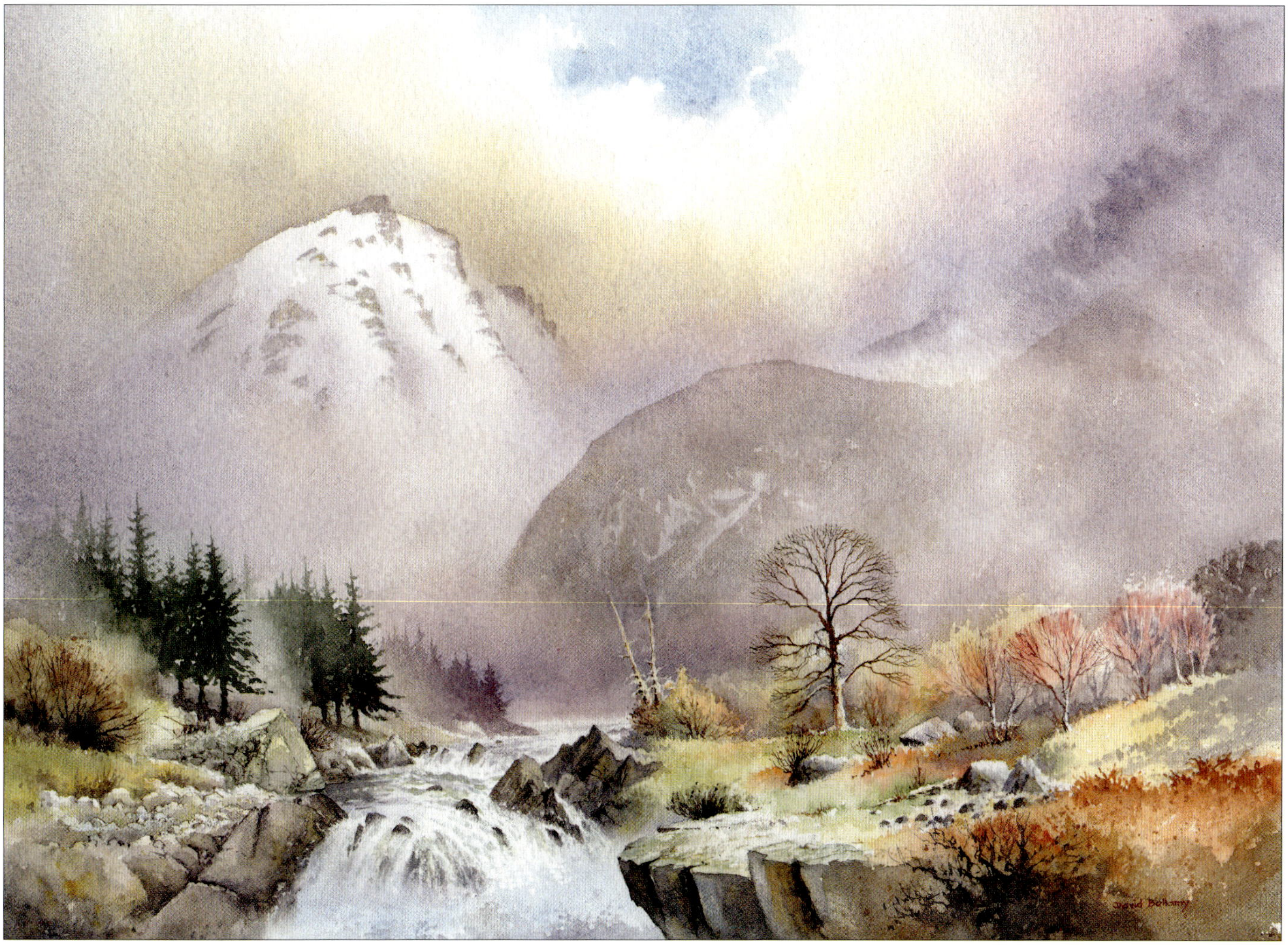

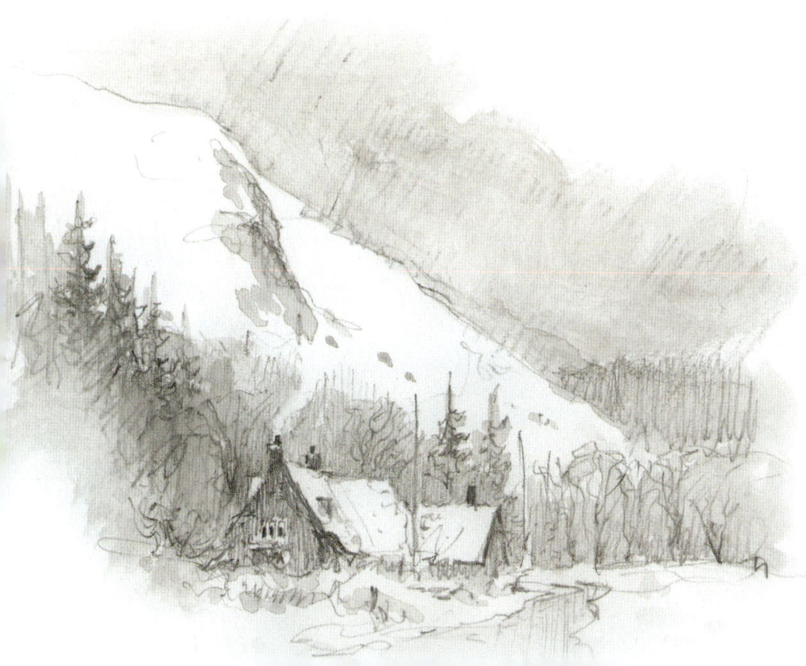

*Elan village under snow*

# Summer

Warm summer days are when the majority of landscape artists enjoy getting outside to seek those subjects that inspire their work, whether in sketches or photographs. Strong sunlight can bring the landscape to life, and many subjects that we might well ignore during the rest of the year are suddenly infused with a much more exciting combination of light and shadow. In this chapter you will learn how to accentuate sunlight in your paintings, engendering a feeling of summer warmth and brightening up your foregrounds with wild flowers and undergrowth. You will also learn how to cope with all those overwhelming greens. Be aware, though, that there are exciting possibilities when the weather is a little bit on the moody side, and these often produce the best paintings.

## MANAGING SUMMER GREENS

Many summer scenes are dominated by greens of many shades, and this becomes quite a challenge to the artist. Do you wish to record every nuance of green exactly as it stands, or maybe paint the same amount of greenery but use fewer greens? Or should you make changes to suit yourself, either reducing the amount of green or completely changing to other colours? The first option is laborious and unlikely to produce an interesting result. Trying to render the scene exactly as it is usually stifles creativity. You need to inject something of yourself into the work, and the other two options offer more excitement and interest. On these two pages you will see a variety of approaches.

COTTAGES NEAR ST DAVIDS
*22.3 x 29cm (8¾ x 11½in), 640gsm (300lb) Not paper*

*If you wish to reduce the effect of overwhelming greenery, you can simply avoid using any green in the distance. In this scene, the area beyond the buildings has been painted in yellow, reds and greys, with the red toned down to suggest distance. I have further reduced the green cover in the foreground by breaking it up with boulders, flowers and patches of strong red. Although these features were actually present, if you wish to diminish the green effect, you can introduce similar objects such as rocks, stones, puddles, patches of gravel, a wide track or whatever might fit into the composition, but try not to overwork the area. Bringing in cut fields not only reduces the impact of the greenery, but also introduces a pleasing variety in the landscape.*

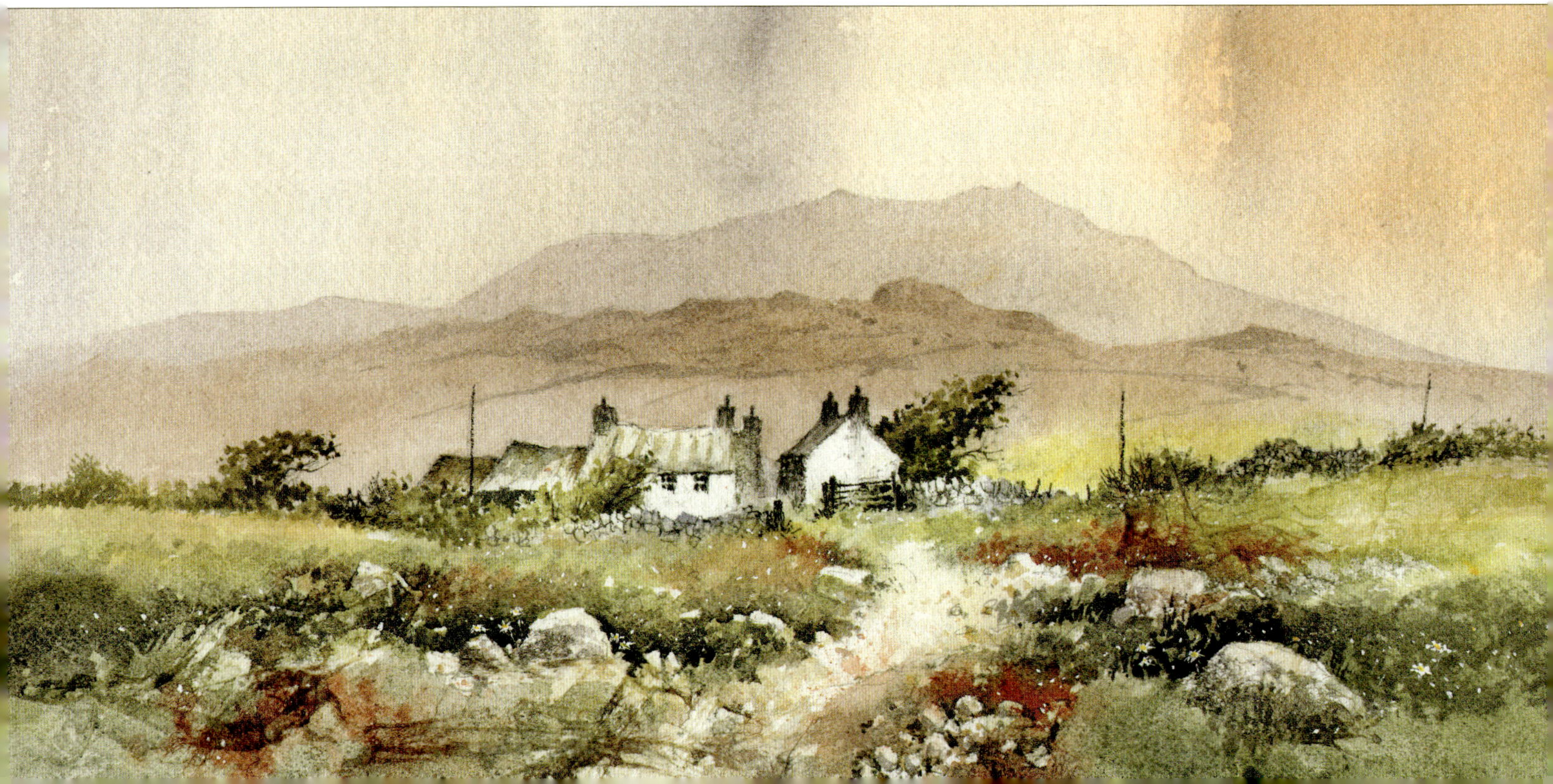

# MIXING SUMMER GREENS

The spring greens chart on page 277 shows some excellent examples for early summer, but for warm greens, mix cadmium yellow pale with French ultramarine, cobalt blue or indigo to extend your range. Substitute cadmium yellow pale with gamboge for even warmer mixes. Adding a touch of cadmium red into these mixtures will give you even more possibilities. Green apatite genuine has become my favourite with its rich colour and strong granulations that suggest foliage without me having to do too much work.

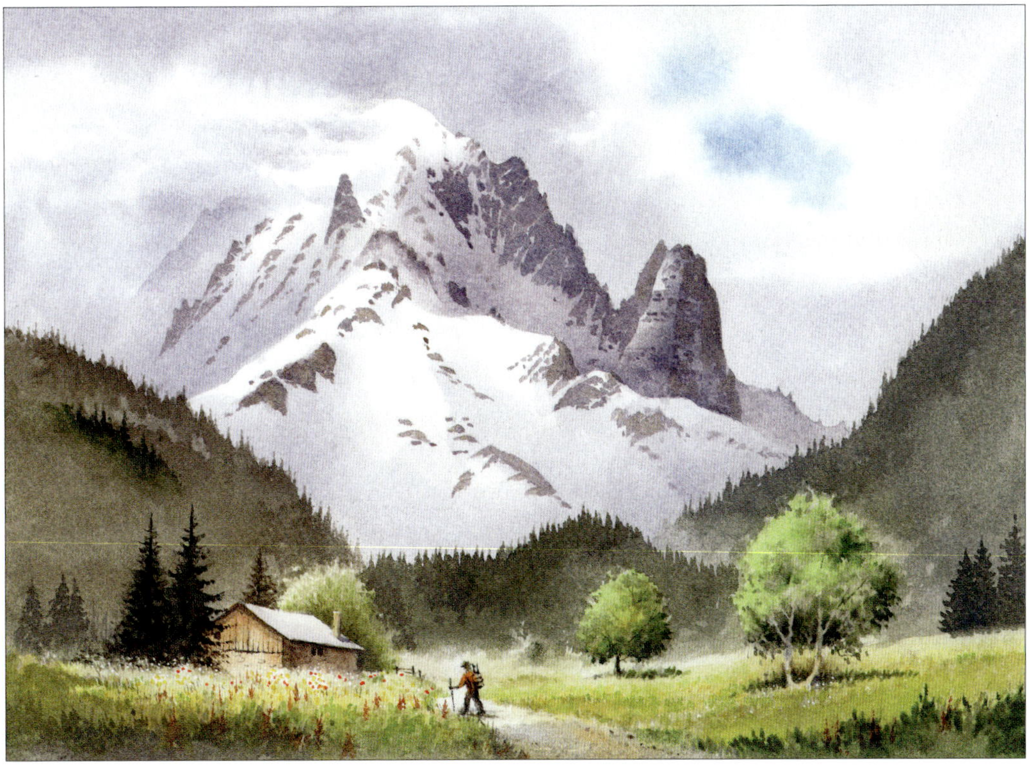

**ALPINE MEADOW**

*23 x 33cm (9 x 13in), 300gsm (140lb) Not paper*

*Using strong tonal contrasts is an effective way of suggesting sunshine. Summer Alpine meadows, resplendent with wild flowers, make excellent foregrounds to the snow-capped distant peaks. There are a number of greens in this painting ranging from almost pure yellow to extremely dark greens. The dark conifers and foreground shadows, together with the cast shadows under the trees, help to emphasize the feeling of sunlight in the lighter parts of the meadow. For the cooler greens on the light trees, I used cadmium yellow pale with cobalt blue, but for much of the warmer grassy foreground, I applied gamboge.*

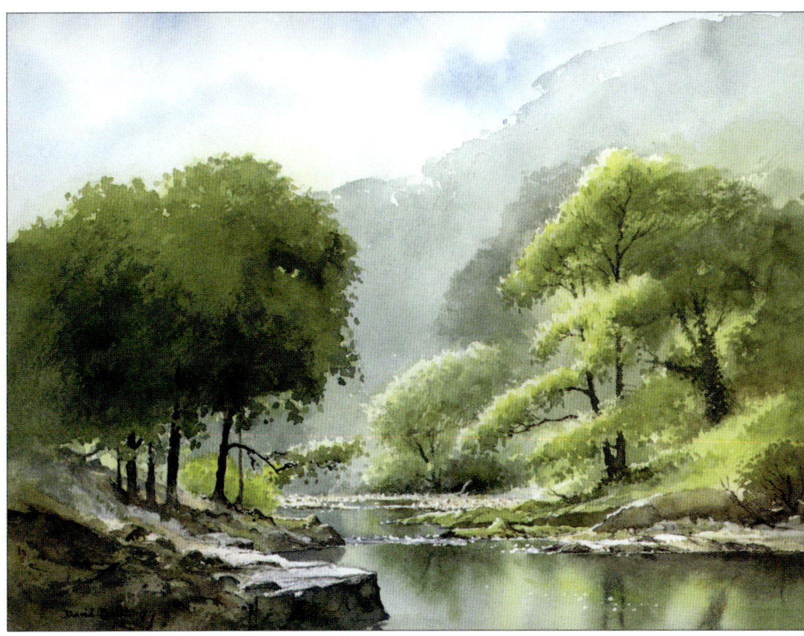

**RIVER MELLTE**

*21.5 x 26cm (8½ x 10¼in), 300gsm (140lb) Not paper*

*The greens here are in three degrees of colour temperature. In order to suggest distance, the background ones are blue-green, a mixture of cobalt blue and yellow ochre. This wash is quite weak for the furthest bank of trees rising up the side of the gorge, but much stronger for the darker foliage just right of centre above and to the left of the tall, sunlit trees. The small tree in the centre is slightly greener: cobalt blue and cadmium yellow pale with more yellow in the mix, while the closer trees on both sides were painted with French ultramarine and cadmium yellow pale, with raw umber and ultramarine for the darker shadows. This gives a sense of depth and space and the overall impact of the massed greens is lessened. The lack of detail in the furthest mass of trees also helps to suggest distance.*

# PAINTING SUMMER TREES

One of the most common failures in painting summer trees is to create what look like lumps of green dough stuck on a matchstick. This is easy to avoid as shown in the examples. Try to find trees where the trunk and several main branches are visible, as these give shape and character. If you can't see any branches, introduce two or three. Trunks and branches often appear as dark silhouettes, but it gives the tree more life if you add colour while the limb is still wet. Reds, pinks, yellows and greens work, and sometimes I even drop a touch of phthalo blue into the dark trunk.

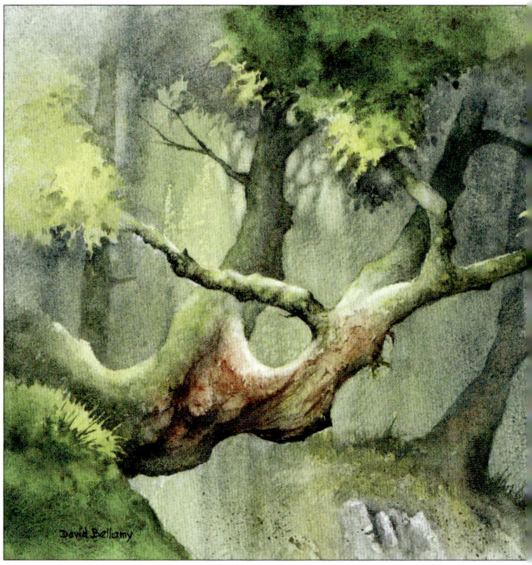

**TWISTED OAK**

*20 x 20cm (8 x 8in), 300gsm (140lb) Not paper*

*Many oak trees look ungainly and awkward, but a lovely mature oak, contorted and with a weathered, textured trunk, can be a gem for the artist. This one grew horizontally out of a bank, then curved upwards, its branches breaking up the strong lines of other trunks and branches. I have simplified the tree by leaving out several less interesting branches: don't hesitate to cut out those that don't suit your purpose. Mosses and lichens gave way in places to naked bark, creating varied colouring. Much of the background was created wet-into-wet, sometimes painting only part of a trunk to enhance a sense of mystery. The wet-into-wet technique is excellent for woodland backgrounds. The composition is overwhelmingly green, painted in the main with a mixture of viridian and bloodstone genuine, with cadmium yellow pale in places. The intense rich greens at the top and the bottom left were painted in green apatite genuine.*

Losing branches into shadow areas gives a natural appearance

Blobs of light gouache help suggest lighter foliage

A sharply defined feature such as a stile helps to counter amorphous foliage areas

Branches and stalks painted negatively provide variation

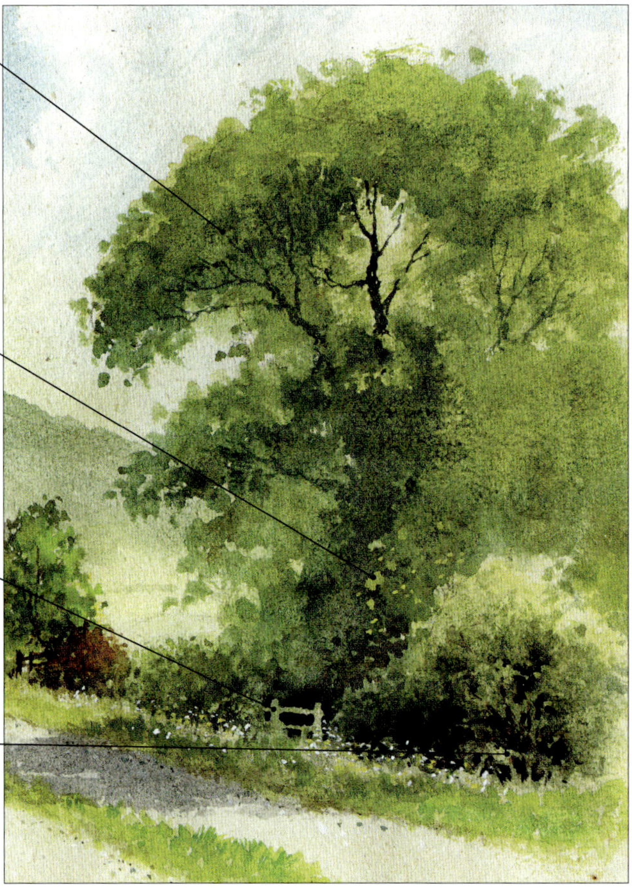

**MATURE TREE IN FULL LEAF**

*You often cannot see trunks or branches in trees with dense foliage, so I add them to give the tree shape. Small blobs to suggest leaves placed just outside the boundary of the main foliage ensure trees don't look like lumps of dough, and here I've added a few in light green gouache near the stile.*

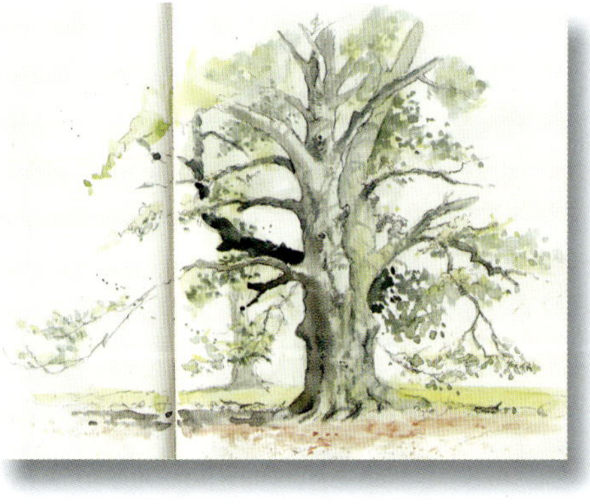

**BEECH TREE SKETCH**

*Sometimes I sketch lone trees where I find good examples, as these can be inserted into a painting. This was sketched as spring was turning into summer, a rewarding time for studying mature trees as you can still view the branches and trunks among the foliage. I love the way sunlight throws the cast shadows of branches across the trunks. These were rendered wet-into-wet on the right-hand trunk and wet-on-dry on the left, to compare.*

## Birch tree

Birches are distinctive, beautiful trees that can enhance a landscape whether as the centre of interest or as a supporting feature. Sketch and photograph good specimens as these can be added to a composition as required. The following two stages will give you an idea of how to tackle them.

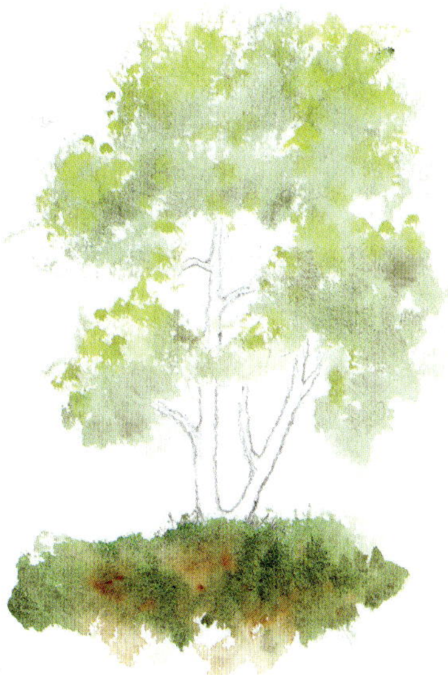

BIRCH TREE STAGE 1

*I drew the outline with a 4B pencil, then applied green apatite genuine with cadmium yellow pale.*

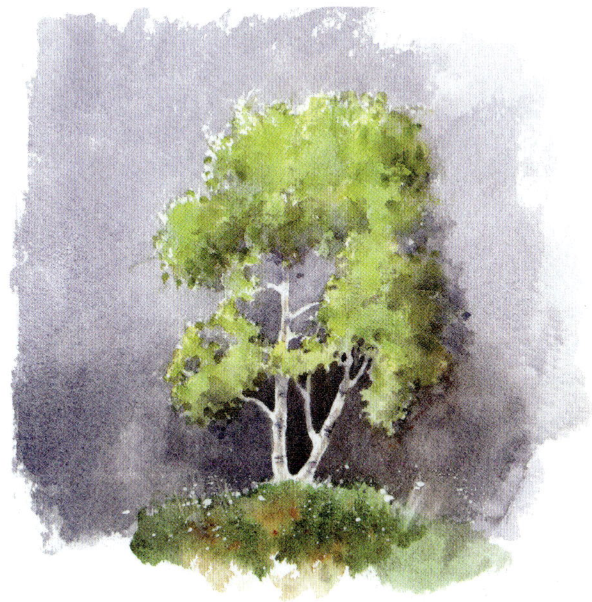

BIRCH TREE FINAL STAGE

*First I wetted the trunks with clean water, then I dragged transparent red oxide down the centres of the trunks, creating a soft effect. A few drops of lunar blue were added here and there. Next I painted a mixture of French ultramarine and cadmium red around the trunks and branches to highlight them light against dark. I added shadows where the trunks go under the foliage and spotted dark flecks of French ultramarine and burnt umber into the trunks in places. The sketch was finished with white gouache spatter.*

## Using the side of the brush for foliage

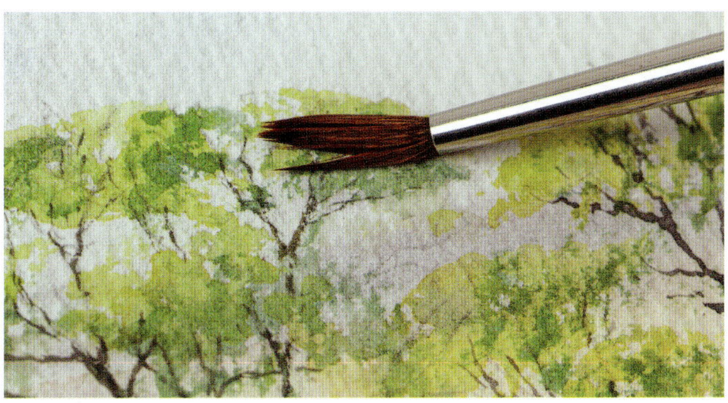

*The brush should not be too wet for this technique. Holding it on its side, drag the belly of the brush downwards over the paper to create textured clumps of foliage.*

## Spotting individual leaves

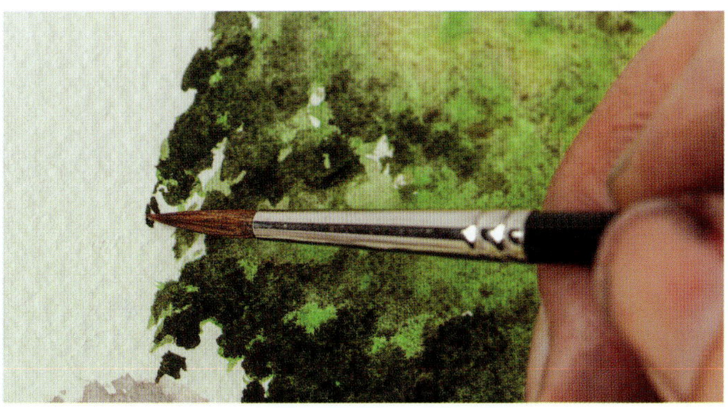

*Using a small brush, dab on individual leaves or clumps beyond the main mass of the tree. This helps to create a much more realistic effect.*

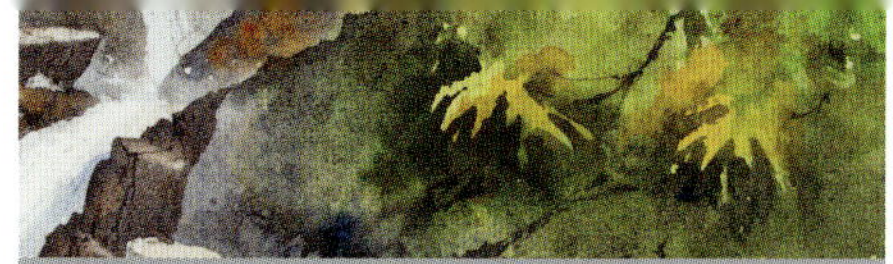

# LAKELAND WATERFALL

Masses of foliage from many trees can create confusion, so here I show how using a combination of misty effects and strong granulating colour can simplify this natural chaos. Often with background mist like this, I hint at wet-into-wet tree shapes in the background, but here I've kept it simple with green apatite genuine. If you don't have this colour, mix French ultramarine and cadmium yellow pale, working a darker colour such as raw umber into the ultramarine where you want a darker area.

**MATERIALS USED**

Saunders Waterford 640gsm (300lb) Rough watercolour paper

Brushes: Squirrel mop, no. 8, no. 6 and no. 10 round, rigger, 13mm (½in) flat

Colours: Green apatite genuine, cadmium yellow medium hue, alizarin crimson, yellow ochre, cobalt blue, burnt umber, French ultramarine, zoisite genuine, transparent red oxide, nickel titanate yellow, Aussie red gold, sodalite genuine

Masking fluid, old brush, 5B pencil

Toothbrush, paper mask, scalpel

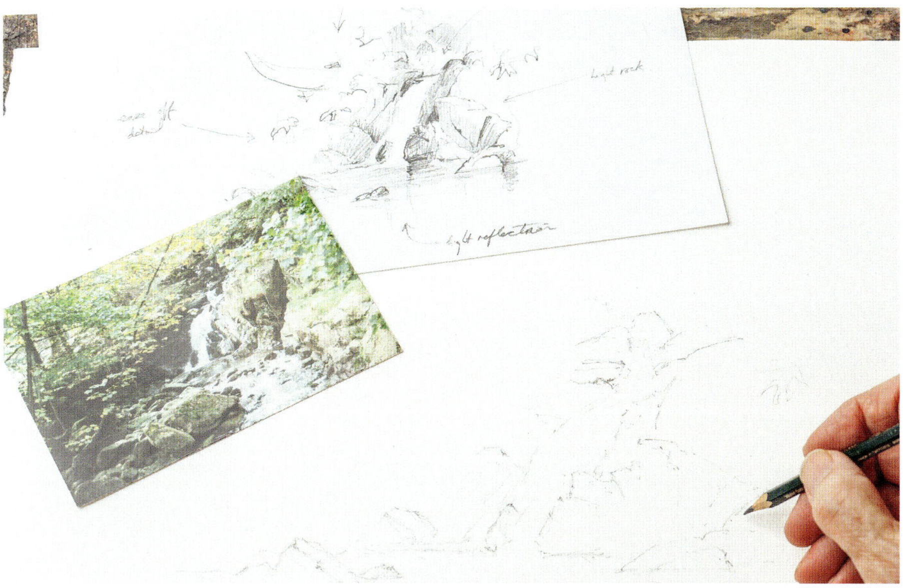

1 Use a 5B pencil to draw the outlines of the scene. I referred to my studio sketch and photograph.

2 Mask some leaves with masking fluid and an old brush. Paint clear water over the background with a squirrel mop, then drop in green apatite genuine, which will granulate, creating textured effects.

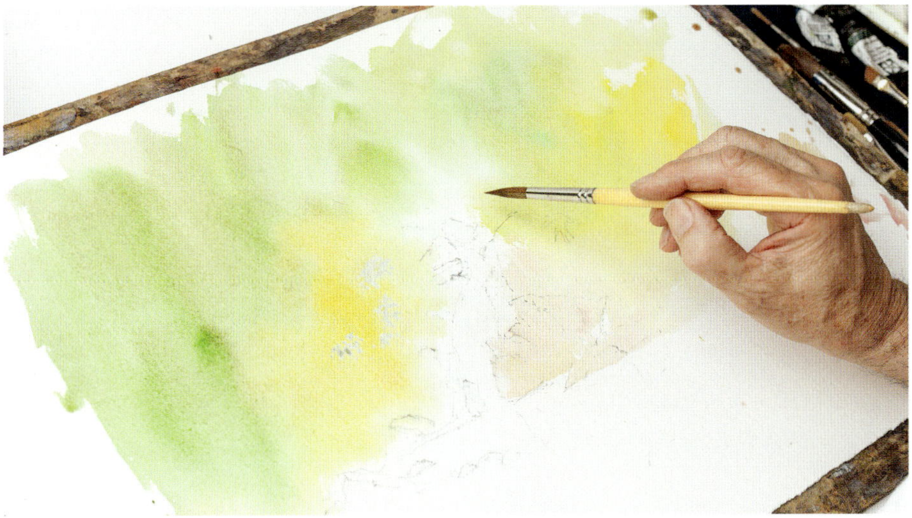

3 Working into the wet background, drop in cadmium yellow medium hue on either side, then use a no. 8 round brush to drop in alizarin crimson and yellow ochre in the centre as a base colour for the rocks.

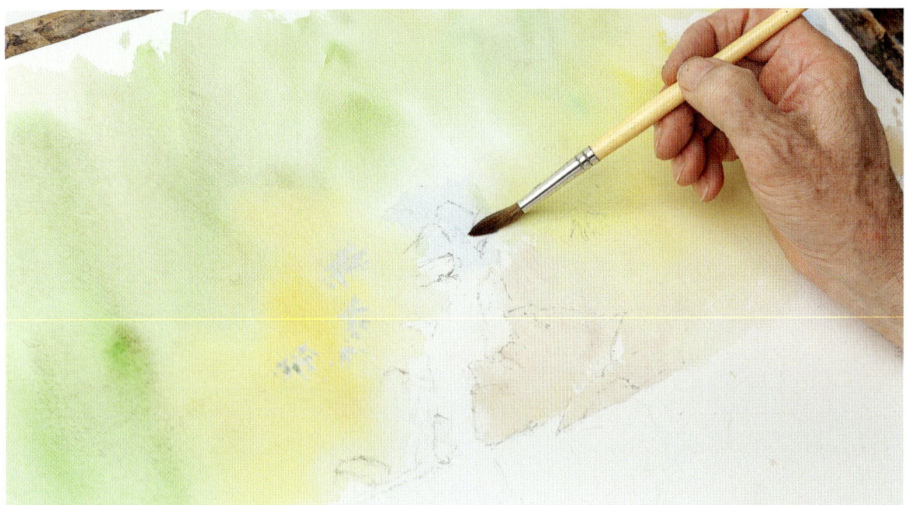

4 Paint a wash of cobalt blue over the distant falling water to make it recede. Fade this out at the top with a damp brush and allow the painting to dry.

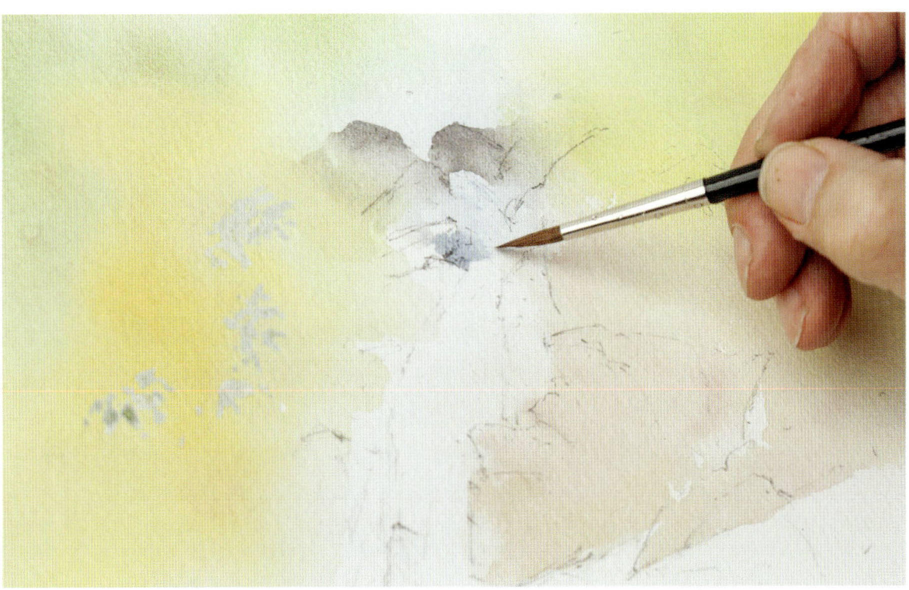

5 Mix burnt umber and French ultramarine to paint rocks at the top of the waterfall. Fade the lower edges. Use the no. 6 round and French ultramarine to hint at falling water.

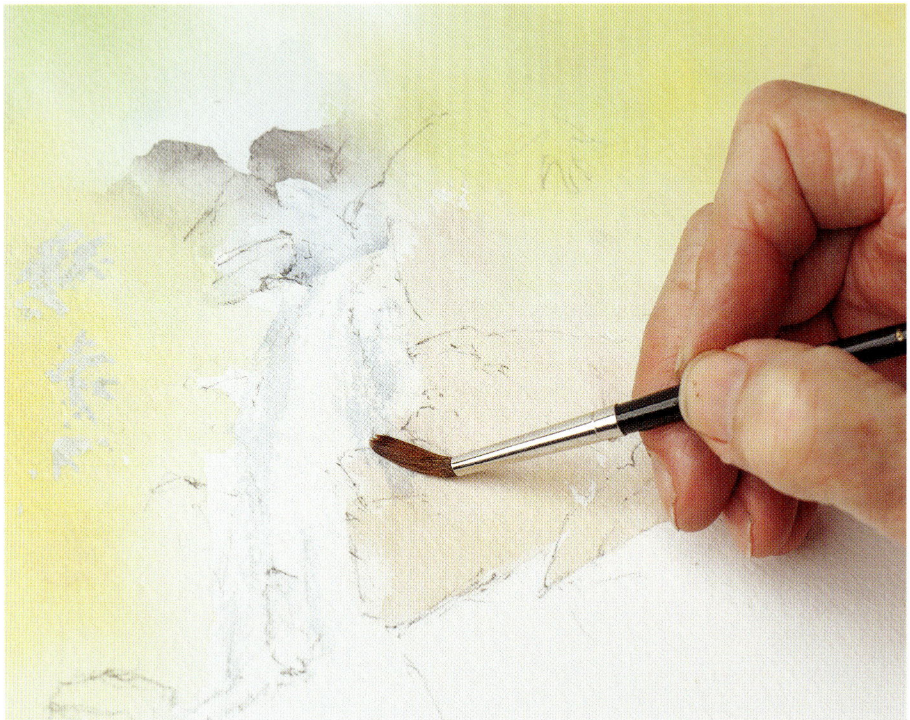

6 With the same mix, drag a dry brush along the edges of the waterfall to suggest rushing water. The dry-brush technique creates a speckled effect with the Rough paper.

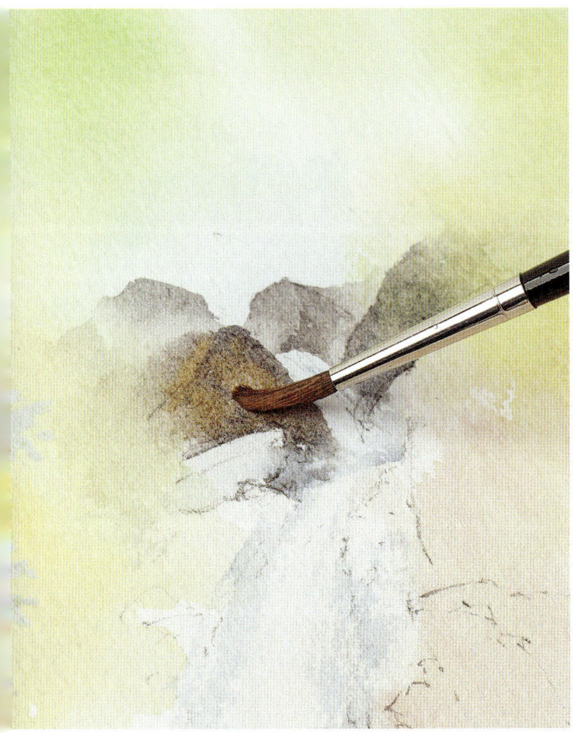

7 Work on the rocks on either side of the waterfall with French ultramarine and burnt umber. Fade off the edges with a damp brush where the rocks enter the water, then drop in yellow ochre to create texture. Allow to dry.

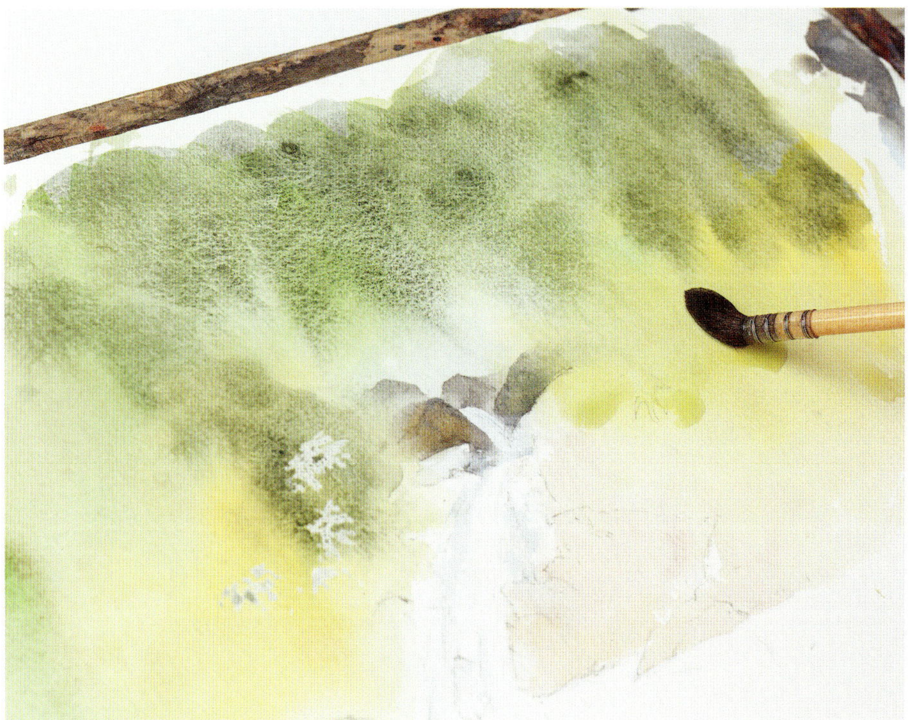

8 Paint over the whole background with a squirrel mop and clean water, then paint on zoisite genuine, which will introduce more granulations as it flows down the paper, creating excellent effects for foliage. Drop cadmium yellow medium hue into the middle ground. Allow to dry naturally.

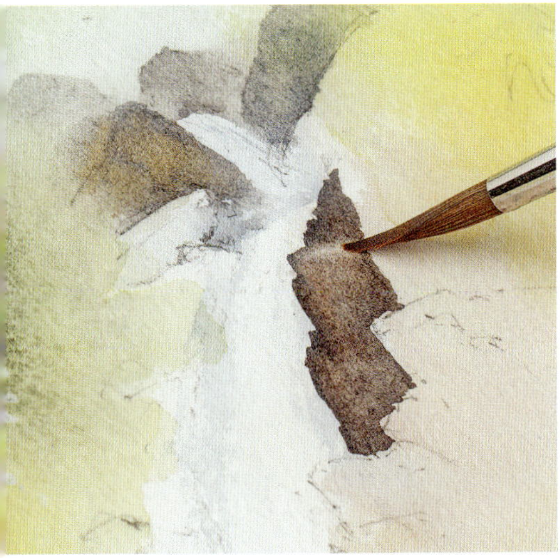

9 Use the no. 8 round brush to paint rocks to the right of the waterfall with French ultramarine and burnt umber. Drop in transparent red oxide while the rocks are wet, then use a damp brush tip to pull out colour where the light catches the rocks.

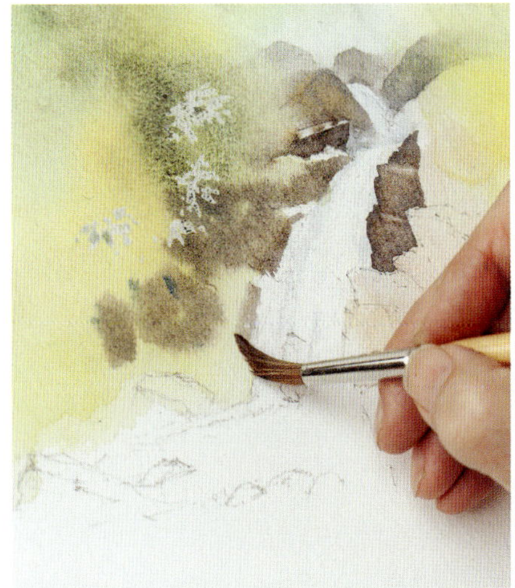

10 Change to the no. 6 brush to paint detail on the left of the waterfall with French ultramarine and burnt umber. Then use the no. 8 brush to wet the area just below this and drop in the same mix.

11 Pick up nickel titanate yellow on the brush and pull back the bristles to spatter this into this wet brown area. Dot in the same colour wet into wet using the masking fluid brush, then spatter on clean water with an old toothbrush to create a mottled effect.

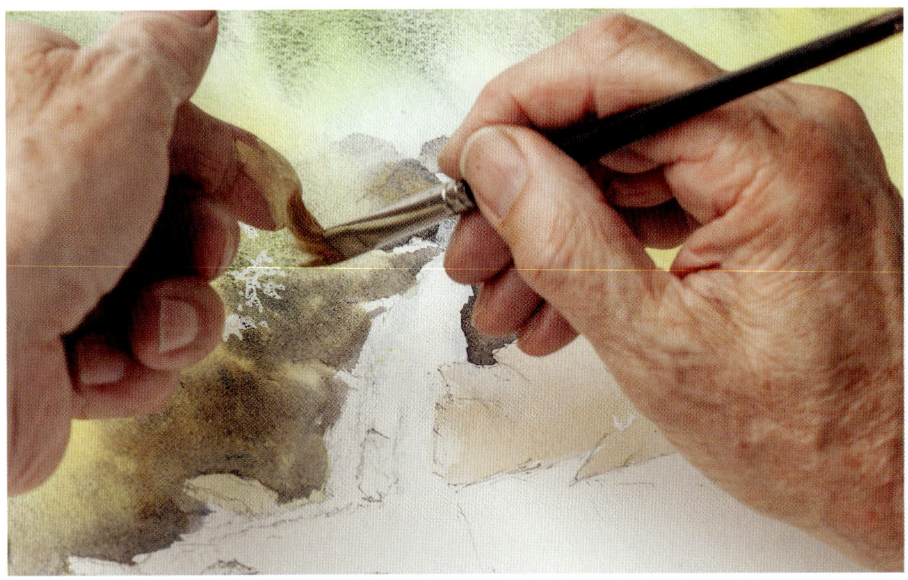

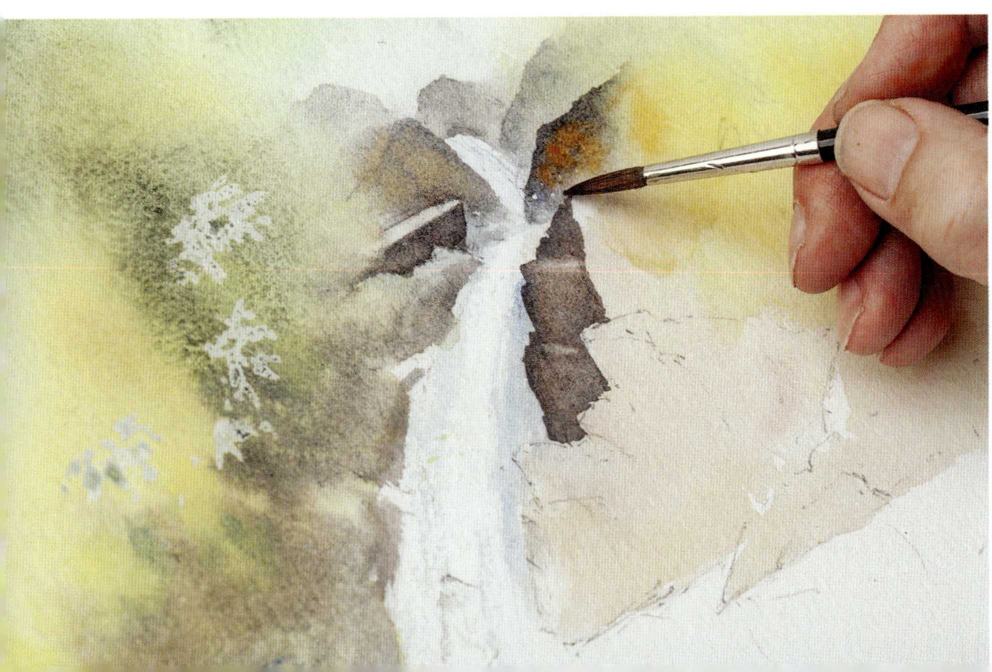

12 Reinforce the falling water with French ultramarine and the dry-brush technique, using an old synthetic brush. Leave most of it as white paper. Paint darker rock on the right of the waterfall with a no. 6 brush and burnt umber with French ultramarine, then drop in Aussie red gold wet into wet to bring this rock forwards, creating depth.

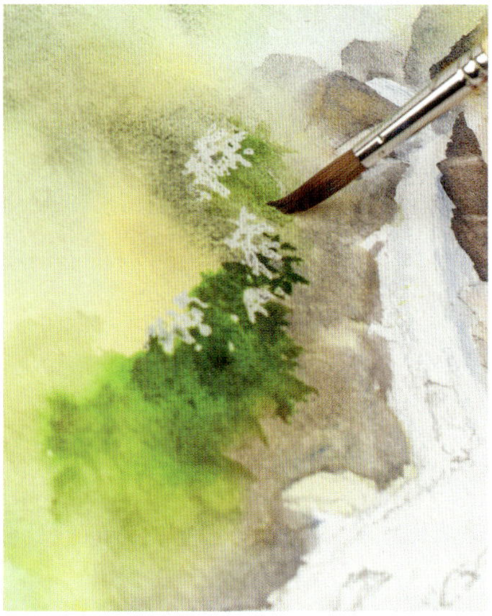

13 Use the no. 8 brush to paint green apatite genuine on the left of the waterfall, around the masked-out foliage.

14 Paint rock detail on the left with the no. 6 brush and French ultramarine and burnt umber. Drop in yellow ochre wet into wet and add this colour to the foliage area too.

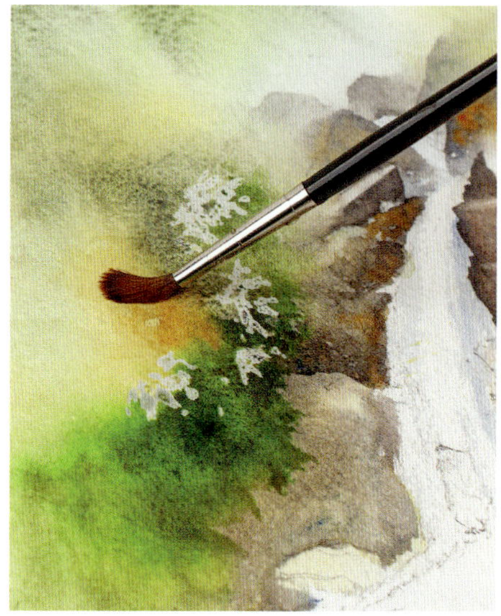

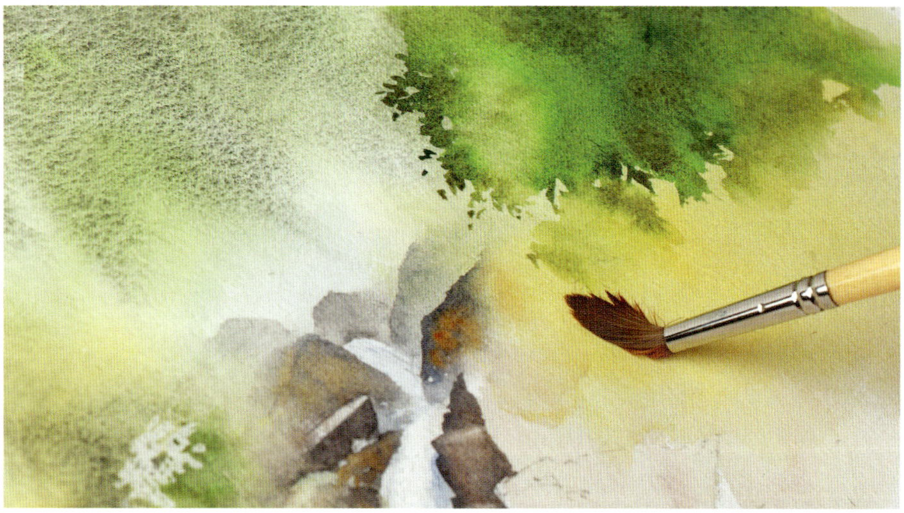

15 Use the squirrel mop to paint green apatite genuine on the right of the painting, then the no. 8 brush to paint foliage detail at the edges of the area. Paint nickel titanate yellow below this area and allow the wet green to run into it.

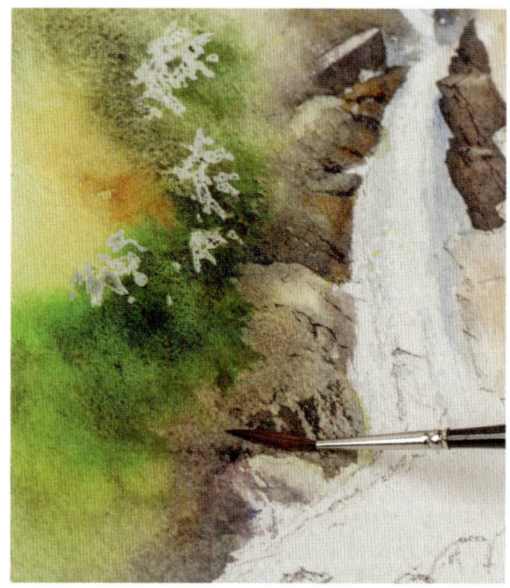

16 With a rigger and sodalite genuine and burnt umber, paint fracture lines in the rocks on both sides of the fall, varying the pressure applied. Use the brush on its side to create texture with dry-brushwork.

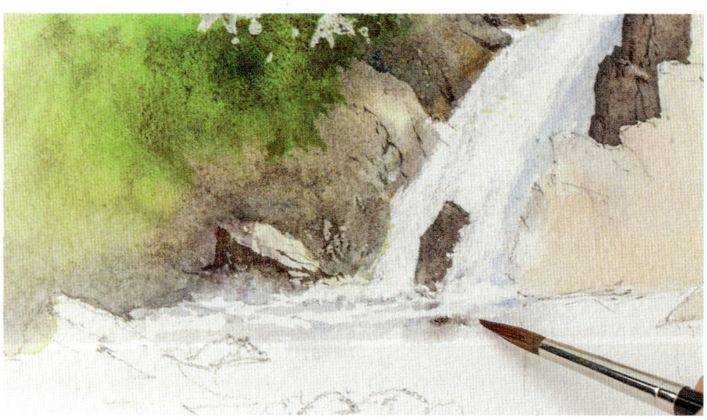

17 Pick up cobalt blue and paint the flat water at the bottom of the waterfall. Use French ultramarine and burnt umber to paint the rock in the middle of the waterfall. Paint the water splashing into the pool with a touch of French ultramarine. Indicate the transition between the foam and the darker pool with French ultramarine, then drop in a reflection with the rock colours wet into wet. Allow the painting to dry.

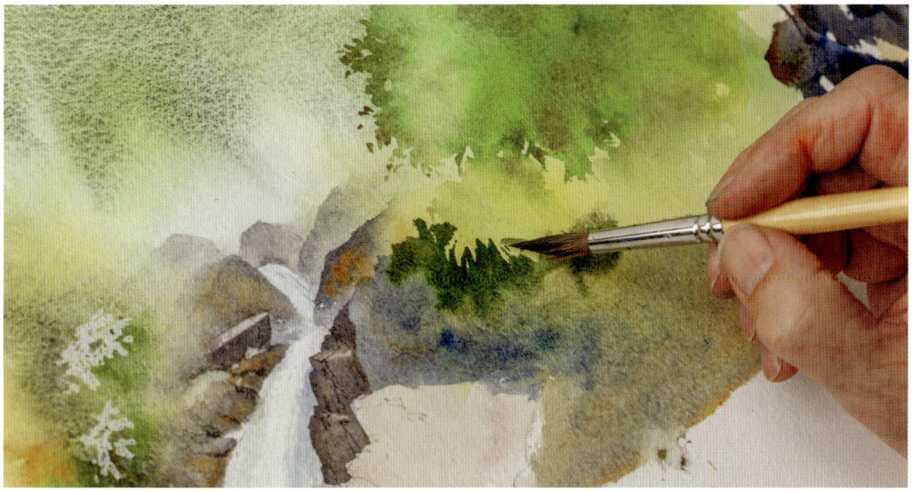

18 Use the no. 8 brush to paint a blue mix of French ultramarine with a little burnt umber to form a contrasting dark area below the light foliage on the right. Drop in yellow ochre wet into wet. Mix sodalite genuine and green apatite genuine and work negatively, painting leaf shapes with the tip of the brush. Lose some edges using a damp brush.

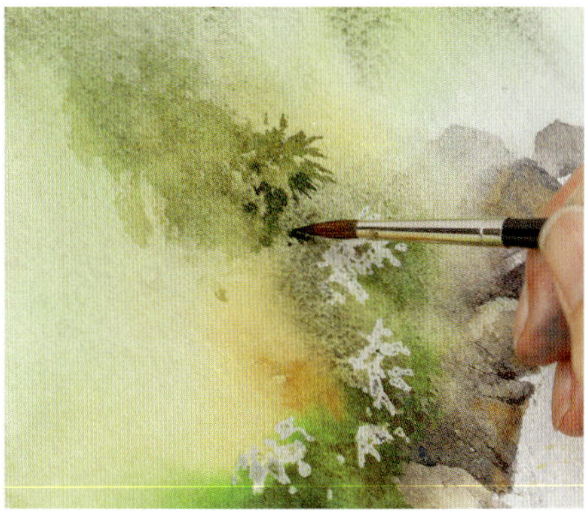

19 Change to a no. 6 brush and paint foliage shapes on the left with the same mix.

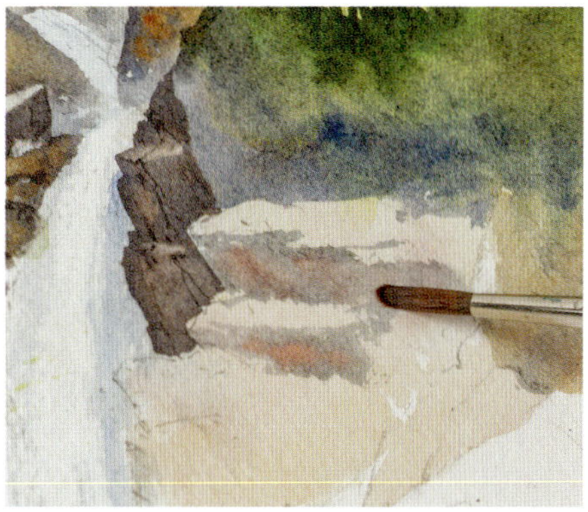

20 Make a weak mix of French ultramarine and burnt umber and paint the shadow and detail on the reddish rock to the right of the waterfall. Drop in alizarin crimson wet into wet.

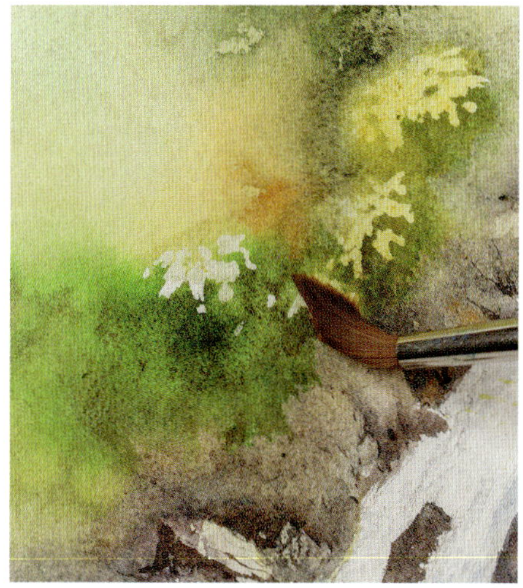

21 Use the same method to model some of the rocks on the left. Rub off the masking fluid in the foliage area. Use a damp 13mm (½in) flat brush to soften some edges, then use a no. 8 brush and cadmium yellow medium hue to colour the previously masked areas. Add green apatite genuine in places. Allow to dry.

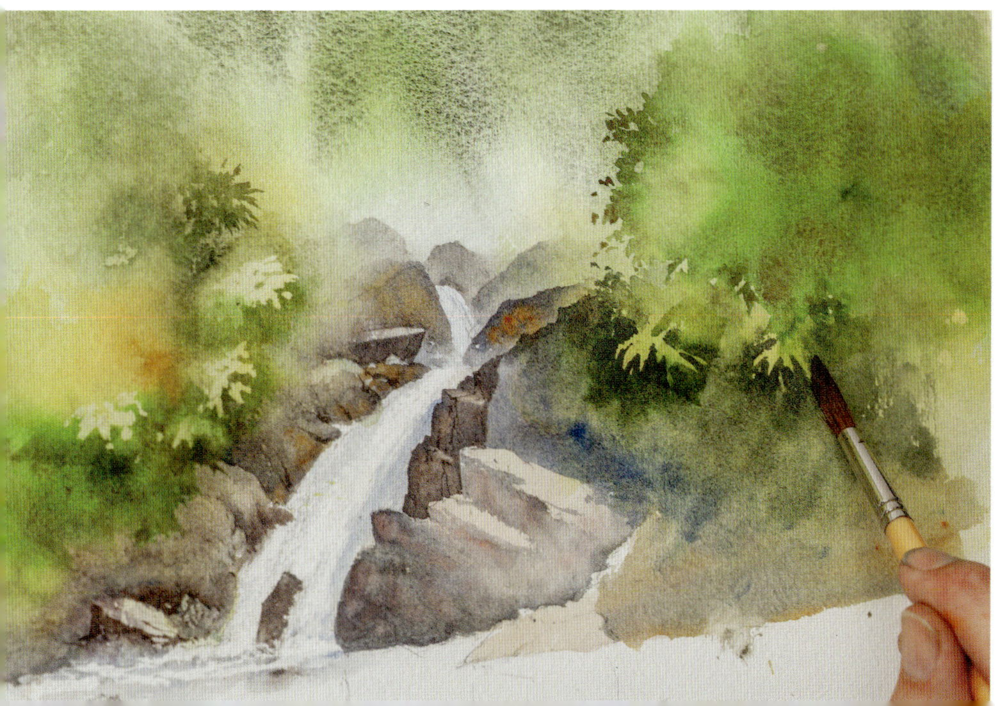

22 On the right of the waterfall, reduce the starkness of the foliage shapes painted negatively with a wash of green apatite genuine.

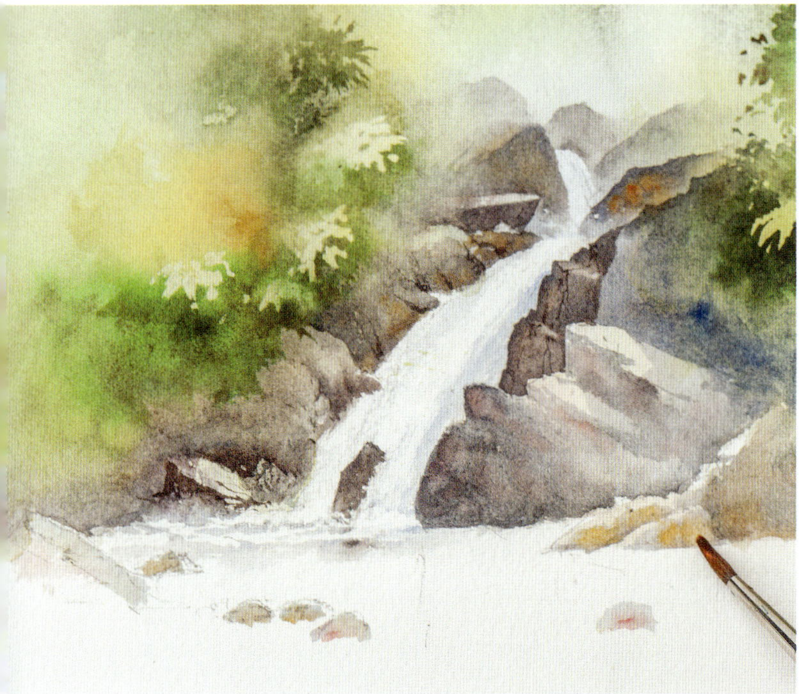

23 Paint the rocks in the stream with the no. 6 brush and a pale mix of French ultramarine and burnt umber. Drop in various colours including yellow ochre and alizarin crimson. Paint the shadow of the rocks at the back of the stream in the same way and drop in Aussie red gold.

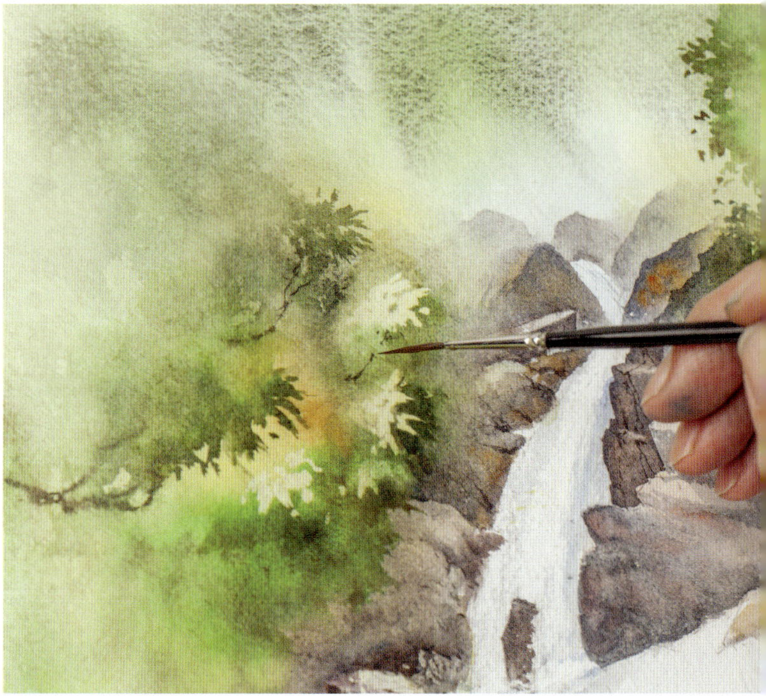

24 Work on the foliage on the left with green apatite genuine, then add sodalite genuine to the mix to tighten up and sharpen details. Mix sodalite genuine and burnt umber to paint branches with the rigger.

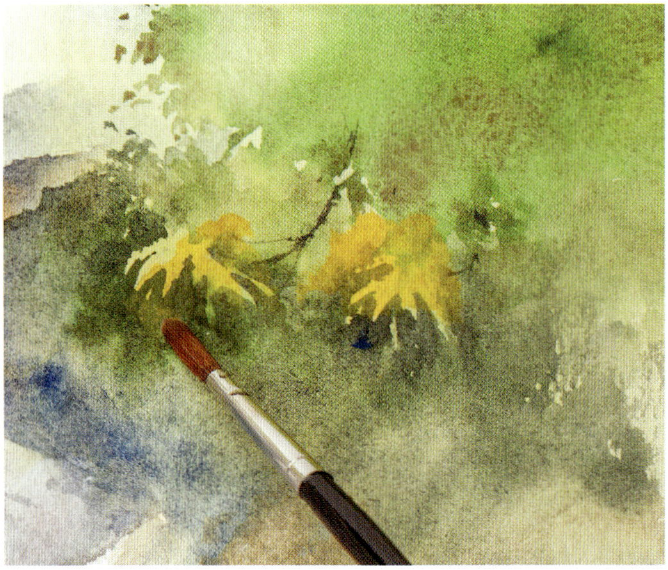

25 Work on the foliage on the left with green apatite genuine, then add sodalite genuine to the mix to tighten up and sharpen details. Mix sodalite genuine and burnt umber to paint branches with the rigger.

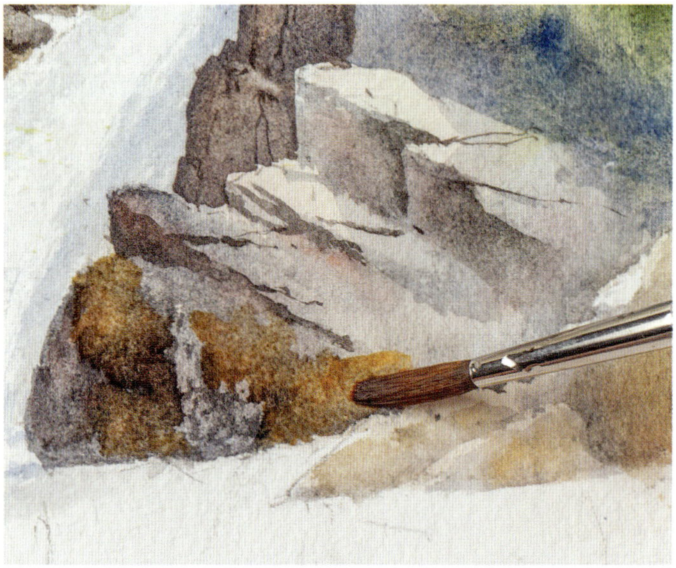

26 Work on details in the rock with a mix of sodalite genuine and burnt umber, then paint fracture lines with the rigger. Drop in Aussie red gold with the no. 8 brush.

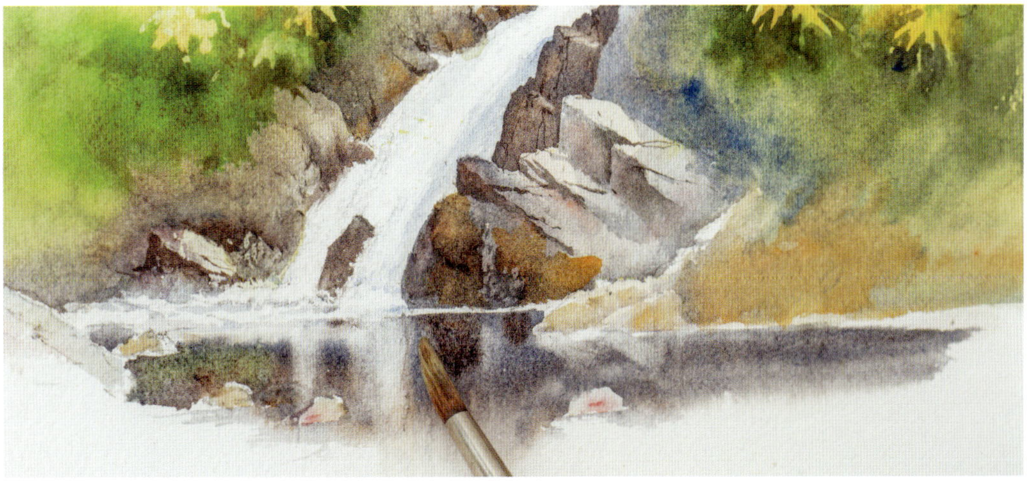

27 Wet the dark area of the pool with clean water, then paint horizontal strokes of burnt umber and French ultramarine. Use a no. 10 brush to drop in touches of colour for reflections: green apatite genuine and sodalite genuine with burnt umber. Work round the light rocks.

28 Paint details on the rocks on the right of the waterfall with the rigger and the same mix, then use the no. 6 brush to paint green apatite genuine to build up the colour of the foliage.

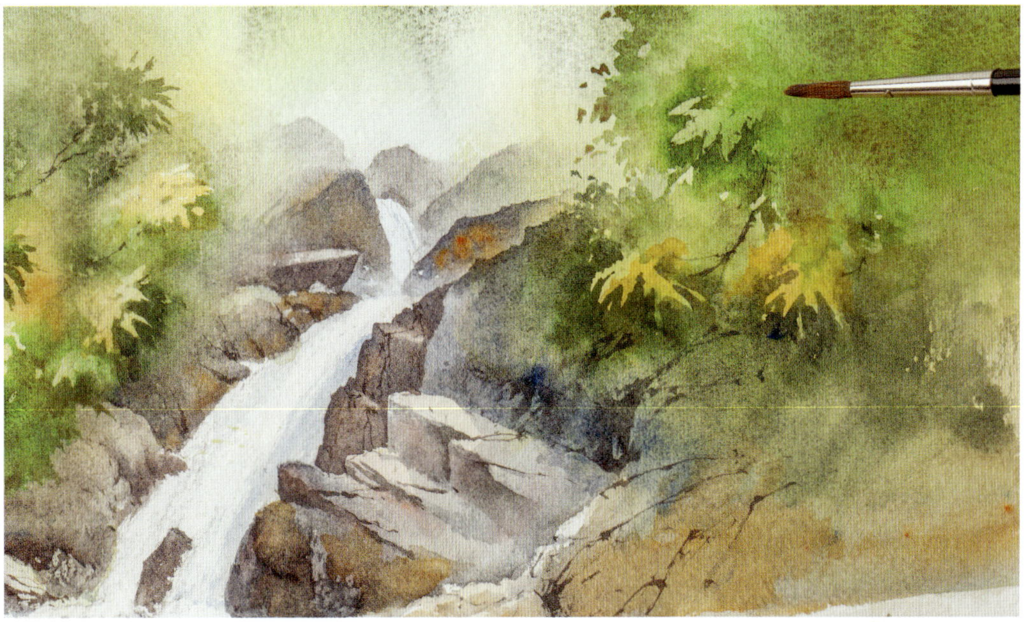

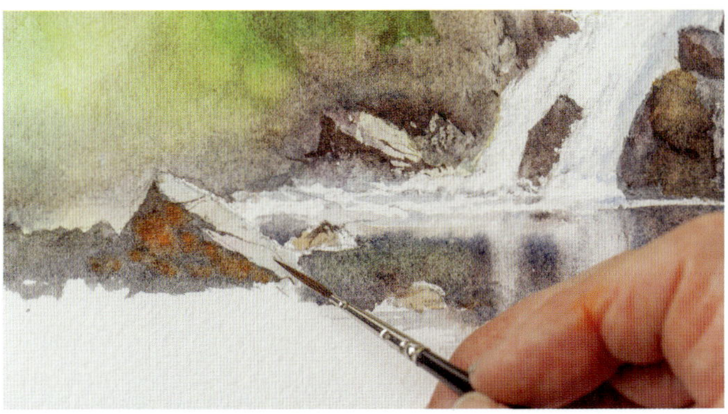

29 Use the rigger with sodalite genuine and burnt umber to paint the rock on the left of the stream. Drop in yellow ochre, then paint the lit side of the rock with alizarin crimson.

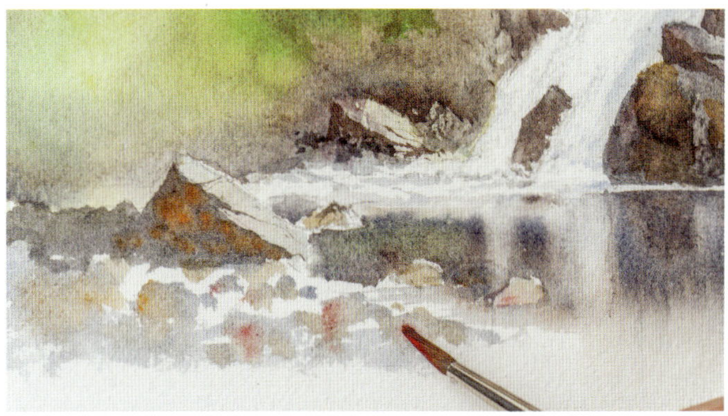

30 With the no. 6 brush, paint stones in the stream with French ultramarine and a little burnt umber, then drop in yellow ochre and alizarin crimson to create variety.

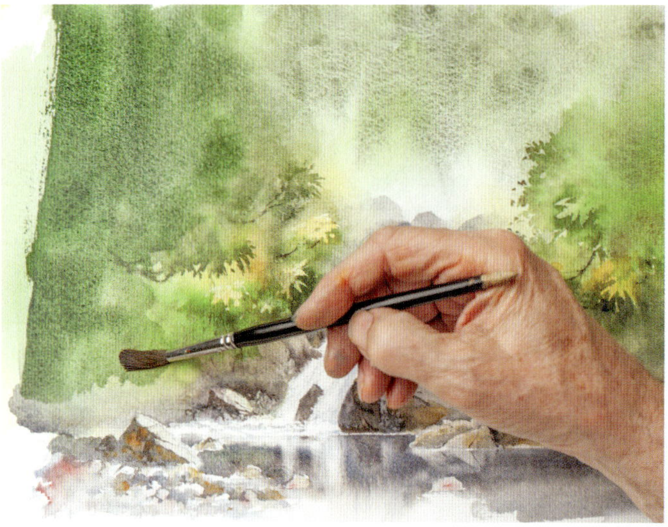

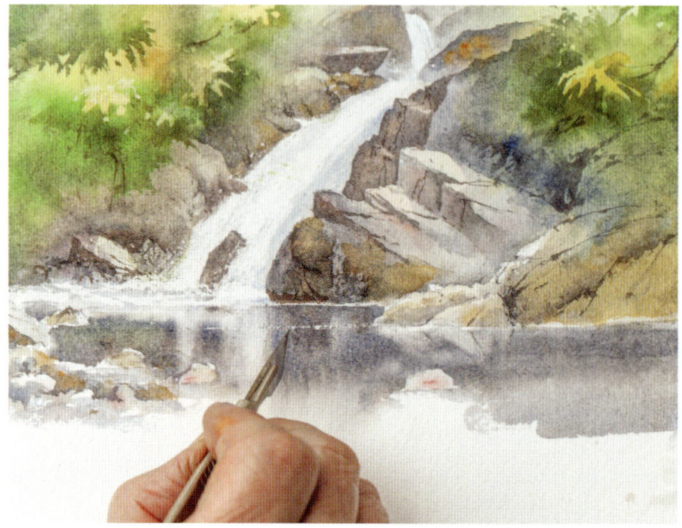

31 Use the rigger with French ultramarine and burnt umber to tighten up details. Use the no. 6 brush to add colour to the left-hand stones. I then assessed the painting within a mount. I decided to extend the dark water to the right by wetting it with a sponge and painting with French ultramarine and burnt umber. I darkened the left-hand foliage with sodalite genuine and green apatite genuine.

32 Use a scalpel to flick out white highlights from the splashing water at the foot of the waterfall, then scratch out horizontal ripples.

*The finished painting.*

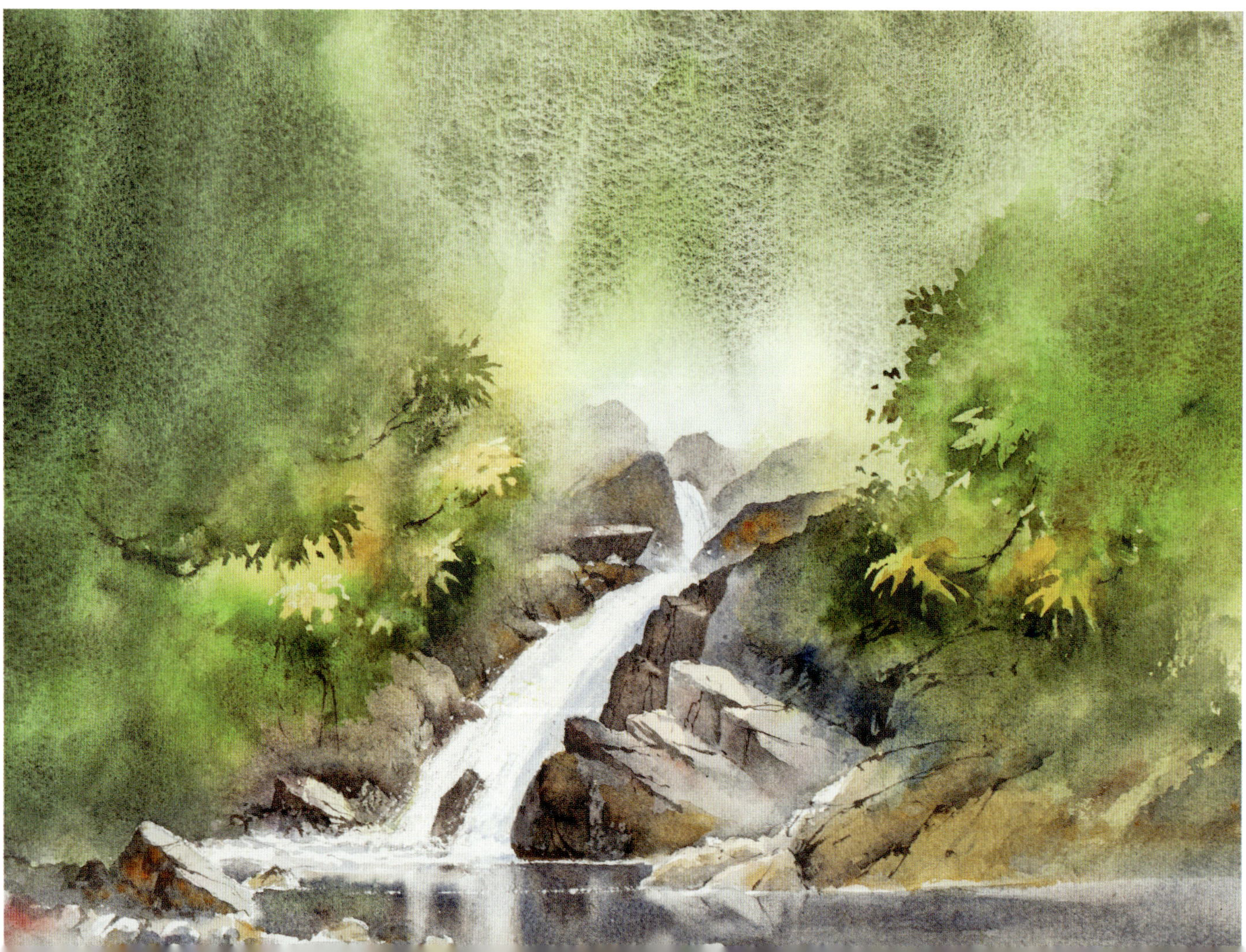

## LIMITED COLOURS FOR MOOD

A limited palette creates a feeling of unity, mood and drama. Backlighting will accentuate this. The painting can appear dull if you are using muted colours. Ensuring that you have really strong tonal contrasts, especially around the focal point, will add interest.

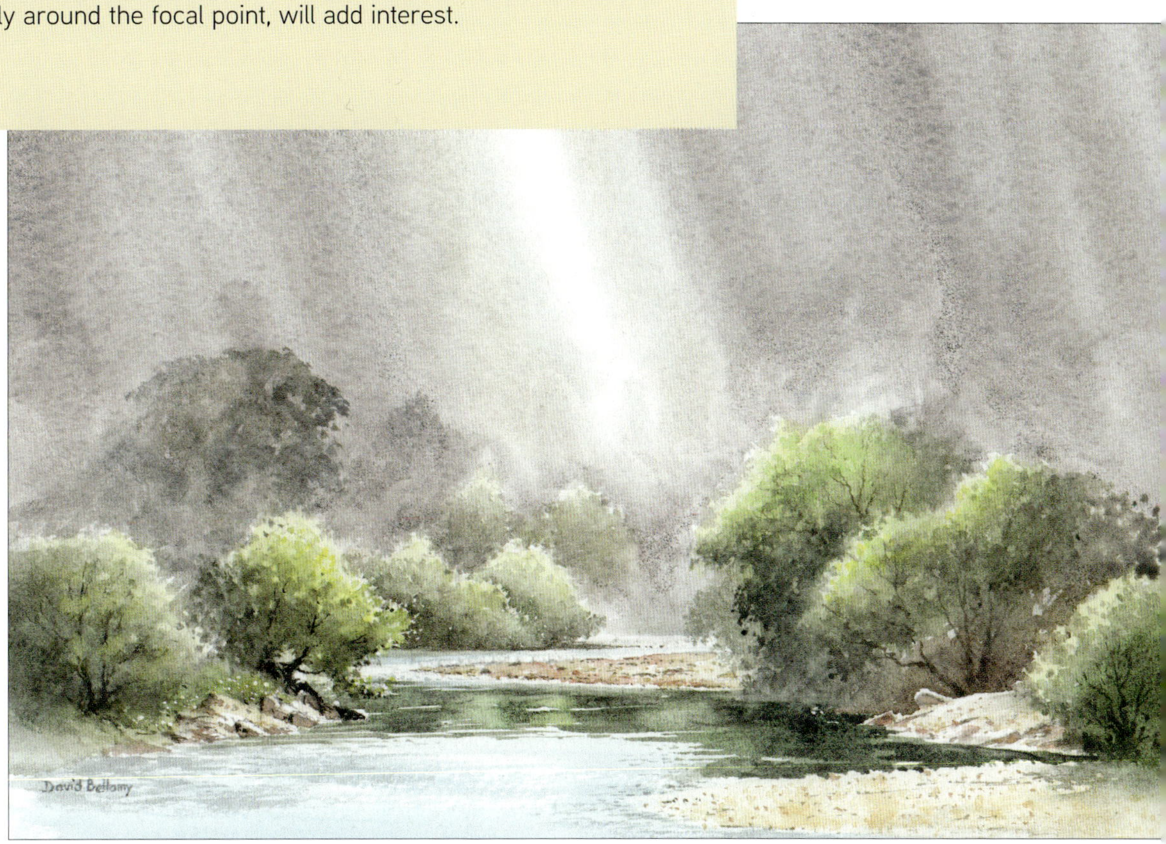


RIVER USK
*18 x 24cm (7 x 9½in), 300gsm (140lb) Not paper*

*The sky was painted with lunar blue and cadmium red, bringing in a touch of nickel titanate yellow down the centre. The misty background hides a lot of distracting detail. I also applied nickel titanate yellow onto the tree masses. The background trees were suggested with lunar blue and cadmium yellow light and the closer ones with green apatite genuine and cadmium yellow light. The shadows were created with lunar blue and green apatite genuine, and the dark trunks and branches with burnt umber and lunar blue. Lunar blue helps create unity in the painting.*

COTTAGES ON THE CLIFFS
*20 x 30.5cm (8 x 12in), 640gsm (300lb) Not paper*

*Here I've used muted colours for mood, but then dropped weak cadmium red into the phthalo blue and yellow ochre background in places. This warms up the landscape without overpowering it. The darker patches are phthalo blue with burnt umber. For the foreground cliffs, I used weak mixes of yellow ochre and alizarin crimson, with French ultramarine and burnt umber in places.*

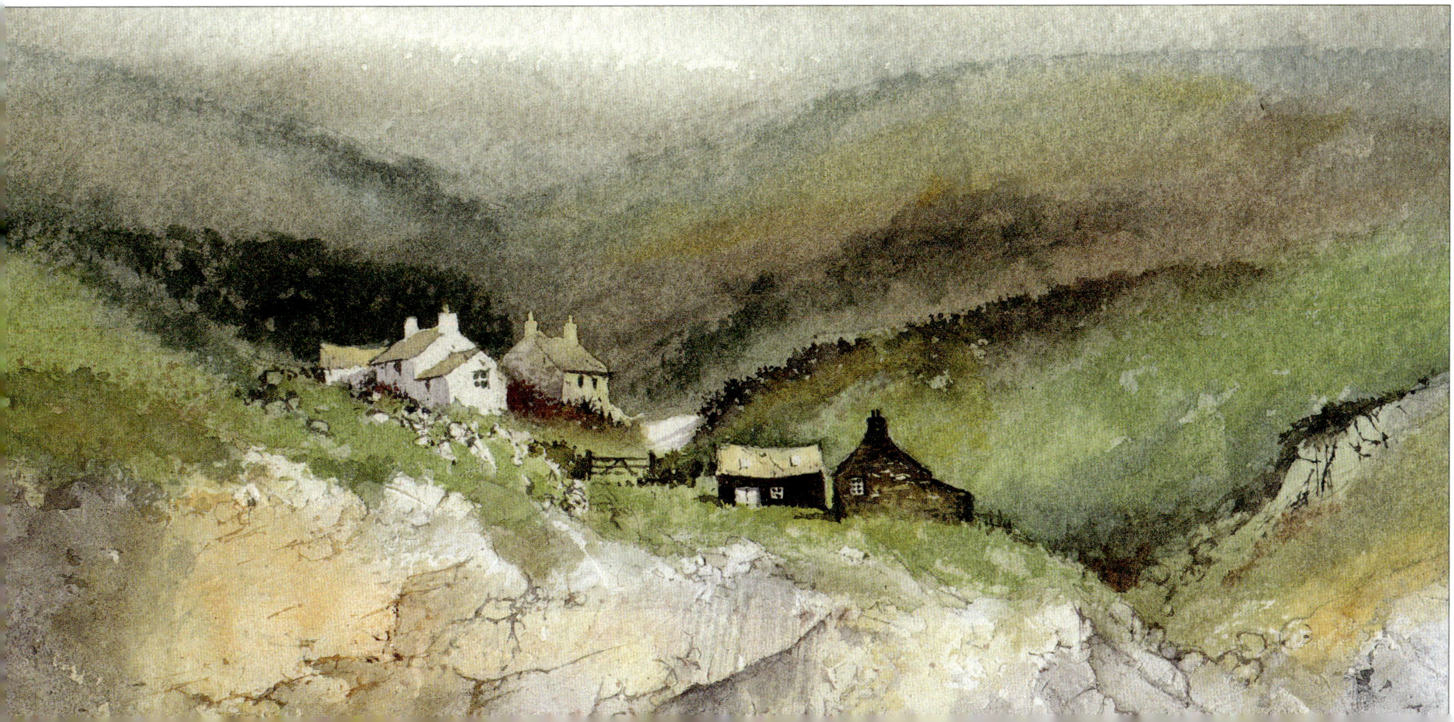

## SPOT COLOUR AND INTENSE LIGHT

Sometimes you may wish to create a warm patch of colour around your focal point, and often a spot of colour will suffice to lift a painting and completely change the mood. Don't hesitate to exaggerate the warmth of the colour.

When you want to suggest a scene bathed in brilliant sunshine, reduce detail, as intense light tends to bleach it out. If you include all these effects for creating a sunny subject, it will suggest a hot day. Strong tonal contrasts and cast shadows also enhance this.

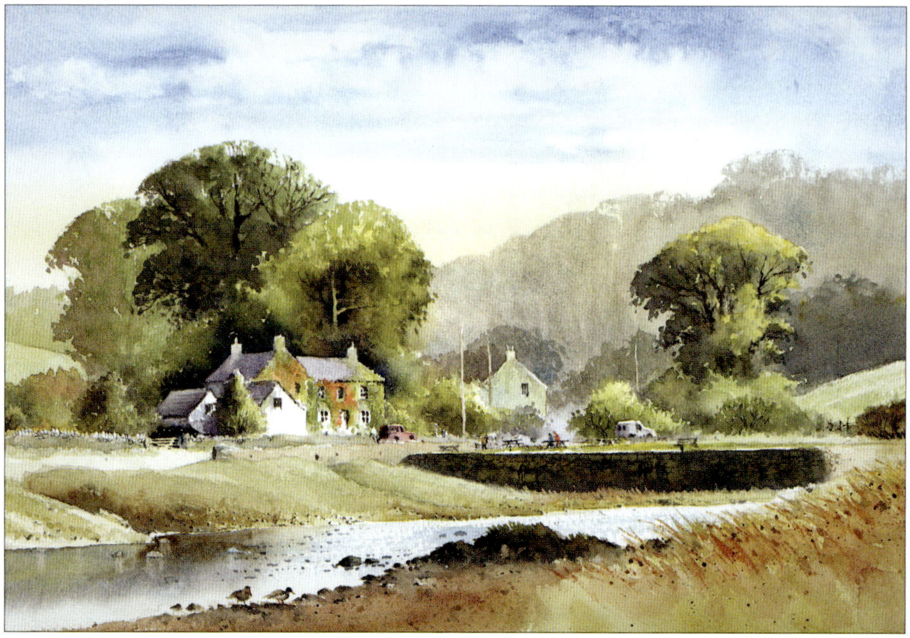

CRESSWELL QUAY
*23 x 30.5cm (9 x 12in), 300gsm (140lb) Not paper*

*Where there is an overwhelming amount of green, it helps to inject a spot of contrasting colour to breathe life into the work. Here the red ivy on the pub does this, particularly as it is a complementary colour to green.*

ABINGER HAMMER

*Nestling below the North Downs, this village is a pleasant spot in summer with lush vegetation breaking up the hard lines of the buildings. I began this sketch with a pen drawing on cartridge paper and then applied watercolour, making the bell tower the focal point. To the left of this, I kept the detail and colour low-key to emphasize the tower and right-hand houses. At the bottom of the bell tower, I slightly exaggerated the red, yellow and green patch to emphasize that spot. I kept most of the greens warm, and the strong shadows suggest a hot and sunny summer's day.*

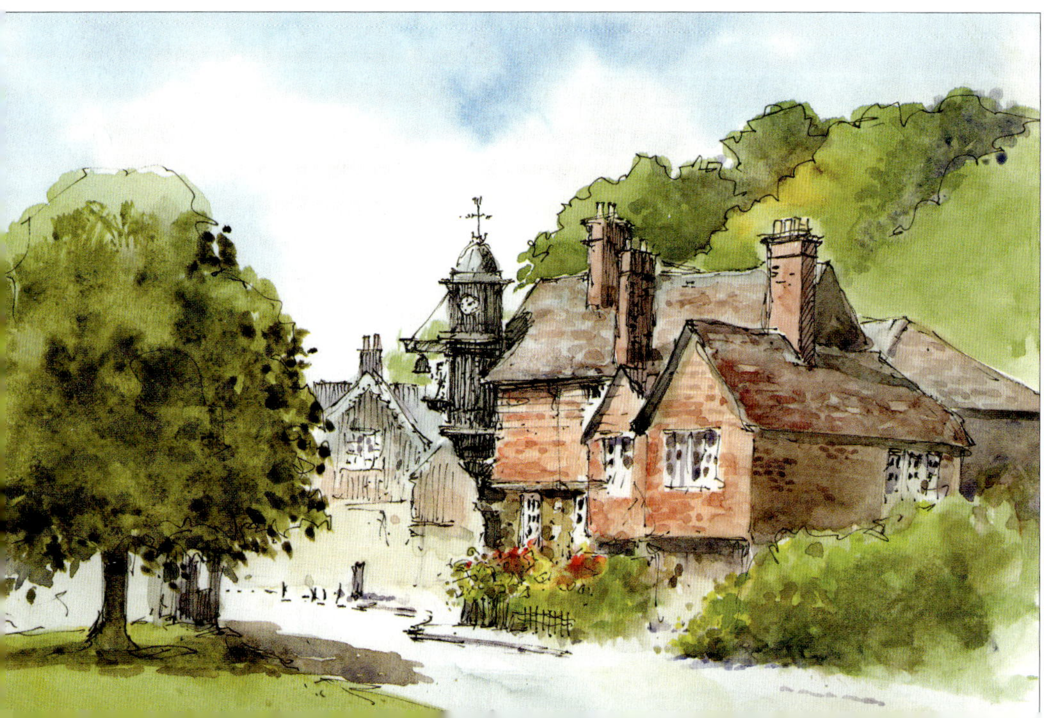

CONTROLLED LIGHTING

*In this small sketch, a spot of colour brings the scene to life as evening light hits sandstone crags high on the Sachsische Schweiz in eastern Germany. This 'spotlight' device adds interest and creates a striking focal point in a dramatic scene of sheer faces dropping into dark shadow.*

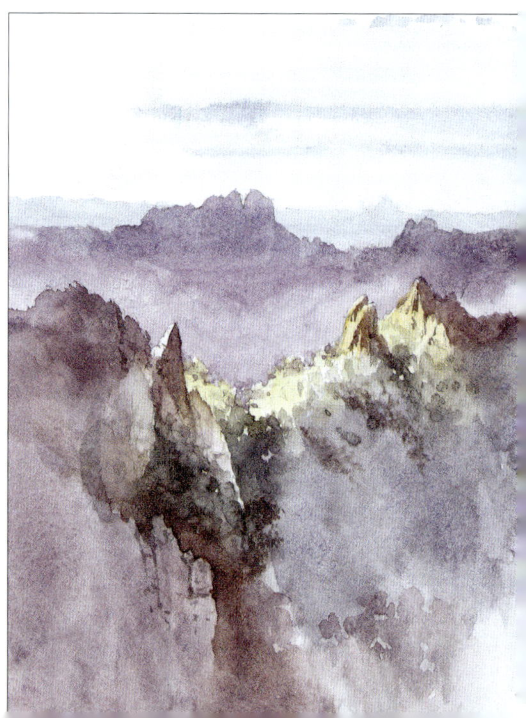

# TECHNIQUES FOR SUMMER FOREGROUNDS

Foregrounds can be simple, complicated or neutral, and many artists insist on hardly any detail here. However, you may wish to concentrate on the foreground, perhaps using it as your focal point with just a vague stand of trees or building in the distance to suggest the setting. If your middle distance is complicated, keep the foreground simple, perhaps just a plain wash and a hint of detail. You can enhance foregrounds with a puddle, wild flowers, rusting farm machinery in long grass, or whatever catches your imagination. Work these in from sketches and photographs from other scenes.

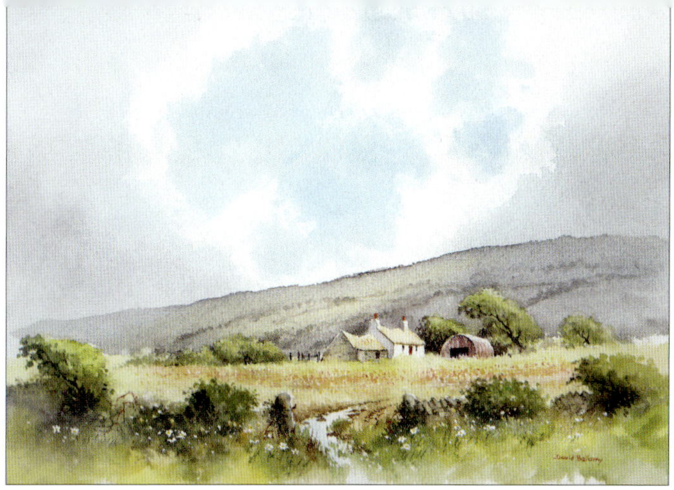

SUNSHINE AND SHADOWS

*23 x 30.5cm (9 x 12in) 300gsm (140lb) Not paper*

*Bringing lush vegetation up to cover walls and other foreground features conveys a sense of summer, and is useful for hiding complicated detail. Keep it simple and avoid covering the whole foreground. Here the long grasses obscure much of the dry-stone wall and the flowers punctuate the mass of vegetation to prevent this passage becoming monotonous. Cloud shadow across the foreground helps to highlight the more distant farmhouse and I have added some red in the field: grass is not always green, so try to observe these minute but effective points. Note how the hedgerows on the hillside are muted and intermittent to suggest distance.*

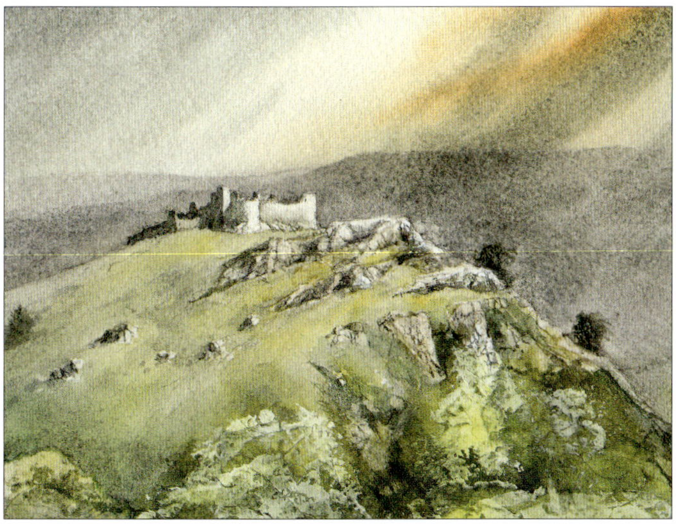

MIXED MEDIA FOREGROUNDS

*Foregrounds are an excellent place to introduce abstract elements or mixed media materials. In this scene I began by sticking a collage of small pieces of tissue-like oriental papers onto the watercolour paper in the immediate foreground. When these were completely dry, I plastered white Daniel Smith watercolour ground (similar to gesso) over parts of the collage with a painting knife, before allowing the area to dry completely for a day or two. I then painted the scene, with the collage and watercolour ground creating striking textures.*

### CREATING STALKS AND GRASSES

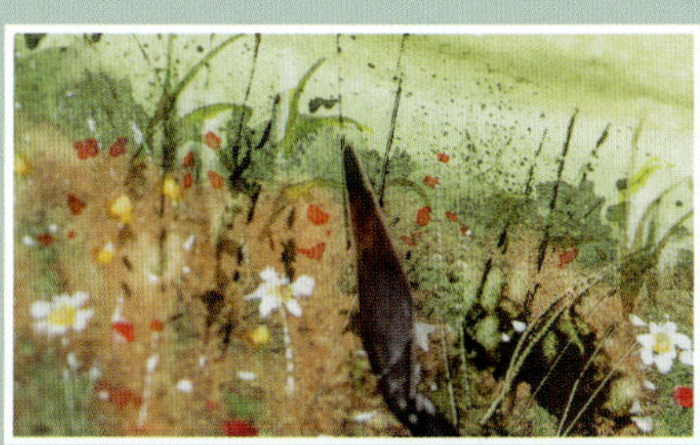

*Pick up paint on the edge of a painting knife, test it first on scrap paper, then press the edge onto the painting and drag it vertically down.*

### PULLING OUT LIGHT GRASSES IN A DAMP WASH

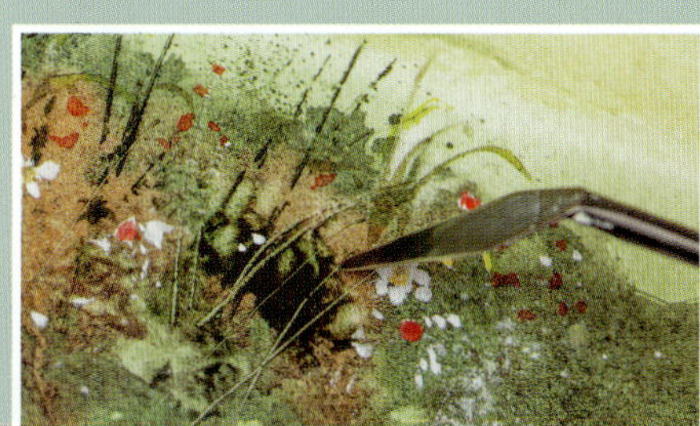

*Scratch out lines in damp, dark paint to create lighter stalks and grasses. The tip of the painting knife will not score the paper like a scalpel.*

### PULLING OUT COLOUR WITH A PAINTING KNIFE

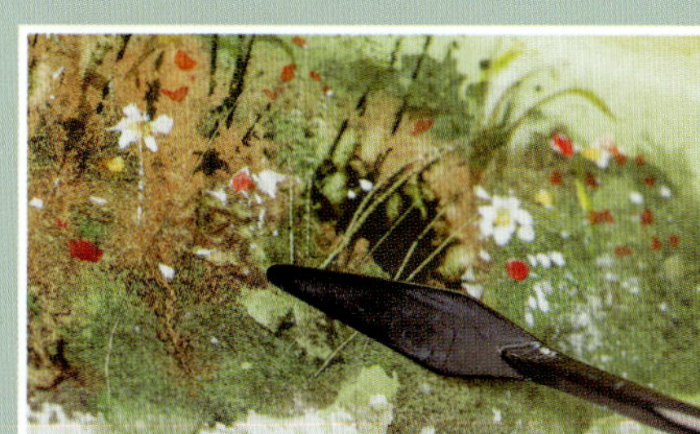

*Here the knife is scraped sideways in a damp, dark wash, removing an area of paint to suggest lighter vegetation or stones.*

# MOOR IN SUMMER

In this demonstration I show a simple approach to a North York Moors scene, with a misty background and weak sunlight falling on the focal point. The majority of buildings in this region have orange-tiled roofs, which I am keen to portray as it illustrates the local character. You may wish to use a lighter weight of paper than the heavy 640gsm (300lb) sheet I have worked on. The composition is based on a pencil sketch I did in an A5 (21 x 15cm/8¼ x 5¾in) cartridge sketchbook.

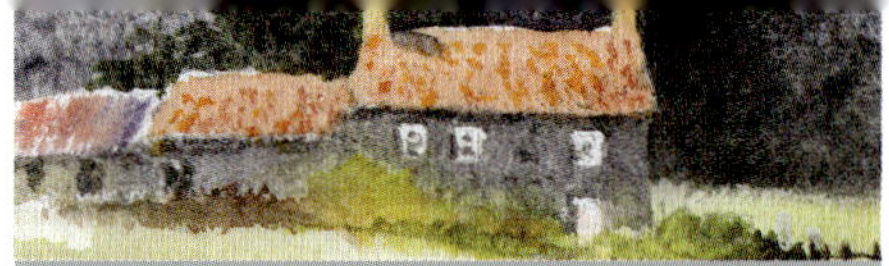

**MATERIALS USED**

Saunders Waterford 640gsm (300lb) Rough watercolour paper

Brushes: Squirrel mop, no. 6, no. 1 and no. 8 round, 6mm (¼in) flat, angled flat, rigger

Colours: Sodalite genuine, lunar blue, nickel titanate yellow, yellow ochre, transparent red oxide, cadmium red, green apatite genuine, cadmium yellow medium hue, cobalt blue, French ultramarine, burnt umber, zoisite genuine, Aussie red gold, alizarin crimson, titanium white gouache

Masking fluid, old brush, 5B pencil, wax candle, toothbrush, paper mask, plant spray bottle

Painting knife and scalpel

1 Use a 5B pencil to draw the main outlines of the scene. I referred to my field sketch.

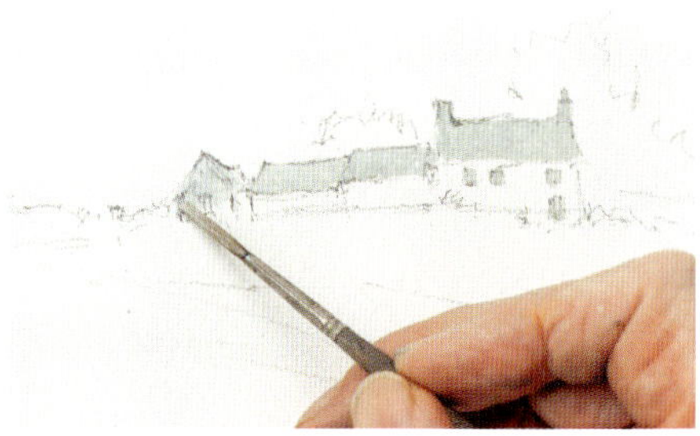

2 Mask the roofs, chimneys and windows and the odd fence post using masking fluid applied with an old brush.

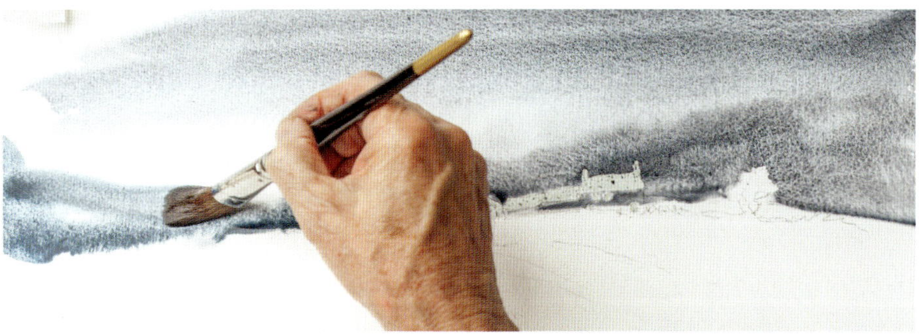

3 Sweep a white wax candle over part of the right side of the moor. The wax catches in the depressions of the Rough paper, creating a speckled resist. Using a squirrel mop, brush clean water over the sky and masked roofs. Paint a wash of sodalite genuine across the sky, leaving a lighter streak, then add lunar blue on the left.

4 Add a touch of nickel titanate yellow to the lighter streak in the sky. Take out any excess water using a barely damp brush, then allow the painting to dry naturally.

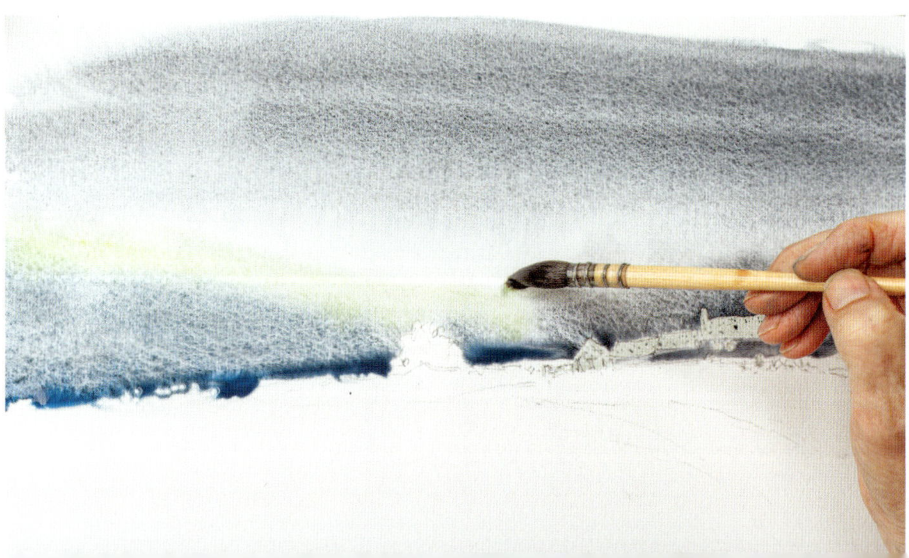

5 Wash nickel titanate yellow across the top of the moor area and float in yellow ochre lower down. While this is wet, dab in rogue colours: transparent red oxide, then cadmium red. The paint reveals the texture created by the wax resist.

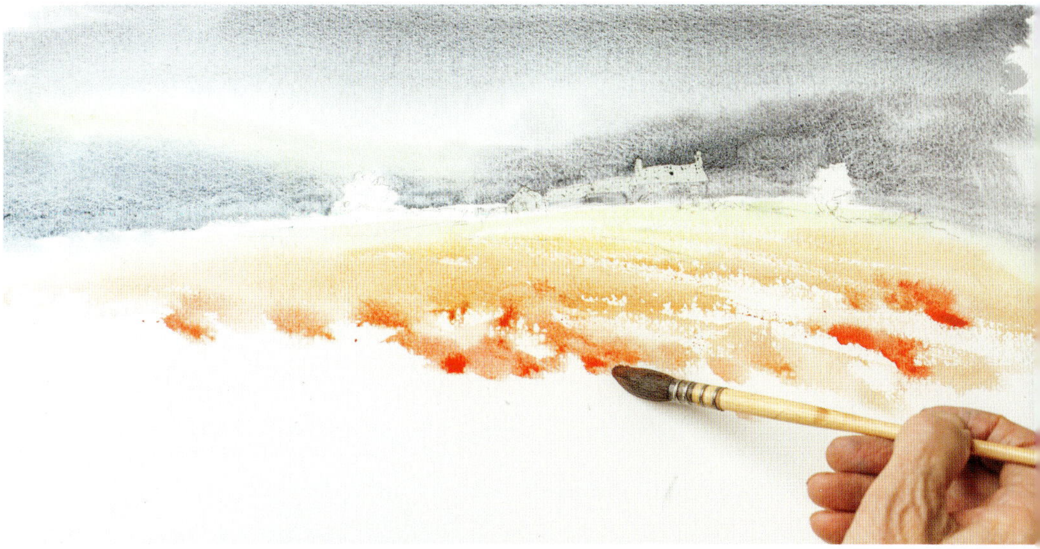

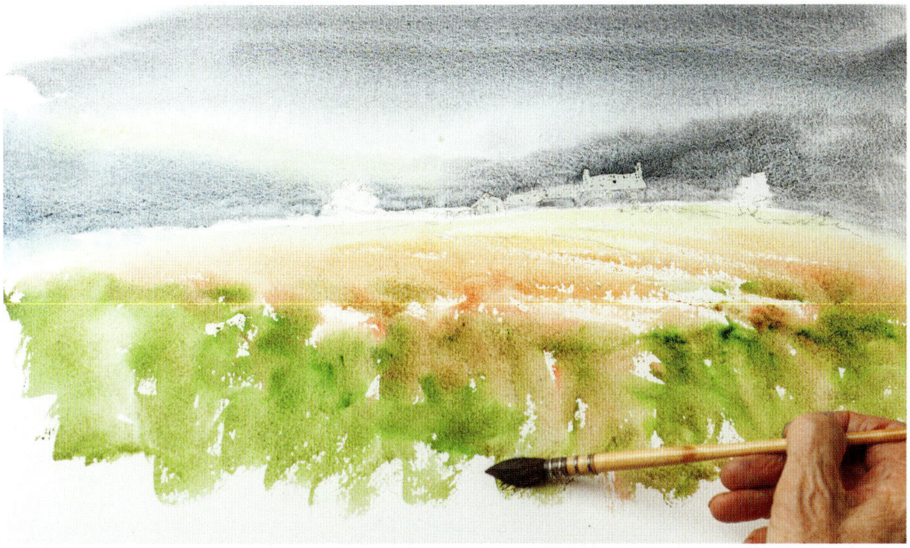

6 Dab green apatite genuine into the area while it is wet. Spray on some clean water from the plant spray bottle to create a speckled texture, then allow to dry naturally.

7 Use the no. 6 brush to paint cadmium yellow medium hue with a touch of green apatite genuine onto the hedgerow in front of the buildings. Paint the trees with the same colour, adding a darker, greener shade to the shadowed sides.

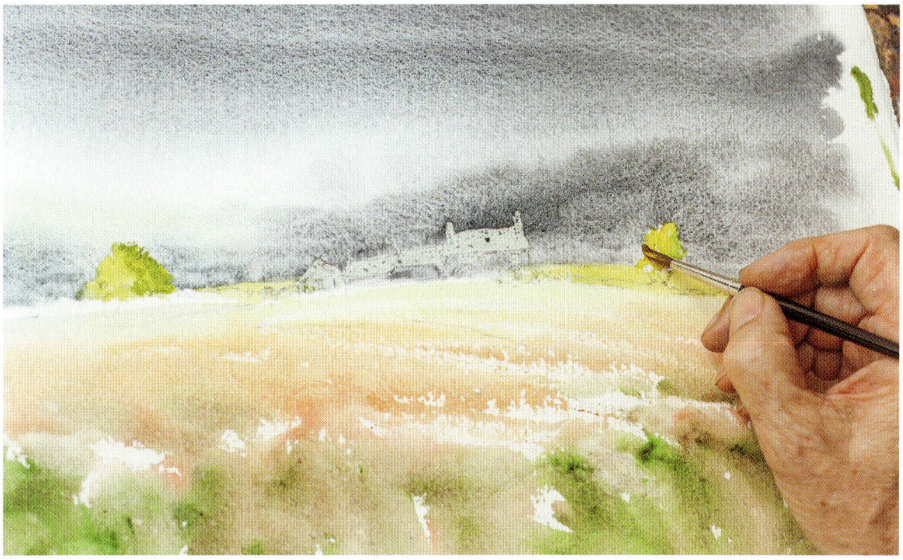

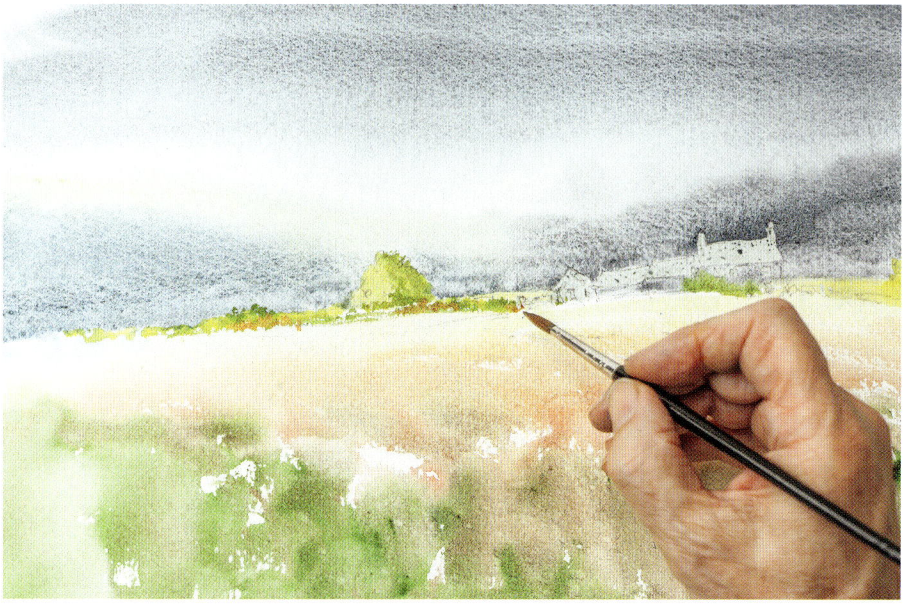

8 Dab touches of the darker green mix into the hedgerow and in front of the house. Drop in a little transparent red oxide in places to vary the effect.

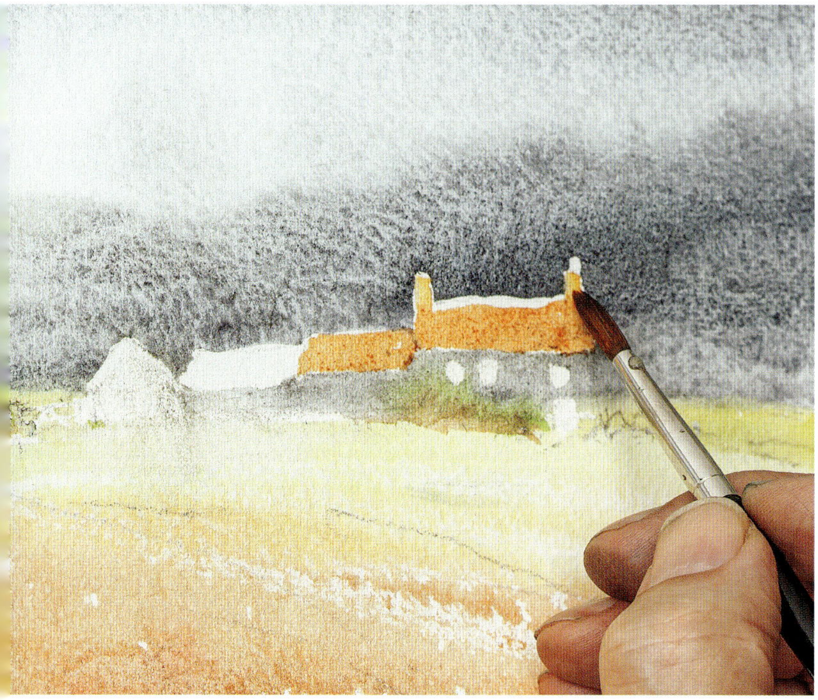

9 When the painting is dry, rub off the masking fluid with a clean finger. Tidy the edges with a damp 6mm (¼in) flat brush. Paint the house roof and chimneys with yellow ochre, then transparent red oxide.

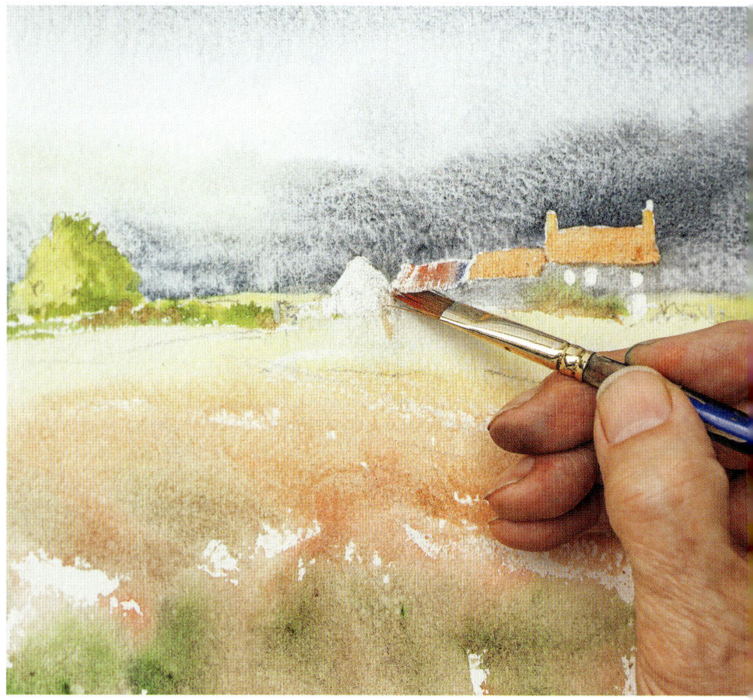

10 Take the angled flat brush and pick up cadmium red on one side and cobalt blue on the other. Separate the hairs and stroke down to create the corrugated iron roof of the building next to the house.

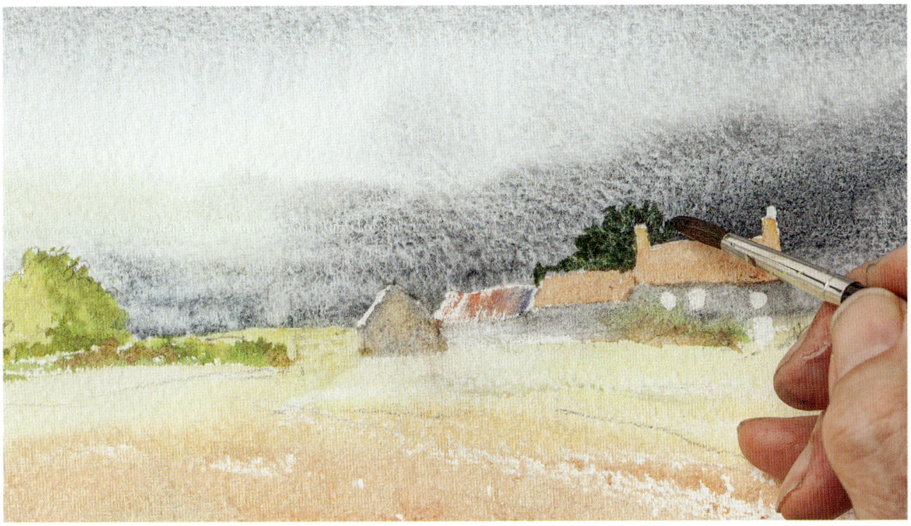

11 With the no. 6 round, paint the building on the far left with a pale mix of French ultramarine and burnt umber, leaving an edge to suggest light catching the roof edge. Drop in yellow ochre wet into wet and allow to dry. Bring out the brightness of the roofs by painting the trees behind with a dark mix of sodalite genuine and zoisite genuine.

12 Paint over the main house again with sodalite genuine and drop in yellow ochre. Shade the right-hand side of the tree with zoisite genuine.

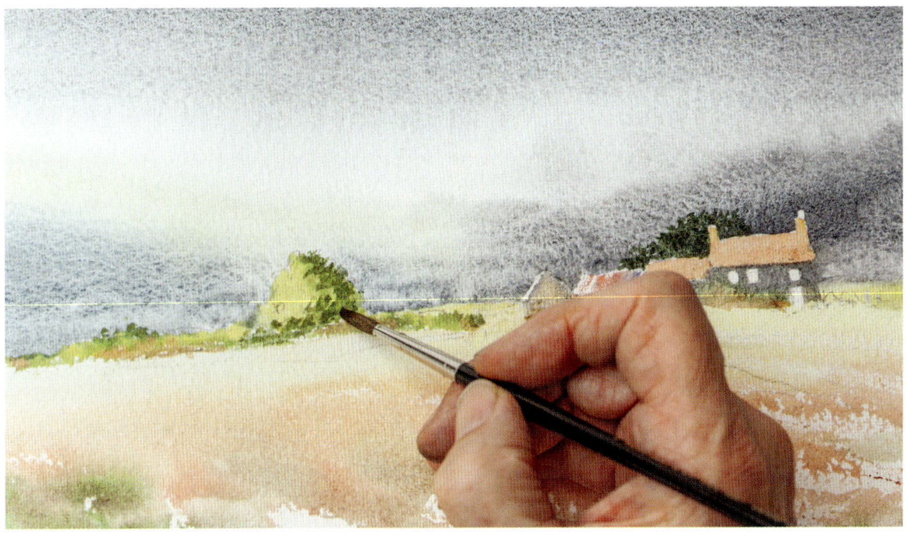

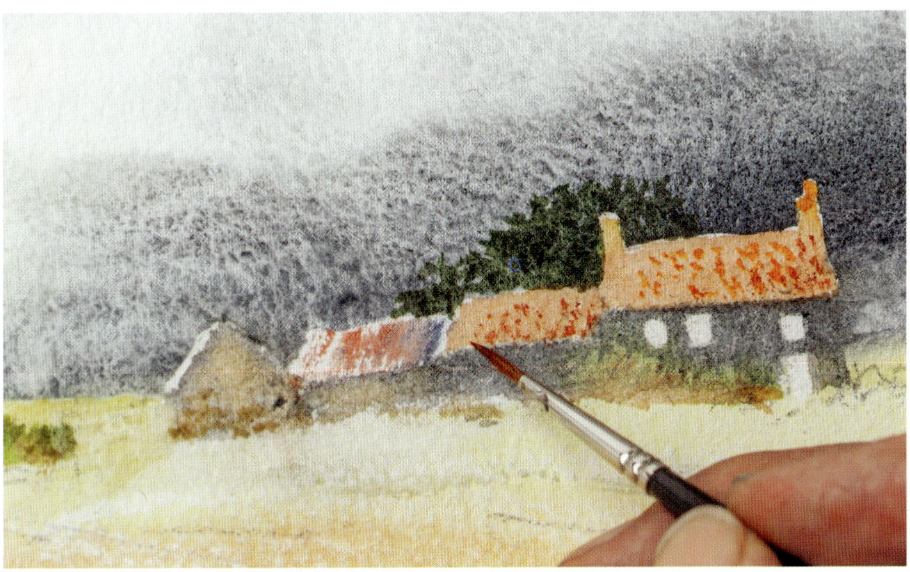

13 Change to the no. 1 brush and paint the chimney pot with Aussie red gold, then add dabs of this and cadmium red to texture the roofs.

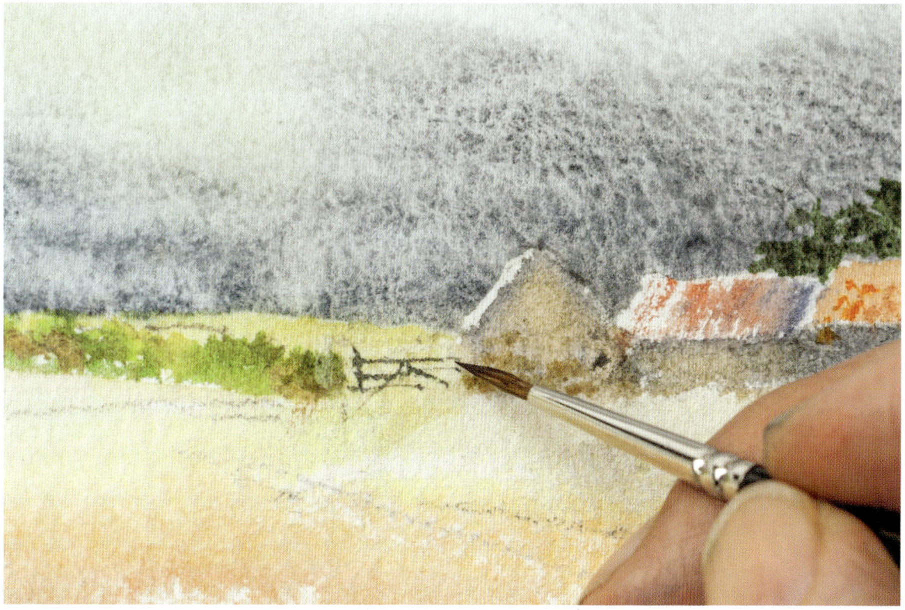

14 At this distance it is fine to suggest a five-bar gate with only two-and-a-half bars or so – do this with sodalite genuine.

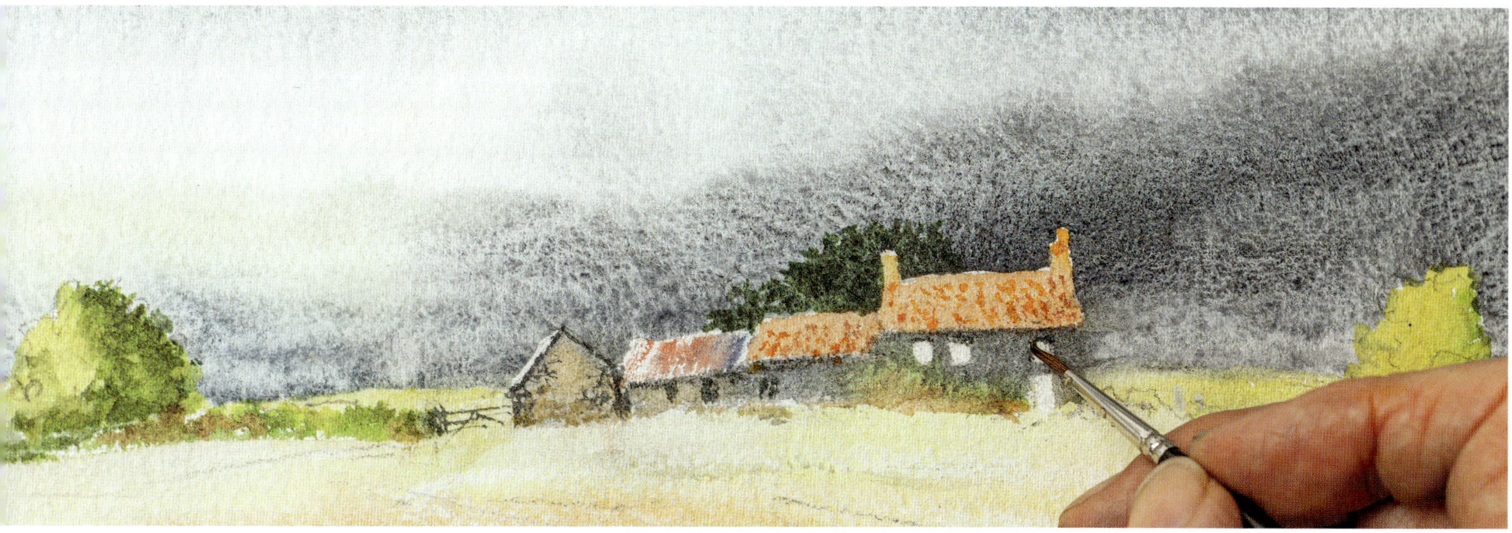

15 Use the tip of the no. 8 brush and zoisite genuine to dot in dark plant shapes in the foreground. Allow to dry.

16 At this point I noted that the bush in front of the house didn't stand out well, so I removed some colour with a damp 6mm (¼in) flat brush. Drop in cadmium yellow medium hue with a no. 8 brush.

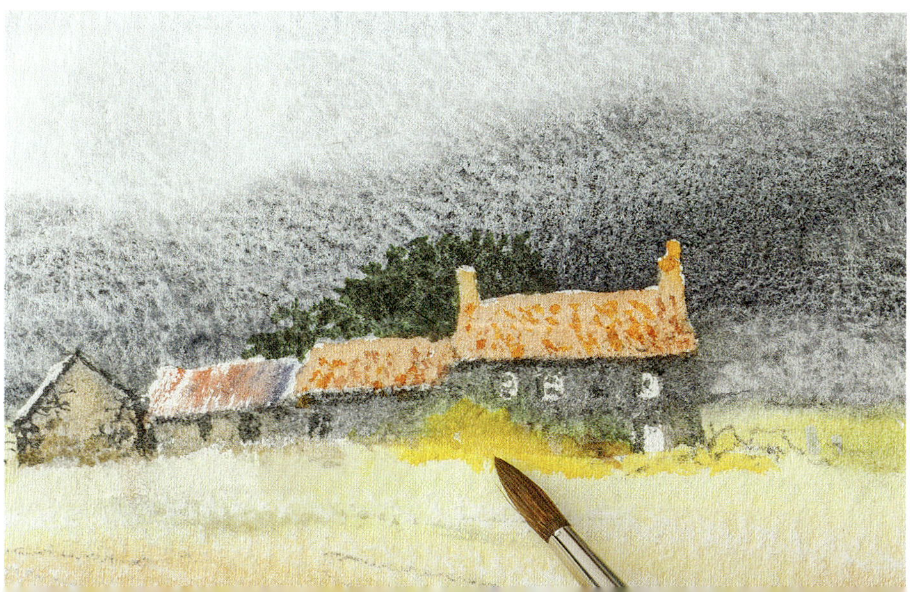

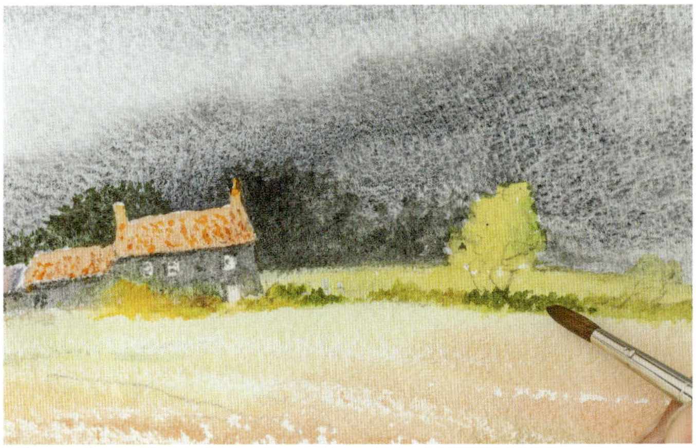

17 Darken the trees in the background with zoisite genuine to make the roofs stand out. Mix cadmium yellow medium hue with green apatite genuine and vary the height and texture of the hedgerow. Add zoisite genuine to darken some areas such as the shadow under the tree.

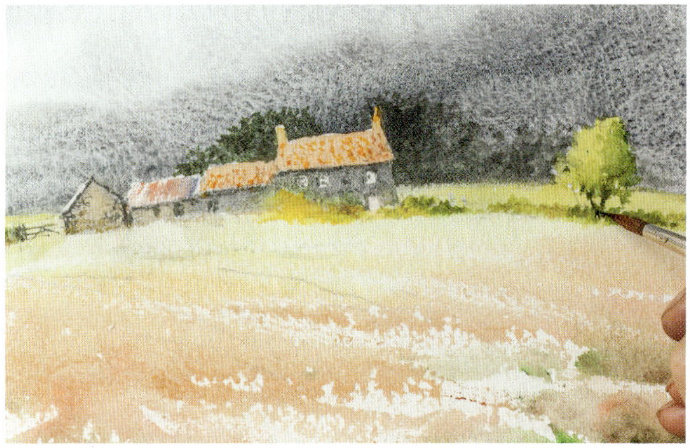

18 Soften the right-hand tree with a damp brush, then paint trunks with sodalite genuine.

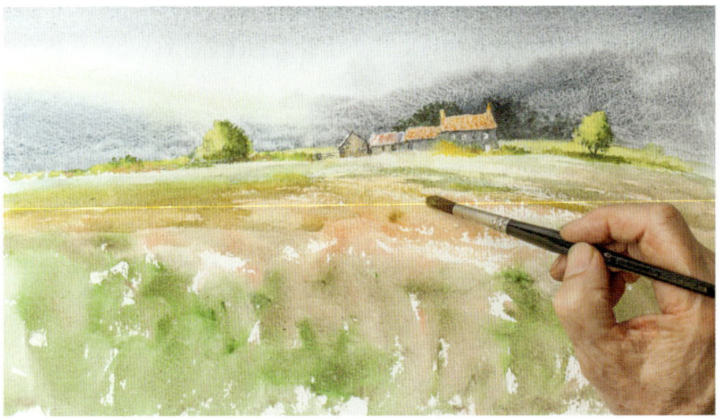

19 Work on the moorland with zoisite genuine and green apatite genuine on an old no. 8 brush. Scrub across the Rough paper surface and wax resist to create texture. Add yellow ochre in places. Subdue the texture elsewhere with water for a varied effect.

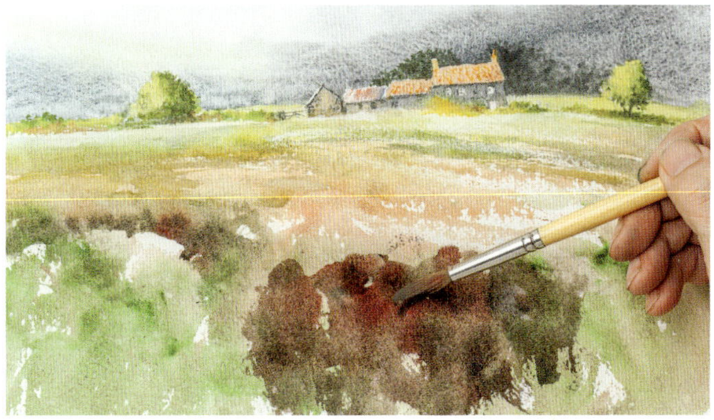

20 Suggest slabs of rock in the foreground by painting negatively around them with zoisite genuine and alizarin crimson.

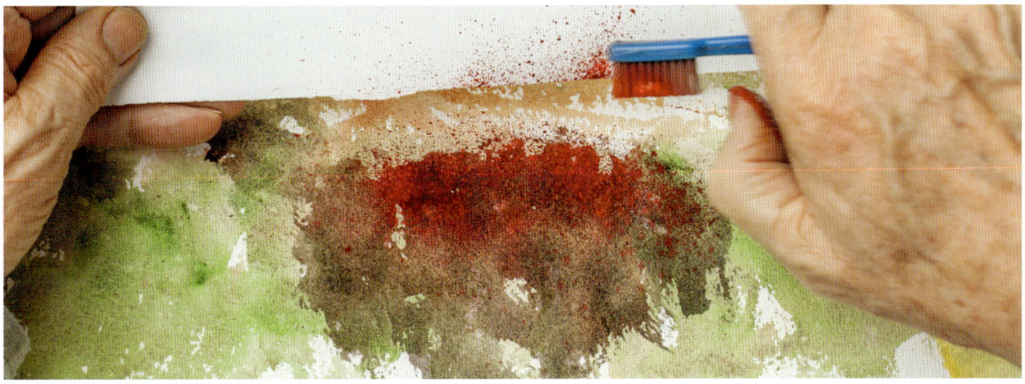

21 Pick up the same mix on an old toothbrush, mask the rest of the painting with scrap paper and spatter the area to add suggestions of small leaves or berries above the red patch.

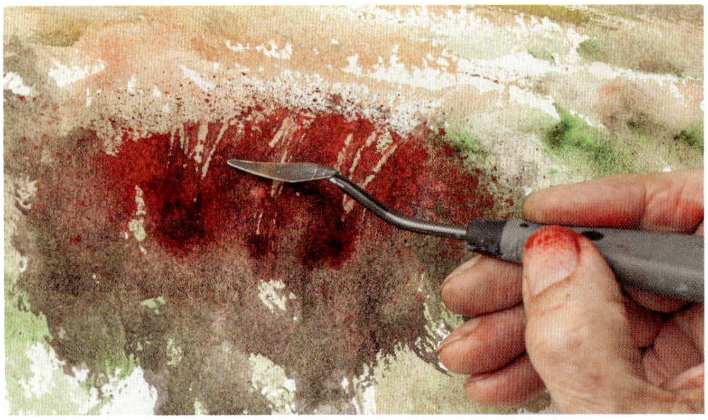

22 Use the point of a painting knife to scratch out more texture.

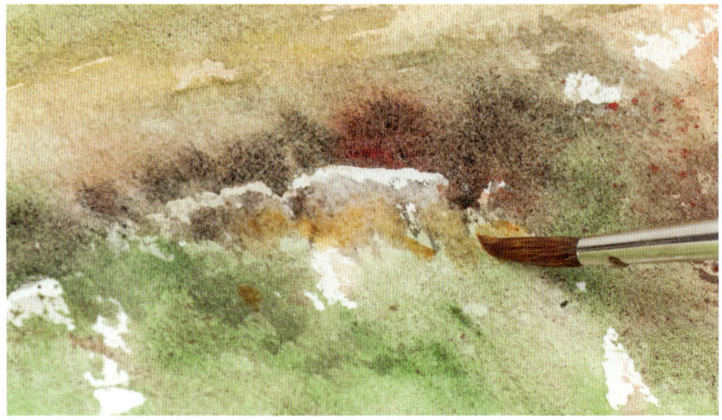

23 Use the no. 6 brush to paint the sides of the rocks you outlined negatively, using French ultramarine and burnt umber and leaving white paper highlights. Drop in yellow ochre, then zoisite genuine wet into wet.

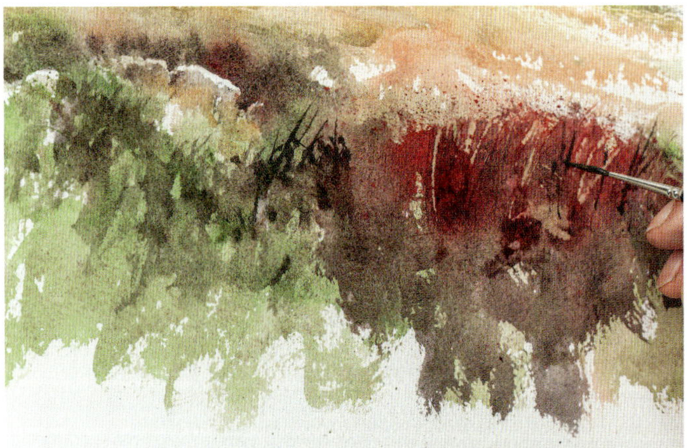

24 Change to a rigger and flick out strokes of the wet colour to create grasses.

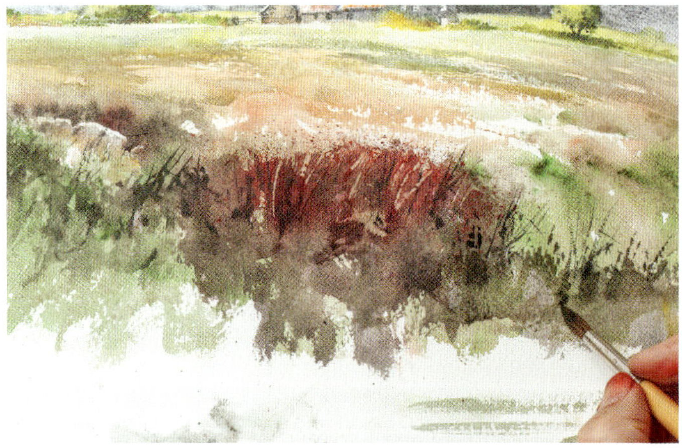

25 Use the tip of the no. 8 brush and zoisite genuine to dot in dark plant shapes in the foreground. Allow to dry.

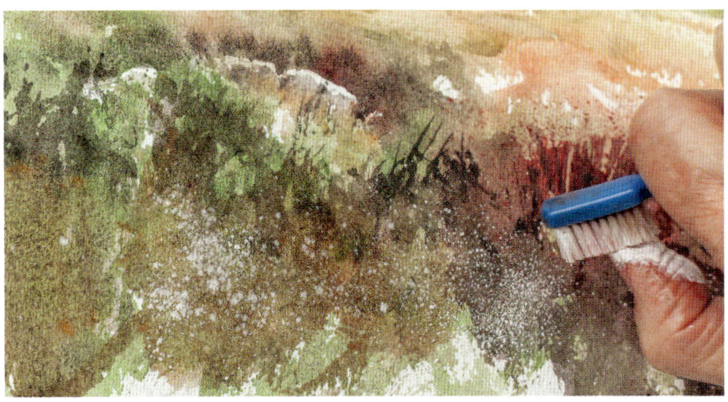

26 Spatter titanium white gouache over both the wet and the dry paint in the foreground, using an old toothbrush. The patchy drying varies the texture achieved.

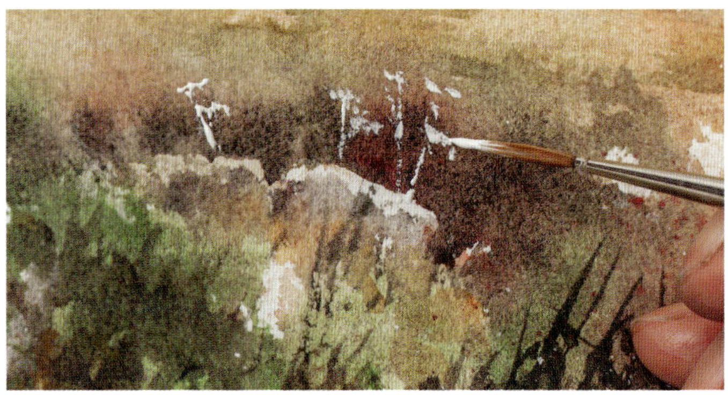

27 Pick up neat titanium white gouache on the tip of the rigger and paint cow parsley stalks on the dark background, then dot in the flowers.

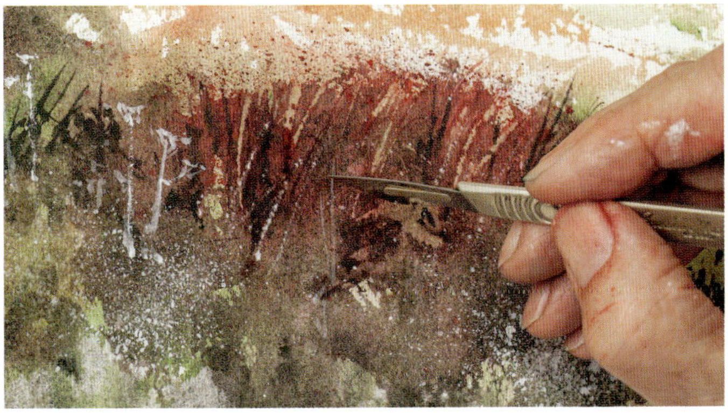

**28** Scratch out grasses with the tip of the scalpel.

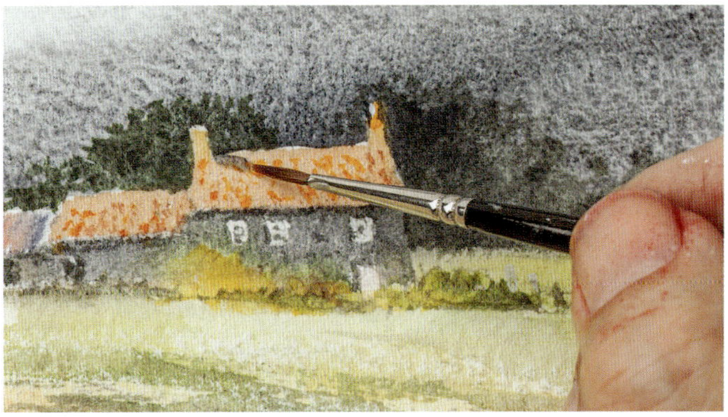

**29** Tidy the windows with the rigger and white gouache. Finally paint a cast shadow from the chimney with zoisite genuine to complete the effect of bright sunlight.

*The finished painting.*

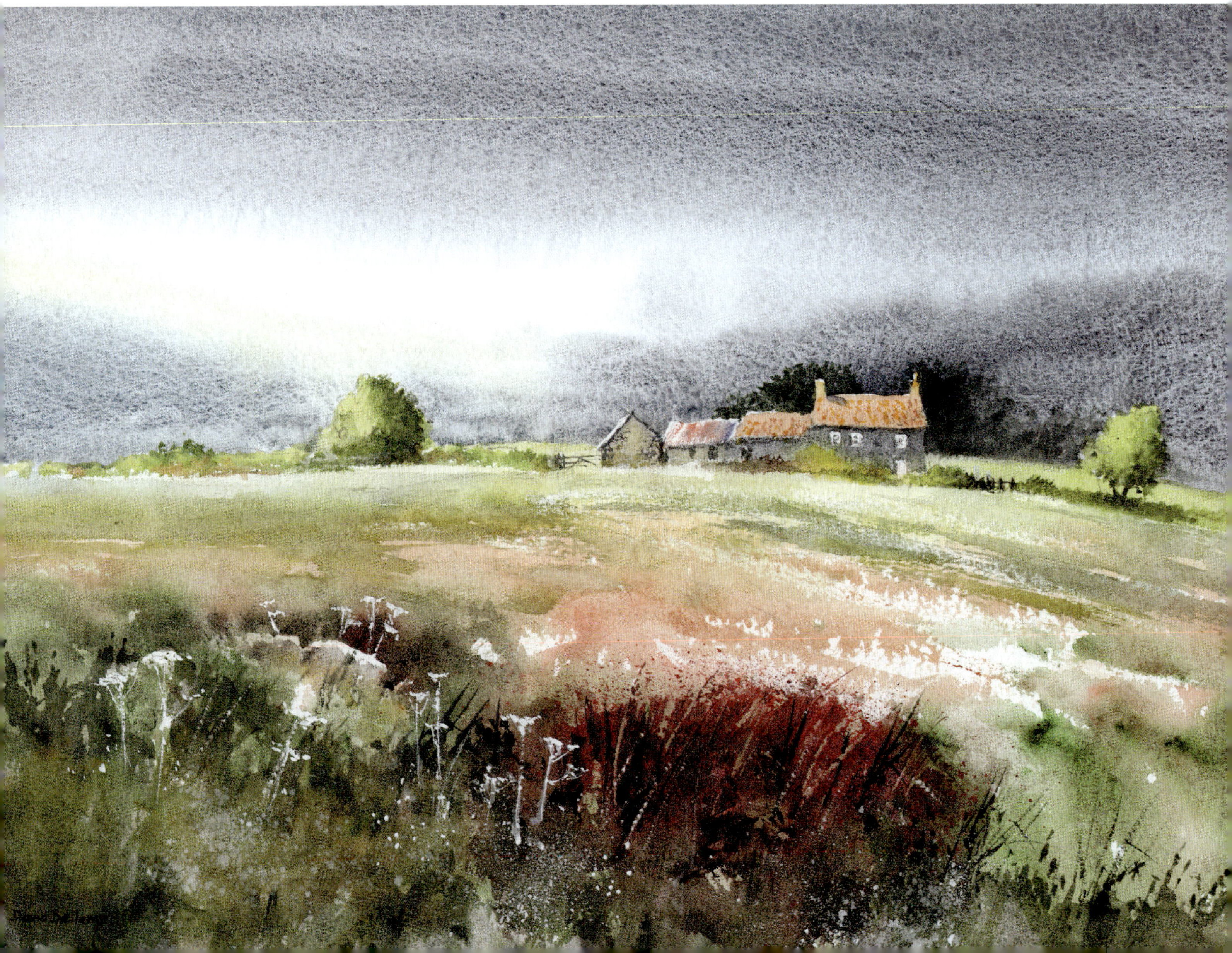

# Autumn

As trees shed their leaves, it is a great opportunity for the landscape artist, with all that massed green foliage being replaced by exciting colours and the interesting bare structure of trunks and branches. Early snowfall can sometimes cloak distant hills and mountains, yet vivid autumn colours are still resplendent in the foreground, providing an exciting combination. It really pays to be ready to capture the transient scenes at this time of year with some potential paintings in mind, as gales and storms can quickly change the state of trees in autumn. Certain local trees can put on a spectacular display of colour every year, so watch out for these. Of course, once you have captured these beautiful days, it is fairly easy to transform your original autumn sketches and photographs into a composition with a snowy background, or vice versa. Changing the season in this way can offer you fascinating new possibilities with a favourite subject. In this chapter we look at these autumn colours which can linger well into the depths of winter. We will also consider some of the lovely atmospheric effects we can encounter at this time of year.

## MISTY SCENES

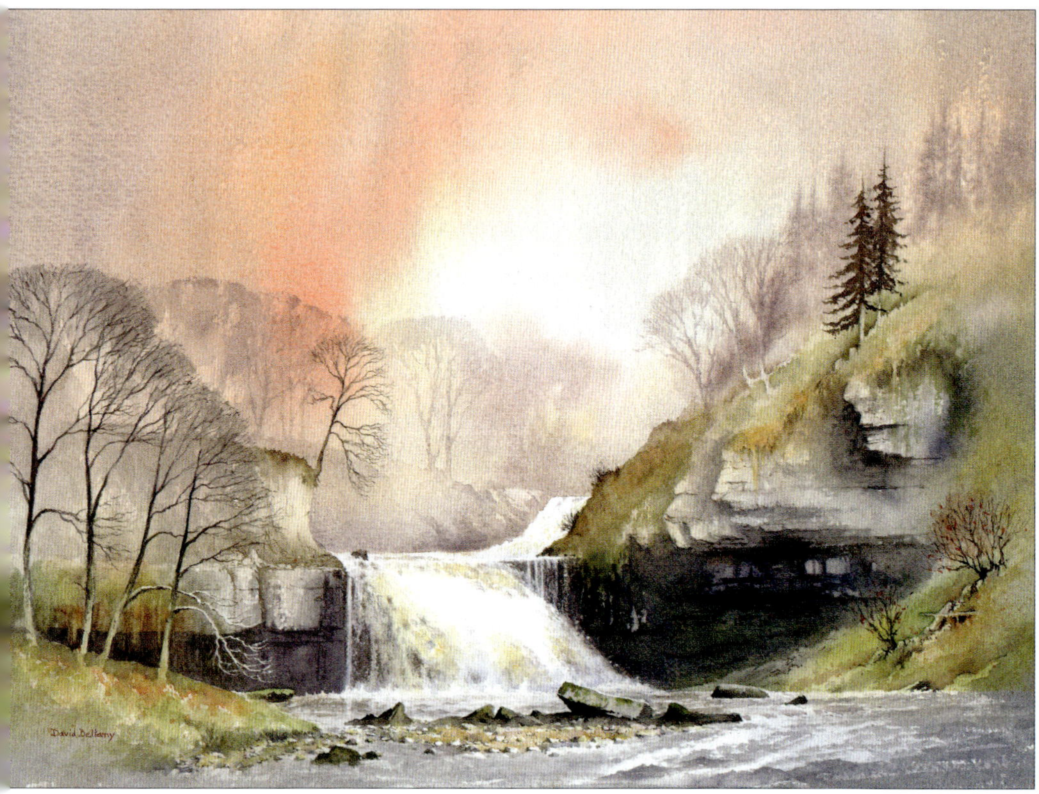

WEST BURTON FORCE
*28 x 35.5cm (11 x 14in), Rough*

*The wet-into-wet method, in which paint is added into a wash that is still wet, is normally the most effective way of suggesting a misty scene, but in this watercolour I have used two techniques as a way of suggesting varying degrees of mist. In the centre, directly above the more distant waterfall, a mixture of cadmium red with a touch of cobalt blue has been applied into a damp background wash of very weak yellow ochre to just faintly hint at the presence of trees in the mist. When the paper had dried completely, I used the same mixture with slightly more cobalt blue added to paint in the two trees that stand centrally above the main falls, while at the same time rendering the bank and rocks below them. I also added trees further to the left in the background. These features all dried slightly stronger than they now appear. Once the paper had dried, I gently sponged over the background trees with clean water and a natural sponge to push them back into the distance, though they are still strong enough to appear in front of those done wet into wet earlier. By combining these two techniques, you can create greater depth in misty scenes. The strongly etched tree on the left that looks as though it is about to fall into the pool adds further depth.*

# COLOURS FOR AUTUMN SCENES

There are endless combinations of mixtures for creating the colours of autumn, but I will just indicate a few of the more exciting examples here to give you a start. Experiment with a variety of colours to find what appeals to you most.

Quinacridone gold + cadmium red

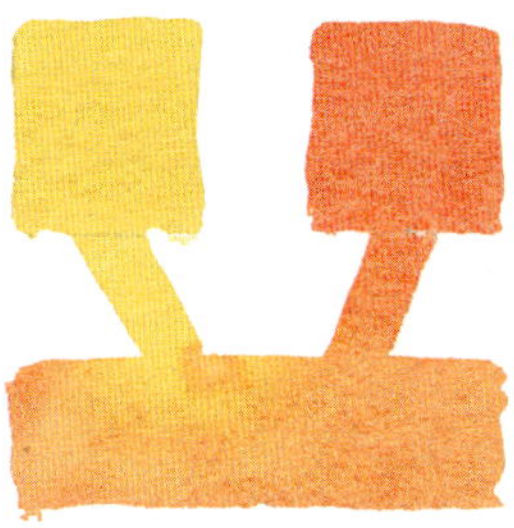

Quinacridone gold + transparent red oxide

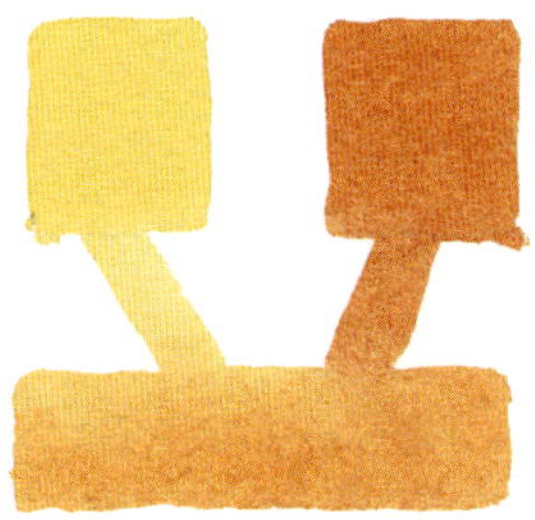

Gamboge + perylene violet

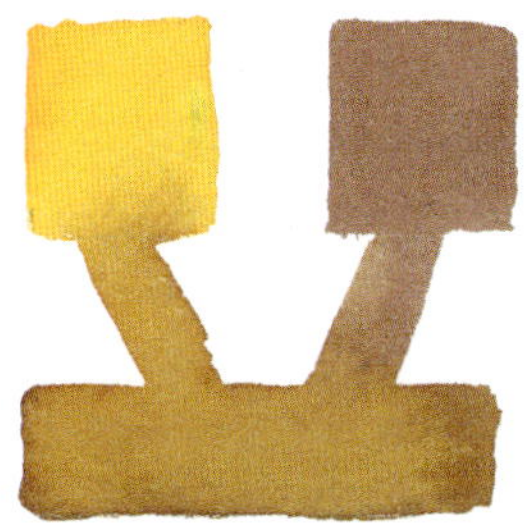

Quinacridone sienna + sodalite genuine

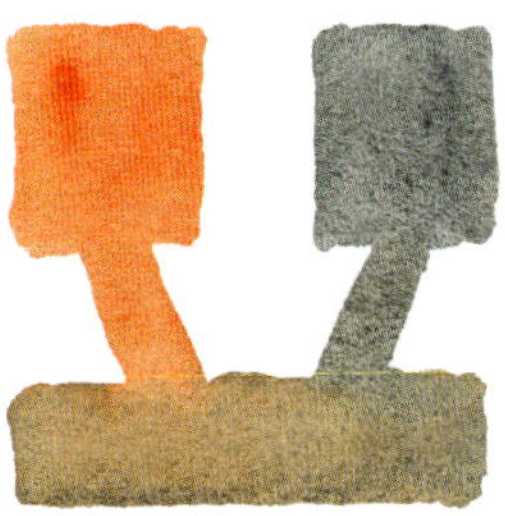

Lunar blue + transparent red oxide

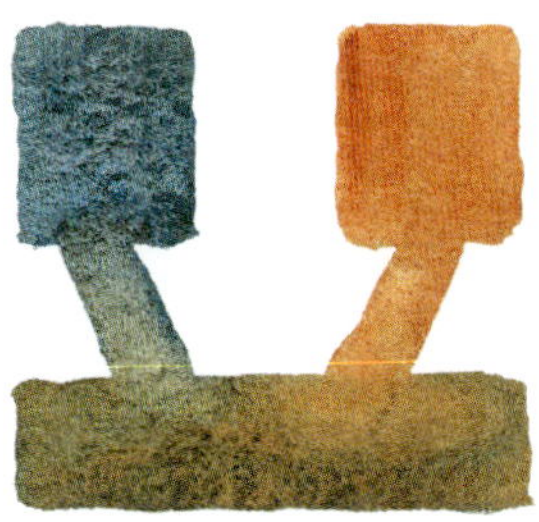

Aussie red gold + sodalite genuine

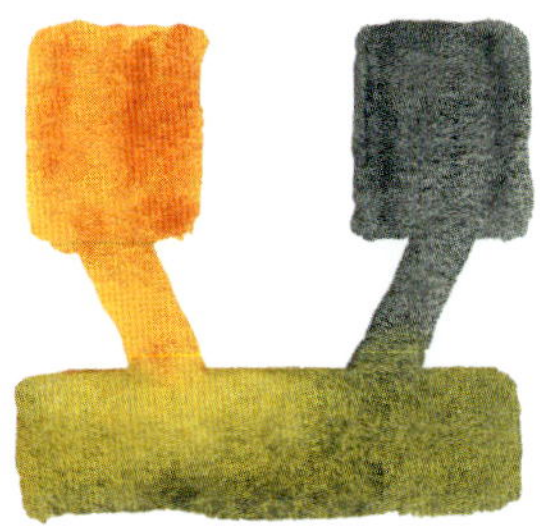

### A SELECTION OF AUTUMN COLOUR MIXTURES

*This is a selection of exciting colours you may like to try for your autumn paintings, but they are by no means the only ones. Although it is not an 'autumn colour,' I have included sodalite genuine to show how it not only darkens the colour with which it is mixed, but also introduces granulations, as shown here with Aussie red gold. Experiment with a wide variety of colours and keep swatches of them for future reference.*

### AUTUMN FOLIAGE WITH INTERMITTENT LEAVES

*Light-coloured flecks of leaves and small clusters against a dark background can be really attractive, but they are difficult to paint in watercolour. Here I spotted masking fluid where I wanted light-coloured individual leaves – mainly at the edges of the foliage. You can also spatter with a toothbrush if you wish. On removing the mask, I dabbed in the bright yellows and reds, allowing them to run together in places. They stand out most clearly against the dark grey.*

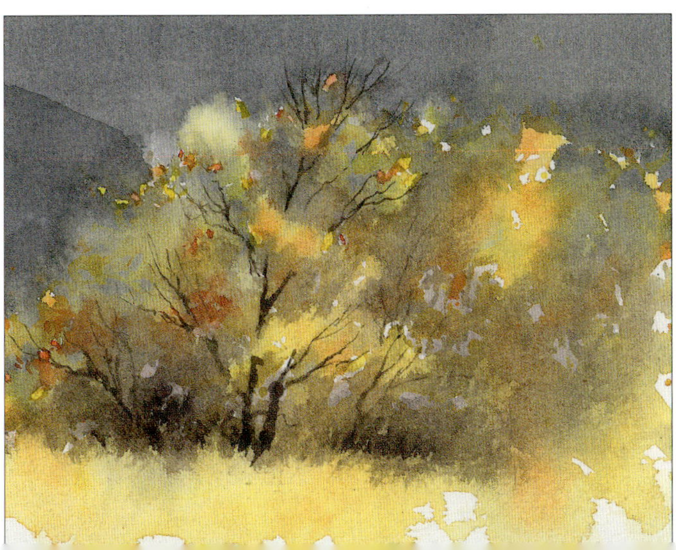

### EMPHASIZING NATURE'S WARM COLOURS

*For these bushes I have used the powerful Daniel Smith colours Aussie red gold and transparent red oxide, then emphasized them by bringing in a background wash of French ultramarine and perylene violet, working round the single leaves quickly with a no. 8 round sable. As purple and gold are complementary colours, this creates a striking combination. Cadmium yellows and reds and gamboge also work well.*

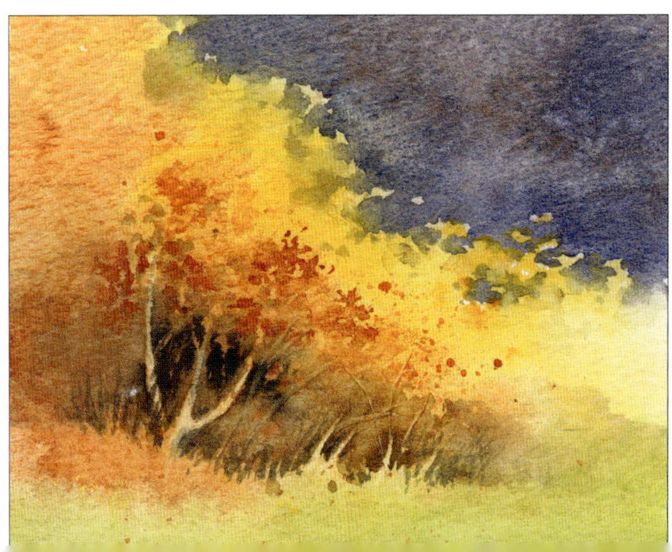

## OBSERVING AND SKETCHING AUTUMN SCENERY

Critical observation and careful analysis of a scene are vital to create an authentic-looking result; try to develop these methods until they become second nature. Whether you are working from life or from a photograph, constantly compare the heights, sizes, tones, colour temperature etc. of each feature. Compare the brightness of adjacent colours and how they react with each other. Consider how you can emphasize the strength of colour or create strong contrasts to ensure a focal point stands out.

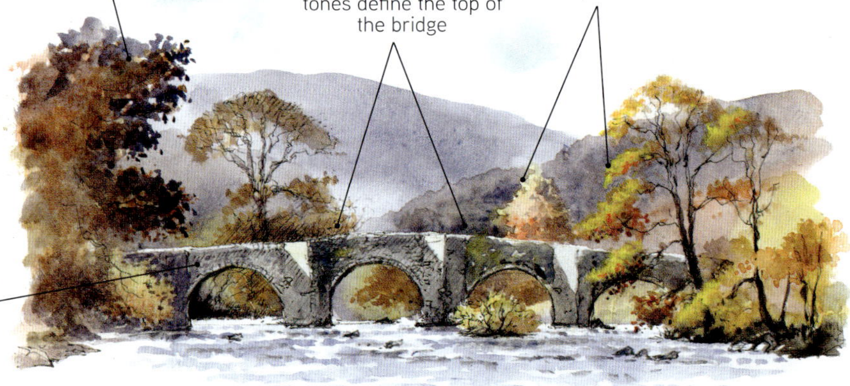


**NOVEMBER COLOURS**

*Sketching colours and their interaction is especially important with autumn colouring. As well as providing a record, sketching in colour shows you which colours work together. When you create a finished painting, you may wish to make changes so that one particular colour is juxtaposed against a different one to that in the sketch. Moving features slightly will achieve this.*

## CAPTURING THE FLOW OF AUTUMN COLOURS

If the whole painting is covered in bright colours, it can be overwhelming. A patch of dullness can add impact to vibrant colours beside it. Splashes of brightness on or beside the focal point can really lift the work.

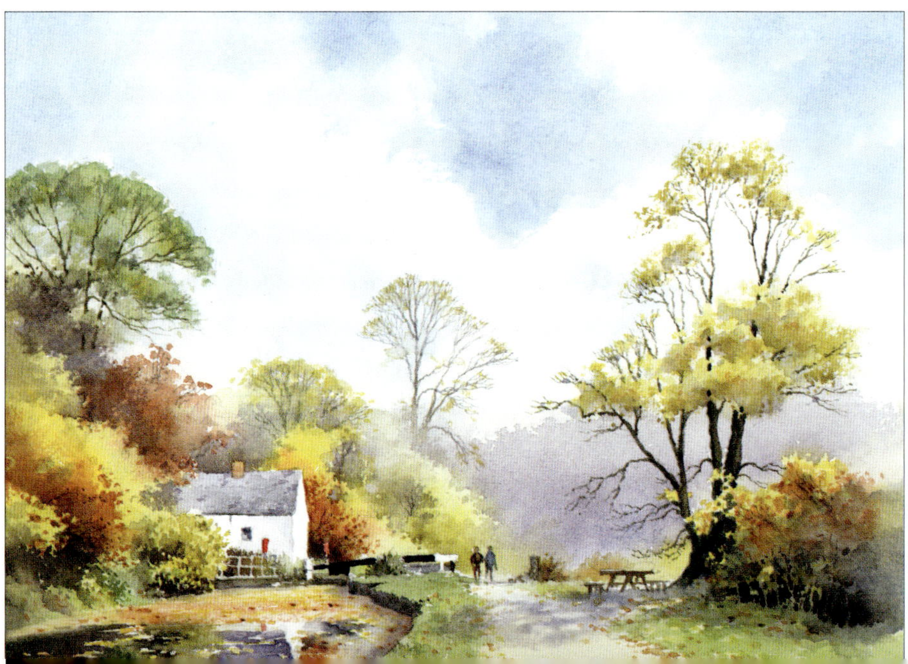

**BRECON-ABERGAVENNY CANAL**

*25.5 x 33cm (10 x 13in), 425gsm (200lb) Not paper*

*I don't often throw the full gamut of autumn colours into a painting as it can become too overwhelming, but in this instance I decided to enjoy a more abandoned approach. Incidentally, this is an excellent idea if you feel that your painting is in a rut. This proved to be a popular painting. Note particularly how those autumn colours set against the pure white of the Saunders Waterford High White paper really stand out well.*

# AUTUMN COLOURS WITH A SNOWY BACKGROUND

The combination of autumn colours with early snow can create a striking composition. In this view above Little Langdale in the Lake District, there are warm autumn colours not just on the trees but also on the ground cover in places.

## Track to Little Langdale

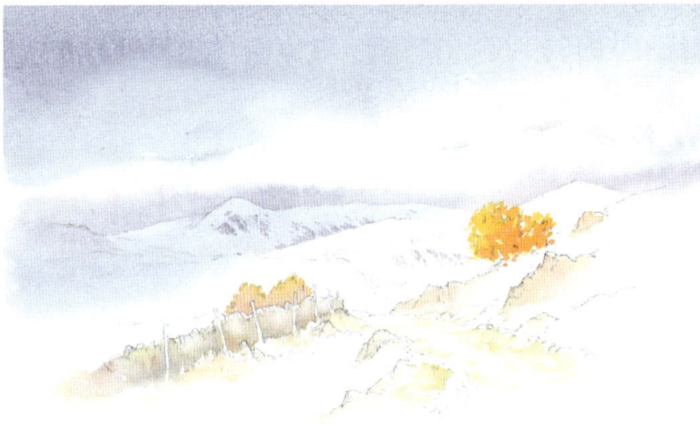

1 I painted the furthest mountain ridge in weak cobalt blue, blending it up into the sky so that the top edge was lost completely and the bottom made a sharp top edge for the white ridge below. The painting was then left to dry. Next, I began the sky at the top with a wash of lavender, a Daniel Smith colour with a gentle granulation. Lower down I introduced Naples yellow in the centre right, with touches of alizarin crimson, and in the lower part of the sky a weak wash of moonglow defined the two peaks and the long distant ridge. Moonglow was also used for rocky outcrops on the ridges. Next I rendered the wall with weak cobalt blue with a touch of cadmium red, and dropped in a little yellow ochre wet into wet. The trees were created with Aussie red gold with touches of transparent red oxide.

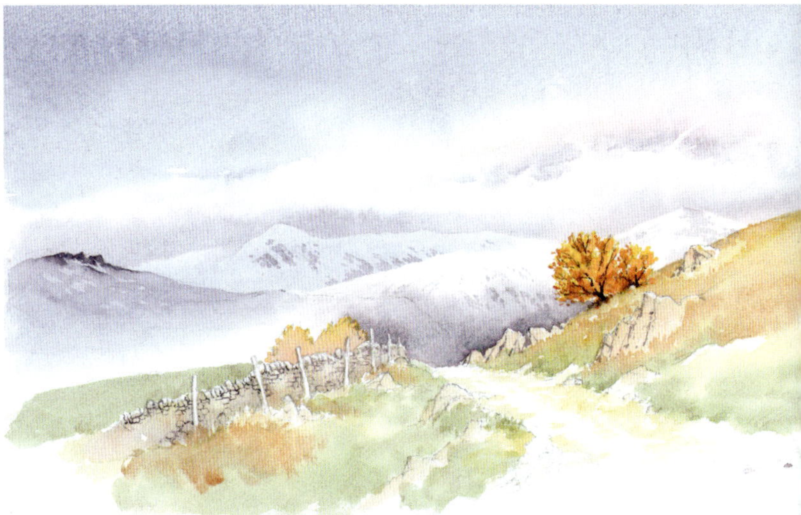

2 I softened some of the distant ridge edges with a damp flat brush, then painted in the dark crags on the left with moonglow. I also used this colour over the lower shadowy valley in the centre, fading it out at the top. Parts of the sky were strengthened to define the clouds. I delineated the trunks and branches on the right-hand trees with French ultramarine and burnt umber. Before finishing this stage I painted weak patches of green apatite genuine and transparent red oxide into the foreground area.

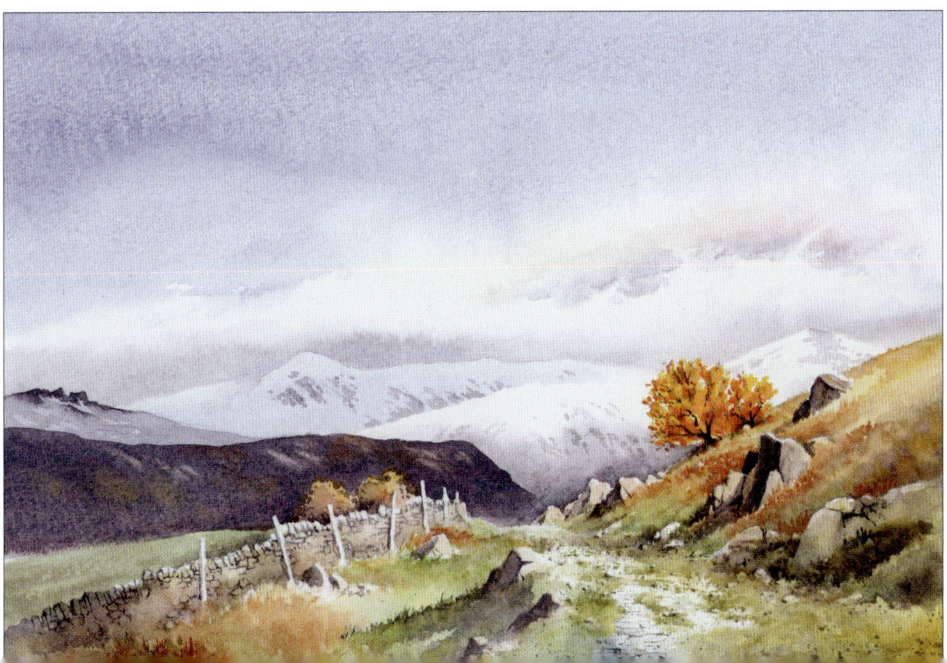

THE FINISHED PAINTING

*23 x 30.5cm (9 x 12in), 300gsm (140lb) Not paper*

*The dark middle ridge was rendered with strong moonglow, working round the small trees, and while it was still wet I pulled out a number of marks to suggest light crags and dropped in some transparent red oxide in places. Finally I tidied up the wall and rocks with detail using French ultramarine and burnt umber.*

# MOORLAND BRIDGE

It can be a challenge to maintain interest in large areas of open moorland. In this demonstration I show how to enliven these various parts of the scene, and throw the main emphasis on to the focal point.

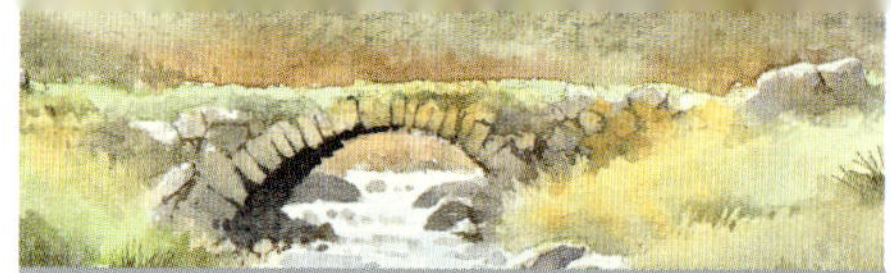

**MATERIALS USED**

Saunders Waterford 300gsm (140lb) Rough watercolour paper

Brushes: squirrel mop, fan brush, no. 7 and no. 4 round, 6mm (¼in) flat, no. 1 rigger and no. 1 round

Colours: Naples yellow, French ultramarine, burnt umber, cadmium red, yellow ochre, raw umber, cobalt blue, viridian, new gamboge, cadmium orange, perylene maroon

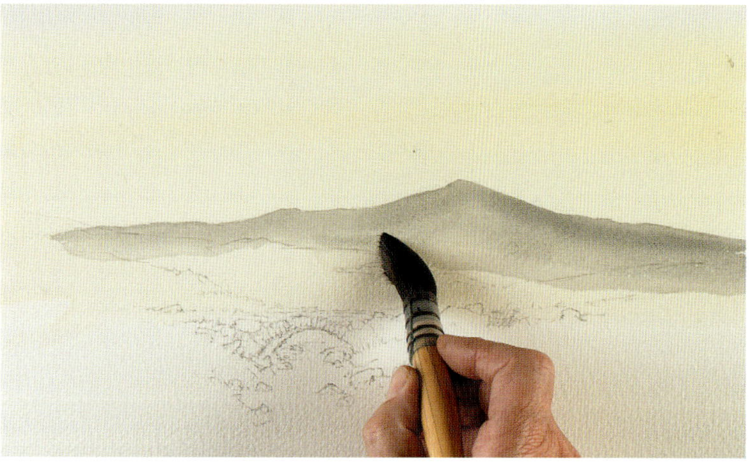

1 Draw the scene. Wet the sky area and distant ridge with a squirrel mop and clean water, then sweep a wash of Naples yellow across the same area. Allow to dry. Paint the distant ridge with a pale mix of ultramarine and burnt umber. Allow to dry.

2 Prop your painting board up at a steep angle. Cover the sky and distant ridge with clean water, then paint a mix of ultramarine and cadmium red into the upper sky. This should run down to create a rain squall. A damp fan brush is effective if you need to encourage its downward progress. Allow it to dry naturally. Lift out colour with a clean no. 7 brush if it creeps too low.

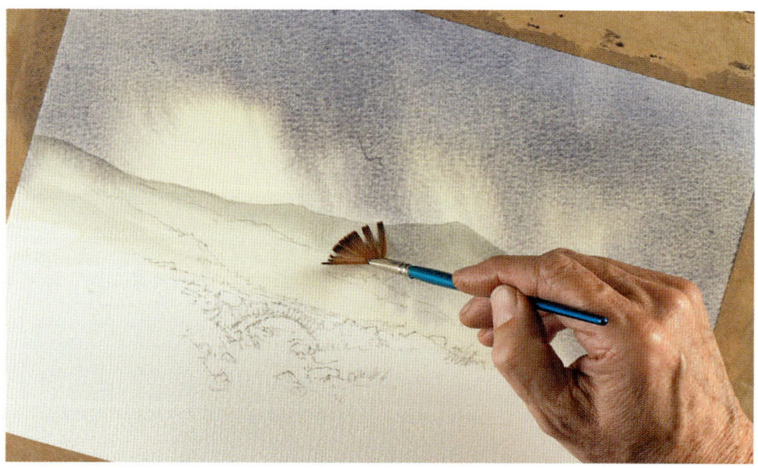

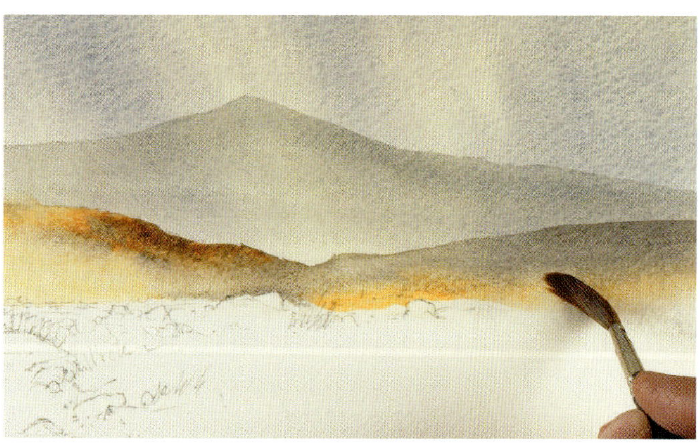

3 Paint the next line of hills in front of the ridge with the no. 7 brush and yellow ochre. Drop in raw umber in places. Paint a mix of ultramarine and cadmium red into the left-hand side, against the light of the sky, then a stronger mix in the middle, in front of the lighter distant ridge, then more of the paler mix to the right. Drop in yellow ochre lower down.

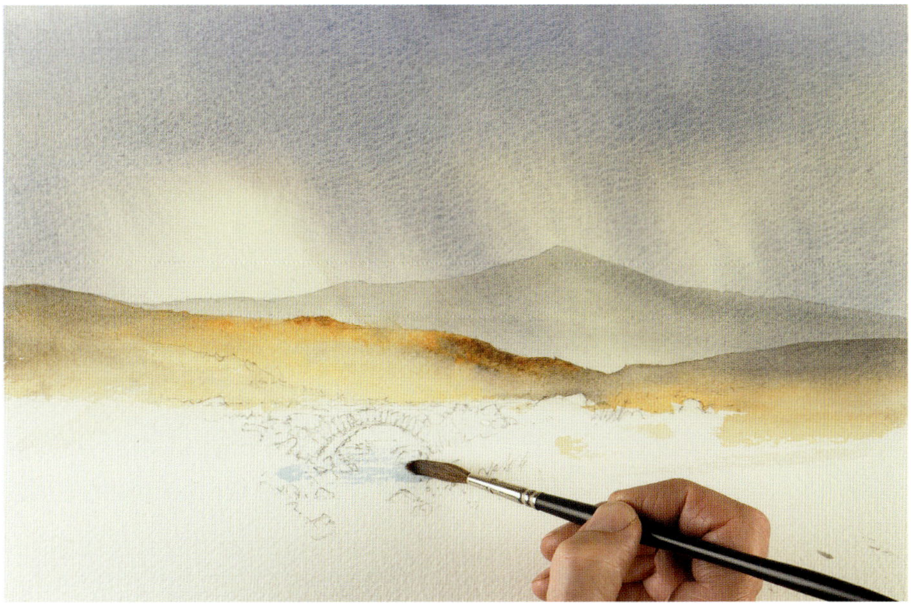

4 Pick up a cobalt blue wash on a dry brush and sweep this across the water area beneath the bridge. The dry-brush technique should create a sparkling effect with the Rough paper.

5 Use the no. 7 brush to paint the green of the grass with viridian and new gamboge, then bring in yellow ochre, down to the bottom, and allow the colours to merge. Use the no. 4 brush to drop in cadmium orange to create brightness here and there. It will lose its intensity in the wet background. Allow to dry.

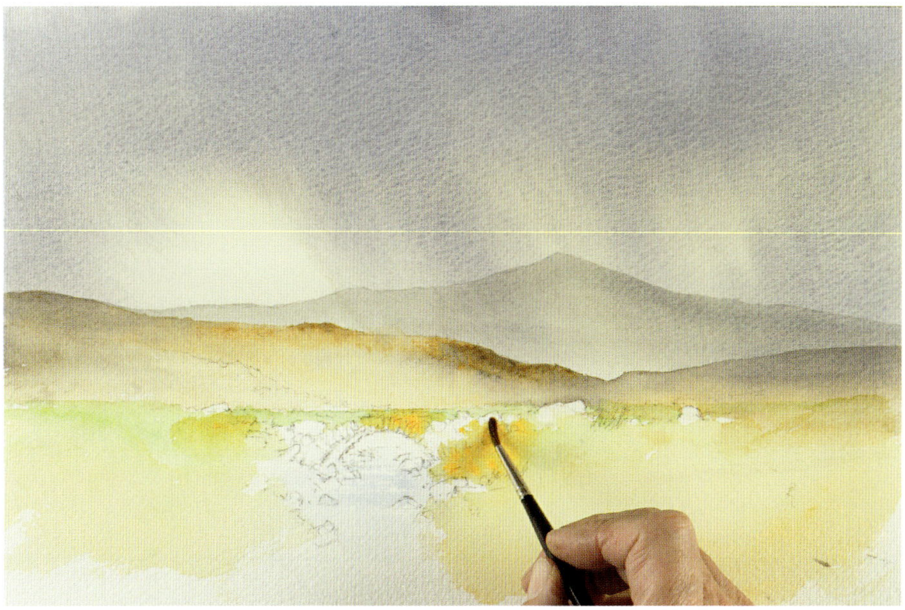

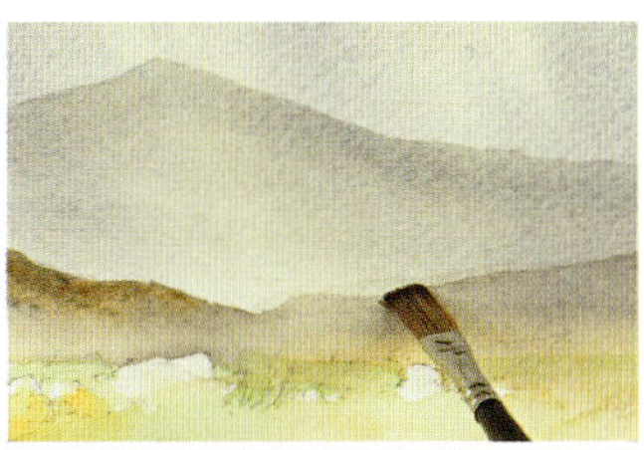

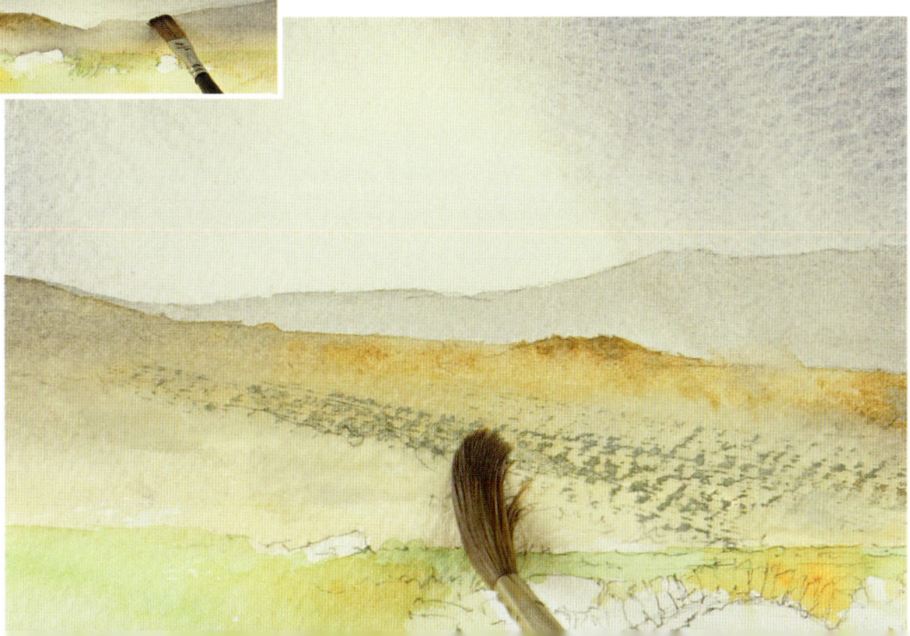

6 To increase the sense of distance, soften part of the middle distant ridge with the 6mm (¼in) flat brush and clean water. Use the no. 7 brush with ultramarine and raw umber to create moorland texture with the dry-brush technique, then soften the edges of this with clean water.

7 Paint more raw umber behind the bridge to highlight the top, then drop in perylene maroon. Vary this with yellow ochre in places and drop in perylene maroon under the bridge.

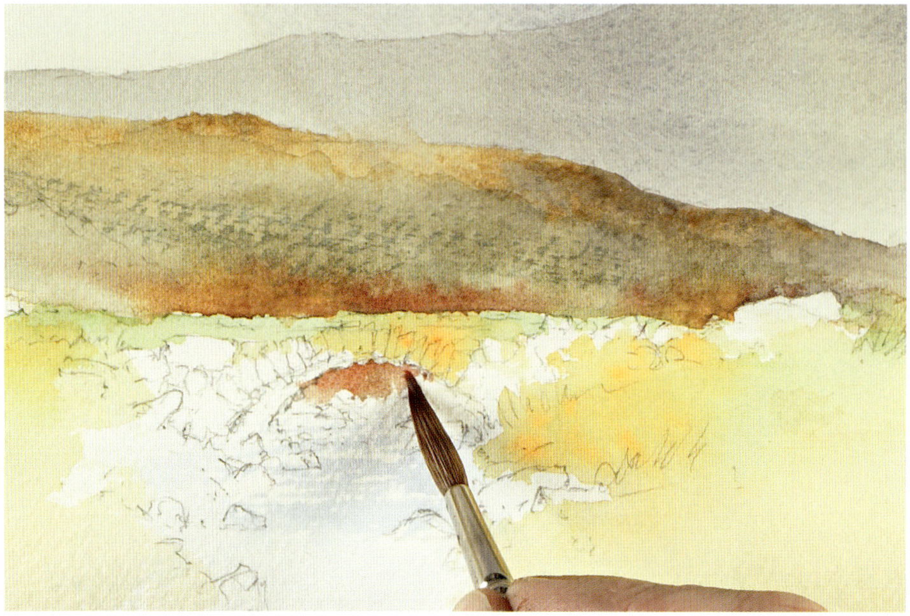

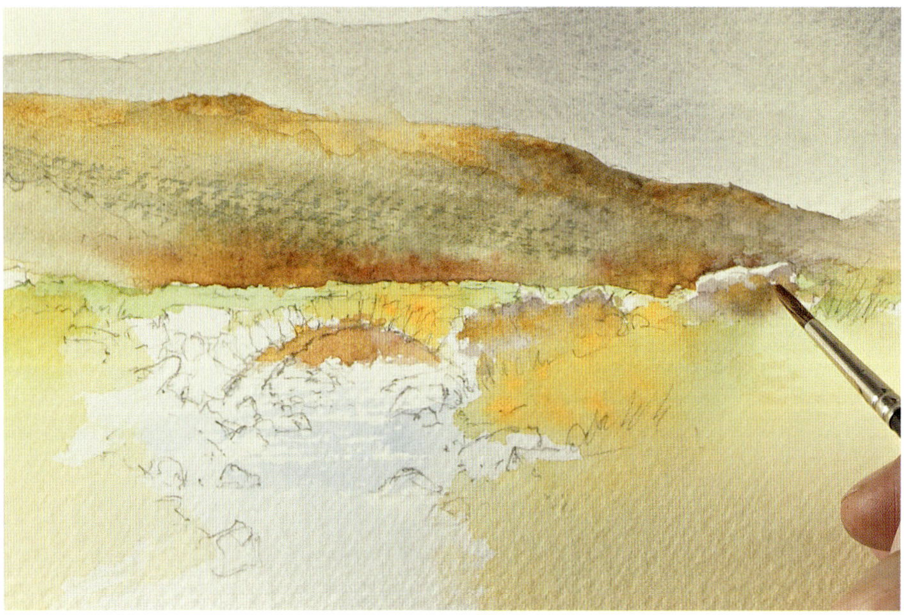

8 Use the no. 4 brush to paint rocks with ultramarine and cadmium red. Soften them at the bottom with clean water, then drop in yellow ochre. Leave white highlights on the tops.

9 Suggest more distant rocks with the same method, blending them into the moorland at the bottom.

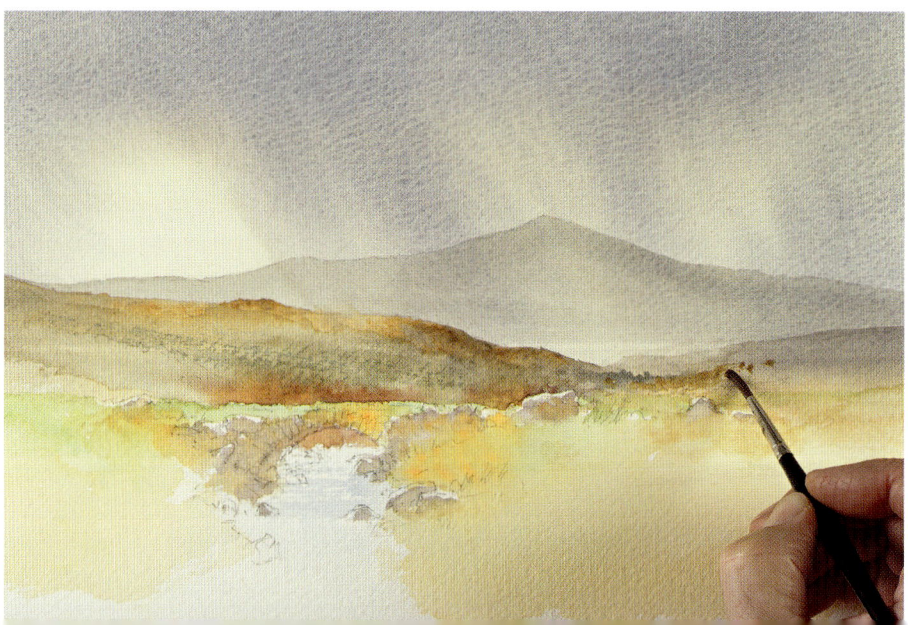

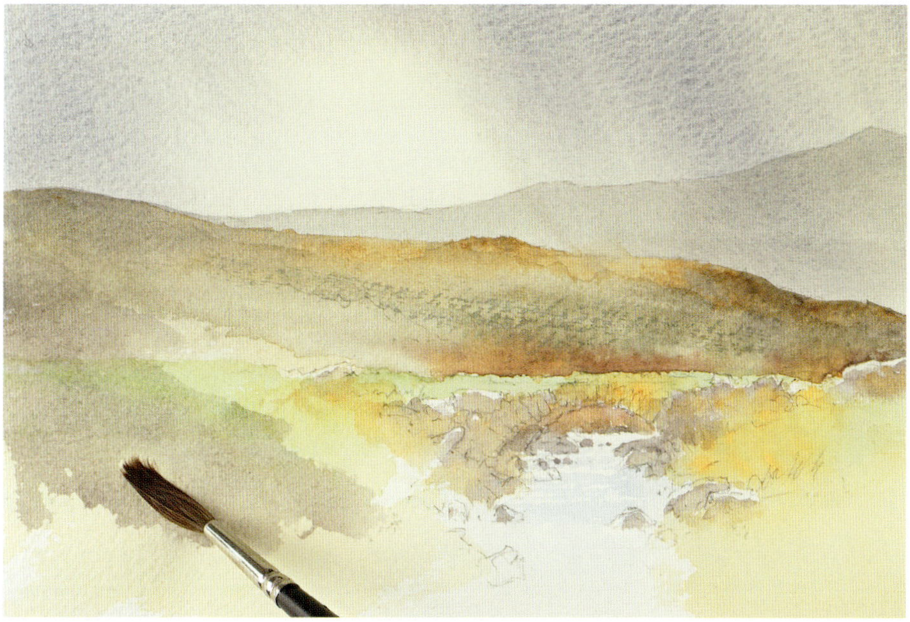

10 Use the no. 7 brush to paint a shadow over the left-hand moorland with ultramarine and cadmium red. Allow to dry.

11 Use the no. 4 brush and a dark mix of ultramarine and burnt umber to paint the strongest tone in the painting: the shadow under the bridge. Add water lower down to suggest reflected light.

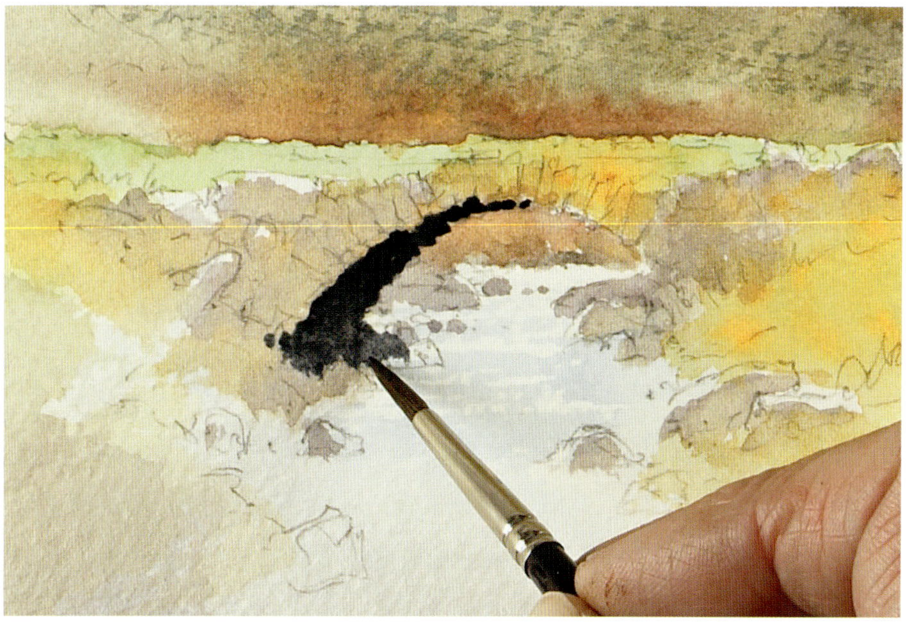

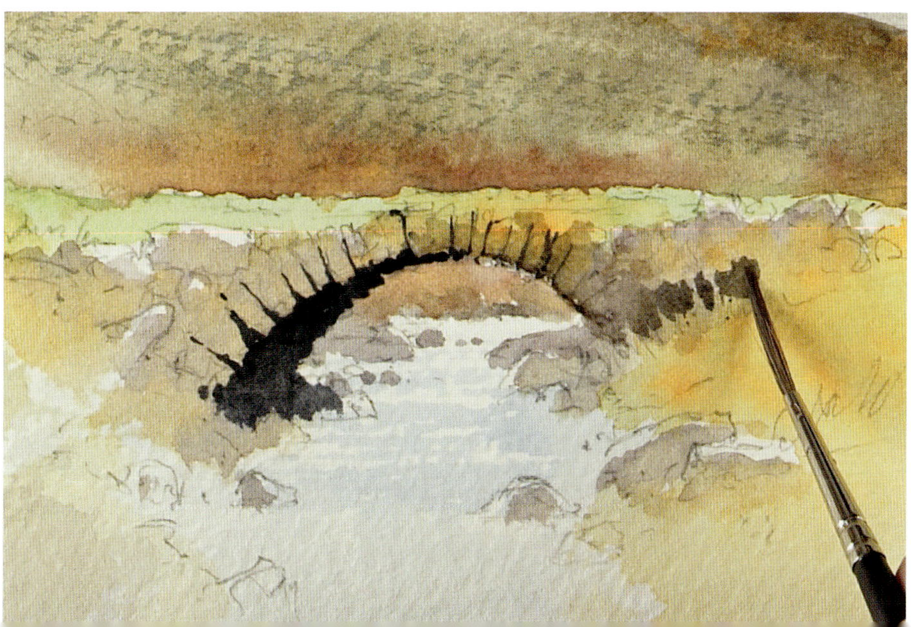

12 Change to the no. 1 rigger. Twirl it across a piece of scrap paper to get a good point and use the same mix to paint the stonework of the arch. Vary the pressure to get a natural look. Darken the right-hand side of the bridge a little with a wash of ultramarine and cadmium red, making it darker still to the right, behind the bright grasses.

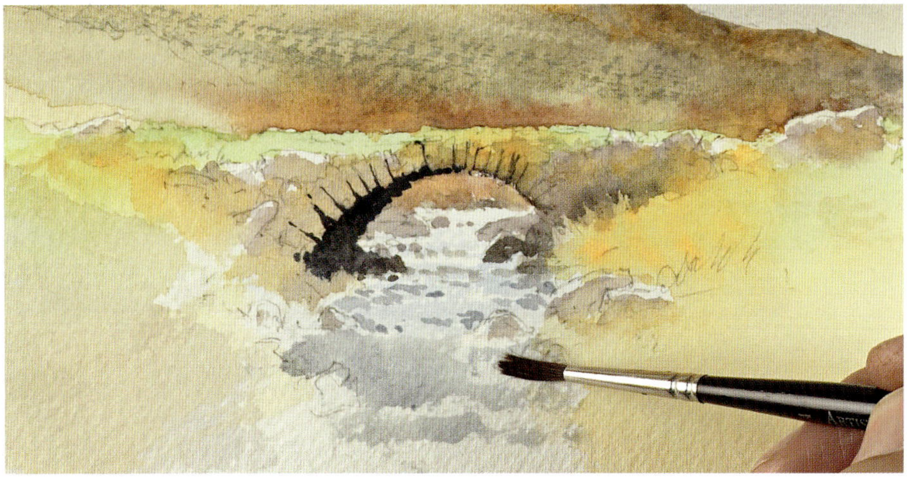

13 Paint rocks under the bridge with the no. 4 brush and a mix of ultramarine and burnt umber. Use the point of the brush and a bluer, paler mix to paint ripples in the water, then use the side of the brush to paint the water.

14 Define the line of the ridge sloping down towards the bridge with a mix of ultramarine and raw umber, then blend this in with clean water.

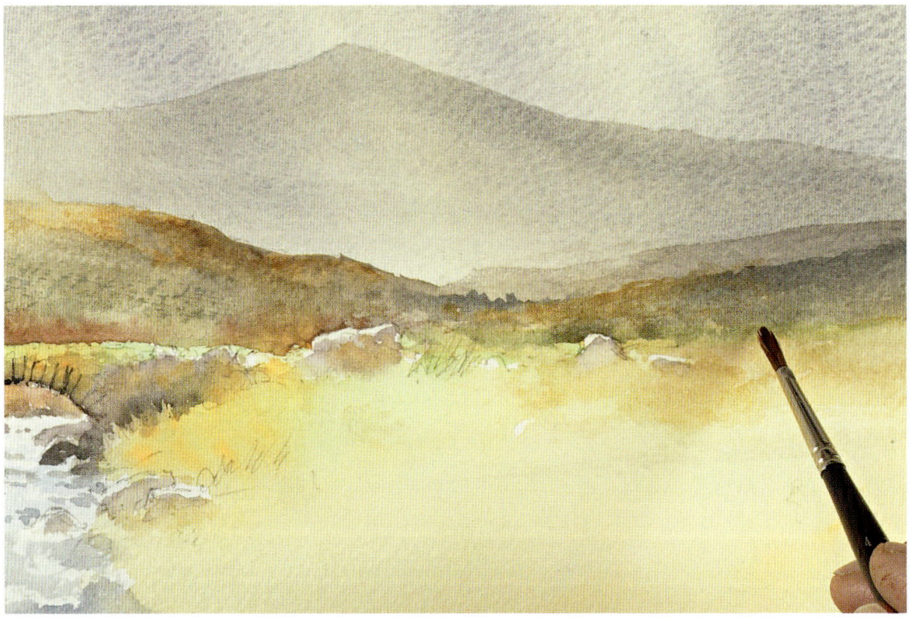

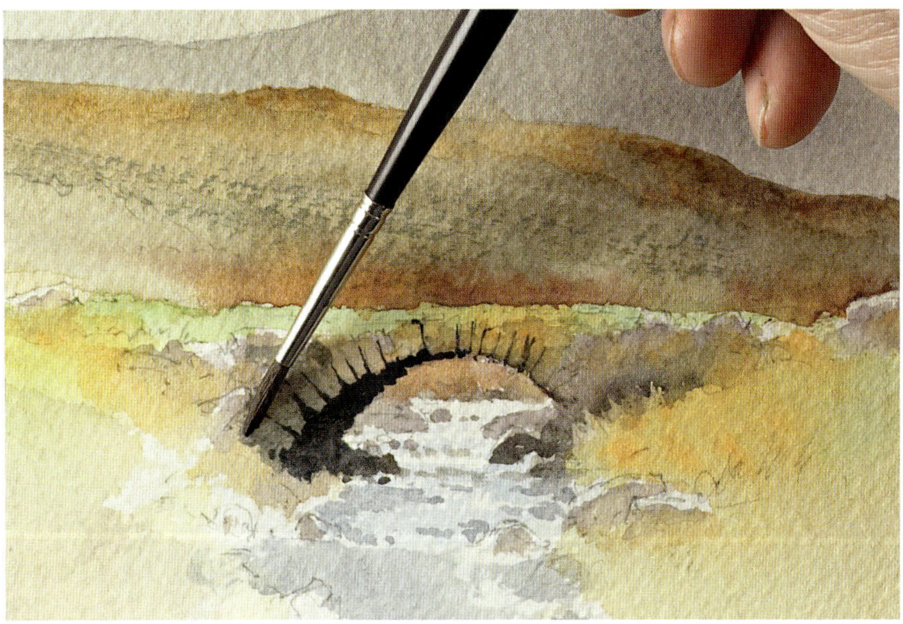

15 Drag the same colour across the lower part of the bridge.

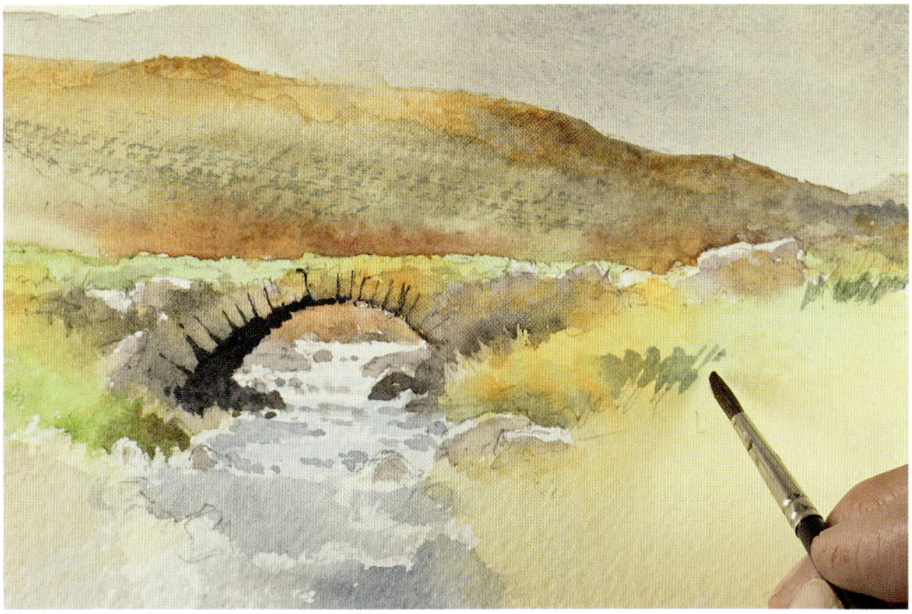

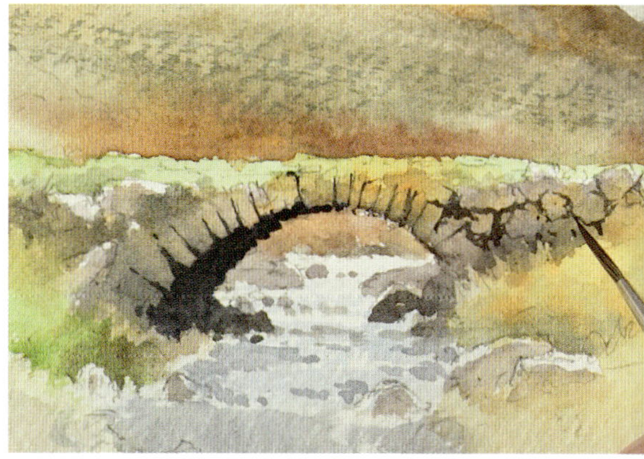

17 Use the no. 1 rigger and a dark mix of ultramarine and burnt umber to paint the remaining stonework of the bridge, varying the pressure to create a natural look.

16 Add bright green to the grass on the left-hand bank with viridian and new gamboge, then paint a little raw umber behind the rocks on the right-hand bank to emphasize them. Suggest grasses with ultramarine and raw umber.

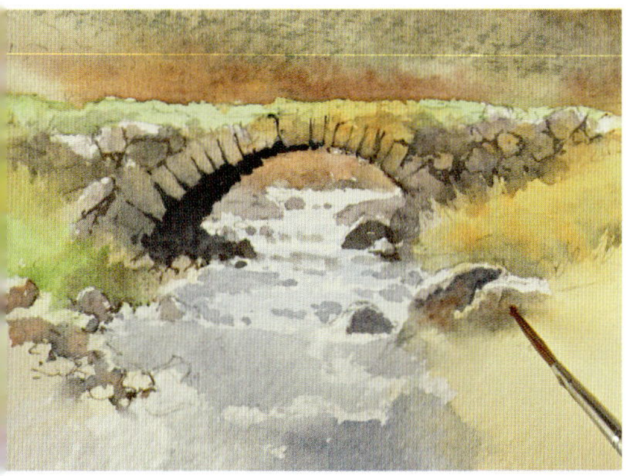

18 Suggest stones on the riverbank in the same way, then add tone with a paler wash of the same colours. Drop in perylene maroon in places.

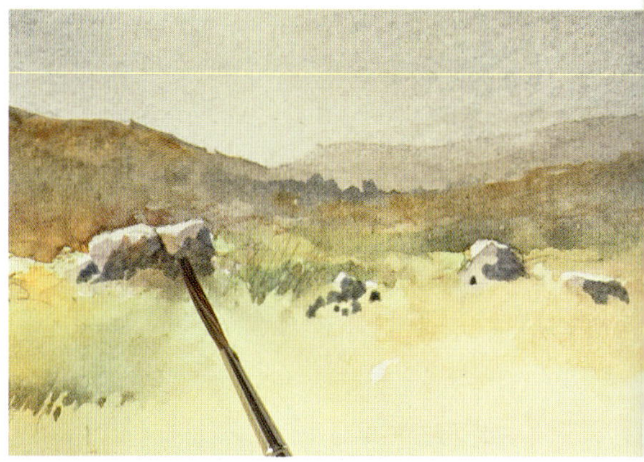

19 Add shadow to some of the more distant rocks with the ultramarine and burnt umber mix.

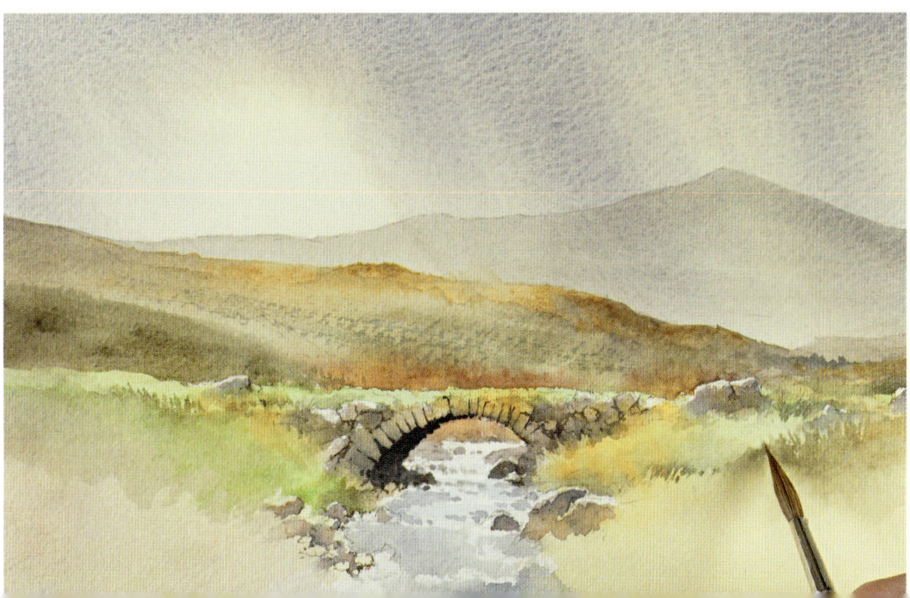

20 Paint the dark ridge on the left of the scene with the no. 7 brush and a mix of raw umber and ultramarine. Add grasses on the lighter foreground green, using the point of the brush. Sweep the brush over the base of the grasses to soften them in. Repeat to add a ridge of grasses on the right-hand side.

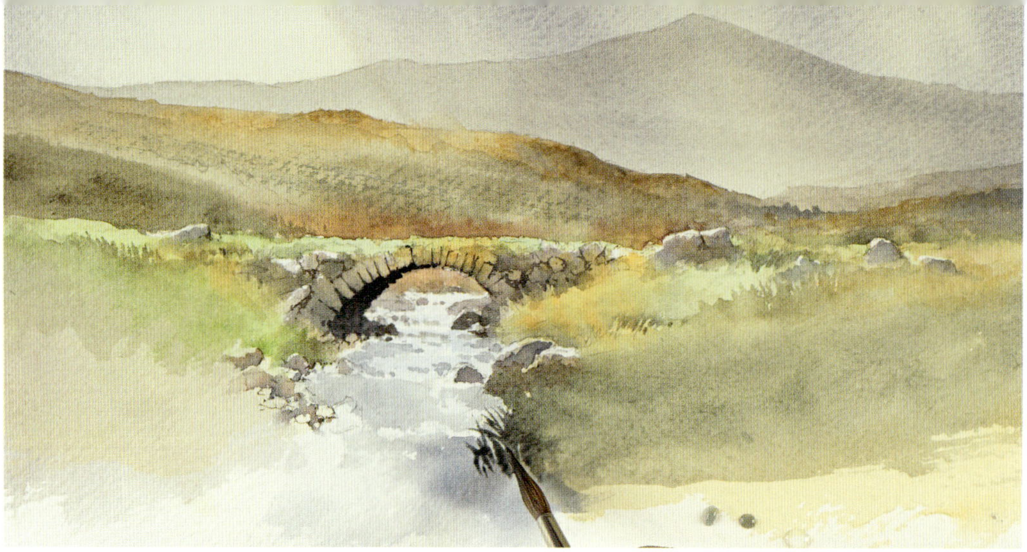

21 Darken the right-hand side of the painting with a wash of ultramarine and raw umber. Use a darker mix and the point of the brush to paint grasses at the water's edge.

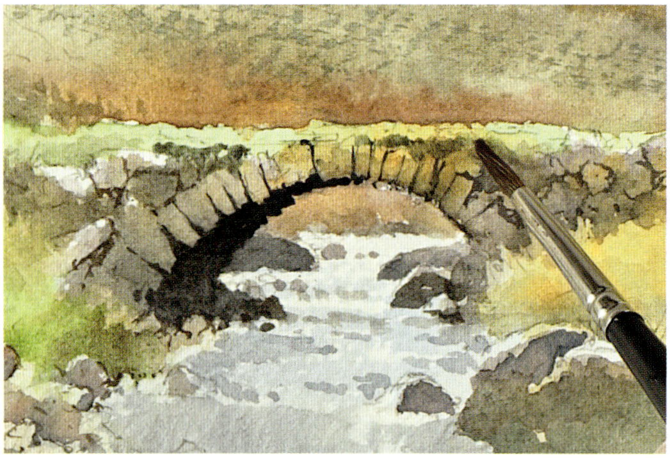

22 Darken the left-hand side in the same way, and drop in yellow ochre. Strengthen the rocky area visible through the bridge with the no. 4 brush and a mix of ultramarine and burnt umber. Add detail above the bridge with the same mix and soften it in with clean water.

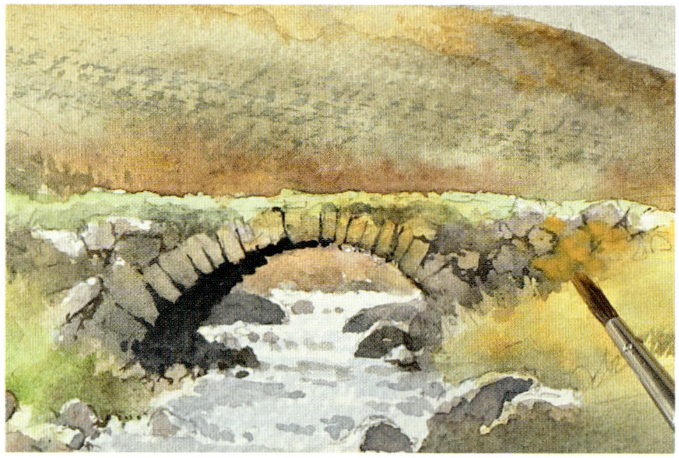

23 Wet the area to the right of the bridge and drop in cadmium orange.

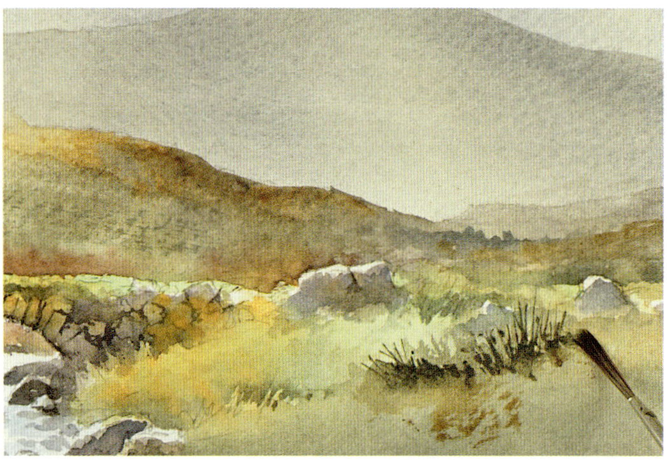

24 Use the no. 1 rigger and a mix of ultramarine and raw umber to paint reeds, and soften them in.

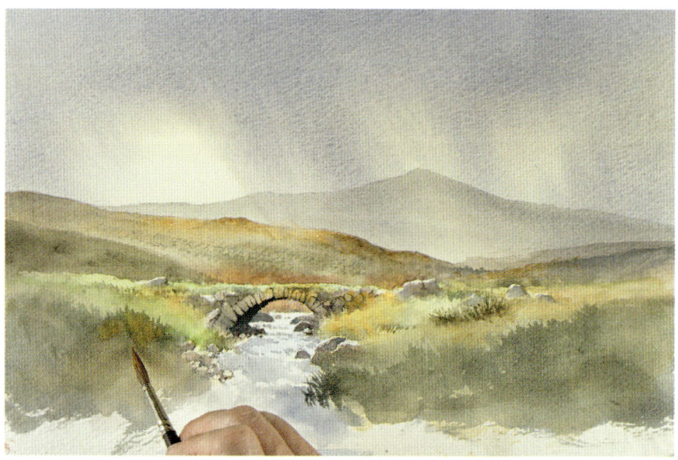

25 Paint a wash of ultramarine and raw umber across both sides of the foreground and drop in cadmium orange on the left.

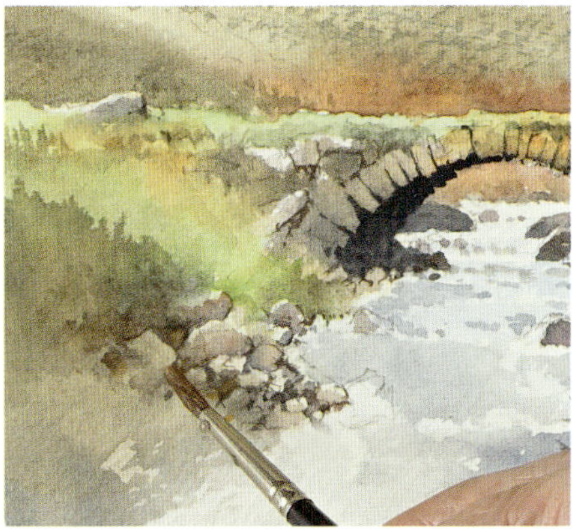

**26** Add dark tone around the rocks on the left-hand bank to emphasize them, using the no. 1 round brush and burnt umber and ultramarine. Drop in yellow ochre.

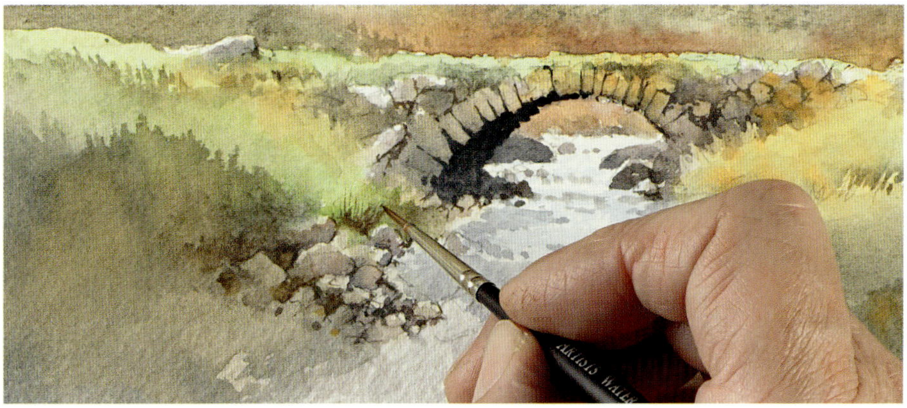

**27** Finally, paint reeds with perylene maroon and burnt umber.

*The finished painting.*

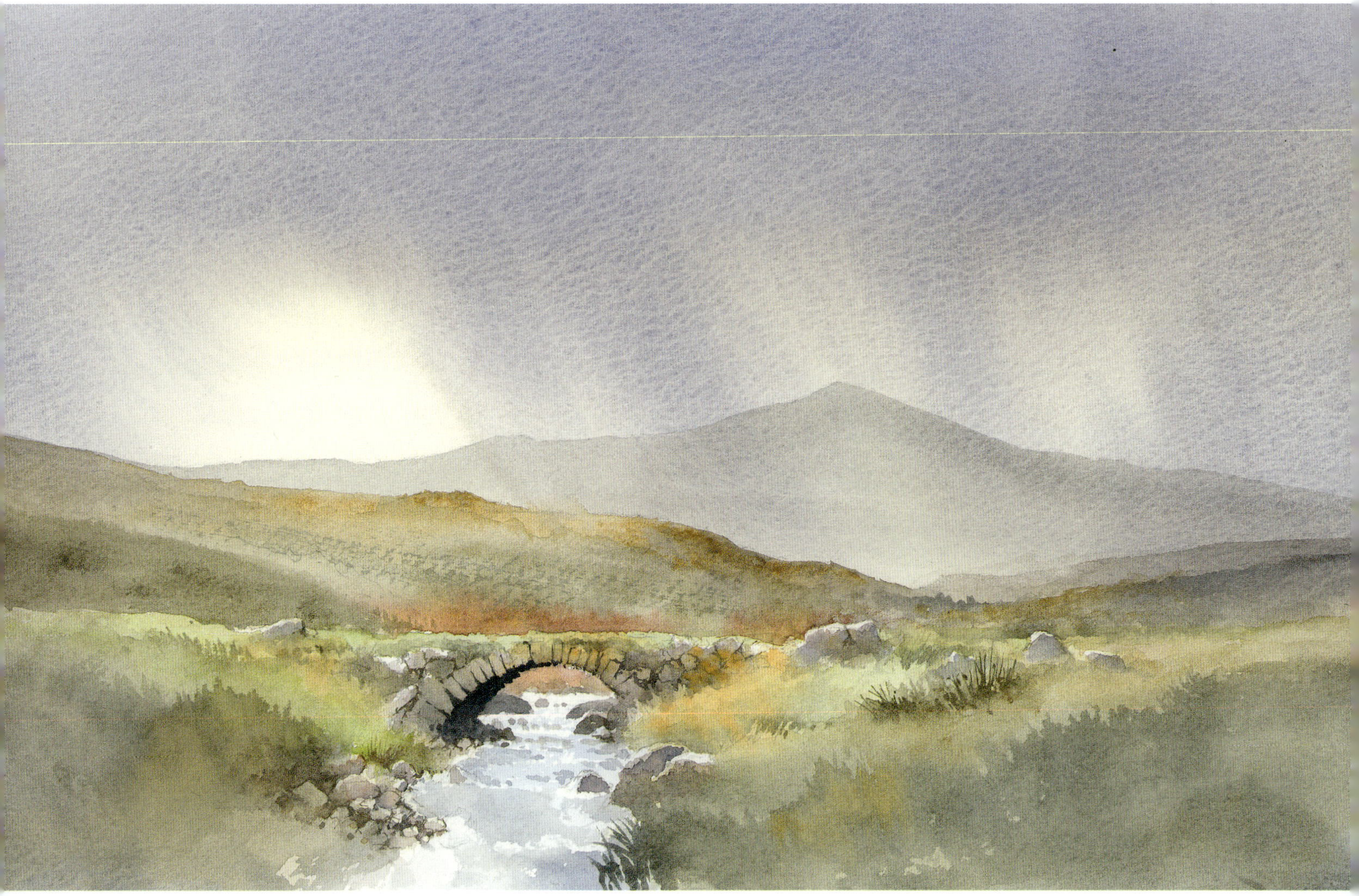

# Winter

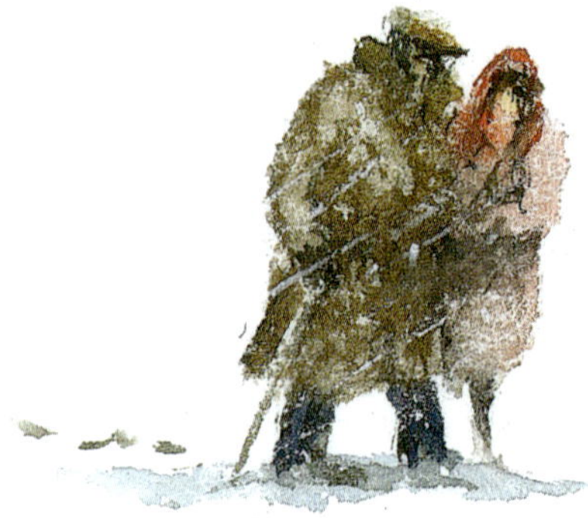

Winter to me is the most exciting of the seasons, and the most varied. Gone are all those greens: we can see features no longer hidden behind foliage, and although daylight hours are fewer, low-angled sunshine creates evocative cast shadows. Fields take on a greater range of colours and textures; tree trunks and branches display interesting colours. When seen as a mass, the branches of birch trees can take on a striking wine colour, especially useful if you wish to bring warmth into a cold snow scene. Dead leaves can be included even if they are not present, as their reds and oranges enliven the landscape and break up the masses of twigs and branches.

A fall of snow brings a complete change: landscape features stand out more clearly against the whiteness. Much of the snow is not white because of shadow areas and colours in reflected light. At twilight, warm-coloured skies create reflections in snowy fields, combined with long cast shadows.

## WORKING OUTDOORS IN WINTER

I have always been an outdoorsman, and aware that without the right clothing, it can be purgatory hanging around outside in the cold. Layered clothing is better than thick garments. Modern thermal underwear that wicks away perspiration, covered with a warm shirt and a lined fleece jacket is excellent, and over this a waterproof and windproof outer shell. A waterproof hood is of great help, but don't forget a woollen hat. Lined trousers are marvellous. Thin but warm insulated gloves allow you to use a brush and pencil easily, although fingerless gloves, some with a flap to cover all while you are not sketching, are also available. Jenny, my wife, often uses hand-warmers in her gloves if it's really cold. Not everyone can tolerate sketching outside, but there is still a lot you can do to obtain reasonable images. Keep your sketching equipment simple and ready for action. Don't forget to take photographs at various angles and zooming distances.

Wind blasting across snowy landscapes can be a real killer, so find some shelter if possible. At times, I have had to dart in and out of the shelter of a boulder or crag to render part of the scene that I can't quite see from my sanctuary, and moving around does help keep you warm. I have often danced round rocks or trees to combat the cold, hoping that no one is watching! Walking and sketching is a superb way to work.

**THE PANTILES, TUNBRIDGE WELLS**

*This pen and wash sketch was carried out over afternoon tea sitting outside a café in Kent, UK. Although winter was just about past, it was cold, but many like to sit outside even in the dead of winter, enjoying the sunshine, and so long as you are well wrapped up, carrying out a sketch while you take refreshments can be rewarding. Just don't dip your brush in the tea.*

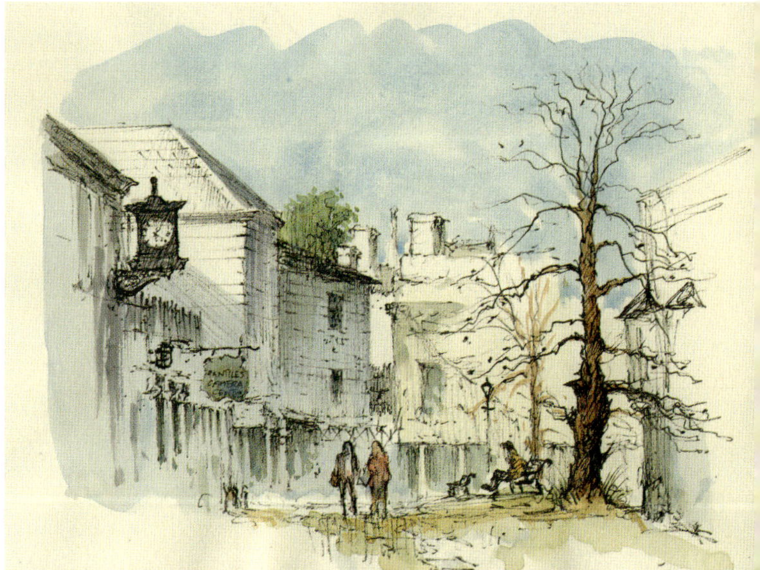

If you become concerned about the cold, then get back into the warm as soon as possible. A few rapid strokes of the pencil may suffice to record the most important aspects of a scene. Once in a car, tent or building, note down any vital bits of visual information, such as colours, that you need to recall later. If there is a line of trees, all of the same species but different shapes and heights, I draw the most important one in detail and then simply create an outline to indicate the others, and I can draw these in details later. I often start off the tone at a critical point in a passage and fill the rest in later. I am often amazed at how clearly I can recall elements in a scene by looking at the mass of sketchy lines I have drawn with this visual shorthand.

When engrossed in a composition, it is easy to forget your situation, so you can become extremely cold without realizing it. Remember to jump up every now and then and walk around vigorously for a minute or two.

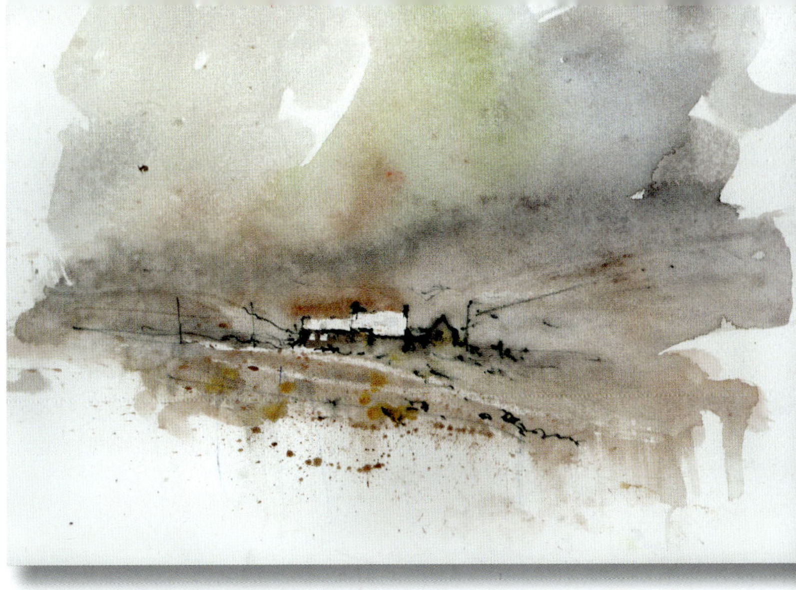

FARM AT SHAW BOTTOM

*Deep snow lay all around, but on the rough moor, much of it had been blown away or fallen into tall grasses and ditches. In this sketch, done on Hot Pressed paper, I rapidly splashed washes on with a no.10 round brush, avoiding the roofs, and immediately began drawing into the wet wash with a black watercolour pencil. I made the background darker in order to make the snow-covered roofs stand out starkly, and could see more of the horizon than is revealed in this sketch. While it was still damp, I pulled out some lighter areas with a flat brush and then spattered other colours over the foreground, some onto damp paper. Working quickly in this way gives a lovely sense of spontaneity, and there is less chance of frostbite for the artist.*

## RAPID WATERCOLOUR SKETCHING IN THE COLD

For this I tend to lay washes down and then draw into them with a dark watercolour pencil as they are drying. This is fast and efficient and usually I can keep painting even when parts of the sketch remain wet, as a strong watercolour pencil line acts as a barrier, containing the wash, provided the angle of the paper is not too steep. By sketching in this way, you learn to simplify a scene, seeking out the most important features and drawing and painting them with bold, confident strokes.

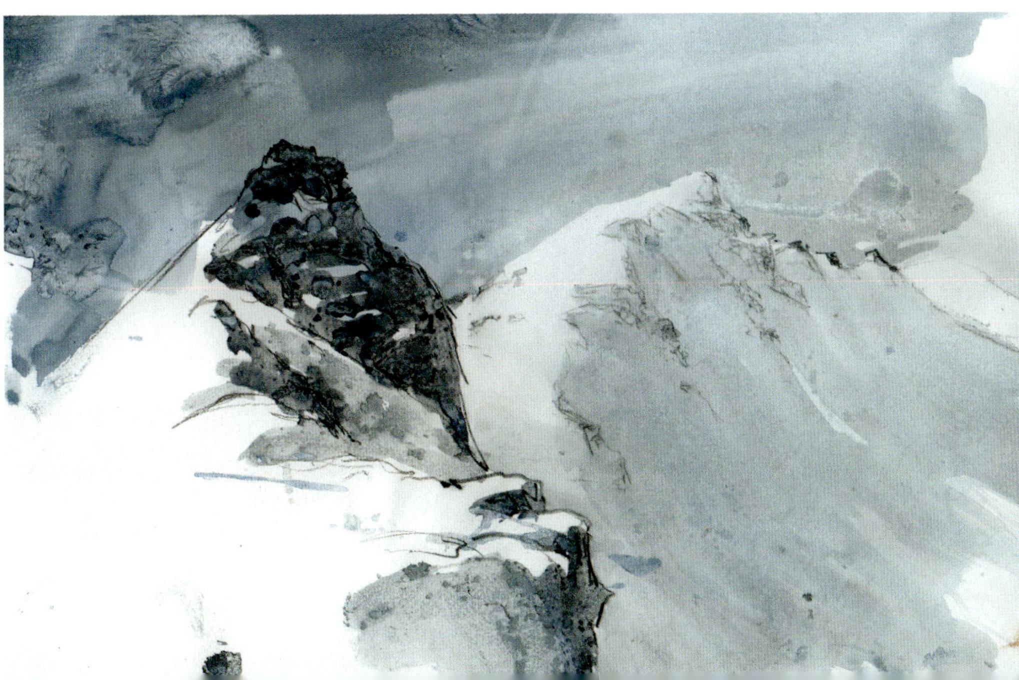

SUMMIT OF PARKHOUSE HILL

*Sometimes the scene is simply too good to miss, whatever the weather conditions, and on this day they were frightful. I include this watercolour sketch because it shows that even with ferocious gusts and below-zero temperatures icing up the wash, you can achieve something that can be used as a basis for a later painting in the calm of the studio. Speed was achieved by using only one colour and drawing with a water-soluble pencil while the washes were still wet.*

# ROGUE COLOURS IN THE LANDSCAPE

There are normally far too many colours in the landscape in front of you, and we need to reduce these to impart a greater sense of unity to the scene. I rarely copy the colours before me, preferring to impose my own sense of colour, whether I feel the need for strongly contrasting colours or more harmonious ones. I always try to take into account the adjacent colours, as this has a strong bearing on how we see the whole effect. One device I constantly use is to drop in what I call 'rogue' colours where I think the composition would benefit. These are often reds or yellows dropped into a wet patch of colour to warm it up. You will see examples of this approach throughout this book. It can be a strong red placed on a prominent tree trunk, a bright yellow field in front of a building, or a patch of Winsor blue amid some warmer blues in a snowy foreground.

GALWAY COAST

*28 x 40.5cm (11 x 16in), 300gsm (140lb) Not paper*

*Although there tends to be more colour in the natural landscape in winter, it is often helpful to exaggerate the warm colours, both to draw the eye to a particular part of a composition, and to counter the coldness in a scene. In this painting of the Galway coast in Ireland, I have warmed up the strip of land below the cottage and the right-hand foreground with a rogue cadmium red, to alleviate the overall coldness of the scene and to give more prominence to the focal point.*

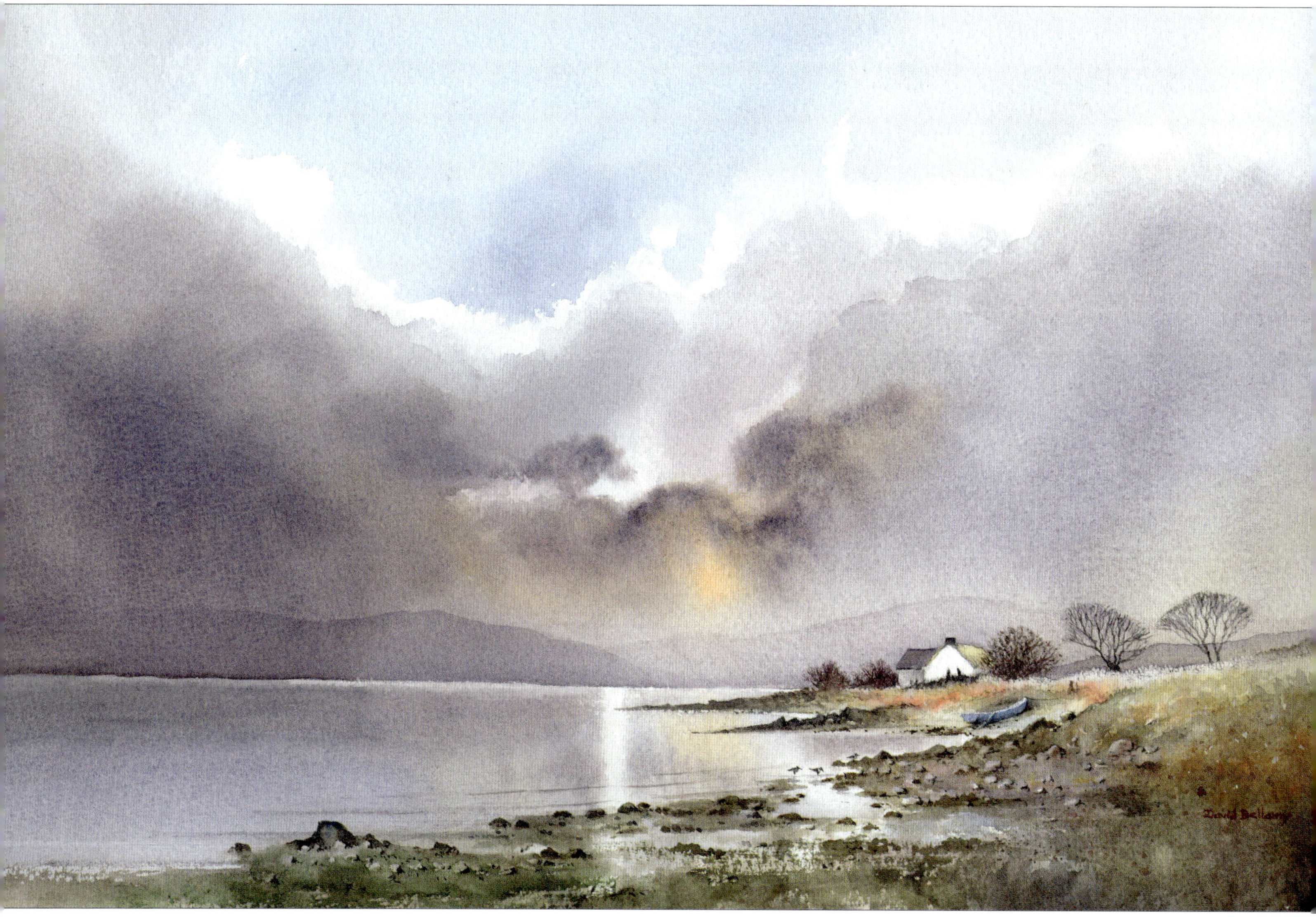

# TAKING ADVANTAGE OF LOW LIGHTING

The lower angle of light during winter creates some wonderfully long and evocative cast shadows. This is especially apparent in early morning or evening, so you can create a lovely sense of evening by lengthening your shadows and combining this with warm light. Here we look at how I have suggested winter light in mid-morning.

**FARM IN WINTER SUNLIGHT**
*28 x 35.5cm (11 x 14in), 300gsm (140lb) Rough*

*Including cast shadows will really emphasize the feeling of sunlight, so take full advantage of long winter shadows, whether they sprawl over a building or field. In this painting the low winter light is coming from the left, throwing shadows from unseen trees across the foreground field. Note that all the fields and hillsides are either pale yellow or pale green – this affords maximum opportunity to make the cast shadows stand out. To accentuate this effect, I sometimes change a dull grey or ochre building into a whitewashed one. I used masking fluid to retain the light cut stalks leading towards the farm. Ruts, furrows and rows of stalks are an excellent way of leading the eye to the focal point.*

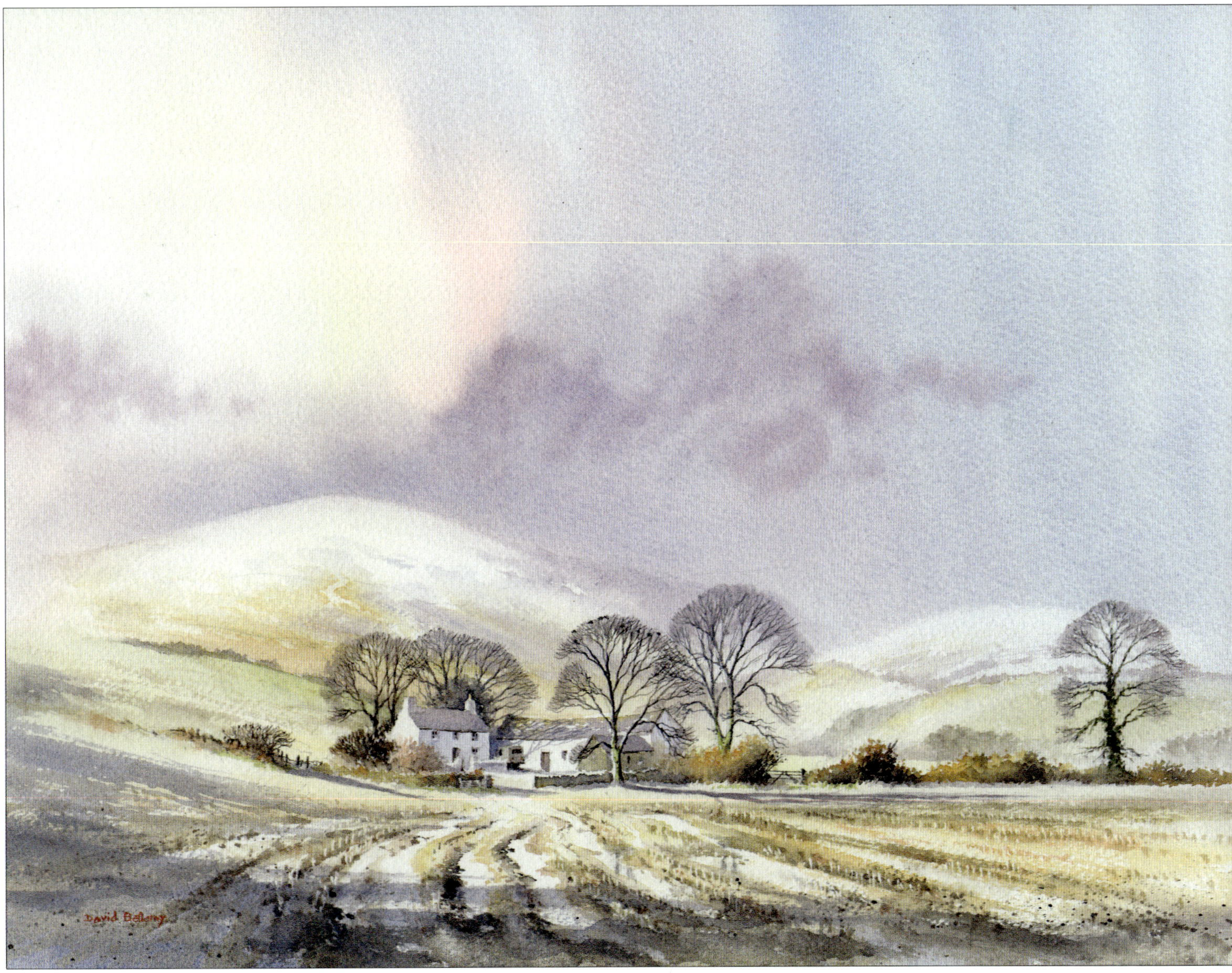

# BARE BRANCHES AND TRUNKS

Winter trees and bushes have a charm and attraction that can enhance any landscape painting, and it is worth spending some time studying their characteristics. Tree trunks can be full of exciting and unexpected colours: reds, pinks, yellows, greens and blues, as well as the more common greys. The closer the tree stands, the more scope you have for including colour. Note, too, how branches hang, droop, curve or entwine themselves into amazing contortions. Here we look at a few examples.

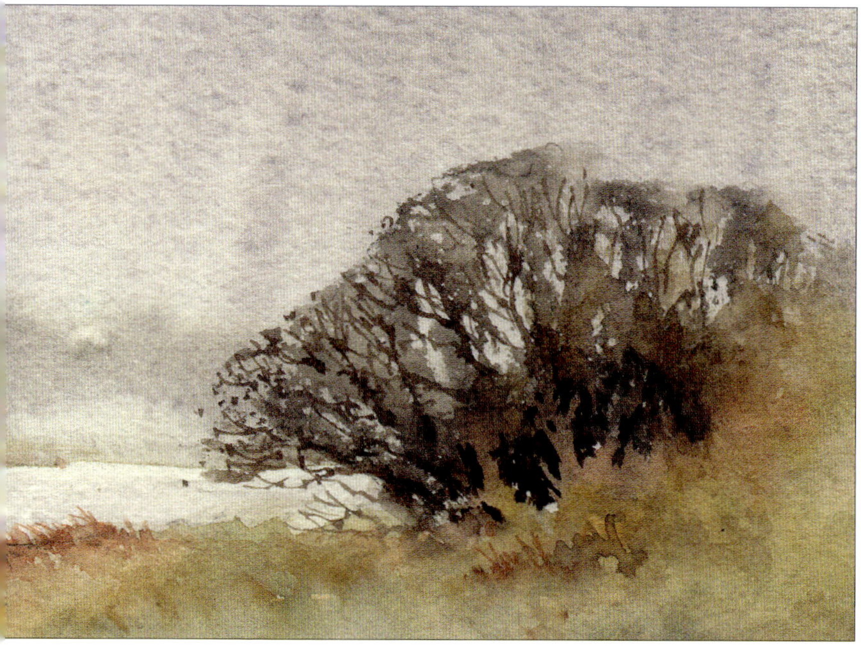

## Negative tree trunks

An effective method with winter trees and bushes is to create a mass of branches and vegetation, apply negative painting into it to suggest trunks, then bring out the massed branchwork at the top. Here, I started with a wash of yellow ochre with a touch of cadmium yellow pale, and immediately dropped in some weak Indian red above this, then a little burnt umber and French ultramarine above that, using the side of a no. 6 brush to suggest a mass of branches and letting all the washes intermingle. This gradual change of colour is simple but effective. When the combined wash had dried, I described more branches with a rigger, over the upper burnt umber and French ultramarine wash. This gave a sense of depth to the branch structure. Finally I painted in the negative shapes between the trunks with a darker French ultramarine and burnt umber mix.

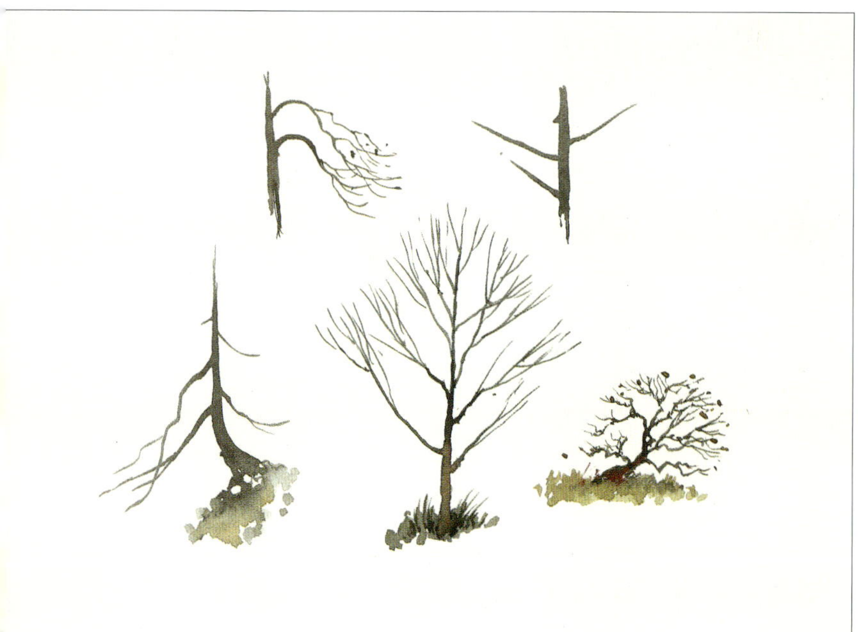

## Angular, sweeping or drooping branches

When you paint bare trees, note how the branches form as they leave the trunk: some shoot straight out, while others, such as thorn trees, are extremely angular. Others change direction dramatically or flow downwards in a graceful curve, like larch branches.

# PAINTING LIGHT TREES AGAINST DARK SKIES AND BACKGROUNDS

Light-coloured trees set against a dark, angry sky or sombre mountain can conjure up real drama, but they are not easy to paint in watercolour. You may be able to see every single branch strongly etched against the darkness, but try to avoid any attempt at putting them all in. Negative painting techniques are almost impossible to render convincingly if you try to emulate a great mass of branches. In these examples I show how masking fluid can work well for this effect.

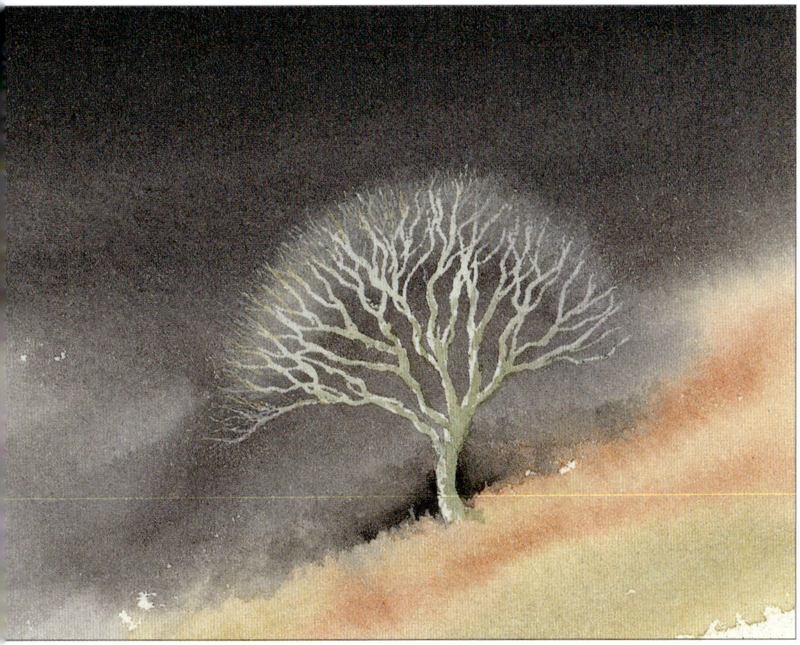

LIGHT TREE AGAINST A DARK SKY

*In this example I have resorted to masking fluid for the main branches, applied with a size 0 rigger with most of the masking fluid removed from the brush, so that a fine line was achieved for the outer branches. You have to waste some masking fluid on scrap paper first to check that it is fine enough for your needs. After the dark sky was painted over the light trees, I removed the masking fluid, then scrubbed the top mass of branches with a small, damp, flat brush. This suggests the mass of light twigs and branches. It also leaves a pleasing fuzzy edge to the extremities. I laid a weak glaze of French ultramarine and cadmium red over the right-hand (shadow) side of the tree, and this also helped to prevent it looking like a cut-out.*

## Choosing those special trees

Tree shapes make a fascinating study, and it is of great value to identify really good specimens and sketch and photograph them to keep as a reference for when you need that special tree. Sometimes the sub-branches leave the main branch in one direction only, as is mainly the case on the far left-hand trunk shown.

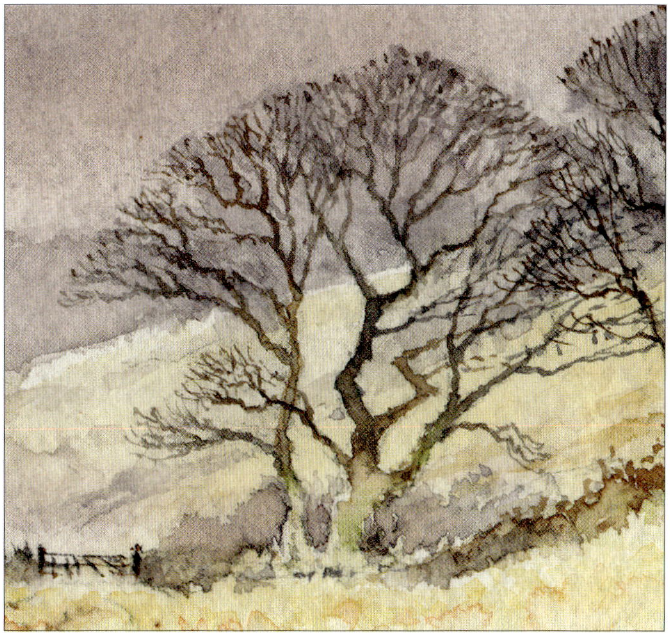

# WINTER MOUNTAINS

In winter, places like Buttermere in the Lake District, UK, are easier to access than in summer, when they can be choked with people and traffic. You don't have to walk far to get a decent viewpoint, and can always retire to the pub if the weather gets too much. In winter, the mountainsides can reveal many warm colours, which you can move to suit your composition. A cool-temperature passage or two works wonders for balance and will make your warm areas appear even warmer.

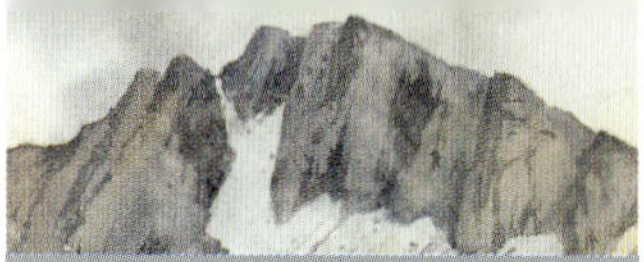

**MATERIALS USED**

Saunders Waterford 640gsm (300lb) Rough watercolour paper

Brushes: Large and small squirrel mops, no. 7 and no. 4 sable round, 13mm (½in) flat, no. 10 sable round, no. 1 rigger

Colours: Naples yellow, yellow ochre, cadmium orange, cobalt blue, French ultramarine, burnt umber, cadmium red, Indian red, light red, quinacridone gold, green gold, raw umber, alizarin crimson

Sponge; paper mask; 6B pencil

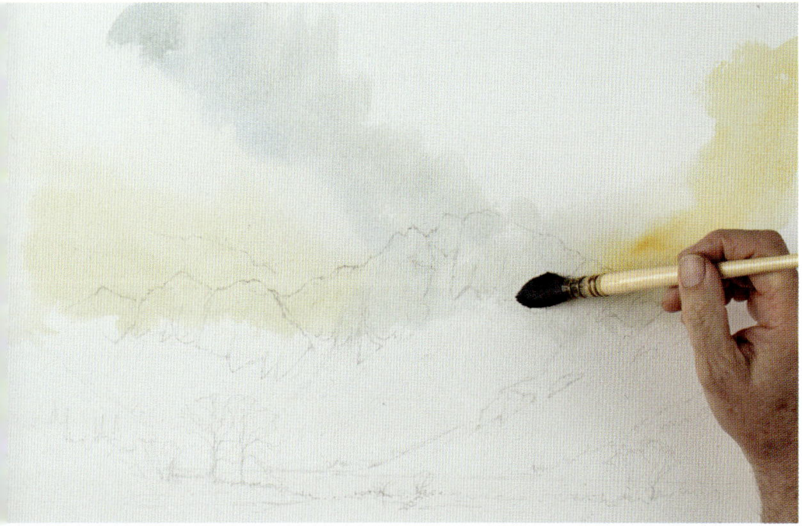

1 Draw the scene with a 6B pencil. Wash the sky and mountains with a large squirrel mop and clean water, then wash Naples yellow and a little yellow ochre over the area, followed by Naples yellow and cadmium orange on the right. Mix a little of the orange with cobalt blue and wash this diagonally across for cloud.

2 Working wet into wet, paint in darker cloud with French ultramarine and burnt umber, leaving hints of white and suggesting cloud boiling up over the mountains. Allow to dry.

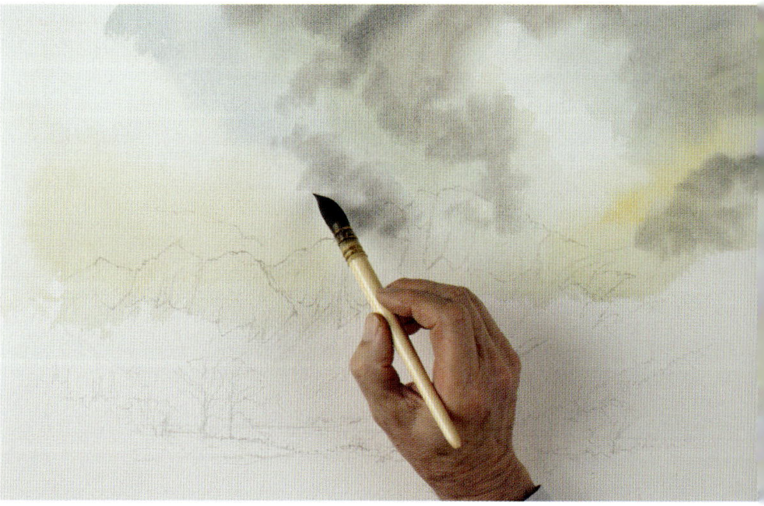

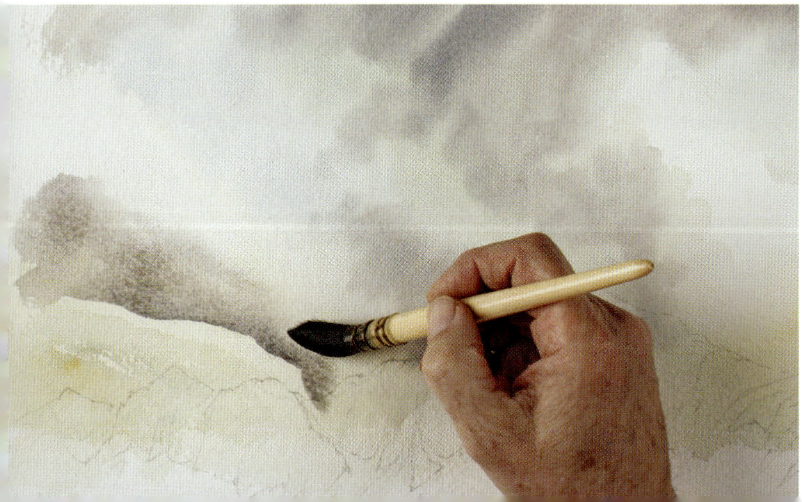

3 Paint the background ridge with pale cobalt blue and yellow ochre, on a fairly dry no. 7 round brush. Use the small mop to rewet the sky behind this and darken it with burnt umber and French ultramarine to highlight the ridge.

4 Use the no. 7 round and dry-brush work with cobalt blue and yellow ochre to paint the scree on the mountain slopes.

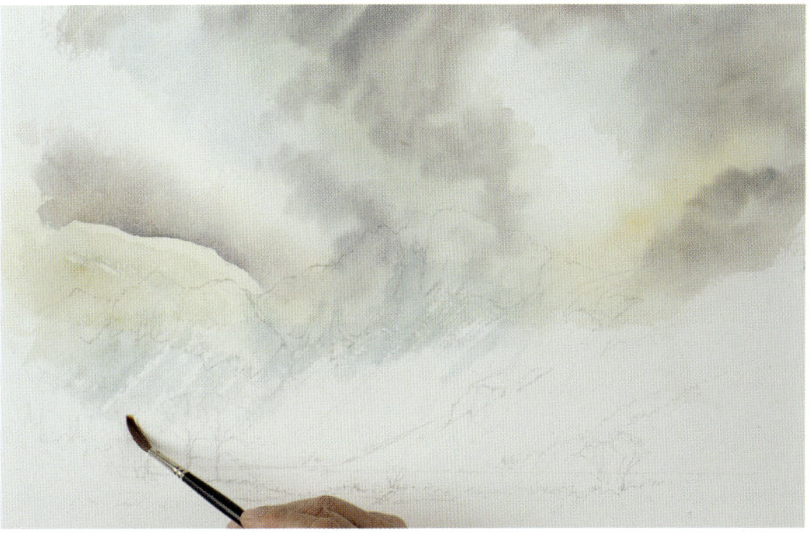

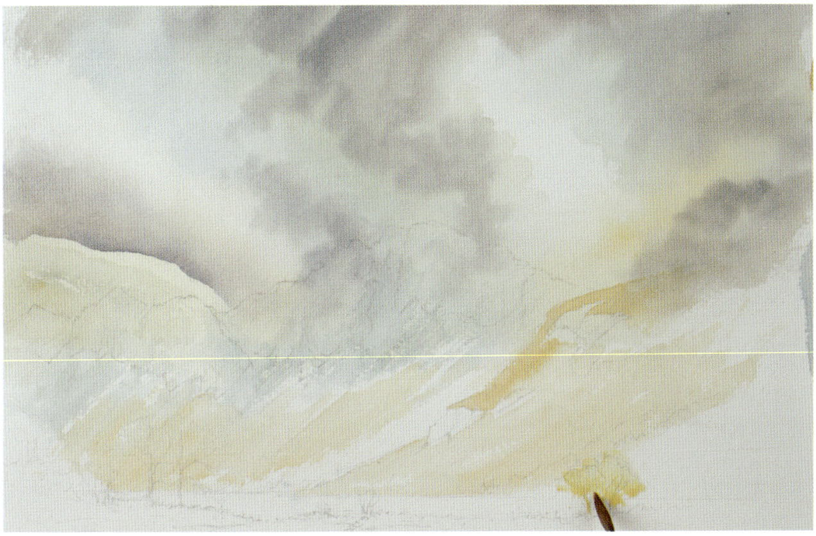

5 Paint the rocky area in the middle ground and foreground with yellow ochre, then paint Naples yellow for the trees on the right, which will be light against a dark background.

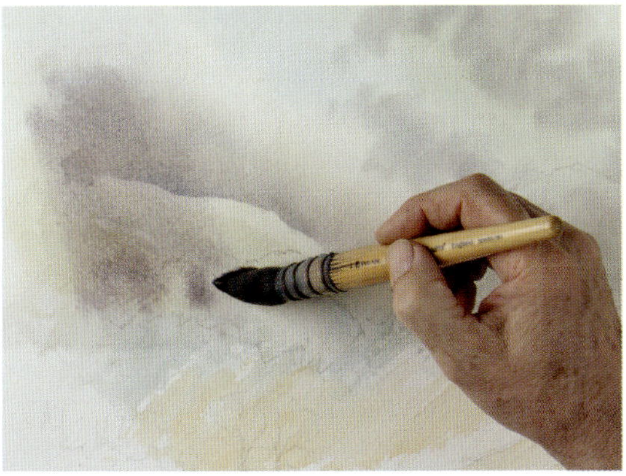

6 Use a damp 13mm (½in) flat brush to soften the hard edge of the background ridge, then use a large mop brush to paint water over the left-hand side of the painting and apply a glaze of cobalt blue and cadmium red. Allow to dry.

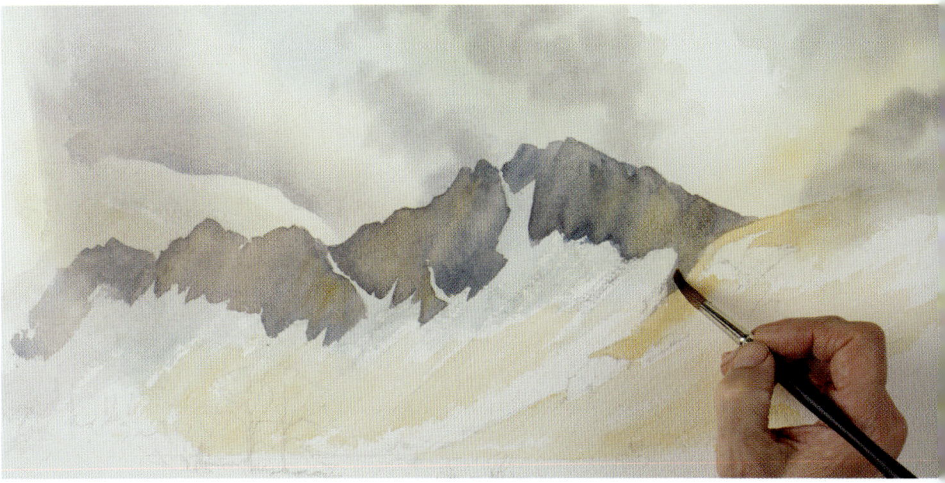

7 Mix light red and ultramarine and use the no. 10 round brush to paint the crags of the mountains wet on dry, then drop in yellow ochre. Continue across the painting in this way.

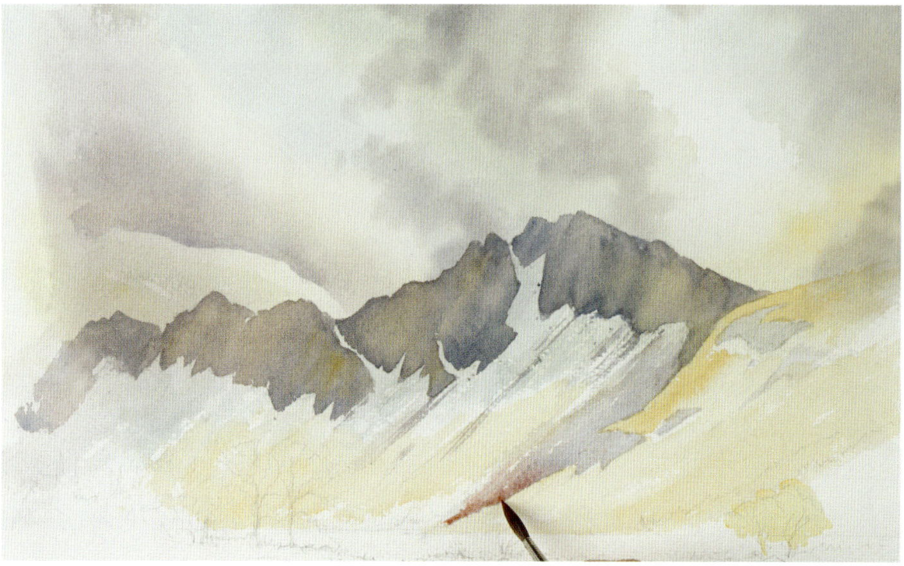

8 Use a paler version of the same mix with a no. 7 brush to paint behind the foreground ridge on the right. Drop in Indian red wet into wet.

9 Rewet the middle area and drop in light red, then Indian red at the bottom. Allow to dry.

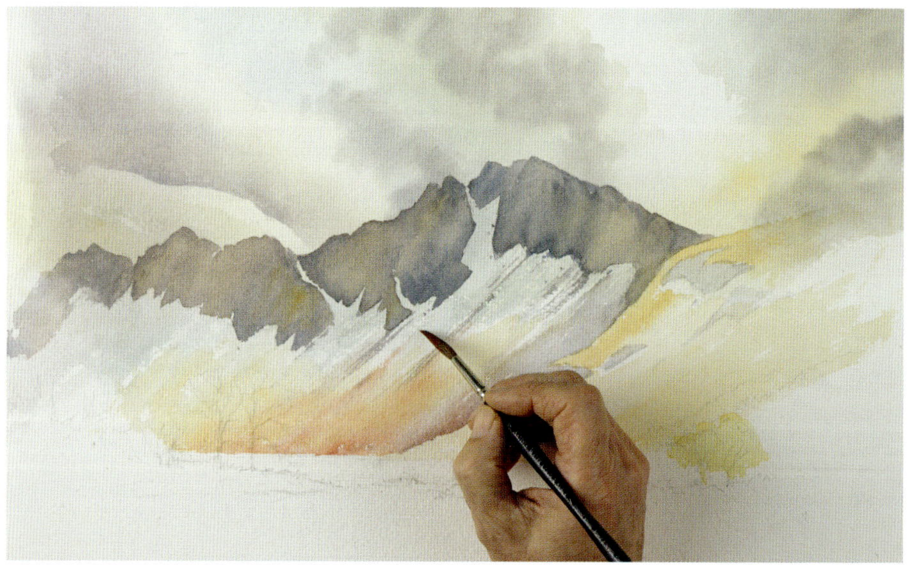

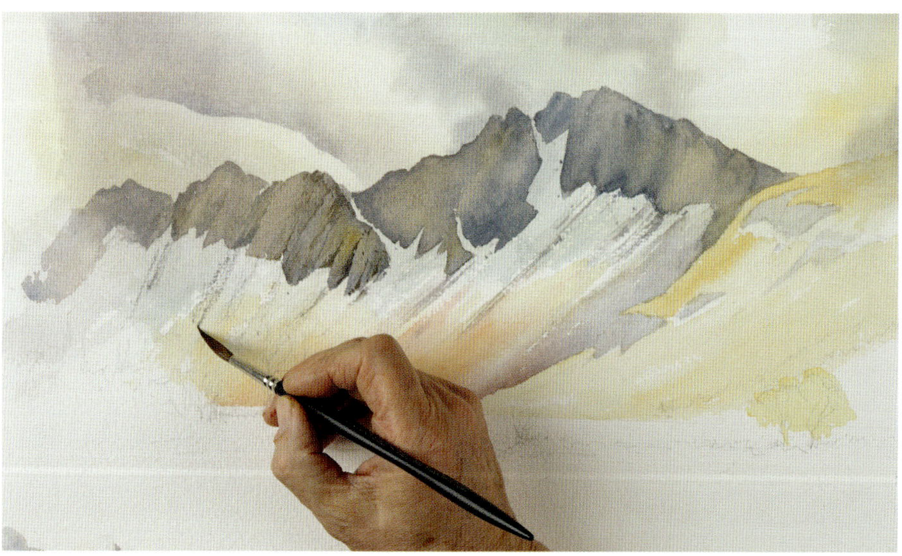

10 Suggest detail on the crags and the lower slopes with the same mix and dry-brush work.

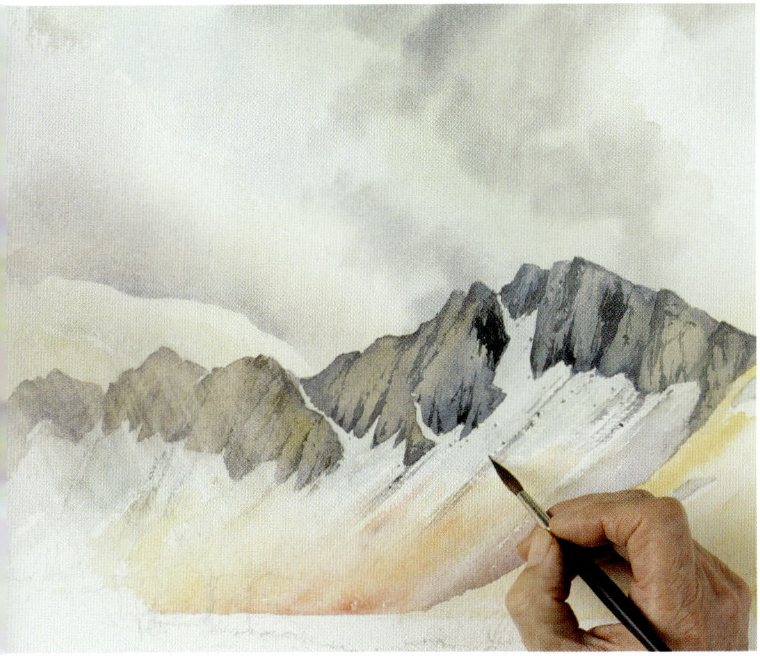

11 Wipe a damp sponge diagonally over the left-hand side of the mountains to subdue them, then use the point of the no. 7 brush to paint detail of the middle crags with French ultramarine and burnt umber.

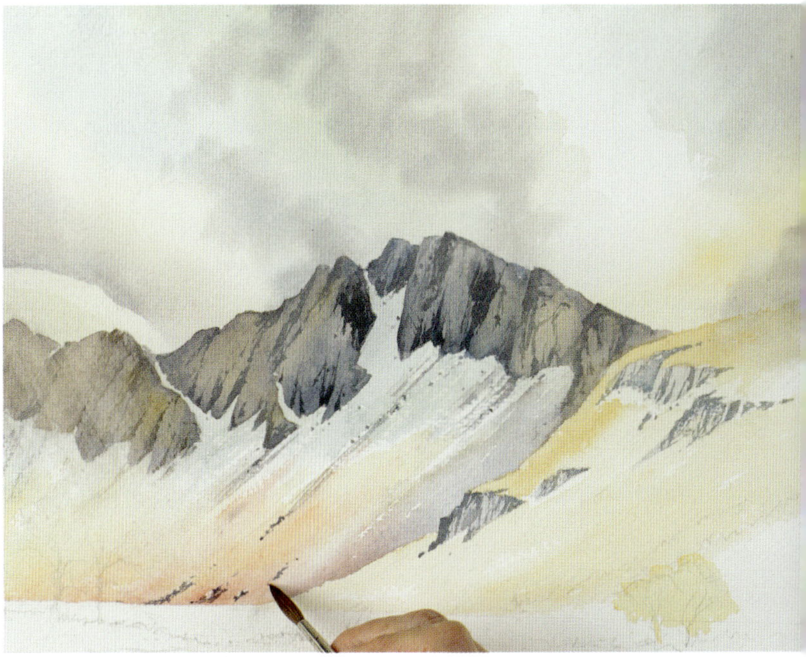

12 Paint more rocky detail on the right-hand side in the same way, and continue on the lower slopes.

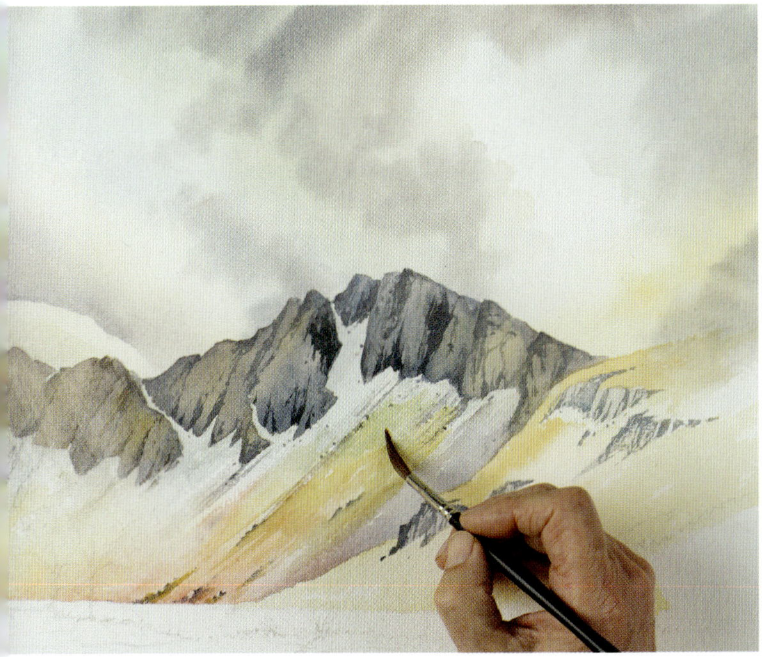

13 Add yellow ochre to the slopes.

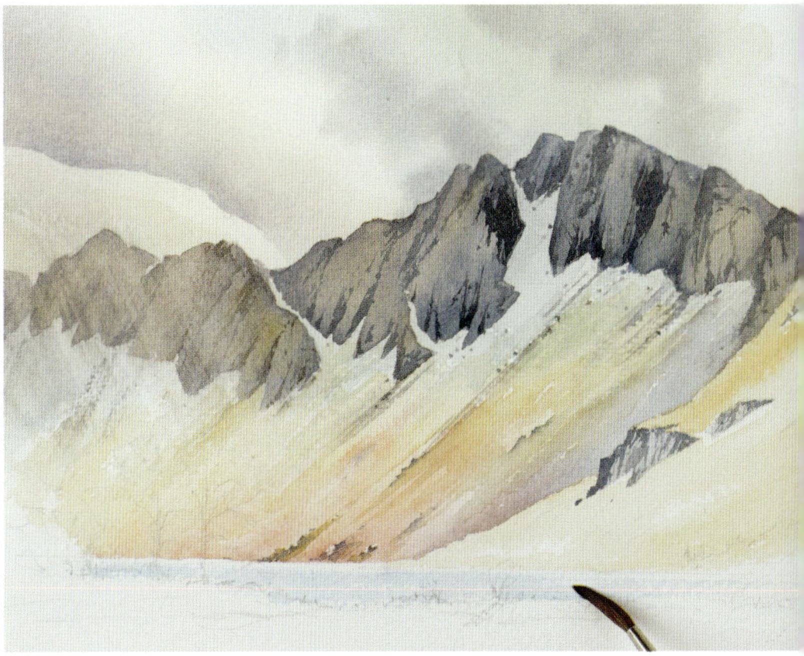

14 Drag a pale mix of cobalt blue across the lake, leaving speckles of white, and allow to dry. This brings out the warmth of the colours behind it.

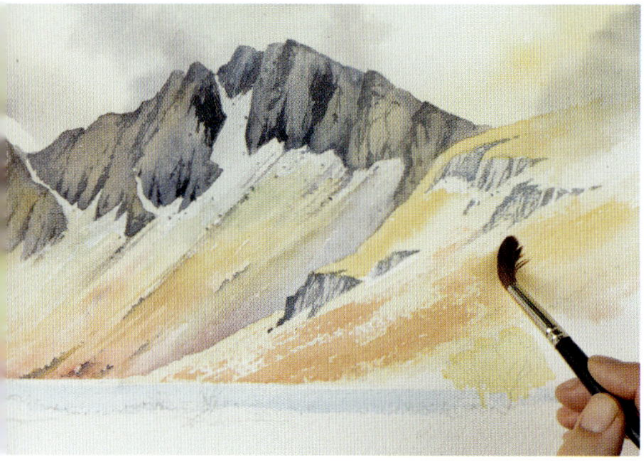

15 Use the no. 10 brush on its side to paint broken colour across the right-hand slope with light red, then soften the edges with water. Add more yellow ochre.

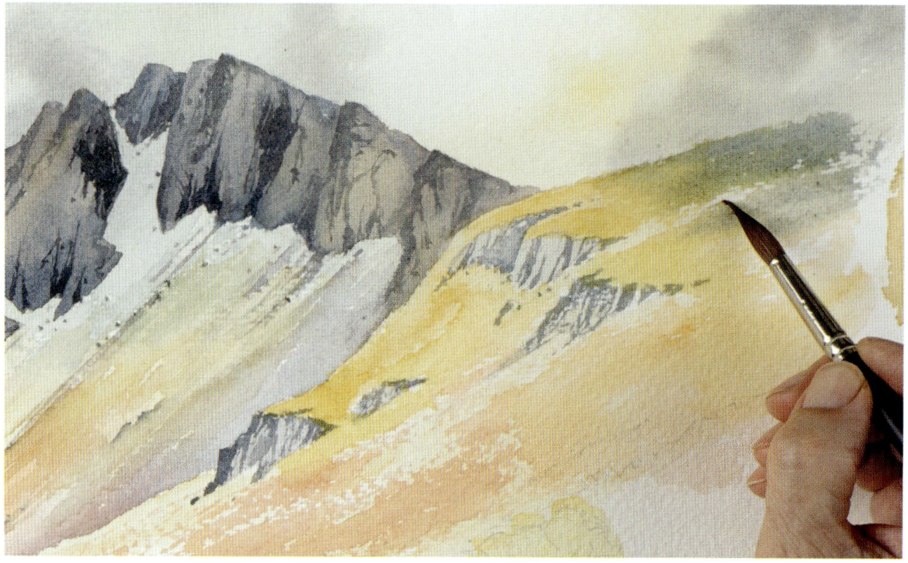

16 Paint quinacridone gold on the surfaces catching the light to highlight them. Blend in a mix of French ultramarine and light red.

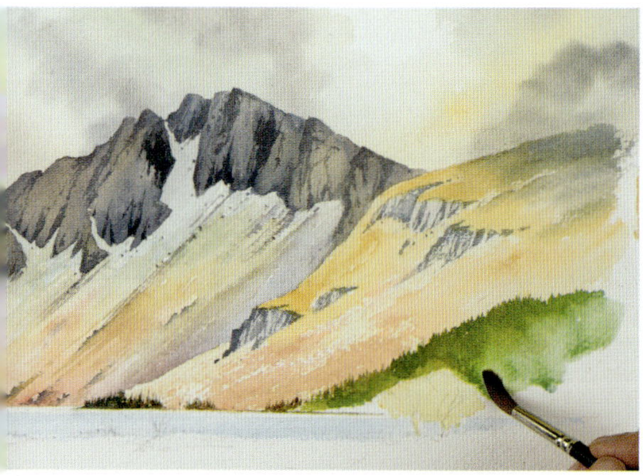

17 Use the no. 7 round and a mix of ultramarine and raw umber to paint conifers on the far shore. Continue them along the lakeside to the right, changing to green gold and cobalt blue. Soften the bottom of the shape with water.

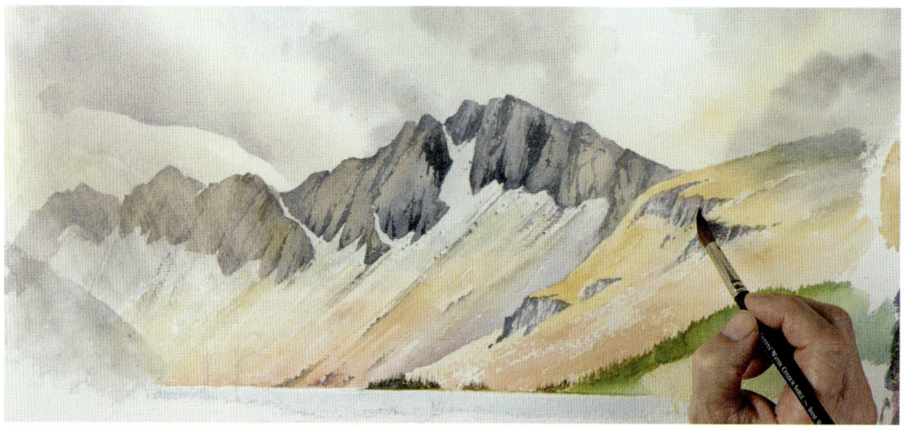

18 Paint a very pale slope of French ultramarine and light red on the far left, then add shadow to the right-hand crags with cadmium red and cobalt blue. Allow to dry.

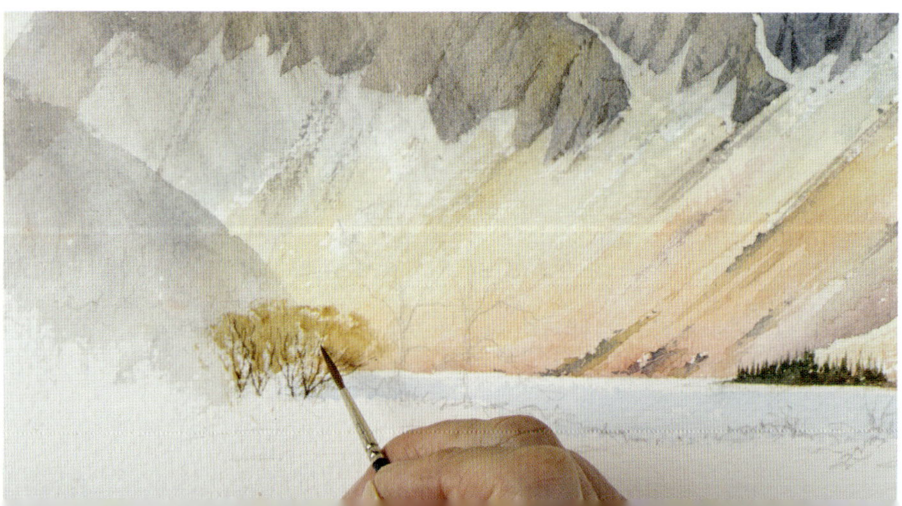

19 Use the no. 4 round brush and raw umber to paint the area of trees on the left, then use the no. 1 rigger and a mix of burnt umber and French ultramarine to paint trunks and branches.

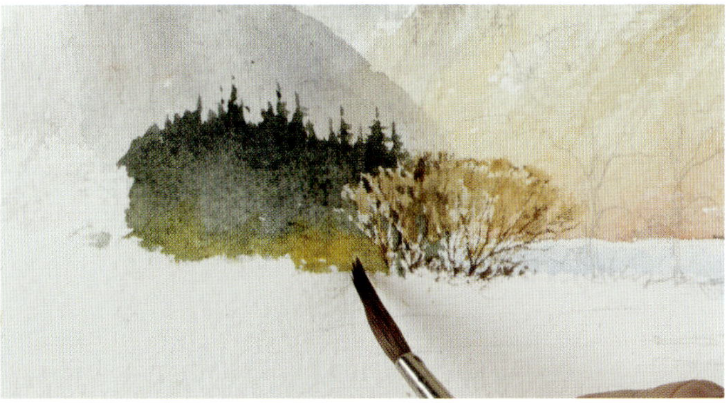

20 Paint conifers to the left using the point of the no. 7 brush and a mix of raw umber and French ultramarine. Paint round the lighter trees. Drop in quinacridone gold.

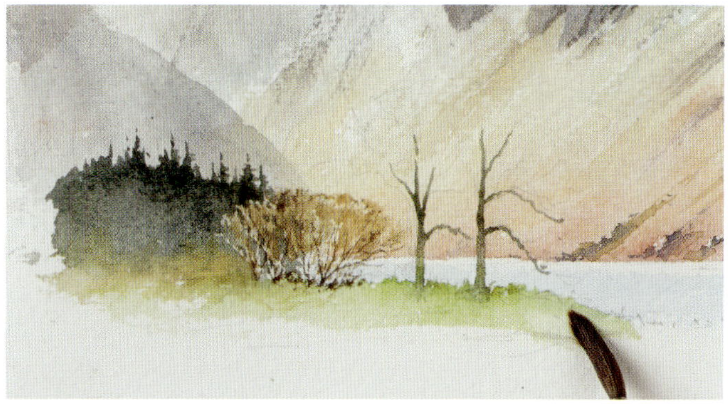

21 Use the same mix and brush to paint the two main trees on the left, then drop in green gold while the trunks are wet. Paint green gold beneath the trees as well.

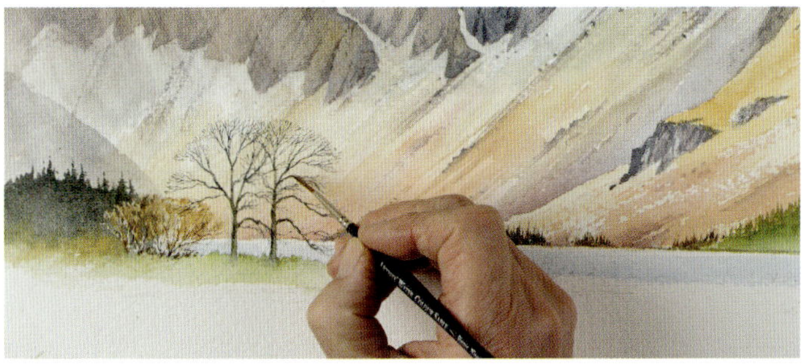

22 Change to the no. 1 rigger and paint the finer branches with burnt umber and French ultramarine.

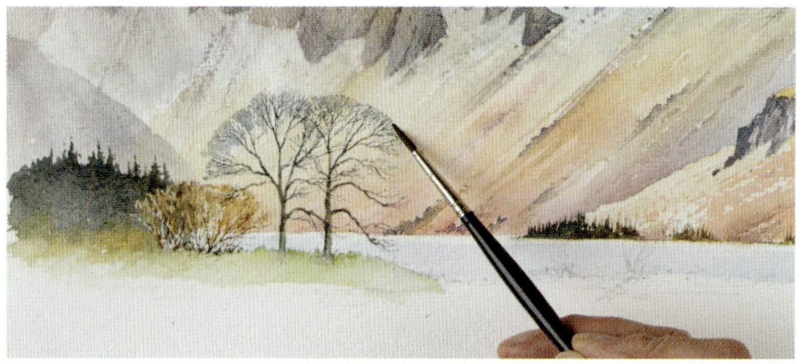

23 Use a weaker mix of the same colours and the no. 4 brush on its side to create the twigwork.

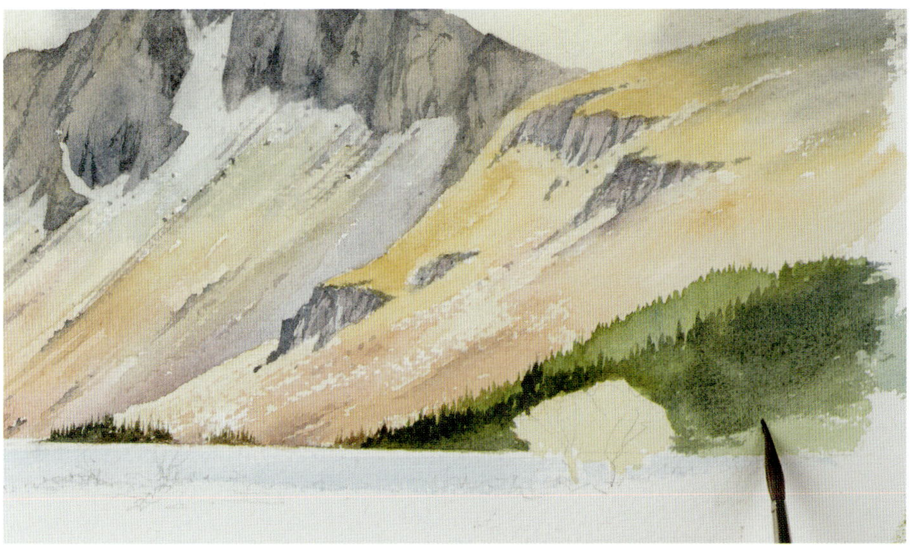

24 Use the no. 7 brush and a green mix of French ultramarine and raw umber to paint the darker conifers on the right-hand lakeside. Paint the pointed tops first, then scrub in the broader area.

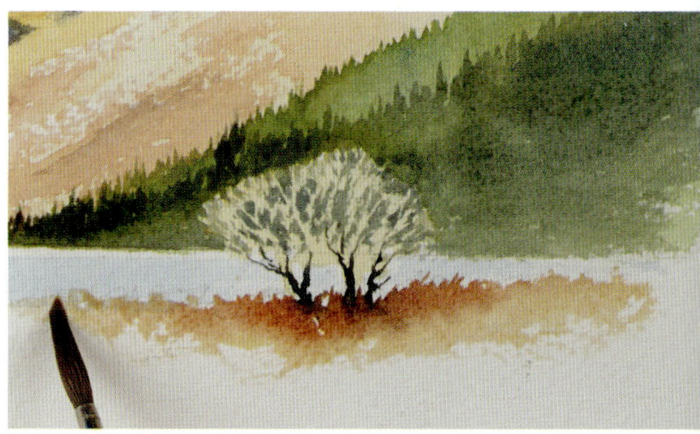

25 Suggest the light winter trees against the dark background with negative painting, then paint the trunks and details with French ultramarine and burnt umber. Drop in light red at the base of the trees, then yellow ochre wet into wet.

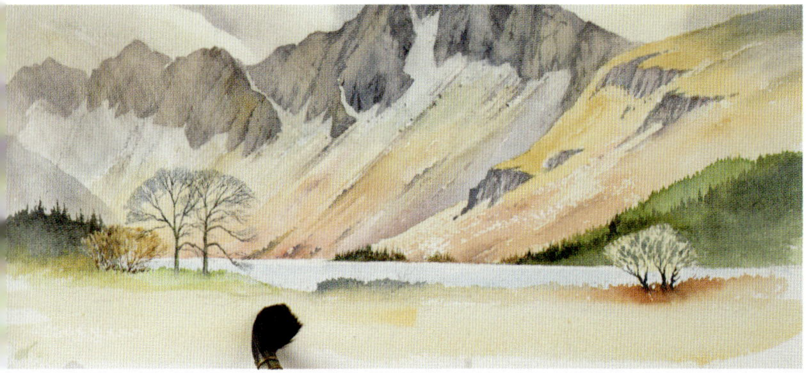

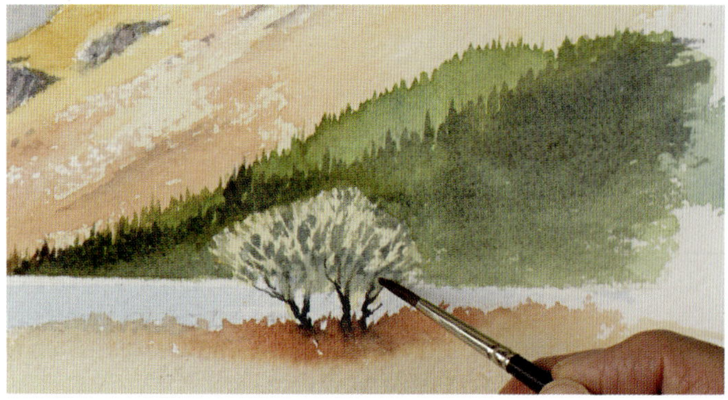

26 Paint the dry-stone wall in the foreground with French ultramarine and raw umber. Use the small squirrel mop to sweep in a wash of yellow ochre in the foreground. Allow to dry.

27 Use the no. 4 brush with a pale mix of French ultramarine and a hint of burnt umber to suggest shadow in the lighter trees.

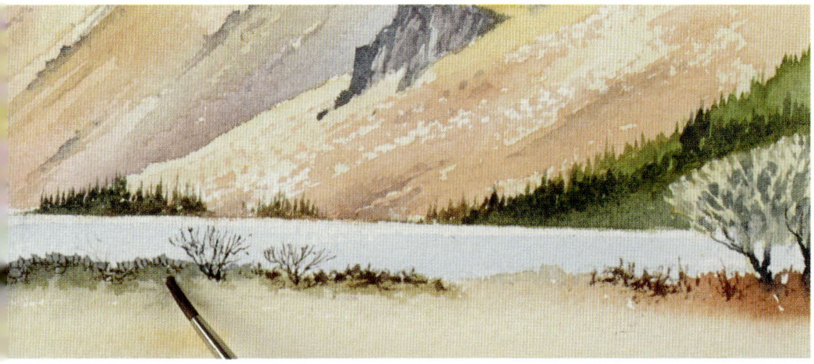

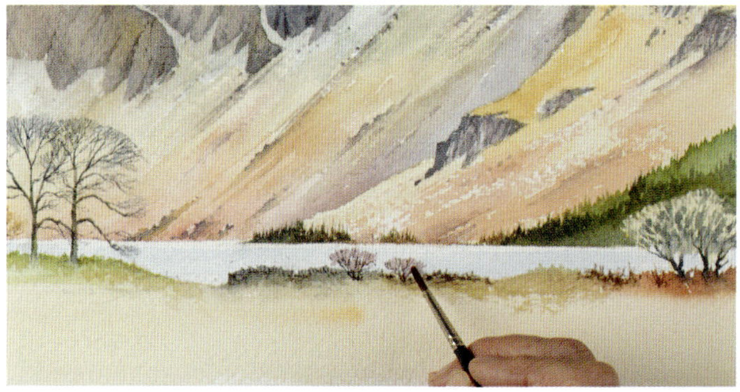

28 Change to the no. 1 rigger and a mix of burnt umber and French ultramarine and suggest bushes against the wall. Hint at stones, especially capstones. Add tone in the wall to subdue the stonework.

29 Darken under the left-hand trees with a little raw umber, then apply alizarin crimson to the bushes for twigwork.

30 Darken the foreground with the no. 10 brush on its side and a mix of cobalt blue and yellow ochre, creating texture. Drop in cadmium red to liven it up, and light red at the edge of the lake. Darken under the trees with French ultramarine and burnt umber.

31 Subdue the right-hand conifers with the small mop brush, first with clean water, then a glaze of cobalt blue and cadmium red.

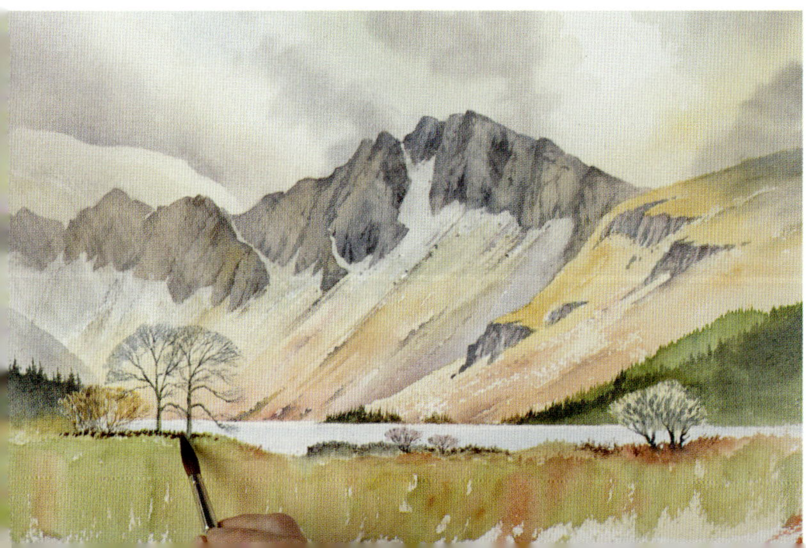

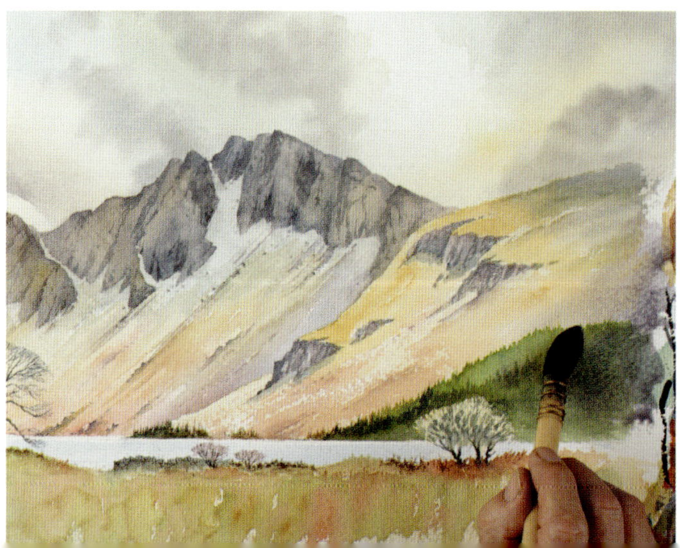

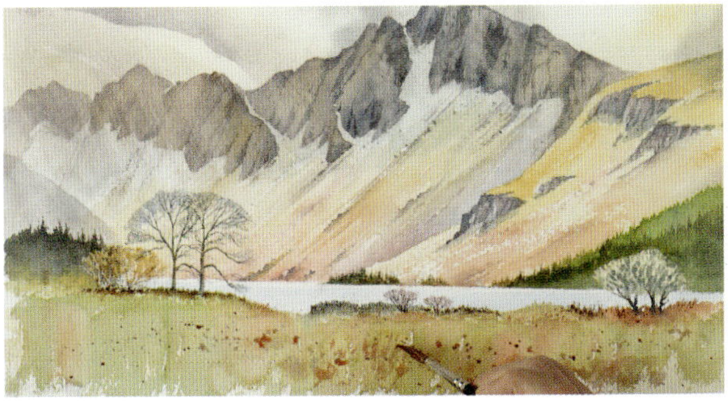

32 Spatter light red and French ultramarine in the foreground from a paintbrush, then drop in more light red and use the no. 7 brush to flick up grasses.

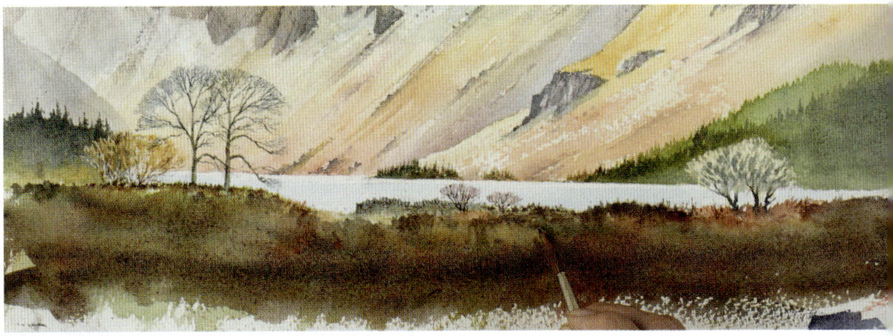

33 At this point I stood back from the painting and decided to darken the foreground. Load the large mop brush with burnt umber and French ultramarine and sweep it over the foreground. Dot suggested detail over the glaze to reinstate it and drop in Naples yellow and light red. Spatter some water across the damp wash to add texture.

*The finished painting.*

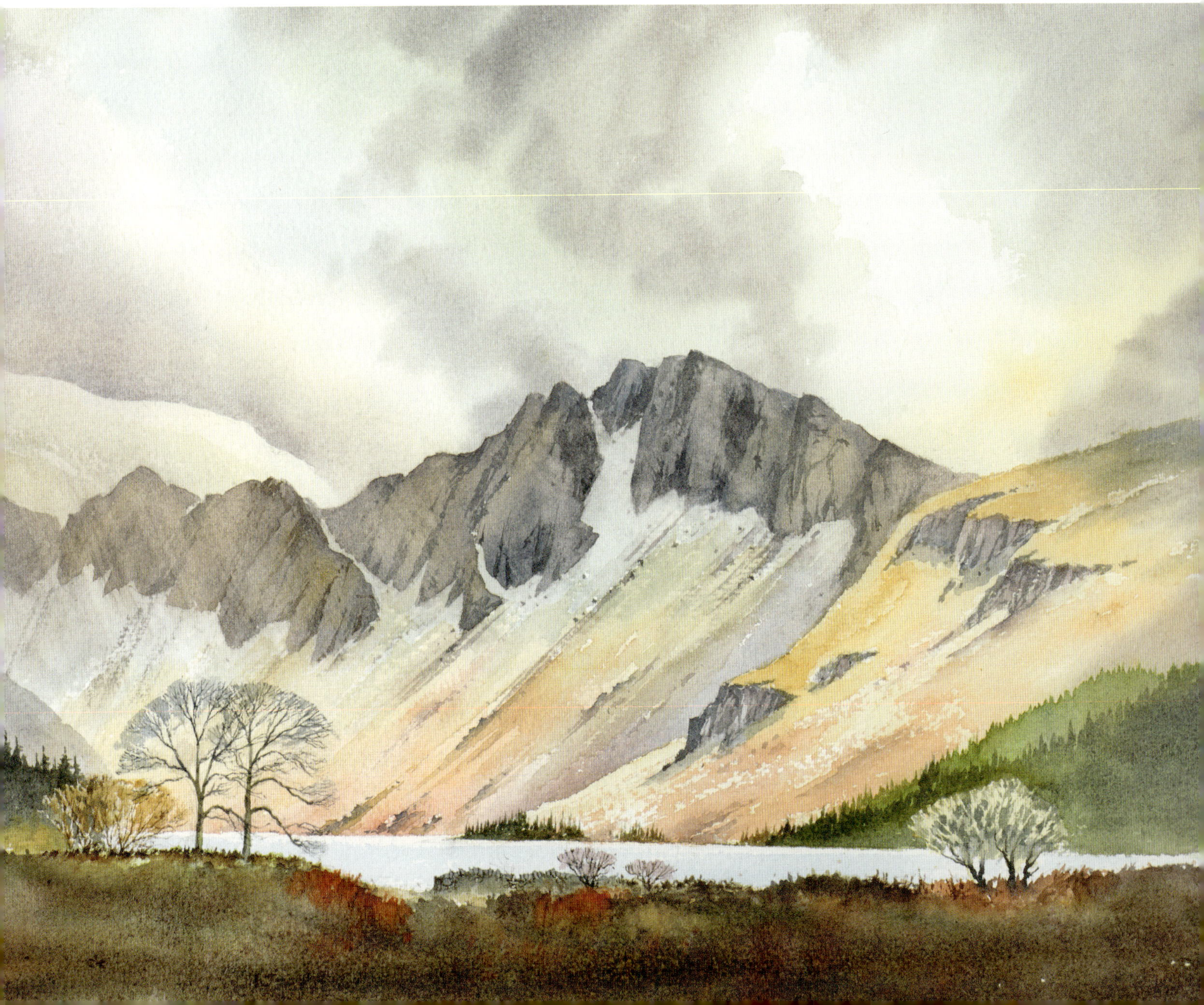

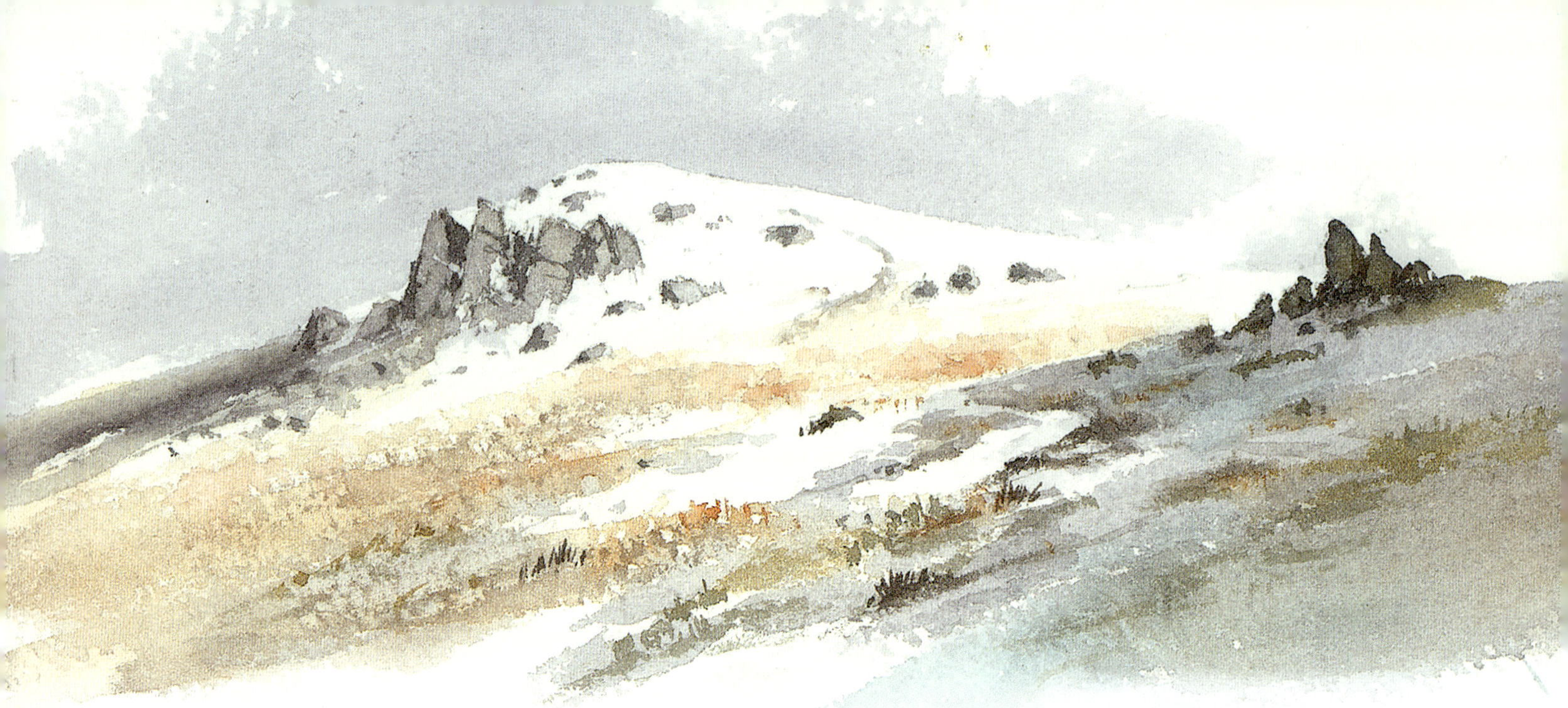

## SNOW COVER

Snow cover can vary considerably from thin, patchy effects to deep snow obliterating almost everything, and the transition from snow-covered hills to the bare ground can cause painters problems. By studying these varied effects, you will be in a better position to alter a scene to your advantage, so when you encounter the next fall of snow, consider how you can render these effects to make the most of the changed landscape.

### THIN, PATCHY SNOW ON OPEN MOORLAND

*A thin layer of snow gives you the opportunity to place your whites and other snow colours where they work best for you, as well as laying in the warmer colours of the bare ground to best advantage. Don't have too many fiddly little patches of snow, though, as it will look messy. Here you will see both hard and soft transitions between snow and untouched ground, and note the winding path which is white in the foreground where snow has accumulated, and dark as it crests the upper slope in the snow. The light red has been applied with a dry brush, blending in some of the edges with a damp brush.*

## TRANSITION FROM SNOW

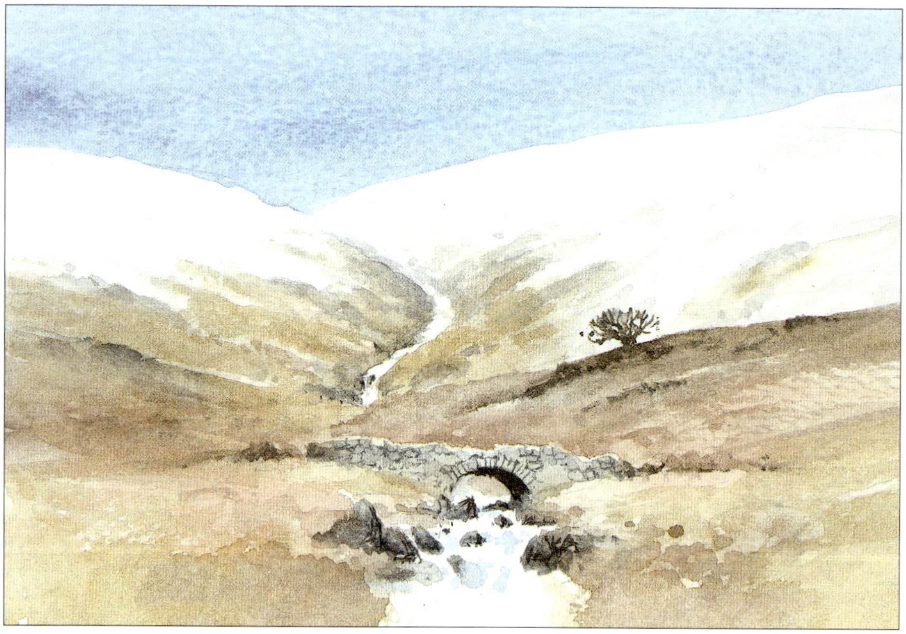

### BRIDGE SCENE

*Painting a snow-covered background of hills and mountains, while retaining a snow-free foreground, can be an attractive way of working. It does not have to be all snow, and sometimes when snow has melted, foregrounds can appear really messy. The transition from snowy areas can be achieved in different ways. On the right, you will see how a dark ridge, painted with light red and burnt umber, stands out hard against the snowy background, while on the left, the transition is more gradual. For this latter effect, you can wet the paper first and then take the ground colour up into the wet area – yellow ochre in this case, tinged in places with a mid-grey made up of cobalt blue and light red. An alternative method is to paint on to dry paper with the side of your brush, or simply to brush upwards with a dry brush, as in the craggy moorland sketch above.*

### USING A WAX RESIST

*Another technique for representing intermittent snow cover is to drag a candle across the required part of the painting, as in this Dartmoor scene. The wax will resist watercolour washes.*

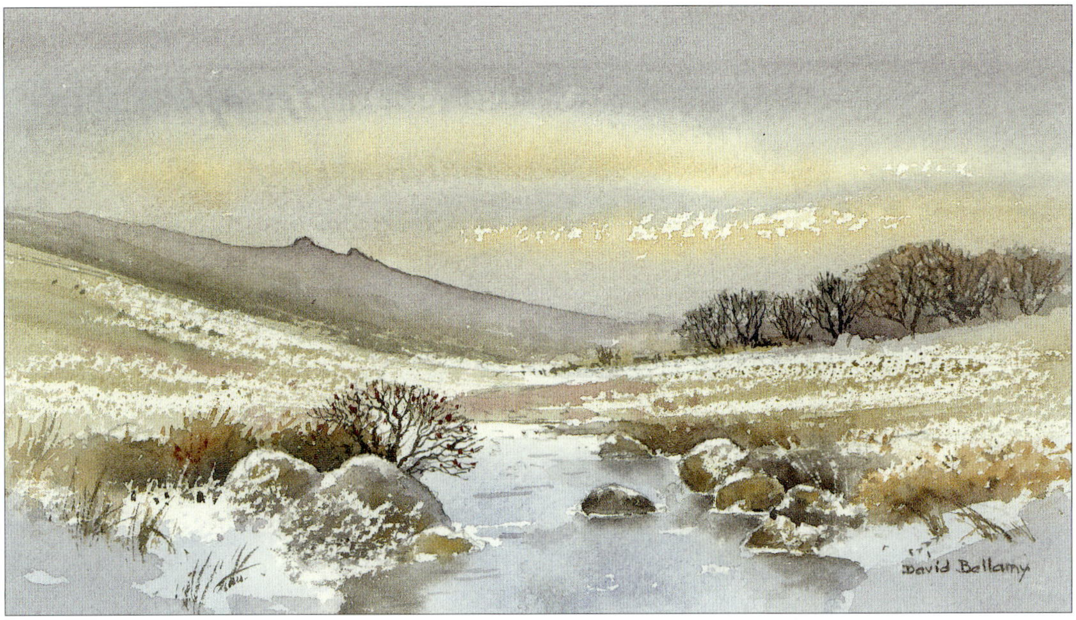

### VIBRANT COLOURS IN THE SNOW – HEREFORDSHIRE LANE

*15 x 20cm (6 x 8in), 640gsm (300lb) Not paper*

*Foregrounds are rarely easy, and often snowy ones can appear almost devoid of any detail, so that we may be tempted to paint in all manner of vegetation sticking out of the blank whiteness. One method I enjoy is splashing in a number of colours – usually different blues, but sometimes even a red, despite it being quite the opposite to anything present in the scene. In this small watercolour, I have added some Winsor blue and permanent rose to join the wash of French ultramarine and cadmium red. The white trees were achieved with masking fluid, with some of the branches washed over after the mask was removed, to create more shadowy branches.*

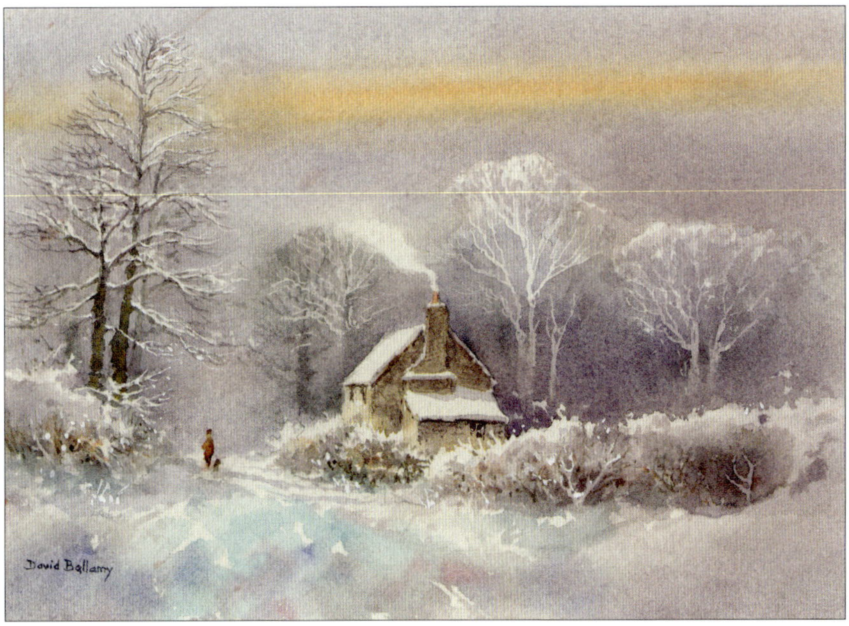

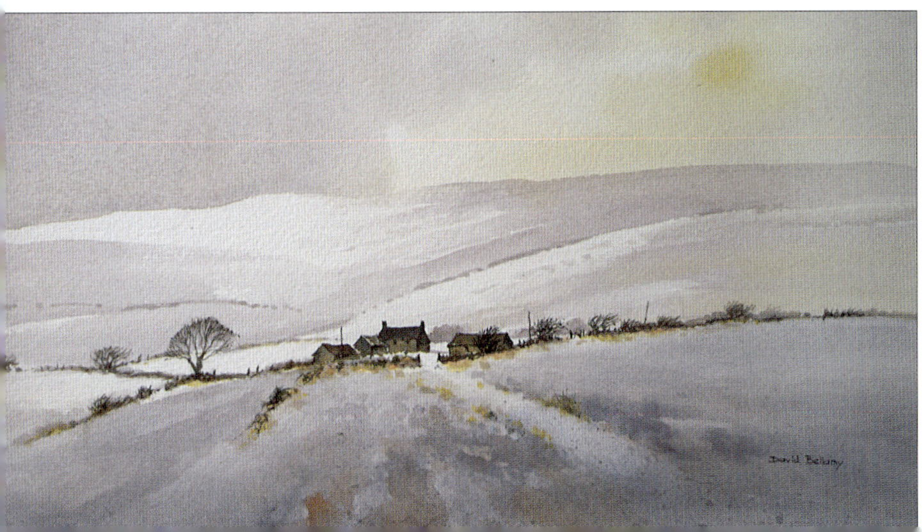

### MOORLAND FARM

*In this composition, you can see various tones on the snow-covered fields, and in particular the change of tone where the hills meet the sky: the hill is simply white paper against a dark sky on the left, and blue-grey against a lighter sky on the right. Planning this out before you start painting will reap excellent rewards. Note how the hedgerows are not continuous. Rather than paint in detailed vegetation sticking out of the foreground snow, I have simply splashed in patches of yellow ochre in a few places, a useful alternative to over-detailing this rather vulnerable part of a painting.*

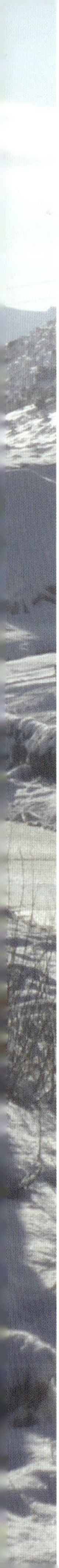

# LANDSCAPE UNDER DEEP SNOW

This scene in North Staffordshire, UK, immediately appealed: deep snow simplified the composition, the road formed an excellent lead-in to the centre of interest, and strong afternoon sunlight created interesting cast shadows and highlights.

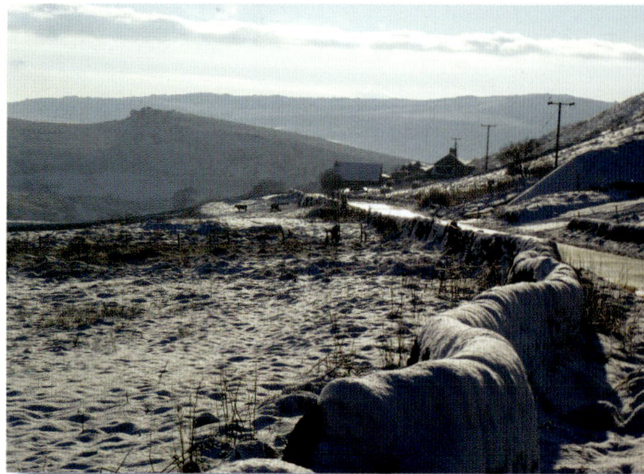

*The actual scene was almost a monochrome and could well have been painted as such. At times, winter presents us with a monochrome, so take advantage of these interesting situations, which can exude a powerful sense of mood.*

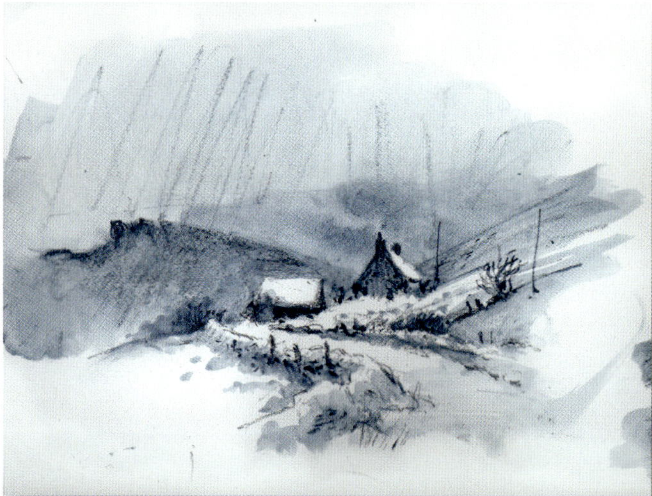

**COLOUR SKETCH**
*With an indigo water-soluble ink block, I drew in the main features, then applied tone in varying strengths, before washing over the sketch with a wet brush. This is a quick way of producing a sketch and the water-soluble ink block encourages you to avoid describing too much detail.*

**FARM AT FLASH BOTTOM**
*15 x 25.5cm (6 x 10in), Rough*
*The lower sky and distant hills were painted with washes of French ultramarine and cadmium red, with the far ridge appearing and disappearing in places. The white parts were left as untouched paper. I added a red muck spreader beside the farmhouse for interest and colour, and the cast shadows gave a strong feeling of sunlight. Blobs of phthalo blue in the foreground create additional variation.*

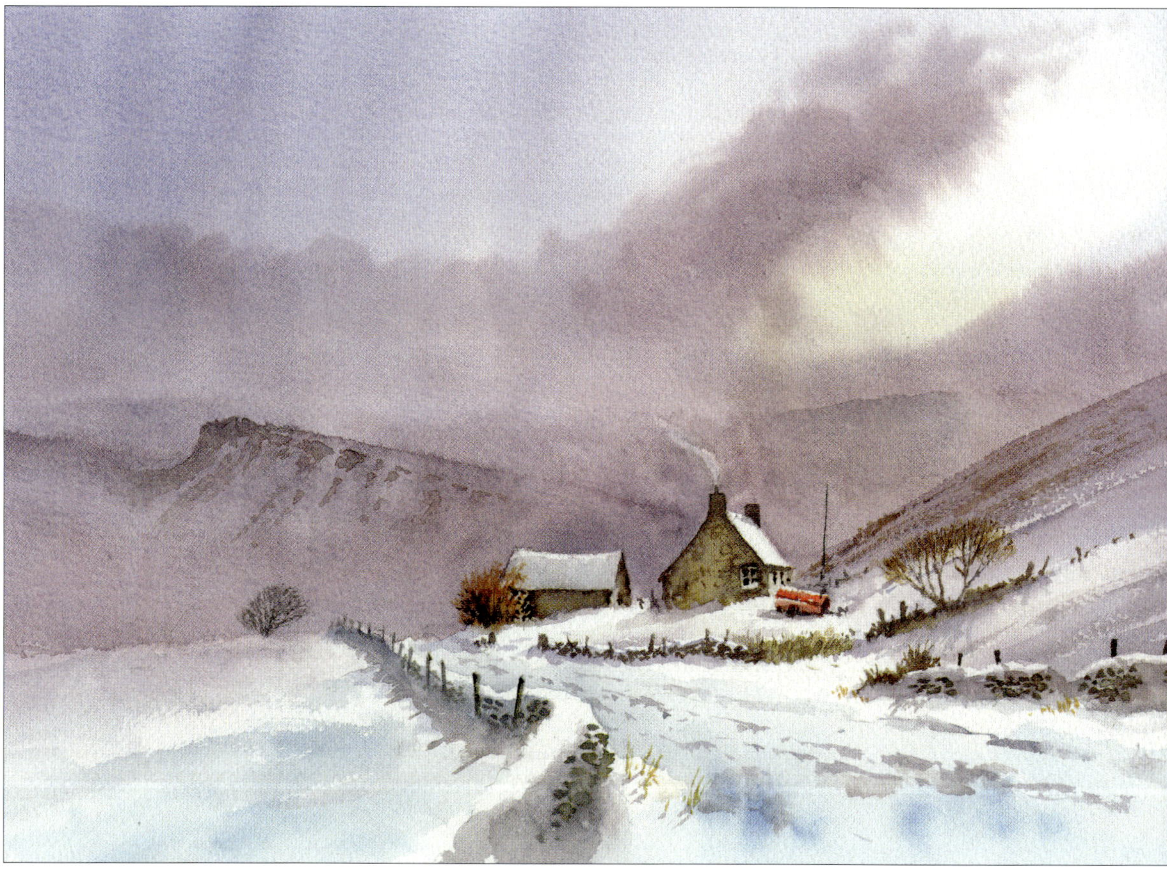

# INTRODUCING COLOUR TO SNOW SCENES

Unless you are intent on portraying a thoroughly cold environment, totally devoid of any hint of warmth, it makes for a more attractive composition if you introduce an element of warm colour into a snow scene. This can be achieved by painting the sky in warm colours, creating warm-coloured reflections in water, ice or snow, or introducing warm-coloured vegetation, figures or objects. Even a small splash of bright colour can make a difference.

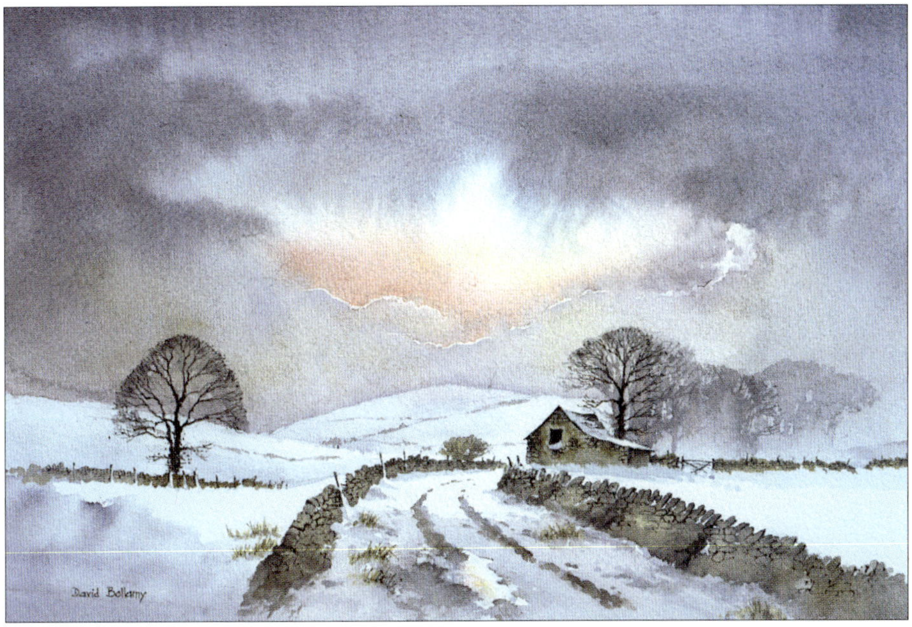

**YORKSHIRE BARN**
*20 x 28cm (8 x 11in)*

*Snow scenes can appear really cold and uninviting if there is a lack of warm colour. In this landscape, the warm colours in the sky, barn, dry-stone walls and smattering of vegetation all add up to a more welcoming snow scene. I deliberately took some time to work out the sort of sky I wanted, and where to place the warm colours. A studio sketch carried out in colour will help you work this out.*

**MASSED TREES AND SNOW**

*A subtle way of increasing the warmer feeling of your snow scenes is by mixing or dropping in warmer colours instead of perhaps more neutral ones. In this landscape, I have dropped light red into the lower half of the massed trees to give it a lovely warm sensation, instead of using a colour like burnt umber to create a cooler, greyer overall effect.*

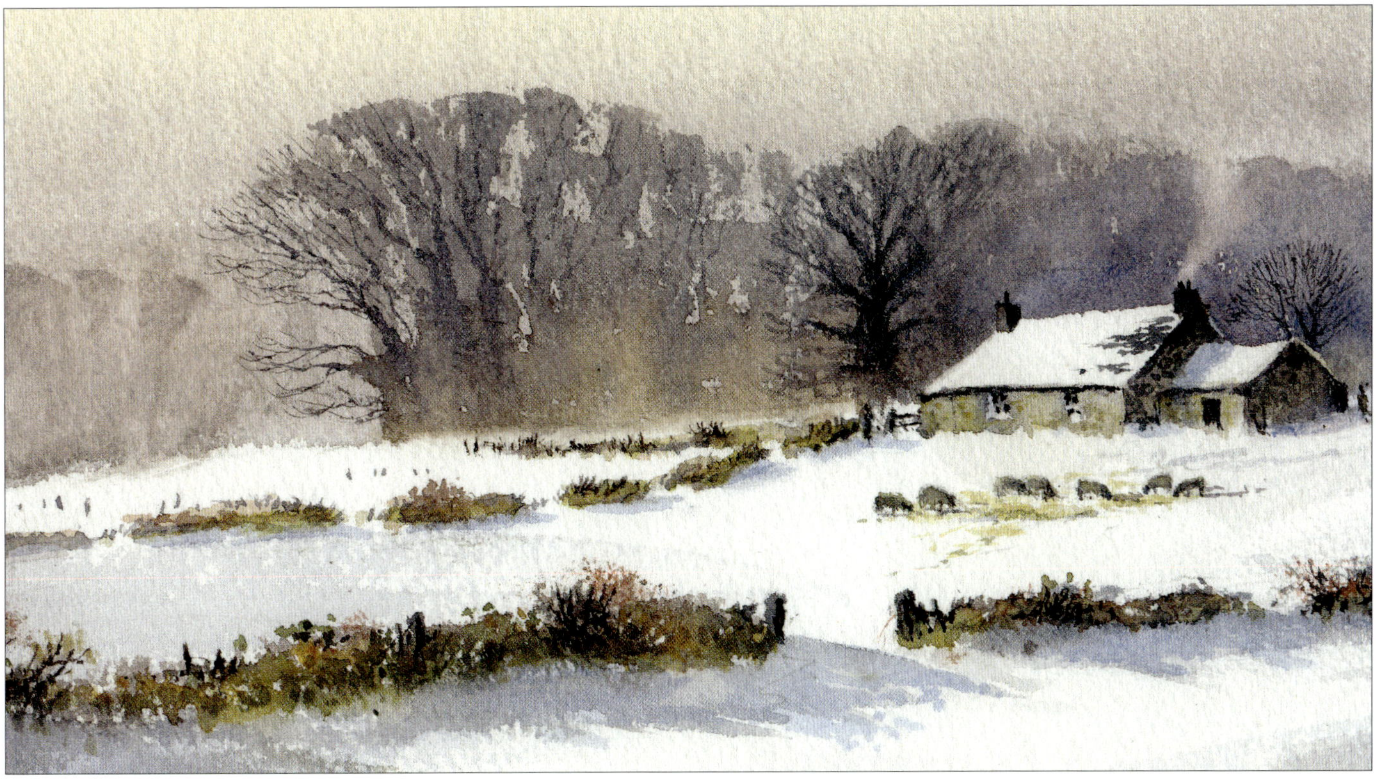

# DEPICTING SNOW AND ICE ON TREES

Ice patterns and snow on trees can range from the ordinary to the spectacular, and they can be further enhanced by the surrounding atmosphere and light. Sometimes the effect of ice-rimed branches can be so overwhelming that any attempt to render such intricate, icy detail will look overworked. Aim for brief glimpses of stunning detail in a lost-and-found manner and use colour and tone as a substitute for detail in places.

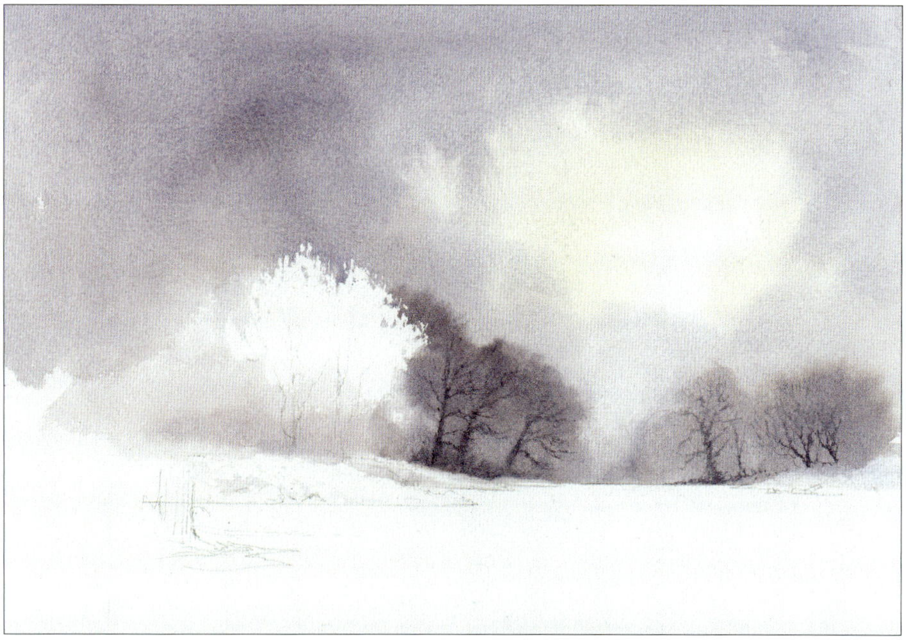

*At this first stage, masking fluid was applied to the top branches of the birch trees. I then laid a fluid wash of Naples yellow on the right-hand part of the sky, then a mixture of French ultramarine and cadmium red over most of the sky. A stronger mix of the same colours, applied wet into wet, suggested the more distant tree mass, then a very strong mixture was applied with a fine rigger to draw in the main trunks. When the paper had completely dried, the masking fluid was removed.*

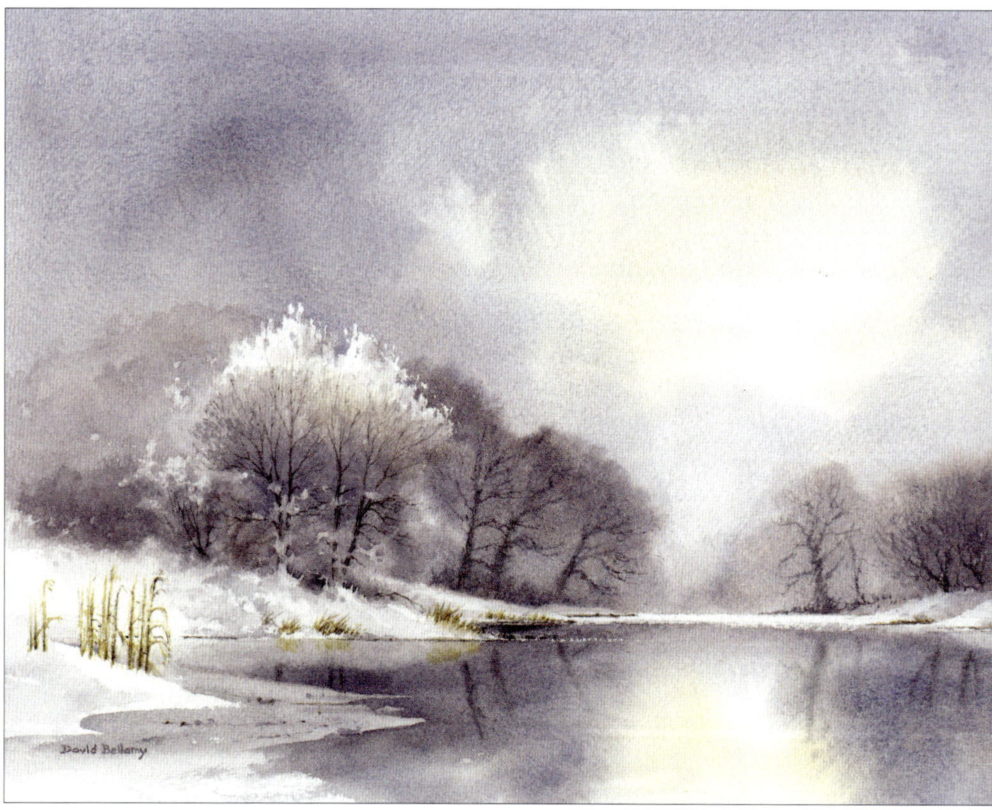


SNOW, ICE AND MIST ON THE WYE
*23 x 30.5cm (9 x 12in), 300gsm (140lb) Not paper*

*I painted more Naples yellow onto the main trees to suggest a slight warming of colour temperature, then the shadow areas with French ultramarine and cadmium red. Yellow ochre was laid over the reeds and vegetation. For the river, after wetting the whole area with clean water, I painted weak Naples yellow in the centre, suggesting some colour reflection from the sky. I then added French ultramarine and burnt umber, running it into the Naples yellow. A light patch of ice was created on the left by working negatively round the shape.*

*Once everything was dry, I re-wetted the river on the left and applied a strong wash of ultramarine and cadmium red into the darkest reflections, thus highlighting the reflections of the lighter snow-covered bank. Finally I scratched out slivers of light with a scalpel.*

# ANIMALS IN COLD CONDITIONS

There is something very appealing and heart-tugging about animals caught in cold snowscapes. Like humans, they often hold themselves in such a way as to show they are suffering from the cold.

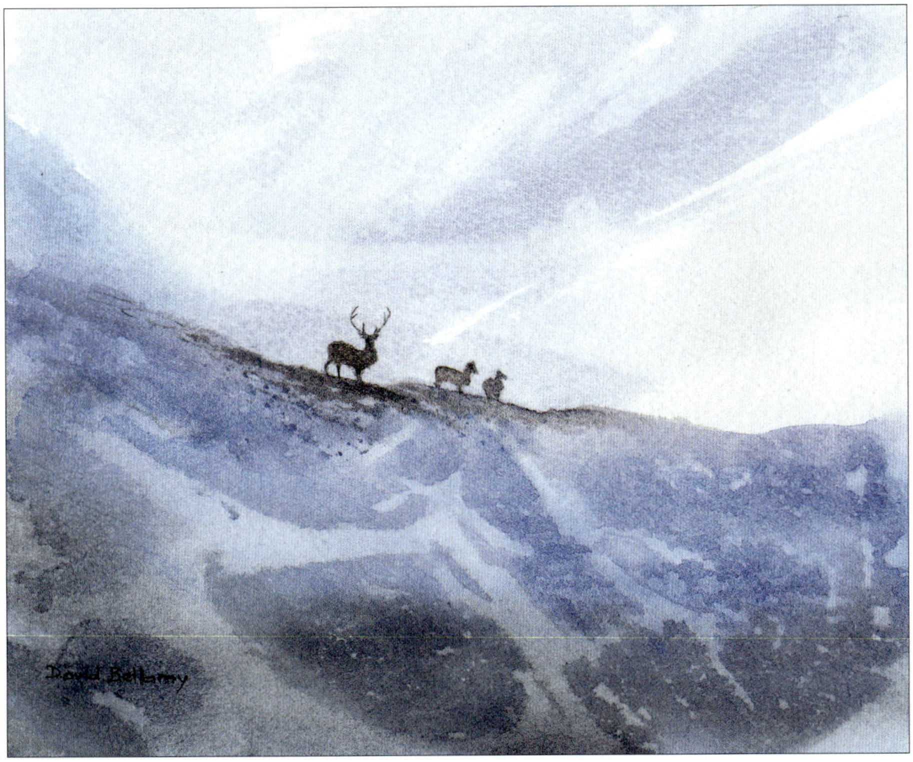


**HIGHLAND DEER**
*15 x 20cm (6 x 8in), 300gsm (140lb) Rough*

*Most artists enjoy trying new techniques. Occasionally, when the subject seems right, I use plastic food wrap to create interesting patterns. This works especially well with snow and ice scenes. Here I applied fluid washes of Winsor blue, at the same time leaving patches of untouched paper to suggest the snow highlights. While this lay wet on the paper, I placed a sheet of plastic food wrap over it and dragged it slightly to the left to suggest a sense of direction. I then left the food wrap in place and allowed the wash to dry. After the paper had completely dried, I removed the food wrap and then painted in the rest of the scene as normal. Sometimes I refrain from doing any pencil drawing until after the washes have dried, thus allowing me to take advantage of how the plastic food wrap has affected the paper.*

**CATTLE FEEDING**
*18 x 25.5cm (7 x 10in), 300gsm (140lb) Not paper*

*Animals make excellent centres of interest, their appeal accentuated when set in a bleak landscape. Note in this work how background features have been deliberately managed to make the animals stand out. The black Friesians to the rear are silhouetted against a purple-grey hedgerow, totally lacking in detail, while the right-hand beast has a light-coloured back that is clearly etched against the dark bush.*

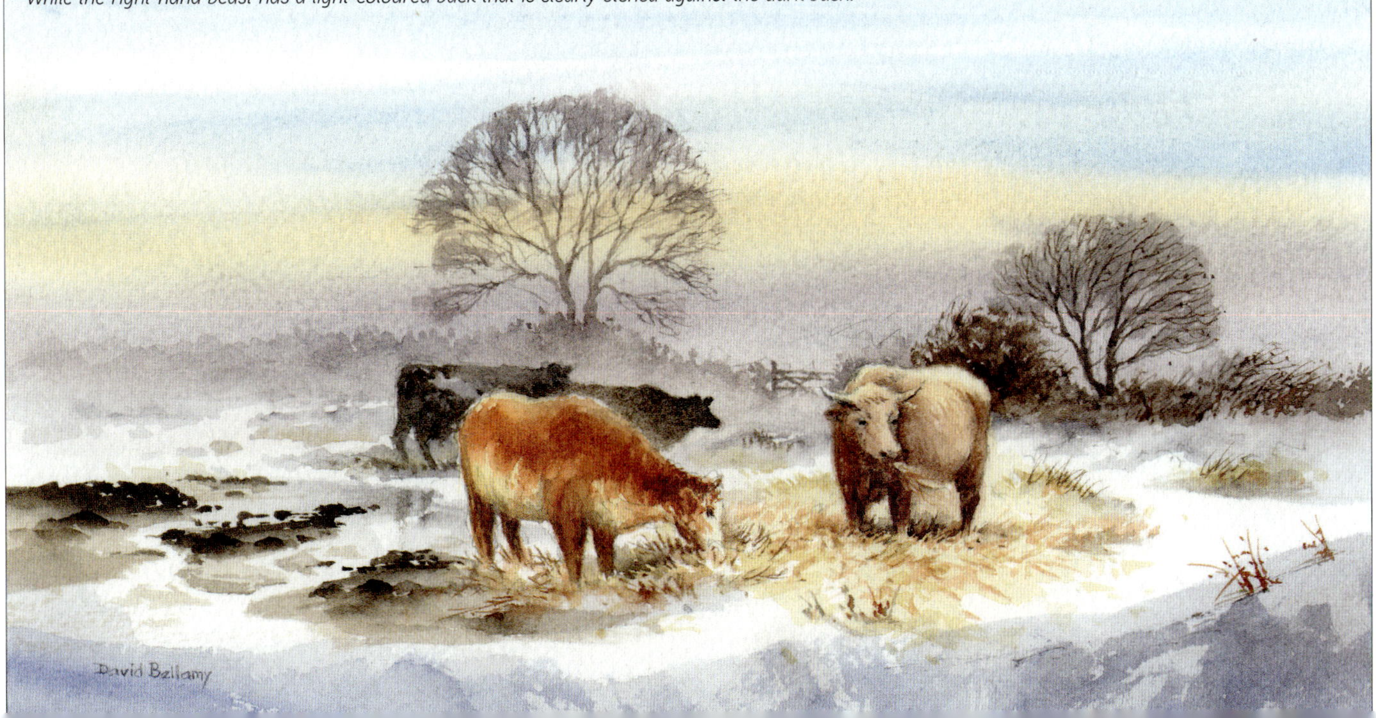

# CAPTURING A CASTLE IN WATERCOLOUR

On this occasion the atmosphere was constantly changing and the washes slow to dry, so outdoor watercolour sketching was challenging, with the great temptation to change my response as conditions altered. That can be fatal to a work, so either do a second sketch or take several photographs as things change.

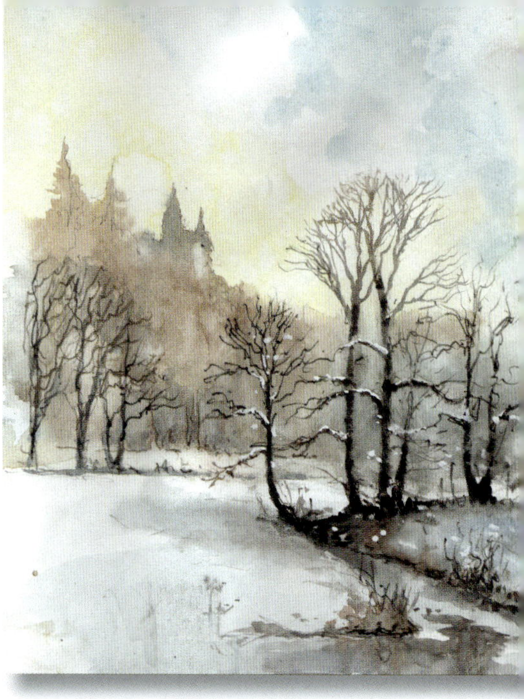

*This viewpoint appealed to me, as the building rose above the trees, all in sunlight apart from the foreground. For this watercolour sketch, I drew into the wet washes with a black watercolour pencil to speed things up. Even so, the sketch took a long time in slow drying conditions, and by the time I had completed it, the sun had disappeared and ground mist created a magical, ethereal atmosphere. In the resulting painting, I decided to incorporate both the sun on the castle and higher trees, and the mist lower down.*

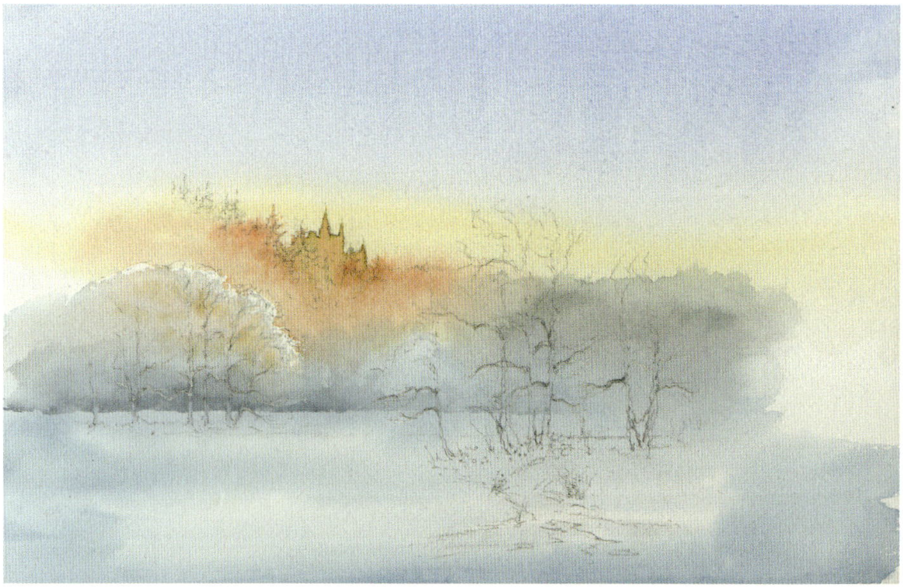

1 I began by laying a wash of cobalt blue over the upper sky, and yellow ochre over the lower part, bringing it down over the trees near the castle. While this was wet, I touched in some weak light red, then allowed it to dry. I painted on masking fluid with an old size 0 rigger for the snow-clad branches, then laid Winsor blue over the lower part of the composition to create a cool effect, though adding in some light red over the left-hand tree mass.

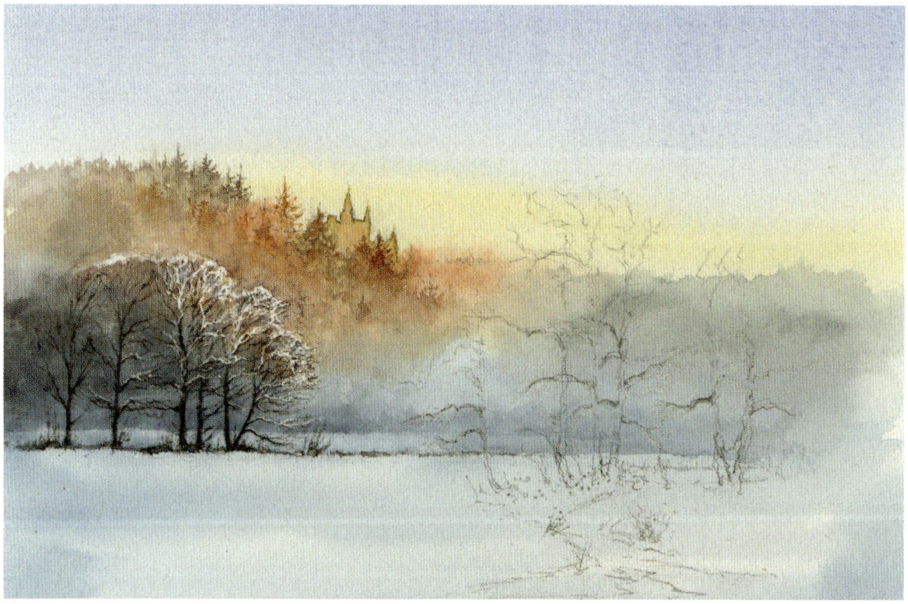

2 I concentrated on the left-hand trees by drawing in the trunks and branches with a mixture of Winsor blue and light red. When this had dried, I removed the masking fluid just from this area, then laid a weak glaze of Winsor blue across the lower section of the left-hand trees.

ALTON CASTLE, STAFFORDSHIRE

*20 x 28cm (8 x 11in) 300gsm (140lb) Not paper*

*With the paper completely dry, I sponged horizontally across the lower part of the left-hand trees to suggest mist, using a soft natural sponge and clean water and dabbing off the excess liquid afterwards. This combination of glazes and sponging is effective for suggesting mist. I then created a shadow band horizontally across the picture, below the band created for the mist, with a weak mixture of Winsor blue and light red. The right-hand tree trunks were rendered with a stronger combination of Winsor blue and burnt umber, followed by a weaker mix of the same colours over the right-hand foreground. To suggest the varied tones in the icy water, I used the same mixture in various degrees of strength. Finally I put in the foreground shadows and vegetation.*

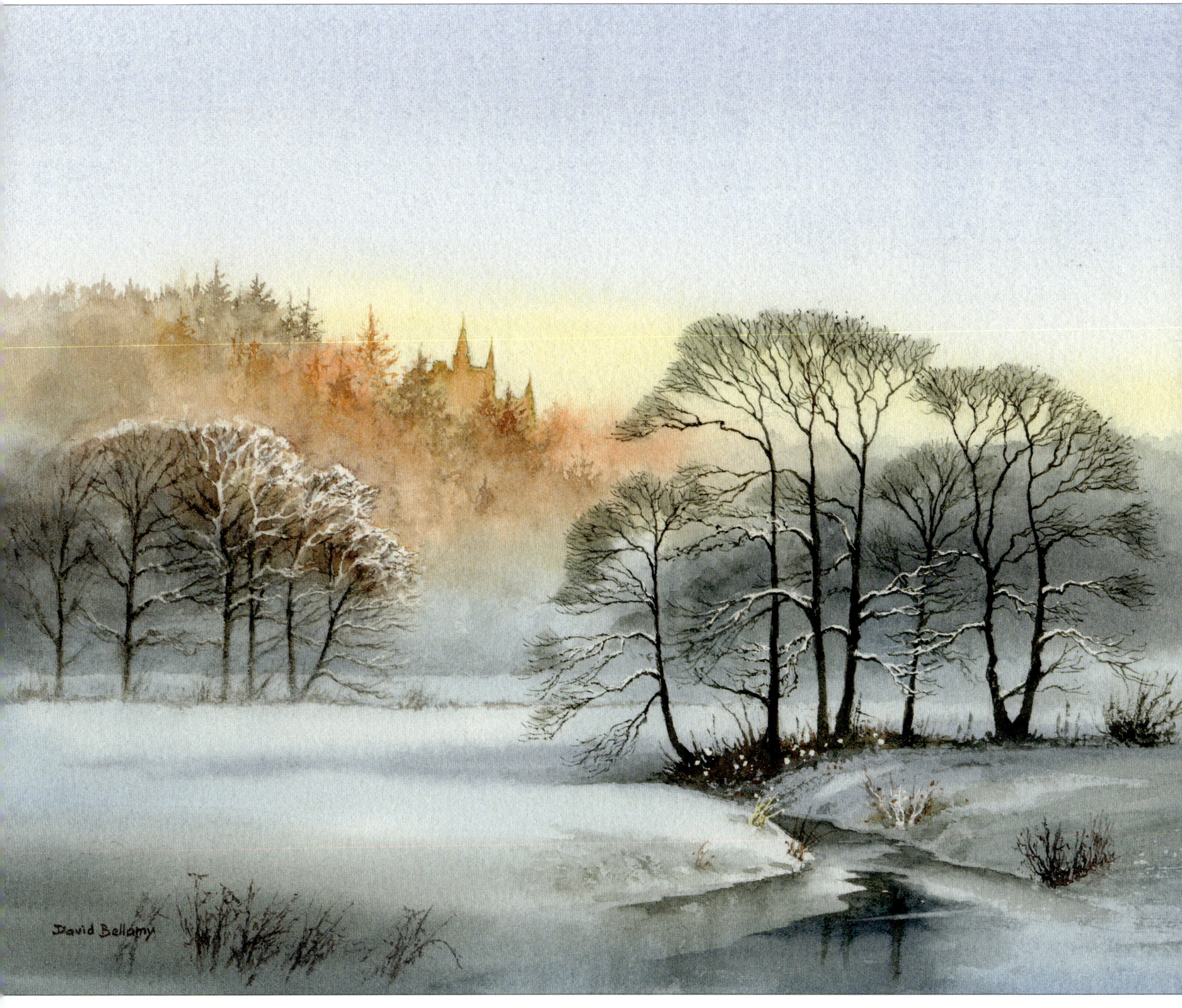

# FALLING SNOW

Gently falling snow is fairly easy to paint. Blizzards are not so easy! These can vary from hard-driven snow to occasional, gentler eddies and flurries against a background of indefinite images. It is fascinating to experiment with these effects.

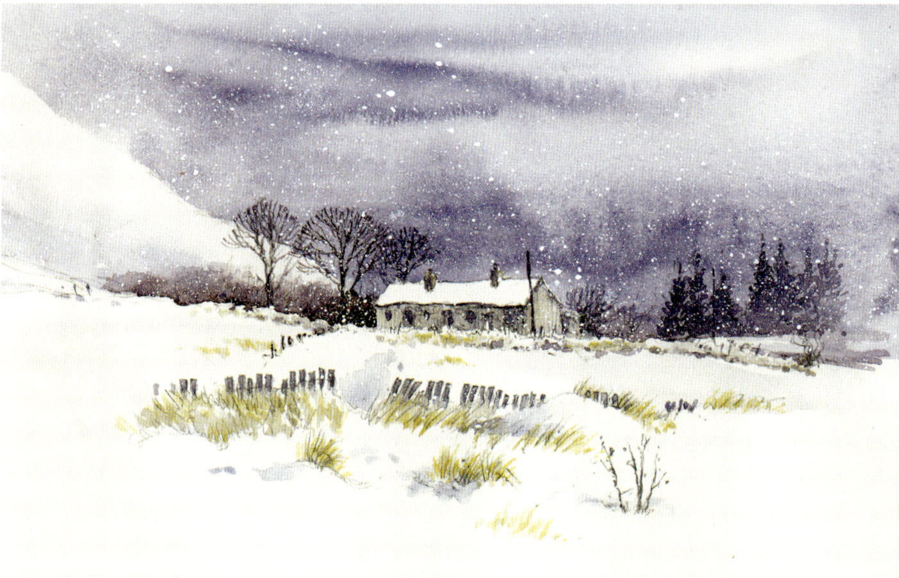

### GENTLY FALLING SNOW

*The falling snow was created by spattering white gouache with a toothbrush – simply load the toothbrush with gouache and then drag your thumb or a palette knife across it. Test it out first on scrap paper with a dark image, as too much water on the brush can result in huge ugly blobs. You may find it helpful to darken certain passages of the composition to a degree so that the white gouache stands out.*

### BLIZZARD IN GLEN FESHIE, SCOTTISH HIGHLANDS

*20 x 25.5cm (8 x 10in), 640gsm (300lb) Rough*

*I began with a wash of water over the sky, then applied Naples yellow above where the trees would appear. I added a weak wash of cadmium orange to warm the sky slightly. A strong mixture of burnt umber and indigo was then laid across most of the sky apart from the area left light, making the right-hand side slightly darker. I waited a few moments before suggesting some pine trees, in two stages to give depth. I waited a further few minutes until the degree of dryness seemed right, then applied the stronger, slightly warmer mixture of burnt umber and indigo to define the main mass of pines.*

*When the right-hand side of the sky was at the right stage of drying, I used a damp 13mm (½in) flat brush without any colour, with short, energetic diagonal strokes, to suggest the violent movement of the blizzard across the sky and pines. I then struck white gouache across the damp paper. Use a 'thin' flat brush for this. When the paper was dry, I spattered it with white gouache on a toothbrush, at a low angle, first using a wettish application for the fainter, falling snow, then gouache straight out of the tube for closer snowflakes, to create depth. I then streaked the flat brush through some of the snowflakes in the same direction.*

*The sheep were rendered in a similar manner, although at the very end I scratched diagonally across them with a scalpel to give the impression of fast-driven snow.*

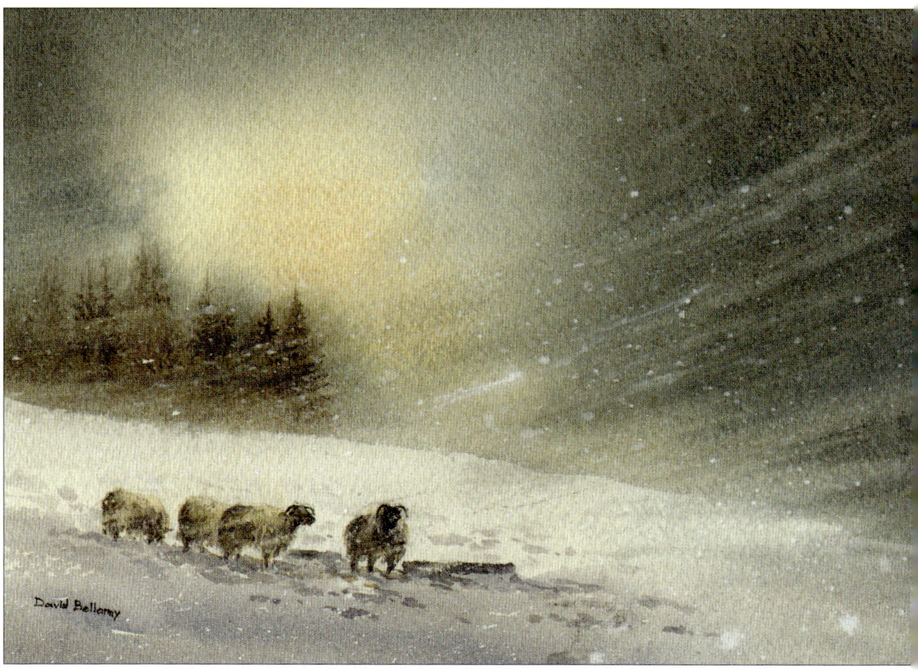

# FARM IN SNOW

Intricate white details in a snow painting can be tricky to achieve, and this is where masking fluid really comes into its own, although it often needs tidying up a bit after removal, especially if it has been applied clumsily. In this demonstration, I show how the white features are created, including the usefulness of having a tube of white gouache handy.

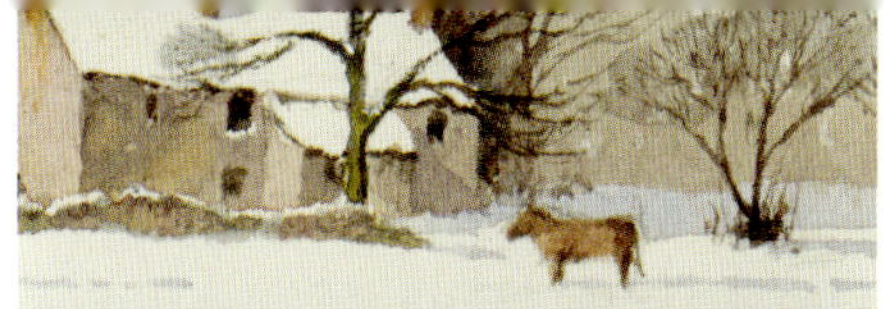

**MATERIALS USED**

Saunders Waterford 640gsm (300lb) HP watercolour paper

Brushes: No. 10 sable round, large and small squirrel mops, no. 7 sable round, 13mm (½in) flat, no. 1 rigger, no. 4 and no. 3 sable round

Colours: Cobalt blue, cadmium red, Naples yellow, cadmium orange, alizarin crimson, burnt sienna, Indian red, burnt umber, yellow ochre, cadmium yellow pale, white gouache

Masking fluid and old brush

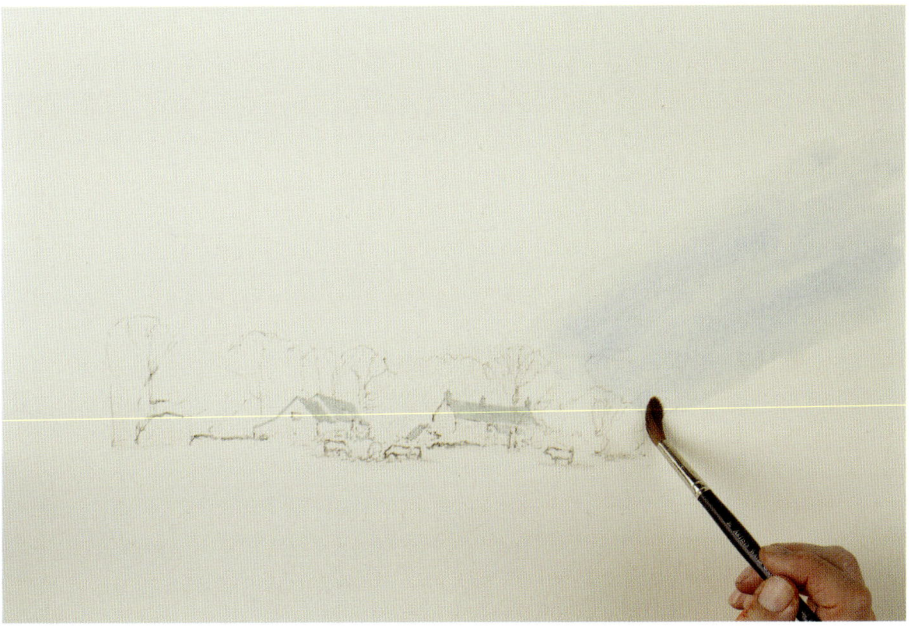

1 Draw the scene and mask the roofs and tops of walls with masking fluid. Add a few dabs of masking fluid to the trees to suggest snow. Use the no. 10 sable round to paint the snowy hillside in the background with cobalt blue and cadmium red. Allow to dry.

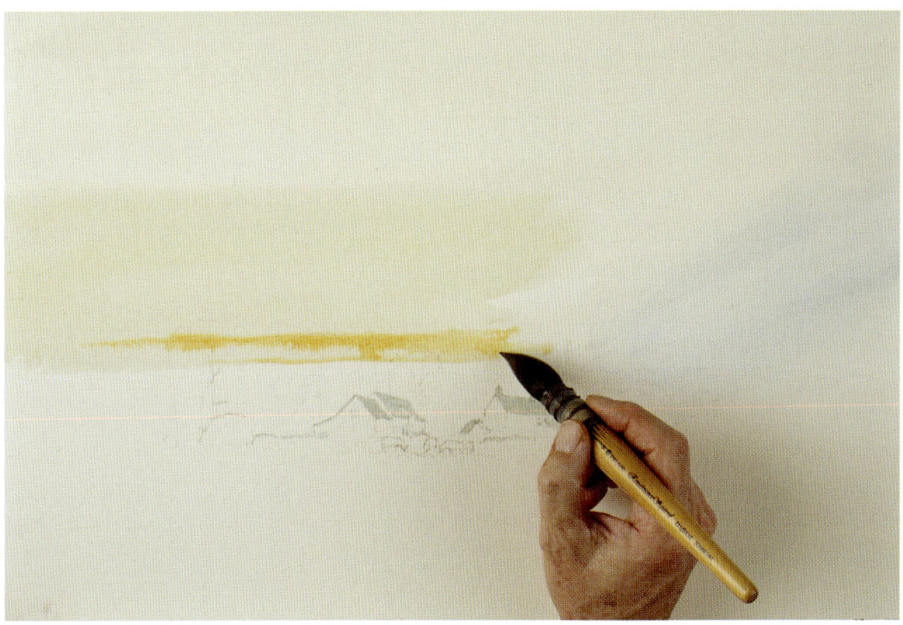

2 Use the large squirrel mop to sweep clean water across the background to just below the tree line and drop in Naples yellow on the left. Paint a line of cadmium orange beyond the trees to suggest a sliver of light.

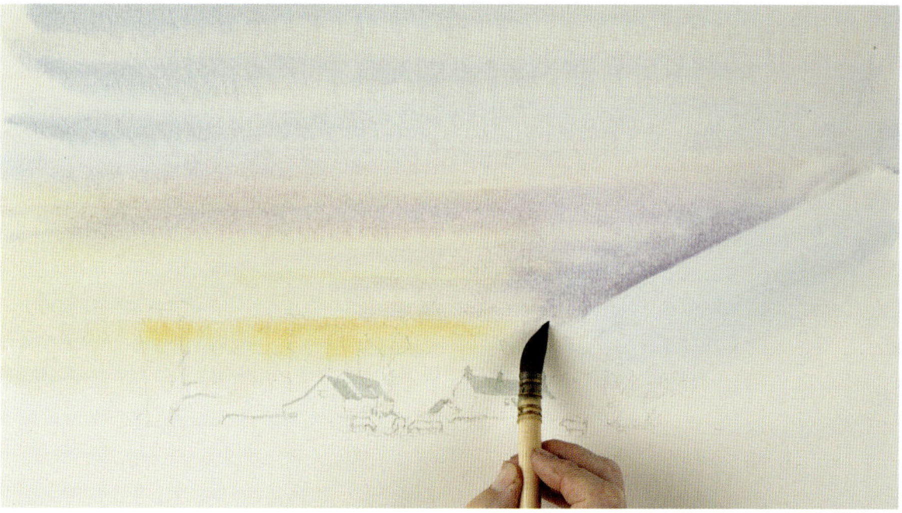

3 Paint cobalt blue and cadmium red wet into wet from the top of the sky downwards to blend with the yellow. Soften any hard edges that appear with a damp brush. Use a smaller squirrel mop with alizarin crimson and cobalt blue to define the mountain ridge, and blend it across the sky.

4 Wait until the sky is just damp and use the no. 7 sable round to dot in clouds with cadmium red and cobalt blue. Test at the edge of the picture to make sure the cloud wash does not spread too far in the damp background.

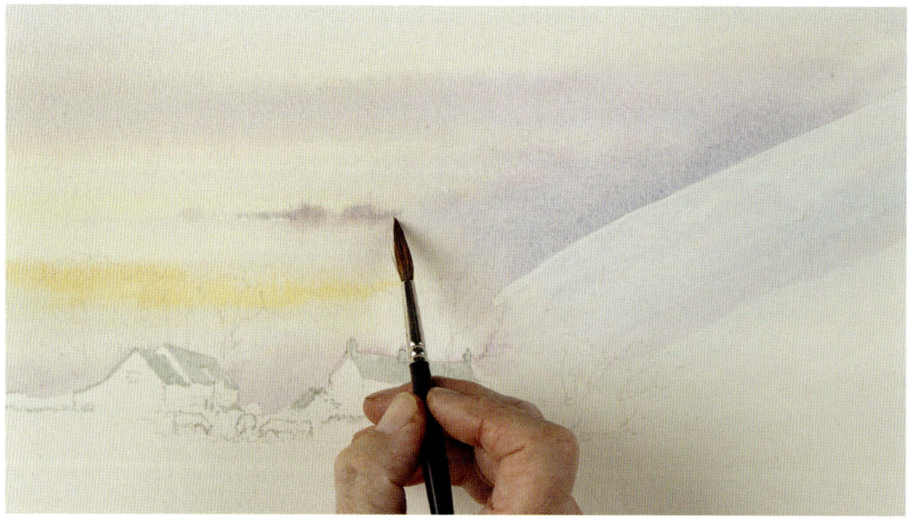

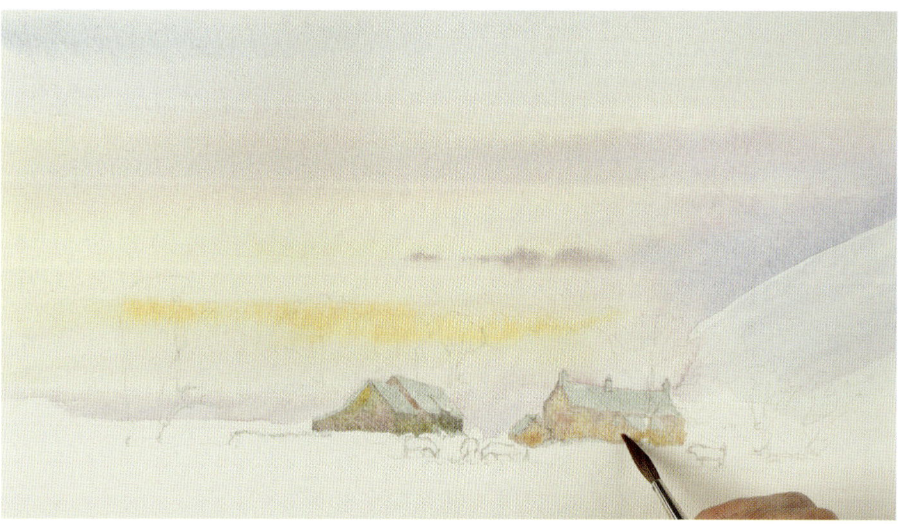

5 Paint the buildings with cobalt blue and burnt sienna, then drop in yellow ochre and alizarin crimson.

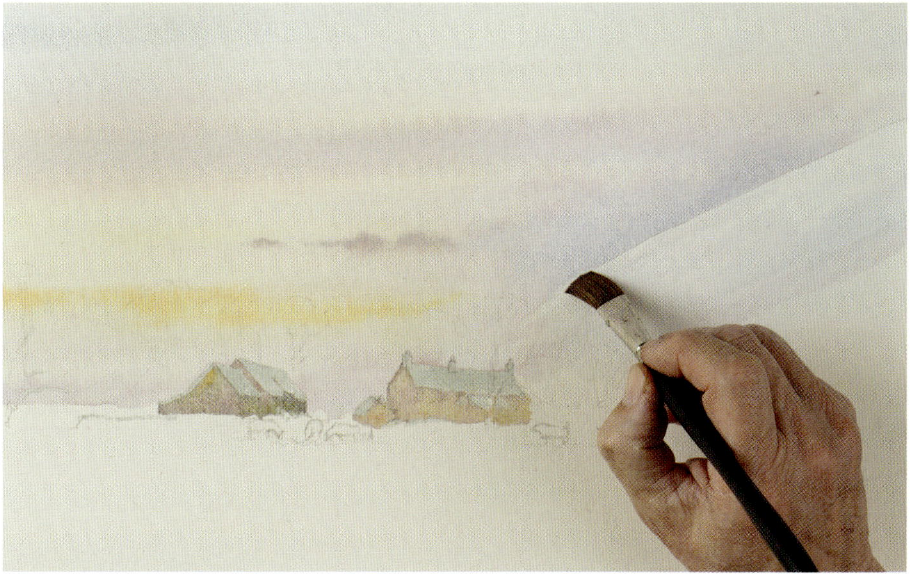

6 Use a damp 13mm (½in) flat brush to soften the line of the ridge.

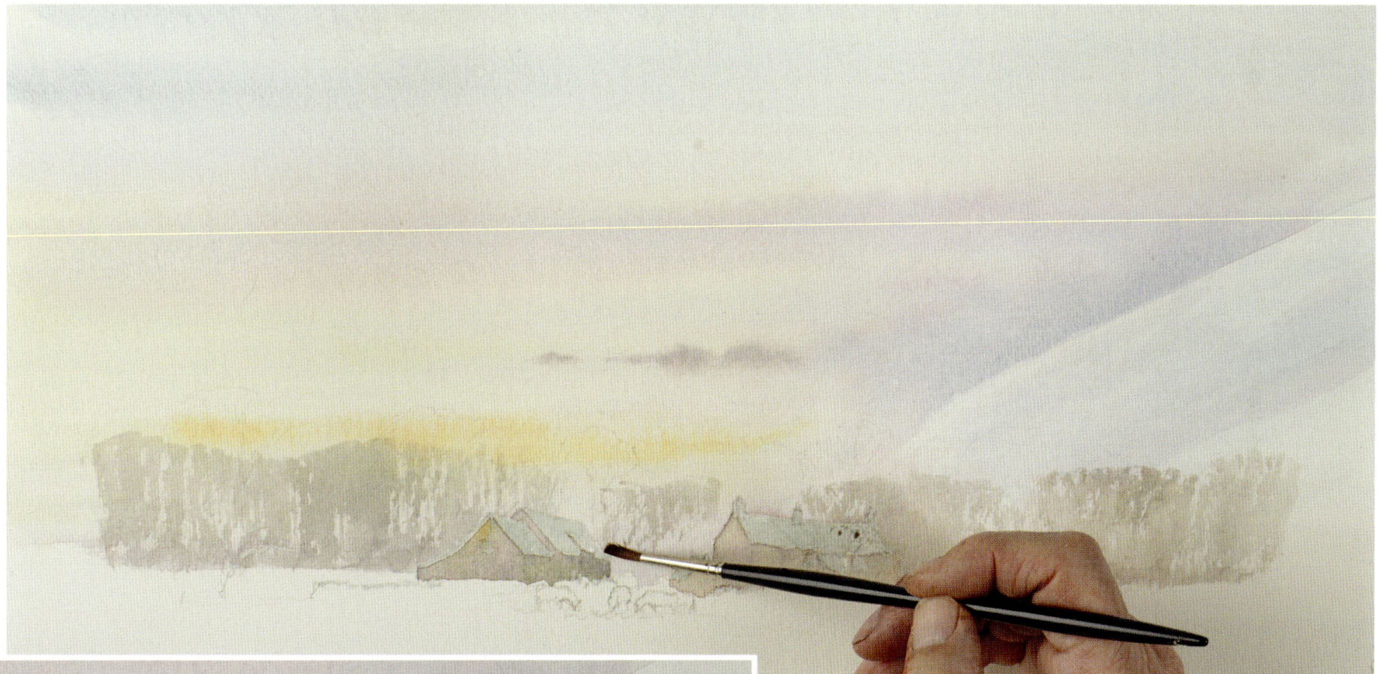

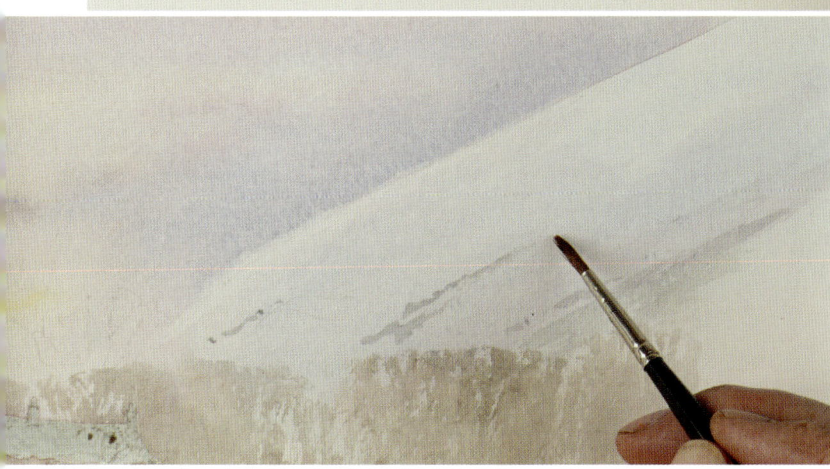

7 Mix burnt sienna and cobalt blue and use the no. 4 round to paint in the background trees. Use the same mix to suggest rocks showing through the snow in the ridge.

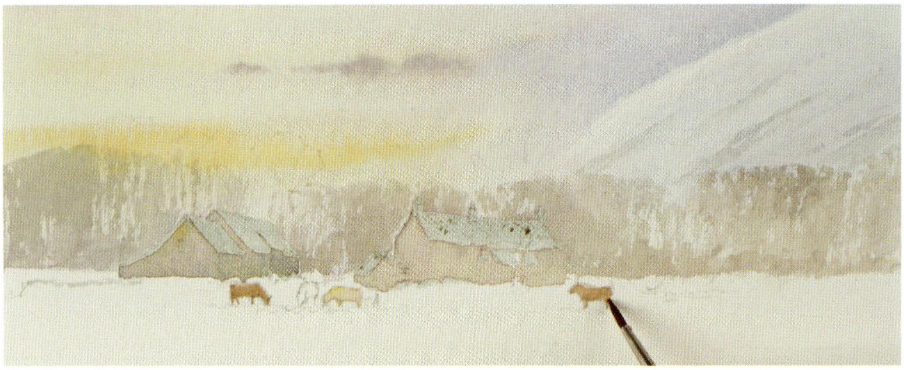

8 Paint some of the cows with Naples yellow with a touch of Indian red, then another two with burnt sienna.

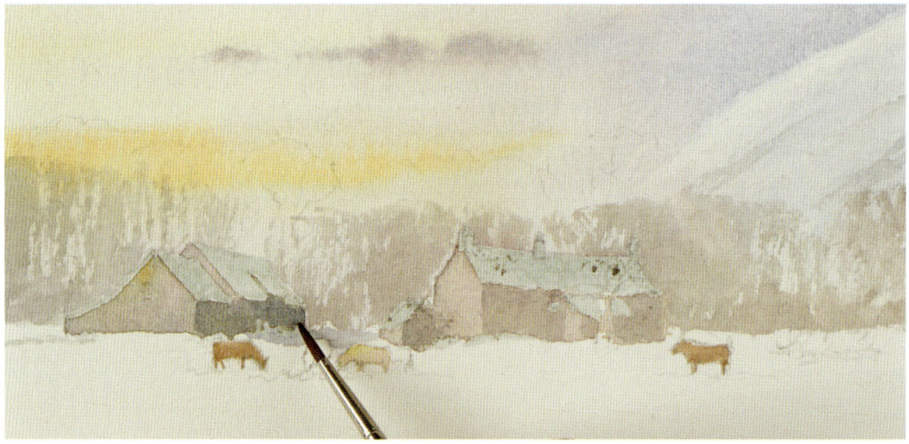

9 Make a shadow mix of alizarin crimson and cobalt blue and paint the area between the buildings, then paint the shaded parts of the buildings with varying mixes of the same colours.

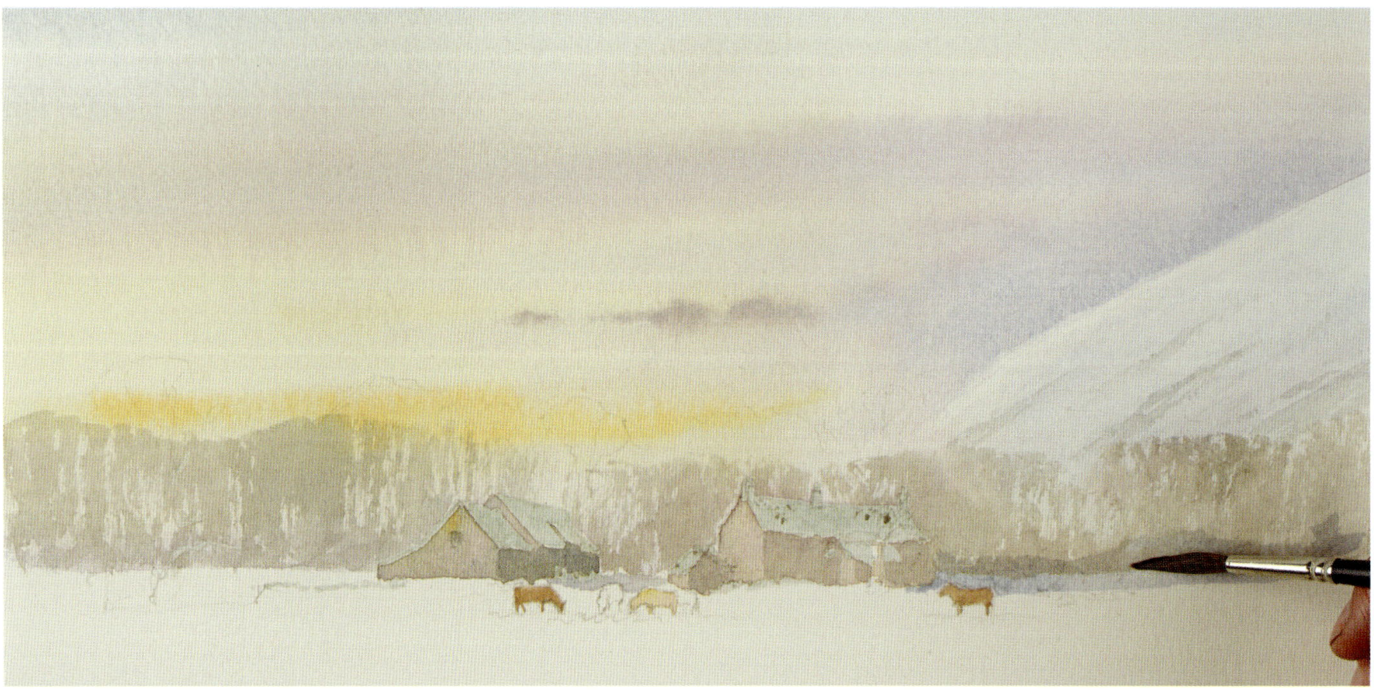

10 Use the no. 7 brush to paint this shadow mix along the treeline to the right of the buildings, and blend it upwards. Repeat to the left of the buildings.

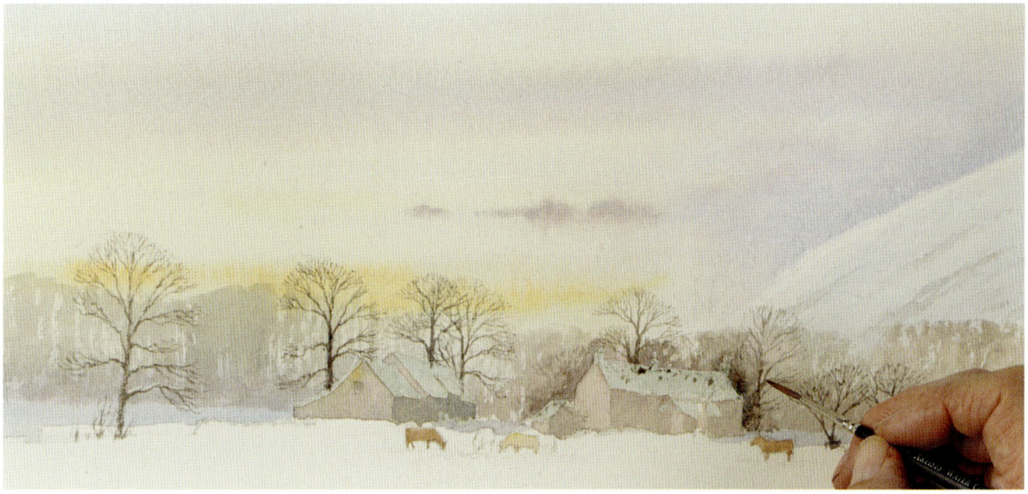

11 Use the no. 1 rigger and burnt umber with cobalt blue to paint trunks and branches on the background trees.

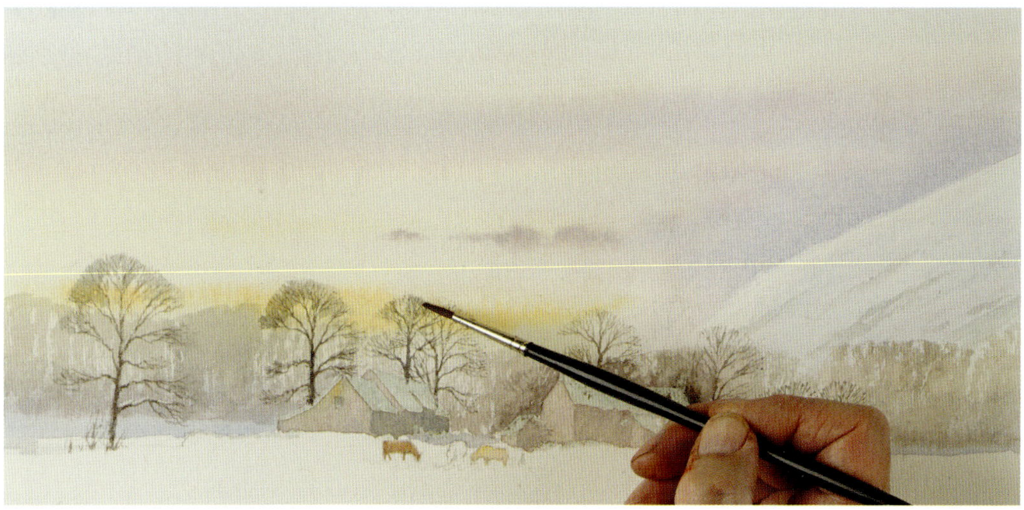

12 Mix cadmium red and cobalt blue and use the no. 4 round brush on its side to paint the twigwork of the trees.

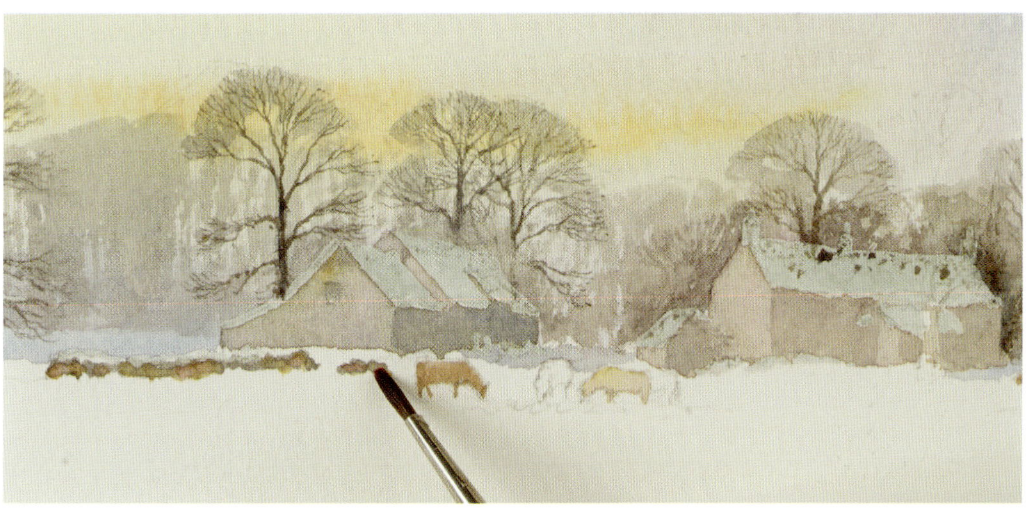

13 Paint the dry-stone wall with a mix of burnt sienna and cobalt blue, then drop in yellow ochre and alizarin crimson wet into wet.

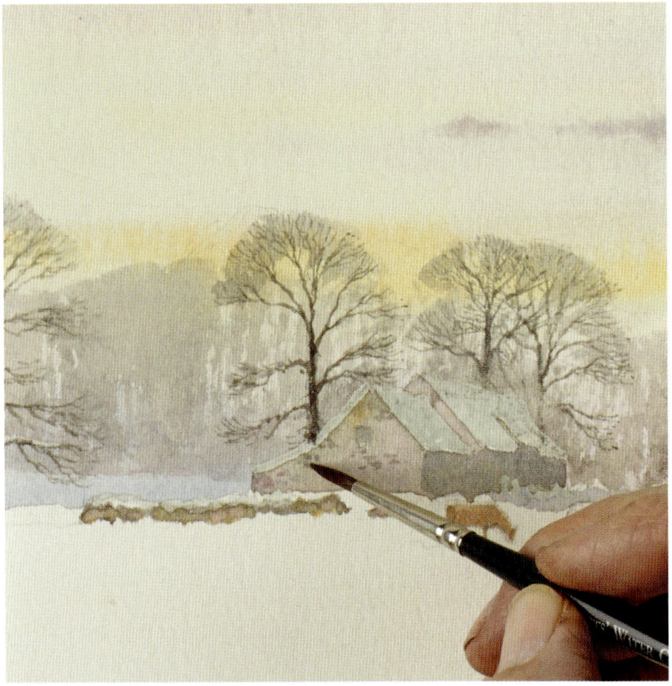

14 Suggest the darker stonework of the buildings with a mix of cobalt blue and burnt sienna, applied wet on dry.

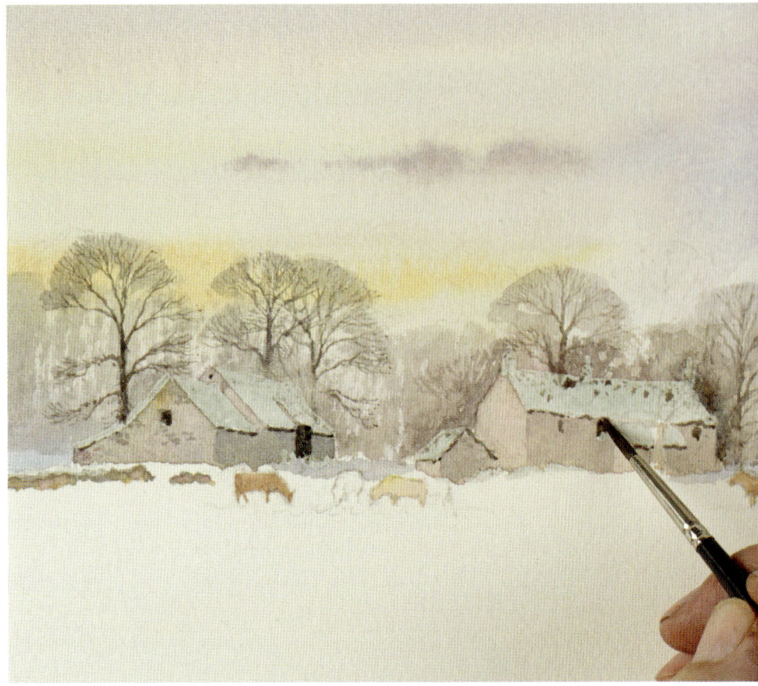

15 Add the darkest details of the buildings such as doors, windows and shadows under the eaves with the same mix.

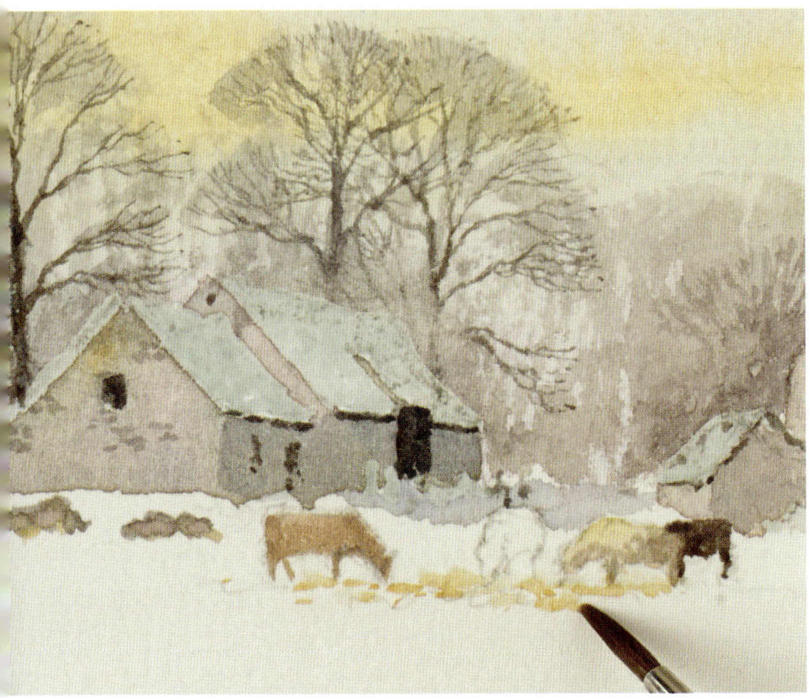

16 Add shade and detail to the cows with the same mix. Allow to dry. Paint yellow ochre under the cows for hay.

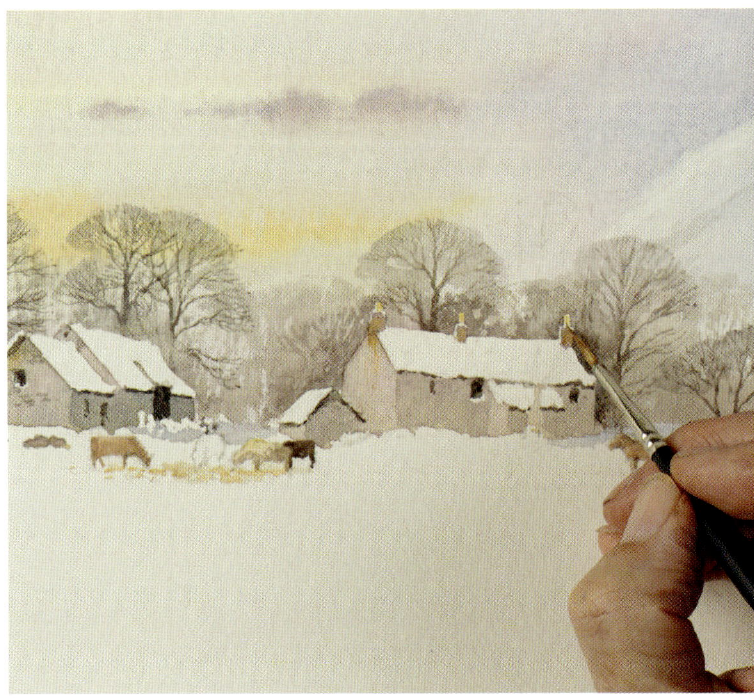

17 Remove the masking fluid. Use the no. 3 round brush to paint the chimneys with yellow ochre and the pots in Naples yellow.

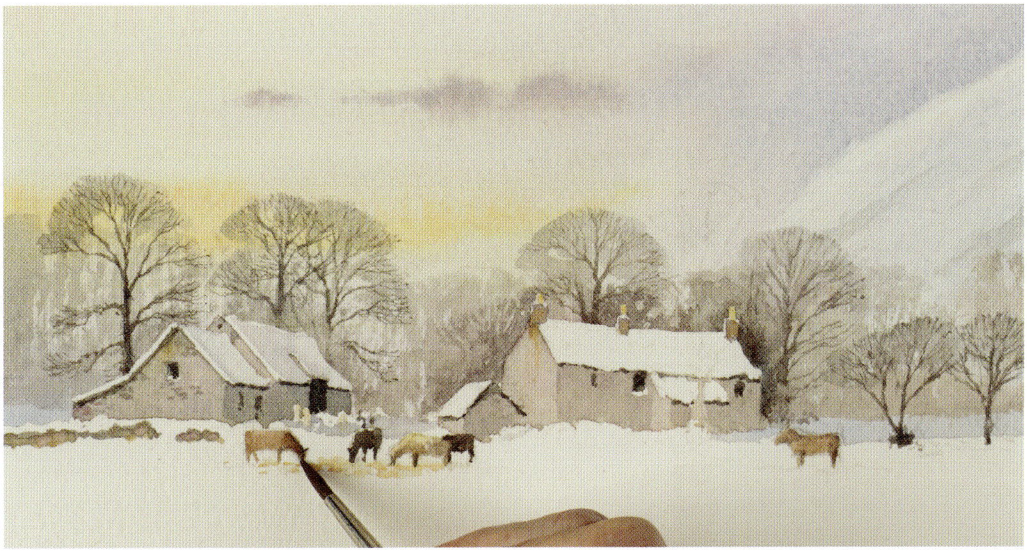

**18** Paint the shadowed snowy roofs with alizarin crimson and cobalt blue. Paint the final cow with burnt umber and cobalt blue and add shadow on the others with the same mix.

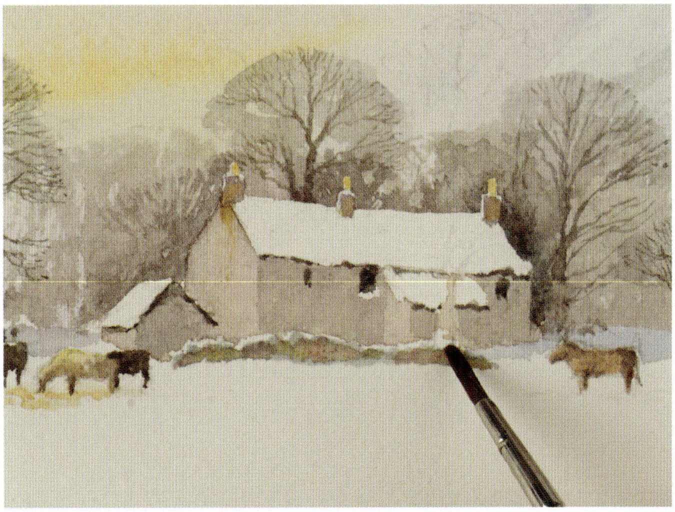

**19** Paint the wall in front of the house with cobalt blue and burnt sienna, leaving white for the snow on top, then drop in yellow ochre and alizarin crimson wet into wet.

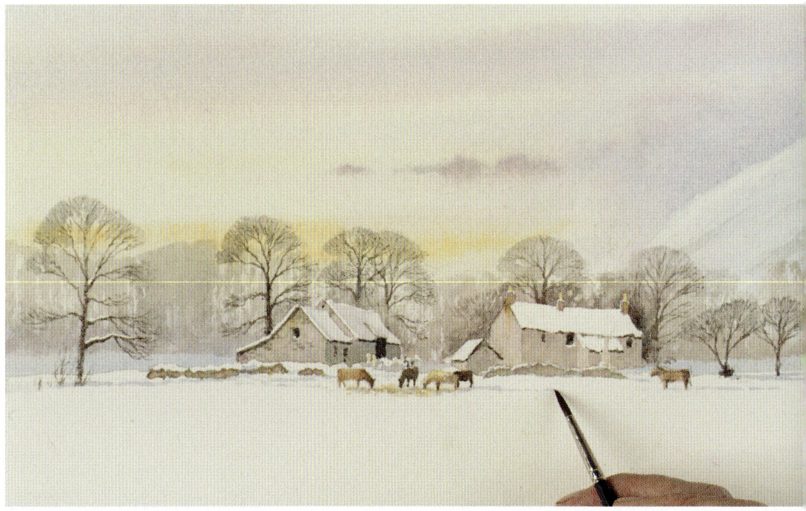

**20** Use the shadow mix of alizarin crimson and cobalt blue to paint cast shadows from the trees, cows and chimneys.

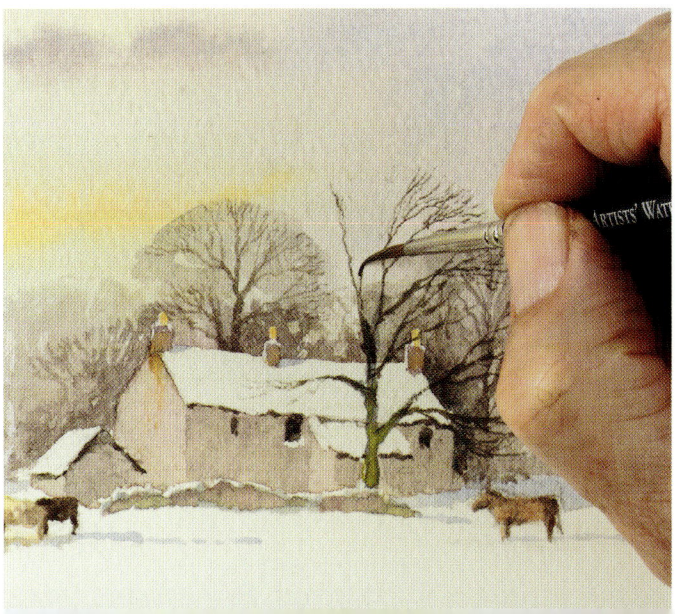

**21** Mix cobalt blue and burnt sienna and paint the tree in front of the house with the no. 4 brush. While this is wet, change to the no. 3 sable round and drop in cadmium yellow pale. Continue painting twigs and branches with the brown mix.

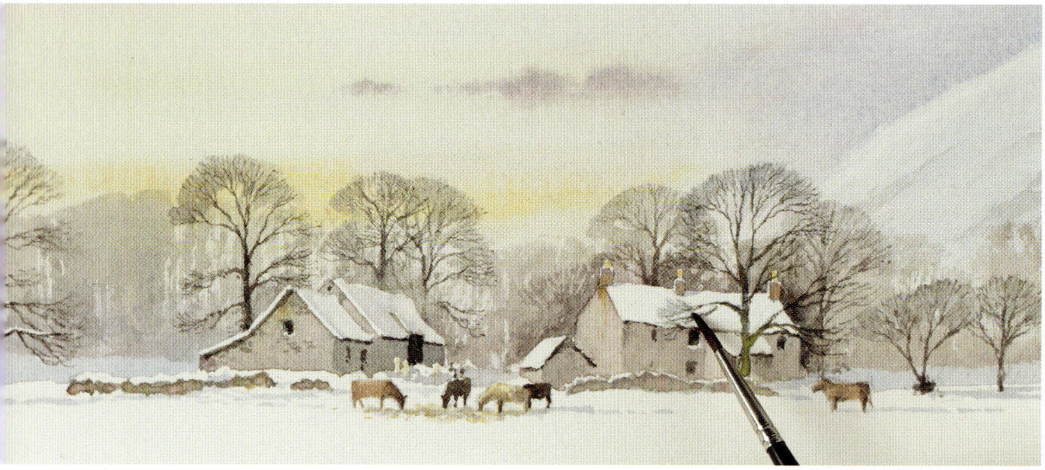

22 Paint the twigwork on the trees with cadmium red and cobalt blue, with the brush on its side and the dry-brush technique.

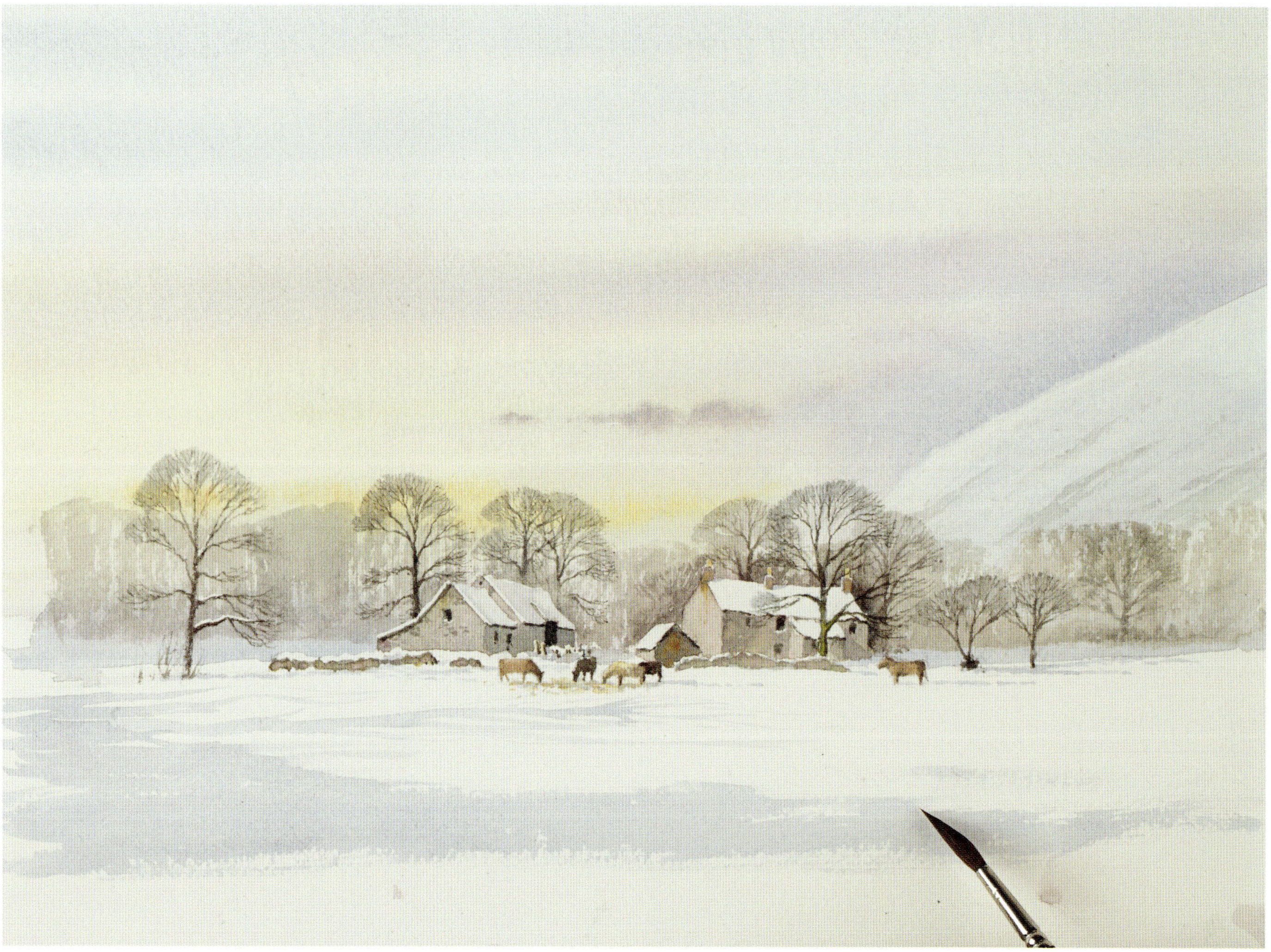

23 Strengthen the shadows beyond the house and on the buildings with a mix of alizarin crimson and cobalt blue. Use the no. 1 rigger to tidy up and add any final details. Change to the no. 7 round brush and paint cast shadows across the foreground snow from some imagined trees to the left of the scene, suggesting the contours of the land.

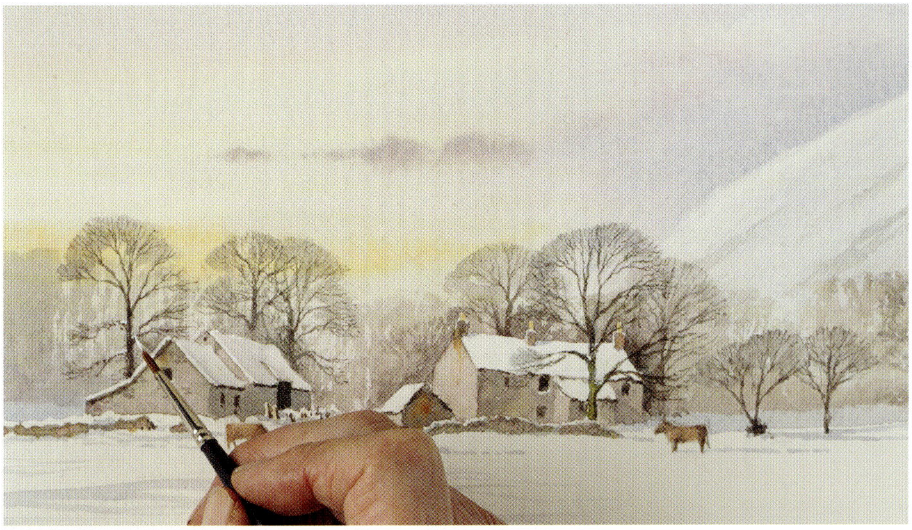

24 Step back from the painting to see what remains to be done. At this point, I darkened behind the snowy roofs with burnt sienna and cobalt blue, then added a little white gouache to suggest snow caught in the trees.

*The finished painting.*

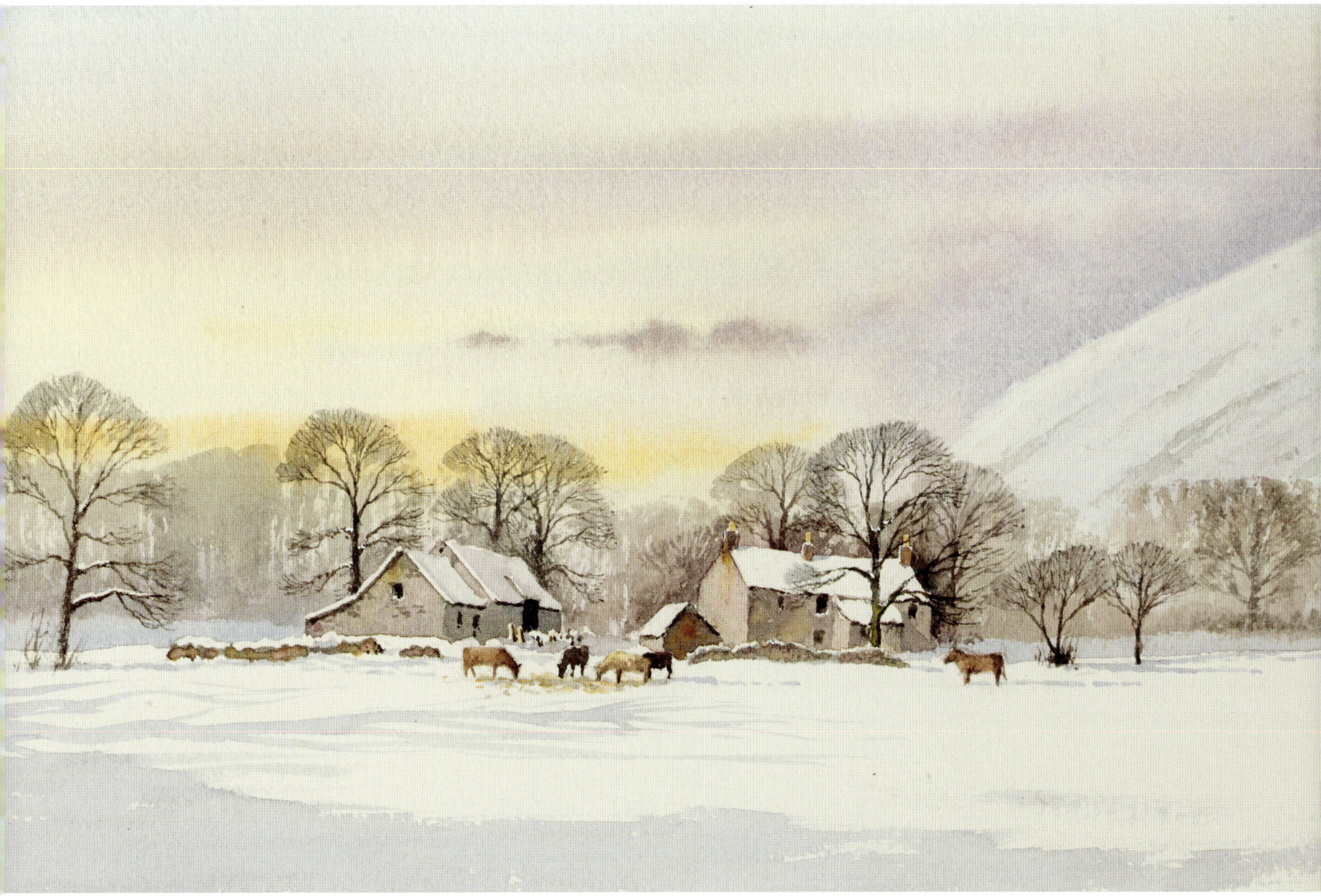

# Spring

Getting outside and recording the fresh colours of the spring landscape is a rewarding and joyful exercise. You can still see the graceful lines of trees as buds emerge, the winter chill recedes and there are longer hours of daylight. The overwhelming greens of summer are still some way off. Choose colours to suggest spring freshness.

Seek out hints of spring: the brighter colours of grass and vegetation and the arrival of spring flowers, often set against the warm colours of dead leaves and branches, creating interesting foregrounds. The sight of lambs in the fields particularly evokes spring, and tree blossom can support a centre of interest.

Vast fields of bluebells have considerable impact, and are often seen at their best when sunlight is pouring through the trees to create patterns of light and shade across the blue masses, a subject we tackle below. Hawthorn blossom can totally transform the lower slopes of mountains, but here I use a couple of bushes to create a centre of interest in a Suffolk field.

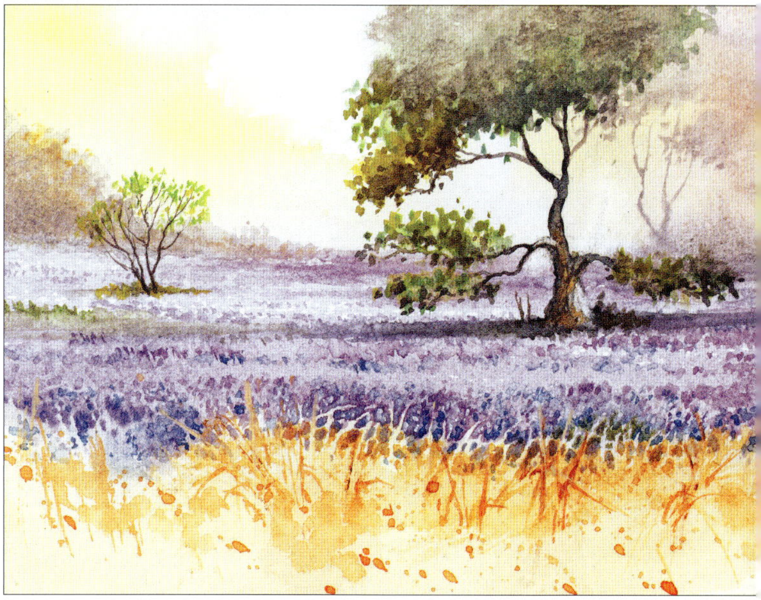

**BLUEBELL FIELD**

*14 x 18cm (5½ x 7in) 300gsm (140lb) Not paper*

*Create an overall impression of the mass of bluebells with just a hint of detail in the closer ones. When these flowers are seen en masse, many tonal variations become apparent through dips in the ground or cast shadows, so use this to inject variety. The bluebells were painted with combinations of cobalt violet deep, ultramarine violet and French ultramarine.*

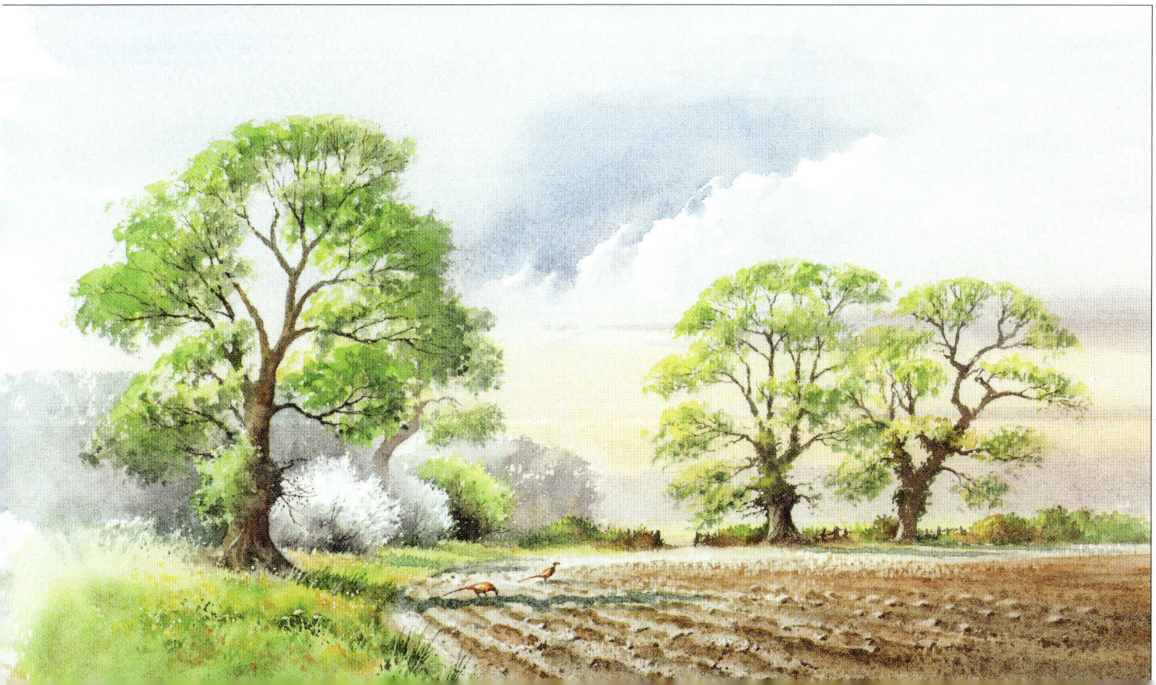

**SUFFOLK BLOSSOM**

*25.5 x 35.5cm (10 x 14in) 425gsm (200lb) Rough paper*

*Blossom not only suggests springtime, but also helps to support a focal point. I have painted the scene much as it appeared on the day, though to create some life, I added a couple of pheasants. As the ploughed field was rather dull in colour, I used burnt sienna to warm it up a little.*

# SPRING COLOURS

Keep your greens and yellows fresh and clean, as in the sketch at the bottom of this page. The chart below gives an idea of some good colour mixes. I have also included a few mixtures of richer and perhaps duller colours, as these can be useful in places to offset the overall brightness. Pink blossom can be painted with a weak wash of alizarin crimson or quinacridone red. Colour in the landscape is affected by light and shade, and cast shadow across bright foliage or a sea of bluebells can dramatically change the way the colour is perceived.

**MIXING SPRING COLOURS**

*The chart below shows colour combinations for spring greens, with a couple of warmer summer versions often prominent in late spring. By including green apatite genuine or lunar blue, you can create granulations which suggest foliage without any help from the artist!*

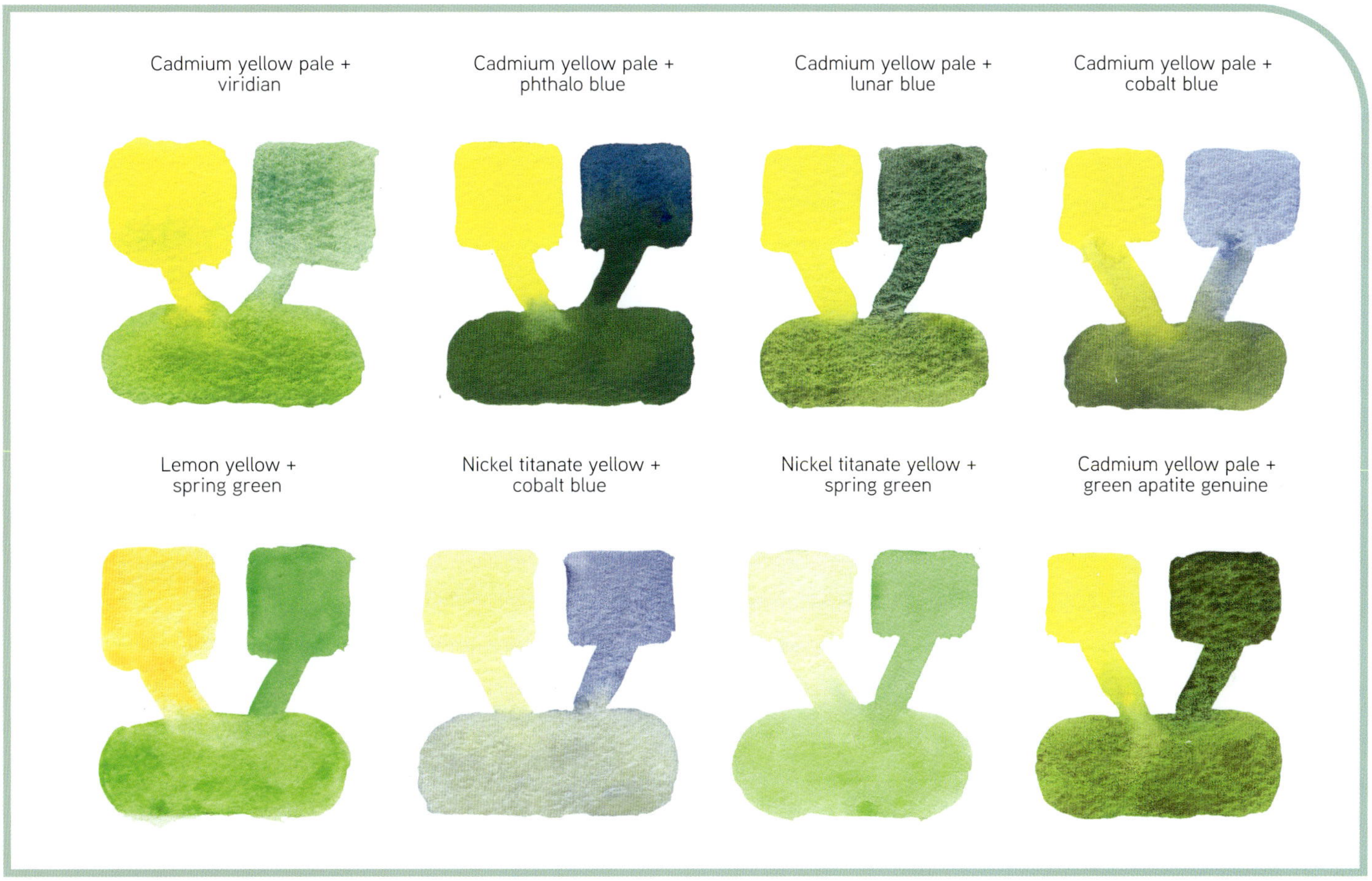


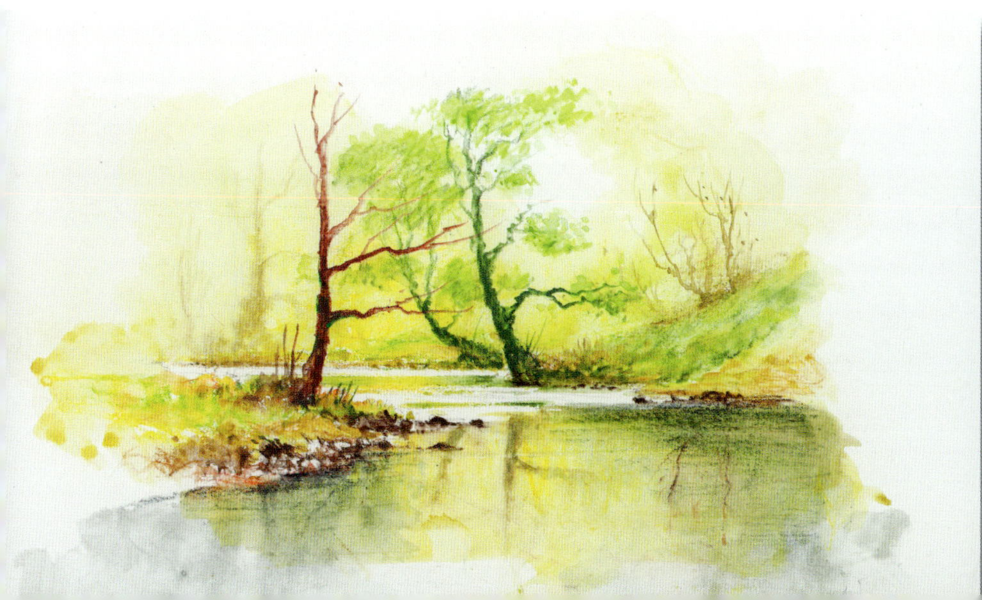

**PLACID STREAM**

*For this sketch, I used Derwent Inktense pencils, drawing first and then washing over with water. The fresh, bright greens give a strong impression of spring, with some trees still bare of leaves. You can combine these pencils with ordinary watercolours if you wish.*

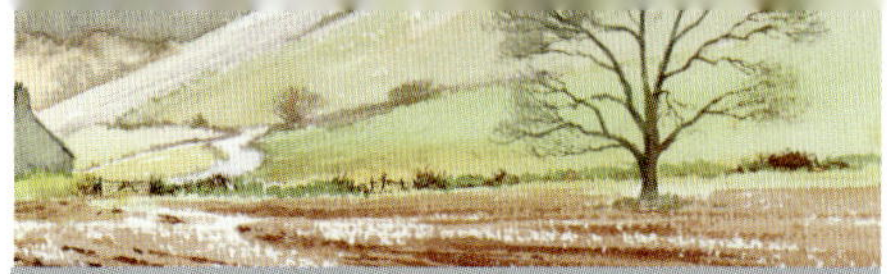

# AFTER THE SPRING SHOWER

There is nothing quite like a spring shower to freshen up the landscape. I take every opportunity to record these effects, as they can give a painting such a lovely sense of mood. One of the main objectives in this demonstration is to show you how to suggest the wet surface of a country lane, and a touch of sparkle on something as mundane as a muddy field.

## MATERIALS USED

Saunders Waterford 640gsm (300lb) Not watercolour paper

Brushes: Small and large squirrel mops, no. 10 sable round, no. 7 sable round, no. 3 rigger, no. 4 sable round, 6mm (¼in) flat, no. 1 rigger, no. 3 sable round

Colours: Cerulean blue, Naples yellow, alizarin crimson, cobalt blue, cadmium red, yellow ochre, cadmium yellow pale, burnt sienna, Indian red, light red, raw umber, new gamboge, cadmium orange, burnt umber, white gouache

Sponge

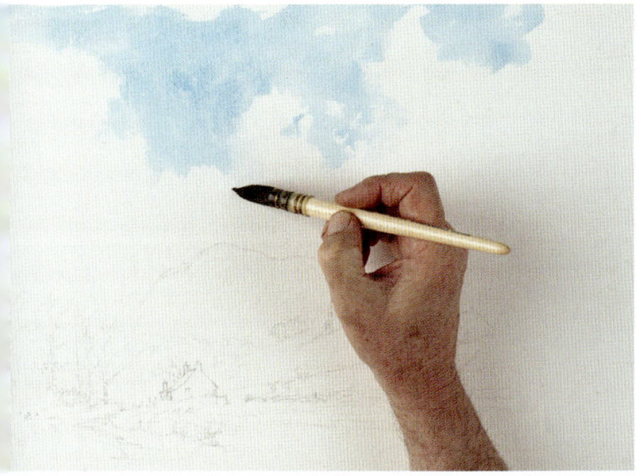

1 Use the small squirrel mop and cerulean blue to paint the sky, leaving lots of white for clouds. Do not apply water first, as you want some hard edges to appear. Soften the left-hand edges with a damp brush as these are away from the sun.

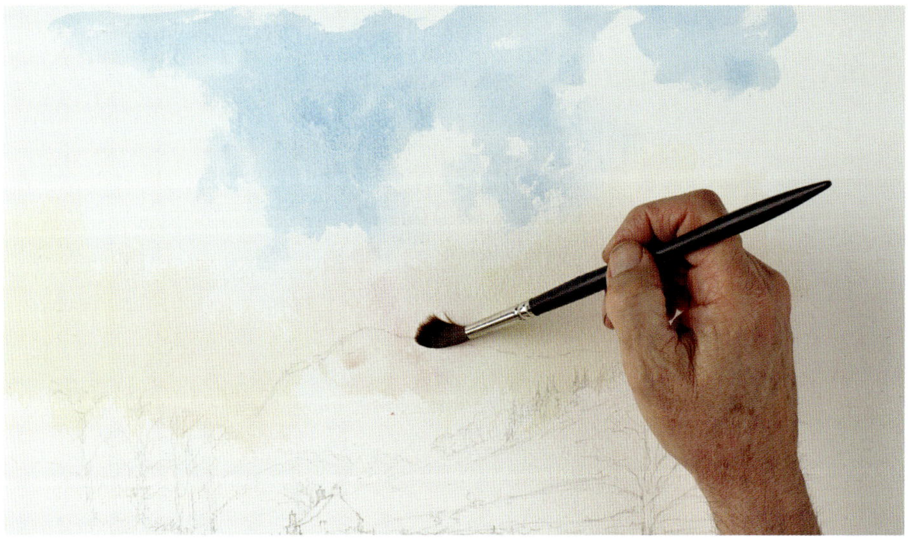

2 Change to the no. 10 sable round and paint a wet wash of Naples yellow in the lower sky and down over the distance. Drop in a little alizarin crimson to warm the colour and allow to dry.

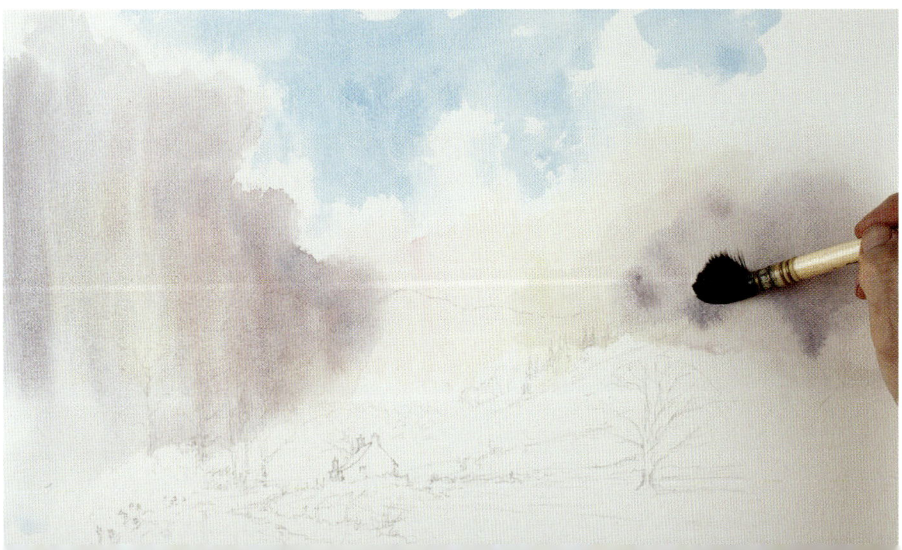

3 Wet the paper in the lower sky and distance using the large squirrel mop, then sweep down a mix of cobalt blue and cadmium red. Soften in places with a damp brush.

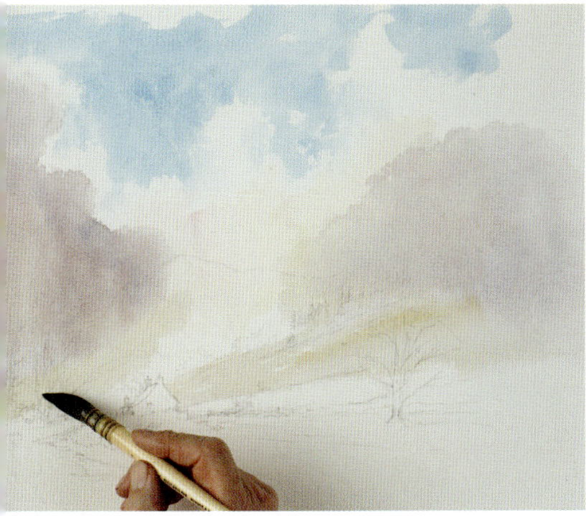

4 Paint yellow ochre from the right-hand cloud down to the building, then on the left over the foliage area. Add cadmium yellow pale in the middle distance.

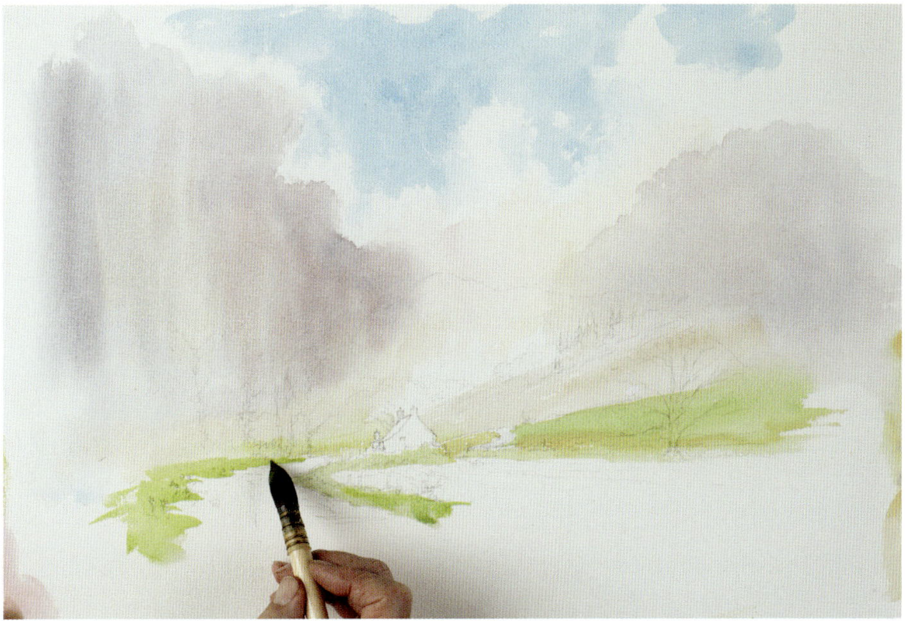

5 Mix cobalt blue with cadmium yellow pale and paint this on the fields near the house. Add Naples yellow below this, then paint the original mix in the area of the daffodils and along the road's edge. Allow to dry.

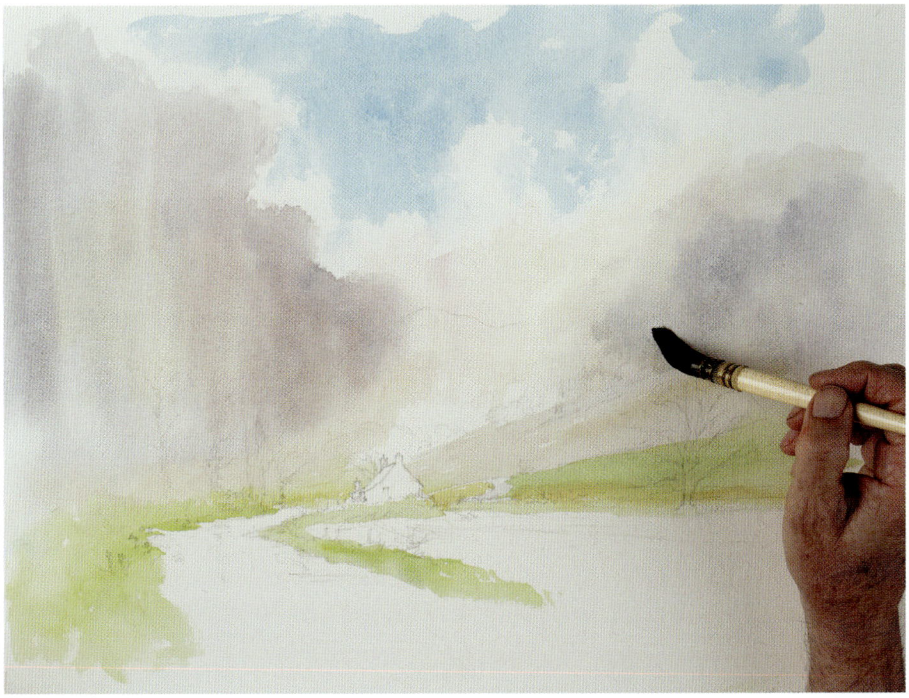

6 Use a damp sponge to soften the edge of the right-hand cloud, then paint on more cadmium red and cobalt blue with the large squirrel mop.

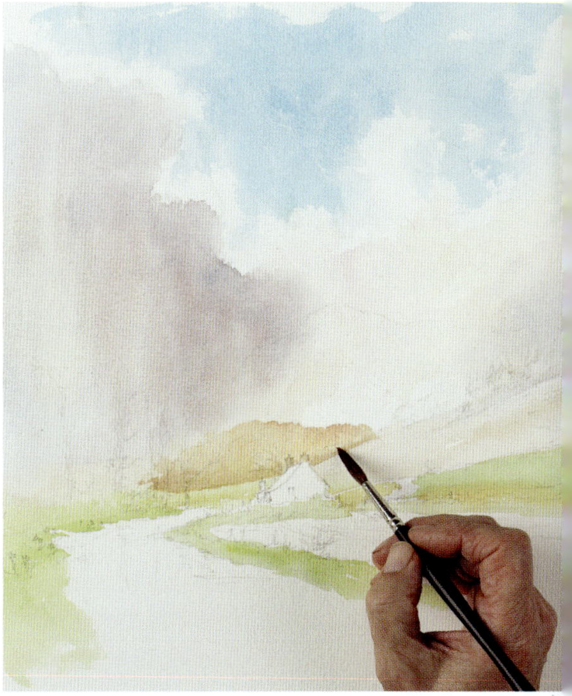

7 Paint the background trees with alizarin crimson and yellow ochre on the no. 7 brush, then add burnt sienna lower down.

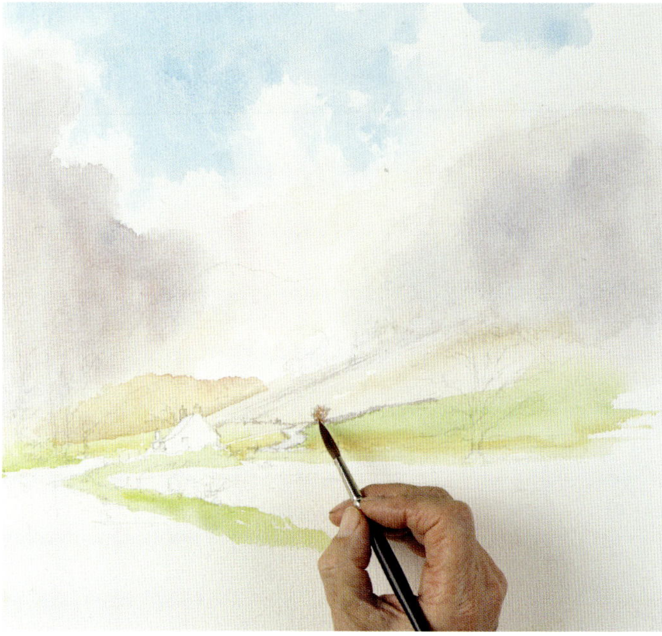

8 Paint a pale mix of cobalt blue and Indian red down the slope towards the house, indicating rough pasture. Drop in light red wet into wet.

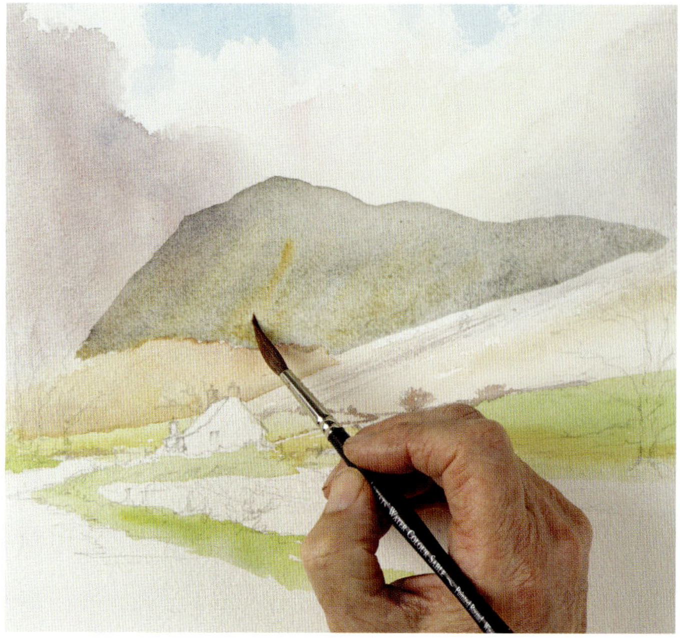

9 Change to the squirrel mop and paint the distant mountain with cobalt blue and burnt sienna with a little yellow ochre. Drop in yellow ochre wet into wet with the no. 7 brush.

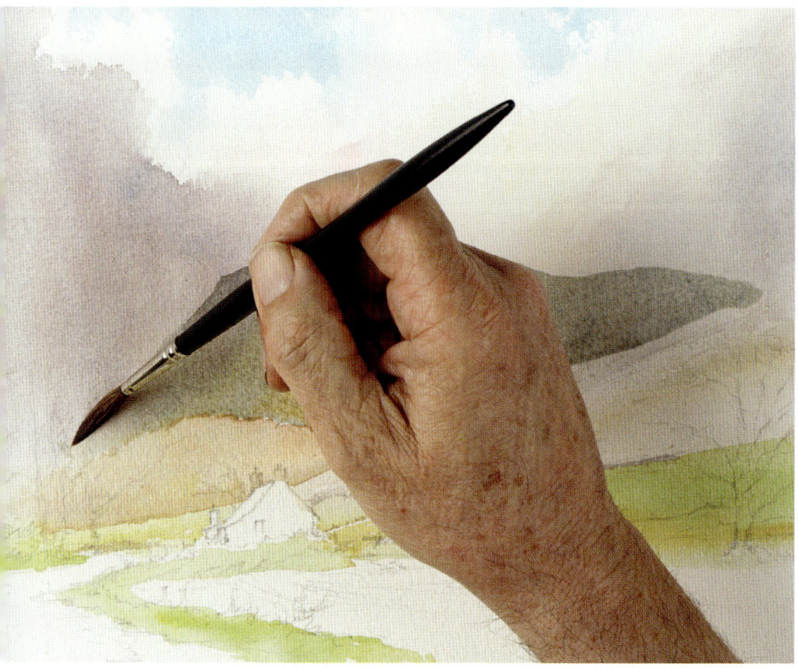

10 Soften the lower edge of the mountain with clean water as it goes behind the trees.

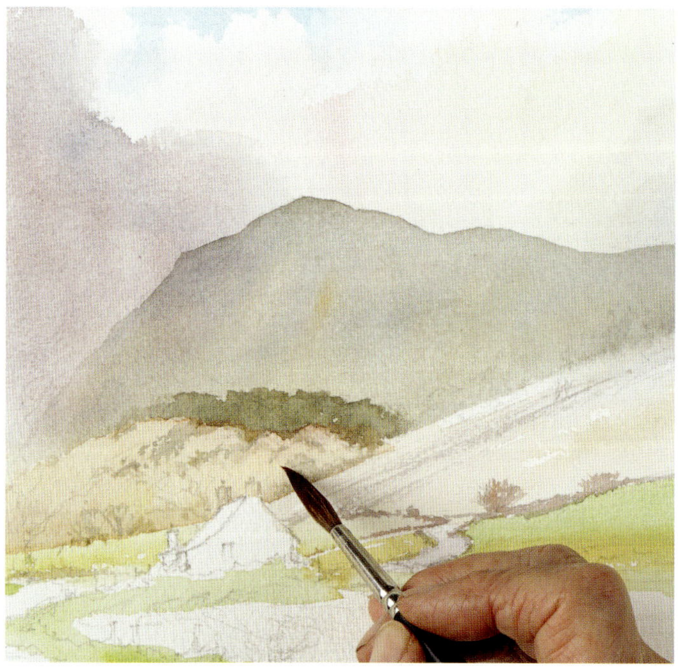

11 Mix yellow ochre and cobalt blue and use the no. 7 brush to paint the darker area of trees, then lift out some of the colour to texture the massed trees in front. Allow to dry.

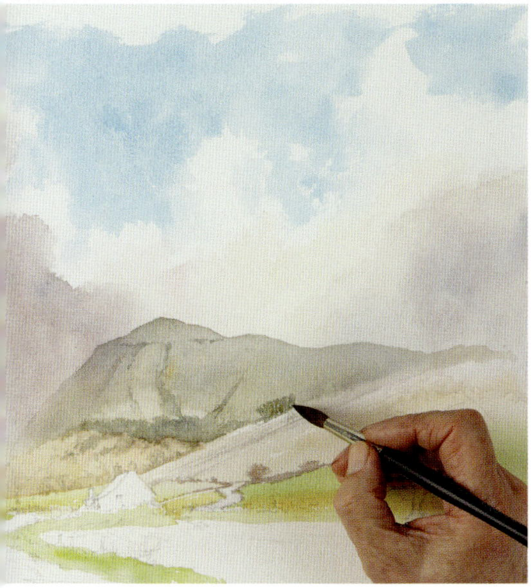

12 Use a sponge to subdue the darker trees, then use the yellow ochre and cobalt blue mix to suggest gullies on the distant mountain. Extend the distant line of trees with the same mix.

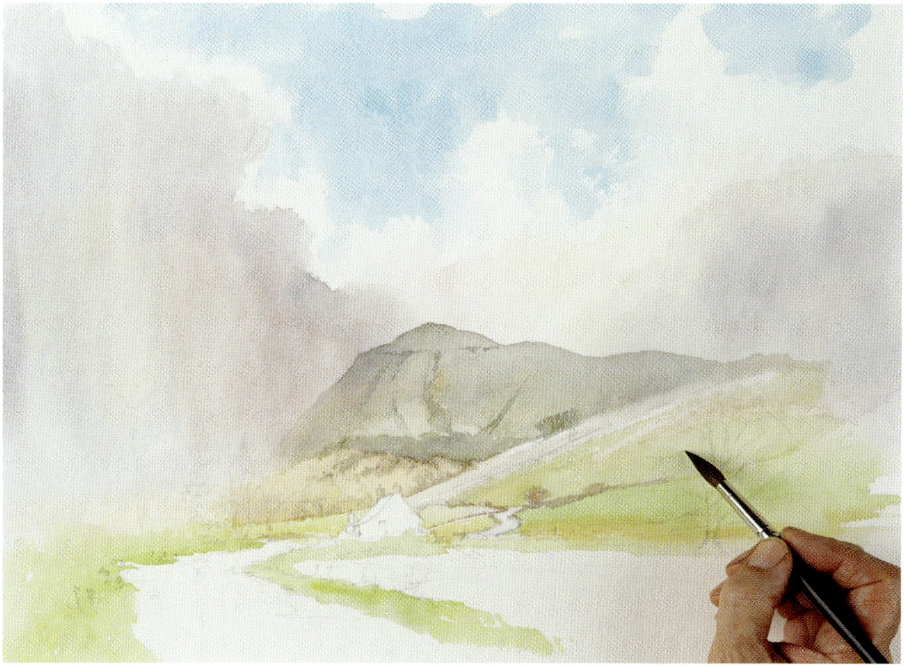

13 Stand back to assess the painting from time to time. At this point I decided that the right-hand slope needed to look more spring-like, so I brightened it with cadmium yellow pale and a little cobalt blue.

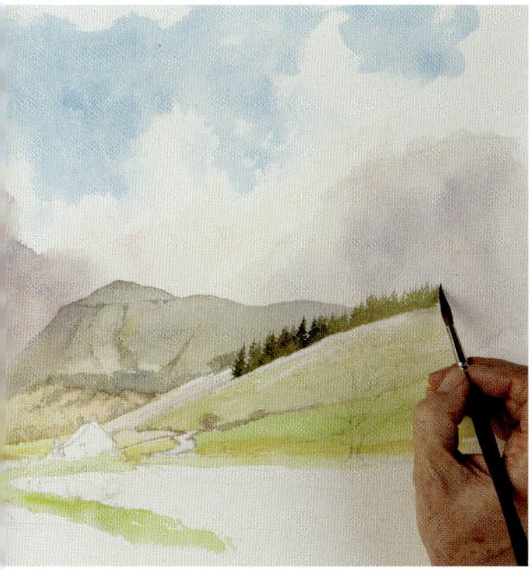

14 Paint the conifers on the right with raw umber and cobalt blue, varying the strength.

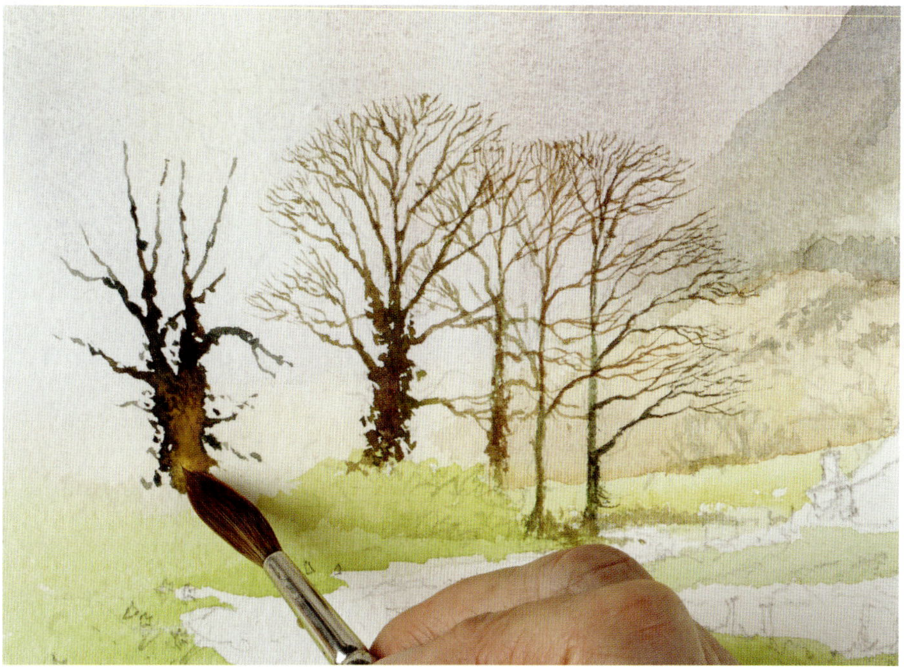

15 Use the tip of the no. 7 brush to paint the trees on the left with raw umber and cobalt blue for the trunks and the branches on the right, and burnt umber on the left. Suggest the ivy on some trunks and drop in new gamboge, then cadmium orange wet into wet.

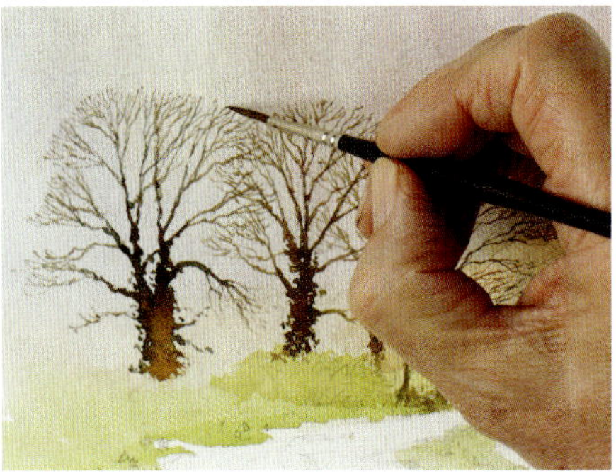

16 Use a no. 3 rigger and raw umber with cobalt blue to build up the finer branches.

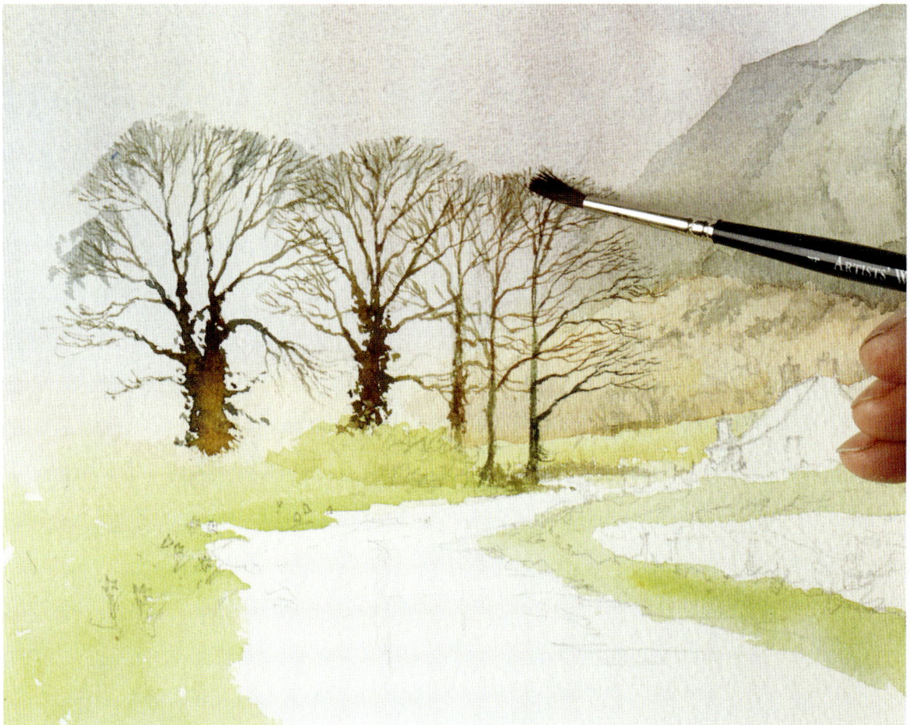

17 Mix burnt umber and cobalt blue and paint the twigwork of the trees with the no. 4 round brush on its side.

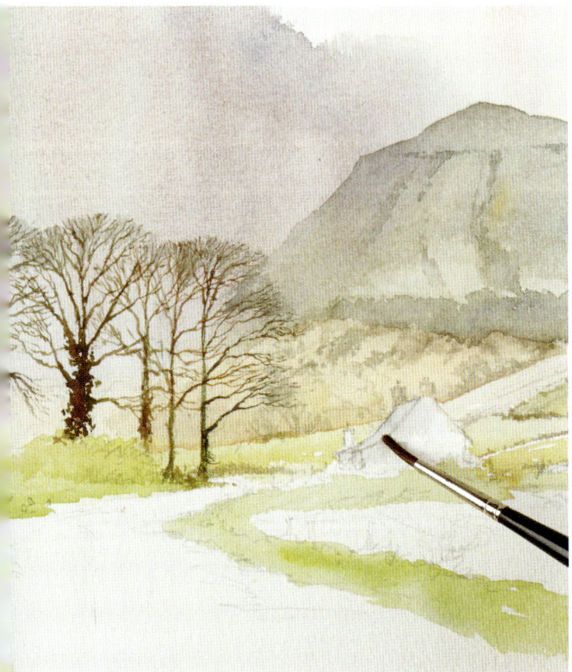

18 Paint the roof of the building with a very pale mix of cadmium red and cobalt blue.

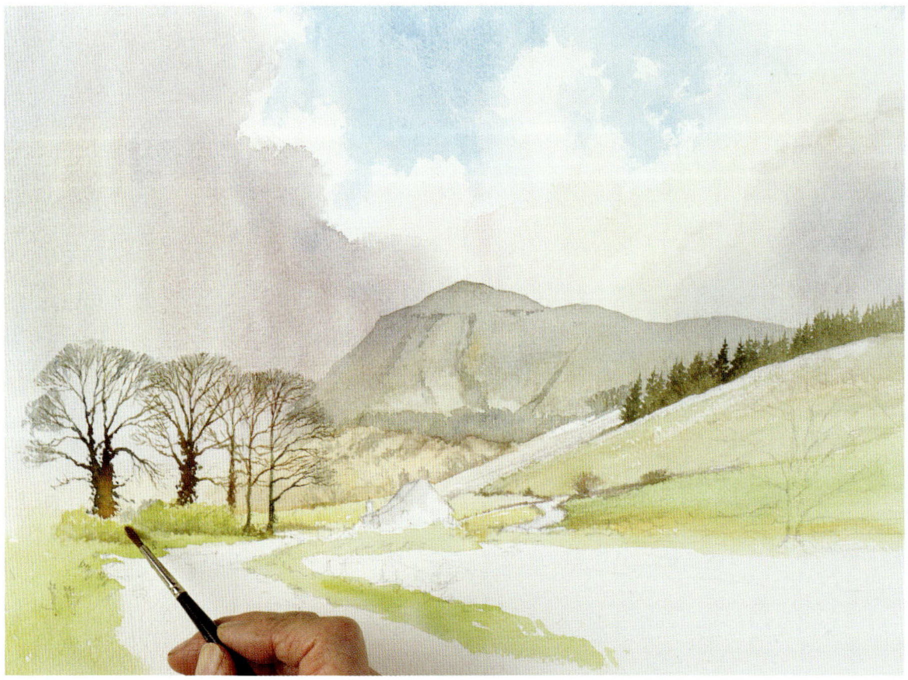

19 Paint yellow ochre and cobalt blue under the trees for the shaded part of the hedge. Add cadmium yellow pale for the lighter part.

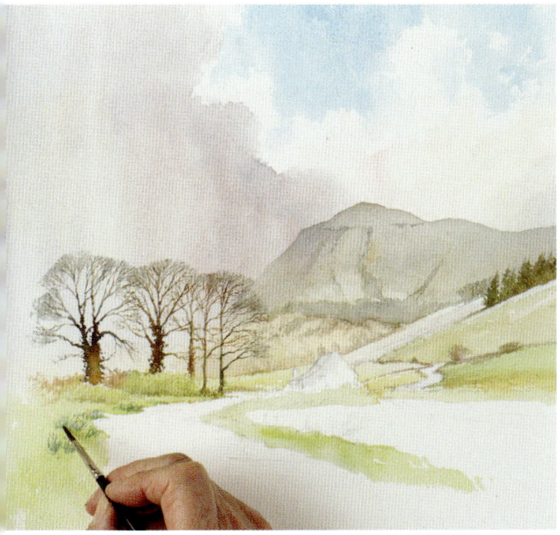

20 Add spots of light red for dead leaves under the trees, then mix cobalt blue with a little new gamboge to create the daffodil leaves coming forwards.

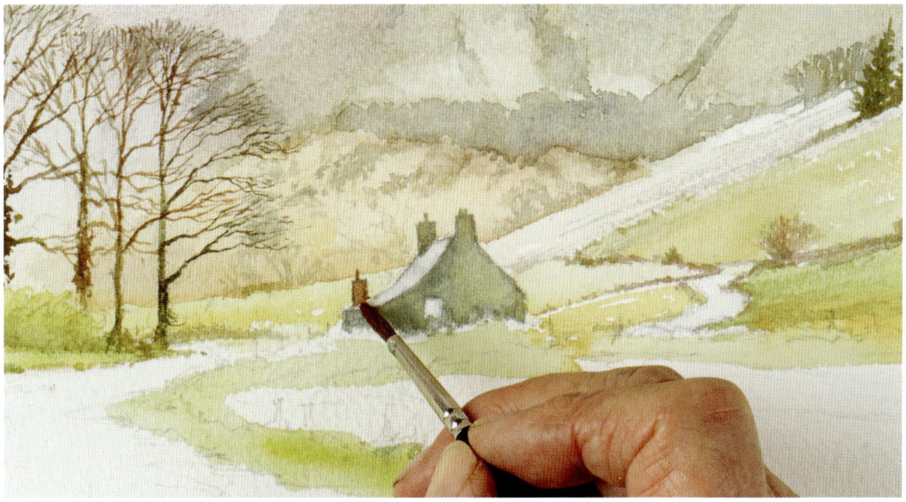

21 Paint the shaded side of the house with burnt umber and cobalt blue, then drop in Naples yellow wet into wet. Paint the chimneys in the same way.

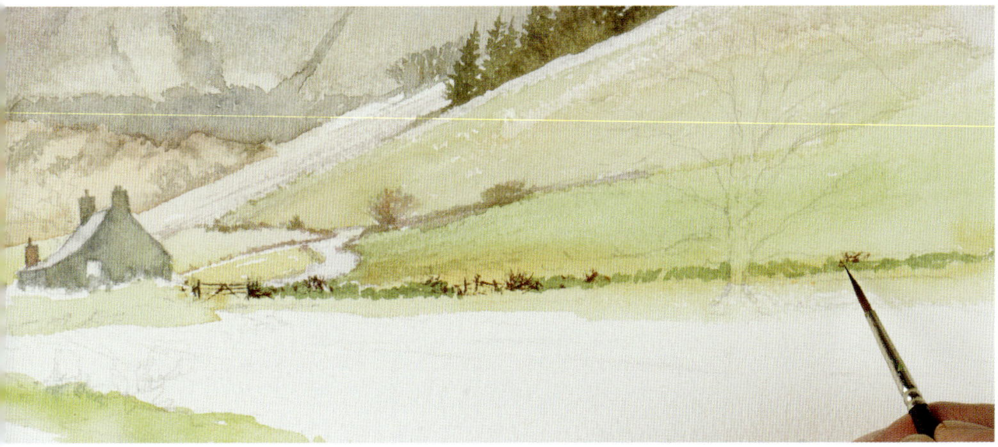

22 Paint the hedge with cobalt blue and new gamboge, then use the no. 3 round brush with cobalt blue and burnt umber to paint the gate, fenceposts and details in the hedge.

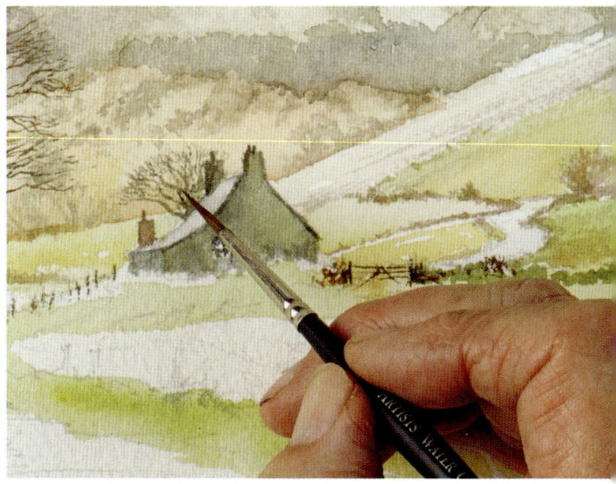

23 Continue painting the posts on the left of the house, the window panes and the tree behind the house.

24 Use the no. 4 brush to paint the tree on the right with raw umber and cobalt blue, then drop in alizarin crimson. Change to the no. 1 rigger and a mix of burnt umber and cobalt blue to extend the branches and twigs. Use the no. 4 brush on its side to paint the twigwork with the same mix.

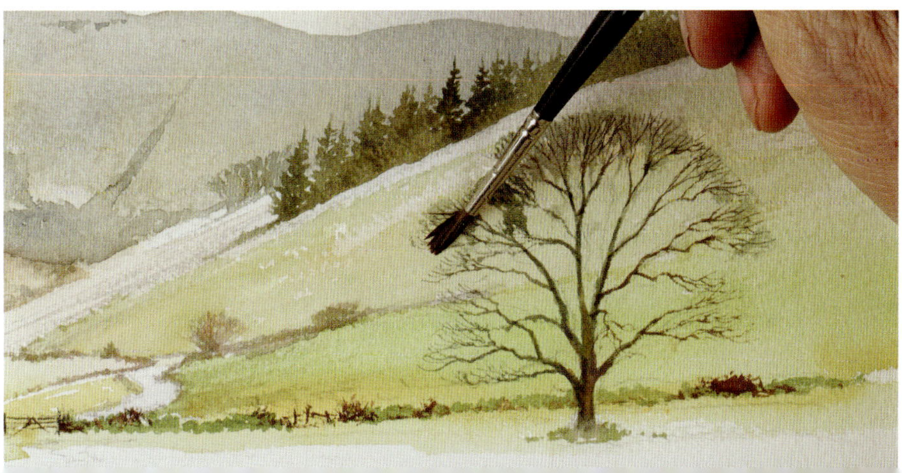

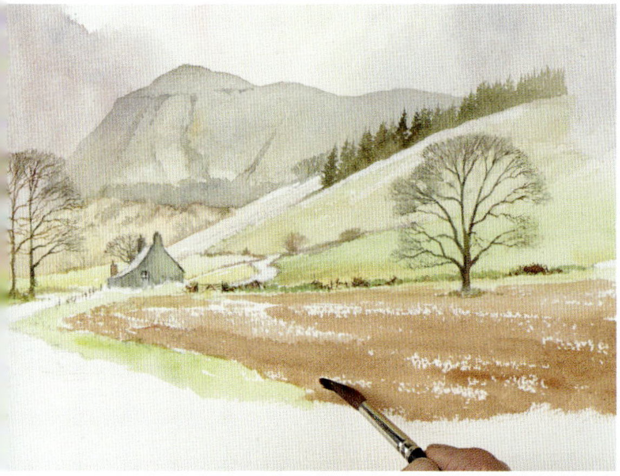

25 Use the no. 10 brush and burnt sienna to sweep in the ploughed field with the dry-brush technique, leaving speckles of white.

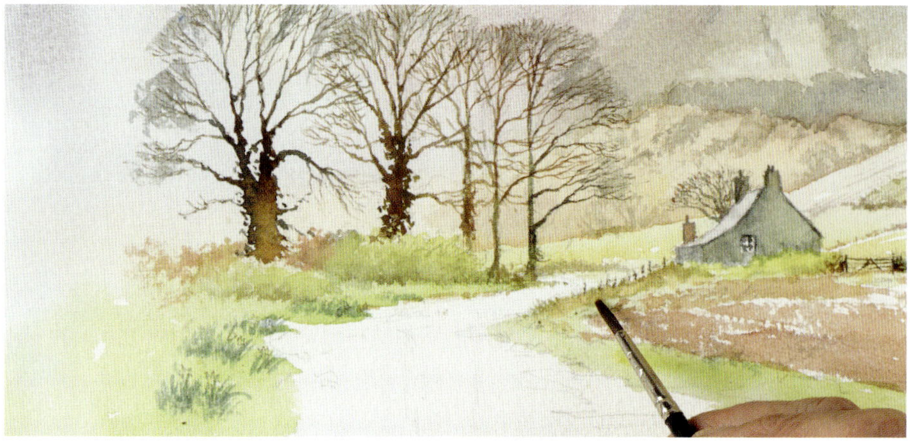

26 Paint the greenery in front of the house and along the fence with the no. 4 brush and cadmium yellow pale, then drop in raw umber.

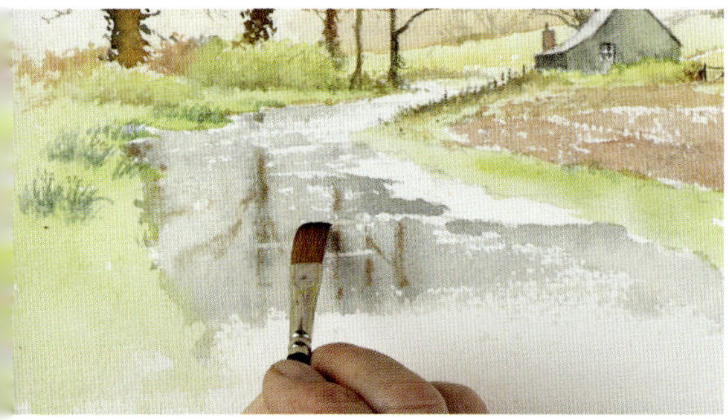

27 Use the no. 10 brush on its side to sweep cobalt blue and burnt umber from side to side across the foreground track, picking up the paper texture. While the paint is wet, paint reflections with a darker mix, then lift out colour with a just-damp 6mm (¼in) flat brush, suggesting ripples.

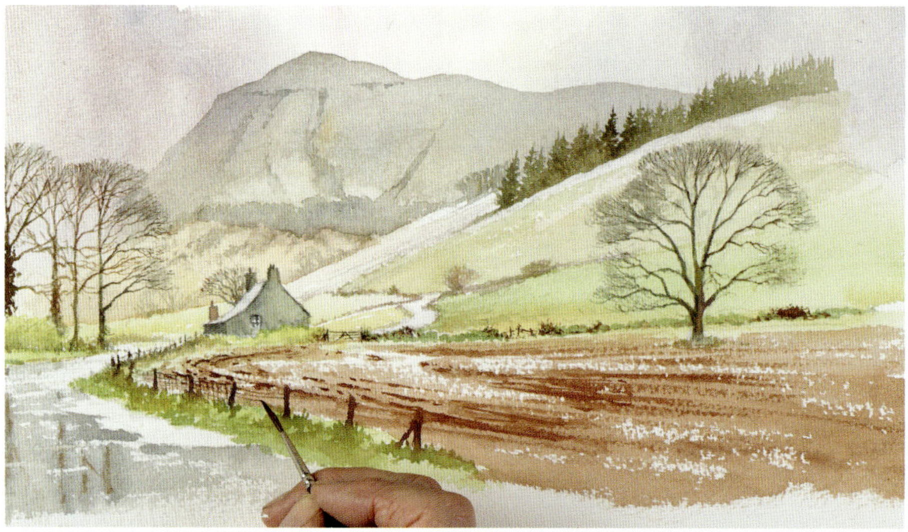

28 Brighten the grass verge beside the track with cadmium yellow pale and cobalt blue on the no. 4 brush, then use the no. 7 brush and burnt umber with a touch of cobalt blue to paint furrows and texture in the ploughed field. Add fenceposts with a darker mix of the same colours, then paint a darker mix of the previous green for grasses. Add netting to the fence with the no. 1 rigger and the brown mix.

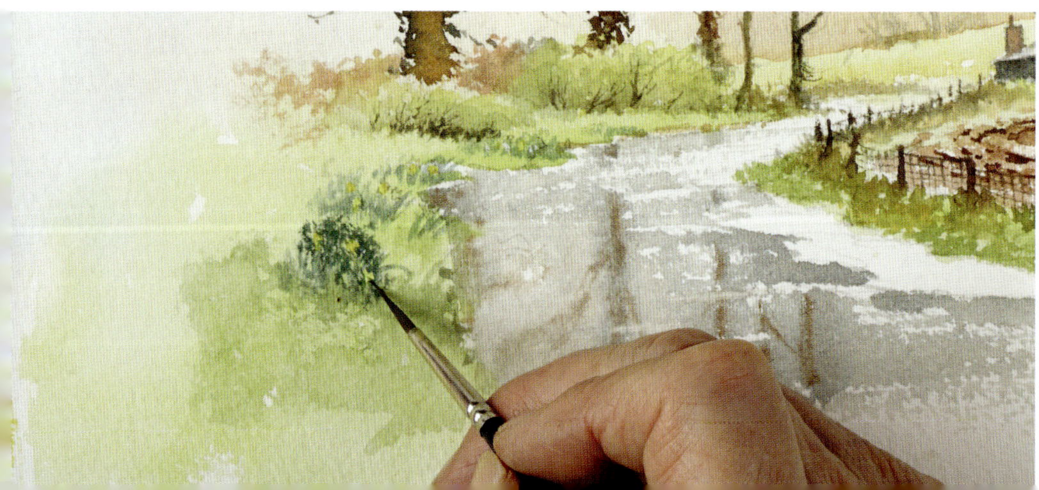

29 Paint the daffodils with white gouache, then cadmium yellow pale. Paint negatively around them with cobalt blue and cadmium yellow pale.

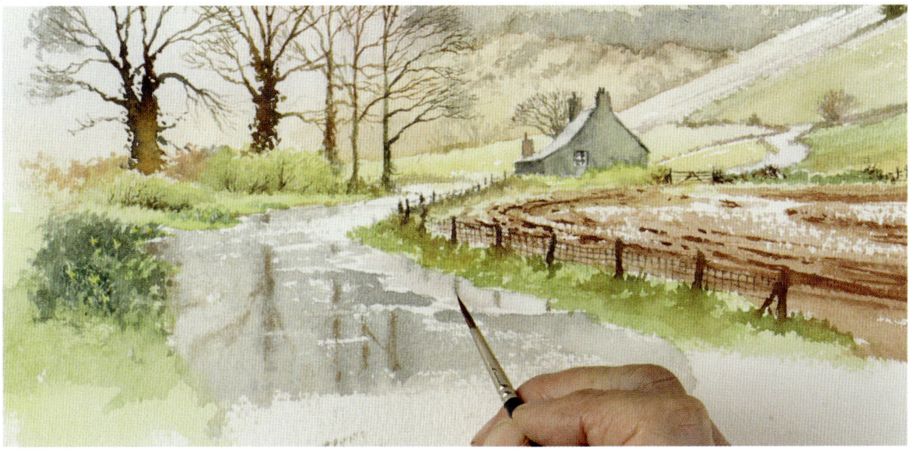

30 Clean up any pencil marks, then use the no. 7 brush and cobalt blue with cadmium red to add dark touches to the puddle, reflecting the sky. Add fencepost reflections to the road with burnt umber and cobalt blue.

*The finished painting.*

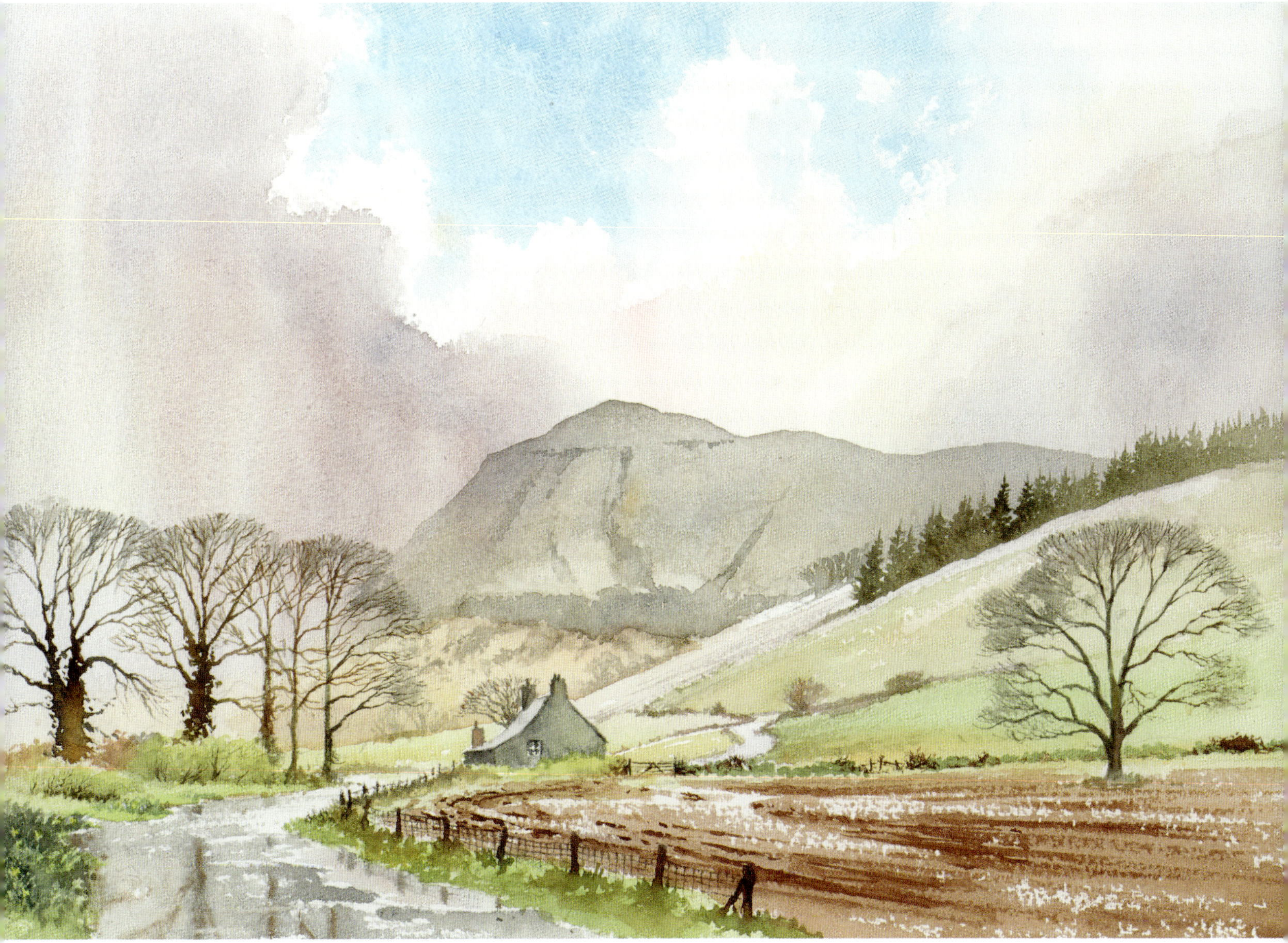

# Index

First published in 2024
Search Press Limited
Wellwood, North Farm Road,
Tunbridge Wells, Kent TN2 3DR

2 3 4 5 6 7 8 9 10

Uses material from the following titles by Search Press:
*David Bellamy's Mountains & Moorlands in Watercolour*, 2010
*David Bellamy's Skies, Light & Atmosphere in Watercolour*, 2012
*David Bellamy's Winter Landscapes in Watercolour*, 2014
*David Bellamy's Seas & Shorelines in Watercolour*, 2019
*David Bellamy's Landscapes through the Seasons in Watercolour*, 2020



Photographs by Paul Bricknell and Mark Davison at Search Press Studios



ISBN: 978-1-78221-678-0
ebook ISBN: 978-1-78126-592-5

**Bookmarked Hub**
For further ideas and inspiration, and to join our free online community, visit www.bookmarkedhub.com

You are invited to visit the author's website:
www.davidbellamy.co.uk

**Publishers' notes**
The Publishers and author can accept no responsibility for any consequences arising from the information, advice or instructions given in this publication.

For errata, please visit our website (www.searchpress.com) or the Bookmarked Hub (www.bookmarkedhub.com).

GPSR information can be found at www.searchpress.com

Printed in China, AP042026

MIX
Paper | Supporting responsible forestry
FSC® C136333
FSC www.fsc.org

## Acknowledgements

I am indebted to Edward Ralph, Sophie Kersey, Juan Hayward and Carrie Baker at Search Press for their enthusiastic help in producing this book, and also to Jenny Keal for checking my original manuscripts.

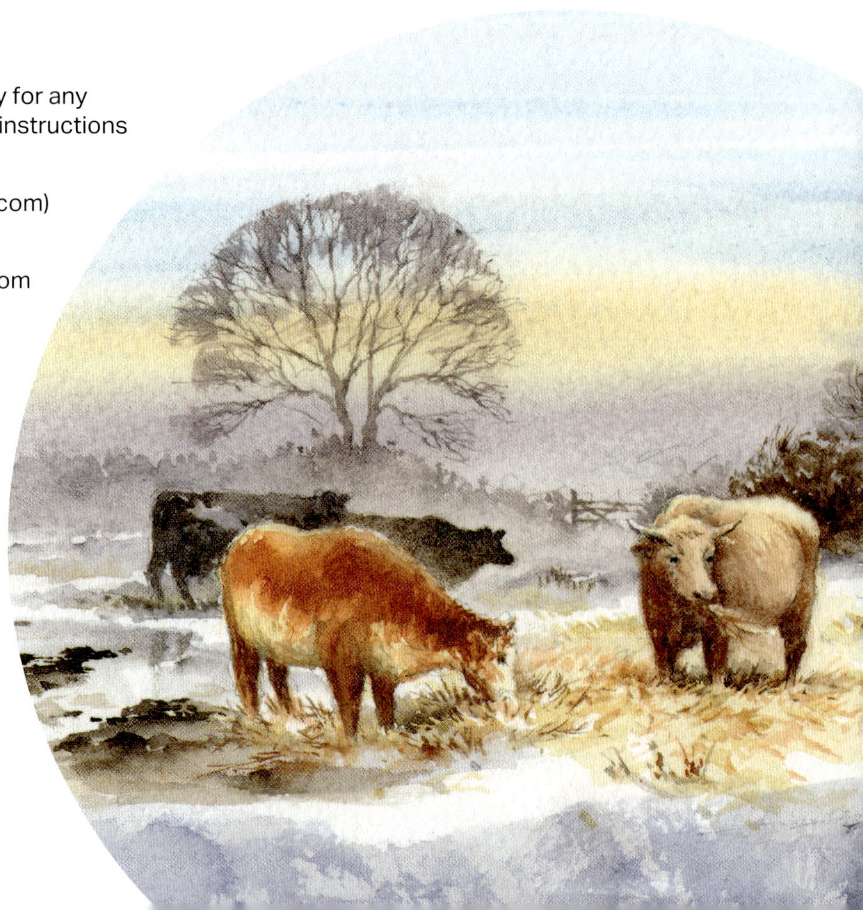